Inside Afghanistan

This book maps out how political networks and centres of power, engaged in patronage, corruption, and illegality, effectively constituted the Afghan state, often with the complicity of the U.S.-led military intervention and the internationally directed statebuilding project. It argues that politics and statehood in Afghanistan, in particular in the last two decades, including the ultimate collapse of the government in August 2021, are best understood in terms of the dynamics of internal political networks, through which warlords and patronage networks came to capture and control key sectors within the state and economy, including mining, banking, and illicit drugs as well as elections and political processes. Networked politics emerged as the dominant mode of governance that further transformed and consolidated Afghanistan into a networked state, with the state institutions and structures functioning as the principal "marketplace" for political networks' bargains and rent-seeking. The façade of state survival and fragmented political order was a performative act, and the book contends, sustained through massive international military spending and development aid, obscuring the reality of resource redistribution among key networked elites and their supporters. Overall, the book offers a way to explain what it was that the international community and the Afghan elites in power got so wrong that brought Afghanistan full circle and the Taliban back to power.

Timor Sharan is an Associate Fellow at IDEAS, London School of Economics and Political Science's foreign policy think tank, London, U.K. He was formerly the International Crisis Group's Policy Analyst for Afghanistan and worked as a Senior Civil Servant for the Afghan government. He completed his doctorate at the University of Exeter and his MPhil at the University of Cambridge, U.K.

Routledge Contemporary South Asia Series

146 Gendered Modernity and Indian Cinema
The Women in Satyajit Ray's Films
Devapriya Sanyal

147 Reading Jhumpa Lahiri
Women, Domesticity and the Indian American Diaspora
Nilanjana Chatterjee

148 Indian Literatures in Diaspora
Sireesha Telugu

149 Identity, Nationhood and Bangladesh Independent Cinema
Fahmidul Haq and Brian Shoesmith

150 Media Discourse in Contemporary India
A Study of Television News
Sudeshna Devi

151 Health Care in Post-Independence India
Kolkata and the Crisis of Private Health Care Services
Amrita Bagchi

152 Inside Afghanistan
Political Networks, Informal Order, and State Disruption
Timor Sharan

153 Bangladesh's Quest for Inclusive Development
Challenges and Pathways
Mustafa Kamal Mujeri and Neaz Mujeri

154 Covid-19 in India, Disease, Health and Culture
Can Wellness be Far Behind?
Anindita Chatterjee and Nilanjana Chatterjee

For the full list of titles in the series please visit: https://www.routledge.com/
Routledge-Contemporary-South-Asia-Series/book-series/RCSA

Inside Afghanistan

Political Networks, Informal Order, and
State Disruption

Timor Sharan

Routledge
Taylor & Francis Group

LONDON AND NEW YORK

First published 2023
by Routledge
4 Park Square, Milton Park, Abingdon, Oxon OX14 4RN

and by Routledge
605 Third Avenue, New York, NY 10158

Routledge is an imprint of the Taylor & Francis Group, an informa business

British Library Cataloguing-in-Publication Data
A catalogue record for this book is available from the British Library

ISBN: 978-1-138-28015-1 (hbk)
ISBN: 978-1-032-33494-3 (pbk)
ISBN: 978-1-315-16161-7 (ebk)

DOI: 10.4324/9781315161617

Typeset in Times New Roman
by Deanta Global Publishing Services, Chennai, India

For Oktay and Keyah Mehr,
whose presence brought light at a dark and difficult time.

Contents

List of tables   xi
List of figures   xii
Preface   xiii

1 Introduction   1

   1.1 What are political networks? 3
   1.2 Networked politics: a new mode of governance 7
   1.3 What contributed to networked politics? 12
   1.4 Post-2001 Afghanistan: a complex global assemblage 14
   1.5 The post-2001 state and informal order 16
   1.6 Political order in Afghanistan's modern state formation 18
   Notes 24

2 Political networks and the state: An analytical framework   28

   Introduction 28
   2.1 Typology of political networks 29
   2.2 What holds a political network together? 31
   2.3 Political networks survival and diversity of power
      resources 33
   2.4 Political networks and levels of engagement 36
   2.5 Political networks and alliance formation 38
   2.6 Political networks and institutional settings 40
   2.7 The safe state position(s) 47
   2.8 International aid and military presence as deterrence 48
   Notes 49

3 The origins and evolution of political networks: Factionalism, violence, and political settlements   52

   Introduction 52
   3.1 The emergence of the PDPA: factionalism and violence 53

3.2 Islamic jihadi tanzims, *insurgency, and the 1992–2001 Civil War 60*

3.3 Failed political settlements and consequences 65

Conclusion 67

Notes 68

4   The Bonn experiment and a flawed foundation: Re-assembling and re-constituting the Afghan state (2001–2004)   74

Introduction 74

4.1 Capturing and re-assembling the state: a fragmented order 79

4.2 Karzai's technocratic network flexing their muscle 102

Conclusion 108

Notes 109

5   Consolidating a political "Empire of Mud" (2004–2014)   118

Introduction 118

5.1 The 2004 presidential elections: projecting power 120

5.2 Power restructuring and alliance-building against Karzai 121

5.3 Restructuring political order: capturing the Lower House and provincial councils 123

5.4 Battling for control of provincial councils 126

5.5 The pre-2009 presidential election dynamics, alliance-building, and a crisis of legitimacy 129

5.6 New administration: new power-sharing 133

5.7 Karzai and the U.S.A.: a turbulent relationship 135

5.8 State institutions and patronage 136

5.9 Alliance-building in the lead-up to the 2014 elections 143

5.10 The post-2014 election crisis: threat of coup and civil war 146

Conclusion 148

Notes 150

6   The National Unity Government: Political order disruption and strains   156

Introduction 156

6.1 NUG power-sharing, ethnicity, and political network restructuring 159

6.2 The underlying source of tension and discord 165

6.3 Concentrating power in the palace 166

    6.4 Centre–periphery relations: disrupting the provincial
      order 168
    6.5 A lost opportunity: crushing revisionist youth protest
      movements 173
    6.6 Ghani: opposition alliances and disorder 176
    6.7 The 2019 presidential election: network dynamics and the
      political settlement 178
    Conclusion 180
    Notes 181

7   Elections for sale: Manipulating identities and bargains   **188**

    Introduction 188
    7.1 The U.S.A., the international community, and the veneer of
      democracy 189
    7.2 Underlying sources of election disputes 191
    7.3 Alliance-building, opportunism, and bargains 195
    Conclusion 209
    Notes 211

8   Parliament as a grand marketplace: Alliance-building,
    auctions, and access   **214**

    Introduction 214
    8.1 Assembling the house: composition, power dynamics, and
      strains 216
    8.2 The 2010–2011 election and the Special Court crisis 223
    Conclusion 234
    Notes 235

9   International money as a "weapons system," rent, and corruption   **238**

    Introduction 238
    9.1 Weaponising international money and its spell on the Afghan
      state 240
    9.2 Customs revenue and extortion 244
    9.3 The Kabul Bank case: a Ponzi scheme 247
    9.4 Contracting, collusion, and profiteering 252
    9.5 The extractive industry: violence and disorder 254
    9.6 Taliban insurgency, illegality, and revenues 261
    9.7 The façade of combating corruption 262
    9.8 Resource flow: upward or downward? 265
    Conclusion 267
    Notes 267

10   The U.S.A. military exit and a spectacular collapse   273

Introduction 273
10.1 International military intervention and state-building in post-
2001 Afghanistan: a self-defeating effort 276
10.2 The U.S.–Taliban deal: demoralising ANDSF and
undermining the already strained informal order 282
10.3 A gamble or horrid intention? The ethnicisation of the
security sector and collapse of central command—the case of
the Ministry of Interior 284
10.4 The networked state and statehood: a summary 285
10.5 Informal order and state survival: its relevance and
applicability 287
10.6 Theoretical considerations for understanding state and
international state-building 291
10.7 The end of an era: uncertainty and instability 293
Notes 294

Bibliography   297
Index   325

Tables

1.1	Distinction between political networks and political organisations	6
2.1	A typology of political networks and power resources	30
3.1	Afghan intra-jihadi war alliances	65
4.1	List of Ministry of Interior ministers (2001–2021)	86
4.2	The post-transitional authority government cabinet	105
5.1	Political networks in the Lower House	124
5.2	The December 2009 cabinet	134
6.1	First round of cabinet nominees	160
6.2	Second round cabinet nominees	162
7.1	The cost of elections in Afghanistan	193
7.2	United Nations and bilateral assistance for 2009 elections (US$ in millions)	193
7.3	Election turnout and fraudulent vote	194
8.1	Political network composition in the Lower House	218
8.2	Four rounds of votes for Speaker of the House	222
8.3	The timeline of events	224
8.4	List of parliamentary groups from 2010 to 2018	228
9.1	U.S. government aid to Afghanistan/amount in billions	241
9.2	Customs duties from imports (million Afghanis, BRT excluded)	245
9.3	Accounts due to the date of conservatorship from the main	248
9.4	Kroll Report: final allocation of the loan book and status of recoveries	249
9.5	Pamir airways beneficiaries	250
9.6	The Kabul Bank list of debtors	252
9.7	Projected and real net revenue contribution in US$, billion	254
9.8	Sample list of politically connected persons and their investments at the national level	255
9.9	Lapis mine in Badakhshan	258
9.10	Price list of MoI appointments (advance one-off payments)	265

Figures

2.1   Power dynamics of political networks and network effectiveness   36
2.2   Levels of engagement/interaction   37
4.1   Regional and provincial strongmen: a fragmented order   80
4.2   Ethnic composition of government bureaucracy at grade 3 (%)—2004   81
4.3   Ethnic composition of four top ministries at grade 3 (%)—2004   82
4.4   Afghanistan national army by ethnic group   82
4.5   Financial flow within the Ministry of Interior   87
4.6   Corruption chain with the Ministry of Interior—contractors   88
4.7   The seven strongmen of the South   97
5.1   The National Understanding Front of the Afghanistan Alliance   123
5.2   Ethnic composition of the Upper House   125
5.3   Political network alliances in 2009 elections   132
5.4   Political networks and their clientele   138
5.5   The cooperation council of political parties and coalitions of
      Afghanistan   144
5.6   The electoral union of the Afghanistan Alliance   145
5.7   The 2014 presidential election alliances   149
6.1   Ethnic composition of key administrative offices (in %)   163
6.2   Ethnic composition of embassies in Afghanistan   163
6.3   President Ghani's technocratic inner circle   164
6.4   Structure of the centre of government   167
7.1   Political network alliances in the 2019 elections   198
7.2   The ethno-regional voting map at provincial level (2019)   209
8.1   Composition of the House in 2018   220
9.1   Visualisation of resource flows (Graeme (2020))   243
9.2   Movement of funds to shareholders   247
9.3   A mapping of the smuggling chain   260
9.4   The circle of corruption and power   266
10.1 Informal order and political outcomes   288

Preface

"More questions?" Kohisaaf snapped. "Your team was here just three months ago. What benefit would your questions bring to me? The river is completely dry, and all our crops are destroyed. We have nothing to eat."

Looking straight into my eyes, Kohisaaf, a farmer in Yamchi village, claimed to be a little over 60 years old but had the deep lines and crevices of a man aged beyond his years by war and poverty. His piercing gaze conveyed a guarded suspicion, but with an undercurrent of kindness, perhaps because of the grandfatherly features carved into his virtuous face. His name, literally meaning *clear mountain*, also set a softer tone to our encounter, one that was at odds with the dry, barren hillside upon which Yamchi village was situated.

An ethnic-Uzbek region in the Sayyad district of Sar-i-Pul province in Northern Afghanistan, Yamchi village is surrounded by predominately *Lalmi* (rain-fed) agricultural land rising over a plain of terraced fields with a few patches of irrigated land on both sides of a seasonal river/stream. The village is home to roughly 100 families and was, at the time of my visit, a bastion of the *Junbish-i-Islami* political network, led by the famous ethnic-Uzbek strongman, Abdul Rashid Dostum. The signs of *Junbish* and its leader's enduring influence were everywhere. The district governor and several former militia commanders who occupied key positions in subnational administrations were Junbish affiliates. When my colleagues and I arrived there in September 2008, to conduct research for a livelihood and food insecurity project, Afghanistan was in the throes of one of its most devastating droughts since the 2001 international military intervention.

On that hot Sunday afternoon, I found myself taken aback by Kohisaaf's recent tribulations. It was mesmerising, and startling, to hear him articulate, in a broken Dari-Persian dialect, the details of his struggle. The family was in a persistent battle with poverty, always on the cusp of tumbling headlong into starvation. Yet despite his poverty, for the past six months he had stubbornly tried to secure his daughter's divorce from an abusive husband.

Kohisaaf spoke of how he had done his best to navigate the sometimes-twisted contours of the "official" government system, regularly bribing provincial judges and failing to comprehend the complex bureaucratic rules and procedures of the fledgling formal justice system. He felt cheated by almost every official he had dealt with. Overwhelmed by the formal system, he instead sought out the support of a distant kinship relation—a former *Junbish-i-Islami* commander in the neighbouring village—to help gain access to the *Junbish* political network and its leader Abdul Rashid Dostum. I will not forget the satisfaction on his face when he said, "while everything else failed, *Waseta* worked."

Waseta is an important informal institution in Afghan society, literally meaning "to connect," a traditional norm in which a person in a position of power or influence is beseeched to facilitate access due to solidarity along with kinship, friendship, or other relational lines. Kohisaaf's *Waseta* had borne fruit: he had secured a signed letter from the *Junbish-i-Islami* leader, Abdul Rashid Dostum himself, instructing the provincial court to assist him. Not surprisingly, Kohisaaf, being illiterate, did not know the content of the letter, but it had given him *access* to the provincial chief judge, a *Junbish* network client, who apparently had urgently worked on the case. Kohisaaf boasted how he had been carrying that letter with him everywhere to show off his connection and social standing.

In the eyes of villagers like Kohisaaf, local officials were first and foremost an extension of their kinship and local patronage system whose primary role was to connect them to the patronage of the Afghan state and international money. Political networks like *Junbish* invested earnestly in facilitating and delivering access to their constituencies for the purpose of legitimation, a model dating back to the jihad years of the 1980s and 1990s. In the highly informal and relationship-based structure of Afghan society, the more political networks generated access and distributed political resources to members and communities, the larger their *posturing* and bargaining power within the state. As this book will show, a political network's survival depends on its ability to provide *access* to power resources.

Indeed, the central role of networked relations and access went far beyond the prosaic demands of local villagers like Kohisaaf, reaching the highest echelons of the Afghan state. I realised this early on in my job as a deputy minister for policy and programme at the Independent Directorate of Local Governance where from May 2017 to September 2019 I observed first-hand how deeply the question of access had become entrenched in the Afghan polity. Anyone who had tapped into a place where power and resources resided soon became the target of *Waseta*-based pleas. And I was no exception.

On a February afternoon in 2018, I received a WhatsApp call from a friend. He was annoyed, and I could feel his frustration. At 3 pm, I was already exhausted and desperate to lie down on the sofa and close my eyes for a few minutes, knowing the working day would go much longer into the evening and night. The exhaustion was not the product of department-related work but the endless unannounced meetings with members of parliament, provincial council representatives, provincial and district officials, and tribal elders who would barge in with requests, demands, and problems—often illegitimate. These calls and meetings were not inquiries; they were clear demands for specific opportunities, or complaints ranging from acquiring access to ministers and the President's Office to getting someone appointed to a position, or caring for an anxious district governor who had hurried to Kabul seeking protection from a purported plot by a rival group. These requests were an everyday practice of *Waseta* that was ubiquitous at all levels of the government.

To many international officials who were working to strengthen Afghan state institutions, some of these requests carried the aroma of illegal demands, and even corruption. However, to many officials and leaders in the Afghan government, enabling *Waseta* was a crucial aspect of a legitimate position of authority and power. In Afghanistan, one's ability to facilitate access is a measure of social capital in a highly informal and *qawm*-based society structured by reciprocal relationships and collectivity, where the gains made by an individual are thought to also benefit their families and the broader community. As this book shows, a political node's networked relations, level of access to the broadest and dominant network in power, and quality of that access are the determining factors for his/her success, standing, and survival.

The friend calling me on WhatsApp was a senior government official who was running a technical commission. He had submitted his travel request letter for an official exchange visit abroad and other supporting documents to the President's Office of Administrative Affairs (OAA) more than two weeks earlier but hadn't heard back. When his office had followed up with the relevant department at the OAA, they had brushed him off saying they hadn't received the letter. This was not unusual; unbending and tedious administrative processes in a corrupt, dysfunctional, and bloated bureaucracy often result in the unequal and unjust treatment of public servants and officials. I called another friend, who was the deputy minister of OAA, for help.

He and I were members of a small technocratic network of young government colleagues—at its peak numbering around 30 civil servants—which functioned mostly as a protective umbrella group against pressure/schemes from members of parliament, rival politicians, and other civil servants. This colleague's stern inquiry over his staff's handling of the incident produced a swift result. By 8 pm, the letter was found and had been signed by the President.

Evidently, my WhatsApp friend was asking me to utilise my contact in the OAA to help him based on our *Andewali* relationship—a reciprocal relationship among friends/comrades with collective interests and responsibilities. *Andewali* had gained political relevance among Afghan networked elites and was considered a key governing rule with which one's political and reputational status was judged and political protection guaranteed. From my experience in the government, mastering the art of *Andewali* within one's political network, and the diverse web of political forces outside it, was key to surviving in the system. Failure to do so meant loss of political protection and eventual downfall. Playing by the *Andewali* rule was key to facilitating the widest political and social *access* to networked associates and constituencies within the Afghan state. This was especially important in the politicised post-2001 bureaucracy and relentless palace politics. Political figures with better access and connections to the upper echelons of power could survive by undermining his/her rival through misinformation, rumours, and manipulation of official reports.

Taken together, the two incidents described above—Kohisaaf's struggle to find justice for his daughter and my own experience in navigating the demands of *Andewali and Waseta*—reveal two important features of governance and statehood in post-2001 Afghanistan: the significance of informal politics and the central role of endogenous political networks like *Junbish*. On that hot afternoon in Yamchi village and in subsequent years through my professional work for the International Crisis Group and the Independent Directorate of Local Governance, I realised that one must go beneath the veneer of formal institutions (both political-cultural and political-economic) to understand the mode of governance in Afghanistan; to understand the last two decades of international intervention and statebuilding, one must examine the power dynamics of political networks and the informal institutional settings in which they operated. The informal cultural-political institutions of *Waseta* and *Andewali* discussed above are important everyday practices of endogenous political networks. As this book demonstrates, in Sar-i-Pul province and large parts of the country in the post-2001 international intervention, power flowed through and was exercised by loosely structured and network-like organisations and their associates, capturing and penetrating formal state institutions and societal structures. Analysing the conflict and competition among rival political networks over the control of the Afghan state and international resources (e.g., political, military, financial) offers us a more nuanced picture of international intervention and statehood.

The two stories also imply a vexing conundrum: how was the post-2001 to August 2021 political order, or at least the façade of an order, maintained when state institutions were so weak and fragmented and struggling to provide basic services for their citizens? One obvious answer was the presence of international coalition forces, which guaranteed political order. Yet, in large areas, such as the Sayyad district of Sari-Pul province, international military forces had virtually no noticeable presence. While this explanation may be partially valid, it does not fully explain how and why the post-2001 Afghan state somehow maintained the illusion of political order and stability despite failing with respect to all criteria of a Westphalian state. Nor does the withdrawal of U.S. troops in itself fully explain the collapse of the Republic in August 2021.

Instead, as this book demonstrates, political networks led by individuals like Abdul Rashid Dostum and their associates who came to constitute the post-2001 state were effective in *performing* as the state through the informal institutions of Waseta, Andewali, and patronage, among others, thus producing the façade of political order. That is, at its core, what this book is about: the last two decades of U.S.-led NATO military and political intervention and the hitherto ignored role of endogenous political networks and their impacts on statebuilding, political order, and violence up until the fall of Kabul in August 2021. It dissects what the international community and the local endogenous political networks and leaders in power got wrong and how, after two decades of military intervention, Afghanistan came full circle, with another Taliban takeover of the country and the near-collapse of the state. In tracing that trajectory, this book addresses three principal research objectives: (a) to investigate the role and power dynamics of political networks and their associates in re-assembling and transforming the Afghan state following the 2001 Bonn political settlement with the help of international militaries and donors; (b) to analyse how everyday political network *institutions* (rules of the game) shaped the nature of statehood and governance; and (c) subsequently, how these power dynamics and informal institutions contributed towards political order/violence and state survival/collapse. As this book shows, informal order was fashioned through and within resource interdependencies among political networks and their day-to-day practices of rent-seeking, coercion, illegality, and instrumentalisation of ethnic identities.

Theoretically, this book offers a network lens through which to analyse international statebuilding and state formation. Its proposed *political network approach* to understanding conflict management and statebuilding differs from the dominant analysis of politics and statehood, which looks at the roles and behaviours of elites and identity-based divisions. Instead, it brings the focus to the networked *character* of governance and statehood. It provides a nuanced explanation for political order and state survival for post-conflict and fragile contexts. This book speaks to three general fields of study: organisation theories and political network studies, political economy of the state, and international statebuilding. Most statebuilding, conflict management, and state formation literatures would acknowledge the existence of political networks but see these as an end—the progressive accumulation of national sovereignty by a hierarchical organisation (the state). They also generally treat networks as a residue of state and civil society rather than an enduring and co-constitutive part of the state formation process. This book brings the *network* aspects of governance and *networked analysis approach* into the fold of state formation and statebuilding literature.

This study draws on my extensive ethnographic fieldwork and hundreds of interviews over several years—first for my PhD thesis from 2010 to the end of 2013 and then while working for several international organisations, including the International Crisis Group as a Policy Analyst for Afghanistan. It also draws on my public service experience at the Independent Directorate of Local Governance (IDLG) from May 2017 to September 2019. The IDLG was positioned strategically between the president's office and over 30 ministries and general directorates in the Afghan government, offering substantial access to formal and informal information as well as granular picture of day-to-day governance across Afghanistan. The stakeholders I interacted with represented a vast network of government officials and politicians including 34 provincial governor's offices, 385 plus district governors' offices, over 450 provincial council members, and many informal community councils and leaders.

This book is structured as follows. The first two chapters (Chapters 1 and 2) develop the book's analytical framework by highlighting the central role of endogenous political networks and the *networked mode* of governance in fragile and post-conflict settings. The introduction (Chapter 1) situates the book's key arguments within the broader literature on network theory, organisational studies, new institutional theory, and international statebuilding. It discusses the key contributing features to the emergence of networked governance in post-2001 Afghanistan and sets out the *political network approach* as the best analytical tool to understand statehood in Afghanistan and other post-conflict and fragile settings. Chapter 2 theorises the relationship between endogenous political networks, the state and informal orders at the intersection of violence, identity politics, patronage, and illegality. It examines and explains the central role of political networks in state formation and statebuilding once a political settlement is reached and their power resources interdependencies in constituting an informal order.

Chapter 3 offers a historical perspective on the origins and evolution of political networks since the 1960s to show how they have evolved over the decades in shaping political order and violence in Afghanistan, including the impact of the two international military interventions: the Soviet Union in the 1980s and the post-2001 U.S.-led NATO military engagement. It demonstrates that most of the key features of statehood and emerging informal institutions (rules of the game) surfaced in the last decades of violence and war economy, on which post-2001 intervention was built and expanded. The next three chapters (Chapters 4, 5, and 6) then map and detail key events, alliances, moments of rupture from December 2001 to August 2021, and their impact on political order.

Chapter 4 details some of the key events and power dynamics of political networks over the control of the Afghan state, including its bureaucracy, army, and police from 2001 to 2004. Chapter 5 demonstrates the consolidation of power by Karzai and his Western educated clients within the state and beyond, which brokered a degree of political stability and order in their interests from the 2004 to 2014 presidential elections. Chapter 6 investigates the shifting power dynamics and tensions during the National Unity Government (2014–2020), President Ghani's divisive policies, and the continuous political crises that surrounded the Afghan state, which at several times nearly brought the country to the brink of collapse.

The following three chapters (Chapters 7, 8, and 9) then expose the day-to-day operation and strategies of political networks by looking at informal institutions of patronage, rent-seeking and opportunism, coercion, and manipulation of Afghanistan's identity-based divisions. Chapter 7 and 8 therefore demonstrate how these strategies became operational through specific moments of contestation and crisis, the four presidential elections (2004, 2009, 2014, and 2019), and the 2010–2011 parliamentary crisis. Chapter 7 shows how competing political networks mobilised their power resources, including discursive, political, and financial resources, to win elections and how elections became another opportunity to renegotiate a political settlement over the control of the state. Chapter 8 demonstrates how the Lower House emerged as the principal "political marketplace" and a platform for alliance-building, where access to national and international power resources (e.g., political, military, and financial) and patronage for political networks and their associates was determined. Chapter 9 highlights the networked practices of illegality, rent-seeking, and everyday corruption by looking at several cases: the Kabul Bank Ponzi scheme and corruption within customs departments, and illegality and profiteering in the extractive industries, namely chromite, timber, and lapis lazuli. It also analyses the impact of international money, including military spending and aid, and its use as a "weapon system" in exacerbating corruption and shaping incentives and behaviours of political networks and Afghan elites.

The concluding chapter (Chapter 10) discusses some of the key factors for the collapse of the Afghan Republic on 15 August 2021. Among other factors, it argues that the hasty U.S.–Taliban exit deal set in motion the rapid breakdown of the fragile informal order among political networks within the state. The increasingly "performative" aspect of political networks by the end of 2020 had made the Afghan state so hollow that when the pressure of U.S. withdrawal was applied, it crumbled like a house of cards. The second part of the chapter explores some of the implications that stem from the theoretical arguments and empirical findings of this book relevant to other fragile and post-conflict settings, while cautioning against making major assertions and encouraging additional studies.

1 Introduction

The 11 September 2001 terrorist attacks in the U.S.A. triggered an international military intervention in Afghanistan, with the backing of over 40 North Atlantic Treaty Organisation (NATO) countries, to overthrow the Taliban, the group that had harboured and aided al-Qaeda. There was overwhelming domestic support within the U.S.A. for a military response to the attacks.[1] As one senior UN official noted, the Bush Administration was keen to have its "fireworks display" to demonstrate to the public that they were taking decisive and robust action.[2]

Certainly, the "War on Terror" carried a strong ideological motivation, influenced by neo-conservatives, and Afghanistan provided an excellent opportunity to "lead a global war of good against evil."[3] Matched against that kind of grandiose rhetoric, however, the scale of the intervention was modest. The military operation, named "Operation Enduring Freedom," was carried out by the Central Intelligence Agency (CIA) and a small deployment of U.S. Special Forces fighting alongside the Northern Alliance (NA, or "Ettihad-i-Shamal") units—a loose coalition of anti-Taliban jihadi *tanzims*, regional strongmen, and militia commanders who had fought one another during the civil war of 1992–1996. The Bush Administration did, of course, get its fireworks in the form of a rapid air bombing campaign.

With the sudden defeat of the Taliban at the end of November, international donors also opted for a "light footprint" approach to peacebuilding; the result was the deployment of a small International Security Assistance Force (ISAF) to Kabul.[4] However, by 2005 the Taliban were back as an insurgency group and the international military involvement quickly grew to an intrusive, long-lasting, and costly mission. At its peak in 2009, it fielded approximately 140,000 international coalition troops on the ground with over 800 military bases of various sizes scattered across the country. Within a few years, what had started as an easy military win devolved into a seemingly interactable struggle with statebuilding and counterinsurgency. Ultimately, two decades later, Afghanistan came full circle, with another Taliban seizure of the country and yet another near collapse of the state.

The journey to that ignominious end arguably began on 5 December 2001, when the international community and the four main Afghan political groupings concluded the Bonn Agreement (officially the Agreement on Provincial Arrangements in Afghanistan Pending the Re-Establishment of Permanent

DOI: 10.4324/9781315161617-1

Government Institutions), a political framework under UN auspices for the re-building of a unitary state in Afghanistan. It set in motion a four-year political process that included the holding of an emergency *Loya Jirga* (grand council) in June 2002 to elect an interim president who would lead a transitional government which in turn would ratify a new constitution in 2003. This would then be fol-lowed by a presidential election in October 2004 and legislative elections a year later. It seemed straightforward enough on paper: by 2005, Afghanistan would have all the trappings of Western-style democracy, complete with a president, a legislature, and a bureaucracy to run it all. The only question was: who would be the powerbrokers and how would their power dynamics shape the future of the Afghan state?

The leading political force at the time was the collection of Northern Alliance jihadis, followed by a hastily assembled batch of Western technocrats associated with the former king, Zahir Shah, referred to as the Rome group. Both the NA and Rome group would come to play leading roles in constituting the Afghan state. The other two, relatively minor, factions were the Peshawar and Cyprus groups associated with Sayed Ahmad Gilani and Humayoun Jareer, respectively, who many believed were included to please Afghanistan's neighbours, in particular Iran and Pakistan. The Rome group was chosen to balance and represent Western interests, while the NA was essentially at the table because they had been effective military partners for the U.S.A.; their battlefield victory against the Taliban, in no small part facilitated by American air support, gave them their legitimacy.

What transpired over the subsequent years of international intervention and statebuilding in Afghanistan is best understood in the context of the continui-ties and changes in power dynamics of these political groups, and their competi-tion and conflict over the control of state power resources. While the 2001 Bonn Agreement offered a framework for conflict management, pact-making, and re-negotiation to end hostilities among warring factions, it failed in some key respects. As Chapter 4 shows, the Conference became yet another high-level, internationally mediated, and ill-conceived settlement, one of several since 1987. It fell short of resolving the root causes of conflict, including the political groups' deep-rooted distrust of each other, and lacked any discernible strategy to overcome the logic of ethno-regional solidarity and networked governance that plagued Afghanistan.[5] Instead, through a grand power-sharing bargain conducted at Bonn, the former jihadi *tanzim* leaders, strongmen, and militia commanders who had assisted in temporarily defeating the Taliban and who possessed the nec-essary coercive organisational capacities, were handed the task of re-assembling and constituting the state and establishing the interim government, which only enabled them to further consolidate their power and gain access to state resources.

But before we can deconstruct how these dynamics operated and contributed to the eventual collapse of the Afghan state, we must first define the analyti-cal tools required. Firstly, I situate the discussion on political networks (Section 1.1) within the broader literature on network theory, organisational studies, new institutional theory, and international statebuilding and offer a conceptualisa-tion of political networks. This is followed by a discussion on *networked politics*

(Section 1.2) as a new and dominant mode of governance in post-2001 statebuilding. Section 1.3 details the key factors contributing to networked politics in post-2001 Afghanistan.

Central to this analysis, much overlooked in statebuilding literature, is the co-constitutive and networked *character* of international statebuilding and state formation as discussed in Sections 1.4 and 1.5. Section 1.6 outlines a more nuanced explanation for the political order in terms of the role and power dynamics of political networks within the state. It then provides a historical account of the political order in modern Afghanistan since its formation in 1747.

1.1 What are political networks?

Situating this work in the theoretical framework of the diverse and fast-expanding literature in organisational studies, new institutional theory, and international statebuilding requires some conceptual clarification.[6] While the studies of social and policy networks have developed over the last half-century, there has been little—and no explicit—attention to the networked structure of political organisations, especially in conflict management, international statebuilding, and state formation studies.

In the broader literature on networks, one can identify two dominant conceptualisations of their utility: network-as-relations and network-as-governance. The network-as-relations approach focuses mainly on individual-level relationships and the structure of these relationships within the network. Early anthropologists explored how individuals and groups were linked and how their relational characteristics affected social outcomes, using such concepts as positions, density, centrality, and links. In the 1990s, sociological studies broadened the focus from a concern with individual relationships among actors to the structural characteristics of networks, introducing concepts such as "structural holes," "social capital," "brokerage," and "enclosure."[7] For instance, the term "network" was used to explain how elites occupy important positions within organisations, how this promotes or hinders access to political and economic opportunities, and how agencies coordinate and integrate their activities for better outcomes.

Recent studies in public policy and management, organisation theory, and international relations have employed the concept of the network as a mechanism of coordination and mode of governance, or what has often been referred to as *networked governance*, and bring our attention to the collaborative aspect of networks.[8] Network-as-governance considers networks to be alternative modes of operation between the Weberian hierarchical state and neoliberal theories of delivering public services through private markets. Networks are treated as units of analysis. In one of the early influential papers in economic sociology, Powell questioned the conceptualisation of the network as a hybrid of market and hierarchy, arguing that networks are distinctive forms of coordinated economic activity.[9] As he noted, it would appear less useful in the 21st century to compare hierarchy and network when hierarchies look less like organisations at this time of emerging bureaucratic organisations.

In a pioneering work on organisational networks, Rhodes asserted that as a form of governance, these networks are replacing traditional hierarchical structures as the task of governing is carried out by flexible, diverse, self-organising, and self-regulating inter-organisational networks.[10] In international relations, for instance, scholars have shown that complex transgovernmental networks of central bankers, government ministers, judges, and legislators are laying the foundation for a complementary world order alongside official global institutions such as the United Nations, the World Bank, and the International Monetary Fund (IMF) to improve coordination and address complex challenges.

This book builds on these network-as-governance studies in conceptualising political networks in state formation and statebuilding. It focuses explicitly on *network structures* and their power resource dynamics rather than individual-level connections and relationships. Political networks are characterised as *distinct open-hierarchical structures whose members are reliant on one another's power resources for political outcomes in an informally structured and continuously renegotiated arrangement*. In its simplest form, a political network is comprised of: (1) a group of actors, (2) actors who are connected by a set of relations (links and ties), and (3) actors who are (inter)dependent on each other's power resources, which facilitate their collaboration. An individual can simultaneously be part of different types of networks (e.g., commercial networks, ethnic solidarity networks, etc.) and utilise them differently depending on their ability to foster a variety of pathways to power resources at any given time. Political networks are goal-directed structures where, as noted by Lake and Wong, members within the network formulate and make utility-improving choices. For members, alternative outcomes have distributional implications, favouring some over others, and members vary in the power or influence that they possess.[11] Political networks are self-organising entities. As Knoke has argued, power in a political network is inherently "relational" and "situational."[12] The nature of power resource dependency can change within a new dynamic and arrangement. An individual's relationships and power within the network can change depending on the nature of the bargains being made among networks within the state at any given time. Also, as shown historically, the goal of a network may change over time; for example, a political network may evolve into a trading network. This appears to be the case with Afghanistan's communists after their relocation to the former USSR.[13]

In fragile and conflict settings like Afghanistan, the organisational theory of group conflict is useful to consider in further advancing the conceptualisation of political networks in statebuilding and state formation. As argued by Abdulkader Sinno in his ground-breaking work on *Organisations at war*, tribes, ethnic groups, social classes, religions, and nations do not engage in conflict or strategic interaction—but organisations do.[14] Historically, it is organisations and their different types of structures (specifically the ones with a relatively hierarchical and decentralised distribution of power) that have shaped and underpinned conflict, state formation, political order, and violence. When Charles Tilly discusses war making and state making in 16th- and 17th-century Europe, he simply infers that organisations that possess the capacity to organise means of violence have facilitated and transformed the formation of nation-states. Twentieth-century resistance and ideological revolutionary groups (e.g., Mao's decentralised guerrilla fighters who later set up one of the most centralised communist parties in history, the Muslim Brotherhood in Egypt, Afghan jihadi *tanzims* fighting against the Soviet invasion) were able to coordinate masses and fighters and mobilise resources not as shapeless ethnic groups or civilisations, but as organisations. Once the war ends, following, say, a power-sharing agreement, it is these organisations that come to compose and transform the post-conflict state and international statebuilding.

In post-2001 Afghanistan, the warring jihadi *tanzims* and strongmen, as decentralised network-like organisations in terms of their institutional arrangements, patterns of exchange, flows of resources, and reciprocal lines of information, came to constitute the Afghan state. During the Soviet resistance, jihadi *tanzims*—except Hizb-i-Islami—were hybrid forms of networks and hierarchies as they were hierarchically structured around a strong leader. In post-2001 Afghanistan, they further splintered into smaller networks. Simultaneously, newly established networks among Afghan expat technocrats, civil society groups, and politician-*cum*-business networks surfaced—empowered by international intervention and statebuilding. The state then became the field within which they contested, competed, and negotiated, underpinning order/disorder and stability/violence (discussed below).

Political networks in statebuilding enjoy several features that distinguish them from traditional political organisations. First, political networks are managed differently in terms of the form and direction of the flow of authority.[15] In a conventional understanding of the political organisation, planning, designing, and leading are centrally controlled by and through a clear command and control structure. In political networks, power and authority are dispersed in hybrid forms (vertical and horizontal) and may not necessarily flow through a precise command and control mechanism. Authority in a political network is collective even though a charismatic leader or several key "structural nodes" might enjoy greater power than others. In a political network, a single central authority, a hierarchical ordering, and a single organisational goal do not exist. There are often several central nodes/actors who sit in positions of extensive opportunity which provides them with greater access to knowledge, financial resources, and authority. Political networks in statebuilding are fluid entities, and membership fluctuates as events unfold, moments of rent-seeking arise, and crises occur; however, they generally present themselves as unitary actors in political arenas. The task of a leader(s) is to *guide* interactions and collaborations, manage the rules of the game, direct resources, and arbitrate conflicts and disputes. Moreover, any one central node has as much authority as the network members allow him or her to possess.

Second, as Mark Granovetter posits in his path-breaking thesis, "The Strength of the Weak Ties," political networks enjoy a higher degree of information-sharing capacity than organisations, enabling them to translate decisions quickly into actions.[16] Loose-knit networks, Granovetter argues, have greater resource-gathering potential for the individual than close-knit networks, because weak ties facilitate the flow of information from otherwise distant parts of a network and help integrate social systems within the network. Some studies have shown that information passing through networks is "thicker" than that obtained from the market and organisations.[17] Networked structures enable members to access information more quickly as shared sources, available to all. Therefore, Afghanistan is one of those societies where information moves most freely.

Third, entry into and exit out of a political network are much easier—determined by the actors themselves rather than mandated by any "higher" authority. Even those faced with some degree of sanctions can exit with little reputational cost. Those with strong connections within a network are likely to feel obligated to stay, whereas someone with weak ties is less likely to feel indebted to stay.

This flexibility, fluidity, and constantly renegotiated arrangement of political networks in post-2001 Afghanistan was their strength as long as domestic and international resources (e.g., political, military, and financial) flows continued. A political actor's strategy of diversifying connections across multiple networks allowed him/her to maximise access and keep exit options open and obligations weak, with little investment in a high-risk and volatile situation. In post-2001 Afghanistan where uncertainty was high, this meant that political networks and their clients' decisions were often governed by shorter time horizons, quick gains, and a mentality favouring low investment. The loose structure of these networks and ability to exit without much personal cost meant that from May 2021, especially when it became clear that President Biden was no longer going to commit U.S. troop presence in Afghanistan, political networks' clients, especially those at the local level, began shifting their allegiance from their patrons and the Republic to the Taliban, sensing the change in the political wind. Evidently as discussed in the concluding chapter, this was one of the key contributing factors to the rapid collapse of the Republic (Table 1.1).

Table 1.1 Distinction between political networks and political organisations

	Political organisations	*Political networks*
Organisational settings	Single-authority structure Exit incurs a significant cost for an individual	A hybrid form of hierarchy and networks Divided authority structure Interdependency Easier exit
Goal structure	Activities are guided by clear goals and well-defined interests	Various as well as a diverse set of goals and interests
Authority	Hierarchical Clear command and control structure Higher efficiency	Dispersed authority Hybrid authority (vertical and horizontal): mediators and powerbrokers Trust and reciprocal relations
Management	Centralised planning and guidance	Co-managing and co-steering Bargaining
Flow of information	Built-in mechanisms of hierarchical information sharing Subject to manipulation	Higher information-sharing capacities. "Thicker" information The strength of weak ties

1.2 Networked politics: a new mode of governance

Most studies on Afghanistan have examined governance and statehood from the narrow lens of elites and their dynamics, identity differences, strongman/warlord power struggles, and patronage politics. While these are important, this book argues that in post-2001 Afghanistan, they are in fact different features of *networked politics* and it is vital to understand the relationships *between* them if one is to understand the shifting geographies of power and governance.

But first, before we move on to the intricacies of their mutually reinforcing relationships and how they come together to foster and reinforce networked politics, we must define what these features are in the Afghan context.

1.2.1 Elite politics and settlement

Influenced by Field, Higley, and Burton's elite paradigm framework, most endogenous indicators for studies of Afghan conflict in the 1980s and 1990s were fixated on factionalism within the communist party, the failure of political elite settlement among jihadi *tanzims*, and the role of spoilers. Field, Higley, and Burton theorised that the examination of national elite structure and transformations are fundamental to explaining patterns of stability and regime outcome. Field and Higley understood elites as:

> People [who are] able, through their positions in powerful organisations, to affect national political outcomes individually, regularly, and seriously. National elites can be said to encompass all those persons capable, if they wish, of making substantial political trouble for high officials (i.e., other elite persons who happen to be incumbents of authoritative positions) without being promptly repressed.[18]

Drawing on Burton and Higley's (1987) categorisation of elite groups (ideologically unified, consensually unified, and disunified), most studies of Afghanistan in the 1980s focused on elite behaviour and elite factionalism to explain the survivability of the communist regime and the continuous failure of political elite settlements for the bloody civil war that followed the collapse of the communist regime.[19]

In the 1990s, the discussion further reduced the dynamics of Afghan politics to the role of elites as "warlords," "strongmen," "militia commanders" or "regional powerbrokers" and to their predatory and "spoiler" behaviour. Others argued for the establishment of strong state institutions that could contain inter-elite competition.[20] Some highlighted that the elite bargain policy pursued by international donors, rather than democratisation as the means through which the spoils of the state were divided, had sustained political order.[21] This study contends that Afghanistan's last four decades of violence and conflict cannot be reduced to an analysis of elites and their orientation for or against an internationally mediated political settlement. It proposes that elites in conflict-driven countries such as Afghanistan must be analysed first and foremost in terms of their political net-works and the hybrid authority structure that these networks represent.

1.2.2 Strongman politics/warlord politics

Since the 1992 collapse of the communist regime and fragmentation of the Afghan state, scholars have brought our attention to the emergence of *warlord politics/strongmen politics*, as the dominant mode of governance in the face of a fragile state, whose greedy and disruptive behaviours, they argued, should be kept in check.[22] As dis-cussed in more detail in Chapter 3, the Afghan jihad against the Soviets produced strong military field commanders inside Afghanistan arrayed against weak political leaders in exile in Pakistan and Iran. Conventional studies have focused on two fea-tures of warlords: (1) bad guys boycotting and spoiling the peace process and under-mining the establishment of a legitimate central state and (2) strongmen motivated by economic profit and enrichment. They are often described as "thugs," "globalised gangsters," "viruses," or "spoilers" of state legitimacy, peace, and statebuilding.[23]

Some recent studies, however, have departed from the traditional understand-ing of strongmen. For instance, Charles King defines warlords/strongmen as "armed agents who wield some degree of civil power and claim some kind of local sovereignty over a defined region while paying allegiance to stronger powers."[24] In post-2001 Afghanistan, as shown by Malejacq, Mukhopadhyay, and Giustozzi, strongmen are an integral part of the state, where they help build bureaucratic institutions in compliance with liberal and democratic processes and deliver ser-vices.[25] These authors conceive of strongmen as "violent political entrepreneurs" and "warlords as bureaucrats" with proven records of building the essentials of the state structure at the periphery, essentially functioning as "state-builders."

There is the linguistic issue surrounding the use of the term "warlord" and its history arising from external intervention in Afghanistan. The term warlord ("Jang Salar") found its way into Afghan political rhetoric through international media and policymakers.[26] Historically and in the daily lives of people, the word "com-mander" was more commonly used. It is also worth noting that the term "warlord" was mainly used by returning expat technocrats as a way of delegitimising people with jihadi backgrounds. One could also argue that the Pakistani spy agency, Inter-Service Intelligence (ISI), played a role in the 1990s in the construction and dis-semination of the term as a foil to their faction of choice, the Taliban. Considering the baggage that comes with it, I avoid using the term "warlord" altogether and instead conceive of them as *strongmen* to reduce the negative burden of the term.

The post-2001 notion of strongmen in Afghanistan must be analysed in its entirety, in terms of the networked structure and power resource dynamics within which it operates. Strongmen-based networks are just one type of political network with links to subnational and national-level network dynamics. Like the rest of the political networks, they do not simply engage in extortion and revenue generation for the sake of personal gains but also reinforce their position through awards, distribution, and patronage to the families and communities they control to maintain legitimacy and expand their allies. They are immersed in the fabric of Afghan society and polity.

1.2.3 *Identity politics*

In the words of one Afghan scholar, Afghanistan is a country of "micro-socie-ties."[27] Over the last four decades, its acutely divided social structures have been further fractured by armed conflict, which has deepened ethno-regional and kin-ship-based solidarities. At numerous moments in Afghanistan's recent history, identity groups have become crystalised, at certain moments, like a powerful "compelling reality" in the words of Brubaker and Cooper.[28]

During the civil war, the jihadi *tanzims* were able to utilise tribal, linguistic, religious, and ethnic markers to consolidate their power.[29] These scholars have argued that the Afghan conflict was not originally ethnic or even ethno-regional but a struggle over control of the state by competing for factional elites. The intense civil war of the 1990s and its violent consequences—the Ittihad and Jamiat's massacre of ethnic Hazaras in Kabul's Afshar neighbourhood in 1994, the Junbish massacre of the Taliban in Mazar-i-Sharif in 1997, and the Taliban massacres of Hazaras in 1998 in the same city—created conditions proximate to an "ethnic security dilemma," as termed by Kaufmann.[30] It produced a powerful and complex bond and symbiotic relationship between jihadi *tanzims* and ethnic and tribal communities that utilised ethnicity to further consolidate their political position in Afghan polity. In such conditions, the appeal of ethnic elites increased conflict further and accentuated ethnic affiliations as the two together provided a rationale for the perpetuation of ethnic divisions.

However, far from resolving ethnic divisions, the post-Bonn process—under conditions of increased external resourcing of the state, inter-elite battles for the state, and a growing Taliban insurgency—provided the basis for the extension of these divisions to the population.[31] In post-2001 Afghanistan, although ethnic and sub-ethnic divisions have a long history, the present levels or scales and functional imperatives are closely related to political networks and their power dynamics within the state. As Ibrahimi has argued, the Afghan state historically has been the chief source for elevating ethnic identities over other categories of social division and boundaries.[32] The empirical chapters in this book (see Chapters 7 and 8) show that manipulation of these divisive identities by competing political networks is a means to guarantee political legitimacy among the population and cover up illegality and rent-seeking practices. Political network competition over the state and international statebuilding resources has become the main driving force for the politicisation of identities, particularly ethnicity. However, it's important to recognise that these modern divisions are borne of networked politics and popular responses to the 40 years of the Afghan war and violence.

1.2.4 *Patronage politics*

Patronage has been a key feature of Afghanistan's modern state formation. Historically, patron-client relationships have persistently helped shape and trans-form the Afghan state, and these have in turn been shaped by their involvement in this process.[33] Patron-client relations take the form of patterns of interactions, in which selective benefits are distributed to individuals or groups in exchange for loyalty or political support, not limited to the electoral process. Scott reveals that this relationship is dyadic and characterised by unequal status, reciprocity, and personal contact arranged hierarchically.[34] As shown by Afghan scholars, patronage in Afghanistan involves complex socio-cultural, political, and economic networks of exchange and association. Shahrani observed that the patron-client relationship emerged from Afghanistan's societal conception of the politics of difference—whether familial, local, regional, tribal, ethnic, or national—structured mainly by the principles of segmentary opposition and ties of patronage between leaders and followers.[35] The ties of loyalty and responsibility are in constant negotiation. The full range of alliances and oppositions were often contingent upon the shifting boundaries of the community in the changing context of various factional struggles within or between contending groups. Maley has described the post-2001 system as a neo-patrimonial political system because it combines formal constitutional and bureaucratic structures with highly personalised patterns of the exercise of power by the political leader.[36] He goes on to argue that such systems are neither purely patrimonial nor purely bureaucratic; it is the entanglement of features of both that gives the neo-patrimonial system its distinctive character.

In post-2001 Afghanistan defined by international statebuilding, patronage continued but its nature and the level of operation were closely combined and interlinked with political networks. It was an everyday practice of networked politics which helped sustain political order; patronage-based networks were one topology of political networks. As such, the post-2001 state can best be seen as a *networked state* where competing political networks were bound to one another in a complex system of resource interdependencies that flowed in multiple directions—not necessarily vertical or top-down, as they often do in neo-patrimonial systems. In Afghanistan, middle-ranking associates within a political network and community elders/tribal elders often obligated and pressured national leaders in Kabul to adopt a particular policy direction or to make appointments that preserved their interests, not necessarily the interests of the national leader(s). As Sarah Chayes pointed out in her book *Thieves of the State*, Karzai was not always distributing money and privileges downwards to buy off potential political rivals. If anything, the reverse was true. Subordinate officials in the network were paying off Karzai or his inner network to secure (1) permission to extract resources for personal gains and (2) protection from repercussions.[37] As part of his network, Karzai's associates could pressure him just as much or more than he could pressure them, utilising different means, including illegality, to control as many power resources as possible for the purpose of redistribution across the network.

As the empirical chapters demonstrate, the most important beneficiary within the network is often not the *leader(s)* but middle-ranking members and power-brokers with the greatest degree of access within the state and society. Unlike the neopatrimonialism description of the state where one or a few select hierarchical leaders are in a position of state resource distribution, in post-2001 Afghanistan the relations, power dynamics, and flow of resources were complex and less hierarchical. It was the power interdependencies within and among political networks that fashioned political order and violence, not the distribution of resources.

1.2.5 Networked politics

All of the features discussed above converged on the nexus of post-2001 Afghan formal and informal politics to empower the political networks that became co-constitutive in statebuilding. Networked politics became the dominant form of governance and the basis for legitimacy. Power flowed through political networks in its daily operation within the machinery of the state, penetrating and transforming institutions, structures, and processes. As such, elites and regional strongmen should be understood within the network-like political structure that they operated in and the power resource interdependency relations that bound them, rather than as autonomous interlocutors who either worked for or against the international statebuilding enterprise. In post-2001 Afghanistan, patronage and identity politics were everyday informal practices, or everyday rules of the game, within which political networks operated to accumulate and mobilise resources, strategise against opponents, and gear up ethnic and tribal support to cover their illegality and criminality. As this work shows, political network competitions and conflict over resources became the main driving force for the politicisation of identities—ethnic, ethno-regional, and tribal—and the application of patronage and opportunistic practices. These divisions were exacerbated by worsening violence and an expanding insurgency.

More broadly, networked politics is an all-encompassing mode of governance through which we can comprehensively understand politics and statehood in post-2001 statebuilding. As post-Bonn international statebuilding attempted to build the modern Afghan state, it concomitantly consolidated and expanded the power of political networks within the state. The power dynamics of political networks, their resource interdependencies, and their day-to-day practices of politicisation of identities and patronage along with ethnicity and tribal lines produced a mutually reinforcing alternative form of politics, *networked politics*, as discussed above and in more detail in Chapter 2. Informal institutions such as illegality and opportunism were not mere "shadows," "informal," or "extra-legal" as suggested by some.[38] As this book uncovers, these were everyday practices applied by political networks which were fundamental to state survival and the production of a complex political order, or at least the façade of it in post-2001 Afghanistan.

A focus on networked politics offers an alternative analytical approach, a *political network approach*, to understand post-2001 Afghan statehood and its international statebuilding efforts, a more nuanced way to account for everyday politics and practices that often go unexamined. Such an approach enables us to go beyond the methodological constraints which limit power politics to dichotomies of state-society, visibility-invisibility, formal-informal, and public-private. It helps us to better understand how diverse types of networks create a web of politicians, insurgents, drug traffickers, arms smugglers, and local powerbrokers and in the process underpin and transform the post-conflict state, its political order, and even the nature of violence. A political network approach to state formation and statebuilding offers two conceptual shifts in the literature: (1) from the institutional and structural effect to the co-constitutive and informal *networked character* and (2) from the behavioural aspects of state formation and statebuilding to its daily *performance* and its effectiveness. Network effectiveness is critical for our understanding of the power dynamics of political networks and their impact on the post-2001 state. Finally, an analysis of political networks requires exploring not only the power relations and practices *within* and *among* competing political networks but also their *links* to local communities. Political networks are, after all, embedded in social contexts that they claim to represent (or manipulate).

1.3   What contributed to networked politics?

Afghanistan's networked politics emerged and was reinforced by the confluence of several factors that are both cultural-political and political-economic. As the case of Kohisaaf in the Preface of this book highlighted, the highly informal, personal, and relationship-based structure of Afghan society and polity is one of the key contributing factors to networked politics. Most Afghans belong to an extended, kinship-based solidarity group known as *qawm*, characterised by multi-faceted ways in which people identify with groups. It is commonly used to refer to any segment of society bound by close ties. Ordinary Afghans use the concept of *qawm* as a mark of distinction vis-à-vis outsiders; it designates solidarity groups of varying sizes (e.g., ethnic group, tribe, kinship network, and even the residents of a particular village and sub-district).[39] It can signify different meanings in different contexts; it can, for instance, even affect researchers and academics, depending on the social/spatial distance between the informant and the person posing questions. In the local context, it can be used to distinguish residents of a village or tribe, but at the national level, it can draw the boundaries between the major ethnic groups of the country. Like any solidarity-based bonding, this produces a degree of *reciprocity* and ensures some level of protection from the advances of the state and other *qawms*.

The second contributing factor to networked politics is the provision of much-needed informal *access* to resources, especially those of the state. Informal access is intertwined and regulated by the norms of reciprocity and obligation. That is why *Waseta*, as discussed in the Preface, is an important informal institution in Afghan societal and political consciousness for facilitating informal access. *Waseta*, as an informal institution, compels people in a position of power and influence to support a relative or a *qawm* member—for instance, in securing a job for a relative, or obtaining an ID card without going through the lengthy bureaucratic and corrupt procedures, or securing a visa for a sick family member for treatment abroad, or leaking company information to a *qawm* member so he/she can win a contract. Here, Pierre Bourdieu's conception of social capital is useful. Unlike Nan Lin, who narrowly defines social capital as the quantity and/or quality of resources that an actor can access or use and its location in a social network,[40] Bourdieu's conceptualisation can be expanded to include other forms of capital/

resources based on the availability and diversity of power—political, economic, coercive, and social. In his view, social capital is about the actual and potential benefits that an individual can gain from the networks they belong to.[41] Ribot and Peluso's definition of *access* is useful: "the *ability* to derive benefits from things— including material objects, persons, institutions, and symbols" in which access is seen as "bundles of powers," interwoven within webs of power sources made up of different material, cultural, political, and economic strands.[42] In Afghanistan, the informal institution of *Waseta* has reinforced a "guilt society" in which the inability to reciprocate might lead to community rejection and in some cases even shame. Access and Waseta are dominant social and political currencies, which help determine an individual's status and position within society and polity.

That is why political networks within the state have invested heavily in facilitating and delivering access to members and followers. The greater the ability of political networks to generate access and distribute resources to members and others in their communities, the greater their *posturing* and bargaining power. Political actors can be members of multiple networks and gain access to different sources of power. Literature on social capital and network theory often measures a person's *access* as the characteristics of an individual's networks and the *size* and/or *intensity* of relations.[43] However, as Ellen Finsveen and Wim van Oorschot found in their studies, the size and intensity of the network connections tell us little about the effectiveness of a person's network in accessing the necessary resources for achieving his/her end goal.[44] In Afghanistan, access, especially political access, is further reinforced among political elites through the informal institution of *Andewali* (a reciprocal relationship among friends/comrades with collective interests and responsibilities) as discussed in the Preface.

Flowing from these cultural-political issues, several political-economic factors play an important role in reinforcing networked politics in post-2001 Afghanistan. Informal access and Waseta, as applied to those who sit in positions of power within the state and its bureaucratic bodies, have become increasingly interrelated with political networks. This is rooted in the 1990s politics of "government-in-exile," which William Maley has called "Peshawar politics." In this "state-free environment," politics was based on continuous alliance-building driven by short-term goals, networking, and patronage relationships.[45] The post-2001 politics has further entrenched networked politics because of the *political* and *institutional setup* it adopted at the Bonn Conference and subsequently at the 2002 Constitutional Loya Jirga. At the time, little attention was paid to what the appropriate role and functions of the state should be rather than simply putting some form of a state together and sharing its spoils in a grand bargain.[46] As discussed in Chapter 3, this had serious implications as it fostered nepotism and corruption in ministries and government agencies, further undermining formal institution-building and democratisation.

The 2003 Constitutional Loya Jirga adopted a highly centralised political setup that gave little voice to communities in the decision-making process. The absence of strong and effective political parties, compounded by the political decision to adopt a voting system that benefitted independent candidates at the expense of political parties (see Chapter 4), created further incentives for networked politics.

The emergence of stronger political parties was actively discouraged by President Karzai, who gave priority to alliance-building and patronage over ideologies or policy agendas. In the absence of a functioning state and political parties, international donors relied on strong networked personalities to achieve their objectives, especially those with coercive and organisational power, which gave primacy to personal relations over institutionalisation and democratisation.

This flawed institutional design was compounded by identity-based conflict and tensions within the state. In a multi-ethnic, divided society like Afghanistan, which experiences low *trust*, effective institutional setups are created to contain identity divisions. The 2001 Bonn Conference failed to achieve this as it distributed ministries among political networks as "positional goods" along ethnic and tribal lines, which then thoroughly politicised state institutions, structures, and processes.[47] In the absence of functioning state institutions and weak citizen-based and rights-based relationships, communities had little choice but to rely on political networks that claimed to represent them for jobs and informal access to other state resources.

Finally, the distorted effect of international aid and the consolidation of a "rentier state" provided additional factors for fostering networked politics. Accessing and controlling the massive flow of international military spending and donor aid money became the driving economic incentive for political networks rather than establishing legitimate tax-based economic activities.[48] Political networks, therefore, were quick to learn how to manipulate international military and donor actors and processes to their advantage. International aid money was consequently divided along the donor country's military geographical responsibilities (e.g., the U.S.A. in the south, the Dutch in Uruzgan province, Germany in Kunduz and the north), which produced a fragmented aid regime benefitting some over others. Massive aid flow also exceeded the absorptive capacity of the Afghan state.[49] As argued in Chapter 9, most of the international military money was used as a "weapons system" to buy loyalties in the war against the insurgency, as shown over the years by Special Inspector General for Afghanistan Reconstruction (SIGAR) reports,[50] going into the pockets of political networks and their clients to purchase additional loyalties and protection, further corrupting the Afghan state and making communities dependant on political networks and regional strongmen for access to state and international resources.

1.4 Post-2001 Afghanistan: a complex global assemblage

International statebuilding that ensued from the U.S. and coalition military intervention, which intensified from 2005 onwards, was essentially a *global assemblage* of international actors, discourses, and practices brought together to serve a *liberal peace* agenda and interests. Ronald Paris has characterised this complex and crowded field as a "loosely structured network" because it constitutes a system that is neither a "market," where interaction is based on pursuing individual goals with little sense of sharing common objectives nor a "hierarchy," a system of top-down command management.[51] The 2001 intervention in Afghanistan led to the import of a diverse network of administrative expatriates (e.g., experts and diplomats), aid agencies (e.g., the World Bank, UN agencies, and others), non-governmental organisations (NGOs), and ethical discourses (e.g., human rights, democracy, freedom of expression, etc.) into one complex assemblage to re-build the Afghan state and its institutions and economy. This meant that diverse actors had to collaborate closely with one another to achieve objectives—what Mandell and others have termed *collaborative governance*.[52] This produced a new mode of governance operation across the broad spectrum of the liberal peace space, which was *networked* in character.

As Eilstrup-Sangiovanni found, governments in international arenas like state-building settings are more likely to operate under networked structures when (1) issues call for quick action, (2) uncertainty is pronounced, (3) their preferences differ from rival domestic agents, and (4) there is a desire to avoid spoilers.[53] In Afghanistan this meant setting up regular ad hoc networked structures such as the "donor discussion group" and "aid coordination committee" to increase governance capacity, improve information sharing, and integrate their diverse approaches and strategies.

Statebuilding settings are also highly political and contested spaces. In Afghanistan, at the peak of international military engagement from 2009 to 2012, more than 40 international donors contributed to security, development, and institution-building efforts, each pursuing their priorities, approaches, and policies. Security provision was carved out along provincial lines among NATO countries with Germany taking the lead in the north and northeast, and Britain and Canada in the south in Helmand and Kandahar provinces, respectively. On the reconstruction front, donor countries shared development priorities and portfolios among themselves with the Italians leading justice sector reform, the Germans and the EU the rule of law and police reform, and the Americans and British taking the counterterrorism and counter-narcotics portfolios. This fashioned a fragmented statebuilding process, pursued in multiple and divided forms, with each donor country pursuing their own separate policies, agendas, and approaches.[54] Despite attempts to bring uniformity across the spectrum through the introduction of networked structures, this remained a major challenge throughout the international intervention in Afghanistan, adversely affecting statebuilding goals. International and local NGOs did not fare much better either as each competed for funds, often duplicating efforts.

Generally, as the experience of post-2001 Afghanistan illustrates, statebuilding spaces are further complicated and politicised because of their interaction with local forces who have their own agendas. Most statebuilding literature overlooks the important role of local forces/actors, and when they do, they are portrayed as powerless, with no agency for themselves, blamed for their predatory and irrational behaviour, and for failing to understand the broader peacebuilding objectives. The dominant literature treats domestic politics as "constraints" and thus fails to fully incorporate the preferences and strategies of local actors.[55] Richmond and MacGinty have argued that *liberal peace*—as a "knowledge system and epistemic community" and the dominant discourse—has subjugated the local actors and discourses by de-politicising its influences, cultures, customs, and histories as well as political, social, and economic systems.[56] They argue that this produces a strained dynamic relationship between international statebuilding actors and local forces. They term this "hybrid forms of peace"—a continuous dynamic of competition and contest between the local and international.

In an interesting study, De Waal suggests that international-local power dynamics take the form of a "patrimonial inclusive buy-in"—a new political rule and statehood.[57] He shows how international peacebuilding creates networked relations with local patrimonial networks in support of agreed constitutional provisions and power sharing. In his analysis, the relationship between international and local resembles a "patrimonial marketplace" where loyalties are negotiated and bought within an "auction of loyalties."[58] He argues that this often takes place without international statebuilding actors realising that they are involved in the political marketplace, helping the winner to take it all while de-legitimising the losers' claim to any share of the national patrimony. In contrast to De Waal's findings, the following empirical chapters show that the international-local dynamic is more complex than merely transactional, subject to the marketplace rule. Local political practices are governed by complex rules of exchange, and informal and reciprocal institutions that are often irrational.[59] In Afghanistan, political networked dynamics are reinforced through different strategies, including resource interdependencies, interfamilial marriages, gifts, partnerships, identity politics, and the reciprocal relationship of *Andewali* and *Waseta*. More importantly, the link between international and local is *co-constitutive* as much as it is conflictive or oppositional. As such, we must pay particular attention to the co-constitutive and *networked character* of statebuilding with an eye to the hitherto ignored local political networks and their role in the process of re-assembling and transforming the post-conflict state.

1.5 The post-2001 state and informal order

There has been no single authoritative account of the post-2001 Afghan state. Many studies of post-2001 international intervention and peacebuilding efforts discuss the state either partially or in passing. Moreover, these studies generally attempt to address the role and impact of international efforts to build formal state institutions. Maley and Goodson highlight the failure of the international community at Bonn to resolve elites' divisions and their impact on state re-building.[60] Suhrke and Clark suggest that donors have created a "rentier state" because of their "tight-embraced" approach to statebuilding.[61] She rightly argues that the Afghan state has become closely tied to the power of foreign troops and capital, which essentially undermines the legitimacy of the state. Ghani and Lockhart assert that the Afghan state suffers from a "sovereignty gap" because of its primary dependence on donors.[62] These studies condition the survival of the state to the continuation of international funds and military presence. In another critique, two practitioners with years of working experience in Afghanistan argue that the perceptions, strategies, and objectives of international intervention conflicted with the Afghan people's own understanding of their country, undermining the democratisation process.[63] They argue that the international interveners risked manufacturing a "narco-state," which maintained itself through the drug trade.

Most of the studies cited above and other recent policy studies have crudely positioned the Afghan state alongside predatory elites and their corrupt practices especially after the August 2021 government collapse, either in competition with (or alternative to) or in the backing of the central state in guaranteeing relative stability.[64] And after the U.S.–Taliban deal in February 2020, there was more emphasis on the regional aspect of the Afghan state, the "bad neighbourhood" effect, and the state's future survival.

Many of the above analyses characterise the post-2001 Afghan Republic state as "weak," "fragile," "corrupt," and even naively as a "narco-state." These characterisations were consistent with the dominant liberal peace evaluation, which measures success in terms of the state's formal institutional capacities to exercise autonomy and sovereignty.[65] Most of these studies ignored the more important informal aspects of statehood, including the role and power dynamics of endogenous forces on statebuilding, stability, and violence. A more insightful account underlined the role of a war economy in supporting the Afghan state.[66] Coburn's ethnographic study in Istalif, a small town in the north of Kabul, found that political order was maintained in rural Afghanistan—where the state seemed a mere "useful fiction"—through the role of informal powerbrokers and community elites.[67]

This book builds on Coburn's and other works that pay attention to the informal aspects of statehood in post-2001 Afghanistan. However, it also suggests that the post-2001 state and statehood must be understood by analysing the continuities and changes in the power dynamics of political networks within the state and beyond and their day-to-day practices. The international intervention helped consolidate the historically and sociologically evolved *networked state* in Afghanistan, as discussed in the next section. The state re-assembling took place in a fragmented and divisive way, reflecting the diverse and often conflicting interests of political networks. This went against the dominant view that sees the state as a cohesive homogenous entity driven by its singular interest. In this sense, this analysis fundamentally questions the way we understand the state in fragile and post-conflict settings like Afghanistan. The state cannot be treated as a unitary entity, exhibiting an unproblematic and uniform organisational structure. This analysis draws on recent anthropology of state studies in Central Asia in seeing the state as a "contested field" subject to material and symbolic competition and conflict between rival political forces.[68] The post-2001 state is essentially a "complex strategic terrain," to use Jessop's phrase, where rival political networks occupy key strategic parts of the state, possessing different sources of power that they then convert into different types of power.[69] Malejacq refers to the Afghan high stake game of *Buzkashi* and the state as its playing field, which is in a constant mode of transformation.[70]

In Afghanistan, the modalities of that contest began to emerge shortly after the Bonn Agreement was signed, when the main networked groups—primarily the Northern Alliance strongmen and the Rome group—carved a safe political position for themselves with the state. And as Chapter 4 demonstrates, once these political networks were in control of key ministries, they began limiting access to resources and privileges to members and communities they claimed to represent. Douglas North's framing of historical state order, what he terms *limited-access* order, is informative for this analysis.[71] North identifies two historically different social orders, which he argues to have shaped historical state formations in most countries: the limited-access state and the open-access state. He asserts that the limited-access state has been the default social order because it aligns the interests of powerful individuals such that they forge a dominant coalition in a way that limits violence. Elite members within the coalition agree to respect each other's political and financial privileges and resources. By limiting access to privileges of the empowered political networks (i.e., patronage, rent-seeking), they create credible incentives to co-operate rather than fight each other, knowing that violence will reduce their rents. Rent creation is a fundamental contributing factor to stability. North understands rent as a return to an economic asset that exceeds the return that an asset can receive in its best alternative use.[72] He treats the state as a single entity or a super-organisation run by a coalition of smaller organisations, which work to safeguard political order and stability. According to North, most Western states are an *open-access* order where the state has been transformed from its natural state as a result of strong social capital development upon which civil societies thrive and formal institutions take root. From North's perspective, one serious shortcoming of liberal peace international interventions and statebuilding is that they treat post-conflict states with an open-access state logic, which is far from the realities on the ground.

This book employs North's historical framing but dives deeper into explaining explicitly how political networks survive within the state and how power dynamics among them shape political order and violence. Also, it shows that resource flows such as patronage and rent are more complex and instrumental in linking vertical and horizontal (bottom-up) dynamics and relations than others have noted. When looking at the day-to-day network practices, political networks were effective in performing and enacting the role of the state. Through the act of "impersonation," network members create the illusion of the state as a singular and vertical entity and subsequently the *façade* of political order in Kabul and the major provincial centres when the state was a mere hollow. This created a complex dynamic where state actors, non-state criminals, insurgents, and donors all thrived from a mix of political order at the macro level but created instability and violence at the micro level. And when the Taliban victory was in sight following the 2020 U.S.–Taliban deal, political networks began disintegrating with clients shifting their allegiances to the Taliban, especially in multi-ethnic and multi-tribal districts and provinces.

1.6 Political order in Afghanistan's modern state formation

Afghanistan's historical state formation and political order is marred by a vicious cycle of political instability and violence, typically characterised by scholars as "try again, fail again, and fail better," one of constant "struggle and survival."[73] Explanations abound, from the sources of political instability in Afghanistan to those who put the fault on the country's resilient socio-cultural "micro-societies" to the topography that makes it difficult to subjugate its diverse population to its strategic position in the Great Game competition to the social organisational dynamics of tribes.[74] Most of these explanations have their merit, but in isolation none can fully explain the entrenched cycle of instability and violence in Afghanistan.

Afghanistan's history of state formation and political order offers insights into the working of the post-2001 networked state. Since its modern birth, Afghanistan was ruled by various types of networked structures, like the networked kingdom founded by the Durrani king, Ahmad Shah Durrani. Moreover, as noted below some of the key features of the statehood including rentier state, patronage, and the segmentary nature of tribal structure as well as historical grievances along tribal and ethnic lines persisted in post-2001 Afghanistan, which continued to threaten political order and state survival.

1.6.1 Founding a "networked kingdom": Durrani Kingdom from 1747 to 1880

The decline of the various Turko-Mongol empires in the 17th century—Safavids in today's Iran, Mughals in India, and Shaybanid Uzbeks in Central Asia and the north of today's Afghanistan—paved the way for the emergence of the Durrani Kingdom ruled by Ahmad Shah Durrani and, subsequently, modern Afghanistan. By 1762, the young kingdom had reached its height when it expanded to Kashmir, Punjab, Sind, and Baluchistan. A century later when Sher Ali Khan (1863–1866 and then 1868–1879) seized power in a bloody power struggle and initiated the "beginning of a new Afghanistan," the kingdom had lost most of its territories and had gone through several cycles of violence and war.[75] Both Timur Shah (1773–1793), Ahmad Shah's son and successor, and later Dost Mohammad Khan's (1826–1838 and then 1842–1863) failure to pass power peacefully to their successor—the former had 24 legitimate sons and the latter had 27 sons in total from 16 wives—brought decades of violence and power struggle among rival royal family lineages for control of the kingdom. Dost Mohammad Khan's reigns coincided with the British invasion of Afghanistan, known as the First Anglo-Afghan war (1839–1842) and Sher Ali Khan (1868–1879) that was overthrown by the British in the Second Anglo-Afghan war (1878–1880) placing the country further under colonial rule.

From 1747 to 1880, successful Durrani rulers guaranteed stability by engaging tribal chiefs, especially ones from the entrenched royal lines, as privileged partners of expansionist policies. Ahmad Shah and his son created an *entrenched leadership* clique among tribes who came to constitute the core of the Durrani Kingdom and marked Pashtun hegemony over other ethno-linguistic groups.[76] The Sadozai and Mohammadzai subdivision within the Durrani confederation and Hotak, Kakar, and Tokhi tribal subdivisions among the

Ghilzai confederation established the "entrenched leading lineage" to rule the kingdom collectively. As Ghubar, the Afghan historian, aptly summarised: the tribal chiefs were *Sharik-o-Dawla* (partners to the state).[77] Ahmad Shah had to consult with a council of nine tribal chiefs called *sardars* ("Amir-i-Lashkar," the head of the army) who acted as the regional strongmen with their own tribal and ethnic army units, collecting revenues from the provinces under their control, while sending only the assigned amount to the king. This was a collective power-sharing enterprise, a "networked kingdom" where competition and conflict over its control by rival tribal leaders and clans shaped and transformed state survival and political order.[78]

The tribal dynamics inherent within the social organisations of Durrani Kingdom also became the main source of political instability. Several historians have made a compelling argument that the internal Pashtun tribal organisational dynamics locked the ruling groups into a vicious cycle of political instability and violence.[79] They illustrate that the dynamics of Pashtun tribal lineage are "segmentary," which means that cooperation or hostility between groups is determined by the scope of the problem at hand. Tapper found the Pashtun tribal structure as the most "pervasive and explicit segmentary lineage ideology on the classic pattern, perpetuated not only in written genealogies but also in the territorial framework of tribal distribution."[80] The segmentary dynamics in Afghanistan have followed a pattern of cousin rivalry (Tarburwali), or jealousy among brothers and half-brothers.[81] This is reflected in the famous Pashtun saying, "Me against my brother; my brothers and me against our cousins; my brothers, cousins, and me against the world." With such dynamics, once a charismatic leader dies or loses influence, the divisive character of the segmentary tribal system impedes the smooth transition of power. Successful successions meant raising the broadest coalitions of tribes and ethnic communities. Barfield observed an inherent tension between the egalitarian Pashtun tribal system and the centrally and hierarchically organised Turko-Mongol government system which the Durrani rulers adopted from the Safavid and the Mughals.[82] He infers that the egalitarian Pashtun tribal organisation is prone to rejecting the centralisation of power because of the instrument of segmentary division. This tension between an egalitarian societal structure and a hierarchical and centralised political structure has been the source of violence and state collapse in Afghanistan.

In summary, the foundation of modern Afghanistan was framed as "networked kingdom" for which political order and state survival were guaranteed by rulers who had the support of tribal chiefs and maintained a balanced power and resources equilibrium among the competing tribes and ethnic groups. Failure to do so paved the way for their eventual downfall. As Chapters 4, 5, and 6 demonstrate, the networked state traits and logic persisted in post-2001 Afghanistan where President Karzai fashioned a relatively stable and balanced equilibrium among competing networks in which they constituted parts of the state. President Ghani, on the other hand, disrupted the delicate balance of power by unsuccessfully undermining and sidelining rival networks, ultimately contributing to the collapse of the Republic.

1.6.2 Centralisation, absolute violence, and
failed modernisation (1880–1929)

With the loss of Indian territory following the signing of the Durand Line Agreement in 1893, Afghan rulers and *sardars* lost the opportunity to wage regular military campaigns into the rich Indian provinces for plunder. One key outcome of the Anglo-Afghan wars (1839–1842 and 1878–1880) was the dependency of Durrani rulers on foreign aid and subsidies for survival. From then on, political order and state survival would depend, among other factors, on foreign subsidies and weapons, which would build "local-imperial power alliances."[83] British aid in the form of grants and subsidies enabled Abdul Rahman Khan (1980–1901) to employ absolute violence at an industrial scale to subjugate tribes and ethnic groups.[84] The violent means employed to suppress the Ghilzai, Nuristani, and Hazara groups were brutal and absolute, as described by Afghan scholars.[85] Louis Dupree (1969) dubbed it "internal imperialism."[86] In crushing the Nuristanis and Hazaras, Abdul Rahman Khan employed Islam as a powerful institution to mobilise the tribes. When suppressing the Hazara revolt, he appealed to the Sunni tribal Pashtuns, Kohistanis, and even the Uzbeks with the offer of land, property, and slaves. Abdul Rahman Khan's centralisation policy had major consequences on the long-term political instability in Afghanistan. As President Ghani once put it to me, "he [Abdul Rahman Khan] set into motion the seeds of ethnic conflict which exploded ninety years after his death."[87] The level of violence of this policy's ethnicising imperative, inciting sectarianism, traumatised state-society relations, which arguably haunt Afghanistan to this day.

The reign of Habibullah Khan (1901–1919) and Amanullah Khan (1919–1929) reconciled Afghanistan with pan-Islamism and modernisation in the Muslim world. In contrast to his father, Amanullah Khan introduced pragmatic reforms and opened the country to new ideas. According to Gregorian, three different ideological networks emerged and competed within the state, all of them anti-British and pro-Turkish in their sympathy: (1) The conservative clerics who sought the re-emergence of Islam, (2) the moderates who wanted Kemalist-style modernisation, with caveats, and (3) the modernist-nationalists who wanted rapid modernisation. Habibullah's assassination was the result of his failure to accommodate the demands of these opposing factions.[88] By the late 1910s, the modernist-nationalists centred on Ghulam Mohammad Tarzi, a prominent scholar who had studied in Damascus and Istanbul and emerged as the dominant force for reform. With the assassination of Habibullah in 1919, Amanullah, a member of the modernist-nationalist group, pushed for a radical modernisation programme.[89] Two reform packages, in particular, taxation and conscription, aimed at reducing the power of tribal chiefs and limiting their allowances and triggered a mass revolt against his rule. The tribal and ethnic chiefs and religious leaders organised a combined revolt but using religious justification. Ideological forces were born and from now on became a source of political disorder with its impact most visible in the last five decades of war and violence including post-2001 Afghanistan. In 1929, Habibullah Kalakani, an ethnic Tajik and a rebel from Kohistan, north of Kabul, seized Kabul and declared himself king. The ability of Habibullah Kalakani to rule for almost a year with the tribes failing to unite around a leader is seen as a confirmation of the segmentary political dynamics of Pashtun tribal societies. The tribes eventually united around Nadir Khan, a former Mohammadzai *sardar* who arrived back in Afghanistan from exile in France. Habibullah Kalakani's defeat brought a new dynasty, the *Musahibans*, which lasted until 1973, fashioning the longest period of political stability in Afghan history.

1.6.3 Rentier state, patronage, and ideological nationalism (1929–1973)

Key to Musahiban survival was the re-adoption of old policies as a means of guaranteeing order, including buying loyalties among tribes and competing for political groupings through patronage and bargaining. Nadir Khan gave tribal chiefs and the religious establishment high-profile positions in the government and maintained a balance among them.[90] His successor, Zahir Shah (1933–1973), pursued similar policies and turned to international systems for resources that could enable him to gradually enlarge state-dominated economic development and political control without confronting tribal chiefs. The Musahibans continued with modernisation and reforms, albeit with pragmatism, caution, and adherence to Pashtun nationalism.[91] Modernisation was aimed explicitly to empower the Pashtun constituency as most development projects were exclusively targeted in the Pashtun regions. Efforts were also made to hegemonise the state, society, and culture through Pashtun nationalism. Pashto was declared the official language in 1936 and attempts were made, albeit unsuccessful, to Pashtunise the predominantly Persian-speaking civil servant class. The *Pashtu Tulane* (Pashto Association) was established in 1937 to research the Pashto language, culture, traditions, history, and way of life. The names of historical cities, towns, and streets were also changed.

From 1960s onwards, the king in an attempt to accelerate the course of modernisation used Cold War superpower rivalries to secure aid and grants but at the cost of transforming the country into a "rentier state."[92] This meant that the foreign patrons could build and expand mutual networks of connections, penetrating different segments of the Afghan state and society. By 1979, around 6000 civilian specialists and 4000 military officers were trained in the Soviet Union.[93] It was these trained officers and fraternity networks of military and police forces who had the necessary institutional base to carry out two successful coups: in 1973, in partnership with Daud Khan, against the king and in 1978, against Daud Khan himself, discussed in more detail in Chapter 3.[94]

1.6.4 Political organisations, internal factionalism,
and violence (1974–1992)

Chapter 3 focuses specifically on the origins and emergence of political organisations in Afghanistan and changes in the power dynamics of political network organisations in the last five decades. Here, I provide a brief analytical summary for the purpose of demonstrating the progression of political order and violence in Afghanistan.

On 17 July 1973, more than 220 years of dynastic rule ended when Daoud Khan, the former prime minister and a cousin of the king, in partnership with the communist Parcham faction of the People's Democratic Party of Afghanistan (PDPA), staged a bloodless coup, overthrowing the monarchy.[95] A significant outcome of the coup was that it brought an end to the historic class of Durrani monarchs and landed gentry (e.g., the tribal chiefs were known as "sardars" and khans). Political order was, thus, no longer shaped and threatened by powerful aristocratic tribal chiefs—the historical model of the uprising against the ruler as noted by Ibn Khaldun—but instead by modern political organisations and the internal factional infighting within them—with links to international and regional patrons—over the control of the Afghan state and international rent.

For political organisations that lacked the capacity to carry out a grassroots revolution, the army provided the quickest way to organise a power grab. During this period until the collapse of the community regime in 1992, Afghanistan experienced four major coups or coup attempts (1978, 1979, 1990, and 1992), which set a precedent for political organisations to use violent means as the main method for acquiring power and controlling the state. These coups were not a product of any demand for revolutionary change on the part of the Afghan population; rather, they reflected a deep division within the political—and mainly Kabul-based—elites.[96] The People's Democratic Party of Afghanistan (PDPA) established in January 1965 carried out a successful coup in 1978, led by the communist army generals and cadres. Once in power, the party split into two hostile factions: *Khalq* (masses) and *Parcham* (banner), named after the titles of their publications, led by Nur Mohammad Taraki and Babrak Karmal, respectively. During this period and since then, governance and statehood has been marred with networked factionalism and mass violence in Afghanistan. First, Khalq faction removed Parchamis from key state positions, especially the army, imprisoning and killing hundreds of Parchamis; then, factions within Khalq turned against each other. Factionalism and internal fighting continued within Parcham throughout the 1980s despite direct Soviet military intervention. The Soviet intervention inspired and empowered jihadi Islamist political-military organisations, known as *tanzims*, to emerge as the dominant force for the next four decades in Afghanistan. The eventual collapse of the Najibullah regime in 1992 resulted in the fragmentation of the Afghan state and society with rival jihadi *tanzims* and associates controlling different parts of Afghanistan. The ten-year bloody civil war in the 1990s brought a more extremist group into power, the Taliban.

The U.S. military intervention in 2001 and the establishment of the Republic state were built on key historical features of a networked state including factionalism, patronage, rentier state, and identity division. Like previous Afghan authorities' attempts to establish formal political order through centralisation and rapid modernisation, in post-2001 through statebuilding, they failed to break the basic features of a networked state upon which Afghanistan was built against persistent resistance from powerful political networks that sustained and entrenched informal rules of the game for their survival. As the empirical chapters (Chapters 4, 5, and 6) in the book show, in post-2001 Afghanistan President Karzai went back to the logic of the networked state to maintain order by balancing power and resource interdependencies among competing forces in which they constituted the state, whereas President Ghani's went against this logic by discriminating and marginating these forces at the time when his own network lacked broad-based support and inclusiveness, which ultimately fashioned the collapse of the Republic.

Notes

1 See Jacobson, (2010).
2 Eide (2012).
3 See Jacobson (2010); and Steuter and Wills (2011).
4 Lakhdar Brahimi, the UN Envoy to Afghanistan, explained a light footprint approach as: "the [UN] interventions should avoid the creation of parallel institutions and dual systems which undermine local authority, hinder coordination and precipitate competition" (2007: 4). See in Suhrke (2009).
5 Previous attempts at reaching a political settlement were the 1989 Rawalpindi accord, the 1991 Peshawar agreement, and the 1992 Islamabad accord.
6 The network as a concept has been understood variously as a "theory" in early anthropology by Barnes (1972) and Mitchell (1969); a "metaphor" in international relations and politics by Emirbayer and Goodwin (1994); a "method" in social network analysis by Scott (2000) and Wasserman and Faust (1994); and as an analytical tool in organisational theory in sociology by Powell (1990) and Podolny and Page (1998). The international politics literature highlights networks as an additional mode of governance that helps coordinate policy outcomes in a complex and globalised world. For public policy studies, see Rhodes (1997, 2006); for public management, see Provan and Kenis (2008), Kickert et al. (1997), Kooiman (1993), Agranoff and McGuire (2003) and Koppenjan and Klijn (2004); for organisation theory, see Powell (1990), Podolny and Page (1998), Wasserman and Faust (1994); for economics, see Burt (1992), Granovetter (1974), and Jackson (2008); for international relations studies, see Kahler (2009), Woods and Martinez-Diaz (2009), Grewal (2008), and Eilstrup-Sangiovanni (2017); for social biology and computer science, see Watts (2003) and Barabasi (2003).
7 See Burt (1992, 2005); Wasserman (1994) and Faust Powell and Smith-Doerr (1994); Podolny and Page (1998).
8 See Slaughter (2004), Kahler (2009); Woods and Martinez-Diaz (2009); Grewal (2009); Maoz, (2010); and Eilstrup-Sangiovanni (2017).
9 Powell (1990).
10 Rhodes (1997).
11 Lake and Wong (2009: 129).
12 Knoke (1990: 2).
13 See Marsden (2016) on the work of Afghan traders.
14 See Sinno (2008).
15 Agranoff and McGuire (2003).
16 See Powell (1990); Uzzi (1997).
17 Kaneko and Imai (1987).
18 Field and Higley (1973: 8). Mosca (1939) and Pareto (1935) argued that elite arrangement and behaviour have significant effects on the form and function of political regimes. However, Burton and Higley (1987) critiqued Mosca and Pareto for over-

looking the nature of political elite settlements and their internal organisations as a mechanism of variability for regimes and brought our attention to political elite settlements.

19 See Maley (1997, 2004, 2006) and Saikal (1998).
20 Chesterman (2004); Paris (2004); Fearon and Laitin (2004).
21 See also Cheng, C., J. Goodhand, and P. Meehan (2018).
22 For studies of warlords, see Reno (1998); Marten (2012); Mukhopadhyay (2009, 2014); and Malejacq (2020); Ahram and King (2012).
23 See Stedman (1997); Lezhnev (2005); and Mueller (2004).
24 Ahram and King (2012: 172).
25 See Malejacq (2020); Mukhopadhyay (2009, 2014).
26 See Schetter, Glassner and Karokhel (2007).
27 See Saikal (2005); Afghanistan's 2004 constitution counts 14 ethnic groups as constituting the "nation of Afghanistan."
28 Brubaker and Cooper (2000: 5).
29 See Roy (1995); Dorronsoro (1995); Maley (1998, 2002); Wimmer and Schetter (2003); Simonsen (2004); Brubaker and Cooper (2000: 5).
30 For some of the atrocities committed by the Mujahedeen, see the 2005 Afghanistan Justice Project Report, *Casting Shadows: War Crimes and Crimes against Humanity: 1978–2001*; US Department of State, "Afghanistan," Human Rights Practices, 1995; Human Rights Watch, *Pattern of Impunity* (New York: Human Rights Watch, July 2001); United Nations Economic and Social Council, Commission on Human Rights, "Report on the Situation of Human Rights in Afghanistan" (E/CN.4/1999/40); The Human Rights Watch report, *The Massacre in Mazar-i Sharif*, was published in November 1998. (Human Rights Watch, Vol. 10, No. 7; Human Rights Watch. *Massacres of Hazaras in Afghanistan*. Human Rights Watch Publications (February 2001) Vol. 13, No. 1(C).
31 Bhatia (2007) and Wimmer and Schetter (2003).
32 Ibrahimi (2017).
33 See Shahrani (1998), Maley (2004), Rubin (2002); Saikal (2005); Noelle (2016).
34 Scott (1972: 92).
35 Shahrani (1998: 220).
36 Maley (2018).
37 Chayes (2015: 59–60).
38 Nordstrom (2001) refers to these as "shadows," Roitman (2003) as "informal," and Duffield (1999) as "extra-legal."
39 For a discussion of Qawm, see Bacon (1958).
40 For a discussion on inequality in social capital see Lin (2000).
41 See Bourdieu (1991); and Coleman's (1990) central argument of his social theory is that actors should be seen first and foremost as beginning with resources over which they have some control and in which they have interest.
42 Ribot and Peluso (2003).
43 A typical measure of *size* is the number of people an individual has contact with, and the intensity is measured using, for example, the frequency of these contacts. It is assumed that the larger a person's network, and the more frequent the person's contacts with network members, the greater the chances that the person can access a resource through his or her network.
44 Finsveen and Oorschot (2008).
45 See Maley (2018); and Christia (2012).
46 On the post-Bonn political setup, see Maley (2018).
47 Hardin (1995) discusses the dangers of state position being used to reward loyal supporters.
48 Farahi and Guggenheim (2020).
49 See Suhrke (2009: 243–4).

50 DOD. 2011. *Money as a Weapon System—Afghanistan (MAAWS-A): Afghanistan Reintegration Program (ARP)*, May (8–14).
51 Paris (2009: 61).
52 On collaborative governance, see Mandell (2002), Stone (2000); Schneider and Hyner (2006); and Ohanyan (2008).
53 Eilstrup-Sangiovanni (2009: 233).
54 See Caplan (2005) on this.
55 See Richmond, Heathershaw, Barnett and Zurcher (2009) for a critique of this.
56 See Richmond (2011b); MacGinty (2010); Lederach (1997); Sending (2011).
57 De Waal (2009: 103).
58 Ibid.
59 Goodhand (2005); Coburn (2011).
60 Maley (2002, 2006) and Goodson (2003).
61 Suhrke (2009: 243–4); Clark (2020)
62 See Ghani et al. (2005). This is a condition characterised by others as "quasi-sovereignty"; see Jackson and Rosberg (1982).
63 Johnson and Leslie (2004).
64 See Giustozzi (2004, 2007, 2009) and Mukhopadhyay (2009, 2014), and Malejacq (2020). Bhatia and Sedra (2007) exposed the central role of local commanders and powerbrokers in the constitution of the Afghan army. See Cordesman (2010) and others.
65 A state is usually considered "strong" if it possesses a combination of state *autonomy* and *capacity*; Evans et al. (1985); Migdal (1988). It must have both infrastructural and despotic power Mann (1986). Autonomy is often referred to as the state's ability to formulate interests of its own, independent of societal forces. Capacity is defined in terms of the state's ability to implement strategies to achieve economic, political, and social goals.
66 Goodhand (2010).
67 Coburn (2011).
68 See Collins (2002); Schatz (2004); Reeves (2009); Rasanayagam (2011).
69 Jessop (2000: 4–9).
70 See Malejacq (2020). Buzkashi is a Central Asian sports game, practised in Afghanistan, in which horse-mounted players compete to seize and retain control of a goat carcass and attempt to place in a goal.
71 North (2009: 7).
72 North (2009: 19).
73 Cramer and Goodhand (2002); and Saikal (2006). Of the 21 rulers (excluding Mullah Omar) of Afghanistan up to 2021, all were either deposed or assassinated, except 5 (Ahmad Shah, the founder of the Durrani Kingdom, his son Timur Shah, and Amir Abdul Rahman Khan, 1880–1901, Burhanuddin Rabbani, 1992–2001, and Hamid Karzai, 2001–2014). Both Dost Mohammad Khan and Shah Shuja ruled twice. The former was first deposed by the British but then reinstalled by them.
74 See Saikal (2006); Kakar (2006); Ghubar (1981), Mousavi (1997); Shahrani (1990); Vogelsang (2008: 233); (Gregorian 1969); Lee (2018).
75 This was a description noted by Gregorian (1969: 93).
76 Noelle (2016). She argues that the Durrani rulers divided the Pashtun tribal structure into the following three categories: (1) *border tribes* who display the dispersion of power typical of segmentary lineage organisation (e.g., tribes in the Khyber pass area and some Ghilzai in Ghazni), (2) *tribal aristocracy* superimposed on a local population of heterogeneous population (e.g., Yusufzai and Tarklanri in Swat, Bajaur, and Dir areas), and (3) *entrenched leadership*, which had crystalised under Safavid/Mughal patronage. Noelle (2016: 122–223).
77 Ghubar (1981).
78 Gregorian (1969: 48).

79 See Noelle (2016); McChesney (1991); Barfield (1990); Rubin (1995); Hopkins (2008); Dupree (1969 and 1973).

80 See Tapper (1983: 43).

81 See Barfield (2012); Johnathan Lee (2018); Saikal (2006).

82 Barfield (2012) identified two different cultural traditions in Afghanistan: (1) the hierarchical Turko-Mongol tribal structure which had dominated the political landscape since the first millennium in Central Asia, Iran, Turkey, and India and (2) the egalitarian Pashtun tribal structure. While the actual units of social organisation among the Turko-Mongols were based on loyalty to successful warrior chieftains, among the tribal Pashtuns it was based on their specific genealogical descent.

83 See Emadi (2010) and Hanifi (2011).

84 In 1882 the British granted the Amir a yearly subsidy of 1.2 million Indian rupees, which was increased to 1.8 after the formal demarcation of the Durand Line in 1893. Saikal (2006: 30); Rubin (2002: 49).

85 Saikal (2006); Emadi (2010); Mousavi (1997). According to one Hazara historian, over half of the Hazara population was either killed or enslaved and their lands were redistributed to Pashtun tribes. For more details, see Dolatabadi (2001), Emadi (2010); Mousavi (1997); and Ibrahimi (2017). Although a realistic estimation is difficult, Dolatabadi uses data from the official court historian, Faiz Muhammad Kateb, in making his estimation. For instance, in one account, Kateb in Siraj-ul-Tawarikh (1858: 1031) says, "out of the 200,000 families of Behsud only 64,000 families in total and only 60 families of the Sultan Mohammad clan survived the war." The state gained the largest share from the selling of Hazara slaves, which became a significant source of their revenue.

86 Dupree (1973, xix).

87 Author's discussion with a leading former academic and politician in 2011.

88 Gregorian (1969).

89 For Amanullah's period, see Poullada (1973). The first Afghan constitution was promulgated in 1923; according to which even the king's actions were, in principle, subordinate to the law. Measures were taken to centralise and improve the effectiveness of administration. A new tax law was introduced and the legal system unified. Universal conscription was imposed. Social reforms included the introduction of universal citizenship, expansion of the education system to include women, mosque schools' reforms, and the banning of polygamy and child marriage. He established the first girls' high school in 1921 and even sent girls to study in Turkey and Switzerland. Poullada (1973: 70–73).

90 See Dupree (1973: 276). For instance, Mojaddadi's brother who had declared jihad against Amanullah, was appointed the minister for justice. Dupree (1973: 276).

91 See Gregorian (1969); Saikal (2006); Emadi (2010).

92 Rubin (2002); Saikal (2006); Gregorian (1969).

93 Ibid.

94 See Giustozzi (2000) and Bradsher (1999) for the details of the first coup. According to Gankovskiy, the second coup was staged by four major military officers who feared that Daud would soon come after them and the entire PDPA leadership. These were Gen. Qadir (Chief of Staff of Air Forces), Watanjar (Deputy Commander of the Fourth Armoured Brigade stationed at Puli Charkhi military base), Gulabzoy (an Air Force Commander who became Minister of Interior), and Mohammad Rafie (would later become Minister of Defence from 1979 to 1984 and 1986 to 1988).

95 The Soviet involvement in the coup is difficult to prove, but most analysts like Kakar (1997), Saikal (2006), and Arnold (1985) contend that the Soviets had at least prior knowledge of the coup.

96 Maley (2021).

2   Political networks and the state

An analytical framework

Introduction

This chapter offers a networked governance analytical framework to analyse the role and power dynamics of warring groups and the newly established political and technocratic networks in shaping and transforming the state, in the wake of an internationally supported political settlement in the form of a power-sharing arrangement—in our case from the Bonn Conference of 2001 to the Republic's collapse in August 2021. Afghanistan's historical and contemporary examples offer important insights into how we think about the relationship between power and the political agents. The key, I frame in this chapter, is not merely the important role of actors in power but the relationships and power resource interdependencies between them, the institutional settings in which these relationships operate and thrive, and how they subsequently advance their chances of survival. It, therefore, unpacks the strategies and practices employed by political networks to fashion stability and political order/disorder and violence.

In this chapter, Section 2.1 offers a typology of political networks by looking at networks' origins and sources of power in post-2001 Afghanistan until the collapse of the Republic. The sources of power could be coercion and violent use of force, financial wealth, ideological authority (including religious and nationalism), constituency mobilisation along ethnic and tribal lines, and political and technical skills. Section 2.2 then disentangles the key factors that enable political network cohesion to understand the strengths/weaknesses of political networks and therefore their chances of survival. Section 2.3 discusses the different types of power resources that political networks enjoy and the diverse interdependencies these produce within a *networked state*, subsequently dictating their power dynamics. Section 2.4 discusses a four-level, mutually interdependent set of interactions that political networks must master to accumulate necessary power resources. These are (1) international statebuilding, (2) the central state, (3) the subnational, and (4) the community level. The higher a network's interaction at all these levels, the greater its control of power resources and chances of survival. Section 2.5 discusses the importance of alliance formation for political network survival and maximisation of power resources. Section 2.6 outlines day-to-day practices (everyday rules of the game) such as patronage, rent-seeking, coercion,

DOI: 10.4324/9781315161617-2

and instrumentalisation of identity-based divisions employed by political networks to guarantee their survival within the state and enact as the state. The final two sections highlight the significance of maintaining a safe state position within the state for networks to continue to survive and the role of international military and financial support as deterrence for intra-network conflict.

2.1 Typology of political networks

I differentiate six types of political networks in war-torn and post-conflict countries by looking at their origins and sources of power.

Most political networks in developing countries in the 20th century originated as either ideological groupings in a shifting global order or as post-colonial nationalist movements, often in response to colonialism and occupation.[1] Most of them initially emerged as networked structures before transitioning into centralised organisations once in power and in possession of the state, including the People's Democratic Party of Afghanistan, the Chinese Communist Party, and the Khmer Rouge. The jihadi *tanzims* in Afghanistan, who had fought the Soviet Union in the 1980s and had enjoyed significant coercive power and international patronage, fractured into smaller *patronage networks* and *strongmen-based* networks in the post-2001 Republic period. *Patronage networks* are structured in an exchange relationship of some private and personal nature in which players have reciprocal needs and expectations but unequal power and status.[2] In Afghanistan, as this book shows over the years the former jihadi networks that were essentially *resistance/insurgency networks* became less ideologically driven and more *patronage networks*. Their militia forces were incorporated into the Afghan army and police while accumulating massive economic resources.

The Afghan jihad produced strong military field commanders against weak political leaders in exile during the jihad. In the post-2001 political settlement, these commanders became powerful regional strongmen, independent of the centre, administering violence and providing security, protection, and other public goods in their territorial domain. Since 2001, strongmen and their networks of vassal and client commanders became an integral part of the Afghan state, functioning as "statebuilders" in helping build bureaucratic institutions in compliance with liberal and democratic processes and delivering services.[3] However, strongmen must be understood, first and foremost, in relation to the networks they governed and resource interdependencies they controlled. *Strongmen networks* generally provide and restrict access to a wider network of actors (for example, parliamentarians, businessmen, armed militia groups, and drug traders) at the subnational level and can function as brokers in a larger political system (Table 2.1).

In traditional societies, *kinship-based networks* are an important additional type of network. Kinship is broadly defined as extended family, including biological relationships, genealogy, marriage, and other self-ascribed associations, beyond the family nucleus of parents and dependent children.[4] Kinship relations can be

Table 2.1 A typology of political networks and power resources

Power resources			
		Low	High
Typology of political networks	Patronage	Ideological Community mobilisation Coercion	Political Financial
	Strongmen	Community mobilisation Ideological	Coercion Financial Political
	Resistance/ Insurgency	Political Community mobilisation	Coercion Ideological Financial
	Technocratic	Ideological Coercion	Political Social
	Civil society	Coercion Ideological	Political Social
	Kinship/ Family	Coercion Financial	Ideological Community mobilisation Political

exclusive to a specific family and its followers or to a more inclusive network of kin, community, and political and business elites in an increasingly complex network connected through marriage and descent relations. In Afghanistan, marriage and kinship have historically been one of the most significant features of political elites' dynamics, helping to maintain alliances, define exclusive privileges, and produce financial capital. For instance, the prominent religious families of Sayed Mansoor Naderi, Sayed Ishaq Gailani, and Sibghatullah Mojadaddi, founded on exclusively religious ground, historically have built connections through marriage, business, and political ties. While in Pakistan during the anti-Soviet jihad, the latter two set up their own *tanzims*. Their main source of power is their historical religious family status and the legitimacy derived from it.

The introduction of international statebuilding projects in post-conflict settings raises the profiles of two other forms of political networks: *civil society* and professional *technocratic networks*. In Afghanistan, these actors took on the role of managers and specialists within the state and international statebuilding structures.[5] These networks emerged as the result of international donor investment in civil society, including significant resource flow to international and local NGOs for service delivery, and the inclusion of the diaspora community in power-sharing processes and post-settlement reconstruction.[6] In the case of Afghanistan, most of the Rome delegation of diaspora Afghans were invited to the 2001 Bonn Conference by the U.S.A. and its allies to represent the interests of the Western countries and were apportioned the second-highest number of seats in the interim government, including the Presidency. In other places, such as post-2003 Iraq and post-1999 Kosovo, an even greater role was given to diaspora community leaders in establishing a power-sharing arrangement.

In fragile countries like Afghanistan, reliant on international aid, NGOs have proliferated, often with significantly expanding their reach and an active role in service delivery to fill the gaps left by weak governments.[7] In Afghanistan, NGOs have helped produce some of the country's best technical elites who have, as Chapter 6 shows, joined the government in key positions since 2014, acting as gatekeepers to President Ghani's network. This isn't the first time Civil Society Organizations (CSOs) and technocrats have made the transition into politics. The role of *civil society networks* in revolutions is well established in places like Georgia and Kyrgyzstan. In Georgia, CSOs influenced the discourse that underpinned the Rose Revolution, helping to de-legitimise the Shevardnadze government. In the process, they themselves transformed into a powerful *political network* to compete in elections.[8] Compared to *technocratic networks*, which possess high political and bureaucratic skillsets, *civil society networks* enjoy mobilisation capacity, especially in urban centres. Both, meanwhile, are beneficiaries of strong international patronage and legitimacy.

As disentangled in Section 2.3, these six types of networks deploy several power resources at any given time, depending on the setting and types of crises, to leverage themselves into political networks and bargain strategically for their benefit. Strongmen-based political networks, centred on strong military figures who possess coercive power through the use of militias and patronage networks, for instance, can also enjoy greater political resources through their embeddedness in the state apparatus. Some political networks, for instance, of the *technocratic* variety, have access to financial wealth while enjoying little connection to constituencies, but they use their wealth to purchase and control strategic parts of the state administration and bureaucracy. Others enjoy strong tribal or ethnic constituency relations (*kinship*), which they can convert into vote banks. Most of these networks, except for *kinship networks*, are inclusive, and members have the ability to exit freely. There is also some room for fluidity between them; all can overlap in certain moments and at times exhibit features of two or more types of networks at once.

2.2 What holds a political network together?

The literature provides four different explanations for what holds a network together: network leadership, mutual interdependency, trust, and common purpose.

For *kinship-based* networks, as well as networks based on economic incentives, including criminality, personal trust is the defining source of network cohesion.[9] As discussed in the opening chapter, trust can impose obligations, expectations, and commitments on others in the network. Axelrod's concept of "the shadow of the future" points to a broader conception of self-interest in which individuals pay attention to the long-term prospect of their reputation.[10] Exiting a network can sanction a higher reputational risk for individuals. Anthropologists have long argued that strong ties based on kinship, families, and friendship build trust and facilitate high-risk activities.[11] For kinship and even some small-scale identity-based networks along with tribes and ethnicities at the local level, trust is considered a key underpinning factor for network cohesion as it helps to build a stronger bond and sense of collective identity. However, more recently, anthropologists have also brought attention to *mistrust* as an important aspect of the functioning of networks, adding nuance to the study of kinship and friendship relations. In fact, kinship relations in Afghanistan have historically often resulted in the opposite of trust: suspicion and mistrust within the clan and tribe.[12] The famous Pashtun Tarburwali norm (a pattern of cousin rivalry) may suggest that this is also an ingrained feature of culture in certain parts of Afghanistan.

In other types of networks, like *civil society* and *technocratic*, having a common purpose, such as fighting corruption or climate change, can be an important source of cohesion. However, even in these networks, in an environment of shifting alliances and uncertainty with significant prospects for corruption and opportunism, common purpose gradually becomes the least potent contributing factor to network cohesion. As the empirical chapters show, most members of a network in an unstable environment are often driven primarily by opportunistic practices of rent-seeking and manipulation for their survival. For instance, the Senior Afghan Government Employee (SAGE) network, a loose network of over 30 young professional public servants and officials close to President Ghani, set up in early 2017, went against its initial goal of promoting and implementing a shared reform agenda to become a source of intimidation and control for its members. The network was hijacked by a few senior officials close to President Ghani, who acted not only as gatekeepers to the president but spoilers—willing to utilise their disruptive power and access against members if they acted against their agenda or voiced opposition.[13]

In contexts marked by decades of war and violence, idealist notions like common purpose are often relegated to the margins. The cold reality is that the most potent cohesive forces are also the most practical: effective leadership (e.g., those who have proven themselves during difficult days of the war) and members' mutual *resource interdependency* (see Section 2.3). Public management literature also supports this conclusion: the success of networks depends mainly on the good management approach of the network leader.[14] In post-power-sharing contexts, political leaders, as the "central node," must build critical linkages externally while simultaneously managing the network internally. A political network leader must know who has the resources within the network (for example, money, information, expertise, and legitimacy) and how to employ them. The most effective role for an individual leader when there is an asymmetry of power resources is to play the role of a "powerbroker" and "facilitator." For instance, in post-2001 Afghanistan, political networks were centred on a strong leader who played the role of both patron and powerbroker, enabling the network to span across "structural holes" within the state and society, negotiating bargains and exchanges, and mobilising support at the community level.[15]

The absence of a strong leader, or a leader who fails to allow for the diversification of authority and mobility within the ranks, can lead to the splintering, weakening, and even collapse of the network. This was nowhere more evident than in post-2001 Afghanistan when the splintering of former jihadi *tanzims* into several patronages and regional strongmen-based networks following the death of the leader became a common feature.

After effective leadership, *power resource* interdependency is the second most important factor in bringing a network together, especially at the coalition/alliance level. Members *within* a political network, as well as political networks *among* themselves, co-exist within the framework of resource interdependency, which shapes the structure of political networks as members need the resources of other actors to achieve goals and survive.[16] At the coalition/alliance level in Afghanistan (discussed in Section 2.5), competing political networks find it advantageous to collaborate strategically with each other in re-assembling and transforming the post-conflict state in their favour and, once the state is re-assembled, to continue working together in maintaining the status quo and limiting access to *power resources*. This brings us to a discussion on the diversity of power resources and interdependencies these produce within a networked state.

2.3 Political networks survival and diversity of power resources

Securing access to some resources is not in itself sufficient for survival. Political networks survive in a resource interdependency context when they possess diverse *sources of power* that they can mobilise and operationalise through a variety of *power resources*. I employ Malejacq's framing of power resources which he employed in relation to warlords' survival to demonstrate how political networks assemble, strategise, and operationalise diverse power resources to advance their goals. Power resources are essentially the medium through which political actors express and exert their power in different settings.[17] He argues that for actors to survive in contexts like Afghanistan, they must accumulate and invest in resources that can be useful to them in the future. A political network's desire to accumulate additional resources is to expand its power and its bargaining position within power resource interdependencies, reward members and followers, co-opt rival members, and reward communities they attempt to represent.

Malejacq draws on the work of Michael Mann to differentiate sources of power, including ideological, political, economic, social, and violent (coercive) powers.[18] He argues that these sources of power produce diverse *power resources* which actors—in our case, political networks and their associates—can rally and operationalise daily to survive and, by investing in other resources, further strengthen and maintain network clientele. In Afghanistan, religious, tribal, and ethnic affiliations remain the most common ideological ground for political networks to claim legitimacy. In post-1992 civil wars, appealing to a specific ethnic and tribal group or Islamic jihad produced a symbiotic relationship between political *tanzims* (military-political organisations) and specific constituencies that feared discrimination and violence. The fear of ethnic violence provided Islamist *tanzims* an opportune source for claiming ideological and discursive legitimacy and representation.

Economic resources take the form of financial wealth—for instance, by securing international military contracts, charging protection fees, accessing development funds, and securing public positions, jobs, and spoils. In post-2001 Republic period in Afghanistan, most financial resources emanated from political networks' partial control of the state administration and bureaucracy and access to international military and donor funding. As Chapter 9 shows, financial wealth is accumulated through licit and illicit activities, including extortion and rents from the key sectors of the Afghan economy, including extractive industries and the drug economy.

Involvement in illegality and rent-seeking requires possessing *coercive power and violent means*. In post-2001 Afghanistan, most patronage and strongmen networks possessed coercive resources either through the use of militias or their embeddedness in the security and defence forces. In the 1980s and 1990s, while some political networks originated as state-sponsored militias like the Naderi family in Baghlan, Abdul Rashid Dostum in Jawzjan, and Abdul Rasul Pahlawan in Faryab province (discussed in Chapter 3), the jihadi *tanzim*'s main source of power was an ideological insurgency against the former Soviet Union which provided them with a significant monopoly over the use of violence in territories they occupied. As shown in Chapter 4, they successfully integrated most of their militia forces in the Afghanistan National Defense and Security Forces (ANDSF) post-2001 through several disarmament, demobilisation, and reintegration programmes over the years. Others set up private security companies, turning their armed men into legitimate service providers, providing security to NATO, embassies, and others.

Social resources, meanwhile, are derived from a political network's ability and strength to mobilise communities and constituencies in moments of contestation such as elections (discussed below in more detail). Some networks enjoy some degree of legitimation with the tribal or ethnic constituencies that they claim to represent. Social resources for these kinship- or religious-based networks include the reputation of one's name and family status (like the Gailani and Mojadaddi families, which were considered pious and religious leaders), as a fighter, trustworthy politician, effective technocrat, and others. As Azoy pointed out, in a tribal society, leaders must prove that they possess two important qualities: *Haisiyat* (character) and *itibar* (credit). The first is established by the behavioural display of "piety, generosity, and wisdom." The second is achieved by the ability to provide and deliver for the community and to create followership. In the absence of one or both, a leader risks abandonment in favour of a rival.[19]

These social resources are often fed and enlarged using *political resources* which come from holding a safe position within the state and the protection it affords, including access to information, securing a contract, international recognition, and political appointments. Those political resources are then in turn reinforced through the strengthening of social resources through the dispensation of political capital. One scholar, for instance, found that over half of the people she interviewed for her research in the Paghman district of Kabul province owed their jobs to local strongmen.[20]

For a political network to survive, it must possess several of these power resources and combine them to acquire additional capital.[21] A political network might possess several resources at any given time and trade them strategically, depending on the situation and the type of crisis. Here, network effectiveness is considered in terms of a political network's ability to survive, sustain, and possibly expand power and resources within the state. Network effectiveness is achieved if political networks can (1) maintain and consolidate political power within the state, (2) accumulate financial gains to buy loyalties and co-opt clients, (3) maintain strong ties to local communities to gain some degree of legitimacy, and (4) enjoy some degree of coercive capacity, including the ability to produce violence and exert sanctions on members and intimidate opponents. In the context of international statebuilding, part of political legitimacy is linked to tacit international legitimacy and their political and financial support for the network. The ability of political networks to perform these functions varies. Some might have excessive financial wealth but a limited political and social power base (for example, constituency mobilisation capacity and ideological authority) and weak coercion and intimidation capacity; others might enjoy higher social mobilisation power and coercion capacity but low financial resources; others might have mastered the political skills needed to navigate the rules of the game better than anyone else, operating in a complex interdependency environment. For a political network to survive and be effective, it must achieve at least two of the above functions in the right combination for specific circumstances. For instance, a combination of wealth and political and administrative patronage can lock political elites and their clients into long-lasting mutual interaction during times of stability but might not be effective in times of major crisis and war. On the other hand, a mixture of high patron–client relations, coercive capacity, and sufficient links to communities is more effective in times of crisis and instability.

In post-2001 Republic Afghanistan, as Chapter 4 shows, while a strongman-based network led by the former Governor Atta Mohammad Noor was primarily motivated by financial and military resource enlargement, Mohammad Mohaqqiq and Abdul Rashid Dostum concentrated their efforts on social and political resources, including ethnic constituency mobilisation, which enabled them to establish themselves as indispensable vote banks. Others like Abdul Rasul Sayyaf and Hamid Karzai proved to be effective political leaders by mastering institutional rules, in large part because they were the key architects of those rules. After the February 2020 deal between the U.S.A. and the Taliban, and the realisation that international militaries would be withdrawing, both Junbish-i-Islami and Wahdat-i-Mardom networks in the north made armed investments in an attempt to re-militarise their former commanders, but as Chapter 10 shows these efforts were too late and with little result. By 2021, the leaders had fractured and fragmented their political networks, essentially powerful political-military networks shrinking into family networks. In a politically fluid context like Afghanistan, where bargains and horse-trading are omnipresent, political networks can operationalise resources at their disposal for the collective goal of the alliance that they have become a member of, which then determines the network's position and access to a share of

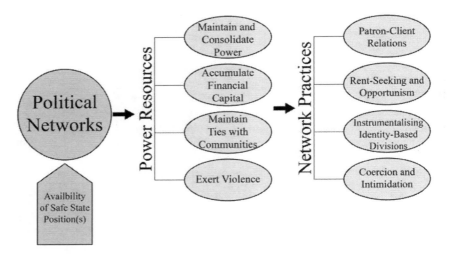

Figure 2.1 Power dynamics of political networks and network effectiveness

future resources and spoils. Strategic calculation of what resources to acquire and collect depends on many factors, including the future of the state, international intervention, the size and strength of the insurgency, and others (Figure 2.1).

2.4 Political networks and levels of engagement

Political networks can engage in four levels of interactions (see Figure 2.2): (1) the international statebuilding level, where they collaborate with—and often become very good at manipulating and exploiting—international actors, securing resources for their own purposes; (2) the central state level, where they collaborate as part of competing alliances within the state with other networks in a power resource interdependency system; (3) the subnational level where they fiercely exploit resources and compete with one another, often with a significant level of violence; and (4) the community level through formal and informal councils, *mullahs*, *maleks* (village elders), school teachers, and others to mobilise constituencies, often along evolving and shifting identity lines, and to secure some degree of public legitimacy. Each level of engagement can be mutually interdependent on the other. The greater a political network's engagement at all these levels, the higher its chances of survival and effectiveness in influencing political outcomes in its favour.

In an environment of resource interdependency and asymmetry of power, each network competes, negotiates, and bargains over the statebuilding process in an attempt to bend and influence processes, policies, and practices in its favour. The ability to engage successfully with international donors provides additional sources of legitimacy—in this case, external legitimacy, which can further

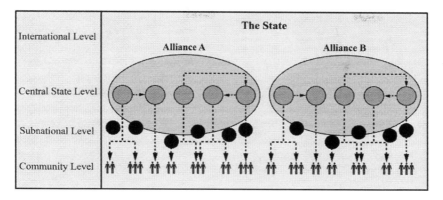

Figure 2.2 Levels of engagement/interaction

empower the network and ensure its relevance. For instance, the U.S. engagement in Afghanistan with some of the regional strongmen and militia-based networks, despite their human rights abuses and association with the drug trade, has given them continuous recognition and legitimacy. In the early years of international military intervention in Afghanistan, Provincial Reconstruction Teams (PRTs) became the main source of patronage for regional strongmen and local networks at the provincial level. As the empirical chapters show, some political networks in Kabul were exceptionally successful in directing aid money and international projects to provinces and districts where they enjoyed strong constituency support. Karzai, in 2011, confirmed that he had been receiving secret money from the CIA, Iran, India, and others (discussed in more detail in Chapter 4).

At the central state level, network members occupy key strategic positions within the state administration and bureaucracy, essentially masquerading as the state. Networks strategically collaborate, if it is to their benefit, over key policies, strategies, and government projects and contracts. At the state level, these networks-in-state play a key role in projecting a façade of political order and state stability by performing as the state and playing along with the established rules of the game. The bigger circle in the picture in Figure 2.2 is the state as the "contested field" among networks. The state, as the main "marketplace" for rent, provides an excellent setting for bargains.[22] At this level, networks ensure internal cohesion, maintain ties with local communities, and provide connections across networks within the state, represented by vertical lines and horizontal arcs, respectively. In essence, they function as intermediaries or powerbrokers, connecting a wide spectrum of actors, networks, and organisations at the international, subnational, and community levels.

The subnational level displays the most significant degree of interaction and power dynamics among a diverse group of network associates and elites (for example, regional strongmen networks, criminal groups, and others). Strongmen networks connect several provinces and districts in their network with a correlation to state-level networks, though not necessarily dependent on state-level networks and centres of power. They enjoy complex relationships and power dynamics with central state networks, local networks, and international agencies. In most cases, the relationships between the local and central state networks are mutually dependent and reciprocal. While central networks provide political protection and support by advocating—within the state and among international supporters— against policies and actions that could harm them, regional strongmen networks control customs, highways, and extractive industries that enable them to disperse some of that accumulated wealth to the central networks.[23] At the same time, by supplying patronage and gifts to local network elites, regional *strongmen networks* can influence the constituency in their control. In some cases, *strongmen networks* might not have any central state support, merited for its own power resources that it controls and ability to purchase loyalty and influence at the national level in key state institutions (e.g., Lower House, Senate, and cabinet). In Afghanistan, the U.S.A. and its allies were the biggest supporters of these regional *strongmen networks* because of their reliance on them for maintaining some of the supply lines for international militaries. When Atta Mohammad Governor Noor, the former governor of Balkh province and the strongman of the North, was removed from office, the main question among members of the international community in Kabul was who was going to keep the North safe. The international- and state-level actors' dependency on regional and local networks (district and provinces) to guarantee logistical supplies, resource flows, or community mobilisation and legitimation was key to maintaining the façade of political order, despite its shallowness.

Finally, networks at both the state and subnational levels are embedded in the communities they claim to represent. This is not to say that each community is tied to a single network; however, several networks might compete in the same community along with identity-based divisions (for example, ethnic, linguistic, religious, and tribal) for ideological and symbolic resources. In moments of crisis when central state-level or regional strongmen networks are under pressure, an appeal to their constituency, along shifting ethnic or tribal lines, is key to showcasing their disruptive power if decisions go against them. Political networks often invest huge amounts of money and discursive resources in their communities to maintain their support. As Chapter 7 shows, during election campaigns, these constituencies become a key source of bargaining for political networks to ensure they have a safe position in the next administration (see Section 2.7).

2.5 Political networks and alliance formation

Alliance formation is tactical, motivated by a concern about survival and the maximisation of power resource return. Christia's work on how survival drives alliance choices and fractionalisation among warring groups during civil wars is informative.[24] This alliance formation logic is still applicable to post-2001 statebuilding among political networks. Here, an alliance is comprised of several competing political networks that are connected by a set of power resource interdependencies, intended either to undermine a rival political network or to prevent it (or a competing coalition) from achieving maximum power with the capacity to exclude others. As Christia argues, ideally all groups want to be in a coalition large enough to attain victory yet small enough to ensure maximum political payoff.[25]

In post-2001 Afghanistan, alliances were often formed on an *ad hoc* and temporary basis in relation to a political situation, response to a crisis, or fear of exclusion. Networks entered an informal resource interdependency bargain in which each network brought multiple resources to the table. Unless a political network was strong enough to co-opt others and establish a monopoly (discussed in the conclusion) over the state, as a regime, coalitions were likely to face constant defection, reconfiguration, and fractionalisation. As Christia aptly shows, in the absence of a credible third-party enforcer, which can ensure that promises are met, the weaker party will often prefer to defect and prolong the war rather than risk being double-crossed at the hands of the stronger ally on the war's conclusion.

This logic dynamically shaped the alliance formation in the post-2001 Republic period in Afghanistan. Additionally, the two key mechanisms driving alliance formation logic which Fotini outlines were also present. The first is the evolution of the *relative power balance* between groups confronted by survival choices both within and across alliances. The post-Bonn Republic state created a relatively stable balance of power and resource interdependencies among competing networks in which they constituted parts of the state. This delicate balance dictated the various networks' choices over the years. President Ghani's attempt to undermine this balance in his favour failed spectacularly after 2014, with political networks constantly building *ad hoc* alliances—relatively strong ones—to ensure he did not achieve significant power.

Counterintuitively, while always seeking to ultimately be on the winning side, political networks sometimes avoided an alliance if it meant it would be the weaker partner and instead shifted to a weaker alliance partner as long as they remained strong. For instance, in the post-2019 Abdullah-Ghani deal in Afghanistan, one of the weaker patronage networks felt it would be excluded from the lion's share of power, with the Junbish network emerging as the dominant force, and therefore defected to Ghani's camp at the last minute. This was despite the huge reputational risk and investment it had made in mobilising its constituency in elections. This defection, on the other hand, significantly weakened Abdullah and his negotiating power.

The second mechanism that determines alliance choice is political network *fractionalisation*. Loss of a safe state position or access to a resource that is important to rivals can foster splintering within the network, often by ambitious members/factions who challenge the existing leader. Fractionalisation can occur when the splintering group sets up its own network or joins a rival network, or when a faction takes over the network with a significant amount of turmoil. The latter has not happened in post-2001 Afghanistan, where most factions have tried to set up their own networks.

Alliances are often temporary, fluid, and spatial. To hold an alliance together, the balance of power resources, interests, ambitions, and authorities must be maintained in a frequently renegotiated dynamic in response to changing conditions. As the empirical chapters show, alliances are constantly evolving and restructuring as events unfold, the crisis continues, socio-political balances change, and positions and resources shift. Exiting is not a major reputational risk; in fact, one could argue that a regular exit is good, as it increases the political network's chances of bargains in a fluid marketplace, but only up to the point where a network begins to develop a reputation for being unreliable/untrustworthy.

The role of a political leader within the alliance is to mobilise and operationalise resources and strategise to achieve the common goal. He/she should also be able to manage internal conflicts that may arise and identify means of achieving necessary outcomes—much of it ad hoc, short term, and situational. However, this is not to say that he/she is capable of dictating terms. While an alliance leader coordinates and facilitates actions, rarely is the real authority granted him/her across the coalition as a whole. Such a move is neither possible nor feasible. Each political network and its leader bring and keep their own authority, thus trying to manage the alliance together. In this situation, leadership is more of a process of co-managing and co-steering.

2.6 Political networks and institutional settings

Political networks operate within a given institutional context in which actors within the network shape their strategies and intentions and help them coordinate complex interactions.[26] Institutions are understood as "humanly devised constraints that structure human interaction. They consist of both informal constraints (sanctions, taboos, customs, traditions, and codes of conduct), and formal constraints (constitutions, laws, property rights)," or simply, the "rules of the game."[27]

In fragile and conflict-ridden countries, existing informal institutions—often overlapping and interconnected with formal institutions—play a key role in regulating the pattern of political network practices, incentive structures, and behaviours. Political networks in fragile and post-conflict settings have every incentive to preserve the old rules of the game, which helped them survive during the warring years. Evidence in post-conflict countries reveals that informal rules such as patronage, illegality, and rent-seeking, in fact, intensify with international intervention and statebuilding and that new rules often build on the existing ones.[28] This institutionalises everyday *practices* that govern the logic of networked governance.

A focus on day-to-day network practices sheds light not only on how competing networks survive but also on how they "perform" and "enact" the role of state. Enactment is the process by which state officials—those who claim to possess legitimate authority—position themselves to represent the state.[29] For instance, how do an army commander, a tribal elder, a village-level community development council member, and a regional strongman whose loyalty is to his/her political network come to make a meaningful claim to an authority that is external to him or her? Through this act of "impersonation," network members, on a daily basis, create the illusion of the state as a singular and vertical entity. In the following subsections, I will outline some of the key practices that political networks utilise to enact and perform as the state on a daily basis.

2.6.1 Patron–client relations

Patron–client relationships are understood as an exchange of a private and personal nature in which dyadic players have reciprocal needs and expectations, but unequal power and status,[30] based on reciprocity of goods and services and hierarchically arranged personal contact.[31] In weak institutional contexts in which the state is fragile, patronage flow acts as basic "political cement," in the words of James Scott, in binding the polity together.[32] Similarly, Putman, in relation to late-19th-century Italy, observes that patronage practices played a more important role in linking the centre to provinces than the formal administrative channels of the state.[33] Patron-client practices are driven by political economy and political culture. Goodhand, in his study of the war-to-peace economy, shows how patronage in post-2001 Afghanistan involves complex socio-cultural and political elements as well as economics of exchange and association.[34] It is often reinforced through strategies of interfamilial marriage, partnerships, and gifts. In relation to electoral politics in Latin America, studies found that it was the contingency of targeted benefits, and not the targeting of goods, that constituted the clientelistic exchange.[35] In one of the early works on patronage, Alex Weingrod highlights electoral patronage as the process in which party politicians distribute public jobs or special favours in exchange for electoral support.[36] As Chapter 7 shows, at one level, voters pledge their votes instrumentally—that is, to politicians who promise to deliver specific goods or who have already delivered a particular mix of goods and services. In the post-2001 Republic period in Afghanistan, patron-client practices are often contingent on the shifting boundaries of the community with the changing context of struggles within or between contending groups, which Professor Shahrani refers to as the "political ecology of particular times, places and spaces."[37] Patronage in post-2001 statebuilding is further complicated by increased bargaining and power resource interdependencies among competing political networks as well as their interactions with the international aid and military industries.

After appropriating a key strategic part of the state, following an internationally mediated power-sharing arrangement, political networks attempt to consolidate and advance their power and access to resources by offering patronage in the form of government positions, contracts, employment, and economic transfers, to their members, clients, and clients' constituencies, to maintain and co-opt key embedded local leaders, district governors, *mullahs*, state officials, and businessmen into their bargaining network. The ties of loyalty and reciprocity—whether economic or political—between the political network and its members within the network and across other political networks are conceived in interpersonal dyadic terms and are subject to constant negotiation, bargaining, and deal-making, especially at the alliance-building level. The ability of political networks to provide privileges, positions, and bargains determines their authority, power, and legitimacy within the re-assembling state. The most important resource within the state is government positions, which Hardin has dubbed "positional goods."[38] The availability of numerous patrons and the clients' ability to defect provides the client with considerable leverage within the network. This of course depends on what a client might be positioned to offer to an alternative patron. As Sinno argues, mid-level patrons can always challenge their own patron if he/she cannot continue to supply them with the resources they need, or if they develop a large clientele or sufficiently accumulate the resources that their patron once supplied.[39]

2.6.2 *Rent-seeking, illegality, and opportunism*

The availability of several networks and the ability of clients to exit to join a rival means that maintaining a political network can be extremely costly. Acquisition of financial resources for distribution to members and clients within the network is instrumental in helping the network survive in competition. In places like Afghanistan, this forced political networks to move towards creating a deeply "entrenched economy" in which small intertwined political and economic networks came to govern economic and political life.[40] With the sudden increase in international aid money, bargaining expanded to include manipulating international donors for rent, thereby creating further opportunities for resource manipulation and extraction. As Chapter 9 notes, a criminal network with links to local and Kabul-based politicians around Bagram airbase, the biggest NATO military camp in Afghanistan, implicitly obtained extortion from international military forces—as well as the Taliban. Even some deadly attacks were reported to be carried out by the criminal network as crude attempts at extortion and rent. The district governor of Bagram district, where the camp is located, outlined to me how this reciprocal game of tit for tat, aid, and extortion worked, making the district the biggest recipient of international aid and its businessmen and former commanders, some of the richest people in the country, as beneficiaries of NATO military transport and logistics contracts.

Rent-seeking is a *process* in which political and institutional dynamics determine the types of rent in play and the efforts put into rent-seeking.[41] Rent-seeking is defined as the "expenditure of resources and efforts in creating, maintaining, and transferring rents" by private and public actors.[42] In countries like Afghanistan, political networks try to capture available rents and to have new ones created to enhance their positions. These efforts could be legal (for example, lobbying, financial and political contribution to political parties) or illegal (for example, paying bribes, illegal political contributions, or expenditures to create and sustain a criminal mafia group). Rent-seeking is closely related to the already established (or being-established) institutions and incentives and the structure of rents in a particular setting. In post-2001 Afghanistan, rents were the power resources identified above that could be obtained legally and illegally, pursued in an established institutional setting with clear rules of the game; the structure of the rent was determined by the resource interdependencies among political networks. Changes to the structure of rents could have serious distributive impacts among networks. In Khan's conceptualisation, not all rents are bad for development and some might be growth enhancing. However, rent-seeking is damaging when the costs are high—that is, when actors must spend a lot of resources on otherwise unproductive (often illegal) activities necessary for securing loans, licenses, a contract, or other privileges. As Chapter 9 shows, in Afghanistan rent-seeking has had a negative effect on the country's economic growth and democratisation.

Studies in other contexts have confirmed that illegality and resource/rent extraction are fundamental in maintaining political networks and state functioning.[43] In his study of illicit border crossings in the Chad basin, Roitman found that illegal resource extraction by state officials was actually seen by many (both locals and state officials) as a "legitimate mode of the exercise of power," fundamental to the survival of the state. Roitman criticised those who he argues misleadingly referred to such practices as an "informal economy," "shadow economy," or "parallel economy," as these activities were fundamentally linked to the state.[44]

Illegality is neither parallel nor captured as suggested; it is an integrated and inseparable process that shapes the nature of governance in these spaces. As such, as some scholars have aptly argued, corruption might actually be necessary to meet the shared objectives of peacebuilding.[45] In the post-conflict settings, where the state is captured by rent-seeking factions, corruption does indeed have a stabilising effect in sustaining political order, in Doughlas North's sense of limited access order, challenging the conventional wisdom arguing that corruption and peacebuilding are fundamentally oppositional. Similarly, as Reeves argues in relation to Central Asian states, illegality is not simply a deviation or corruption of the state; nor is it incidental to its constitution; it is an everyday function.[46] In places like post-1998 Bosnia, post-2001 Afghanistan, and post-2003 Iraq, political networks and the state thrive on illegality, as resource extraction through illegal means such as rent, land grabbing, kidnapping, and extortion are fundamental everyday practices that ensure the survival of the networks and the state.

In some instances, political networks engage in criminality and build relations with criminal networks. As Chapter 9 shows, illegality and criminality in some instances are intertwined and entrenched. Criminality and rent-seeking work best when using a combination of weak and strong ties. Podolny and Page highlighted that networks enable criminals to build positive relations with the political groups on which they depend for protection and to build functional, mediated, and varied connections with non-criminal actors whose expertise is of value to them.[47] For instance, traffickers use strong intimate ties with local residents to maintain an inward trust base to build the trafficker's leadership role while limiting the local roles of weakly tied state officials and still using contacts with those officials to obtain funding and build political support. As one study found, traffickers form social connections with government officials to reduce risk and uncertainty.[48]

However, wealth accumulation is not an end in itself for political networks that engage in (or are indirectly involved in) illegality, criminality, and rent-seeking; rather, it is often a means for political and social ends in purchasing loyalties, expanding political support, gaining prestige, or simply reciprocating as part of informal institutions of *Waseta* and *Andewali*, discussed in the Preface of this book. The combination of patron–client practices and rent-seeking locks political networks and their clientele into long-lasting interactions. Failure to redistribute the accumulated wealth will damage the reputation of network leaders in the long run among the members and communities they claim to represent. As discussed in Introduction, the expectation among communities is high. Scholars have found that most communities in Afghanistan consider their elected and state representatives first and foremost an extension of their local patronage system, whose primary role is to connect them to the patronage aid provision of the Afghan state and international statebuilding.[49]

The greater the ability of political networks to generate access and distribute resources to members and others in their communities, the greater their *posturing* power when it comes to bargaining within the state. The community perceives them as being able to deliver greater benefits, therefore improving their position within an interdependent political system. Worth noting is that, as the empirical chapters show, in societies where access to resources is the definition of statehood, it is often the followers who push provincial- and national-level actors and networks to utilise all means necessary—including, in some cases, illegality—to generate as much control over resources and redistributable income as possible. The bottom-up pressure to provide on the networked elites is huge. It is the power resources in possession of a network and the relevance of these resources for a particular setting that are key to survival.

2.6.3 Coercion and intimidation

Political networks, especially those in possession of violent means, on occasion do exert some degree of coercion and intimidation (often in the form of threat), though not always successfully, especially at the subnational level where the reach of the central state is weak. In the wider dynamics, most political networks—depending on their degree of military resources—are involved in the business of private protection, using violence to provide political protection to members and businessmen, provincial contractors, and others outside their group.

Coercion is conceived of as a kind of activity by a powerful agent who creates and then utilises significant disparities in power over another to constrain or alter the latter's possibilities for action.[50] Anderson argues that this power differential may be used to put pressure on the coercee's will, but additionally, it might work by simply prohibiting or disabling agents or more systematically disrupting various possibilities for action. Coercion depends on the existence of a credible threat of punishment.[51] It results from the direct use of force or violence. While the coercee might not always comply, the threat should be credible and enforceable to ensure a businessman or local commander thinks twice before engaging in non-compliance.

Within political networks, the patron should be able to monitor, prevent, and suppress dissent before it materialises into a well-organised rebellion that threatens to splinter the network. Threat and intimidation can be effective additional tools engaged by networks to exercise discipline and loyalty. The distribution of resources and positional goods might not be enough on its own to ensure loyalty. In other words, the patron must be able to use a mix of patronage and coercion to achieve compliance and loyalty. In general, the more centralised a political network is around a leader, often strong and charismatic, who possesses the means of violence, the higher the coercive discipline within the network and subsequently network cohesion.[52] Discipline and order within the network are key for establishing the ability to accumulate wealth, share information, and better organise against a competing network. However, within a context of multiple competing networks and patrons, harsh disciplinary action and sanctions can be seen as unjustifiable by other members and can be counterproductive, encouraging members to splinter or switch to a rival network. The most effective means, such as limiting access to resources, sanctioning resources, or reshuffling members within the network, seem to be indirect measures to instil discipline effectively.

The use of threats and intimidation, as much as it is a tool for exerting discipline and control over members, especially among militia-based and strongmen networks, and at the local level, is also about increasing one's bargaining position or a way of projecting power. Malejacq has shown how warlords project their power as a strategic tool to ensure their survival by portraying themselves as the strongest actors on the local scene to the international community, central elites, and local population. This is what Pierre Bourdieu termed symbolic power, a power which exists because the person who submits to it believes that it exists.[53] As Noah Coburn notes in his work, reputation is indeed "a man's [sic] greatest weapon and greatest vulnerability" in the eyes of communities that one claims to represent or international backers who bestow external legitimacy to political networks. And as Hobbes asserted, "Reputation of power, is power."[54] However, political networks must occasionally display their violent capacity and intimidation on the field by subduing a local rival militia or by conducting killings (both judicially and extra-judicially) to maintain their reputation.

In the post-2001 Republic period in Afghanistan, except for civil society and technocratic networks, most political networks utilised some degree of violence and other tools to make conditional threats, indirectly, strategically, and selectively. Those networks in possession of greater military resources were successful in coercing international statebuilders to rent them for services where their disruptive power was seen as a threat to the stability of the country (or parts of the country) and their fight against international terrorism and insurgency. As Chapters 8 and 9 illustrate, coercion and intimidation exacerbated criminality, illegality, and opportunistic practices. They created an intertwined and complex opportunistic system within which armed men were available for hire to criminal groups and businessmen who paid them to engage in disruptive activities, such as kidnapping travellers on highways to force people to take airplanes, or blowing up telecommunication towers to increase insurance fees. Ordinary investors were forced to hire armed militiamen to construct residential towers in metropolitan cities against government regulations because that was cheaper than following lengthy bureaucratic processes. As Chapter 9 shows, some political networks established their own militia groups, which fought under the banner of the Taliban insurgency and were utilised to silence opponents and control drug trafficking routes and trade, and subsequently as tools for bargains with international statebuilders and the central government. During my work at the Independent Directorate of Local Governance (IDLG), the National Security Council identified more than 1200 illegal armed groups across the country that had between 10 and 2000 armed men whose use of violence, threats, intimidation, and illegality was an everyday norm in the periphery.

2.6.3.1 Instrumentalising identity-based divisions

Most political networks invest symbolic, political, and financial resources into maintaining close ties with local communities to satisfy their needs and expectations in order to gain a degree of political legitimacy. Studies suggest that community elites are strongly affected by their proximity to the network of informal social relations.[55] Legitimacy is key to the long-term survival of political organisations and their status and viability.[56] While wealth might help them buy loyalty, political networks also need communities as an additional bargaining resource in political exchange, especially in moments of high contestation such as during elections and crises (see Chapter 7). Legitimacy in post-conflict statebuilding is often achieved alongside a combination of service provision and traditional means such as religious, tribal, and ethnic support.

In divided societies, identities provide a powerful means through which political networks and their clients can mobilise communities. Prolonged conflicts often produce an environment of "complex security dilemmas," in which ethnic and tribal divisions provide opportunities for political networks to claim representational legitimacy for the communities in which they are embedded.[57] In such conditions, the appeal of identity elites further accentuates identity affiliations, as the two together provide a rationale for the perpetuation of identity divisions. This produces a symbiotic relationship between political networks that wish to advance their own bargaining position within the state and their constituencies who fear political domination. However, this is not to imply that identities are fixed and stable in post-conflict countries. As Barth argues in his classic work, identity is not a quality of a social group but, rather, a relationship between social groups.[58]

As such, identities are multiple and overlapping forms. This is why Russell Hardin argued in his 1995 book that one should speak of "identifications" rather than "identities," crosscutting families, villages, and regions.[59] Similarly, Rogers Brubaker shifts our analytical focus from identity to "identifications," from groups as entities to group-making projects. For him, ethnicity, race, and nation are not things in the world but perspectives on the world: ways of seeing, interpreting, and representing the social world.[60] Individuals are self-categorised or categorised by others depending on different types of social relationships in different situations. As such, identities are multiple and overlapping forms, crosscutting families, villages, and regions. Identities provide a powerful terrain on which symbolic and discursive battles could be contested among political networks. In Afghanistan, while none of the political networks came to power through identity structures, once in power they pursued every effort to maintain a certain degree of influence over the ethno-regional and tribal systems.[61]

In summary, it is the combination of these rules of the game and daily practices that ensure networks survive and sustain themselves within the state as well as enact as the state. This in turn ensures that political order and stability are guaranteed, as is the potential for disruption. In these governing rules of the game, the non-cooperation—or refusal to participate in the above-highlighted practices—comes with strong sanctions. The alternatives to not playing along for members within the networks are exclusion, isolation, and, in some cases, ridicule. During my work in the government, many of the professional technocrats in senior government positions were ridiculed and bullied for failing to play and master the game. They were often labelled weak and ineffective. For these professionals, non-conformity often meant exclusion from important behind-the-door decision making and a lack of political protection against rivals. For a businessman in the North allied with Governor Atta Mohammad Noor meant the loss of access to domestic markets and, in some instances, kidnapping and even loss of assets, when his patron's relations deteriorated in 2017 with President Ghani.

2.7 The safe state position(s)

The contingency that would have a significant influence on political network survival is the network's control of a safe state position(s).[62] A safe state position(s) refers to the political network's strategic control of a key position within the state (that is, presidency, vice-presidencies, ministerial positions, directorates, governorships) from which it could contest against potential rivals both materially and symbolically. The safe position is important because it provides political networks with the necessary legitimacy to make a claim to the state and enact themselves as the state. Once in power following a power-sharing arrangement in which state positions are distributed as positional goods, political networks utilise state resources and the legitimacy given to them by the state to expand and consolidate their power within the state (this is discussed further in Chapter 5). The state provides these networks with the opportunity to accumulate wealth, gain access to national and international projects and contracts, and shape policy. More importantly, it offers them first-hand access to information. For instance, a friend working for President Karzai's office explained to me how knowing about the government's housing policy a few months before the release of the policy to the public had enabled a particular construction company, with links to the first vice-president, to win a contract. The state position gives political networks the capacity to project power and relevancy. That is why, for some networks, it is so important to secure a cabinet position, seen as symbolic prestige in the eyes of the public, which puts them in a particular category, even though it may be a materially toothless office that does not improve its broader position in bargains.

But safe positions are rarely safe for long within the state because, in a "contested field" dictated by the asymmetry of power and resources, competing political networks continuously try their best to undermine their rival's safe position. It might also allow new networks that are more capable of organising members and more able to offer technical and political expertise to emerge within the state bureaucracy and administration with the external backing of international statebuilders. To survive, a network that gains control of a safe position(s) within the state must strengthen its grip by pursuing at least two, if not all, of the key network practices outlined above. Failure to do so will result in the collapse and disintegration of the network, resulting in members switching to a rival.

2.8 International aid and military presence as deterrence

International military money and aid provided an excellent opportunity to political networks in the post-2001 Republic period for rent-seeking and resource extraction, enabling them to accommodate actors in their network, purchase loyalties, and partly deliver services for their communities. It created a symbiotic interdependency between the U.S.A. and allies and a small group of Afghan elites within the state, civil society, and business community, where they pursued their collective and country-specific agendas and interests. The U.S.A. in particular used money as a weapon system to pursue its "War-on-Terror" objectives and procuring loyalties for short-term gains. This is discussed in detail in Chapter 9 and conclusion of this book. The overall result was a *fragmented statebuilding* effort with each country responsible for key statebuilding tasks and pursuing their own approach and practice in achieving them. And in doing this, each international donor and international military produced their own local clients at the national and local level who were readily available for hire. The Australian relationship with Matiullah Khan in Uruzgan was a classic example of such a relationship, discussed in detail in Chapter 4.

There is a general assumption that the presence of international troops can help deter interstate conflict among governments and intrastate war among domestic political forces. A Rand Corporation study of U.S. military presence since 1945 found that a large U.S. troop's presence may reduce the likelihood of interstate conflict in two ways: by deterring potential adversaries from initiating interstate war or by restraining allies from initiating militarised behaviour.[63] However, military presence may increase interstate militarised activities short of war. Contrary to the assumption during the post-2001 Republic period in Afghanistan, U.S. presence did not reduce the risk of intrastate conflict or change actors' behaviours. As detailed in Chapter 6, the post-2014 presidential election crisis nearly produced a coup, and rivalry among political network clients at the subnational level produced daily violence over resources and territories which were often overlooked as long as Kabul and major cities were secure to produce the façade of political order. As the concluding chapter (Chapter 10) in this book argues, it seems that international aid and military expenditure, as important sources of patronage for political networks, were more important in deterring national political disorder and instability than having U.S. troops stationed in the country as a means of deterring war.

Notes

1 Kwon (2010) challenges the notion that the Cold War was a global struggle fought uniformly around the world. In reality, in large part of the developing world, it was marred by vicious civil wars and other exceptional forms of violence. To name a few political and military organisations: the Muslim Brotherhood in Egypt, the Afghan communist and Jihadi groups, Mao's guerrilla fighters (before transforming themselves into a centralised military organisation), and other nationalist movements like the National Liberation Front in Algeria and Palestine Liberation Organisation.
2 See Johnson and Dandeker (1990).
3 Malejacq (2020), Mukhopadhyay (2009 and 2014).
4 The classic anthropological work on kinship dates back to Morgan and Levi-Strauss (1969); Schweizer and White, (1997).
5 Civil society includes a wide range of associations, people's movements, citizens' groups, consumer associations, small producer associations and cooperatives, women's organisations, indigenous peoples' organisations, and, of course, development NGOs.
6 See Alger (2005), Barnes (2005), Belloni (2001), and Paffenholz (2010).
7 According to recent data, as of October 2016 and since 2005, there were 4001 registered local NGOs in Afghanistan and 434 international NGOs registered with the Ministry of Economy which provided one of the biggest job markets in the country. See http://www.icnl.org/research/monitor/afghanistan.html.
8 See the edited volume Stewart (2012).
9 This is more the case with "face-to-face" trust than with "civic" or "anonymous" trust: see Maley (2003).
10 Axelrod (2006).
11 See Schneider (1984), Sahlins (2013), Curtin (1984), Monsutti (2004), and Marsden (2015).
12 See Marsden and Anderson (2020), and Monsutti (2014).
13 Author interview with the Senior Afghan Government Employee (SAGE) network members, July and August 2020.
14 Agranoff and McGuire (2003); Huxham and Vangen (2005); Klijn and Koppenjan (2000).
15 Burt (2005) provides a rich account of social capital in networks. He shows how brokers fill structural holes to connect different clusters, help bridge differences and work towards cooperation. Network entrepreneurs identify lucrative structural holes in a market or organisation and secure an advantage by managing the work of patching up the hole. A structurally autonomous group has a strong reputation mechanism aligning people inside the group, and the advantage of a broader vision as a result of brokerage outside the group. They have a creative view of valuable projects, whom to involve, and with whom to work together to make it happen.
16 This explanation in public policy was advanced by Rhodes and Marsh (1992) and Rhodes (1997).
17 See Malejacq (2020: 47–50).
18 Mann (1986).
19 Azoy (1982).
20 Murtazashvili (2016).
21 See also Malejacq on power conversion, (2020:49–50).
22 The concept of marketplace is explained below in network practices section.
23 Chayes (2015)
24 Christia (2012: 6–7).

25 Ibid.
26 On the relationship between institutions and networks, see Scott (2008) and Owen-Smith and Powell (2007) studies; and Hodgson (2004); North (1990); Ostrom (1990).
27 North (1990: 1–2).
28 Narten (2009); Sending (2011).
29 Reeves (2007).
30 Johnson and Dandeker (1990).
31 Scott (1972).
32 Ibid.
33 See Putnam (1993).
34 Goodhand (2004).
35 Kitchelt and Wilkinson (2007); and Shahrani (2002).
36 Weingrod (1968: 379).
37 Shahrani (1998: 220); Ladwig III (2017).
38 Hardin, R. (1995).
39 Sinno (2008: 39).
40 For recent studies of economic entrenchment theory, see Faccio (2006) and Fisman (2001). Empirical studies that analyse the effect of political connections and rent-seeking activities on firm performance (Faccio, 2006; Fisman, 2001) suggest that such connections represent an integral firm asset. Burt (1992) and Granovetter (1985) found that these connections have a social capital component, which affects both firms' strategic choices and their performances in the market.
41 The concept of rent-seeking dates back to the work of Gordon Tullock in 1967 and Anna Krueger in 1974 in the field of economics. Since then, the concept has been further developed in economics, political science, and law. See Krueger (1974) and Tullock (1967).
42 See Khan (2000).
43 See Roitman (2003), Nordstrom (2001) and Reno (2001).
44 Roitman (2003: 192–93).
45 See Cheng and Zaum (2011) and their edited volume on corruption and peacebuilding.
46 Reeves (2007: 134).
47 Podolny and Page (1998).
48 Kahler (2009).
49 See Weinbaum (1972 and 1977).
50 See Anderson (2010). The literature on coercion in international relations and institutions is diverse across sociology and sexuality studies. For philosophical discussion on coercion, see Nozick (1969) and Zimmerman (1981). For international relations and politics studies, see edited volume by Reidy and Riker (1996).
51 One of the earliest conceptualisations of coercion was developed by Robert Nozick (1969) which provided an intuitive picture of how coercion works. Coercion occurs when (a) person P threatens person Q, (b) thereby altering Q's perceived rational self-interest, (c) all in order to alter/increase the likelihood that Q will do what P wants him or her to do, and (d) Q complies as a result of P's threat. In his view, coercion results only from certain "conditional threats" which Q complies with voluntarily. This understanding has come under great scrutiny because it inadequately assesses the social and political significance of coercion as it limits it to *conditional threats* which assumes the coercee will comply voluntarily. However, coercion also results from the direct use of force or violence, and coercee might not always comply. Scott Anderson (2010) makes a distinction between the *enforcement approach* and the *pressure approach* to understanding coercion.
52 For studies that look at the connection between forms of organisations and coercion, see Du Picq (2013); Marks (2013).
53 Bourdieu (1991).

54 Hobbes, (2017)
55 For community elite networks and collective actions studies, see Laumann and Pappi (1976), Laumann et al. (1977).
56 Suchman (1995) asserts that there are two types of legitimacy, internal and external. External legitimacy is bestowed by an international intervener's support to political networks. The international invitation of several networks to the Bonn Conference in 2001 provided Jihadi political networks with the necessary external recognition they needed. External legitimacy is gained on a daily basis in the process of statebuilding. Tsai (2001) argued that external links are crucial to the survival and expansion of networks. As outlined in Chapter 5, external support and legitimacy was a key factor in enabling Karzai and his emerging political network to pursue repression and accommodation policies.
57 See Kaufman (2000: 441).
58 Barth (1969).
59 Hardin (1995)..
60 See Brubaker (2006) and Brubaker and Copper (2000).
61 See Wimmer and Schetter (2003); Roy (1995); Dorronsoro (1995); Simonsen (2004).
62 I draw on Sinno's idea of a "safe position" contingency at war.
63 O'Mahony (2018).

3 The origins and evolution of political networks

Factionalism, violence, and political settlements

Introduction

This chapter is a historical account of the origins and evolution of Afghanistan's political networks since the 1960s to understand continuities and changes in the power dynamics of political networks and sources of power in the post-2001 Republic period. By doing so, it shows how the post-2001 Republic state was built with extensive and integral rudiments of conflict deeply rooted in the last four decades of intra-network rivalry, factionalism, war, and violence.

Most of the prominent political networks and their leaders in the post-2001 Republic period in Afghanistan, including jihadi Islamists, had their origins in the *constitutional decade* spanning the early 1960s to the early 1970s when Cold War ideologies found fertile ground among Kabul elites. Factionalism, governance, and statehood were interlinked with the role of power dynamics of political organisations and their sub-networks. They also became clients of rival international and regional stakeholders in the Cold War struggle, making Afghanistan a proxy battleground, which continued in the post-2001 Republic period in different formats under the U.S.-led NATO military intervention. The country was rapidly transformed into a "rentier state," with "rentier political organisations" acting as agents on behalf of international and regional patrons, a key feature of the networked state that will remain in the post-2001 Republic period.[1] Competing foreign countries built and expanded their client networks within the state and society, penetrating key state institutions with political groupings' loyalty and accountability lying outside the country than to the Afghan population.

Soviet Union-trained leftist officers staged two successful coups—first in July 1973 against Zahir Shah and then in April 1978 against Daud Khan—carrying on the long tradition of violence and insurgency as the dominant method for capturing the state and transforming state-society relations. Jihadists and later the Taliban would employ insurgency as the means to overthrow the state and in the post-2001 period blame American military intervention to justify their violence against the Afghan state and population. Since the collapse of the communist regime in 1992, Afghanistan has remained a "regional conflict complex," with rival countries fighting their competition inside Afghanistan and enabling Islamist

DOI: 10.4324/9781315161617-3

jihad and later Taliban insurgency to sustain themselves against different foreign military interventions.[2]

In this chapter, I first examine the period of communist rule (1978–1992) and the enabling political environments for the emergence of leftist political organisations and their sub-faction networks to show how the nature of statehood was transformed. The impact of factionalism on the stability of the People's Democratic Party of Afghanistan (PDPA) and their sub-networks within the communist party leading up to and after the 1978 coup, particularly between the Khalq and Parcham factions, set the tone for what was come; elite disunity, factionalism, and violence since then became key features of statehood in Afghanistan including in the last two decades of the Republic. The second part of this chapter then switches focus to the other side of the coin—the intricate roots and evolution of Islamist groups and their intra-network dynamics within the so-called "government-in-exile" in Peshawar, Pakistan. Finally, I tackle the consequences of previous failed political settlements to overcome political network disunity, division, and fragmentation with the ultimate goal of situating the 2001 Bonn Agreement in the context of other internationally mediated and highly flawed power-sharing arrangements which had serious repercussions for post-2001 Afghanistan including its eventual collapse in August 2021.

3.1 The emergence of the PDPA: factionalism and violence

The roots of transformational politics in Afghanistan trace back to the reformist and pro-democratic movement that began with the liberal parliament of 1949–1952 but gained momentum between 1964 and1973, known as the "constitutional decade." During this period, Afghanistan, like many other nations, was exposed to radical Cold War-era political and ideological thoughts and forces.[3] In 1949, the parliament provided a useful platform for reformist leaders to air grievances against the royal ruling family and their mismanagement and corruption, as well as to preach their new and radical political ideas. This indirectly had an immense impact on the Student Union at Kabul University, established on 4 April 1950—the first student organisation in the country's history.[4] Soon it became a hotbed for university and high school student activism and mobilisation, providing a platform for debate and recruitment for reformists calling for parliamentary democracy from both the left and right of the political spectrum. Despite the student union's short life—banned after seven months—political liberalisation fashioned some of the future political leaders within the communist and Islamist parties and planted the seed of a transformational political consciousness. Prime Minister Daud's resignation in 1963 led to the introduction of a series of democratic reforms under a constitutional monarchy. The new constitution bestowed a string of political freedoms which galvanised small underground ideological networks, leading them to emerge as political parties of four competing strands: leftists (both Marxism-Leninism and Maoism), Islamists, royalists, and liberal-democrats, inspired by and modelled on their international counterparts.

A bill formalising political parties was never decreed by the king, but this did not, of course, prevent political parties from pursuing activities and setting up demonstrations, recruiting members, and publishing pamphlets and newspapers to promote their ideologies. There is a broadly accepted argument that the king did not sign the proposed Political Parties' Bill for fear of parliament's dominance by radical parties, especially the left.[5] Although this fear might have been genuine, as Bezhan (2013) convincingly argues, there was no real reason for the monarch to fear the emergence of political parties because none of the parties could have obtained a majority. Both Islamists and leftists had little constituency in the countryside, evident from how few of them won seats in the 1965 elections. PDPA won only four seats in the 1865 parliamentary elections. The king's allies did attempt to set up parties, but because of a lack of support from the king, those attempts failed and quickly disintegrated.[6] Their members were a liberal, reform-minded political brotherhood, mainly Western-educated members of the royal family who once the communist came to power left the country to return after the fall of the Taliban in 2001 and to join Karzai and other technocratic networks, some taking important positions in the future cabinet and in police and army.

The leftist groups initially formed as small networks in semi-secrecy around charismatic leaders; they identified themselves as "study groups." Of the seven main active leftist networks, six came to establish the PDPA on the evening of 1 January 1965.[7] The force of networked politics led by strong personalities would remain a major contributing factor to factionalism and internal infightings within PDPA for the next two and a half decades. Nur Mohammad Taraki was elected as Secretary-General and Babrak Karmal as Party Secretary.[8] Taraki's group received three positions in the seven-member Central Committee, while the Karmal group received one member. Division of power along networked lines so early in the process, without even drafting a constitution and agreeing on key ideological positions, would come to plague the party, embedding division, distrust, and factionalism into its very DNA. Eighteen months after its establishment, the PDPA split into two hostile camps, *Khalq* (masses) and *Parcham* (banner), led by Taraki and Karmal, respectively, after the names of their publications. Both retained the PDPA designation, each calling the other the splinter group.

The divisions were network based and rooted in the full spectrum of Afghanistan's socio-political categories, from kinship ties to educational and fraternal backgrounds. Rubin's mapping of the communist elites at the politburo, central committee, and cabinet levels is telling.[9] His dataset highlights that the Parcham faction was comprised of mainly urban elites, Persian speakers (even among the Pashtuns), and a significant number from Kabul, often well-off, from different tribes and ethnicities that generated a network of clientelism through marriage.[10] The Khalq faction was from rural Afghanistan, with a stronger network of connections to their tribe and clans within the party. The social composition of the middle- and lower-ranking officers was mostly Ghilzai Pashtuns from rural Afghanistan, which gave *Khalq* a recruiting advantage over *Parcham*.[11] Also, the same dataset on primary and secondary educational backgrounds reveals that at least half of the Parchamis had attended Kabul's elite schools. Most had studied at Kabul University and were recruited from there. About a quarter of both Khalq and Parcham members had attended the Soviet-funded Kabul Military Academy. By 1983, over 50% of party members were in the armed forces, which produced its own intricate fraternity networks.[12] By 1979, a third of the party membership worked within the state, reaching 82,000 by 1987, dominating both the state bureaucracy and the armed forces.[13] Lacking the capacity to carry out a grassroots revolution, the army provided the quickest way to organise a power grab—carrying out two successful coups in 1973 (in partnership with Daud Khan) and 1978 (against Daud Khan).[14] As rightly noted by Professor Maley, the leftist revolution and subsequent coups were not a product of popular demand to transform state-society relations; rather, they reflected severe divisions within the political, and mainly Kabul-based, networked elites.[15] The military takeover of power through coups set a precedent for political organisations to use violent means as the main method for acquiring power and controlling the state. The jihadis in the 1990s and the Taliban in the two decades of American military intervention employed similar mass violence to overthrow governments, despite the opportunity for political settlements as discussed in Section 3.3.

3.1.1 Factionalism, violence, and the state

Once in power in April 1978, the *Khalq* and *Parcham* factions and their sub-networks began a fragile power-sharing settlement within the state. Initially, what they set up was a delicate "networked regime" with the strength of each faction and their networks carefully balanced within the cabinet, central committee, the politburo, and security sector. Both leaders, Taraki and Karmal, reclaimed their original posts of Secretary-General and Party Secretary. However, this did not last long. A few months into their power-sharing agreement, the *Khalqis* being in control of the presidency and politburo saw an opportunity to start purging Parchamis, especially those in the army. Of 62 army generals from the old regime, 60 were killed, removed, or forced to retire.[16] And out of the original 18,000 members of the party, and the 28,000 who had joined before the end of 1979, half had died or had been purged by the time the Soviet Union invaded.[17] Once the *Parchamis* were weakened, internal division shifted within the *Khalq* faction between rival networks around two networks led by Taraki (who was its general secretary) and Hafizaullah Amin (the prime minister). In a failed attempt by Taraki to assassinate Amin, the latter's network clients staged an internal coup and killed Taraki.[18]

As discussed in Chapter 2, Khalqis only relied on coercive and political sources of power within the state; the Khalq faction failed to accumulate social, ideological, and international patronage sources of power. Out of the four levels of interactions that were identified in Chapter 2 (international, central state, subnational, and community levels) for it to remain effective, it depended only on state level and international level interactions. It quickly lost international patronage and forced the Soviet Union to invade Afghanistan in 1989 as well as alienating the local population. Its leaders' avowed atheism, killing of thousands of innocent people, as well as pursuing radical and provocative policies to shape state-society relations, including an unpopular land reform policy, pushing local communities into the arms of the Jihadi groups, with an increasing number of them taking up arms against the regime. It, therefore, lost both international and domestic legitimacy. And as asserted in the previous chapter with the logic of networked politics, instead of building alliances with other political networks within the state to maximise power resources and ensure its survival, the Khalqis selfishly excluded and alienated others before its grip over the state was secure. As shown below, the Parchamis would make similar mistakes and fail to broaden its political base despite the Soviet pressure and when President Najibullah tried to do this, it was too late and not considered serious enough.

In many ways, the Soviet intervention, which began on 27 December 1979, was an extension of this internal factional fighting within Afghanistan's leftist politics. The ten-year Soviet occupation began with the violent removal of Khalqi leader, Hafizaullah Amin, and his replacement by Parcham leader Babrak Karmal. At the same time, the Soviet action inspired the Islamists and gave legitimacy to their cause as well as deepening the *Khalq-Parcham* factional divide. The policy of accommodation and compromise in relation to both the *Khalqis* and the rural countryside was just lip service, each network faction tried to empower and appoint their own members and secure a safe position within the state. Actors' loyalty and allegiance remained to the networked patron who has secured them the job. Each network even within the Parcham faction worked against the other, trying to undermine the other in the eyes of their Soviet patrons. A Soviet Union main security agency (known as KGB) officer visiting Afghanistan in the early 1980s reported that it was almost impossible to create a single effective army unit because of factional infighting.[19] Continued inter-network fighting and factionalism undermined the capabilities of the state and army central command to plan and operationalise troops, which negatively impacted its performance on the ground against jihadi *tanzims*.

By 1985, the Soviet leadership had realised that its troops were trapped in a quagmire facing an increasingly stronger insurgency and an unreliable Afghan partner that was consumed with party infighting and rivalry. In November 1986, the Soviet Politburo, under the influence of the new General Secretary of the Communist Party of the Soviet Union, Mikhail Gorbachev, decided to withdraw from Afghanistan. The Soviet exit plan was (1) to negotiate with the United States and neighbouring Pakistan to sign a non-intervention agreement—known as the Geneva Accords (detailed below)—and (2) at the Afghan level to bring to power a new leader who would be more willing to reform the party structure to widen the political base, thereby improving the regime's legitimacy before reaching a political settlement with the jihadi *tanzim* leaders in Peshawar.[20] Ironically, three decades later and after two decades of military intervention in Afghanistan, the U.S.A. and its allies would pursue a similar exit strategy and withdraw without an intra-Afghan peace deal, and an Afghan leadership in charge that resists broadening its political base.

As part of the Soviet plan, Karmal was replaced by Dr. Mohammad Najibullah in 1986 as head of the party but was also pressured by the Soviets to pursue a

National Reconciliation Policy—*Siyasat-i-Mosaleh-i-Millie*—to reach out to different segments of Afghan society.[21] To appeal to non-communists, Dr. Najibullah changed the name of the party to *Hezb-i-Watan* and sought to bring non-communist elites into the cabinet. The regime also held several ethnic Loya Jirgas (for instance, the first ethnic Hazara Loya Jirga was organised in 1989) to appeal to different communities to support the regime against the mujahedeen. However, the "national reconciliation" policy was seen by many as being too narrow and too late. And it upset hardliners within the party, especially the Karmalite network.[22]

3.1.2 PDPA militia policy and the origins of militia and strongmen networks

The Parchamis' policy, especially Dr. Najibullah's, to utilise *ethnic and tribal-based* militias against the jihadi insurgency groups facilitated the emergence of militia and strongmen networks that would come to play a key role in the 1990s civil war and post-2001 international statebuilding. The militias were recruited to help close the mujahedeen's infiltration routes, limit their movement, and maintain security in their region in exchange for fees and other government privileges such as titles, etc. This was an expensive bargain, with "containers" of banknotes being sent to regime supporters to rent their loyalty.[23] The militias played a key role in fighting for and sustaining the regime. In 1988, of 55,000 troops in Herat, 30,000 were militias. The 17th Infantry Division counted 3400 regular troops and 14,000 militiamen while the entire 53rd Division, commanded by Abdul Rashid Dostum, was militias.[24] In the short run, these militias helped Najibullah survive for almost two years but eventually led to his sudden downfall once Soviet funds dried up. Militia commanders like Dostum had become too powerful and politically ambitious.

With the access to financial patronage, a monopoly over violence, and control of safe territories, state-sponsored militia leaders evolved into powerful autonomous strongmen with access to other vessel networks of commanders increasingly realigning themselves along regional and ethnic lines. For instance, Juma Khan led the Andarabi militias, Sayyed Jaffar Naderi and his family ran the Ismaili Hazara militias in Baghlan province, Abdul Rashid Dostum controlled the Jawzjan Uzbek militias, and more marginal commanders like Rasoul Pahlawan, Ghaffar Pahlawan as vessel commanders, and Malik Firdous Khan operated in two districts of Faryab and Sar-i-Pul provinces, and the Ghoshta district of Nangarhar, respectively. The most effective pro-regime militia was the 53rd division, established in 1988 under the command of Abdul Rashid Dostum in Jawzjan province. It had a force of 40,000, mainly ethnic Uzbeks, and was so effective that the government dispatched it to the south to fight the mujahedeen in an area extending from Kabul to Kandahar. Dostum was also a charismatic leader with political ambitions. As doubts grew about the regime's survival, Dostum successfully convinced his fellow Uzbek militia commanders in the neighbouring provinces of Sar-i-Pul and Faryab to bring their forces under his central command and act as his vassal clients.[25] He also established close relations with other militia brigade leaders such as Sayed Jaffar Naderi in Baghlan and Amanullah Khan (nicknamed "Gilamjam," or carpet grabbers) in Balkh, as well as with other regular regime army officers.[26]

Ultimately, as the collapse of the regime became more manifest in early 1992, this alliance of militia forces, provincial *tanzim* commanders, and former PDPA army officers would assemble around Dostum in setting up first the Harakat-i-Shamal (the Movement of the North) and then the powerful Junbish-i-Milli-Islami of Afghanistan (National Islamic Movement and hereafter "Junbish-i-Islami"). By March 1992, Dostum's forces had captured Mazar-i-Sharif, which ultimately and swiftly led to the fall of the regime.[27] Junbish-i-Islami organised its first congress on 1 June 1992, and elected Dostum as its leader with Atta Mohammad Noor—his future arch-enemy—as its deputy. Its 31 Executive Council members were comprised of 10 former members of leftist groups, 2 from the Ismaili community, and 5 military officers of the former regime; the remaining 14 were jihadi and militia commanders, with a roughly equal distribution between jihadi and former PDPA officials.[28] Dostum and his newly established strongmen network emerged as the most powerful force in the country, controlling the northern regions. During the civil war, he could boast that he had a more effective and functioning diplomatic environment in Mazar-i-Sharif than in Kabul, as the UN had moved its major offices and seven countries had established consulates in the city.[29]

In post-2001, Dostum, the Naderi family, and Commander Noor emerged as prominent political strongmen in charge of an extensive network of commanders, politicians, and businessmen. Governor Noor emerged as the strongman of Balkh, while Dostum became the most prominent ethnic Uzbek leader; he ran for the presidency in 2004 and then became the First Vice President to Ashraf Ghani in the post-2014 National Unity Government. Naderi and his family led a small constituency of Ismailis in Kabul city and Baghlan province until the fall of the government in August 2021, holding government positions in the cabinet and a significant share in the mining sector.

3.1.3 PDPA and ethnic realignment

As the 1989 Soviet withdrawal ended and the survival of the regime came into question, networked factions began realigning themselves increasingly along ethnic lines as another power resource, especially after the reduction of international patronage. This policy was largely driven by President Najibullah's policies to bring change to the organisation of the state, the army, and the economy, which accentuated the ethnic realignment.[30]

Najibullah, a Pashtun, appealed to the Khalqis based on Pashtun solidarity while balancing their power in the army with non-Pashtun militias outside the regular chain of command (discussed in Section 3.2).[31] The pro-Najibullah and pro-Karmal divide became more prominent with pro-Karmal networks favouring jihadi commander Ahmad Shah Masoud, in part due to ethnic solidarity and in part to the belief that Masoud would be more willing to compromise with them in a power-sharing arrangement. In an environment of uncertainty and survivalism, national and regional officials, district and provincial governors, among others, started building contacts and securing assurances from various jihadi *tanzim* commanders outside the state along similar ethnic and opportunistic lines.[32] For instance, in May 1990, *Khalqi* Defence Minister Shahnawaz Tanai staged a coup, as part of a deal with Hekmatyar, to overthrow Najibullah and open up the security cordon to the south of Kabul city so Hekmatyar's Hizb fighters could enter the city. The coup failed and Najibullah ordered the arrest of 127 Khalqi military officers. Twenty-seven of them fled to Pakistan, where they appeared at a press conference with Hekmatyar denouncing the regime. But for Tanai, the move paid off in terms of the political capital he accumulated from the attempt: Hekmatyar appointed him commander of his army, the Lashkari-Isar, or the Army of Sacrifice.[33]

Once the regime collapsed, jihadi *tanzims* were able to absolve many of the PDPA generals and officials in their networks of guilt associated with their former communist alignments along ethnic and tribal lines. Ethnic solidarity determined the destination of defectors. Most pro-Karmalis, primarily ethnic Tajiks, surrendered to Jamiat and Wahdat *tanzims* and aided them in controlling strategic parts of Kabul city.[34] The pro-Najibullah Pashtuns, for the most part, gravitated towards Hekmatyar's *Hezb-i-Islami. With the help of Khalqi* Interior Minister Raz Muhammad Pakteen and Defence Minister Aslam Watanjar, *Hizb smuggled fighters into downtown Kabul, especially around the* Ministry of Interior and the Palace.[35]

These realignments, often counter to the logic of ideology, suggest a much deeper and perhaps more fundamental set of motivations operating in Afghanistan during a period of severe uncertainty and instability. Most of the leaders and officials attempted to consolidate their original networks and then build alliances with relevant jihadis for their survival. Hatred and division within both factions and the networks were so deep that until the last day, different factions plotted against one another. Pro-Karmalis thwarted Najibullah's departure from the country, as agreed and facilitated by the UN, forcing him to seek asylum at the UN compound.[36] A few days before the regime collapsed, in another last-ditch attempt to save their own skins, the pro-Karmalis led by Gen. Azimi, commander of Kabul Garrison, carried out a "silent coup" to overthrow Najibullah.[37] Later, this over-reliance on ethnic and tribal militias facilitated the emergence of strongmen and militia networks during the civil war. The collapse of the Najibullah regime resulted in the fragmentation of the Afghan state and society. Ethnic and tribal lines, more so than ideology, played an important role in building networked alliances between former PDPA officials and jihadi *tanzims*. A new power dynamics emerged and consolidated whereby political networks run by jihadi leaders and commanders, militia-based strongmen networks, and religious kinship families came to dominate Afghan politics and the state. On April 28, Sebghatullah Mojadiddi, the head of the two-month transitional government, arrived by car in Kabul, as head of a new Islamic government, and took power from the Military Council, ushering in what would be the bloodiest period in recent Afghan history.

3.2 Islamic jihadi *tanzims*, insurgency, and the 1992–2001 Civil War

Like their leftist cousins, jihadi *tanzims* were formed in the crucible of politics on the Kabul University campus in the late 1950s, centred on some of the professors and students of the theology department and its leaders, including Prof. Ghulam Muhammad Niazi, the Dean of the Faculty, Prof. Sebqatullah Mojadiddi, Prof. Burhanuddin Rabbani, and student union members like Abdul Rasul Sayyaf, Ahmad Shah Masoud, and Gulbuddin Hekmatyar.[38] Niazi is considered the Godfather of political Islam in Afghanistan, heavily influenced by the Muslim Brotherhood in Egypt. In 1968, with greater political freedom during the *constitutional decade*, the Muslim Youth Organization (Sazman-i-Jawanan-i-Musulman) was founded as an alternative to other ideological circles prominent on campus, especially communism. Prof. Burhanuddin Rabbani, a lecturer at the Sharia faculty of Kabul University who had completed his post-graduate studies in Egypt, was chosen as the leader, and the leadership council named the party the Jamiat-i-Islami (the Islamic Society).

In 1973, the Islamists attempted a poorly coordinated failed coup against Daud Khan, forcing the leadership to escape to Pakistan.[39] The blame game over who was responsible for the failure led to the fracturing of the Jamiat-i-Islami, with Gulbuddin Hekmatyar setting up his own *tanzim*, the Hizb-i-Islami in 1975. In Peshawar, the Pakistani government regulated the number of Afghan Islamist parties, allowing only seven Sunni and one Shia *tanzims* to operate in their country to better control the flow of military aid and their activities.[40] Almost all U.S. and Saudi funding was channelled through the Pakistani Inter-Service Intelligence (ISI), which, for a variety of reasons, favoured Hizb-i-Islami and allocated most funding to them.[41] These funding flows created a complex set of power relations based on patronage both within and between *tanzims'* clienteles in Pakistan, Iran, and beyond, helping to re-order access to power resources and establish new rules of the game.[42]

By the time the Soviets invaded in 1979, the stage was already set for a complex and fractured network of resistance emanating from Peshawar and Iran, guided by the interests, often conflicting, of a variety of foreign backers. Islam, the only umbrella that could unite all communities in Afghanistan, provided the jihadi insurgency groups with a powerful symbolic tool against the PDPA and the Soviets. However, the causes of insurgency varied from one part of the country to another with the primary motives being political and personal rather than ideological.[43] As Roy notes, the rise of Islamist *tanzims* was as unnatural and distasteful to most Afghans as the communists, insofar as they piggy-backed off jihad for legitimacy. In other words, organising resistance in the name of Islam was indigenous; Islamism and the Islamist *tanzims* were not. As such, it was primarily the funding, weapons, and external financial and military aid which fostered the *tanzims*, not popular mobilisation. Almost all of the refugees in camps had to be a de jure *tanzim* member to receive a ration and services including a support letter for immigration documentation. If commanders wanted weapons, they had to be a member of the seven in Peshawar or cosy up to the Iranians. In Iran, some had to fight in the Iran-Iraq war for months to qualify for weapons from Teheran. The Pakistani and Iranian overlordship of refugees had a significant impact on shaping and transforming Afghan constituencies for organising cross-border resistance.

3.2.1 Networked insurgency and jihad

The jihadi insurgency *tanzims*, except for *Hizb*, were mapped along the lines of de-centralised political-military organisations because of their network-like organisational structures, mode of operation, and communication lines. Mendel (2010) described such insurgency groups as "networked insurgency."[44] At the ground level, given the Soviet and communist regime's harsh and brutal retribution, jihadi insurgency activities were carried out through trustworthy and reliable personal associates. Their command, coordination, and communication could be implemented only through an informal social structure of personal network ties. Therefore, *tanzims* had to build an extensive web of connections with tribal chiefs, village mullahs, commanders, and community leaders to coordinate their fighting power and achieve military objectives. In fact, many have argued that the network structure of insurgency groups—which enabled them to be highly adaptable at the operation and tactical level—was the principal factor in making them a formidable resistance force and ultimately responsible for their success.[45] These groups were also linked to international patrons who provided them with funding and facilitated the recruitment of tens of thousands of foreign fighters in global Jihad efforts.

Hizb-i-Islami, by contrast, built up the most centralised *tanzim*—much more akin to Marxist-Leninists and some of the Arab Islamists—which seriously undermined its ability to build fluid alliances that could ultimately enable it to establish a territorial base inside the country. Despite defections by key PDPA *Khalq* officials and generals, Hizb's hierarchical structure meant that these former communists could not be absolved of their past alliance with the Soviets. Consequently, their skillsets and networks went unused. Jamiat and Wahdat *tanzims* were more effective in establishing safe geographical territories in the northeast, west, and central highlands of the country, primarily because of their network-like structure and their active policy of alliance-building with other groups, including secular elements within society. Accordingly, their commanders enjoyed, if not a monopoly, then at least an oligopoly of the means of violence. This arrangement meant that the military commanders were able to accumulate and access their own resources and build an expansive force, which eventually facilitated the emergence of *strongmen* and *militia networks* during the civil war of 1992–2001.[46] As the empirical chapters show, the military wing of Jamiat, Shura-i-Nizar (Supervisory Council), and Wahdat came to dominate their parties' core power; its commanders-turned-politicians found it tactically effective to appeal to the notion of the party and, more broadly, of "Mujahedeen" solidarity while setting up their own patronage networks in post-2001 Afghanistan.[47]

3.2.2 *The government-in-exile and the origins of civil society and technocratic networks*

As mentioned earlier, the *tanzim* leadership in Peshawar functioned as a "government-in-exile," performing administrative tasks for millions of Afghan refugees using the prerogatives of the former central state.[48] Each *tanzim* had its own shadow committees dealing with health, culture, education, and other services. In some instances, they were collecting taxes using their own judicial power; some even issued passports. In the 1980s, Peshawar was also serving as the hub for humanitarian operations for Afghan refugees inside Pakistan and Afghanistan, hosting 66 NGOs—then the densest such concentration anywhere in the developing world.[49] NGOs and Donor Coordination Assistance—a 16-member country donor group initiative that included The United States Agency for International Development (USAID), Germany, Scandinavian countries, and others—were essentially an "aid delivery regime" for the government-in-exile to provide humanitarian services to Afghan refugees.[50] Over time, these same NGOs went beyond merely tending to the needs of Afghan refugees in Pakistan and vulnerable Afghans inside Afghanistan; they were also co-opted into a campaign of regime change against the Soviet-backed Kabul government.[51] The post-1992 mujahedeen-led government subcontracted most of their services to these NGOs, which in turn facilitated the emergence of young Afghan technocratic and civil society leaders who would not only become the backbone of the Afghan bureaucracy in the post-2001 state but also emerge as influential politicians and officials.

For some well-educated young Afghans who could speak English well and were ambitious, NGOs, the United Nations, and donor missions provided excellent job opportunities and careers. As their skillsets in organisational management and networking expanded, some set up their own NGOs, which became giants in service delivery inside the country, assembling aid infrastructures that employed thousands of people. In the post-2001 reconstruction and state re-assemblage, these young NGO elites became key strategic and policy advisors and managers, including during the 2002 Emergency Loya Jirga and Constitutional *Loya Jirga*. With the increase in international aid, the number of NGOs mushroomed in Afghanistan. By 2003, aid workers became a key component of the Afghan economy.[52] As of October 2016, there were 4001 registered local NGOs, not all of them legitimate, in Afghanistan and 434 international NGOs registered with the Ministry of Economy.[53] In post-2001 Afghanistan, civil society elite interests and goals merged with those of international partners and Western-educated Afghan expats, creating new networks of interests, often in confrontation with militia-based and strongmen networks. As Chapter 6 shows, most of the key officials and the inner circle around President Ghani in his first term in office had a background in NGOs.[54] These were the same people who had played an important role in helping President Ghani get elected in the 2014 elections.

3.2.3 *Jihadi commanders and the emergence of powerful strongmen networks*

During the Soviet occupation, jihadi commanders and those of the communist regime-sponsored militias emerged as influential players at the provincial and district levels. Most of the jihadi commanders saw themselves as independent agents bound more to the population of the region, province, or district in which they fought than to the leadership in exile. As Roy aptly argued, jihadi *tanzims* suffered from a growing discrepancy between a would-be state from below (the field commanders) and a would-be state from above (the Pakistan and Iran-based political leadership and their bureaucracies in exile). This produced tensions between political leaders and field commanders, with the latter facing immense pressure from local communities to respond to their needs and perform as the state in delivering justice and services.

The creation of the Commanders' Council ("Shura Sar ta Sari") was a prime example of this tension. Frustrated by the Peshawar-based political leaders' lack of unity and continued personal rivalry, especially after the failed 1989 Rawalpindi Accord, which excluded *tanzim* commanders, several prominent figures, including Ismail Khan, Amin Wardak, Abdul Haq, Mullah Malang, and Ahmad Shah Masoud, set up the Commanders' Council. Around 1200 commanders participated in its first gathering, from 11 July to 23 July 1989 in Ghor province—a clear show of force. The second meeting took place in Paktia in May 1990, the third in June in Kunar province, and the fourth and final meeting in Badakhshan in October 1990, which denounced as unacceptable any future formulation of a political settlement without representation by commanders.[55] Although the Council did not succeed in achieving its purpose of coordinating tactical operations, it served to affirm the strong position of the commanders, which elevated them to centre stage with international backers. The most successful Military Council was the Shura-i-Nizar (Supervisory Council), set up by Masoud inside Jamiat in 1987. The civil war further consolidated the council's position, undermining the status and influence of its political arm, headed by Prof. Rabbani. As one Jamiat political leader put it: "the war increased Prof. Rabbani's dependency on them [commanders]. The war did not give space to Rabbani to exert and expand his political influence."[56] But while real power rested with the commanders, Rabbani retained a measure of authority stemming from his spiritual, intellectual, and Islamist credentials, not only facilitating his role as titular head of Jamiat but assuring him a position in the government post-2001.[57]

Meanwhile, some of these *tanzim* and militia commanders emerged as *strongmen* with their own expansive networks during the civil war. This led to the fragmentation of the Afghan state, with competing *tanzims* and strongmen commanders controlling different locales and carving out separate state administrations and bureaucracies. According to data collected by Fotini (2013), on the list of commanders in Kandahar, Nangarhar, and Balkh provinces, out of the 131 who participated in the jihad against the Soviets, 102 continued fighting during the civil war. Ninety-four percent of these commanders enjoyed close political, tribal, and ethnic links with their local communities, which enabled them to survive. The weakest link was in Kandahar, which might explain why the Taliban movement sprang up in the province.[58] In the north and northwest, Junbish-i-Islami, led by Dostum, emerged as the undisputed dominant force in the country. His strategic control of the northern provinces bordering Central Asia and its airports, roads, and fuel depots financed his army and provided salaries and career prospects to many different groups, including former communist generals and officials.[59] In Nangahar province, Haji Abdul Qadir (representing Hizb-i-Islami of Mauwali Khalis), a prominent member of the Arsala family which also included the Kabul-area Pashtun commander Abdul Haq, emerged to head a local jihadi shura (a 22-member council), which controlled the city.[60] However, among them, five major powerbrokers emerged who competed with each other: Hazrat Ali (an ethnic Pashai also representing Mauwali Khalis),[61] Shamali Khan Kuchi (representing Mahaz-i-Milli), Commander Malinyar (representing Ittihad-i-Islami), Haji Munjai (Mahaz-i-Milli), and Haji Zaman (Hizb-i-Islami Gulbuddin). In Kandahar province, various commanders belonging to *Jamiat*, the *Ittehad,* and Gailani's *tanzims* initially fought one another over control of the city. Eventually, Gul Agha Shirzai emerged as the undisputed strongman. The *Jamiat* leader, Mawlawi Naqibullah, ultimately surrendered Kandahar to the Taliban without a fight, prompting suspicions that he had been bought, though there is also evidence that he was following Rabbani's instructions.[62] In the Central Highlands, commanders from Wahdat—a newly unified Shia *tanzim* formed after the merger of several smaller groups to balance the Peshawar Sunni tanzims' power in future power-sharing arrangements/negotiations—established their control. In the West, particularly in Herat province, Ismail Khan, a Jamiat-i-Islami commander, successfully established a monopoly by eliminating rival militia commanders and collecting substantial customs revenues from the Islam Qala border with Iran.

3.2.4 *The civil war,* tanzims, *and alliance-building*

Following the collapse of the Najibullah regime in April 1992, for the next three years, the *tanzims* fought a bloody civil war on the streets of Kabul, committing mass violence and atrocities. It's worth noting that there had been internecine conflict between jihadi groups before 1992 which had produced significant distrust and in some cases bloodshed—e.g., the Nasr and Pasdaran infighting in the central highlands and west Kabul, and Hezb versus Jamiat outside Kabul.

Despite their ethnic and tribal flavours, both Fotini and Dorronsoro aptly demonstrate that the Afghan civil war during 1992–2001 was not "primitive," "ethnic," or "tribal," in nature but strongly political.[63] As framed in Chapter 2 in relation to networked governance, alliance formation and alliance shifting were two of the main survival strategies utilised by political tanzims, with warring groups constantly changing allegiances to maintain the balance of power. Fotini's mapping analysis of shifting alliances between the *tanzims* during the civil war years is revealing (Table 3.1). She found that the relative power distribution between and

Table 3.1 Afghan intra-jihadi war alliances

Year	Alliance one	Alliance two
1992	Pashtun	Tajik, Hazara, Uzbek
1993	Pashtun + Hazara	Tajik + Uzbek (Shura-i Ahl-e Hal va Aqd)
1994	Pashtun + Hazara + Uzbeks (a new alliance, called Shura-i Hamahangi ["Council of Coordination"])	Tajiks
1995–1996	Pashtun (Taliban) + Hazara (Mazari and Khalili) + Uzbeks	Tajiks + Hazara (Akbari) + Pashtuns (Hekmatyar)
1996	Pashtun (Taliban)	Tajiks + Hazara + Uzbeks
1997	Pashtun (Taliban) + Uzbeks (Malik)	Tajiks + Hazara
1997	Pashtun (Taliban) with defectors	Tajiks + Hazara + remaining Tajiks + Uzbeks + Hazara Islamic United Front for the Salvation of Afghanistan (Jabha-i Muttahid-i Islami bara-yi Nijat-i Afghanistan)

Source: Fotini (2012)

within the warring groups was the primary driving force behind alliance formation, alliance changes, and group split and takeover. She mapped the evolution of power and alliances from 1992 to 1998 and found seven instances of alliance shifts. As such, alliance formation in this period confirms the logic of networked governance as discussed in Chapter 2 those of *relative power balance* and *fractionalisation*. *Tanzims* were tactically motivated by a concern with victory, a fear of defeat, and the maximisation of return in a future power-sharing arrangement to ensure the group is not the weakest force with little bargaining power. As Chapters 6 and 7 show, the same alliance-building logic and constant alliance shifting continued in post-2001 Afghanistan within the networked state framework.

3.3 Failed political settlements and consequences

There has never been a successful political settlement in Afghanistan's modern history. The failed political settlement in the 1980s and 1990s period, and even the most recent one impelled by the Americans, is no exception. As discussed in the next chapter, this is because these attempts never went beyond the question of distribution of power and how to divide the state as a prize, rather than addressing the root causes of state failures such as how to bring power closer to the people, address historical grievances among communities, outline key functions of the state, and subsequently create best structure for it. The logic of a networked state as a limited-access order prevailed in these settlements, limiting power resources and privileges to members and a small group of people in communities. In this period, the diversity, fragility, and distrust among *tanzim* leaders and commanders made any chance of political settlement unlikely. Each saw all politics as war. These qualities would dictate the terms of the Bonn Agreement in 2001, which would plant the seed of political network division and competition, and the eventual collapse of the Republic.

The shifting alliances among Afghan *tanzims* did not, of course, play out in a vacuum. Even as the Jihad raged on, it became clear by October 1985 that the Soviet Union was preparing for a face-saving exit from Afghanistan. The Geneva talks, facilitated by the UN and led by Diego Cordovez, between the Afghan government and Pakistan (Iran refused to take part), with both the Soviets and the U.S.A. in the background, hammered out an agreement on a timeframe for Soviet withdrawal, including a guarantee that outside elements would not interfere and a final settlement among the warring groups. The Geneva Agreement was signed on 14 April 1988, but it quickly disintegrated. The jihadi groups that were excluded from the negotiations refused to accept it because it kept Najibullah in power; Iran called it "legally invalid," and members of the PDPA saw the process as a betrayal of Soviet commitment and nothing short of a military exit agreement.[64] Both the Soviet Union and the U.S.A., meanwhile, which agreed to play the role of the guarantor and end interference in Afghanistan, continued to provide support to their respective clients.[65] Pakistan showed no interest in ensuring a political settlement among Afghans because of the general belief that the communist government would collapse soon.

As the Soviet exit advanced, the Peshawar groups began their effort to agree on an interim government that could take over from the communists. On 10 February 1989, a 519-member Shura (council) representing seven jihadi *tanzims* was set up and convened with the help of the Pakistani and Saudi governments in Rawalpindi. Negotiations with Iran and the Soviets failed to produce a formula for the representation of both Shia and "good Muslims" from Kabul, as government delegations were called.[66] In the words of one scholar, the process began with "prejudice" and was conducted in "secrecy and corruption," which produced "bitterness, and ended in worse than futility by making a peace settlement more difficult."[67] The Shia, royalists, Kabul regime, the Commanders' Council representatives, as well as others were excluded.[68] Mojadaddi was named President because he was the weakest *tanzim* leader, influenced heavily by the ISI and Saudi Arabia (the latter's intelligence agency spent USD 26 million during the Shura to influence the outcome in their favour).[69] To please the Saudis, the position of Prime Minister was offered to Sayyaf; a plan to make Hekmatyar the Defence Minister collapsed in the complex deal. Rabbani, the leader of the Jamiat *tanzim*, received the symbolic position of Minister of Reconstruction. The key positions of Prime Minister, Minister of Defence, and Foreign Affairs were given to the Pashtuns. The Shia groups, as well as the Commanders' Council, rejected the outcome immediately.[70] In response to what they called an unfair and prejudiced outcome, the eight Shia *tanzims* came together on 16 June 1990, to establish the *Hezb-i-Wahdat-Islami* (the Islamic Unity Party). Feeling excluded, the commanders reinforced their efforts to consolidate their Commanders' Council and pushed for military victory.

With the announcement of President Najibullah's resignation on 18 March 1992, Pakistan quickly pushed to get the jihadi groups to reach an agreement, forcing one through on April 26, known as the Peshawar Accord. It agreed on the formation of the Transition Council (*Shura-i-Intiqali*) led by Mojadaddi and comprised of 10 nominees of the main Peshawar groups, 10 *ulama*, and 30 field commanders to take over from the Military Council in Kabul. After two months, Rabbani would take over as President and Head of the *Shura-i-Qiyadi* ("Leadership Council") for a further four months. This was followed by a Council of Supreme Popular Settlement (known by the Islamic legal term *Shura-i Ahl-e Hal va Aqd*) to form an interim government which would organise elections to be held after 18 months. According to the Agreement, the position of prime minister would go to Hekmatyar or his nominee; the Defence Ministry would go to Jamiat and the Foreign Affairs Ministry would go to Gailani's party. However, representatives of both Hizb Islami and Wahdat *tanzims* walked out of the final meeting, arguing that they had been under-represented.[71] Subsequently, Hekmatyar refused the offer of prime minister for his party and instead denounced the new administration as "communist";[72] he resorted to a strategy of spoiling.[73] Dostum and the Northern Military Council were excluded from the deal, with many jihadis justifying this on the basis that Dostum was a communist who had fought against them.

Once in Kabul and in power, Rabbani stayed in power after his agreed four-month term by holding a Loya Jirga in December 1992, composed of mainly Jamiat-i-Islami and Junbish-i-Islami representatives; he was elected president for an additional 18 months.[74] At the height of the Kabul civil war, there was one more attempt in Islamabad in March 1993 to reach an agreement and resolve the difference. The agreement, which came to be known as the Islamabad Accord, agreed that Rabbani would continue to be president until his 18-month term was over. Under intense pressure from Pakistan to compromise, Hekmatyar this time accepted the prime minister's position and Masoud stepped down as minister of defence. In June 1993, Hekmatyar was sworn in with a cabinet but did not leave his headquarters in Char Asyab district; the cabinet meeting would take place there.[75] However, the real power was still with Shuray-i-Nizar commanders within Jamiat led by Panjshiri commanders like Ahmad Shah Masoud, Qasim Fahim, and Yunos Qanuni, and other groups like Junbish-i-Islami did not receive any major positions. The existence of two executive offices (presidency and prime minister's office), and little clarity over the role and authorities of each did not help, either, as it created exceptional tensions and further misunderstandings.

Conclusion

The main thrust of this chapter has been to develop a schematic of the various groups that would come to represent the networked politics of post-2001 Afghanistan and highlight the key features of networked governance that the post-2001 period inherited. Indeed, the post-2001 Republic period was built around the entrenched informal institutions of the war economy of the 1980s and 1990s, internal factionalism, and failures of political settlements to overcome political network dynamics, ethno-regional solidarity, and patronage relations in Afghanistan. In fact, it is arguably the victim of those same failures, with the 2001 Bonn Agreement being only the most recent example of a badly designed internationally mediated pact.

Internally, meanwhile, Afghanistan has been the victim of geopolitical realities and Cold War dynamics that plagued many nations in the 20th century, particularly those—like Afghanistan—situated in the penumbra between Soviet and U.S. interests. Political factionalism and rivalry among different factions of the PDPA and their sub-networks over control of the state resulted in several coups and mass violence and ultimately the collapse of the regime. The state provided the political framework for factional and sub-network infighting where each faction used state coercion and violent capacities to eliminate its rivals. As the next chapter shows, the post-2001 state would be re-assembled for the same purpose: to function as a political framework for political network competition and conflict. In the 1980s and 1990s, mass violence emerged as the determining tool for securing power and controlling the state. That's what the Jihadis and the Taliban would use to take control of the Afghan state by military force rather than a negotiated settlement even when the opportunity to avoid bloodshed existed.

In the 1990s, the jihadi tanzims would viciously fight one another and committed mass killings with the bloody civil war displacing over six million Afghans. The war would further ethnicise Afghan polity and society and led to the emergence of a fundamentalist group, the Taliban. New rules of the game, including patronage, the instrumentalisation of identities, criminality, and violent coercion, would emerge as the dominant informal institutions and features of statehood. It would lead to the emergence of strongmen, militia, and technocratic networks that would come to play an important role in the post-2001 Republic period. The following chapter shows how the internationally sponsored statebuilding that followed the Bonn Conference sparked an extensive built-in element of conflict, deeply rooted in the last four decades of intra-network rivalry, factionalism, war, and violence.

Notes

1 Rubin (1992); Saikal (2006), Gregorian (1969), Emadi (2010).
2 See Buzan and Weaver (1990) on the discussion of regional conflict complex.
3 See Bezhan (2013); Farahi (2001); and Rutig (2020).
4 Some of the early leaders were Mir Ghulam M. Ghobar, Abdul Rahim Mahmudi, Mir M. Seddiq Farhang, Abdulhai Habibi, M. Karim Nazihi, and Gul Pacha Ulfat.
5 Three reasons prevented the king from fully supporting it: Firstly, Zahir Shah wanted a purely monarchist party to be established around his image, whereas Demokrat-e-Motaraqi was founded around the leadership and political authority of Maiwandwal. Secondly, the monarch was not impressed with the slogans of the party, particularly socialism as a method of economic progress. Thirdly, there was strong resentment against Maiwandwal among some influential members of the royal family, including Abdul Wali Khan, the king's chief advisor and son-in-law. Wali regarded Maiwandwal as a protégé of Muhammad Naim Khan and Daud Khan. The king actively suppressed the party through various means. For more details on the activities of political parties during this period, see Weinbaum (1972); and Bezhan (2013).

6 The first attempt was by Khalilullah Khalili, the famous Afghan poet who had served in the cabinet and was an advisor to the king, who founded the Wahdat-e Melli (National Unity). After their poor performance in the 1965 elections, he was appointed as the Ambassador to Saudi Arabia. The second attempt was pursued by Hashim Maiwandwal in 1966 who was the head of Wesh Zalmayan (Awakened Youth Party), setting up a new party name, Demokrat-e-Motaraqi (Progressive Democratic). The Awakened party had been set up before 1947 at the time of Prime Minister Shah Mahmud who dominated the Liberal Parliament of 1947–1953 and took modest steps towards preparations for a free election, free at least relative to the past elections.

7 For a more detailed list of leftist parties, see Arnold (1983); Roy (1988).

8 See Bradsher (1999: 7), Adamec (2005) and Dupree (1979: 7) for details of this meeting. The meeting took place in secret at Taraki's house. Those present unanimously elected Taraki Secretary-General. They also elected a Central Committee whose regular members were Nur Mohammad Taraki, Babrak Karmal, Ghulam Dastigir Panjsheri, Nur Ahmad Nur, Dr. Saleh Mohammad Zeri, Shahrullah Shahpur, Sultan Keshtmand, Dr. Shah Wali, and Taher Badakhshi. Alternates were Abdul Mohammad, Bareq Shahfiyee, Hakim Shahrayee, Ismail Danish, Abdul Karim Misaq, Wahab Shafie, Zaher Ofaq, Dr. Zaher, Hafizullah Amin, and Sulaiman Layeq.

9 Rubin (1995: 93–100).

10 For instance, according to Abdul Wakil's memoir he was second cousin to Babrak Karmal from the father's side; Ghulam Jilani Bakhtari was the son of his aunt who was a close friend of Prime Minister Hassan Sharq; and Jilani was then related to Karmal. Politburo members such as Mir Akbar Khaybar and Suleiman Laiq were close friends of Hassan Sharq. Anahita Ratibzad married her two sisters to Karmal's brother Mahmud Baryalai and politburo member Nur Muhmmd Nur. Mir Akbar Khaybar married Suleiman Laiq's sister; Laiq was another Politburo member. Some of the leaders had married to the aristocracy and prominent religious elites. See Wakil (1396)

11 See Rubin (2002a) for the full details of the dataset.

12 One such secret army network was the Armies' Revolutionary Organization or the United Communist Front of Afghanistan. General Abdul Qadir, the leader of the group, had reportedly recruited nearly 800 officers by the April 1978 coup with the help of the Soviet Defence Ministry's Main Intelligence Directorate. See Bradsher (1999: 10); Akbar and Azimi memoire, and others.

13 See Arnold (1994: 51); and Giustozzi (2000: 16).

14 See Giustozzi (2000) and Bradsher (1999) for the details of the first coup. According to Gankovskiy, the second coup was staged by four major military officers who feared that Daud would soon come after them and the entire PDPA leadership. These were Gen. Qadir (Chief of Staff of air forces), Watanjar (Deputy Commander of the Fourth Armoured Brigade stationed at Puli Charkhi military base), Gulabzoy (an Air Force Commander who became Minister of Interior), and Mohammad Rafie (who would later become Minister of Defence from 1979 to 1984 and 1986 to 1988).

15 Maley (2021).

16 Bradsher (1999).

17 Giustozzi (2000: 4).

18 For the detailed account of the coup, see Arnold (1985) and Kakar (1997).

19 Giustozzi (2000: 83).

20 Karmal was no longer considered an asset for the Soviet exit plan for two reasons: (1) he was hesitant to broaden the party's base to include non-PDPA members and (2) he favoured the withdrawal talks to be directly between Islamabad and Kabul—something Soviet leaders were not interested in pursuing. Eventually under Soviet pressure, Karmal reluctantly resigned on 4 May 1986, just hours before the eighth round of Geneva talks began. Relations between Karmal and his Soviet bosses had been strained for the previous year. According to Soviet archive documents, in October 1985, after a heated exchange between Gorbachev and Karmal in Moscow, Gorbachev

decided to send a strong 'recommendation' to the Afghan government that 'with or without Karmal, we will firmly carry out policies that must lead to withdrawal from Afghanistan in the shortest possible time' (Cordovez and Harrison 1995: 202). It was announced to the 27th Party Congress on February 27, 1986, that the Soviets would exit from Afghanistan through a "phased withdrawal" in accordance with the proposed UN settlement. (Cordovez and Harrison 1995: 202). According to Cordovez, the Soviets went as far as favouring the former king to be the Head of any future government.

21 It brought some non-communist moderate Afghan groups in exile into the political structure; the most notable change was the appointment as Prime Minister of Mohammad Hassan Sharq, who had been a deputy prime minister during Daud Khan's presidency.

22 It created a serious division within PDPA with network elites loyal to Karmal allegedly sabotaging it and others for fear of losing their jobs and positions opposing it. During this period, there were rumours in Kabul that Karmal, through his brother Baryalai, was creating a rift within the party. Karmal was eventually sent into exile, some alleging that he was first arrested and then banished.

23 Rubin (1995: 161).

24 Giustozzi (2000: 213–24).

25 Giustozzi (2008: 103–105).

26 Some of the former regime officials that Abdul Rashid Dostum maintained close relations with were Gen. Momin of the 70th division in Hairatan; Gen. Hilal of the helicopter regiment based in Balkh; and other high-ranking pro-Karmal associates in Kabul.

27 Events leading up to Abdul Rashid Dostum's decision to switch sides are fascinating and reveal the weakness of the militia policy. In January 1992, based on an assessment by Gen. Manokay Mangal, Najibullah ordered the replacement and sacking of several key generals, doubting their loyalty. These included Gen. Juma Nazimi (commander of 18 Division in Balkh) with Gen. Rasool (Bekhuda) and Gen. Momin (commander of 70 Brigade Division in Hairatan) with Sattar Basharmal. He also ordered Gen. Hilal (commander of Air Force in Balkh) and Gen. Ahmad Yar (Balkh Provincial Police Chief) to relinquish their positions and report to Kabul. In early Feb., Najibullah ordered Gen. Juma Atchak (the 9th Army Corps Commander) to implement these changes. The result was the breakdown of Central Command: Gen. Momin refused to relinquish charge and instead imprisoned D.W. Sattar Basharmal, while Gen. Hilal relinquished his position but joined Gen. Momin. Both generals joined Dostum and Sayed Jaffar Naderi (Commander of 80th militia division). In Kabul, the Politburo was divided on how to handle the crisis. Fida Yunas, the Pakistani *chargé d'affaires*, provides an account of the secret meetings between Karmal and Dostum from 1989 onwards. He also suggests that there was collusion between pro-Karmal networks in Kabul and Dostum in the North to set up a northern safe zone as a contingency plan aimed at enabling PDPA leadership to retreat to Mazar-i-Sharif if they lost Kabul to the Mujahedeen. The PDPA certainly strengthened the administration and infrastructure of northern Afghanistan in 1988, creating a military command structure for the northern zone. This is confirmed by the author's interview with several former PDPA officials in April 2020. After a month of negotiations and several delegations (first Gen. M. Rafie and then Gen. Azimi), eventually in early March Najibullah dispatched Gen. Mangal along with a team of generals to mobilise troop forces against Momin and Dostum. They bombed Sheberghan and Hairatan, but the campaign failed. By March 18, Mazar-i-Sharif city was surrounded. According to Walwalji, based on advice from Gen. Azimi, Dr. Najibullah allowed Dostum's militias to enter the city first. With the collapse of the strategic city of Mazar-i-Sharif, rapid disintegration of the state and breakdown of central command and party ranks occurred. The UN five-point peace plan forced Dr. Najibullah to announce his resignation on March 20, 1992, and declared his departure after the establishment of an Interim Government in Kabul, transferring all powers and all executive authority to the Interim Government.

28 Giustozzi (2008: 107).
29 Rubin (1994).
30 See Rubin (1995: 150–53).
31 Rubin (1995: 150).
32 See Rubin (1995: 148); Maley (2018); Giustozzi (2000); Fotini (2012: 118–19).
33 See Giustozzi (2000); Rubin (1995: 151); Maley (1997 and 2002).
34 On 25 April, Hekmatyar forces captured the Palace and other key installations in the city. They failed to capture the Radio and TV station. Hekmatyar claimed control of Kabul, denouncing the new Peshawar-agreed administration as 'communist' (see Fida Yunas 1997 and 2002). During fighting from April 25 to 27 in Kabul, Gen. Azimi, along with forces loyal to Masoud, Dostum, Wahdat, and Harakat attacked Hekmatyar forces and successfully drove the Hizb out of the city.
35 450 Hizb-i-Islami fighters were smuggled into the MoI compound and some around the Palace with the help of Pakteen loyalists. Also, 500 Masoud fighters led by Abd-ur-Rahman, Deputy Shura-i-Nizar arrived in Kabul. Masoud accused Hekmatyar of a coup attempt against the Peshawar negotiation efforts. Author's interview (22–24 April 2020).
36 See Yunas (1997 and 2002) for a detailed account of what happened the early morning of April 16 when the UN convoy tried to evacuate Dr. Najibullah to the airport and from there to India. I was also shown a letter written by Dr. Najibullah in which he explains that pro-Karmalis had done nothing less than to orchestrate a coup to put all the blame on Najib and make a deal with the Mujahedeen. This letter was obtained from Dr. Najibullah's daughter, Heela Najibullah.
37 The pro-Karmalis were Gen. Muhammad Nabi Azimi (commander of Kabul Garrison), Abdul Wakil (foreign minister), Asif Sarwari (the army chief of staff), and Farid Mazdak, Mahmud Baryalai (Karmal's brother), and Suleiman Laeq (politburo members). Dr. Najibullah's allies were Yaqubi (intelligence), Watanjar (Minister of Defence), Pakteen (Interior), and Gen. Manokay Mangal.
38 For Islamist groups during this period, see Edwards (2002); and Roy (1984); and Tawana (1989).
39 My interviews with several Jamiat and Hizb officials in March 2020 reveal that there was an internal division within Jamiat whether to carry out a coup. Reportedly, Rabbani was against the idea but was pushed by younger leaders like Hekmatyar who argued in favour of a military solution. The argument the latter group had proposed was that before Daud found the time to strengthen his position, they must strike. Apparently, distrust between Masoud and Hekmatyar started from here as the former did not join the coup on time, for which Hekmatyar blamed him personally for the failure of the coup.
40 The only Shia *tanzim* operating from Pakistan was Harakat-i-Islami led by Asef Mohseni which was operating from Quetta city in Pakistan. Harakat maintained contact with Iran and Peshawar groups.
41 See Coll (2004).
42 For instance, Gulbuddin Hekmatyar was supported by Pakistan's Inter-Services Intelligence (ISI), Abdul Rasul Sayyaf by Saudi Arabia, Ali Mazari by Iran, and Abdul Rashid Dostum by Uzbekistan and Turkey.
43 See Roy (1990); Shahrani and Canfield (1984).
44 In that sense, the tanzims' structure is not very different from the Taliban Mahaz (front) military structure. General Stanley McChrystal, the 2009 International Security Assistance Force (ISAF) commander, categorised the Taliban along the same lines, asserting: "it takes a network to defeat a network." See Mendel (2010: 734); and McChrystal (2011).
45 See Roy (1990); and Sinno (2008).
46 See Roy (1990), Sinno (2008).
47 See Tchalakov (2013).

48 See Roy (1990) and Maley (1998).
49 Nunan (2016).
50 See Nancy Dupree (1989) for this period of humanitarian INGOs. INGOs including France's Médecins Sans Frontières, the Stockholm-based Swedish Committee for Afghanistan and Norwegian Church Aid.
51 Nunan (2006).
52 Ghafour (2003). The inflows of international aid fuelled price bubbles in food and real estate as well as urbanisation, attracting people to Kabul, particularly with the promise of improved livelihoods.
53 See http://www.icnl.org/research/monitor/afghanistan.html.
54 These included people like Salam Rahimi, the President's former Chief of Staff; Jelani Popal, former Head of the Independent Directorate of Local Governance (IDLG); Haneef Atmar, the former National Security Council Advisor; Nader Nadery, the President's former Chief Advisor on Strategic Affairs and Public Relations and the Head of the Independent Administrative Reforms and Civil Service Commission (IARCC); Akram Ekhpelwak, the President's former Chief Advisor on Political Affairs; and Masoum Stanekzai, the former Head of National Directorate of Security. Ghafour (2003).
55 See Maley (2018).
56 Author's interview, April 17, 2020.
57 Roy (1990:112–113).
58 Christia (2013: 129–37).
59 See Giustozzi (2008); Rubin and Malikyar (2002); and Dorronsorro (2012).
60 Dorronsoro (1995: 5).
61 It was not until Mawlawi Khales defected to the Taliban, prompting Haji Hazrat Ali to switch his allegiance from HIK to Jamiat-e Islami, that the Jamiat gained strength in the district. He was involved in the assassination of Commander Shamali Khan.
62 Davis (1998: 49–50).
63 Dorronsoro (1995: 37); and Christia (2012).
64 Afghan Jehad (April–June 1988: 37–38).
65 The Soviets continued to send aid and weapons to their clients, valued by Western sources at USD 3–4 billion a year until the end of 1991 (see Rubin: 2002a:147). The U.S. and Saudi aid to mujahedeen increased from USD 700 million in 1988 to USD 715 million in just three months from December 1989 to February 1990 (Bradsher 1999: 334).
66 The Shia delegation had demanded 120 members. Mojadaddi was in favour and had worked hard because he wanted to gain the support of Iran-backed Shia to get elected as president. The main resistance came from Hekmatyar, Khalis, and Sayyaf. See Afghan Information Centre.
67 Bradsher (1999: 326).
68 The Iran-based Shia tanzims advocated for a 20% representation in the future government, based on population. According to Roy (1989: 80), the Sunni jihadis' rejection of this was not so much based on the disagreement on population distribution or the Saudi-Iran rivalry but the strong anti-Shia and Hazara discrimination that existed among other ethnic groups, rooted in Afghanistan's historical state formation.
69 Rubin (2002a: 250). Some claimed that each member received 25,000 USD.
70 IRNA from Tehran, 9 March 1989.
71 Bradsher (1999: 383); Rubin (2002a).
72 Mainly because of Dostum's position.
73 Maley (2002).
74 Hizb Islami Khalis refused to take part, Harakat Islami (Mohseni) did not take part because of the Chindawool issue, Mahaz Milli Islami (Gialani) opposed and did not participate, and Jabhe Nijat Milli (Mujaddadi) did not join. Wahdat (Mazari) opposed

because of the position of the State Security. Junbish (Dostum) boycotted but accepted the result.

75 A number of cabinet officials expressed how difficult it was to go to Charasyab for the cabinet meetings and that Hekmatyar would use them as political campaign tools criticising Rabbani and Masoud. Author interview January 2020.

4 The Bonn experiment and a flawed foundation

Re-assembling and re-constituting the Afghan state (2001–2004)

Introduction

"This meeting is the path towards salvation," the thin, hesitant voice emanating from the satellite phone intoned. "We are one nation, one culture." Earlier, Lakhdar Brahimi, the United Nations special representative for Afghanistan and Iraq, had told the gathering of delegates in Bonn, Germany, with a flair for the dramatic, that an important tribal elder from Southern Afghanistan would be joining them via satellite phone to deliver a speech.

"We are united, not divided," the voice, gaining in volume and depth, was now telling the gathering. "We are a strong people who would like to assert our will and sense of self-determination."[1] The surprise phone call gambit had been played by James Dobbins and Zalmay Khalilzad, members of the U.S. delegation, to raise the profile of their relatively unknown candidate to lead Afghanistan's interim administration—or at least this is how most of the delegates saw it. Before and during the conference, the Americans had worked tirelessly to garner support among Afghanistan's neighbours of their choice: Hamid Karzai.[2]

The theatrics behind the phone call had created a sense of anticipation. While this unknown personage was being connected to the conference audio system, a bated stillness had descended over the large conference hall, and as soon as the speech had ended, the conference room had erupted with whispers. One delegate asked, "Who was he?"; another questioned, "Why did he address us? What does this mean?" The susurrations continued for the next few days, accompanied by a steady stream of speculations and suspicions that hung like an electric charge in the empty halls and corridors of the hotel. In a week's time, Lyse Doucet, the BBC correspondent, would inform Hamed Karzai about his appointment as the Chairperson of the Interim Administration via satellite call.

The Americans, of course, were known for their flair for the dramatic, and the setting for the conference only amplified the mystique. The Hotel Petersberg was a grand, ostentatious location for a conference bringing together Afghanistan's powerbrokers in the aftermath of the fall of the Taliban regime at the end of November 2001. Being the official guesthouse of the German government in Bonn, the former capital of West Germany, the hotel had hosted international dignitaries, including Queen Elizabeth II and the Shah of Iran, and had been the

DOI: 10.4324/9781315161617-4

headquarters of the Allied High Commission for Germany after the Second World War, dubbed the "German Camp David." Located on top of a mountain outside the city, the Petersberg offered a breathtaking view of the Rhine valley, and a much-needed break for the participants, who could wander its luxurious grounds between the meeting sessions, which ran from late in the day and ended late into the night to allow participants to observe the Ramadan fast. The conference began on 27 November under immense diplomatic pressure amidst a rapidly evolving situation on the ground in Afghanistan, with the Northern Alliance (NA) in control of Kabul and the major cities. The U.S.A. and its allies, especially Germany and the UN, had quickly put together the conference, inviting the four main Afghan political groupings, along with international and regional countries, with the goal of agreeing on a power-sharing arrangement and a roadmap for the future of Afghanistan.[3]

As the negotiations dragged on, optimism and courtesy promptly gave way to old rivalries and suspicions over the two hotly contested issues: the deployment of peacekeeping forces to Kabul and the choice of leadership for the interim government. The Shuray-i-Nezar commanders led by Yunus Qanuni naturally favoured an all-Afghan peacekeeping force given that they were already in possession of Kabul city.[4] Others under the NA umbrella, and the three other groups attending the conference, advocated for an international force under the auspices of the UN. By December 4, talks had stalled. The Rome Group, representing the former king and Western-educated Afghans, had twice voted for Abdul Sattar Sirat as their choice for interim leader, an ethnic-Uzbek and a former minister of justice under the king, but were overruled by the Americans who favoured Karzai, an ethnic-Pashtun.[5] Sirat consequently walked out of the Conference in protest.[6] President Rabbani, who had refused to attend, insisting that talks should take place inside Afghanistan, was using all his diminishing authority in Kabul to sabotage the process.[7] As it became clear that the self-interests of the Shuray-i-Nezar commanders were undermining the entire process, Haji Abdul Qadir, the head of the Eastern Pashtun leader of Arsala family network and a member of the NA, left in disapproval, while Karim Khalili, the leader of Wahdat-i-Islami, and Abdul Rashid Dostum, the leader of Junbish-i-Islami, began to publicly question the inclusiveness of the conference. Time and momentum were running out.

Amidst fears that the talks would collapse, Powell, the U.S. secretary of state, reportedly instructed his team to "not let them break up. Keep them there. Lock them up if you have to. We do not want this to go anywhere else. We're almost there, and this is the time to grind it out on this line," an approach Powell credited to Richard Armitage, his deputy at the time.[8] Certainly, most of the delegates remembered the heavy-handedness of Dobbins, Khalilzad, and Brahimi in shaping the process and achieving American policy interests. The last-minute agreement came out on December 5 at 6:45 am after an exhausting night of bickering and horse-trading.[9] However, not everyone was happy, and not everyone signed the final agreement, including Sirat and Haji Qadir, who had walked out, Enayatullah Wasefi, Abdullah Wardak (Sayyaf's representative), and Ghulam Mohammad Eylaghi. *De jure*, the four main Afghan political groups agreed to a "broad-based, multi-ethnic, politically-balanced, freely-chosen Afghan administration."[10] *De facto*, however, power was largely concentrated in the hands of the NA and within them, the military wing of *Jamiat* (the Shuray-i-Nezar), predominantly comprised of ethnic-Tajiks of the Panjshir valley. The conference proved to be a "grand bargain" in which the state's ministerial positions were treated as "positional goods" and "spoils" for distribution. The number of ministries for the interim administration was deliberately increased to accommodate and award attendees for their participation.[11]

These incipient grievances along the political network and ethnic lines set the stage for deepening distrust, exclusion, and conflict, which would shape and transform the post-2001 state, its institutional setup, and the overall political order. On that majestic mountain top, surrounded by the grandeur of the Hotel Petersburg, a precedent was set that, in the new era, signalled Afghan politics would once again be divided along the political network and ethnic lines and that concepts of democratic representation and a fair balance of representation were only to be found in the rhetoric of internationals. The pantomime of Afghan nation-building had begun.

A week later, on 12 December 2001, on a cold winter night at Bagram airbase North of Kabul city, a high-profile delegation including most of the Bonn Conference attendees was waiting to greet the newly appointed head of the interim government, Hamid Karzai, and his two companions.[12] Among the delegation was the 42-year-old Commander Mohammad Qasim Fahim, the military leader of the Jamiat *tanzim* and one of the most feared strongmen of the Shuray-i-Nezar, who was appointed as defence minister at the Bonn Conference. Beside him was Yunous Qanuni, another Shuray-i-Nezar commander, appointed at Bonn as Interior Minister, and a large crowd of mainly Jamiat members and commanders, including those who had housed and dined the delegation at the village next door to the base while waiting for Karzai's arrival. It was after 8 pm when the plane landed alongside a long row of vehicles that had lined up to light the runway, their headlights tracing out long, foreboding shadows from the discarded and broken Soviet tanks and helicopters scattered over the base. This had been a gruelling journey: the American military C130 aircraft had picked up the guests from Kandahar, transferring them to Manas airbase in Kyrgystan first—a newly opened U.S. transit centre near Bishkek to support military operations in the war on terror in Afghanistan—before flying them into Bagram.

As Karzai exited the plane, wearing his now-famous *karakul*[13] hat and a beige-coloured *patu* around his shoulders, Fahim approached him, opened his arm, and gave the newly minted leader a seemingly warm and welcoming Afghan hug. But as he embraced Karzai, Fahim sarcastically muttered, "where are your bodyguards?," a mean and deliberate gesture to remind him that it was he who wielded real power in Kabul, to which Karzai reportedly countered, "when I have you, do I need bodyguards?" Before his trip to Kabul, some of Kandahar's elders, including members of Karzai's Popalzai tribe, had pressed him to take at least 2000 fighters along with him to Kabul to guard the Palace.[14] He had refused. Karzai would humourously describe this encounter with Fahim years later to his close aides, perhaps to boast about his survival skills against impossible odds—possessing no military force, organisational structure, or power base behind him.[15] That is arguably why the Shuray-i-Nezar commanders chose Karzai at Bonn, because he was perceived as weak and flexible, little more than a figurehead to appease ethnic-Pashtun opinion.

From Bagram, the 50-minute drive to the Presidential Palace in downtown Kabul felt longer engulfed in the darkness of the countryside. When the delegation arrived at the Palace, it was already quite late. They were greeted by President Burhanuddin Rabbani, who still worked and resided in the Palace and considered himself the legitimate president of the country. He remained bitter about the outcome of the Bonn Conference, considering it a deal for the Shuray-i-Nezar commanders, and a personal betrayal, as well as a betrayal of the Jamiat *tanzim*.[16] After much congratulatory speech-making and exchange of pleasantries, Azizullah Karzai, Karzai's uncle, asked for a *chapan* on the pretext of keeping warm. It was a shrewd diplomatic move, forcing the host to informally acknowledge his guest's authority by draping a large, Afghan long coat over his shoulders—a customary gesture of acknowledgement when transferring power from one elder to another. As the guests made their exits, the inner Haram Saray Palace, with its high ceilings and windows, was left bare, airy, and cold, enveloping the new occupants with a feeling of abandonment and vulnerability. The occasional chatter of Fahim's men guarding the outer walls punctuated the silence, a grim reminder that danger was never far away. Rumours in the weeks ahead would circulate that Karzai's suitcase, filled with CIA cash, was stolen from the Palace, allegedly on Fahim's orders. It would take another 10 days, on December 22, the day on which Karzai was sworn in along with his cabinet, for Rabbani to vacate the Palace and its offices. Karzai and his aides would find themselves powerless in the face of hostility, stuck in the Palace compound, and at the mercy of powerful Panjshiri Shuray-i-Nezar commanders.

Meanwhile, the Americans and their allies concentrated their attention on the main objectives, the "war on terror" against al-Qaida, renting out security to political networks, powerful strongmen networks, and their associates, with statebuilding a mere afterthought. In 2002, Jack Straw, the then-British foreign secretary, aptly described this strategy: "the more we can get people who have occupied positions of force and strength in the past but who now say, 'we're committed to a political process' … the better the future of Afghanistan will be."[17] What he really meant was by allying with those in possession of military power resources, the Western interests would be better guaranteed. Donald Rumsfeld, then-U.S. defence secretary advised Karzai to govern like the infamous 1960s' Chicago mayor, through patronage.

> It was not a perfect analogy, but I was convinced Karzai needed to learn to govern the Chicago way. In the 1960s, Mayor Richard J. Daley ruled Chicago—a city of many diverse and powerful elements—using manoeuvre, guile, money, and patronage, and services to keep the city's fractious leaders from rebelling against his authority …. My point was that instead of giving

Karzai the freedom to throw around the weight of the U.S. military, he should learn to use patronage and political incentives and disincentives to get the local Afghan warlords, governors, and cabinet officials in line.[18]

In other words, the Americans and their allies threw Karzai into the ring and expected him to survive on his own against powerful political networks and centres of power, with no other weapons except his political skills and charm. When Karzai took power on December 22, he inherited a hollow state. Ironically as the subsequent chapters show, the state arguably remained hollow until its collapse in August 2021 with political networks effectively enacting the state and fashioning the façade of a functioning state and order. There was no central police or army at his command to keep his rivals at bay, and the state administration, which had almost completely collapsed, was being re-assembled by the jihadi networks in Kabul and its periphery. In the early days, those few Afghans from the diaspora who had arrived to work with Karzai provided a harrowing account of the lack of basic office equipment and skills, ubiquitous political strains and confrontations, and fear over their political survival. One Karzai aide accounts how they had to borrow blankets from a friend's house for Karzai and his two first nights in the Palace. The first three years, until the 2004 presidential elections when Karzai was elected president through a popular vote, is a tale of a power struggle between Karzai and his technocratic clients and NA political networks and regional strongmen over control of the state.

This chapter accounts in detail the power struggle over the Afghan state and key power resources from December 2001 to the presidential elections in 2004 by different and competing political networks at the national and subnational levels. It examines how the national and subnational administration including its bureaucracy and security institutions came to be re-assembled, re-constituted, and transformed by Kabul-based patronage, regionally operating strongmen-based and their militia clients, and kinship networks (family and tribal). Section 4.1 details how *Jamiat* network, and within them several principal political nodes of Shuray-i-Nezar commanders mostly from Panjshir, captured important national institutions including key provinces and districts surrounding the capital. They then proactively empowered and protected their regionally based loyal clients and representatives in the provinces against rival networks such as Jamiat, Hizb-i-Islami, Wahdat, and others. Section 4.1.2, for instance, unpacks the conflict and competition within one ministry, the powerful Ministry of Interior, to offer insights into the operation and strategies of political networks to survive within the Afghan state. Section 4.1.3 unpacks the fragmented order that emerged in post-2001 with regional strongmen, ethno-regional entrepreneurs, and provincially based family and tribal networks that came to constitute Afghanistan's provinces.

Section 4.2 examines key events, including the 2002 emergency and 2003 constitutional Loya Jirgas, to show how Karzai and his Western-educated network aides came to utilise these platforms to flex their muscle against mainly Jamiat network and its clique of powerful Shuray-i-Nezar commanders. It's worth nothing that Jamiat, Wahdat, Junbish, and other major political networks had maintained some degree of political cohesion and unity until the end of 2003; however, they began fracturing into several patronage networks and regionally based strongmen networks following their subsequent setbacks in key political stages, including the 2003 constitutional Loya Jirgas and the 2004 presidential elections. Some of these networks lost their constituency support and were able to sustain themselves through the accumulation of financial and military resources both inside and outside the formal state and market. By the end of 2004, Karzai and his aides were able to consolidate power in the periphery by pursuing a mixed strategy of repression and accommodation, utilising his position in the internationally sponsored state and his network's access to international resources and legitimacy to vigorously undermine and oust his adversaries.

4.1 Capturing and re-assembling the state: a fragmented order

The early post-Bonn period resembled the situation of post-1992: a *fragmented state* where competing *tanzims*—political-military networked forms of organisations—and their regionally and provincially based military commanders carving out different geographical territories performed as the state and fashioning a "fragmented order" as one of the four political order outcomes that is analytically discussed in the concluding chapter of this book. Rival political networks that had defeated the Taliban in 2001 and were allied with the U.S.A. in its counter-terrorism efforts re-merged the winners. They were awarded by being tasked with re-assembling, constituting, and re-building the state: utilising their coercive and organisational resources and capacities, they thereby captured different strategic parts of the national and subnational state as safe positions within a networked state (Figure 4.1).

4.1.1 Jamiat network and Shuray-i-Nezar of clique: masters of the state in Kabul and its neighbouring provinces

With the help of devastating U.S. airstrikes, Jamiat and its Shuray-i-Nezar group—the former military wing of Jamiat network set up by Ahmad Shah Masoud in the 1990s—forces made swift progress against the Taliban in their stronghold of Parwan and Kapisa provinces and other provinces and districts surrounding Kabul on November 11.[19] Defying U.S. appeals, on November 13, they marched into Kabul city as the Taliban retreated without a fight. Being the first major anti-Taliban forces to enter the capital put them in a strategically advantageous position vis-a-vis other groups at the Bonn Conference. After Bonn, Jamiat under the military command of Mohammad Qasem Fahim (the leader of Shuray-i-Nezar group) refused to evacuate their militias from the city, as was agreed they would at the conference, making NATO's International Security Assistance Force (ISAF) mission seem redundant—except maybe to help give the façade of a stabilising effect.[20]

In Kabul city and the three provinces north of it known collectively as the *Shamali* plains (comprised of Parwan, parts of Kabul province, Kapisa, and

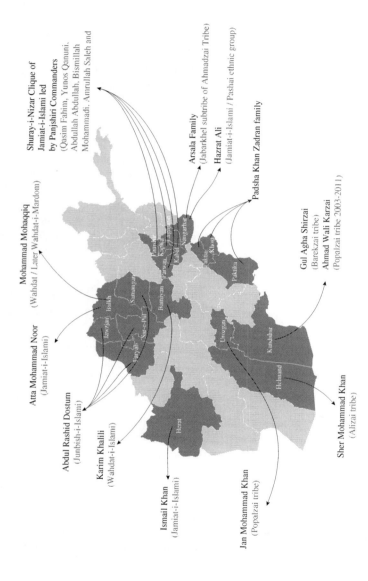

Shuray-i-Nizar Clique of
Jamiat-i-Islami led
by Panjshiri Commanders
(Qasim Fahim, Yunos Qanuni,
Abdullah Abdullah, Bismillah
Mohammadi, Amrullah Saleh and

Arsala Family
(Jabarkhel subtribe of Ahmadzai Tribe)

Hazrat Ali
(Jamiat-i-Islami / Pashai ethnic group)

Padsha Khan Zadran family

Gul Agha Shirzai
(Barekzai tribe)
Ahmad Wali Karzai
(Popalzai tribe 2003-2011)

Mohammad Mohaqqiq
(Wahdat / Later Wahdat-i-Mardom)

Atta Mohammad Noor
(Jamiat-i-Islami)

Abdul Rashid Dostum
(Junbish-i-Islami)

Karim Khalili
(Wahdat-i-Islami)

Ismail Khan
(Jamiat-i-Islami)

Jan Mohammad Khan
(Popalzai tribe)

Sher Mohammad Khan
(Alizai tribe)

Figure 4.1 Regional and provincial strongmen: a fragmented order.

maybe Panjshir), Jamiat network and, in particular, the Shuray-i-Nezar command-ers swiftly re-asserted their presence and influence over the central government and provincial administrations, as they had done after the collapse of Najibullah's government in 1992. In 2001, Shuray-i-Nezar prominent members included Qasim Fahim (intelligence chief and later Masoud's successor, and post-Bonn minister of defence), Yunus Qanuni (minister of interior), Abdullah Abdullah (minister of foreign affairs), Bismillah Mohammadi (later minister of defence and interior), Arif Sarwari (intelligence chief in interim and transitional government), and Amrullah Saleh (intelligence chief after the post-2004 elections). The bonds that tied this close-knit clique together were a combination of the shared solidarity of calling the same narrow valley, Panjshir, home, marriage, and most importantly political and financial interdependencies dating back to jihad. There were other important Shuray-i-Nezar commanders from other provinces than Panjshir, but they were never given prominence and leadership access throughout the Republic period. That's why after the 2014 elections (Chapter 6) most non-Panjshiris set up alternative patronage networks and alliances to survive and remain relevant such as the Shuray-i-Bozorg-i-Shamali (Ground Council of the North).

Jamiat network members, most of them ethnic-Tajiks, dominated the state bureaucracy and administration in Kabul and its provinces. Data collected by the Office of Administrative Affairs (2006) confirms that monopolisation, not just at the ministerial level but at all levels of the Afghan state—bureau-cracy, army, and police—was consolidated under Bonn (Figures 4.2, 4.3, and 4.4).[21] It also shows nepotism, especially along ethnic lines, and as Chapter 6 shows, that nepotism became an entrenched part of pre- and post-election cycles over the next two decades. Figure 4.2 shows that even in 2006, after the formal elimination of most Jamiat network leaders from the government, ethnic-Tajiks still comprised 53% of the government bureaucracy at grade 3

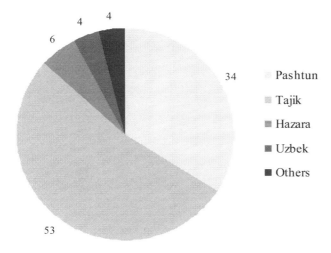

Figure 4.2 Ethnic composition of government bureaucracy at grade 3 (%)—2004.

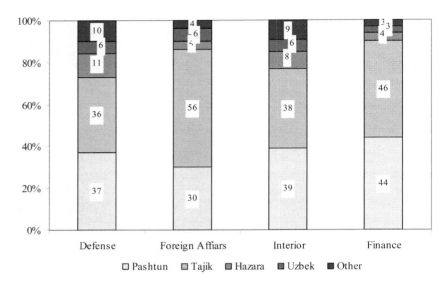

Figure 4.3 Ethnic composition of four top ministries at grade 3 (%)—2004.

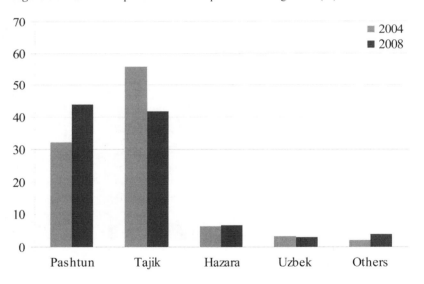

Figure 4.4 Afghanistan national army by ethnic group.

and above, compared to Pashtuns at 34% and Hazara and Uzbek, respectively, at 4% each.[22] The ethnic-Pashtuns were predominantly represented by techno-crats, former Hizb-i-Islami members, and different family and tribal networks, while Hazaras were primarily represented by Wahdat and Harak-i-Islami net-works; and Uzbek largely by the Junbish network.

The ethnic composition of the top four key ministries of Defence, Foreign Affairs, Interior, and Finance also cleaved to this over-representation of ethnic-Tajik in the early post-Bonn period (Figure 4.3). All except Finance were captured by Jamiat and Panjshiri Shuray-i-Nezar commanders. Under the Disarmament, Demobilisation, and Reintegration (DDR) programme, Jamiat network was also able to successfully re-integrate their militias into the army and police across the country, especially in Kabul and the three provinces north of it. The Jamiat network had the highest integration into the Afghan National Police (figure 4.4).[23]

The arrival of NATO forces at Bagram airbase, the biggest military camp in Afghanistan, created the most expansive war industry machine (e.g., logistical contracts, security provision, transportation, and criminality, including kidnapping and extortion) the country had ever seen, with Jamiat associates becoming the primary beneficiaries. Jamiat and, in particular, Shuray-i-Nezar successfully portrayed itself as the natural and strategic partner to the U.S. military in their counter-terrorism objectives, which ensured that Panjshir, Parwan, and Kapisa provinces had the highest employment rate in and around U.S. military camps and some of the most lucrative security and logistics contracts in Afghanistan. To the very end, even as Kabul fell to the Taliban in August 2021, the CIA station in Kabul employed exclusively Panjshiri security personnel to guard and defend its compound. Their hegemony over these resource flows further advanced their claim to political legitimation and representation over the population and the politics of these four provinces.

The non-Panjshiri vessel commanders who were protected by the Shuray-i-Nezar commanders-turned-politicians were entangled in criminality to secure additional sources of power: intimidation, threat, and financial capital. The result was the formation of some of the worst criminal groups in Afghanistan. Since 2001, people like MP Shir Ali, MP Qais Hassan, and M. Daood Amin in Bagram district; Dawat-i-Islami Commander Mumtaz and former Jamiat Commander Mullah Ezzat with links to Qasim Fahim in Paghman district; Amanullah Guzar linked to Bismillah Mohammadi, the former minister of defence in Kabul; Mullah Taj Mohammad and Commander Lotfullah in Shakar Dara district; and Sufi Raziq (a former Jamiat commander) and Bashir Khan (former Hizbe-Islami) in Estalef district were all entrusted by former Shuray-i-Nezar commanders-turned-politicians to regulate and extract licit and illicit resources in Kabul city and its surrounding districts and provinces.[24] In 2017, over 100 illegal armed groups were operating in Parwan province, most of them affiliated with key powerbrokers and politicians in Parwan and Kabul.[25] In June 2014, U.S. forces close to Bagram base destroyed the personal weapons cache of a former Jamiat commander, Jan Ahmad Khan, Abdullah's provincial campaign manager for the presidential elections, reportedly caught with thousands of weapons. That same year, the National Directorate of Security recorded 152 incidents of serious criminal acts, including kidnapping, attributed to several armed criminal groups linked to Jan Ahmad Khan and another criminal network based in Mir Bacha Kot district of Kabul.[26] His associate, known as "Hasho," was considered one of the most notorious criminal leaders in Afghanistan, accused of extra-killings and kidnappings, among other crimes, in Charikar and Kabul. After several failed attempts, on 19 May 2016, a team of Afghan Special Forces, without informing Parwan officials, were finally successful in killing "Hasho" and 13 of his associates in an operation in Charikar city.

Violent criminal enterprises remained not the only sources of financial resources for Jamiat and its powerful Shuray-i-Nezar cliques in Kabul, even after Jamiat splintered into several smaller patronage networks from 2004 onwards. Land grabbing was another means to consolidate their power and wealth and continue to purchase loyalties from rival clients. According to an investigation carried out by Afghanistan's Lower House, over 1279 jerabs of land (2000 square metres) were confiscated in Kabul alone by 15,000 individuals.[27] According to the Ministry of Interior's list of the most egregious land grabbers, out of 126, 56 were from Kabul and the 3 provinces north of Kabul, and most of them senior government officials and members of parliament.[28] For instance, in the Kabul district of Deh Sabz, Allah Gul Mujahed (a former Jamiat commander) and Mulla Tarakhel (an ethnic-Pashtun local strongman) were accused of grabbing thousands of jerabs of land, charging protection fees to the brick factories in their areas of control and engaging in illegal cement extraction. A 2017 report compiled for IDLG revealed that Mujahed had at one point hired over 500 armed men to disrupt and extort money from the New Kabul City project, paying them 500 afghanis a day (just less than 10 U.S. dollars).[29] Reportedly, Mujahed's brother was the head of the brick industry association that regulated extortion, while Mullah Tarakhel's brother, Shah Wazir, the former district 21 police chief in 2018, was also accused of extortion and extra-judicial killings.

Over the years, these middle-ranking networked anchors became exceptionally adept at securing political rewards and compensations from the central government and Kabul-based political network leaders by threatening to generate disorder and chaos using their violent and financial power resources. In the post-June 2014 presidential election debacle, for instance, Amanullah Guzar and Jan Ahmad Khan threatened to stage a coup if Abdullah Abdullah was not declared the winner.[30] The severity of their threat reflected how intimately their fortunes were connected to specific political networks. Ministries and departments, and the politicians and bureaucrats who occupied them, had become so deeply entangled in the web of patronage networks and accumulation of power resources for survival and expansion that the fates of the two had, for all intents and purposes, become one.

Jamiat network remained essentially captured by the powerful Shuray-i-Nezar clique led by Panjshiris from 2001 to 2004 and arguably to the end of the post-2001 Republic in 2021, controlling and regulating access to both national and international power resources. Prof. Burhanuddin Rabbani remained the symbolic and spiritual leader of Jamiat with little actual authority. This power dynamics within Jamiat and the limited access to power resources frustrated many ambitious mid-ranking network anchors and regionally based strongmen that from 2004 they began fracturing into several smaller political networks around key figures. Most of the national-level splintered groups became mere patronage networks focusing on accumulating financial and military resources, losing social sources of power including ethnic and constituency support. As argued in Chapter 2, social capital is key to political network survival in times of crises and uncertainty. Jamiat along with other former powerful networks such as Wahdat and Jamiat lost significant support among the population towards the end of the Republic and therefore lost the state they had constituted to the Taliban in August 2021.

4.1.2 The Ministry of Interior as contested playing field for power resources: a case study

A closer look at the Ministry of Interior (MoI) reveals the extent to which state institutions were captured by competing political networks and how contests over state resources became an everyday part of network politics. It is a prime example because of the central role the ministry played in domestic security and policing, control over which paves the way for acts of criminality with impunity. In fact, ever since its establishment, the MoI and its provincial and district offices were utilised by rival political networks to win votes and provide political protection to engage in illegal resource extraction, smuggling, and narcotics trafficking. The ministry was, as one former official described it, a "honeycomb" for the flow of resources and illegality. Indeed, it's no surprise that after the Taliban takeover of Kabul in August 2021, the MoI was turned over to the Haqqani network, a notoriously corrupt organisation with massive stakes in smuggling networks between Afghanistan and Pakistan.

MoI's initial setup suited and advanced the interests of the powerful Shuray-i-Nezar Panjshiri commanders, functioning as the violent arm of Panjshiri commanders-turned-politicians, to intimidate and silence opposition and to access and regulate state resources, both licit and illicit. As such, over the years, the ministry became a *contested playing field* between two competing broad political networks: (1) Jamiat and its Shuray-i-Nezar Panjshiri commanders-turned-politicians and (2) the presidency including the National Security Council Office led by ethnic-Pashtun technocrats (first by President Karzai and then by President Ghani). This also reflected the broader norm of delicately balanced power sharing in the security sector—the National Security Council (NSC), Ministry of Defence (MoD), MoI, and National Directorate of Security (NDS)—between the former Jamiat network primarily led by Panjshiris, and ethnic-Pashtun networks led by the President's Office. For instance, in May 2021, the appointment of Bismillah Khan as MoD (ethnic-Tajik) and Ahmadzai as Chief of Army (ethnic-Pashtun) and Minister Mirzakwal (ethnic-Pashtun), Haroon Shirzad as deputy minister (DM) of Security (ethnic-Pashtun), and M. Ayub Salangi as First DM (ethnic-Tajik and) at MoI reflected this pattern of balancing act.

And as Table 4.1 shows, out of 15 ministers after the Bonn Conference in 2001 until the collapse of the Republic in August 2021, there were 7 ethnic-Tajiks (except 1 all others from Panjshir province and except 2 the rest were Shuray-i-Nezar affiliates) and 8 ethnic-Pashtuns (all affiliated to Pashtun technocratic network led by Presidents Karzai and Ghani—even though some of them

Table 4.1 List of Ministry of Interior ministers (2001–2021)

	Full name	Period	Political affiliations	Ethnicity
1	Yunus Qanuni	Dec 2001–June 2002	Jamiat—Shuray-i-Nizar from Panjshir	Tajik
2	Taj Mohammad Wardak	19 Jun 2002–Jan 2003	Jihadi and a member of Commanders' Council	Pashtun
3	Ali Ahmad Jalali	Jan 2003–Sept 2005	Technocrat	Pashtun
4	Zarar Ahmad Moqbel	Sept 2005–Oct 2008	Jamiat—Shuray-i-Nizar from Parwan	Tajik
5	Mohamad Hanif Atmar	Oct 2008–July 2010	Technocrat	Pashtun
6	Bismillah Mohammadi	Jul 2010–Sept 2012	Jamiat—Shuray-i-Nizar from Panjshir	Tajik
7	Mujtaba Patang	Sept 2012–July 2013	Communist/affiliated with technocrats	Pashtun
8	Mohammad Omar Daudzai	Sept 2013–Dec 2014	Jihadi/affiliated with technocrats	Pashtun
9	Nur ul-Haq Ulumi	Jan 2015–Feb 2016	Communist/affiliated with technocrats	Pashtun
10	Taj Mohammad Jahid	Feb 2016–Aug 2017	Jamiat—Shuray-i-Nizar from Panjshir	Tajik
11	Wais Barmak	Aug 2017–Dec 2018	Technocrat—from Panjshir	Tajik
12	Amrullah Saleh	Dec 2018–Jan 2019	Jamiat—Shuray-i-Nizar from Panjshir	Tajik
13	Masoud Andrabi	Jan 2019–Mar 2021	Technocrat—former Jamiat	Tajik
14	Hayatullah Hayat	Mar 2021–June 2021	Technocrat	Pashtun
15	Abdul Sattar Mirzakwal	June 2021–Collapse	Former communist affiliated with technocrats	Pashtun

were former communist Khaliq and Parcham networks).[31] From 2015 onwards, President Ghani tried to disrupt this balance and tilt the power in favour of his younger, technocratic clients, almost all of them ethnic-Pashtuns.[32]

The Ministry of Interior (MoI) also became a locus of financial resources in post-2001 Afghanistan for political network survival. Figure 4.5 shows the financial flows within MoI which became a major source of tensions and conflicts between the two key political networks highlighted above. An ethnographic study of MoI in May–June 2021 revealed that the top 20 MoI contractors were well-connected traders with connections to political networks affiliated with MoI officials and the President's Office, especially its Office of National Procurement Authority, with access and protection to key echelons of state (Figures 4.5 and 4.6). Each network and its cliques were competing for a piece of the pie.

MoI as an important "political marketplace" within the networked state meant that valuable positions were often "auctioned" to the highest bidder. The most desired positions and provinces were in high demand.

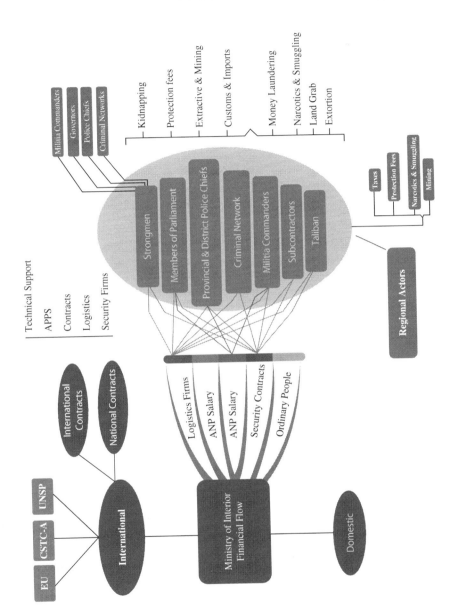

Figure 4.5 Financial flow within the Ministry of Interior.

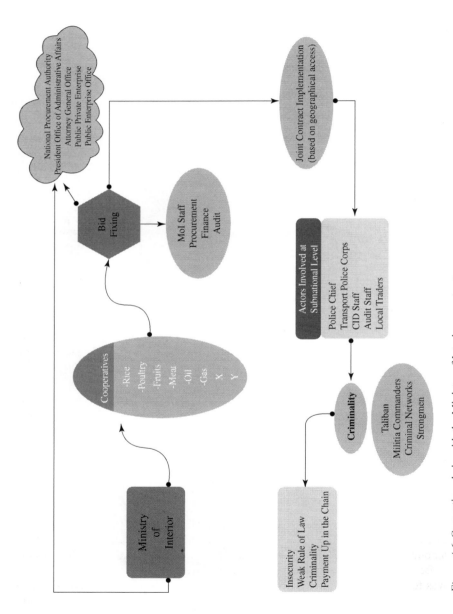

Figure 4.6 Corruption chain with the Ministry of Interior—contractors.

The price list of some of the key MoI positions were as follows:

- Provincial Chief of Police: $150,000–$300,000
- District Chief of Police: $30,000–$100,000
- Director-General of Border Police: $200,000–$500,000
- Director of Crime Investigation Department: $150,000–$250,000
- Customs post Commander: $100,000–$250,000

As the case study of MoI illustrates, key ministries and state institutions in post-2001 Afghanistan became a contest and a "political marketplace" between competing political networks who used them as "safe positions," argued in Chapter 2, to consolidate and ensure their survival. Nepotism and corruption created a "self-perpetuating system" in which political patronage and money ensured appointments and promotions along with protection (immunity from prosecution), which then enabled the "extortion and recycling of resources into the system and its continuous perpetuation."[33] This cycle created strong incentives to engage in corrupt practices to maintain a safe position within the re-emerging networked state and to survive against competition. Such corrupt practices became everyday practices, illustrated with more detailed case studies in Chapters 8 and 9 and, therefore, major obstacles to police professionalism and reform.

4.1.3 Who ruled Afghanistan's regions: strongmen and kinship networks?

This section shows how during the period from the 2001 Bonn Conference to the 2004 presidential elections, Afghanistan was governed by regional strongmen, ethno-regional entrepreneurs, and provincially based family and tribal networks with international military and funding assistance. This was a *fragmented order* that experienced a significant degree of violence and elements of the war economy in the provinces. The façade of political order was maintained by their political network leaders in Kabul as the state was being re-assembled and state institutions divided among them as a prize.

4.1.3.1 Jamiat led by Atta Mohammad Noor: the strongman of Balkh

The immediate post-2001 fragile order was seriously tested in the strategic province of Balkh in the North. The city of Mazar-i-Sharif was liberated on 9 November 2001, a month before Karzai arrived in Kabul as the head of the interim government. Preliminary order was maintained with a political settlement among provincial leaders and commanders of the three major political networks in Balkh: Jamiat, Junbish, and Wahdat networks. A provincial leadership council was formed—comprised of the three strongmen commanders of Junbish-i-Islami led by General Rashid Dostum, Jamiat-i-Islami led by Atta Mohammed Noor, and Wahdat-i-Islami led by Mohammad Mohaqiq—dividing the provincial administration and revenues proportionally to reflect their political network's control over the stockpiles of military supplies and armed men.[34] According to a

UN report, the customs' revenue from the Hairatan border with Uzbekistan on the Amu Darya River, the primary source of revenue in Balkh province, was shared among the competing strongmen networks, with Jamiat-i-Islami receiving 50%, Junbish-i-Islami 37%, and Wahdat-i-Islami 13%.[35]

This balance of power, however, quickly tilted in favour of the Jamiat network led by Commander Noor within the leadership council when he was appointed the seventh Corps Commander of Northern Afghanistan by his fellow Jamiat colleague in Kabul, Defence Minister Qasim Fahim. Ishaq Rahguzar, another Jamiat commander, became the provincial governor.[36] The shift in the power balance sparked open conflict. In the violent battles that took place between the three competing tanzim networks throughout 2002–2003 over the control of the province, the Jamiat network led by Commander Noor emerged as the undisputed winner. In the last battle over Mazar-i-Sharif in the fall of 2003, Junbish forces attacked the city, reportedly encouraged by Karzai.[37] However, once it became clear that he could not win, Karzai switched his support for Jamiat, imposed a ceasefire, and demanded full disarmament of the warring groups. Throughout 2002 and 2003, Commander Noor received political and military support, including weapons and armed men from his fellow Jamiatis in Kabul and Balkh's neighbouring provinces.[38] Jamiat established its hegemony in Balkh province and large parts of the North.

Commander Noor quickly established himself as the strongman of Balkh by appointing his Jamiat network colleagues and ethnic-Tajiks as state officials in key directorates. He also exploited the DDR process, in part because the Ministry of Interior was at that point controlled by his Jamiat network comrade (see Section 4.1.2), to re-integrate his militias and strongman network client commanders into the army, police, and intelligence services.[39] Until his removal as governor of Balkh in 2017, 90% of the 60-plus leadership positions in the provincial administration were ethnic-Tajiks loyal to Commander (who later became the provincial governor – hereafter governor Noor) Noor's network. In 2011 when I was doing my fieldwork for my Ph.D. study, at least 15 of the 19 provincial council members were associated with Governor Noor.

By 2003, his monopoly over licit and illicit trade, government contracts as well as extortion in the province was acutely entrenched, with most traders involved in the lucrative construction and fuel business paying a protection fee directly or indirectly to Governor Noor and his associates, including the highway police chief, Hairatan's customs head, and the director of commerce and trade.[40] Allegedly, most provincial government contracts were given to companies connected to Governor Noor, like the AFTECH group, which was run by his son, or his business partners.[41] In April 2012, I documented more than 30 land-grabbed housing towns associated with commanders-turned-politicians in Mazar-i-Sharif, including Abbas Ibrahimzada, Alam Khan, Ibrahim Ghazanfar, Haji Abdu, Juma Khan Hamdard, Ashraf Ramazan, and others, an excellent method for laundering their illicit money.[42] Most of them were affiliated with Governor Noor. Coercive provincial institutions were at his disposal to intimidate rivals. According to the U.S. embassy cables, Governor Noor was reportedly involved in planning and financing the assassination of 22 political opponents in Balkh between 2003 and 2005.[43]

By 2004, Governor Noor would emerge as one of the most powerful regional strongmen in the country with his power and influence burgeoning across state institutions, including in the *Wolesi Jirga* (Lower House), opening up access to state resources and partnerships with smuggling and criminal networks in Kabul, Kapisa, and Parwan provinces. He established himself increasingly independent of the Jamiat network, and acted independently as a strongman with his self-governing vessel commanders, allies, and independent sources of power resources.

American support for Governor Noor was key to his survival, and, in retrospect, he ensured to promote American interests in the North in its "war against terror." The Americans saw Governor Noor as the stabilising force in the North, and any attempts to remove him, as one U.S. embassy cable described it, would be "worse than the disease."[44] This was in stark contrast to Dostum, whom the Americans described as a "war criminal" and a "brutal warlord" who would upset the balance of power in the North if permitted. Not without some irony, along with the U.S.A., Governor Noor remained Iran's favourite client as well and received political and financial support from the regime in Tehran in the form of market access, at least until 2018 (see Chapter 6).

4.1.3.2 Junbish-i-Islami and Abdul Rashid Dostum: war criminal, ruthless warlord, or beloved ethno-regional leader?

With the collapse of the Taliban in 2001, the Junbish-i-Islami network led by Gen. Dostum carved out a safe geographical territory for themselves in the North and Northwest of the country. Junbish militiamen entered the city of Mazar-i-Sharif victorious on 9 November 2001, with support from the U.S. Special Forces.[45] In the immediate power-sharing arrangement in Balkh province, Dostum was chosen as the Head of the Leadership Council. He swiftly appointed the provincial governors of Jowzjan, Faryab, Sari-Pul, and Samangan provinces, as well as their district governors and police chiefs with Junbish clients.[46] In Faryab province, Junbish reinstated Gen. Hashim Habibi as provincial division commander, even though he had sided with Abdul Malik in 1997 and remained with the Taliban until nearly the last hour before their fall.

Junbish realising its weakness, including its lack of military assets and weak organisational structure—which were obliterated first in 1997 by Rasul Pahliwan's brother, Abdul Malik, and then finally by the Taliban in 1998— it agreed to make some compromises.[47] Although Junbish leader, Dostum, did not take a formal administrative position in Kabul, he appointed Shaker Kargar, a young Junbish-i-Islami cadre, as one of the deputies to Karzai in the interim government. Kargar, however, proved to be ineffective in safeguarding the interests of the Junbish. Junbish then was forced to the appointment of Ishaq Rahguzar as governor of Balkh and Governor Noor as corps commander, despite initial resentment. The early infusions of cash from the Americans did keep Junbish afloat, but its rival, Jamiat led by Governor Noor, had greater access to resources, which constrained Junbish's ability to buy loyalty.[48] Although initially Dostum confiscated USD 8 million in revenues stored at Hairatan customs, he agreed in the end to a lower financial share from the border.[49] And with the publication of an article in *Newsweek* in 2002 titled, "The Death Convoys of Afghanistan," which claimed that hundreds of captured Taliban prisoners of war had been massacred by Dostum's men, his well-tended image as a secular strongman and an ally of the U.S.A. was irrevocably tarnished.[50] From then on, Junbish leader would be depicted by Western media and policymakers as a brutal warlord and a challenge to the stability in the North fostered by Governor Noor.[51]

To overcome these setbacks, in 2002 Junbish-i-Islami held a National Congress inviting Uzbek intellectuals as well as commanders and political figures from other *tanzim* networks, allocating more seats on its Executive Council to liberal and educated factions to broaden its appeal.[52] Junbish appealed to ethnic-Uzbeks from other political networks such as Jamiat and Hizb-i-Islami officials and local commanders along ethnic solidarity lines, including Ahmad Khan in Samangan, Lal Mohammad in Balkh (his second in command during the Mazar-i-Sharif campaign), and Piram Ghul and Abdul Mottaleb Beg in Takhar province. However, the rivalry between Jamiat and Junbish over the control of the North quickly erupted into violent conflicts in 2002–2003. In Kabul, the Jamiat-dominated security ministries actively undermined Junbish's influence. For instance, the Ministry of Defence (MoD) and Ministry of Interior leadership appointed, armed, and supported anti-Junbish forces in Faryab province. By 2003, half of all local administrations were ethnic-Tajiks, loyal to Jamiat-i-Islami—a vast over-representation considering Jamiat's minor influence in the province.[53]

Meanwhile, Junbish's hold on Balkh was also tested. In February 2003, soon after taking office, Interior Minister Ali Ahmed Jalali, under pressure from Jamiat, named new governors for Jowzjan and Faryab, on either side of Balkh. When the new governor of Jowzjan tried to take up his post, Junbish-i-Islami militiamen chased him out. In another incident in April 2004, a popular demonstration against the Faryab governor, Enayatullah Enayat, possibly orchestrated by Junbish attacked the city and provincial divisional commander led by Gen. Hashim Habibi, who was accused of being unwilling to confront Jamiat's expansion in the province and had reportedly switched allegiances. Junbish forces took the provincial capital and its surrounding districts.[54] Fighting in the North subsided when Dostum travelled to Kabul for talks with Karzai on April 19.

Despite the machinations against him, the Junbish network repeatedly over the years proved to be a force to be reckoned with. Dostum remained de facto Chair of Junbish and the undeniable ethnic-Uzbek strongman of the North, thriving on continuous crises and disorder, claiming a commanding strength in terms of ethnic support, the loyalty of armed militia groups, and a solid organisational network cohesion compared to any other political networks. In the 2004 presidential elections, his charismatic ethnic appeal among the local population in the North rejuvenated his position after he secured 9% of the national vote on the back of his Uzbek and Turkmen constituencies, establishing himself as the most sovereign "vote bank" leader.

4.1.3.3 A family network: the Arsala family in the East

In Nangarhar, the largest province in Afghanistan's Eastern region, and the seat of the regional capital, Jalalabad, the Arsala family—the head of the powerful Jabbarkhel subdivision of the Ahmadzai tribe—had been the dominant force since the early 1980s.[55] Within the family, the prominent jihadi commanders were Abdul Haq and Haji Abdul Qadir, representing the Mawlawi Khales network during the jihad against the Soviet Union. Both were killed in 2001 and 2002, respectively. In post-2001 Afghanistan, Din Mohammad (Qadir's brother) and Zahir Qadir (Qadir's son) rose to replace them.

With the fall of the Taliban in Nangarhar in 2001, a Council of former jihadi groups was established to agree on a power-sharing arrangement. In this local political settlement, Haji Qadir was named governor of the province, Eng. Ghaffar (a former Hizb-i-Islami Gulbuddin commander) as mayor of Jalalabad city, Hazrat Ali (an ethnic-Pashai who had switched to Jamiat from Mawlawi Khales) as the provincial police chief, and Haji Zaman Khugyani (a former Hizb-i-Islami Gulbuddin commander) as the provincial military division commander. Haji Qadir's son, Haji Zahir, served as the frontier force commander for Nangarhar, giving him access to a lucrative smuggling network of goods across the border as well as control over the narcotics trade.[56]

In July 2002, Abdul Qadir was assassinated in Kabul. Many blamed the Shuray-i-Nezar leader and Minister of Defence, Qasim Fahim. Qadir's brother, Haji Din Mohammad, became the governor and stayed in that position until 2005. As a result of the killing, the rivalry between the Arsala family and Hazrat Ali, the leader of Jamiat network in the Eastern region, turned violent, shaping the struggle for dominance in the Eastern region. Jamiat continued to exert influence in the Eastern region through Hazrat Ali who was appointed as the provincial police chief by his fellow Jamiat network colleagues in the Ministry of Interior (see Section 4.1.2), further consolidating his coercive resources as well as Jamiat's access to other sources of financial resources. While Haji Zahir was accused of narco-trafficking and smuggling, Hazrat Ali and his associates were known to be involved in kidnapping, land grabbing, and other illegal activities.[57] From 2005, Hazrat Ali found protection in the *Wolesi Jirga* (Lower House) as an MP while maintaining a strong connection in Nangarhar, first through his brother-in-law, Gul Karim, and later via his son in the provincial council. Jamiat network enjoyed considerable support from Hazrat Ali's Pashai tribe, as he helped the tribe rise significantly from their historically marginal position in the province, securing key posts for Pashai members in the army and police as well as contracts and jobs on international military bases, cashing in on being a client of Jamiat.[58]

Despite these significant challenges to its authority, the Arsala family remained influential, even after the split within the family in 2005, led by Haji Din Mohammad and Haji Zahir factions who were able to use their financial and social resources to convert themselves into state-level actors in Kabul and build powerful alliances that sustained their political power. These network resources provided protection to provincial-level network elites as well as access to intimidation and coercion that continued to shape local politics for the next 15 years. In the 2009 provincial council elections, two members of the Arsala family won seats and served as chairs of the council from 2009 to 2010 (Nasrullah Arsala, son of Din Muhammad) and 2010 to 2011 (Haji Jamal, son of Haji Zahir's brother), an indication of their political and patronage influence.

Nationally, the family supported Karzai in the 2004 presidential elections. But while Haji Din Mohammad remained a key Karzai ally, serving in the High Peace Council, the senate, and as the incumbent president's 2009 campaign manager, Haji Zahir's relations with Karzai soured following the appointment of Gul Agha Shirzai, a Kandahari Pashtun strongman, as the provincial governor of Nangarhar (see Chapter 5). In 2006, Haji Zahir was exiled to the Northern Takhar province as the Head of Border Police. In 2007, Haji Zahir's cousin and secretary, Bilal Wali Mohammad, and several partners were arrested with 120 kg of heroin worth approximately USD 3 million.[59] They were jailed but later pardoned by Karzai out of respect or pressure from the Arsala family. Haji Zahir rose as Karzai's archenemy after the 2009 presidential election, leading the *Support for The Rule of Law* coalition during the 2010–2011 parliamentary crisis (see Chapter 8), which successfully challenged Karzai's authority.

4.1.3.4 Padsha Khan Zadran and the tribal network in the Southeast

In the Southeast, Padsha Khan Zadran and his tribal militias—estimated at around 3000 fighting men—governed major villages and district centres around the Khost-Gardez highway.[60] In November 2001, the CIA had provided cash to Zadran, who was living in the tribal areas of Pakistan, to recruit militias, mainly from his own Zadran tribe who populated the major districts around the main highways connecting Paktia and Khost provinces.[61] During the jihad, he was a Mahaz-i-Millie network commander and had fought the Soviets and the Taliban. During the civil war of the 1990s, he became the head of the Paktia provincial military division and, for a short period, was acting as the head of the regional army corps.[62] Zadran, a passionate supporter of the former king, was the only member of the Rome Group who attended the Bonn Conference from inside Afghanistan, for which his brother, Amanullah Zadran, was awarded the post of Minister of Border and Tribal Affairs.

On 14 November 2001, the Taliban in Paktia negotiated the surrender of the strategic city of Gardez to the Paktia Tribal Council—a loose coalition of diverse tribal elders in the province, before Zadran and his men could reach the city. This was the first instance where locals had mediated the Taliban's handover, and this council was subsequently running the local administration, as caretakers, when Zadran and his tribal militias arrived.[63] A few days later, the Taliban in Khost also handed over power to the Khost Tribal Council, which set up its own administration. In January 2002, Karzai appointed Zadran as governor of Paktia. However, the tribal council opposed his appointment. Zadran's attempt to enter Gardez city in Paktia with around 2000 of his militiamen led to a bloody fight with forces loyal to the tribal council leader, Haji Safiullah, an Ahmadzai tribal leader, and his commander, Abdul Matin. They chased Zadran's forces out.[64] Similarly, in Khost, the tribal council blocked the Zadran brother's Kamal Khan militias from entering the city and raised tribal forces against them. In retaliation, Zadran took matters into his own hands and fired rockets into Gardez from two hills overlooking the city, killing 38 civilians. The Karzai administration responded by calling Zadran a disruptive warlord who was working to destabilise the country.[65]

Zadran's relations with the U.S.A. also deteriorated when he sold weapons to al-Qaida affiliates who then shelled the American base near Khost city.[66] In March 2003, U.S. Special Forces killed one of Zadran's sons and forced him out of the province.[67] On a request from the Americans and the Karzai administration, in November, he was arrested in Miranshah by Pakistani security forces and jailed. He was freed in 2004, reportedly after making amends with Karzai, and was able to run for a seat in the Lower House in 2005, which he won.[68] His son, Abdul Wali, became the district governor of Wazi Zadran, the family's home district. His brother, Sardar, became the head of the notorious Khost Protection Force (KPF)—a contingent force of over 5000 men who were trained and instructed by the U.S. Central Intelligence Agency accused of many human rights violations— for a brief period before he was removed.[69] Ironically, according to a report compiled for the U.S. Congress, Zadran's three sons (Sediq, Rauf, and Dawlat) continued to provide security and trucking services to NATO via their security companies, arguably awarded as part of the U.S. strategy of using money as a weapon system in its "war against terror."[70] Intimidation by their men made it impossible for anyone to operate in the region without paying them and their companies' protection fees.

Zadran family's political influence gradually waned, mainly because they limited access (political, social, financial, and military) to their extended family and their tribal affiliates instead of leaving it more accessible to other tribal elders and networks, contrary to what I argued in Chapter 1 is a necessary adaptive feature in unstable environments for a network's long term survival. In the 2010 parliamentary elections, he failed to win his seat in Paktia, making the family almost politically irrelevant.

4.1.3.5 *Ismail Khan: the Amir of the West*

Thus far in this chapter, we have seen three different kinds of networks that proliferated in Afghanistan after the 2001 Bonn Agreement: strongman, ethnic entrepreneur, and kinship (family and tribal). Each relied on different strategies— sometimes converging, sometimes diverging—to maintain their positions in a networked state where access to resources was contested. The fourth category of network was established in the West of the country by Ismail Khan, who returned to power as the governor of Herat province, bordering Iran, setting up his absolute fiefdom in the form of an Emirate—a conservative administration controlling all aspects of society, which went against the Jamiat's moderate Islam. He run Herat and neighbouring provinces by a small number of religious aristocratic families, the backbone of his patronage network—mainly residing in the city and of Mir, Khoja, Sayyad, and Hazrat religious titles/origins—which alienated many Jamiat affiliates and powerful families.[71]

Jamiat network through Ismail Khan had ruled the region from 1992 until the collapse of Herat city in September 1995. Originally from the Shindand district, Khan had become famous because of his leadership in the anti-communist army mutiny of 1979 and later for being appointed the provincial leader of the Jamiat-i-Islami *tanzim* in 1982.[72] In 2001, when Jamiat retook power, Khan had an estimated 20,000-member militia at his disposal and good relations with neighbouring Iran, which reportedly provided him direct financial and logistical support in the early years. He quickly established himself as an *Amir* with an administrative reach, private militias, and a network of loyal Jamiat network supporters stretching to Ghor, Badghis, Nimruz, and Farah provinces. His power was further bolstered, among other things, by the huge inflow of customs revenues from two of Afghanistan's main transit ports: Islam Qala (bordering Iran) and Torghundi (bordering Turkmenistan), which he refused to channel to central government coffers.[73] The customs money enabled Jamiat and Khan to deliver relatively quality services for which many people in Herat still credit him to this day.

Unlike other strongmen, Khan's approach to governance was absolute monopolisation of power and centralisation of authority around him, which did not win him a lot of friends and went against the logic of open-access network membership and alliance-building.[74] And although he was not as brutal, or as personally corrupt, as other strongmen, his defiance of the Jamiat network in Kabul, in particular Shurayy-i-Nezar, absolute centralism of regional administration, and radical religious discipline became a source of growing concern and discomfort for his Jamiat backers in Kabul. That is why, partly, when Karzai attempted to unseat him in 2003, his Jamiat colleagues in Kabul, urban Jamiatis in Herat city, and rural comrades in Ghor and Badghis provinces did not come to his rescue. His Chief of Staff, Gen. Abdul Wahab Qatali, arguably with the approval of Khan to accumulate financial resources, built a massive financial empire. Their group of companies, the Faizi Group, set up in 2003, would control key transport, construction materials, and food markets in Herat, and their Arya Security Company would win profitable contracts from NATO to provide security for its convoys on the road to Kandahar.[75] The family's prominent son, Sayed Wahid Qatali, became the chair of the provincial council in Herat with the help of other pro-Ismail members, then director-general of the President's Office of Administrative Affairs, and finally, in 2020, the governor of Herat province.

In 2003, Karzai successfully unseated Khan (discussed below) by first provoking his rival ethnic-Pashtun militia commander in Shindand, Amanullah Khan. In the ensuing battle over the control of the city, Ismail Khan's son was killed, and with the U.S. intervention, he was forced to leave Herat and join Karzai's government as minister of energy. Khan's influence waned in Herat and within the Jamiat over the years. But he found protection after the 2009 presidential election by associating himself with Abdul Rasul Sayyaf, the influential powerbroker, and leader of Dawat-i-Islami network.

4.1.3.6 The seven strongmen of the South: a resource-dependency tribal confederation

In the Southern provinces, seven authoritarian chiefs emerged following the defeat of the Taliban in 2001. The South being Hamid Karzai's home base meant that he had to directly intervene in guaranteeing his clients cemented their power to reinforce his authority, agenda, and interests. He was, after all, chosen at the Bonn Conference for his Popalzai Durrani tribal background and for being from Kandahar.

Gul Agha Sherzai, a Barakzai tribal chief affiliated with Mahaz-i-Millie network during the anti-Soviet jihad, was in Pakistan in hiding when the Americans and the ISI approached him with cash and weapons to mobilise his tribe and others to help topple the Taliban.[76] Surrounded on all sides, Taliban leaders agreed to evacuate Kandahar following negotiations with Karzai through Mullah Naqibullah, an Alokozai tribal chief affiliated with the Jamiat *tanzim*. For playing an instrumental role in negotiating the Taliban's surrender, Mullah Naqibullah was promised the position of governor.[77] However, when Kandahar fell in early December, Shirzai and Naqibullah forces fought on the street for the control of the city. Under U.S. pressure, and Shirzai's threat of an all-out war, Karzai and Mullah Naqibullah backed down. A deal was reached in which Shirzai became the governor and Mullah Naqibullah his deputy.[78] However, Mullah Naqibullah, who was in his late sixties, declined to accept the post on the grounds of advanced age. Instead, he stated that he would nominate someone else from within his tribe for the position. In the end, however, it did not matter who was appointed to the deputy position; the real powerbroker in Kandahar would be the U.S.-favoured Shirzai. Once again, the U.S.A. had played an instrumental role in tilting the balance of power, this time in favour of Shirzai (Figure 4.7).[79]

In Kandahar, tribal dynamics played an important role in the capture of key state institutions. By early 2003, out of 60 heads of department directorates in the province, all but 8 were from Governor Shirzai's Barakzai tribe.[80] Karzai's Popalzai

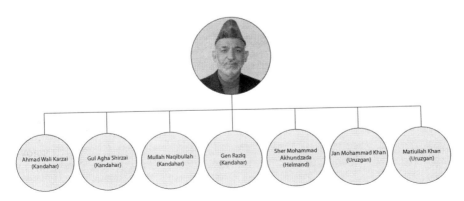

Figure 4.7 The seven strongmen of the South.

tribe dominated district administrations because of the chairman's power of appointment in Kabul, while the Alokozai were over-represented within the police force because of their strongman, Akram Khakrezwal, who was serving as police chief. Meanwhile, the Achikzai tribe controlled the important Spin Boldak border crossing and its customs revenues and procured militia forces for Governor Shirzai. Other tribal elders, including Governor Noorzai, Ishaqzai, and Ghilzai, were excluded from post-2001 spoils. Subsequently, most of them joined the Taliban.

Shirzai and his cousins, Yousaf Pashtun and Khalid Pashtun, taking advantage of their tribe's close relationship with the Americans, produced fake intelligence to eliminate their political and economic rivals, including Mullah Naqibullah.[81] For instance, Shirzai's brother, Major General Raziq in the Afghan army, ran much of the contracting at Kandahar airfield through his son's construction company, tapping into the influx of the international military's flow of resources.[82] According to Chayes (2007), the family came to provide everything from gravel to the leasing of Kandahar airfield to the international forces stationed at the airport. They were charging the U.S. Provincial Reconstruction Team outrageous prices. For example, gravel used to repair the runway was sold at USD 100 a truckload compared to USD 8 in the open market.[83] Chayes estimates that Shirzai and his family associates made a net profit of USD 1.5 million per month for providing fuel, building materials, and other items to the international militaries,[84] plus an estimated USD 8 million from the Spin Boldak customs border.[85]

Hamid Karzai saw Shirzai and the expanding power of other actors in his home province, and their increasing control of the South's resource flows, as a threat to himself and his Popalzai tribe. Ahmad Wali, Karzai's half-brother, was appointed as the chief of the Popalzai tribe and the head of Kandahar Reform Council in 2002—a coalition of tribal elders to oversee governance in the province. Exploiting his position within the Council and his brother's international patronage and position in Kabul, Ahmad Wali began challenging and unseating his rivals. First, in 2003, through the DDR process, Akram Khakrezwal was removed as chief of police, and Khan Mohammad Mujahed, the powerful Alokozai commander and deputy to Mullah Naqibullah, lost command of the Second Army Corps when it was disbanded.[86] Amir Lalai, Karzai's Popalzai rival, and Habibullah Jan, an Alizai militia commander, were also removed from their military position and their militias demobilised. In 2003, Shirzai was forced to take a ministerial position in Kabul while his ineffective cousin, Yousef Pashtun, as a last-minute compromise was appointed as the new governor.

However, after the fall of Governor Shirzai, real power stood with Ahmad Wali. Among the marginalised Governor Noorzai tribe, Karzai promoted Arif Governor Noorzai, related to him through marriage, first as the minister of border and tribal affairs and, when he was elected to the Lower House in 2005, as deputy speaker of the House. Within the Achikzai militias, the young Gen. Raziq emerged as the main violent actor in Spin Boldak district. His position was further cemented when Achikzai militias were integrated into the Afghan National Border Police and the 358th border brigade allowing him to play an instrumental role in the security of the province.[87]

From 2005 onwards, the political order in Kandahar centred on two key network leaders: President Karzai's family and their Popalzai tribe, first led by Ahmad Wali Khan and later, after Ahmad Wali's assassination in 2010, by his brother Shah Wali Khan; and Kandahar Police Chief Gen. Raziq. When the latter died in 2017, his brother Tadin Khan took over as provincial police chief and head of the Achikzai militia forces, overseeing their vast illicit financial networks. Ahmad Wali would enjoy close relations with the CIA, renting them properties and private militias in exchange for money and thus building one of the most expansive financial and political networks in the South. In 2005, his election as the head of the Provincial Council gave him further legitimacy.[88]

In Helmand and Uruzgan provinces, Sher Muhammad Akhundzada as governor and chief of the Alizai tribe in Helmand, and Jan Muhammad Khan as governor and key Popalzai leader in Uruzgan, would emerge as the unchallenged strongmen. The latter's nephew, Matiullah Khan, and his private militia of 2000 armed men responsible for the security of the Kandahar-Uruzgan highway became the family's violent capital. The five of them (Ahmad Wali, Gen Raziq, Sher Muhammad, Jan Muhammad, and Matiullah Khan) would constitute President Karzai's core Southern network (see Chapter 5).[89]

Together, these seven chiefs enlarged and strengthened their tribally based strongmen networks and controlled most of the South's resources. They established a resource-dependent tribal network alliance which would govern the South. In Kandahar, tribal chief-based dynamics determined stability and violence rather than strong *tanzim* groupings around a strong ethnic leader, which had happened in the North.[90] By 2003, with the departure of Gul Agha Shirzai and marginalisation of Mullah Naqibullah, Karzai's ring of five set up virtually unchallenged control of the licit and illicit resource flows in the South, including the drug trade, contracts with the American military and Afghan government, land and real estate, and others. For instance, all Host Nation Tracking NATO contractors and subcontractors paid between USD 1500 and 3000 per truck to Matiullah Khan's men for safe passage of supplies from Kandahar to Uruzgan's Tirin Kot.[91] In another case, Mark Dodd and Jeremy Kelly, writing for *The Australian*, documented that in April 2008, Khan received USD 340,000 per month—nearly USD 4.1 million annually—for ensuring two convoys from Kandahar reached Tirin Kot safely each month for the Australian and the Dutch armies alone.[92] Also at the time, 600 of his men were being paid by the Ministry of Interior to provide security for the main highways.[93]

As framed in Chapter 2, building alliances and maintaining a balanced equilibrium among key tribal networks became the principal blueprint to guarantee informal order in the South, despite a defiant insurgency from 2005 onwards. Collectively, these seven tribal network leaders reinforced Karzai's legitimation and guaranteed political order and the sustainability of the post-2001 state. While they were awarded and were tasked to maintain stability, other tribes were marginalised and excluded from national and provincial power and representation such as Governor Noorzai and Ishaqzai in Kandahar and Helmand, Kakars in Uruzgan, and Tokhi in Zabul who then found sanctuary with the Taliban from 2005 onwards.

4.1.3.7 Karim Khalili: the "feeble" strongmen of the Central Highlands

In early November 2001, Karim Khalili, an ethnic-Hazara and the political leader of the Wahdat network, and his militia forces (numbering some 2500 men stationed in Dar-i-Suf and Yakawlang districts) began their offensive on Bamiyan city from several directions.[94] They were aided by a small group of American advisors, numbering between 15 and 20 men. With American cash, weapons, and initial aerial bombardment of Taliban positions, Khalili's forces captured the city on November 11 without much resistance, a month before Karzai reached Kabul as head of the interim government.[95] Although Bamiyan was not considered an al-Qaida haven or Taliban stronghold, the capture of the provincial capital, the political and administrative heartland of the ethnic-Hazaras, was a symbolic victory and legitimation for the Wahdat network and the U.S.A.[96] Other neighbouring provinces in the Central Highlands, including Daikundi, Ghazni, Wardak, and Ghor, also quickly fell. However, Khalili and his forces scrambled towards Kabul, the ultimate prize in the fast-moving military offensive against the Taliban, to secure a foothold in the capital, leaving local commanders in charge, and also because the leader of Wahdat network, Karim Khalili, was selected as one of the four vice-chairmen to Karzai.

Unlike other tanzim networks and strongmen commanders, Khalili waited for the interim government to form before filling in key administrative positions in Bamiyan. In agreement with chairman Karzai and interior minister Qanuni, a delegation made up of four key *tanzim* representatives was sent to Bamiyan to carry out an assessment and make recommendations on a power-sharing arrangement.[97] As a result of their recommendations, Wahdat received most government positions, including governor (commander Aliyar), police chief (commander Fahimi), and command of the army's newly approved 34th division (commander Jawhari), because of its stockpile of military and political resources. Even though other *tanzims* had almost no, or little, role in the defeat of the Taliban in Bamiyan, the 24-plus provincial directorates were divided equally among the four groups. For instance, Harakat-i-Islami took over the directorate of National Security and five others; Jamiat received Mustufiyat (Ministry of Finance Directorate), Labour and Social Affairs, Justice, Public Works, and two others. Out of six district governors, four went to Wahdat and two to Jamiat.[98] This inclusive approach to political settlement and order would prove more sustainable and one of the key reasons that Bamiyan province remained the most peaceful province in the country until the collapse of the Republic in August 2021.

Also, unlike other regions, the provincial administration had no access to customs revenues or any other international funds to enable it to accumulate wealth, which may partly explain why Bamiyan remained relatively peaceful. The U.S.A. made no substantial military investment in the Central Highlands, and the few New Zealand troops stationed in Bamiyan saw active combat. The only major source of illicit activity was illegal excavation and trade of antiquities which was nothing compared to the billions of "money as a weapon system" that went to other regions.[99] However, in Kabul, Khalili's brother, Haji Nabi Khalili, became one of the many jihadi officials involved in land grabbing and other dubious activities, which again was minor compared to other players.[100]

Khalili's policy of including other *tanzims* in the local administration, without obtaining any concessions, put him at odds with his Wahdat commanders who had helped him regain the province. However, it ensured a long-lasting balance of power in the province. Khalili's astringent pressure on his commanders to hand over their weapons in the DDR process, as the chair of the DDR Commission, further disfranchised many of them.[101] By the end of 2004, most of them sided with his main rival, Mohammad Mohaqiq. With the appointment of Habiba Sarabi, the first female governor of Afghanistan, Khalili gradually lost his stature and influence over the province, and his influence among his constituency gradually declined.[102] This was because Wahdat network failed on acquiring at least two of the four key resources (discussed in Chapter 2): accumulate enough wealth for distribution to members and fend off competition, control significant safe positions within the state to supply political patronage, and exercise coercion and intimidation against clients that desire to exit the network.

Not surprisingly, Wahdat splintered into at least four main patronage networks in 2002 and 2003: Hizb-i-Wahdat Islami Afghanistan led by Karim Khalili, Hizb-i-Wahdat-Islam-i-Mardom led by Mohammad Mohaqqiq, Wahdat-i-Millie led by Mohammad Akbari, and Wahdat-i-Millet led by Qorban Ali Erfani—now deceased. Bypassing Wahdat altogether, Karzai promoted Sadiq Modabber from among the Hazaras, a former Harakat-i-Islami commander, to the prominent position of Head of the Office of Administrative Affairs of the President. He subsequently set up his Ensejam-i-Millie network (National Harmonisation) with its members occupying key positions in the central government and central highland provinces, further undermining and weakening Khalili. With little international money flowing in and a relatively balanced order among the competing *tanzims*, the region did not see the level of violence and strongman politics that the rest of Afghanistan experienced. Given the scarcity of resources it received, one could argue, as some have, that the lighter international footprint in the region produced more order and less violence.

To conclude this section, provincial commanders-turned-strongmen, kinship-based networks (family and tribal), and ethno-regional political networks proliferated and cemented their power in their geographical territories. By using their "hybrid authority" as state officials and informal strongmen, they were able to monopolise the use of violence and employ it to consolidate their power.[103] Many saw governing the subnational administration as their legitimate right, autonomous of the centre, as they had ruled their geographical safe havens during the 1992–2001 civil war. They, therefore, refused to send customs revenues to the central government's coffers until May 2003. It was only towards the end of 2004 that Karzai, through the use of a carrot and stick strategy, with the backing of the international military forces, was able to incorporate them within the larger state administration. Resource extraction and rent-seeking became the principal rules of the game, leaving formal institutions to play only a marginal role.

International military forces had a key role in empowering and transforming political networks as part of their counter-terrorism mission at the expense of nascent institutions.[104] The U.S.A. and its allies pursued a multiplicity of agendas, interests, and practices that produced an array of contradictory policies and tools. For instance, throughout the American military intervention, while the State Department was condemning strongman behaviour and corrupt practices, the U.S. military and CIA pursued a protectionist policy, considering them "assets." In this period what we inherited was a "fragmented order" and a "fragmented state." As the concluding chapter outlines, the influence of political networks would diminish over the years as they go against the logic of the networked state outlined in Chapter 2 by limiting power resources (political, social, financial, and military) to their extended family and their tribal affiliates instead of leaving it more accessible to broader communities and groups.

4.2 Karzai's technocratic network flexing their muscle

During this period, Karzai in Kabul was surrounded by a cabinet of powerful political networks especially Jamiat and its Shuray-i-Nezar clique, circumscribed in his own office, including the Office of Administrative Affairs, by aides loyal to his vice-chairman Qasim Fahim.[105] In those early years, many Western diplomats and Afghan officials felt sorry for Karzai, whose power they described as nothing more than the "mayor of Kabul."[106] Until July 2002, Karzai's security guards were provided by and loyal to Qasim Fahim. After a credible threat to his life, he replaced them with 46 American contractors who remained with him for two years.[107] In February 2002, the Civil Aviation Minister, Abdul Rahman, was killed at Kabul Airport, allegedly by men loyal to Fahim. Karzai described it as a "premeditated assassination plot ... stemming from a personal vendetta" and indirectly accused Fahim.[108] In July, Karzai lost his close aide, deputy head of interim government and minister of public works, Haji Abdul Qadir; many pointed the finger at Fahim. On the anniversary of Mujahedeen Day, 27 April 2002, Karzai was forced to promote Fahim to the position of Marshal and officially bestowed on Ahmad Shah Masoud the title of "National Hero." It was in this context, feeling increasingly frustrated with his lack of authority, that Karzai and his technocratic aides saw platforms such as the 2002 emergency Loya Jirga, 2003 constitutional Loya Jirga, and the 2004 presidential elections as excellent opportunities to flex their muscles. Karzai came to realise the importance of setting up his own patronage network which naturally meant allying himself with Western-educated technocrats, Rome Group members who had cabinet positions, ethnic-Pashtun former Jihadis in Hizb-Islami, and others. As Chapter 5 shows, he mastered the art of building alliances and co-opting middle-ranking clients from other networks, as the highest bidder in the network state in control of state resources.

4.2.1 Emergency Loya Jirga and the transitional authority

The emergency Loya Jirga was held in June 2002 to elect the head of the Transitional Administration and the cabinet, as had been agreed at the Bonn Conference. About 1600 members attended the Jirga representing all districts of the country, including representatives from intellectuals, *ulema* (religious leaders), women, religious minorities, and traders.[109] Two major issues dominated the Jirga: (1) the role of the former king, as he had expressed interest in being elected as the head of state in the future government[110] and (2) breaking the Shuray-i-Nezar commanders' monopoly over the security sector ministries.[111]

The king, who had returned to Afghanistan in April, had shown political ambitions. It didn't help when more than 800 of his supporters signed a petition urging his nomination as the head of state, if only as a figurehead.[112] The Jamiat network leaders had expressed their discontent with the idea of the king taking on a formal position, both in Bonn and in Kabul. As a sign of their opposition, prominent jihadi leaders, including former president Rabbani, did not go to the airport to greet the king when he arrived in Kabul.[113] To resolve the crisis, the Jirga was postponed for more than a week, claiming technical reasons. Zalmai Khalilzad, the U.S. Special Presidential Envoy for Afghanistan, who would later be named ambassador, held several meetings with the former king, and eventually, a day before the Jirga, he held a press conference at which he announced that the king had decided not to stand as a candidate and that he instead was supporting Hamid Karzai for the post of the head of state.[114] On the same day, the king held a press conference in which he reiterated that he was not a candidate for any position, with Karzai sitting next to him. The king settled with the symbolic title of the Baba-ye-Millat (Father of the Nation), and former president Rabbani also withdrew his candidacy under U.S. pressure. The Americans were going to have their man, Hamed Karzai, as president and if required they would use muscle and finances to get their wish.

The second issue which was more serious and controversial was the composition of the future cabinet, especially Pashtun technocrats' demand to relinquish one of the security ministries which the Shurayy-i-Nezar Panjshiri network was controlling. It brought Jamiat into direct confrontation with Pashtun technocratic led by Karzai. Under international pressure, they eventually gave up the Ministry of Interior, but this further soured relations within Shurayy-i-Nezar and that is why Qanuni splintered from them to set up his own patronage network, Hizb-i-Nawin Afghanistan. Qanuni was replaced as minister of interior by Taj Mohammad Wardak, an ethnic-Pashtun, and was offered the Ministry of Education instead. However, Wardak was blocked from entering his office by Qanuni's men for several days. Later, another compromise was reached by establishing a marital connection between the two families, among other things.[115] In January 2003, Wardak was removed after only a few months and replaced by Ali Ahmad Jalili, a Western-educated Pashtun technocrat. Political networks whose power and legitimacy were primarily centred on religion with little coercive and community resources demanded that Afghanistan be called the Islamic Republic. During the Jirga, Abdul Rasul Sayyaf (leader of Dawat-i-Islami network) and Sheikh Mohseni (leader of Harakat-i-Islami) advocated and even blackmailed the assembly to adopt the additional title "Islamic" for the new Afghanistan Transitional Administration, counter to what had been stipulated in Bonn.[116]

Despite serious intimidation and threats by the Jamiat-controlled National Directorate of Security during the Jirga, and with the heavy-handed tactics of Khalilzad, Karzai was elected as the chair of the Transitional Government with 80% of the vote, which provided him with much-needed legitimacy.[117] International funding for the Jirga, which was channelled through the Interim Authority, had also enabled Karzai to buy votes or discourage others from undermining him. It is difficult to verify the back-channel fund, but this seems to have been discussed among international partners.[118] On June 19, following intense horse-trading with key patronage, kinship, and strongmen networks, Karzai announced the names of 14 ministers and 3 vice-chairmen, who were subsequently endorsed by the Loya Jirga. His cabinet was a compromise between stability and pushing for a degree of change to please his Pashtun and technocratic constituency.[119] The final cabinet was composed of 5 vice-chairpersons, 3 special or national advisors with cabinet status, and 30 ministries. The ethnic balance changed slightly from the Northern Alliance that controlled 17 of the previous 28 ministries, with Pashtun representation increasing to just under 50% (15 ministries from 11 in post-Bonn, plus the chief justice), and Tajik and Hazara representation reduced. Karzai was able to bring in several Western-educated technocrats, including Ashraf Ghani as minister of finance, Ali Jalali as minister of interior (in 2003), Abdul Haq Ahadi as head of central bank, and Hanif Atmar as minister of rural development, who comprised the core of his political network in his struggle against the Jihadis. Junbish-i-Islami and Wahdat-i-Mardom networks were the biggest losers. Karzai appointed Abdul Rashid Dostum, the leader of Junbish, as his special advisor on military affairs of the North, a mere symbolic appointment (Table 4.2).

4.2.2 The constitutional Loya Jirga

The January 2003 constitutional Loya Jirga offered yet another opportunity for Karzai and his technocratic network clients to consolidate their institutional power. Tensions rose between the non-Pashtun-dominated political networks and the Pashtun-dominated Karzai team over the modality of the political system, among many other issues. The Constitutional Review Commission's draft included a directly elected president, a prime minister, a two-chamber parliament, and a constitutional court.[120] However, a last-minute change, most probably by President Karzai and after buying off key elites, who wanted a strong presidential system, dropped the position of the prime minister.

An influential group of younger and educated Jamiat network reformers, led by Abdul Hafiz Mansur and Mohiuddin Mehdi, tried to rouse the Jirga into an opposition force against Karzai with their lobbying for a parliamentary system.[121] There was significant opposition to a strong presidential system among ethnically mixed liberals, Jihadis, and Pashtun royalists advocating for limiting the authority of the president. Among the non-Pashtun networks and centres of power, there was also an underlying ethnic with Junbish and Wahdat networks advocating for a more decentralised form of governance, possibly federalism, and Jamiat to keep their status quo lobbying for a parliamentary system with substantial authority to

Table 4.2 The post-transitional authority government cabinet

Name	Position	Ethnicity	Political affiliations
Hamid Karzai	President	Pashtun	Technocrat
M. Qasim Fahim	Vice President and Defence Minister	Tajik	Jamiat
Karim Khalili	Vice President	Hazara	Wahdat
Abdul Qadir	Vice President and Minister of Public Work	Pashtun	Arsala Family
Hedayat Amin Arsala	Vice President	Pashtun	Technocrat/Karzai
Nematullah Shahrani	Vice President and Head of Constitution Commission	Uzbek	Technocrat/Karzai
Fazal Hadi Shinwari	Chief Justice	Pashtun	Dawat/Karzai
Yunus Qanuni	Special Advisor on Security and Minister of Education	Tajik	Jamiat
Ashraf Ghani	Finance	Pashtun	Technocrat/ Karzai
Abdullah Abdullah	Foreign Affairs	Tajik (Herat)	Jamiat
Taj M. Wardak/later Ali Ahmad Jalali	Interior	Pashtun	Karzai
Arif Sarwary/later Amrullah Saleh	National Security Directorate	Tajik	Jamiat
M. Mohaqiq	Planning	Hazara	Wahdat-i-Mardom
Mustafa Kazimi	Commerce	Hazara/Sayyed	Wahdat
Habiba Sarabi	Women Affairs	Hazara	Technocrat
Saeed Mohammed Ali Jawad	Transport	Hazara/Sayyed	Harakat-i-Islami
Hanif Atmar	Rural Development	Pashtun	Technocrat/Karzai
Juma. M. Mohammadi	Mines and Petroleum	Pashtun	Karzai
Inayatullah Nazeri	Refugee	Tajik	Jamiat
Yunus Qanuni	Education	Tajik	Jamiat/ Shuray-i-Nezar
Nur M. Qarqin	Social Affairs	Turkmen	Junbish
Sharif Faez	Higher Education	Tajik	Jamiat
Ahmed Shakar Karkar	Energy and Water	Uzbek	Junbish
Abbas Karimi	Justice	Uzbek	Junbish
	Narcotics		
Fahim Farhang	Economy and Reconstruction	Pashtun	Technocrat/Karzai
Masoom Stanekzai	Telecommunication	Pashtun	Technocrat/Karzai
Yusuf Pashtoon	Urban Development	Pashtun	Technocrat/Karzai
Sayed Hussain Anwari	Agriculture	Hazara/Sayyed	Harakat-i-Islami
Makhdoom Rahim	Culture	Tajik	Jamiat
Sohaila Sediqi	Health	Pashtun	Technocrat/Karzai
M. Amin Naziryar	Religious Affairs	Pashtun	Karzai
Arif Noorzai	Tribal Affairs	Pashtun	Karzai
M. Alim Razm	Industries	Uzbek	
Abdullah Wardak	Martyr and Social Affairs	Pashtun	Technocrat/Karzai
Ahmed Yusuf Nuristani	Irrigation and Environment	Nuristani	Technocrat/Karzai
Mirwais Sediqi	Transport and Aviation	Tajik	Jamiat/Ismail Khan son
Zalmai Rassoul	National Security Advisor	Pashtun	Technocrat/Karzai
	Administrative Affairs Office	Pashtun	Technocrat/Karzai
	Chief of Staff	Pashtun	Technocrat/Karzai
Anwar ul-Haq Ahadi	Governor of the Central Bank	Pashtun	Technocrat/Karzai

the prime minister's office, which they demanded for themselves. Both suggestions received a strong reaction from some ethnic-Pashtun delegations as they argued this would break up the country and empower warlordism/strongmen networks.[122] President Karzai's network and allies (Karzai's technocratic group such as Qayum Karzai, Ashraf Ghani, Hanif Atmar, and their Islamist ally, Abdul Rasul Sayyaf) played the ethnic card, exploiting the deep mistrust that many Pashtuns felt for the Northern Alliance groups that had dominated power in post-2001 Afghanistan.[123] The president's team seems to have bribed the delegates—a pattern that would encompass all aspects of political life in Afghanistan for years to come. According to a UN staffer, a delegate's vote would cost USD 300 and up, with some receiving as high as USD 5000.[124]

Finally, a compromise was made in which Dari was accepted as the official language along with Dari and Uzbeki, in exchange for accepting the presidential system. The newly approved constitution adopted a strong presidential system with the president serving as both head of state as well as head of government, enabling him/her to appoint Supreme Court judges, one-third of the upper house members, and act as the head of the three branches of government, blurring the balance of power.[125] The Jirga and the process, instead of bringing consensus, enabling debate, and finding a mechanism to reinforce national solidarity, exacerbated ethnic tensions and seriously undermined national unity—one of the many occasions that political networks would use ethnic and tribal cards to appeal to their constituency and mobilise support. Other networked practices of patronage, corruption, and co-opting rent were visible, albeit at a very small scale. As the subsequent chapters show, these network practices would become more prominent and costly at moments of contestation like elections.

These network practices were further aggravated by President Karzai's adoption of a repression strategy, discussed below and in the next chapter, to go after regional strongmen and kinship networks (family and tribal) after the Jirga. This was a high-risk strategy that led directly to significant outbreaks of political violence in the periphery.

4.2.3 *Confronting regional strongmen: stretching beyond Kabul*

With the legitimacy bestowed on him at the emergency Loya Jirga in 2002 and the new constitution in 2003, Karzai felt more secure in his position to exert his authority beyond Kabul. American support was crucial for Karzai to win, especially that of Zalmai Khalilzad, now the U.S. ambassador. At the time, the general perception among many Americans at the embassy was that Khalilzad was the one calling the shots, sarcastically referring to him as the "Second President" or even "President Khalilzad."[126] Karzai had to prove to his predominantly Western-educated and technocratic network and allies that he is able to reward patronage and exploit his position as the head of state to expand his networked destarkhan, "tablecloth" for a broader category of political grouping and constituencies.

Karzai's calculation to weaken political networks was to go first after their clients and strongmen in the provinces. To achieve this and before a direct attempt to suppress subnational clients of political networks, Karzai took two important decisions. First, on 20 May 2003, Karzai summoned ten provincial governors, one deputy governor, and two military commanders to Kabul and arm-twisted them into signing a 13-point declaration in which they would agree to "follow and implement the laws, regulations and legislative documents of the country and their job descriptions."[127] Most of them are either the leader of strongmen networks or clients of Kabul-based patronage networks. They pledged not to interfere in the affairs of other provinces and to obey central government-directed policies. They also committed to transferring all provincial revenues to Kabul, which they had refused until then. Second, on 14 July 2003, Karzai issued a decree which banned government officials from holding both military and civilian posts. These two acts allowed Karzai to find excuses to go after strongmen in the periphery.

His first target was Jamiat in Herat by galvanising anti-Jamiat forces. Throughout 2003, Karzai had been provoking and helping Amanullah Khan, a powerful Pashtun commander in Shindand district, as well as other local commanders, to challenge Ismail Khan, the Jamiat leader in the West of the country.[128] Using his July decree, in August he removed Khan from his command of the fourth army corps. In March 2004, an assassination attempt was made on Khan's life, which he survived. Fighting erupted when Khan's son and aviation minister, Mirwais Sadiq, was killed as he led an advance team on the headquarters of General Zahir Nayebzada and his brigade, the 17th division, whom he blamed for the assault on his father.[129] In the ensuing battle, over 100 people were killed, one of the worst outbreaks of violence since the fall of the Taliban.[130] In August 2004, in a final battle between Ismail Khan and the pro-Karzai commanders, the government sent more than 1500 members of the U.S.-trained national army and 300 German-trained police to Herat.[131] Khalilzad flew to Herat to meet Ismail Khan and other antagonists. In a press conference the next day, he announced on television that Ismail Khan had agreed to leave the city and join the Karzai government as minister of energy and water. The political backing of Khalilzad and the U.S. military signalled to patronage networks in Kabul and strongmen that the U.S.A. was fully behind Karzai.[132]

On 21 May 2003, in another attempt to weaken Jamiat in Balkh, another Jamiat network stronghold, Karzai issued a decree appointing Dostum, the leader of Junbish-i-Islami network who was the deputy defence minister, as his special advisor on security and military affairs.[133] Formally, he was to advise and present recommendations to the Afghan Transitional Administration on security affairs of the Northern provinces including assisting the central government with downsizing and ultimately dismantling the seventh and eighth army corps stationed in the North. However, this was merely a pretext; the real motive was to empower Junbish-i-Islami and give authority to Dostum against Governor Noor, a Jamiat strongman.[134] Throughout 2003, skirmishes broke out between Junbish and Jamiat networks and commanders. During the last battle between them in May 2003, possibly encouraged by Karzai, he offered his military support as Junbish-i-Islami attacked the city of Mazar-i-Sharif. Once it was clear that Jamiat would hold to Balkh and emerge the winner, Karzai switched his support for

Governor Noor, imposed a ceasefire, and demanded the containment of heavy weapons under DDR.[135] It became evident that Jamiat-i-Islami network leaders in Kabul, who were in control of MoD and most of MoI directorates, undermined Karzai's plan and indirectly channelled arms and support to their fellow Jamiat Governor Noor. Junbish-i-Islami's relations with Karzai were strained from then on. While Governor Noor gradually emerged as the strongman of the Northern region, Dostum had to take a symbolic position in Kabul. The seeds of hostilities between Junbish and Jamiat in the North were planted, and each would use their militias, from 2007 onwards in the name of Taliban and later Daesh, to attack the other. Karzai was also able to send a strong signal to the Jamiatis that he could go after their clients if they crossed the certain line and the established rules.

In Kandahar, Paktia, and Nangarhar, Karzai pursued similar strategies. In Kandahar, he used several skirmishes in the city in 2002 and 2003 between Governor Gul Agha Shirzai (head of Barekzai tribe) and his main rival Mullah Naqibullah (head of Alokozai tribe) as a pretext to remove Shirzai from his stronghold and appoint him as minister of urban development before exiling him to Nangarhar province in 2004 as governor, at the same time weakening the Arsala family network by removing Haji Zahir from the governor position and appointing him as border police chief in Takhar. Shirzai's removal helped Karzai's younger half-brother, Ahmad Wali Karzai, emerge as the undisputed strongman of Kandahar and the South. In Paktia, Karzai allied himself with the tribal councils against Padsha Khan Zadran family network and, with help of the Americans, successfully uprooted him from the region. Zadran family had to escape to Miranshah in Pakistan and was later arrested. It was only with Karzai's blessing that he was allowed to run for a seat in the 2005 parliamentary elections. In Nangarhar, with the help of the powerful Arsala family, Karzai effectively removed Hazrat Ali, a Jamiati, from his position and weakened his influence.

Finally, on 26 July 2004, after much speculation, President Karzai made the audacious move to dismiss his powerful minister of defence, Mohammed Qasim Fahim, and his former vice president. Karzai had waited to the very last of the deadline for registering his presidential candidacy to remove Fahim, to make sure that the Jamiat, in particular, Shuray-i-Nizar, could not regroup in time or promote a candidate for the election. Karzai's victory in the 2004 presidential election sealed his authority throughout the country.

Conclusion

This chapter showed in its counter-terrorism pursuit, the U.S.A. enabled and aided former tanzims and ethno-regional and provincial commanders to emerge as the dominant force in Afghan politics. They were tasked to re-build and re-assemble the Afghan state, which was multiple and fragmented in nature. The U.S.A. needed a functioning Afghan state and its army and police and effective political networks as partners in its counter-terrorism mission. As others have pointed out, the U.S. mission was never about statebuilding even though most often this was masked as the reason for the U.S. military involvement.

The Afghan state was re-assembled to exhibit a combination of weak capacities with excessive functions that perform little and became a *contested playing field* for competing political networks. Once again, as in the 1980s and 1990s, the post-2001 state came to provide the framework for political network competition and endowed the networks with symbolic and material resources. These networks and the regime together represented and, in turn, constituted the state itself and its bureaucracy, army, and police, enacting the state as officials with access to state resources and thus maintaining a degree of legitimation. The actions and strategies of political networks in those early days set the foundations of an inter-network conflict and clientelistic features of Afghanistan's state and society. These rules of the game undermined democratisation and institution-building.

This was a fragmented order. By the 2004 presidential elections, Karzai network that had established his own political network centred on technocrats, former Peshawar NGO elites, and former members of Pashtun jihadi networks, was able to strengthen his authority throughout the country, thanks to American support and a centralised political system that gave him incredible power. This excessive power in the office of the president would become a curse in itself as a source of political networks and ethnic tensions in post-2004 Afghanistan. At the same time, the democratic cycle of elections and the need for votes and the mobilisation of constituencies exposed the limits of the president's authority and his interdependency on other political networks and their power resources. Thus, as Chapter 5 shows, Karzai pursued a policy of appeasement, acting as a balancer/stabiliser of networks, moving towards a balanced order.[136] He saw his role as the "primus inter pares" to protect and safeguard their interests. Distrust and division further splintered major jihadi *tanzims* including Jamiat-i-Islami, Wahdat-i-Islami, and Hizb-i-Islami giving Karzai room to manoeuvre.

Notes

1 Wedeman and Bittermann (2001).
2 Dobbins (2008) in his book notes it was Abdullah Abdullah, the NA commander, who first suggested Karzai's name as the head of the interim government and the Turks, Iranians, and Ehsan ul-Haq—then head of Pakistan's Inter-Services Intelligence—indicating their blessing for Karzai. For more details on shuttle diplomacy before and during the Bonn Conference, see Fields and Ahmed (2011); and Maley (2008) in his chapter, "Looking Back at the Bonn Conference". In Hayes and Sedra (2008) eds.
3 Despite differences over the process and the participants' interests in advancing their proxy groups' positions, there was genuine cooperation and consensus among major international and regional powers, including Iran and Pakistan, that a new and inclusive government with broad-based legitimacy needed to be established quickly, though Iran opposed any future role for the king. The Russians, meanwhile, were pessimistic about achieving a deal in a single conference, envisioning a lengthier process over several months. For more details of these countries' positions, see Dobbins (2008: 70–76).
4 Known as the Shuray-i-Nezar-i-Shamal (Supervisory Council of the North) became the main military arm of the Jamiat Tanzim, set up in 1985 by Ahmad Shah Masoud,

who drew most of his military base from Panjshir, Parwan, and Kapisa provinces in the North of Kabul.

5 Author's interview, Kabul. October 2010.

6 According to participants, there were two rounds of votes for the head of the interim government. Abdul Sattar Sirat, the head of the Rome delegation, won both rounds, but this was not accepted. In the third round, the Americans ensured that Karzai was elected. Author's interview, 17 June 2009; also see Abdul Sattar Sirat's interview with *The Guardian*.

7 In a press conference in Kabul he told the press that he had instructed his head of delegation, Yunous Qanuni, to walk out "if under pressure, [saying] 'I have no authority'". See "Filling the Vacuum: The Bonn Conference", *Frontline*, 28 November 2001.

8 "Interview with Colin Powell", *Frontline*, June 7, 2002.

9 Erlanger (2001).

10 United Nations (2001).

11 Maley (2008).

12 Karzai's uncle Azizullah Karzai, who served as an ambassador to Poland during the Rabbani government, and an Uruzgan elder.

13 Karakul hat is a fur hat made of newborn lambs of the Karakul breed of sheep traditionally worn by Northern ethnic groups. Later Karzai would wear a *chapan* which is a coat with very long sleeves worn traditionally by Turkic communities in the North. The hat and chapan would become the most recognised symbol of Afghanistan identity around the world with British Museum displaying Karzai's chapan.

14 Author's interview with President Karzai, September 2020. Karzai's clothes earned him plaudits from fashion experts around the world. Tom Ford even praised him as "the most chic man on the planet today."

15 In his interview with the author on August 2020 in Kabul, Karzai confirmed that such an encounter had taken place, but he was not sure if this was Fahim or Qanuni.

16 See James Dobbins (2008). Dr. Abdullah Abdullah of the NA had warned that persuading Rabbani to transfer power was going to be a difficult task.

17 Cited in Edwards (2011:148).

18 Rumsfeld (2011:407–408).

19 The *Shuray-i-Nizar* (Supervisory Council) was the military wing of the Jamiat *tanzim* that was set up by Commander Masoud within Jamiat in 1985. Its core members were predominantly from the Panjshir province.

20 On 20 December 2001, the United Nations Security Council Resolution (UNSCR) 1386 authorised the establishment of an International Security Assistance Force (ISAF) for Afghanistan to provide security for Kabul city and its surrounding districts, responding to the request of Afghan authorities on 14 December 2001.

21 According to the Office of Administrative Affairs, the study aimed to come up with a more inclusive bureaucracy to include more minorities in the government. The margin of error is estimated at 10%.

22 This shows a significant over-representation of Tajiks and a serious under-representation of Hazara and Uzbeks when compared to the estimated overall ethnic composition of Afghanistan. There are 8 grades in the Afghan bureaucracy (1–8), with 1 being general-director and director-level bureaucrats. Above this is deputy ministers and ministers—almost all were political appointees.

23 See Giustozzi (2008); Bhatia and Sedra (2008).

24 Suroush (2017).

25 Internal National Directorate of Security report, May 2014.

26 Ibid.

27 Afghan Voice Agency. 1392. "Ghazb Yak Million va 279 Hazar Jirib Zamin Tawasot-e 15 Hazar Nafar". 13 Jawza 1392.

28 Leaked Ministry of Interior Report. 2019. "Khabare Taza: List-e Ghazibin Tawasot Wezarat Dakhela Efsha Shod". 14 January 2019.
29 Internal IDLG Commissioned Report. 2017. "Political Economy of Kabul Province". May 2017.
30 Author's conversation with several people close to Karzai and Ghani in October 2020 in Kabul.
31 Minister Andarabi was not Abdullah and Jamiat's first choice in 2018 but was imposed on them at the last minute.
32 The Disarmament, Demobilization, and Reintegration programme (DDR, 2003–2005) process ensured that jihadis, and in particular ethnic-Tajiks and Panjshiris, were overwhelmingly present in the structure and composition of the MoI leadership and police force and thereby expanded their patronage and nepotism within the Afghan police. Karzai and his ethnic-Pashtuns relied on former communists to balance the jihadis.
33 Ishaqzadeh and Giustozzi (2015).
34 See Fishstein and Wilder (2012).
35 Malikyar and Rubin (2002).
36 At the time, governors' appointments were the mandate of the Ministry of Interior, controlled by Yunus Qanuni, with Karzai probably having no say in the process.
37 Author's interview with Junbish Deputy Chairman in Kabul, Fayzullah Zaki, 14 September 2009. Giustozzi (2004) makes the same claim.
38 According to Giustozzi (2009: 150), the Defence Minister, Gen. Fahim, dispatched troops and military vehicles from Kabul to Mazar, officially for the celebration of annual mujahedeen day but was seen by some as a warning sign to Dostum that Kabul would support Governor Noor at all costs.
39 Author's interview, April 2012. See also Mukhopadhyay (2009), Hakimi (2012), and Giustozzi (2009).
40 Author interviews and observations at Hairatan during 2–3 March and 15–19 April 2012. As one Transparency International officer described it: "To run your business you must have the blessing of the governor and pay his protection money. The risk is high. He has removed his key opponents out of the energy market. His rivals cannot compete because the governor uses the Hairatan storage facilities and his own security companies to reduce his costs and win contracts."
41 For instance, Abbas Ibrahimzada was a business partner in the petrol trade with the governor as well as having several Shahrak [property development projects] in Elmarab area. Ahmad Ramazan, who accused Governor Noor of assassinating his brother in 2005, became his business partner, especially in the property sector.
42 Interview with civil society organisations, Interviews from 15 to 19 April 2012.
43 U.S. Cables, 22 March 2006 ("PRT/Mazar-e Sharif: Balkh Governance Politicians Demand Atta's Ouster", March 22, 2006, Wikileaks U.S. Cables (https://wikileaks.org/plusd/cables/06KABUL1250_a.html).
44 Ibid
45 See also Brian Glyn Williams' article which provides a detailed account of the Mazar-i-Sharif campaign in which Dostum played an instrumental role. He also stayed with the general for a few months. Williams (2010).
46 The governor of Faryab Jowzjan was Sayed M. Hassan Hashimee (2002–2004); Faryab (Mohammad Saleh Zari from 2001–2003); Sar-i-Pul (Taj Mohammed Kohi, an ethnic Aimaq and a former Hizb-i-Islami commander proposed by Dostum) and Samangan someone loyal to Ahmad Khan. Author's interview with two senior Junbish officials. 8 April 2020. IDLG internal document on governors, accessed in July 2017.
47 This included abandoning former PDPA generals and leaders who constituted the backbone of the Junbish military and political leadership from 1992 to 1998.

48 Ibid.
49 Malikyar and Rubin (2002).
50 "The Death Convoy of Afghanistan". *Newsweek* (25 August 2002).
51 For more on Dostum's depiction in the Western Media, see Williams, B.G. 2013. The Last Warlord: The Life and Legend of Dostum, the Afghan Warrior who Led US Special Forces to Topple the Taliban Regime. A human rights report published by Physicians for Human Rights had documented in detail these brutalities. See Physicians for Human Rights, "Preliminary Assessment of Alleged Mass Gravesites in the Area of Mazar-i-Sharif, Afghanistan," 2002. Also, this image of Dostum was largely promoted by both Jamiat network officials and ethnic-Pashtun technocrats in Kabul. Dostum's actions also did not help him either as videos emerged of his soldiers heartlessly killing captured Taliban prisoners.
52 Giustozzi (2009: 105–108).
53 See Gompelman (2001).
54 Astill (2004). President's spokesman at the time, Jawid Ludin, condemned this, saying, "Abdul Rashid Dostum is an advisor to the President. However, that does not give him the right to deploy forces or get involved in any military operational issues." Ibid.
55 The *Arsala* family is a prominent Ahmadzai clan from the Eastern Ghilzai Pashtuns. Historically they have been Khans (similar to lords) of the Ahmadzai tribe. The great great-father of the *Arsala* family was known as the Redbeard who had earned himself the Governorship of Jalalabad for his slaughter of British troops in the First Anglo-Afghan War in 1842.
56 He played an instrumental role in mobilising Pashtun support for Karzai in the emergency Loya Jirga and was made minister of public works and vice president in the transitional government.
57 Author's ethnographic fieldwork in Jalalabad city in July 2012.
58 See The Liaison Office report: *Justice and Security: Practices, Perceptions, and Problems in Kabul and Nangarhar*, May 2004.
59 Stockman (2009).
60 See Ruttig (2009) who notes that later six hundreds of them were hired as auxiliary troops within the Afghan security forces.
61 See Profile of Pacha Khan Zadran, GlobalSecurity.org, available at http://www .globalsecurity.org/military/world/ Afghanistan/zadran.htm. In terms of tribal structure, he remained pro-government, supporting the Rabbani government and fought the Taliban, whereas his other famous tribal rival, Jalaluddin Haqqani, the former head of Haqqani network, aligned himself with al-Qaida and other foreign terrorist groups with a base across the border in Miranshah.
62 Author's interview with several former government officials in Kabul, 12–17 April 2020.
63 Author's interview with several former government officials in Kabul (12–17 April 2020) revealed that in 1995, the Khost tribal council had reached an agreement with the Taliban to hand over the city to them on the condition that the Taliban would not disarm fighters and that the people would not be forcibly conscripted for the Taliban cause. The reason for the prominent role of tribal councils in the Southeast dates back to the 1929 uprising. The tribes rose up and helped Nader Shah, the Durrani leader who was exiled in Paris, to overthrow the ethnic-Tajik Habibullah Khan in Kabul. As a result, they received privileges that others did not, including honorary military titles, property, monitory gifts, and political advisory jobs in Kabul. They were exempt from military service and could practice their traditional customs without state interference. During Taliban rule, they also enjoyed these privileges.

64 Radio Free Europe/Radio Liberty. 2002. "Afghanistan: Karzai to Announce Decision on Paktia after Pakistan Trip". February 8, 2002. The main tribal council members represented seven different tribes: Ahmadzai, Tutakhel, Mangal, Zurmati, Gardizi, and Jaji. Haji Saifullah was later appointed governor of Wardak province.

65 Ibid.

66 In an operation, U.S. Special Forces captured a stockpile of weapons belonging to Zadran. In a separate incident, the Americans killed 65 tribal elders from the Ahmadzai tribe who were on their way to see Karzai in Kabul, mistaking them for al-Qaida members. The wrong information was provided by Zadran and many accused him of deliberately using U.S. airpower to get rid of his enemies. "*Killing you is a very easy thing for us*" (PDF). *Human Rights Watch*. July 2003, 40. Retrieved 2007.

67 See Ruttig (2009).

68 *Pakistan Hands Over Afghan Rebel*, BBC (February 5, 2004).

69 Khost Protection Force was set up by the Americans initially to provide security to American bases in Khost and Paktia. However, it expanded over the years to carry out two additional tasks: (1) responsible for border protection, i.e., controlling the movement of Taliban fighters across the border and (2) special operations against Taliban targets. Consequently, its numbers increased dramatically. Over the years, the force was used in as far-off provinces as Takhar and Faryab.

70 *Warlord, Inc.: Extortion and Corruption along the U.S. Supply Chain in Afghanistan* (2010). Report was prepared by the Majority Staff of the Subcommittee on National Security and Foreign Affairs of the Committee on Oversight and Government Reform.

71 Ibid. and Giustozzi (2009).

72 Giustozzi (2009). In April 1992, provincial PDPA military officials decided to hand over power to Ismail Khan, with whom they enjoyed ethnic affiliation and had established contacts, rather than Hizb-i-Islami. This helped him consolidate his position against other rival *tanzims*.

73 On 20 May 2003, President Karzai called a meeting of 12 provincial governors who were refusing to send customs revenues to the central government of Kabul, including Ismail Khan. They signed an agreement after the meeting to pledge to deliver millions of dollars owed to the central government. Radio Free Afghanistan RFE/RL, May 20, 2003 (https://www.rferl.org/a/1340620.html). See also Giustozzi (2009); Malejacq (2020).

74 See Giustozzi (2008, 2009) for Ismail Khan's troubled relations with other military commanders.

75 See Foschini (2011)

76 See Chayes (2006: 28–84).

77 See Giustozzi and Noor Ullah (2007).

78 Shirzai was the governor of the province after the collapse of the Najibullah regime in 1992 until the capture of the city by the Taliban in September 1994. He had done a terrible job of governing the city by inflicting much of the chaos that eventually contributed to the emergence of the Taliban in 1994.

79 See Forsberg (2009).

80 See Giustozzi and Noor Ullah (2007).

81 See Gopal (2014); Smith (2013); and Chayes (2006).

82 See Aikins (2010).

83 Rashid (2000).

84 According to Chayes (2006) Kandahar airfield initially housed 8000 soldiers, but it grew to support 32,000 soldiers by 2010. See also Motlagh (2010).

85 See Forsberg (2010).

86 See ICG Asia report no. 65, pp. 19–22; United Nations disarmament, demobilization and reintegration resource centre, "country programme: Afghanistan," under "DDR

strategy and approach," http://unddr.org/countryprogrammes.php?c=121. Khan Mohammad Mujahed became the provincial police chief and was later killed.

87 Ibid.

88 Ibid.

89 Jan Mohammad Khan was the governor from 1992 to 1994 until the Taliban took over. He was one of the first people who accompanied Karzai in his battle to take over Uruzgan and remained a senior advisor to Karzai until he was assassinated on 17 July 2002. After his downfall from his position as governor of Uruzgan in 2006 under Dutch pressure, because he was suspected of running, or associated with, the drug trade and human rights abuse; his nephew, Matiullah Khan, carried out the legacy in the province. Both U.S. and Australian Special Forces contracted Matiullah Khan's private army, called Kandak Amniante Uruzgan, with 2000 armed men, to provide security services for their bases. The Afghan government also paid 600 of his men to provide security for the main highway from Uruzgan to Kandahar. Matiullah's compound sits about 100 yards from the American Special Forces compound in Tirin Kot. See also Dodd and Kelly (2009).

90 Roy (1990); Rubin (2002), 243–46; Matthieu Aikins provides an interesting story which highlights the prominence of tribes over political affiliations. In the early years after Bonn, the Taliban kidnapped a civil servant from the Barakzai tribe and took him to neighbouring Panjwai district where the Noorzai tribe was the dominant group. In response, a large group of armed men from the Barakzai tribe took a few dozen men from the Governor Noorzai tribe as hostage from the villages of Nakhonay. The Governor Noorzai elders then went to the local Taliban commander and pleaded with him to release the men, which he did.

91 See *Warlord, Inc.*, 94.

92 Ibid. Kelly (2009); see also "The Netherlands Pays Afghan Warlord Millions for Protection". *Radio Netherlands Worldwide* (January 7, 2010).

93 Filkins (2010).

94 Author's interview with senior Wahdat commanders involved in the Bamiyan offensive. Kabul city. 11–12 April 2020.

95 According to the author's interviews with commanders involved in the fight, the Americans provided only light weapons—around 1600 AK47s and some cash, which went directly into Khalili's pocket. They accused Khalili of failing to distribute the cash among the commanders. Also, see Coll (2004); Human Rights Watch, "The Forgotten War", 125–30.

96 Taliban atrocities against ethnic Hazaras are well documented by Human Rights organisations. In August 1998, when the Taliban took control of Mazar-i-Sharif, they massacred at least 2000 people, mainly Hazara civilians. In another incident, in January 2001 in Yakawlong district, the Taliban burned houses and killed at least 178 who have been provisionally identified, of whom 175 were civilians and 3 were *hors de combat*. See Afghanistan Justice Project.

97 These were Wahdat, Harakat, Pasdaran (led by Mohammad Akbari and Mustafa Kazemi), and Jamiat.

98 Khorrami became the district governor of Kahmard district. But the real power was with Commander Nabi Tofan, an ethnic Tajik, who had fought alongside Wahdat to defeat the Taliban. Hadi Saighani, a Jamiat influential elder became the district governor of Saighan district. The other four district governors of Wahdat were: Naser Sharifi (Yakawlang district), Sarwar Jawadi (Waras district), M. Hussain Ibrahimi (Panjab district), and Abbad Rasa (Shibar district). Except for Naser Sharifi, the other three were involved in the final battle to defeat the Taliban.

99 Author's interview. Individuals like Haji Feda and Jawad Zuhak have been mentioned by several officials with direct links to Karim Khalili.

100 Pajhwok News. 2011. "Khalili Denies Playing a Role in Land Grab by ONYX". April 21, 2011. https://www.pajhwok.com/en/2011/04/21/khalili-denies-playing-any-role-land-grab-onyx.

101 One famous commander complained about the pressure exerted by Khalili that they had to buy 60 AK47, in which the community provided only 40 and they bought the rest. Author's interview, 12 April 2020.

102 Despite its decline, the party's staunch supporters held key leadership positions to the very end, including Deputy Governor Fahimi, the head of the Provincial Council Pooya and deputy chief of police. Their base of power lay in Bamyan and Yakawlang districts.

103 Bhatia and Sedra (2008: 229) found that in the immediate post-2001 period, a commander's strength was expressed less in terms of offensive capability against an opposing unit, rather than his ability to acquire supporting contracts, maintain armed units, and integrate them into official and quasi-official security structures.

104 See *Warlord, Inc.*

105 Muhammad Yusof Etebar, a Jamiat affiliate, received the powerful Office of Administrative Affairs (OAA). The OAA was the administrative office of the president, known among civil servants as the "roundabout of the state administration" with everything passing through this office for the president's approval. The creation of the OAA was a legacy of the centralised communist regime that wanted to keep tight control over state administration.

106 See Ignatieff (2002).

107 Beaumont (2002).

108 Synovitz (2002).

109 See Fange (2002) for a detailed report on the emergency Loya Jirga (ELJ) composition and process.

110 U.S. embassy cable. His officials told the Americans and the Italians that he would prefer a French system in which he could be the head of the state or the president of the country with a prime ministerial position.

111 Author's interview with a former senior Afghan advisor for UNAMA, 26 April 2020.

112 His former chief of staff and the minister of civil aviation in the interim government, Zalmai Rassoul, and Zadran, among many, had hoped he would stand. Amanullah Zadran, the minister of frontier and tribal affairs, went public saying that the former king would be chosen as the next head of state: see Ruttig (2012).

113 Incidentally, when the king arrived, there was reportedly a deliberate power cut and live media coverage broke down. There was no announcement of his return on radio and TV. The power was also switched off at the Loya Jirga at the start of his speech. Many blamed the Northern Alliance because the power ministry was in the hands of NA supporters. And Hafiz Mansoor was the minister of information and culture responsible for radio and TV broadcast in Afghanistan (see Ruttig 2012).

114 Interviews with a number of Afghans involved in the Jirga revealed that Khalilzad had even written the former king's statement himself; see also Khalilzad (2010); and Tomsen (2011).

115 Ruttig (2012)

116 Ibid. Also, interviews revealed that the organisers had not allocated a VVIP sitting arrangement for prominent jihadi leaders. When Karzai arrived and saw this, he asked to set up additional front rows and asked people like Sayyaf to come to the front. On one occasion, one of the female participants, Malalai Joya, stood up in protest and shouted that they are criminals.

117 See UN Security Council Report. 2002. "Loya Jirga a Truly Representative Sample of Afghan Society". SC/7429 (21 June 2002). There were reports of intimidation by the Jamiat-controlled National Directorate of Security during the Jirga against some outspoken participants. Interviews with participants revealed that at the night of the

Jirga, there was a genuine fear in Kabul that retaliation might follow. For instance, there was a report of intimidation against Dr. Sima Samar, the newly appointed chairperson of Afghanistan Independent Human Rights Commission, who had taken an anti-jihadi stand in the Jirga. Her house in Wazir Akbar Khan came under attack. She was taken out of her house in a UN vehicle and sheltered at the UN compound that night. Author's interview, 26 March 2020.

118 In a visit to Italy on 11–12 March 2002, the U.S. Deputy Director of State, Steve McGann, and Italian MoFA official exchanged views on the future role of the former king and the upcoming emergency Loya Jirga. According to the cable, the Italians advised the U.S.A. to consider making funds available to counter the former president, noting: "the reality in Afghanistan was that those who continued to receive outside support, such as former President Rabbani, would also be able to continue to seek and obtain inside support: Simply put, to buy Loya Jirga votes" (see 3 April 2020 cable, titled "Afghanistan: Zahir Shah's future plans, closing out ESF Grant to Zahir Shah Foundation").

119 See Johnson (2006).

120 In this, the president would have extensive executive powers that included appointing the prime minister, the judges of both the supreme and constitutional courts, and one-third of the members of the Upper House. The prime minister was to have responsibility for enforcing laws, protecting the national interests and sovereignty of Afghanistan, managing financial affairs, and reporting to the National Assembly at the end of every fiscal year. See ICG Afghanistan: the Constitutional Loya Jirga, 12 December 2003.

121 Ruttig (2012).

122 See International Crisis Group report, "Afghanistan: the Constitutional Loya Jirga", 12 December 2003.

123 Ibid.

124 Ibid.

125 See International Crisis Group. 2013. "Afghanistan's Flawed Constitutional Process". 12 June 2013.

126 See Jon Lee Anderson's profile article on Hamid Karzai; "The Man in the Palace", 30 May 2005, and Khalilzad (2010).

127 Tarzi, A. 2003. "A Victory for Karzai or a Masked Plea for Help?". *Radio Freedom*, 23 May 2003,

128 Interviews with a number of Herat's influential leaders reveal that there was an ethnic tension here, especially in Shindand as most local government officials appointed by Ismail Khan were ethnic Tajiks and Jamiat, ruling over a 90% Pashtun population of the district. Author's interview with two influential local tribal leaders, 31 April 2020.

129 When Nayebzada carried out the attack, his claim was that he was taking orders from MoD. He later revealed that had not consulted the ministry regarding the outbreak of violence earlier in the day. See Free Radio Europe/Radio Liberty, "Afghan Report", March 25, 2004. Volume 3, Number 12. See also Waldman (2004).

130 Hersh (2004).

131 See Dietl (2004).

132 All of this happened when Karzai was in Europe to receive an award. Khalilzad flew to Herat to meet Ismail Khan and other antagonists. In a press conference the next day, he announced on television that Ismail Khan had agreed to leave the city and join the Karzai government as minister of energy and water. See Khalilzad (2016).

133 Radio Free Afghanistan RFE/RL, 20 May 2003, https://www.rferl.org/a/1340620 .html.

134 Giustozzi (2004).

135 Giustozzi (2004).

136 This study draws on my fieldwork in 2009 in Afghanistan, carrying out participant observation in three districts of Kabul (Dashte Barchi, district 13; Chaharrahi Sarsabzi and Shamali, district 11; and Karet Naw, district 8). In addition, 24 in-depth interviews with key political informants such as ethnic-regional clients, leaders of political parties, and campaign directors were conducted.

5 Consolidating a political "Empire of Mud" (2004–2014)[1]

Introduction

"We have now left a hard and dark past behind us, and today we are opening a new chapter in our history, in a spirit of friendship with the international community," said the newly elected President Hamid Karzai in his 15-minute inauguration speech.[2] Almost precisely three years had passed since Karzai's first address to Afghanistan's power brokers through a crackly satellite phone in Bonn. On 7 December 2004, at his swearing-in ceremony as Afghanistan's first democratically elected president, the audience was arguably even heftier, attended by over 150 foreign dignitaries, including some political heavyweights from the U.S.A.: Vice President Dick Cheney, Defense Secretary Donald Rumsfeld, and President George W. Bush's trusted advisor, Karen Hughes. The significant American presence was a clear measure of the event's importance to the Bush administration. During his own 2004 election campaign, Bush had touted bringing democracy to Afghanistan as a key foreign policy success. In Kabul, Karzai was seen as the American candidate who had to secure a convincing victory; his rivals had accused the U.S. Ambassador, Zalmay Khalilzad, of elbowing them out of the race, offering them political rewards during candidate registration.[3] In the second row of the audience, the all-powerful Jamiat and Shuray-i-Nazar leader and former defence minister, Qasim Fahim, sat beside Ahmad Wali Masoud another Shuray-i-Nazar leader, both with smug looks on their faces, unaware of the cameras filming them. The event was later watched by millions of Afghans across the country on the recently established Tolo TV network. In a theatrical speech, Karzai promised a better future for Afghans, and to please his foreign audience, he vowed to crack down on opium cultivation and the drug trade, calling it a great threat to Afghanistan's future. A survey, released a month earlier by the United Nations Office on Drugs and Crime, had warned of Afghanistan becoming a "narco-state."[4]

Less than a decade later, as he neared the end of his second term in office, the shift would be stark: Karzai would not only be abandoned by the U.S.A., but his political empire of mud would be on the verge of collapse, facing an increasingly buoyant and expanding insurgency, incompetent and corrupt administration, and an increasingly divided polity along political and ethnic lines. His domestic

DOI: 10.4324/9781315161617-5

opponents and international donors, including the U.S.A., were relieved to see him go; many had condemned him for being an unreliable partner. As early as July 2006, in leaked U.S. diplomatic cables, Karzai was depicted as "weak," "vacillating," "inept," "out of touch" with ordinary Afghans, and often "paranoid and conspiratorial."[5] In his final years, the president interpreted the Afghan war and the U.S engagement in it as part of a "conspiracy," against him personally, if not the country.[6] He countered corruption charges against his administration by blaming the U.S.A. for being the driving cause of corruption and using the Afghan state as a convenient scapegoat to suit its agenda of expansionism and regional domination. The U.S.A. and its allies, meanwhile, described President Karzai's 12 years rule as a "self-organised kleptocracy," a charge that was later validated by documents leaked to the Washington Post in 2018. In 2014, the newly elected technocratic president, Ashraf Ghani, and his associates chastised Karzai for governing like a tribal *khan* (chief), lacking statesmanship and a vision, and a fair assessment in many respects. His excessive reliance on old political networks, informal practices of patronage and *Waseta*, and alliance-building and deal-making with political networks was castigated for undermining formal institution-building and democratisation. His most significant legacy would be "political unity" and a "balanced order," at least amongst political networks and their elites, with Karzai himself as patron-in-charge.

Ironically, Karzai's adeptness at managing the lion's den he was thrust into after Bonn came as a surprise to many Afghan observers. As I note in the previous chapter, Karzai was an acceptable interim leader to Afghanistan's power brokers because he was seen as weak and ineffectual. Instead, he proved much more of a challenge than anyone had anticipated. As this chapter will show, he proved skilful in directing political networks towards a new political order, which he was the patron of, by his canny knack for manipulating the rules of the game established at the 2001 Bonn Conference. Between 2004 and 2014, Karzai oversaw key events that transformed and consolidated Afghanistan into a "networked state" that ensured the survival of the networks that had come to dominate the political landscape.

How he accomplished this, brokering political stability and order within the state and beyond, offers a fascinating glimpse into how networks were operated and were managed. As this chapter highlights, the multifaceted dynamics of the post-2004 Afghan state was not a narrow top-down system of patronage dependency in which Karzai, as patron-in-charge, would simply dictate terms; subnational networks often drove, pulled, and forced Karzai and other state-level networked leaders to adopt policies and strategies that enhanced their interests. However, Karzai remained the political architect and master tactician of the game and the playing field.

The first section of this chapter discusses the outcome of the 2004 elections and its impact on the power dynamics of political networks. It then examines several rounds of cabinet appointments and shuffles to show how Karzai skilfully maintained a power equilibrium by balancing out competing political networks within the state. The subsequent sections highlight the various alliance-building efforts in the parliament and provincial councils by those outside the state to advance their bargain with Karzai pre- and post-2009 and 2014 elections. Section 5.6 shows how Karzai exploited international military and financial resources including that of the formal state institutions to strengthen his grip on the state. The final sections unpack alliance-building and power dynamics of political networks before the 2014 presidential elections, leading up to the formation of the National Unity Government (NUG) after the disputed election, another political settlement attempt amongst key networks, negotiated by the Americans.

5.1 The 2004 presidential elections: projecting power

The first presidential election in post-2001 Afghanistan took place on 9 October 2004. The election was widely considered a success despite doubts about its feasibility.[7] It was also considered a significant accomplishment for its high turnout (at 70%, of which 40% were women) and credibility. A total of 23 registered candidates were on the final ballot announced by the Joint Electoral Management Body—19 independent candidates, including Hamid Karzai, and three serious contenders representing specific political networks or alliances.[8] The May 2004 election law had proposed a simple majority to win an election—if no candidate won an outright majority in the first round, the election would go to a run-off.

Karzai emerged as the winner in the first round of voting? With 55% of the vote, followed by Qanuni (representing most of the Jamiat network), Mohaqqiq (standing for Wahdat-i-Mardom network), and Dostum (representing Junbish network), who received 16.3%, 11.7%, and 10%, respectively.[9] Karzai secured the backing of some influential political networks and centres of power: his First Vice President, Ahmad Zia Masoud and, by extension, the former president Rabbani within the Jamiat network, Wahdat-i-Islami network led by Karim Khalili as his second deputy, newly rebranded Dawat-i-Islami (formerly known as Ittihad-i-Islami) led by Abdul Rasul Sayyaf, and other minor networks. America's tacit backing for Karzai certainly tilted the balance in his favour. Several other candidates had spoken out against Ambassador Khalilzad for meddling in the election, accusing him of arm-twisting one candidate into dropping his campaign, and working out a deal with Karzai.[10] Over the years, this precedent of horse-trading would be further formalised and emboldened.

Karzai's key political network opponents ran solely on ethnic grounds, their logic being that they needed to successfully determine and demonstrate the size and strength of their constituencies for future bargaining over the cabinet, provincial and district governors, and embassy positions, among many others.[11] Qanuni as the broader Jamiat network candidate ran to champion the ethnic Tajik votes with an appeal to his former Jamiat colleagues, which had splintered into several smaller patronage networks around key personalities (e.g., Fahim, Qanuni, Ahmad Zia Masoud, and Rabbani). Qanuni had formed his political network in 2003, called the New Afghanistan (Afghanistan-i-Nawin), and Masoud and Fahim, who had initially established an alliance under the Nehzat-i-Milli-i-Afghanistan (Afghanistan National Movement) fell apart when Masoud dropped out to become Karzai's running-mate. Politically, the election provided an excellent contingency for political networks and their ambitious elites to demonstrate their power base and to reinvent themselves as irrepressible political network "vote bank" brokers.[12] Both Junbish-i-Islami leader, Abdul Rashid Dostum, and Wahdat-i-Mardom leader, Mohammad Mohaqqiq, the ethnic Hazara strongman, saw elections as an opening to reassert themselves in national politics given that both had been weakened in the north. Junbish and Wahdat-i-Mardom networks appealed to their ethnic and regional constituencies by claiming to have defended their interests, thereby characterising the general vote as an ethnic/tribal one (more on this in Chapter 7). Thus, according to Fayzullah Zaki, the Deputy Chairman of Junbish:

> This was the first time in the history of this country that an opportunity had risen which gave ethnic groups like Uzbeks the chance to contest in the political process. Throughout history, the Turkic groups were deliberately estimated at only 2 or 3 per cent. Despite knowing we would not win, Abdul Rashid Dostum contested in the election to prove the size of our ethnic group. Dostum won ten per cent of the vote. Now, nobody can deny that Uzbeks are any less than ten per cent in the country.[13]

The tactic proved wildly successful. For instance, in Faryab, where Junbish was battling with Jamiat, Dostum won 73% of the vote, followed by Qanuni at 13% and Karzai at 10%. And in the northeast in Takhar province where some of the most powerful former Jamiat Uzbek commanders, like Abdul Mottaleb Beg and others, had sided with Karzai, Junbish won 39.5% of the vote.[14] The relative success of these political networks led by ambitious leaders sent a clear message to Karzai that networks such as Jamiat, Junbish, and Wahdat-i-Mardom had to be taken seriously in a democratic system, or at least in the façade of one, that operates on election cycles—a valuable bargaining resource which he would need later. The power of these networks, in general, would be further reinforced a year later during parliamentary and provincial council (PC) elections where they would win significant seats, forcing Karzai to adopt a more accommodating and reconciliatory policy towards them.

The 2004 presidential election and subsequent parliamentary election in 2005 suggest that political networks are an extension of the democratic rules established at the 2001 Bonn Conference where political network leaders as power brokers were rewarded for participating in the democratic process. From then on, as illustrated below, they felt they were entitled to their places for supporting these processes and for maintaining order, if not more, within the networked state.

5.2 Power restructuring and alliance-building against Karzai

After the elections, Karzai warded his technocratic clients with key cabinet positions: Ashraf Ghani (Finance), Rahim Wardak (Defence), Anwar ul-Haq Ahadi (Finance, and a member of the Afghan Millat party), Ali Ahmad Jalali

(Interior), Hedayat Arsala (Reconstruction), Amin Farhang (Economy), and Hanif Atmar (Rehabilitation and Rural Development). Karzai's other political network allies within his election alliance also received important positions in subnational administrations. These included the two-moderate family-based networks: Nazhat-i-Hambastagi (the National Solidarity Movement) led by Pir Gailani and Jabha-i-Nijat-Milli Afghanistan (Afghanistan National Liberation Front) led by the former president Mojadaddi, and among others Dawat-i-Islami led by Abdul Rasul Sayyaf and Hambastag-i-Milli Jawanan-i-Afghanistan (National Youth Union of Afghanistan) led by Jamil Karzai, along with his two vice presidents (splintered Jamiat networks led by Ahmad Zia Masoud and President Rabbani and Wahdat-Islami led by Karim Khalili).[15] For instance, in mid-2005, Karzai awarded Dawat-i-Islami with three provincial governorships: Zabul, Kandahar, and Ghazni (Mullah Khel Mohammad, a former Taliban minister, Asadullah Khalid, and Sher Alem, respectively).

Feeling left out, the three political networks and other minor patronage networks and nodes—some of whom were with Karzai during the elections but were disgruntled with his failure to offer them a government position in the new administration—retaliated by setting up an opposition alliance against Karzai and his team, with Qanuni emerging as their leader.[16] This ballooned into an 11-political network alliance called Jabha-i-Tafahom-e-Melli-i-Afghanistan (the National Understanding Front of Afghanistan), which was, smartly, welcomed by President Karzai in an official statement.[17] The Front's ultimate aspiration was to win a decisive majority in the upcoming 2005 parliamentary election and amend the constitution from a presidential political system to a parliamentary one.[18] The first blow to the alliance came from some of the leftist leaders, Pedram and Neda'i, who alleged that Qanuni might be following a separate internal agenda.[19] Qanuni was guilelessly caught having secret meetings with Karzai just two weeks after the formation of the coalition which raised eyebrows—in this case, with the Palace possibly double-crossing Qanuni by leaking the information to the press.[20] As the parliamentary election date approached, more internal differences emerged within the alliance around the group's objectives, priorities, and strategies. There were also tensions between the three leading networks—Jamiat, Wahdat-i-Mardom, and Junbish—who dominated the coalition and the junior partners who felt omitted from key decision-making processes. Within the logic of *alliance formation*, outlined in Chapter 2, once weaker and minor networks realised that their advances were limited by a coalition under Qanuni, and Karzai controlled most of the state power resources and patronage, they unsurprisingly defected to the stronger side. And the leading networks also went through a *fractionalisation* process as the result of mistrust and more importantly fear that Qanuni might double-cross them at the last minute (Figure 5.1).

Two other alliances emerged in 2005 but had little success in influencing the process and challenging Karzai's authority. None of their leaders became significant in post-election politics, with the exception of Rangin Dadfar Spanta, who joined Karzai's cabinet in 2006 as Minister of Foreign Affairs. The first group was the National Democratic Front, composed of 13 smaller and less forceful liberal

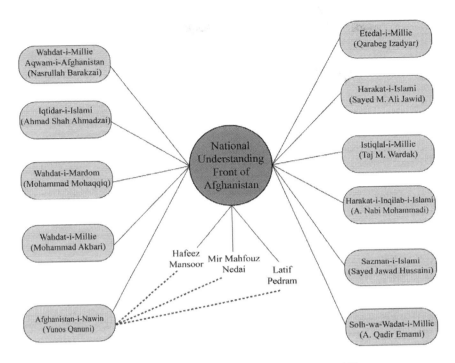

Figure 5.1 The National Understanding Front of the Afghanistan Alliance.

and democratic parties that received some funding and technical support from the Washington-based National Democratic Institute (NDI).[21] The second was an alliance of former leftists and Maoist networks and nodes, called the Payman-i-Kabul (Kabul Accord), which included SAZA (Sazman-i-Inqilab-i-Zahmatkashan-i-Afghanistan; Revolutionary Organisation of the Toilers of Afghanistan), Wolesi Millat (People's Nation), a faction of Afghan Millat, and Shuray-i-Democracy (Council of Democracy), led by Spanta.

5.3 Restructuring political order: capturing the Lower House and provincial councils

On 18 September 2005, more than 6 million people went to the polls to elect representatives to the Lower House (Wolesi Jirga) and provincial councils, ending the transitional political process outlined at Bonn.[22] A total of 2,835 candidates (344 women) competed for the 249 seats in the Lower House and 3,201 candidates (285 women) for the 420 contested seats in the 34 provincial councils. In the absence of a national census, the Joint Election Monitoring Body (JEMB) allocated seats based on wildly inaccurate Central Statistics Office estimations of provincial populations. Kabul received 33 seats, the largest, while the allotment for Panjshir, Nuristan, and Nimruz was only two seats each.[23]

Some of the powerful state-level political network leaders and their subnational clients, regional strongmen, and family and tribal network patrons including Mohaqiq, Qanuni, and Sayyaf in Kabul, Padsha Khan Zadran in Paktia, and Haji Zahir in Nangarhar provinces ran for seats in parliament, which provided them with the safe state position they had lost by not being included in the cabinet or provincial governorships. The Lower House effectively provided a new platform, a more purposeful and safer one, to defy President Karzai and his policies. At the provincial level, for instance, in Nangarhar Province, the former *tanzim* commanders Haji Ghaffar, Haji Zahir, and Hazrat Ali became members of the national assembly while Haji Zaman along with other family members won seats on the provincial council. The only major non-networked outsider was Mirwais Yasini, an ally of Karzai, who won a seat in the national assembly and became the Deputy Speaker of the House.

A National Democratic Institute report provided an estimate of the different network members elected to the House.[24] The biggest winners were the former jihadi *tanzim* networks, including former president Rabbani's Jamiat-i-Islami, Qanuni's Afghanistan-i-Nawin, Wahdat-i-Mardom led by Mohaqqiq, Junbish-i-Islami, Dawat-i-Islami led by Abdul Rasul Sayyaf (see Table 5.1). According to an Afghanistan Evaluation and Research Unit analysis of the composition of the House, approximately 133 of the 249 members fought in the anti-Soviet jihad and 113 were affiliated or belonged to Islamist parties.[25] They were able to utilise the strength of their networks and leverage identity politics to mobilise their constituencies. The election of 23 candidates with leftist or communist backgrounds,

Table 5.1 Political networks in the Lower House

Political groupings	Leader	Estimated no of seats
Jamiat-i-Islami	B. Rabbani	25–30
Junbish-i-Islami	R. Dostum	23–25
Wahdat-i-Mardom	M. Mohaqqiq	20–25
Wahdat-i-Islami	K. Khalili	5–6
Afghanistan-i-Navin	Y. Qanuni	22–26
Dawat-i-Islami	R. Sayyaf	10–12
Muttahed-i-Milli	Ulumi and other leftists (Ulomi, Ranjbar, Tanai, Aryan)	10–12
Afghan Millat	Anwar ul-Haq Ahadi	7–8
Nazhat-i-Hambastagi	Gailani Family	6–7
Jabha-i-Nijat-Milli	Mojadaddi family	3–4
Other Shia groups (Iqtedar-i-Millie, Harakat, Hizb Wahdat)	M. Kazemi, M. Akbari, S. Jawed	5–6
Paywand-i-Millie	S. Masur Nadery	2

Source: Mainly NDI, 2005 and AREU reports.[27]

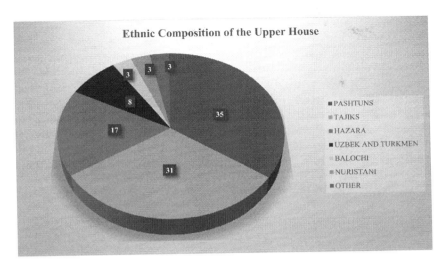

Figure 5.2 Ethnic composition of the Upper House.

including 15 who were formerly affiliated with the People's Democratic Party of Afghanistan, such as Ulumi and Gulabzoy, was a surprise to many.[26] However, continued personal rivalries and grievances dating back to the 1980s factionalism meant that they could never unite as a coalition. Their power was reduced in subsequent elections (Figure 5.2).

For all practical purposes, former jihadi leaders essentially captured the parliament (both houses) and were able to launch a series of attacks against President Karzai and his allies. This is roughly the same estimate that the Afghanistan Research and Evaluation Unit (AREU) analysis records of the composition of the House, which divided MPs into three categories: pro-government (81), pro-opposition (84), and "non-aligned" or with no clear network alignment (84).[28] In terms of ethnic composition, Pashtuns comprised 43% (including 10 seats allocated for Kuchi nomads); Tajiks and Aimaqs 29%; Hazaras 16%; Uzbeks and Turkmens 10%; Baluchs 8%; and Nurestanis 4% of the Lower House.[29] The Upper House had approximately the same ethnic distribution as the Lower House (35% Pashtun; 31% Tajik; 17% Hazara; 8% Uzbek and Turkmen; 3% Baluch; and 3% Nurestani) (see Figure 5.2).[30]

These fault lines became important in the election of the Speaker of the Lower House, which was prefaced by weeks of horse-trading and alliance-building. Two opposing alliances were built around the pro-Karzai candidate, Sayyaf, and the opposition candidate, Qanuni, the former leader of the National Understanding Front, discussed above. In a surprise deal with the government, Mohaqqiq, the leader of Wahdat-i-Mardom, agreed to support Sayyaf's candidacy in exchange for the position of deputy speaker for himself. However, this did not go over well with his ethnic Hazara MPs and wider clients who increasingly saw it as a betrayal of their cause.[32] Therefore, many of his Wahdat-i-Mardom network MPs sided with Qanuni, a good example of the limit of the power of a political network leader and the ability of networked members to exit if their personal interests are not aligned and guaranteed. After three rounds of the vote, Qanuni was elected the Chair of the Lower House with 122 votes, against Sayyaf's 117. Along with Sayyaf's defeat, the Mohaqqiq-Sayyaf alliance suffered another setback when Mohaqqiq was defeated by Arif Governor Noorzai, an ally of Karzai.[33] Fawzia Koofi, an ethnic Tajik from Badakhshan and a member of Jamiat, was voted in as the second deputy speaker. In an internal deal, reportedly to gain the support of former president Rabbani, Qanuni and Ahmad Wali Masoud gave up their positions as heads of the Afghanistan Nawin and Nehzat-i-Islami, which they re-merged with Jamiat-i-Islami under Rabbani's leadership; not that this was sustainable and made much difference in practice except in name. In the Upper House, with Karzai's support, Mojadaddi easily secured the position of the Speaker of the House while Karzai's other ally, Hamed Gailani, Pir Gailani's son, became the first deputy. Using the Harmony Group, a collection of 25–30 MPs, he would galvanise support for the president in the Upper House.

In the Lower House, Qanuni proved an effective and astute leader who controlled parliamentary affairs to ensure the body kept a check on the powers of the president and to maximise his group's interests. He was able to shore up support among political networks including parliamentary groupings (see Chapter 8) against Karzai on most key issues, blocking and undermining Karzai's policies inside and outside parliament. He often side-lined Karzai's political appointees in the secretariat and kept tight control over parliamentary dealings, including its relations with diplomatic missions.[34] He was also considered an effective "fire-fighter" who could put out the flames of discord before they got out of control. At one point in 2008 for instance, Qanuni was quick to exploit this. For instance, in a show of force, in September 2008, he gathered two-thirds majority support among MPs to override all of Karzai's veto powers.[35] This was a huge defeat for the president just a year before the 2009 presidential elections and further bolstered Qanuni's position in the United Front coalition (see below section for more on this coalition) which was positioning itself to put forward a presidential candidate.

Karzai, meanwhile, didn't help himself when he refused to form a de facto political network or a de jure political party, based on his view that parliament should be subservient to the executive branch, and became overly reliant on the state ministry of parliamentary affairs led by Minister Farook Wardak (and other powerbrokers such as Sayyaf) to advance his interests. As outlined in detail in Chapter 8, Karzai preferred expensive and ad hoc alliances in the Lower House with some political networks whenever he needed them compared to setting up a serious political network in the Lower House. Most of the independent MPs, roughly 100, were subject to some sort of patronage and co-optation by Karzai.

5.4 Battling for control of provincial councils

In the 2005 provincial council (PC) elections, Karzai's authority was further challenged by state-level patronage networks and regional strongmen networks who saw an opportunity to flex their muscles and shape local politics, including resource flows. The PCs were seen as an additional platform for legitimation and an important political commodity. Of which 3,027 candidates (including 248 women) competed for over 440 allocated seats for the 2005 PC elections.[36] Article 139 of the Constitution and, subsequently, the 20 August 2005 provincial council's law furnished only advisory and advocacy authorities and negligible resources for these bodies.[37] The elections produced a decisive victory for regional strongmen and their affiliates, who captured most of the seats and won most of the PC leadership positions (Head, Deputy Head, and Secretary). This subsequently created further power dependencies with which Karzai and his allies in Kabul had to contend, complicating political network dynamics and horse-trading. Also, the contest over control of PCs sets the scene for power struggles between subnational administration officials (provincial, district, and municipal) appointed centrally by Kabul and democratically elected provincial bodies affiliated with provincial and district strongmen networks.

The impact of the provincial council election was most visible in the Nangarhar Province. The Arsala family network led by Haji Zahir established in the provincial PC, Karzai's foes, enjoyed if not complete dominance, then significant authority over the leadership and decisions of PCs. The Arsala family network won two seats in the PC with Nasratullah Arsala becoming chairman and Haji Qadir's son, Jamal, another powerful member. With the latter's father in the Lower House, the reach of the Arsala family now stretched beyond Nangarhar to play an important role in national politics as the case of the 2010–2011 parliamentary crisis shown in Chapter 8.[38] In order to challenge the Arsala family's hegemony in Nangarhar and to remove Gul Agha Shirzai from Kandahar, Karzai appointed the latter as the Nangahar Governor in 2005. This gave rise to a new dynamic competition around key power resources, including provincial administrative positions, customs revenues, and access to smuggling networks and goods. Americans provided Shirzai with lavish funds for development projects, which allowed him to improve security, standards of governance, and infrastructure, which gave him leverage to co-opt rival clients into business partnerships, thereby weakening the Arsala family and others.[39]

In an attempt to reassert themselves in Nangarhar in 2010, Haji Zahir and Jamal Qadir emerged as the main rivals to Karzai and Governor Shirzai's authority. They levelled public allegations of corruption against Shirzai and sought to undermine him in other ways. During my visit to Nangarhar to conduct fieldwork for my PhD in June 2012, a skirmish took place between Jamal Qadir and governor Shirzai's allied local businessman Haji Farough. Jamal attacked Farough at his home for not paying his protection fee for a contract he had won.[40] The fact that Jamal Qadir had carried out such an attack on Haji Farough's house illustrates the extent of power he enjoyed in Nangarhar. A month later, on Shirzai's insistence, the Attorney General's Office and the Ministry of Interior arrested Haji Jamal in Kabul. However, he was released a few days later and was warmly welcomed back to the city by his supporters.[41] Also in 2012, Haji Zahir and Hazrat Ali reconciled their differences to unite against governor Shirzai in an attempt to unseat him, using all means available to them.[42] During another visit to the province in 2012, I witnessed a land dispute erupt between the Khugyani and Mohmand tribes leading to a weeklong tribal conflict. Interviews with Provincial Council and *Wolesi Jirga* representatives uncovered that Haji Zahir's affiliates had stirred up and exploited existing tensions to destabilise the province.[43] Most of these efforts were directed at Karzai, in retaliation for the 2010–2011 Special Court Crisis following the disputed parliamentary elections in which Karzai tried to unseat 62 sitting MPs (see Chapter 8). Haji Zahir established himself as the leader of the opposition to Karzai during the crisis.

In other provinces, Karzai's opponents were also elected as heads of their respective PCs, including Jamiat associates in Kabul, Allah Gul Mujahed; Jamiat and Shuray-i-Nazar clients specifically Qasim Fahim's ally in Parwan and Panjshir; Jamiat provincial leader Ismail Khan's son, Mir M. Yasir Saadiq, in Herat; Jamiat strongman Atta Mohammad Governor Noor's affiliate, Dr. Afzal Hadeed, in Balkh; Junbish members in Sheberghan, Faryab, and Sar-i-Pul provinces; Wahdat-i-Islami's client in Bamiyan, Khalili's ally Muhammad Ishaq Poya. Karzai had success in the south through his brother Ahmad Wali (assassinated in July 2011). His brother was elected as the Chairman of Kandahar PC, but de facto he was the "super-governor" of southern provinces. In Kandahar, he shaped and reinforced his own policy towards the tribes, often independently of Kabul along with six other tribal network leaders highlighted in Chapter 4.

In Balkh, the provincial council was beyond the reach of Karzai.[44] During my visit to the province in 2011, at least 15 of the 19 provincial council members were associated with strongman Governor Noor, and he had no qualms with flexing his muscle openly. When, for instance, it was time to select who the council chairman and his deputy should be, members acceded to his wishes.[45] "Governor Noor warned us that nobody should campaign in the internal provincial council election," the deputy chairman, Ghulam Abbas Akhlaqi, told me. "He proposed Dr. Mohammad Afzal Hadid as the chairman, myself as deputy chairman, and Mahbooba Sadat as secretary."[46]

Herat, meanwhile, became a contest between the Jamiat network led by Ismail Khan, on the one hand, and Karzai's allies led by Mawlawi Khudadad, the powerful head of the Provincial Religious Assembly (Shuar-i-Ulama), joined by moderate liberal leaders like Spanta and the Afzali family. Pashtun leaders such as Dr. Azizullah Ludin, Humayun Azizi, later the state minister for parliamentary affairs, and some Afghan Millat members such as Jelani Popal, the head of the newly established Independent Directorate of Local Governance also joined. In the provincial-level politics, this meant constant political skirmishes, blocking of access to resources to rivals, and manipulation and undermining of provincial administrations if he/she is not a member of your network. That is why, the Jamiat network took every opportunity before the 2014 presidential elections to undermine Karzai-aligned provincial governors, including Sayed Ali Anwari (2006–2009) and his successors, Nurestani and Daud Shah Saba.[47] In the 2013 provincial council leadership election, Jamiat was able to secure Sayed Wahid Qatali's election, a family relative and Jamiati associate, as the chair. A few months later, the

Jamiat network led by Khan mobilised the combined strengths of its members (the Qatali family and his allies in Herat's PC and MPs) to force Governor Saba to resign.[48]

As these local dynamics show, Karzai was not always able to dictate terms and had to concede to patronage and subnational strongmen networks to project a degree of political order and legitimation. Certainly, the writ of the central government held little sway in provinces controlled by Karzai's rivals and even when the president was successful in projecting central government power, it was through his provincial allies and clients. Subnational strongmen and their affiliates manipulated events in their provinces not only to exert authority but also to gain compensation from Kabul. The PCs, instead of serving their intended goal—at minimum to oversee the local administrations' performance in service delivery—became a disruptive thorn in the side of Kabul-appointed provincial and district governors and subnational administration officials. They were also instrumental as vessels of national patronage and regional strongmen networks in promoting rent and illegality, including illegal resource extraction, kidnapping, extortion, drug trafficking, and so on. In 2007, according to the Government Independent Directorate of Local Governance (IDLG) data, 13 PC chairmen had criminal or corruption cases filed against them. Attempts, by myself included, to bring these cases to court by working closely with the Attorney General Office failed because of the sweeping political protection granted to them by key political network leaders, including the president.[49] Consequently, at least one-quarter of all PC members throughout the country were involved in some form of illegal activities.

5.5 The pre-2009 presidential election dynamics, alliance-building, and a crisis of legitimacy

In preparation for the 2009 presidential elections, the United Front (Jebha-i-Millie) coalition was formed to introduce a unified candidate. The Front was dominated by former Jamiat splinter networks: the former president Burhanuddin Rabbani, the Speaker of the Lower House, Qanuni, Mohammad Akbary, an MP from Badakhshan, Qasim Fahim, the former Ministry of Defence (MoD) minister, Ismail Khan, Governor Noor in Balkh, and others. Mustafa Zahir (the former king's grandson) as well as some former People's Democratic Party of Afghanistan (PDPA) leftist figures like Nurul Haq Ulumi (Mutahed-i-Millie) and M. Gulabzoy, in addition to dozens of other smaller networks. They tried to court the two important vote banks—Junbish-i-Islami led by Abdul Rashid Dostum and Wahdat-i-Mardom led by Mohammad Mohaqqiq—and former president Sebqatullah Mojadaddi. However, they refrained from making a firm commitment even though their representatives were attending senior leadership meetings. Their hesitation was perhaps driven by two factors: waiting to see whom the Americans would support, and not wanting to be on the losing side.[50] They were also "testing the water" and sounding out constituency responses to ensure that they were not too far-removed from their electorate's mood.

After months of internal debate within its 50-member executive council over the choice of presidential candidate, in March 2009, the first crack appeared within the coalition.[51] Qasim Fahim and Rabbani (Ahmad Zia's father-in-law) advocated for Abdullah Abdullah while Yunos Qanuni was backed by Ahmad Zia Masoud's network. Frustrated by a lack of unity around a candidate, second-tier ethnic Tajik members such as Amanullah Payman (the second Deputy Speaker to the Lower House), MP Qadria Yazdanparast, and Amrullah Saleh began separately reaching out to other rival candidates. Among ethnic Hazara groups, Akbari (Wahdat-i-Islami), Ali Kazimi (Mustafa Kazimi's brother who was assassinated in 2006), and Qurban Ali Erfani (Wahdat-i-Islam-i-Millie Afghanistan) sought out alternative camps. Eventually, Mustafa Zahir left the coalition and other leftist groups followed suit.

Sensing disunity, Karzai, with the help of his close allies such as Sayyaf and Mojadaddi, reached out to key United Front (UF) executive members with the offer of government positions and privileges. This included an appeal to support Fahim, for whom Karzai offered the position of first vice president. He proposed Sadiq Chakari as Minister of Hajj and Religious Affairs in a post-election government.[52] Karzai also suggested giving the position of the second VP to Mohaqqiq (the Wahdat-e-Mardom leader) though this may have been a ploy to make sure Mohaqqiq did not fully commit to the UF; most observers at the time knew that Karzai preferred Karim Khalili for the position.

To gain the support of Junbish-i-Islami, an important vote bank bloc, in August 2008, President Karzai hinted at his openness to resolve the Junbish leader's exile problem in Turkey. Six months earlier, in February 2008, Abdul Rashid Dostum had allegedly ordered his militia guards to raid and abduct Akbar Bai, his ethnic political rival, in Kabul who was then badly beaten up.[53] Under international pressure, Karzai had ordered the Afghan police force to surround Dostum's house. After a tense few days, and with the Turkish government's mediation, Dostum was sent into exile to Ankara.[54] The then-Attorney General, Abdul Jabbar Sabit, prepared criminal charges against him but the government never brought them forward, much to Bai's frustration. In October 2008, Karzai asked his trusted ally, Sebqatullah Mojadaddi, to reconcile between Dostum and Akbar Bai. Under pressure from Karzai, on October 26, Bai appeared at Mojadaddi's house in front of the press alongside Dostum, giving a brief statement saying the dispute had been resolved. A deal was struck in which Junbish-i-Islami joined Karzai's election alliance to line up the ethnic Uzbek vote, which made a huge difference in the north (see map in Chapter 7).

In order to remove the final hurdle to his election bid, in May 2009, Karzai arm-twisted Shirzai, his fellow ethnic Pashtun strongman and famed governor of Nangarhar, to withdraw his candidacy. In early 2009, Shirzai had expressed his interest in running, even choosing his running mates. He had gained popular support in Kandahar and Nangarhar and was widely nicknamed the "Bulldozer" for his rapid implementation of reconstruction projects and development. In a dinner meeting that took place on May 1 in the Palace, Karzai first deployed political persuasion to convince Shirzai not to run, arguing a lack of support from the international community and southern tribes. When this did not work, Karzai allegedly shifted to threats, anger, and intimidation, forcing him to withdraw his candidacy.[55] Karzai feared that if Shirzai stayed in the race it would split the ethnic Pashtun vote, disadvantaging him. By June, Karzai had successfully secured the backing of heavy-weight vote banks: Junbish-i-Islami and Wahdat-i-Mardom—a major blow to Abdullah's campaign strategy to consolidate the anti-Pashtun ethnic vote.[56] In addition, as Figure 5.3 shows, he also secured the backing of influential religious figures such as Abdul Rasul Sayyaf and family-based networks such as Sebqatullah Mojadaddi, the leader of the Upper House, and Pir Gilani, the leader of the Mahaz-i-Millie, who were then utilised for their networking abilities and connections among religious groups.

After months of bickering and delay, on April 15, Abdullah Abdullah was chosen as the Front's candidate, losing most of its powerful clients. To boost in-house cohesion, the Front launched a series of attacks against Karzai when the election was postponed for a few months. Qanuni and other Front members in the Lower House, also launched a well-coordinated attack on Karzai, questioning his intention to remain in office beyond 22 May 2009, the day when his government's constitutional mandate would come to an end. The Front announced two possible options for resolving post-May 22 presidential continuity: (1) transitional mechanisms based on political consensus; and (2) a caretaker government based on the presidential succession articles of the constitution.[57] On 15 February 2009, Ahmad Zia Masoud mounted a deliberate, and public, condemnation in the Panjshir Province of Karzai's record on service delivery, governance, security, and anti-corruption. The next day, Karzai confronted Masoud at a cabinet meeting about his remarks, reportedly yelling at him and saying, "take your dirty laundry and get out."[58] Masoud responded that he would wait until May 22 to resign, reinforcing his belief that Karzai would lose his constitutional legitimacy after that date.

In the end, the attempts to de-legitimise Karzai after his constitutional mandate expired on May 22 failed. President Karzai was able to buy the loyalty of a few key players in Abdullah's camp with an offer of seats in the cabinet and provincial governor positions. The final result, which was announced two months after the August 20 election, put Karzai at 49.67% (just short of a majority), Abdullah at 30.59%, Dr. Ramazan Bashardost at 10.46%, and Dr. Ashraf Ghani at 2.94%.[59] The election was marred by widespread fraud (see Chapter 7). Karzai had initially declared victory but after two months of disputes and interventions by the U.S.A., the European Union and United Nations Assistance Mission in Afghanistan (UNAMA), the UN-backed panel of election monitors found nearly a third of Karzai's votes fraudulent.[60] Elections went to a run-off between Karzai and Abdullah as neither candidate had reached the 50% majority. However, on 1 November 2009, surprising many, Abdullah announced his decision to withdraw from the race, officially stating that all his demands, including changing the Independent Election Commission (IEC) commissioners and its administrative leadership, and the suspension of government ministers among others who were involved in the election fraud, had been rejected by Karzai.[61] His speech was critical of Karzai and the IEC but he stopped short of declaring a full boycott

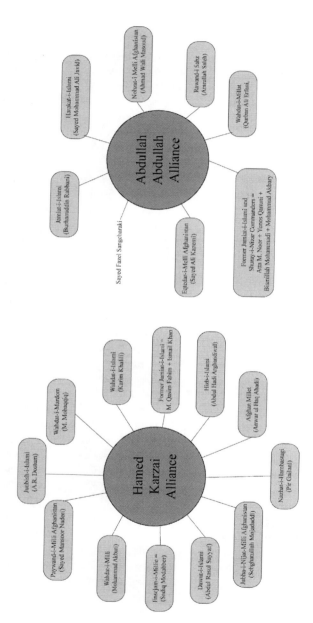

Figure 5.3 Political network alliances in 2009 elections.

and calling the new administration illegitimate, as many of his followers were demanding. Karzai was declared the winner the next day.[62] To many, it remains a mystery as to why Abdullah withdrew from the race, though rumours abound.[63]

Despite the victory, Karzai's authority was weakened by the fraud allegations. Many opposition figures immediately questioned the legitimacy of the government. For instance, Ahmad Wali Masoud, Abdullah's ally, said, "Whatever he does he will not be legitimate."[64] The Americans were quick to congratulate Karzai as they saw a new government in Kabul as essential to their war aims. Obama was planning to send 40,000 troops as part of his surge strategy, the first step in preparations for a full military withdrawal from the country.[65]

5.6 New administration: new power-sharing

Under domestic and international pressure to form a new government before the planned 28 January 2010 international conference on Afghanistan in London, UK, and to quickly restore his legitimacy, Karzai introduced his first cabinet list of 24 ministers on 19 December 2009.[66] Spanta, the foreign minister, would stay on the job until the London conference. The list was the product of bargains between Karzai, key ethno-regional strongmen, and state-level powerbrokers who had secured the vote for him, with some concessions to the international community, which wanted some of the top technocrats to remain in government. On 2 January 2010, the Lower House voted on the proposed ministers. Only seven of the 24 were approved (Farough Wardak, Atmar, Zakhilwal, Shahrani, Asef Rahimi, and Rahim Wardak). All except one were sitting ministers from Karzai's network. His network-client leaders complained that Karzai had left them high and dry to defend their ministers and make their own bargains with MPs rather than have access to state resources (e.g., buying off the vote, intimidation, dealing for other positions and contracts). His second cabinet, introduced on January 9, also saw only seven candidates approved, and again mostly those with access to state resources. Chapter 8 goes into detail about how aides loyal to Karzai and future president Ashraf Ghani manipulated, bought off, and intimidated parliamentarians to secure the approval of their cabinet people. Suffice to say for now that the new cabinet saw a resurgence of ethnic Pashtun dominance with Karzai apportioning almost all key positions (Finance, Defence, Interior, and Foreign), including key security posts—except the head of the Directorate of National Security—to his ethnic Pashtun supporters at the expense of other groups.

Some ethnic Hazara and Uzbek MPs argued that the first cabinet list was a sacrifice list, a strategy to propose cabinet ministers from his rival groups knowing they would not be approved so Karzai could then appoint his own men in the next round. It was also suggested that the move was intended to demonstrate to power brokers that he had fulfilled his campaign promise without giving up too much. Regardless of his true intentions, Karzai got his key allies elected to top positions in the first round. This annoyed many of the powerbrokers, who retaliated by joining the opposition (Table 5.2).

In addition to Defence, Interior, and Finance, another ethnic Pashtun, Jilani Popal, was appointed as Head of the powerful Independent Directorate of Local

Table 5.2 The December 2009 cabinet

Name	Ministry	Ethnicity	Political affiliation	Votes
Hazrat Omar Zakhilwal	Finance	Pashtun	Technocrat/Karzai	141
Rahim Wardak	Defence	Pashtun	Former Jihadi/Karzai	124
Hanif Atmar	Interior	Pashtun	Technocrat/Karzai	147
Dadfar Spanta–	Foreign	Tajik	Technocrat/Karzai	No vote
Asif Rahimi	Agriculture	Pashtun	Technocrat/Karzai	136
Farouq Wardak	Education	Pashtun	Former Hizb/Karzai	155
S. Amin Fatehi	Health	Pashtun	Mojadaddi family/Karzai	102
Anwal ul-Haq Ahadi	Economy	Pashtun	Afghan Millet	91
Yusuf Pashtun	Urban Development	Pashtun	Gul Agha Shirzai	88
Wais Barmak	Rural Development	Tajik	Technocrat/Qasim Fahim	90
Obaidullah Obaid	Higher Education	Tajik	Fahim	94
Sayed Makhdoom Rahim	Culture	Tajik	Close to former king	120
Ismail Khan	Energy and Water	Tajik	Former Jamiat	111
Enayatullah Nazari	Refugee	Tajik	Technocrat/Fahim	82
Amirzai Sangeen	Telecommunications	Pashtun	Afghan Millet	92
Sarwar Danesh	Justice	Hazara	Wahdat (Khalili)	96
Enayatullah Baleegh	Haji and Religious	Tajik	Sayyaf	108
Banou Ghazanfar	Women Affairs	Uzbek	Ghazanfar business family/Dostum	115
M. Batash	Transport	Uzbek	Junbish-i-Millie	82
Gholam Aylaghi	Commerce	Hazara	Wahdat-i-Mardom	76
Hamed Gailani	Border Affairs	Pashtun/ Sayed	Gailani Family/Karzai	70
Ismail Munshi	Social Affairs	Turkmen	Junbish	39
Gen. Khodaidad	Counter-narcotics	Hazara	Wahdat-i-Islami	36
Abdullahi	Public Works	Hazara	Wahdat-i-Islami	33
W. Shahrani	Mines	Uzbek	Shahrani family/Karzai	
Sadiq Modabber	Office of Admin Affairs	Hazara	Ensejam-i-Millie/ Sadiq Modabber	No vote
Omar Daudzai	Chief of Staff	Pashtun	Former Hizb/Karzai	No vote
Rangin Spanta	National Security Advisor	Tajik	Technocrat/Karzai	No vote
Jelani Popal	Independent Directorate of Local Governance	Pashtun	Afghan Millet	No vote

Source: Afghanistan Analyst Network.[31]

Governance. There was only one female minister, Banou Ghazanfar from the Ghazanfar Group, which had contributed a significant amount of money to the President's campaign. In addition, in 2009, Ghazanfar Bank had written out a two million dollar interest-free loan to Karzai for his election campaign.[67] On January 2, the Junbish party released a statement saying that this was not an outcome they had expected from their deal. They made a toothless warning that "those who believe in tactics more than solidarity and political partnership will face consequences."[68]

For the next five years, President Karzai continued with his strategy of maintaining a balance of power among subnational and state-level networks, all to ensure that no single one grew too strong to become a threat to his rule. This ensured that political networks remained dependent on his largesse and benevolence. Whenever there was a crisis, of which there was never a shortage in Afghanistan, often of Karzai's own making, he would facilitate and build short-term—and short-sighted—alliances. The first two years of his term were occupied by the parliamentary elections of 2010 and the subsequent crisis in which he tried to unseat 62 sitting MPs (almost a quarter of the parliament) by establishing a special court to investigate election fraud. Many saw this as a direct attempt by Karzai and his network clientele in the executive to control and influence the legislature (see Chapter 8). From 2012 onwards, politics was dominated by the emergence of several alliances focused on finding a suitable candidate for the 2014 presidential elections. Karzai's second term in office was also defined by a worsening relationship with the Americans following the 2009 elections during which the U.S. mission in Afghanistan led by the late Richard Holbrooke, the Obama administration's special representative for Afghanistan and Pakistan, tried to oust Karzai (see Chapter 7).

5.7 Karzai and the U.S.A.: a turbulent relationship

In the early years following Bonn, the U.S. political and financial support was critical to Karzai's ability to project power and expand his authority beyond Kabul. Much of those resources were spent suppressing strongmen networks and their commanders. Karzai's relationship with Ambassador Khalilzad was essential to his ability to consolidate power. But by 2006, the U.S.A. had come to question Karzai's competence and state of mental health.[69] In 2008, the new Obama administration publicly criticised him for failing to deal with corruption and improve security and governance. After the 2009 presidential elections, three significant issues came to encapsulate his strained relationship with the U.S.A.: corruption, the Central Intelligence Agency (CIA)-linked special forces night raids, and the Bagram prisoner release. On 31 May 2011, Karzai chastised the U.S.A. for its aggressive night raids and air campaign in which civilians were killed. He stated that the way foreign forces were acting closely resembled "the behaviour of occupation, and Afghan people know how to deal with that."[70] A year later, in March 2012, he lashed out at North Atlantic Treaty Organisation (NATO) over civilian deaths.[71] And in September 2012, he asked the U.S.A. to transfer the American-built

Bagram prison facility to Afghans. In November, he ordered Afghan forces to take control of the prison, accusing the U.S.A. of violating Afghanistan's national sovereignty and an agreement to fully hand over the facility to Afghan control.[72]

The Obama–Karzai relationship was damaged during the 2009 presidential elections when Richard Holbrooke openly interfered in the process to tilt the 2009 election against Karzai.[73] In his memoir, Robert Gates, the former U.S. Defense Secretary, accuses Holbrooke and the then U.S. Ambassador, Karl Eikenberry, of attempting to unseat Karzai.[74] Gates notes that Holbrooke was doing "his best to bring about the defeat of Karzai. What he wanted was to have enough credible candidates running to deny Karzai a majority in the elections, thus forcing a runoff in which he could be defeated." Karzai had for some time accused the Obama administration of trying to secretly engineer his downfall and he found evidence during the 2009 elections in Holbrooke's man at UNAMA, Peter Galbraith, who had openly accused Karzai and his team of "wholesale" fraud (see Chapter 7). Following this, Karzai saw American hands in everything that went wrong, which further reinforced his conspiratorial thinking. This explains why his post-2009 inner circle was mostly made up of anti-American former Hizb-i-Islami figures, including his chief of staff, Karim Khurram, and Omar Daudzai who urged him to move closer to Iran and Pakistan.[75]

From almost the beginning to the very last day of his presidency, Karzai was sceptical of U.S. motives and agendas and as years passed the rift between him and the Americans widened. The last year of his presidency focused almost entirely on the politics of the U.S.–Afghanistan Bilateral Security Agreement, which he refused to sign, despite the November 2013 Consultative Loya Jirga overwhelmingly approving it.[76] Perhaps Karzai wanted to leave office brandishing evidence that he was not a U.S. stooge. As Kai Eide, former UN Special Representative to Afghanistan said, Karzai faced a relationship between "partnership and occupation—a difficult dynamic but one U.S. actions made worse than necessary."[77] And as Ronald Neumann, the former ambassador to Afghanistan, aptly expressed, "Karzai's failings were steadily exacerbated by unclear and changing U.S. policies, a frequent disconnection between stated U.S. policies and actions and blindness to how Afghanistan perceived statements by U.S. officials."[78] At first, the U.S.A. had advised Karzai to rely on power brokers and use patronage as a tool of governance but later demanded he fire those same power brokers. The confused policy, exacerbated by a radical shift in American leadership with the end of the Bush years and the beginning of the Obama era, left Karzai bewildered by the notion of American exceptionalism and democracy. In the end, he believed in neither.

5.8 State institutions and patronage

The perceived betrayal of the U.S.A. was especially irksome to Karzai because he believed he had done exactly what the U.S.A. had expected of him. Throughout his presidency, he had exploited the state's formal institutions and resources to exert control over the country. State ministries such as parliamentary affairs, the IDLG, tribal affairs and borders, Hajj and religious affairs, rural rehabilitation and development, among others, were at his disposal in the process of containing and quashing rival leaders and networks. Officials within these state institutions, however, were not mutually exclusive of the political network but overlapped with it at certain moments. Also, this was not an exclusively top-down, Karzai-dependent patronage network, as the clientelism literature suggests, rather it was a complex interplay of resource interdependencies in which regional strongmen networks and power brokers enjoyed their agency and were able to influence and manipulate Kabul on policies, fund allocations, and appointments. As Chapters 6 and 8 demonstrate, local forces were often successful in manipulating political strategies, the flow of resources and patronage relations—which were as much bottom-up as they were top-down. Karzai's advantage lay in the fact that, as the head of state, he possessed substantial financial and coercive resources through the bargains he had made with his allied networks. In other words, he had inter-twined some political networks and state officials with an extensive bargaining and interdependency system that defined the rules of the game, making it difficult for those networks to disentangle themselves. Among the seemingly indecipher-able web of interdependencies were key institutions which operated as hubs in these networks, which Karzai used to consolidate his political empire.

5.8.1 The IDLG and subnational administrations

The centralised nature of the political system Karzai developed gave extensive power to the president to appoint most provincial and district governors, or use them to horse-trade with political networks and other centres of power, and grade one and two line-ministry directorates (Can you explain what those directorates are? It sounds a bit too insider-y here.) The latter were often appointed with the recommendation of the ministry, which the president could overrule.[79] Provincial and district governors often acted as local "gatekeepers," especially those with the direct backing of the president. Thus, as the president's representatives, their influence often far surpassed what was constitutionally allotted to them.[80]

At the end of 2007, when President Karzai's relations with the Americans deteriorated, the Americans advocated for the establishment of a separate directorate to keep an additional tab on the power of the President in the provinces.[81] Karzai was also in favour of the plan, but he had other intentions: to streamline and institutionalise subnational appointments, making sure these officials knew that the president himself had appointed them and could keep a close eye on them. This would help guarantee his success in the 2009 elections. Karzai appointed Ghulam Jelani Popal, an ethnic Pashtun from the same tribe as the president and Millet network leader, as the head of this new department—the Independent Directorate of Local Governance—with his two deputies, Barna Karimi and Abdul Malek Sediqi. Karimi was a former deputy to Karzai's previous chief of staff, Jawed Ludin, who was known for his competence. The word "independent" was added to the name to project the illusion of independence and to legally protect the minister from going through the parliament for a vote of confidence. Maintaining control over the IDLG was crucial for Karzai: it would play an instrumental role in mobilising subnational governors, mayors, village elders, provincial councils, and informal community councils to garner votes for the incumbent, including during the 2009 presidential elections.[82]

A 2012 Killid Group study showed how this reciprocal relationship between the president and key political networks and powerbrokers played out with respect to the appointment of governors in Afghanistan through the IDLG. In the bargains that followed the 2009 presidential elections, political network leaders introduced their clientele as provincial governors (Figure 5.4). This was not very different

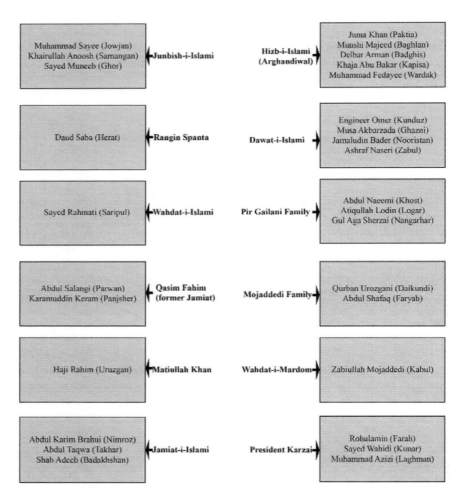

Figure 5.4 Political networks and their clientele.

from the early Durrani governance system in the 18th and 19th centuries where tribal chiefs were given spheres of influence in the form of territorial regions to control resource extraction and distribution as long as they remained loyal to the ruler. In the 21st-century version, this also included 387 district governor positions and more than 165 municipalities. (I'm pretty sure you did it in an earlier chapter but is there any way to note again here how you ended up working with the IDLG?) My quick assessment of four central highland provinces at the IDLG in 2018 highlighted that 90% of district governors in these provinces had been in their position for more than 10 years with entrenched connections to local- and state-level networks.[83] That same year, instructed by president Ashraf Ghani, I announced 16 new positions, with the help of the Independent Administrative Reform and Civil Service Commission of Afghanistan (IARCSC), which created a tsunami of political reactions. I subsequently received calls and visits from influential leaders and their associates, including members of parliament, arguing for or against the move, threatening, and even attempting to blackmail me as well as others at the IDLG. This created a complex interplay of power politics, resulting in a web of negotiations, bargaining, and promises. Each network and its associates tried to undermine their rivals, questioning their opponent's personality and background. While the appointment of provincial governors and mayors often happened as the result of state-level negotiations and bargains, the selection of district governors and mayors was often subject to the twin dynamics of localised power contests and state-level political network influences.[84] As Figure 5.4 illustrates, the trend with Karzai's appointment of provincial officials was primarily driven by the logic of maintaining balance among political networks and regional strongmen. This became less and less the case with Ghani, as the next chapter shows, which often led to political and ethnic tensions in the periphery, costing the new president serious problems of legitimacy.

The IDLG remained one of the most powerful institutions in Afghanistan until the end of the nation-building experiment. One former director-general labelled it the "prime minister's office," reporting directly to the president. In 2014, President Ghani used the IDLG as an extension of his own Office to manage subnational affairs. The IDLG's *de jure* arms and authority could stretch and connect the president to all subnational administrations, including the more than 45,000 villages in Afghanistan. The village administration was run by a *malek* (village elder) who was essentially the president's representative in the village even though he was elected by the villagers. *Maleks* were important as they could function as village powerbrokers. They exerted independence and agency and often connected provincial and district networks and power brokers with local communities. Above I discussed the importance of provincial councils and how they were captured by key regional and provincial leaders or their affiliates. The IDLG could play a vital role in overwhelming or intimidating PC members administratively, financially, and politically. This would often turn into a "tit for tat" game in which councils would spark public demonstrations against the local administration, in some cases even encouraging supporters to block highways, coerce the centre to respect their agency and demands, and force it to play by their rules.

5.8.2 *State ministry of parliamentary affairs and parliament*

While at the subnational level, the patronage game was characterised by this intricate web of local networks and the sometimes-messy game of mass mobilisation, on the national stage, the game took on much more sinister dimensions. It's hard to discern which was more or less responsible for the ultimate collapse of the state—the Swiss cheese of local patronage networks which left the foundation weak, or the spectacular corruption at the state level which arguably encouraged and extended subnational decay. At the national level, the central agencies enabling Karzai's agenda and exerting influence on MPs were the state ministry of parliamentary affairs, and to some degree the National Security Council (NSC) and the National Directorate of Security (NDS), when intimidation was needed. The position of state minister of parliamentary affairs was always occupied by someone close to the sitting president. As highlighted in Chapter 7, the ministry was responsible for whipping MPs into line, purchasing loyalty, and making bargains with MPs for passing Karzai's agenda. Reportedly, payments were often made by the department run by Ibrahim Spinzada—Karzai's long-time aide and the Deputy National Security Council chief who was known to be the president's confidante for some of his more suspect and secretive projects.[85]

Interviews with several senior officials at the Ministry of Finance and other line-ministries revealed the extent of appropriation of public resources for personal gain. In 2010, the presidential palace accounted for the highest amount of illegible budget (unaccounted for money) spent in the country at around US$300 million, nearly 2% of the country's GDP, followed by parliament at around US$50 million.[86] Although it is difficult to establish conclusively how this money was spent, one could plausibly summarise, based on key informants' statements, that a substantial part of it went to buying loyalties and making bargains. The quote below, by a senior official at the Ministry of Finance and the Office of Administrative Affairs, reflects the overall level of bargaining that became entrenched in post-2001 Afghanistan. This money was paid to influential elders and others to buy loyalties.

> I cannot tell you exactly how this money is being spent but we are constantly under pressure by the presidential office and the minister [Minister of Finance] to provide money … Most of this money is being channelled as extra payments to key individuals. This is not something new. But this is having serious consequences. This year, the World Bank under the Afghanistan Reconstruction Trust Fund cut $70 million of our funds.[87]

Of course, this did not include other unaccounted for money that Karzai and his clients received from neighbouring countries. In 2009, Karzai publicly admitted to receiving suitcases of money from neighbouring countries for his office expenses.[88] He also confirmed in 2013 to have received payments from the U.S. intelligence service over the previous decade, known as "ghost money," that "came in secret and left in secret," which he claimed to have spent on his office expenses.[89] These statements also suggest that international donors were not only aware of these illegal practices but in some instances fostered them, violating their own rhetoric of liberal peacebuilding and transparency.

In the Upper House, Karzai enjoyed a greater control due to his constitutional power to appoint one-third of representatives.[90] Also, given that district council elections never happened in 2004, the president had superior manoeuvring power and space to sell off, or bargain, seats to loyal allies.[91] He was able to secure the election of Mojadaddi, his mentor and former boss, who put his weight behind the president's agenda from 2005 to 2010.

5.8.3 Managing and manipulating tribes: The Ministry of Border and Tribal Affairs

The preceding pair of patronage networks represent the institutional bookends, so to speak, of Afghanistan's political landscape. The IDLG was the proverbial meeting place of the masses while the Upper and Lower Houses circumscribed the echelons of the elite. In between, however, was what might be considered Afghanistan's most complex and difficult to manage the system of power distribution: the communities, tribes, and diverse ethnic groupings. Fortunately for Karzai, Afghanistan's modernising King, Amanullah Khan, had set up an institution in 1921 which would evolve into a ministry to manage them: The Ministry of Border and Tribal Affairs. In Afghanistan's tribal south and southeast, where Karzai's constituency was largely based, he relied on this ministry to systematically manage his relations with tribes and to galvanise their support in moments of contestation, such as the 2009 and 2014 elections and the 2013 Bilateral Security Agreement crisis with the U.S.A.

As an ethnic Pashtun, growing up in the tribal society of the south, with a deep awareness of the tribal governance structure and the historical role of tribes in governance, Karzai recognised that managing tribal dynamics was key to his survival. In a 1988 essay analysing Zahir Shah's relatively peaceful reign, Karzai concluded that political order and stability were produced as the result of "absolute support, confidence, and trust" of the tribes to the king.[92] He further explained that statesmen who lost touch with the tribes, preferring to govern through formal institutions, did not stay in power long.

Chapter 4 showed how Karzai had relied on six strongmen to administer the south on his behalf. They exerted extensive tribal power which had the ripple effect of forcing Karzai to appoint their men to key positions in Kabul. The Ministry of Border and Tribal Affairs (MoBTA), however, provided an additional mechanism to exert influence over tribes. Using the ministry, Karzai was able to pursue a "carrot and stick" strategy vis-à-vis tribal leaders by rewarding those who supported his agenda in the local government whilst excluding those who did not. This required concentrated coordination between the ministry and the six southern strongmen. For instance, in Kandahar, the key tribes who were well-presented in the provincial administration were the Popalzai, Barekzai, Alokozai, and Mohammadzai, whereas Governor Noorzai, Eshaqzai, and Ghilzai tribes and sub-tribes were excluded. In Uruzgan, Jan Mohammad Khan appointed most of the provincial team from his Popalzai tribesmen, monopolising administrative power. His rival Mullah Shafiq, from the underdog Ghilzai tribe, who had lobbied hard in a tribal jirga to become governor in 2002, was excluded. He joined the Taliban and became a leading commander, once again.[93] The president's office also used the budget code 92—an operative code used at the discretion of the president for secretive operations and functions—to regularly pay tribal elders and communities, with recommendations from the ministry. In the uncertainty generated by a regime/state where the rule of law was absent in most of the tribal areas, the fear of punishment was high. Human rights organisations widely documented the level of intimidation and abuse by government officials in the south, especially under Ahmad Wali and General Raziq.[94] Some of these tribal-cum-provincial officials were accused of having personal prisons where they tortured their opponents and anti-government forces.[95] Tribal leaders were consistently reminded that if they did not support the government and the president they would be excluded from the local government: meaning the loss of jobs, aid money, and privileges. Coghlan (2009) provides an insightful account of the rivalry between the different tribes (Governor Noorzai, Alikozais, Alizai, and Ishaqzai) in the Helmand Province and lays out how both the Karzai network and the Taliban used these rivalries to strengthen their power in the province.[96] Excluded tribes turned to the Taliban for protection. This created a symbiotic relationship in which the Taliban provided protection against the state and state-aligned tribes—especially when this was intertwined with opium cultivation and illegality—to tribes supplying fighters and hospitality.

5.8.4 Other state institutions as network resources

In the end, it would take the combined resources from multiple state institutions for Karzai to exert his influence over the Afghan grassroots. Other key ministries used to accomplish this task were the Ministry of Rehabilitation and Rural Development (MRRD), to help connect with village-level Community Development Councils (CDCs), which offered funding for community-level development projects, the Ministry of Interior, which appointed district, provincial, and urban police chiefs, and the Ministry of Hajj and Religious Affairs to connect with and drum up support amongst religious leaders across the country. On the development side, in addition to IDLG, MRRD was key in terms of development programmes and service delivery in making sure that the president's agenda reached every single village in Afghanistan and that villagers knew it was the President himself who initiated national poverty-reduction projects, such as the National Solidarity Programme, worth over US$1 billion, funded by the World Bank and other donors. By 2012, the MRRD had established over 100,000 CDCs across villages in Afghanistan, implementing small-scale development projects.[97] During the 2009 elections, the MRRD was one of the central platforms through which Karzai and his campaign appealed to CDCs at the village level to win votes. The entire provincial reconstruction fund eventually came under the supervision of the MRRD, which enabled Minister Atmar to emerge as an influential player in helping Karzai link Kabul to the provinces. During this period, several ministries emerged as financial hubs based on the influx of development funds, often associated with president Karzai's clientele, with donors and the Afghan government allocating billions of dollars, giving them huge power. These included the IDLG, MRRD, MoI, MoD, Energy and Water, and Mines and Petroleum, opening up space for contracts and bargains. The Ministry of Interior and the appointment of provincial and district police chiefs would become a source of patronage through which Karzai would reward power brokers, as discussed further in Chapter 9. Contracts within the Ministry of Mines became another source of bargains and patronage, as Chapter 9 explains further. For instance, over 40 members of parliament in 2016 were involved in the mining sector, and it was impossible to secure contracts without significant access to the president or his aides, or power brokers who had horse-traded with the president.

5.9 Alliance-building in the lead-up to the 2014 elections

As the end of Karzai's constitutionally mandated two terms as president approached, negotiations over what the post-Karzai period would look like began to take shape. The first indication that the idea of an Afghanistan without Karzai was already being contemplated came two months after the assassination of Burhanuddin Rabbani by a suicide bomber on 11 November 2011. In its aftermath, some of the former UF leaders announced the re-launch of the alliance. Wahdat-i-Mardom, Zia Masoud, the brother of Ahmad Shah Masoud who had a few clients in his small network, and Junbish-i-Islami along with their associates and several smaller patronage networks and prominent members of parliament held a press conference to outline their strategy for radical reform. Their declaration raised the spectre again of a prime minister position, changing the political set-up to a parliamentary system, increasing the authority of provincial councils and governors—without offering specifics, and introducing a proportionate electoral system.[98] However, this time around the UF did not have the remaining former Jamiati leaders such as Qanuni, Fahim, and Ismail Khan on board. Also, the UF turned out to be more of a reaction to the death of Jamiat's spiritual leader than an organised effort to withstand opposition to Karzai.

Less than a year later, around 20 political networks joined together to establish a new coalition—the Cooperation Council of Political Parties and Coalitions of Afghanistan.[99] On 23 September 2012, during the launch of its programme, the coalition distributed what it called the "Democracy Charter" calling for reforms and amendments to the electoral system, the election law, and changes in the leadership of electoral institutions. The Coalition also hinted that soon they would introduce their candidates for the upcoming elections. They also warned that a delay in the 2014 presidential elections would lead to a serious crisis.[100] There was a genuine fear that Karzai would prolong his stay in power after 2014, or at least try to manipulate the election framework, including election date, electoral laws, and IEC leadership appointments to serve his interests and those of his camp. As

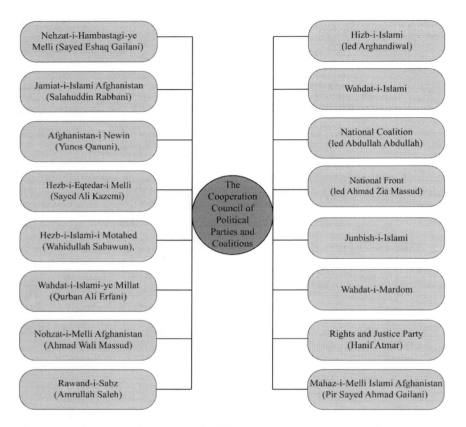

Figure 5.5 The cooperation council of political parties and coalitions of Afghanistan.

Figure 5.5 shows, Coalition members included most of the former jihadi networks, including the children of their leaders, as well as members of Karzai's own government, including first and second vice presidents, Qasim Fahim and Karim Khalili, Ahadi, Pir Gailani, Arghandiwal, and Bismillah Muhammadi. The Coalition was not only an effort to prepare for the 2014 elections; it also expressed a desire in the government to change course in the post-Karzai era and offered a chance for aspiring presidential hopefuls to test the waters, dipping a toe in Afghanistan's tumultuous political seas to see how warm it was to their participation.

In a more serious effort to agree on a candidate, mainly headed by former Jamiat leaders, on 29 August 2013 a new alliance of parties and networks announced their formation, naming themselves the Electoral Union of Afghanistan.[101] After months of meetings and negotiations among members, they failed to agree on a candidate—the self-declared reason d'etre for the group's establishment. According to an Afghanistan Analyst Network (AAN) report, the alliance turned out to be "somewhat meagre,"[102] divided once again between the competing

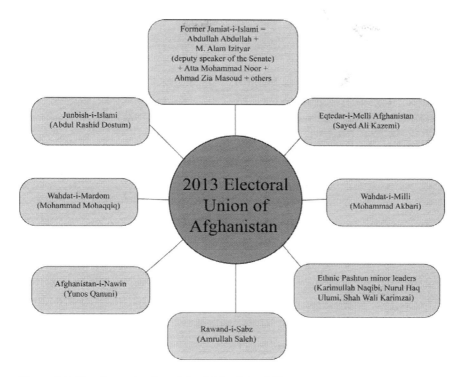

Figure 5.6 The electoral union of the Afghanistan Alliance.

presidential aspirations of Abdullah Abdullah (National Coalition) and Ahmad Zia Masoud (United Front). However, as elections neared, two important vote bank networks, Wahdat-i-Mardom and Junbish-i-Islami, left both the United Front and Electoral Union of Afghanistan, making themselves available to the highest and safest bidder. As the logic of alliance-building and fracturing outlined in Chapter 2 dictates, no one wanted to pick the losing team or be the one to gain the least from an alliance. Thus, network leaders and power brokers would wait to the last minute, cynically sizing up which candidate had the most convincing edge before throwing in their lot with them (Figure 5.6).

Using this logic, Mohaqqiq joined Abdullah's ticket as the second deputy when he failed to get a clear signal from President Karzai about who his favoured choice was. Arghandiwal stayed on and introduced Eng. Khan Mohammad, a former MP, Hizb commander and relative unknown, as the first deputy. This alienated other former Hizb members. His colleague, Qutbuddin Hilal, ran as an independent candidate while Ghairat Bahir (Hekmatyar's son-in-law) described Arghandiwal's decisions as personal, which had nothing to do with the party.[103] The Electoral Union of Afghanistan was divided between three tickets: (1) Ahmad Zia Masoud and his disgruntled ethnic Tajik network, who joined Zalmay Rasoul; (2) Abdullah, who was joined by Wahdat-i-Mardom leaders, Mohammad Mohaqqiq, and Khan Mohammad; and (3) Junbish-i-Islami and its leader Dostum joined Ashraf Ghani's ticket as first running-mate, in a surprise, and controversial, political manoeuvre. Ghani had once described Junbish-i-Islami leaders as a "known killer," but political expediency, and Junbish's ethnic vote bank, trumped past pugilism.[104] Karzai later argued privately that he made this choice not only to win but also to capitalise on Uzbek grievances by promoting them in the power hierarchy.[105] In a deal with Wahdat-i-Islami (Karim Khalil), he accepted Sarwar Danesh, a senior of Wahdat-i-Islami as his second running-mate. Other Pashtun technocrats, such as Hanif Atmar with his Rights and Justice network and Jalali, among others, joined the Ghani team. Pashtun networks such as Afghan Millet network leader, Anwar ul-Haq Ahadi, and other technocrats including Rahim Wardak, and Azizullah Ludin registered their candidacies. Qayum Karzai, the president Karzai's brother also registered with an ethnic Uzbek, Wahid Shahrani, along with Ibrahim Qasimi, a close ally of Sadiq Modabber, the leader of Ensejam-i-Milli network. Qasim Fahim, the powerful Jamiat commander, backed Abdullah in the campaign.

The 2014 election line-up had all the hallmarks of Karzai: the political architect and tactician. As the sitting president, he certainly had influence over electoral institutions and still had state resources under his control to engineer advantages for his favoured candidate (see also Chapter 7). Interviews with several Karzai insiders revealed that he encouraged the Junbish-i-Islami network to join Ashraf Ghani's team while he left the Wahdat-i-Mardom network guessing to the last minute, which then forced them to join the Abdullah team as a desperate last resort. Also, when the leader of Dawat-i-Islami leader Abdul Rasul Sayyaf proposed to run, Karzai apparently encouraged him to do so and persuaded Ismail Khan, the strongmen of Herat, to join his ticket. Evidently, Karzai kept his strategy ambiguous.[106] For instance, he indicated that his favourite candidate was his protégé, the Kandahar-born former minister of foreign affairs, Zalmai Rasoul.[107] But interviews with several key insiders suggest that he privately facilitated and lobbied the Junbish-i-Islami (ethnic Uzbek) and Wahdat-i-Islami (ethnic Hazara) to join the Ghani camp.[108] The only plausible explanation is that he wanted to "muddy the water to fish," as one Afghan proverb says, to strengthen his position in the post-2014 political environment. His political architectural design was such that it ensured the election went to the second round with no candidate winning a majority. Arguably, such a situation would have strengthened his hand and helped him remain relevant in a post-2014 Afghanistan where the U.S.A. had less influence and manpower, and whomever he backed would be dependent on his largesse. Thus, in the second round, and during the post-election crisis negotiations, there was ample evidence to suggest that he actively advocated for and favoured Ghani over Abdullah (see Figure 5.7 for the alliance formation during the elections).

5.10 The post-2014 election crisis: threat of coup and civil war

The 2014 electoral crisis, resulting from fraud, not only undermined the legitimacy of the Independent Election Commission and candidates, but also threatened to split the country along ethno-regionally contested lines. Just as in 2009, the 2014 elections were marred by accusations of "industrial-scale" fraud. The IEC's July 7 preliminary results put Ghani at 56.4% and Abdullah at 43.6%, which infuriated Abdullah's powerful supporters.[109] Allegations, verified by taped recordings, of ballot stuffing by Ghani's camp jeopardised the entire electoral exercise.[110] In July 2014, a faction of the National Directorate of Security leaked tape recordings in which Ziaulhaq Amarkhel, the then IEC Chief Executive Officer instructed IEC provincial directors and personnel to stuff-ballots for Ghani.[111] In one recording, Amarkhel instructs provincial staff to "take the sheep to the mountain and bring them stuffed," using the code term "stuffed sheep" as a reference to ballot boxes.[112] After immense national and international pressure, much to the dismay of Abdullah, only 1964 polling stations (out of the 20,561 nationwide) were audited and 810 recounted, with a total of 918 station results disqualified.[113] This became the core of the dispute between the candidates and gave the impression that Karzai-appointed IEC commissioners were favouring Ghani over Abdullah, widening the dispute along ethnic lines and agendas, between Pashtun-dominated state machinery that tried to maintain its grip on power at all costs versus an ethnic Tajik challenger.

In a political system in which elections produce a "winner-take-all" outcome—which goes against the logic of network politics and governance in Afghanistan—where the president and his cabinet have the power to appoint more than 2,000 positions nationwide, including mayors, district, and provincial governors as well as most of grade 1 and 2 directorates, there is no acceptable consolation prize. The system leaves very little for others to take credit for, especially when political parties are absent and can show little for their members and constituencies. As such, the stakes are higher for the loser. Thus, it logically makes sense for the losing side to aggravate and harden its position and challenge the results at all costs. This is exactly what happened during the 2009, 2014, and 2019 presidential elections.

By July, Abdullah's supporters, including some hardliners like former National Security Agency (NSA) Director, Amrullah Saleh, threatened to form a parallel government.[114] Prior to this, on June 27, in the second such protests, Abdullah's supporters organised massive demonstrations in the city, blocking roads and demanding elections fraud be addressed. A few days after the demonstrations, there was a serious threat of violence and, by many accounts, a real risk of some kind of soft coup with the formation of a parallel government.[115] Reportedly, some armed groups supporting Abdullah began to seize government centres in three provinces north of Kabul and threatened to storm government offices in the capital, including the presidential palace.[116] Conversations with several senior officials close to Abdullah revealed that there was a last-minute phone call by President Obama warning Abdullah and his supporters to back down.[117] With the threat of all-out chaos looming, the U.S. Secretary of State, John Kerry, was forced to make three unannounced visits to Kabul to resolve the dispute.[118] According to some sources, he made over 30 phone calls to top Afghan officials after the run-off vote.[119] Also, President Obama called each of the candidates three times.[120] The bulk of

Abdullah's network resources for the use of violence were concentrated in Kabul and its surrounding provinces to the north, as explained in detail in the previous chapters. He had the military capacity and financial resources to stage a coup and mobilise his majority ethnic Tajik and Hazara supporters within the city, Kabul's historical vulnerability that had led to the quick collapse of governments in the past.

The political compromise was the formation of the NUG—with Abdullah as the "Chief Executive Officer (CEO)" after more than three months of horse-trading and negotiations. On 21 September 2014, both leaders signed the National Unity Government Agreement, committing to a "genuine and meaningful partnership" to govern together.[121] Later the same day, the IEC announced Ghani as President but not the official "winner" under immense pressure from Abdullah's camp.[122] The Agreement committing them to govern together included an "equitable" distribution of ministerial appointments and other key positions in Kabul and subnational administrations, the holding of a Loya Jirga in two years for legalising the position of CEO, and reforming the electoral as well as other laws.[123]

Conclusion

During his two terms in office, President Karzai and the political networks firmly consolidated a regime state. Karzai and his allies occupied powerful government positions, using their formal state positions and state institutions, along with informal power brokers, to extend their authority throughout Afghanistan. Karzai orchestrated a power balance amongst and between political networks in which he acted as "patron" within the political system. From 2010 to 2014, he further consolidated institutional settings (rules of the game) within which political networks entrenched their dominance within the state, as the playing field. The period from 2005 to the 2009 presidential election can largely be explained in terms of active state network extension by Karzai, on the one hand, and efforts by competing political networks to transform themselves into successful patronage, family-based, and ethno-regional client networks, on the other. Steadily, a new informal political order emerged in which the political networks' sphere of influence within and outside the state became sharper and more transparent. Subsequently, Karzai extended authority by relying on some of the former patronage and family-based networks, who largely acted as mediator clients, to maintain a complex patronage system connecting commanders, tribal leaders, and local power brokers. As detailed, these patronage connections functioned both ways, from top to bottom and vice versa.

Karzai's 12.5 year presidency was closely entangled with the American military, diplomatic, and financial support. From 2005, Karzai would come under constant criticism by the U.S.A. and its allies for failing to go after corrupt officials and networks. During his second term, after the 2009 presidential elections, Karzai became deeply opposed to the Americans, seeing American's hand in everything that threatened to undermine him. There was certainly some truth to this as the Americans did spread rumours about some of his damaging habits, which included the rumour that his behaviour was erratic

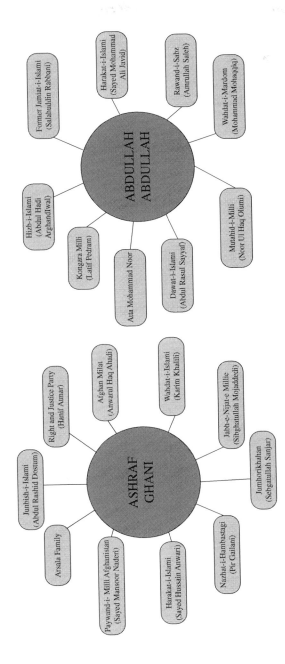

Figure 5.7 The 2014 presidential election alliances.

because of a hashish dependency.[124] Towards the end of his administration, Karzai told *The Atlantic* magazine: "I didn't see a war in Afghanistan—I saw a conspiracy. And my effort was to repel the conspiracy in which Afghan blood was shed. So, my purposes were different from those of the Americans and NATO."[125] His successor, inheriting a National Unity Government in which he had to share power, would struggle to counter the entrenched networks and transform the established rules of the game in his mission to strengthen formal state institutions. He tried to rely on international support, which was not often forthcoming. He would disrupt the foundation of the informal political order and rules of the game prematurely, before strengthening his position within the state, mobilising political networks against him while he was still vulnerable. As the next chapter shows, the disastrous power-sharing agreement would become the primary cause of tension between the two political camps, disrupting the carefully engineered political order formed under Karzai and subsequently producing immense political disorder and instability within the Afghan state at a time when the Taliban, driven by the 2014 U.S.-led NATO military exit, was intensifying its insurgency.

Notes

1   The "Empire of Mud" title was used by Antonio Giustozzi for his book, *Empires of Mud: Wars and Warlords in Afghanistan.*
2   Schmitt and Gall (2004).
3   Watson, P (2004).
4   UNODC (2004).
5   "Karzai: A Lame Duck President." U.S. Diplomatic Cables, July 17, 2006, https://wikileaks.org/plusd/cables/06KABUL3198_a.html.
6   Mashal (2014).
7   See Reynold and Wilder (2004) for details of the logistical challenges the election faced.
8   The Joint Electoral Management Body was an 11-member hybrid body, consisting of six Afghan members appointed by the president and five international experts selected by the UN Special Representative of the Secretary-General to plan and implement the election process. For the final list see Afghanistan 2004 Presidential Election Results, IEC, http://www.iec.org.af/public_html/Election%20Results%20Website/english/english.htm, 3 November 2004.
9   "Afghanistan 2004 Presidential Election Results." IEC, November 3, 2004, http://www.iec.org.af/public_html/Election%20Results%20Website/english/english.htm.
10   Watson, P. 2004. "U.S. Hand Seen in Afghan Election." *Los Angeles Times*, September 23, 2004. According to the same article, one of the candidates, Mohammad Mohaqiq, accused Khalilzad of putting immense pressure on him to quit. He even facilitated negotiations with the palace to agree to a deal in which he would be offered two ministerial positions, two deputy minister spots in other ministries, and one governorship. The negotiations eventually collapsed.
11   Author's conversation with Mohaqqiq and some of the people in Junbish central political committee.
12   See Bijlert (2009); Wilder (2005).
13   Author's Interview, Kabul, September 14, 2009.
14   See Gompelman (2001).

15 Jamil Karzai is the president's nephew who acted in parliament more as a salesman with minor influence than a power broker.

16 International Crisis Group (2005).

17 Presidential Office, press release, April 1, 2005, In *Anis* (Kabul), April 2, 2005.

18 "Head of Afghan Opposition Front Outlines Platform, Goals, Membership." In *Anis* (Kabul), April 6, 2005.

19 Ibid.

20 Ibid.

21 See International Crisis Group (2005) for detail of these coalitions and parties.

22 National Democratic Institute Report (2005).

23 An interview carried out by International Crisis Group in 2005 with Joint Electoral Monitoring Body chairperson Bissmillah Bissmil revealed that, at the time, he admitted that there was widespread dissatisfaction with the allotment of seats but defended the process in light of the difficult circumstances and lack of time. ICG (2005).

24 National Democratic Institute Report (2005).

25 Wilder (2005)

26 Ibid 6.

27 National Democratic Institute Report (2005).

28 Ibid

29 Ibid.

30 With the delay in district council elections, on October 27, 2005, the Cabinet passed a decree in which two members from the Upper House were elected from each provincial council and on December 11, 2005, President Karzai announced his 34 appointees. For the percentage of ethnic composition see National Democratic Institute Report (2005).

31 See Bijlert (2009).

32 Author's interview and observations, August 2011. Many saw this as a betrayal as Sayyaf was responsible for starting the civil war against Wahdat in the 1990s and had committed atrocities against the Hazara Shia community in West Kabul.

33 He was also related to Karzai's family as his sister was reportedly married to Karzai's younger brother.

34 "Karzai's Ineffective Parliamentary Outreach." U.S. Embassy Cable. October 6, 2008.

35 Ibid.

36 Background Briefing: Wolesi Jirga and Provincial Council Elections 2005, JEMBS.

37 Article 139 of the constitution stipulates that "the provincial council takes part in securing the developmental targets of the state and improving its affairs ... advises on important issues falling within the domain of the province ... performs its duties in cooperation with the provincial administration." The 2005 Provincial Council Law left the councils' authorities vague by noting that the councils work at the provincial level with the "purpose of establishing a system that guarantees the participation of the people and civil society in local governance and that gives advice to the local governmental institutions." It did not clarify how the PCs would take part in provincial affairs (e.g., security, development planning, budgeting, and oversight). However, after intense lobbying in 2014, they gained oversight authority and by 2019, when the author left IDLG, their power and privileges, including their budget, had expanded significantly. See below section.

38 Author's fieldwork visits to Nangahar in 2012.

39 See Mukhopadhyay (2014); Foschini (2011).

40 Author's interview, Jalalabad city, April 12, 2012. Also, see Pajhwok Afghan News. 2012. "Traders Seek Action against Extortionist Gunmen." January 16, 2012. The news reported that 30 to 40 men stormed the factory belonging to Haji Farough, destroying machines and injuring workers. Haji Farough then accused Haji Jamal,

claiming: "The Council Head is involved in taking extortion money from traders. Anyone refusing to pay extortion will meet the same fate as I did."

41 Pajhwok Afghan News. 2012. "Ex-Head of Provincial Council Arrested in Nangarhar." March 12, 2012.

42 Ibid.

43 As one MP from the Ahmadzai tribe described, "These incidents happen all the time. The Khugyani and Mohmand tribal dispute was over a Khugyani purchasing land in the Mohmand district. Haji Zahir used this issue to create rife between the two tribes. They manipulated the elders. It was an attempt to create chaos and instability and a way to find an excuse to threaten the governor Shirzai. The underlying incentive for these powerbrokers is economics." Author's interview, April 12, 2012. There were several other rounds of high-profile protests against governor Shirzai orchestrated by his opponents. The first was in 2011 after an attack on Kabul Bank by the Taliban for which the Haji Zahir, Hazrat Ali and other rivals spurred protests. The last was in April 2013 with protestors blocking the major roads, accusing him of land grab and allowing the infiltration of Pakistani military into the border districts. For more details see Foschini and Ali (2013); Jackson (2014).

44 There were several attempts by Governor Noor's rival to try to unseat him. In March 2006, representatives of four main parties (Junbish, Wahdat, Hizb, and others) met with Karzai and U.S. embassy officials stressing the need to replace Governor Noor, even threatening a civil war in the province. None of these threats paid off.

45 Author's interview, April 21, 2012.

46 See Sharan (2014).

47 Leslie (2015).

48 Foschini (2013).

49 Author's collection of data at IDLG. The same list of cases must exist in AGO central Office in Kabul.

50 Author's conversation with a senior Junbish official and Mohammad Mohaqqiq, Kabul, February 2010.

51 "More Fractures in the United Front." US Embassy Cables. 2009. March 10, 2009,

52 Ibid.

53 Wafa (2008). Bai was a former Dostum ally who broke away in 2007, setting up his party, the Turkic Council of Afghanistan.

54 Author's interview with senior Junbish officials, Kabul, May 5–6, 2020.

55 "Shirzai Aide Claims Karzai Strong-Arms Shirzai out of the Race." US Embassy Cables. 2 May 2009,

56 Reportedly, a last-minute deal was reached between Karzai, Mohaqqiq, and Dostum in which they had agreed on the number of cabinet seats, governor positions, and a reform package. Author's interview with Mohaqqiq and other Junbish officials, Kabul, May 5–6, 2020.

57 https://wikileaks.org/plusd/cables/09KABUL789_a.html.

58 "Karzai-Massoud Tensions Highlight Executive Authority Disagreement." US Embassy Cables. February 20, 2009,

59 "IEC Final Certified Presidential Results." Independent Election Commission Website, May 10, 2020,

60 See Chapter 7 for details of these interventions.

61 Boone, J. 2009. "Afghan Election Chaos as Abdullah Pulls Out of Run-Off." *The Guardian*, November 1, 2009.

62 "Karzai Declared Elected President of Afghanistan." CNN, November 2, 2009; "Afghanistan Election Challenger Abdullah Abdullah Pulls Out of Runoff." *The Guardian*, November 1, 2009,

63 These ranged from pressure by the U.S.A., to getting paid up to US$50 million by Kabul Bank, to payments by the European Union of US$16 million. The Karzai team explained that the president was unwilling to make the necessary compromises. It is argued that Abdullah knew the odds were against him, especially with a pro-Karzai Election Commission and no measure in place to reduce widespread fraud (see Chapter 7).

64 Boone, *The Guardian*, November 1, 2009.

65 CNN, November 2, 2009.

66 Brulliard, K. 2009. "In Nod to the U.S., Karzai to Keep Current Ministers in Top Cabinet Jobs." *Washington Post*, December 19, 2009. Dadfar Spanta was left in his position and unlike other sitting ministers was not on the list sent to the parliament.

67 Chatterjee, P. 2009. "Afghanistan: Paying Off Warlords, Anatomy of an Afghan Culture of Corruption." *TomDispatch*, November 17, 2009.

68 "Parliament Rejects Most of Karzai's Cabinet Nominees." U.S. Embassy Cables, January 3, 2010,

69 "Karzai: A Lame Duck President." U.S. Embassy Cables, July 17, 2006,

70 Partlow, J., and C. Whitlock. 2011. "Karzai Demands NATO Stop Bombing Homes." *Washington Post*, May 31, 2011.

71 Also, see Rosenberg, M., and H. Cooper. 2012. "Karzai Lashes Out at NATO over Deaths." March 16, 2012; see also the Human Rights Watch report on abusive night raids carried out by the U.S.A., "They've Shot Many Like This: Abusive Night Raids by CIA-Backed Afghan Strike Forces," October 2019.

72 Sukhanyar and Norland (2014).

73 It seems Karzai suspected something as early as March 2009. According to a U.S. diplomatic cable leaked to WikiLeaks, on March 25, 2009, Karzai confronted Deputy Special Representative Paul Jones about rumours that the U.S.A. was backing one of his opponents and that it had two objectives: (1) to create and support an opponent to him; and (2) to divide the Pashtun vote ("Karzai Raises Questions on U.S. Role in Afghan Election", U.S. Embassy Cables. March 25, 2009).

74 Gates (2014).

75 Most Wikileak cables related to Hamid Karzai and portray him as weak, corrupt, and prone to believing in conspiracy theories.

76 See Afghanistan Analysts Network (2013) documenting the details of the last day of the Jirga. For a copy of the BSA document, see the UN Afghanistan website (https://www .afghanistan-un.org/wp-content/uploads/2012/05/AFGAN-US-PartnershipEnglish .pdf). Retrieved April 5, 2020.

77 Eide (2014).

78 Neumann (2015).

79 Article 64 of the Constitution.

80 See World Bank, "Service Delivery and Governance at the Sub-National Level in Afghanistan"; The Asia Foundation, "An Assessment of Subnational Governance in Afghanistan".

81 According to several international staff working on the stabilisation program the U.S.A. wanted to set up these offices, with connections to the U.S. embassy, not only to limit the power of the President by appointing professional staff but also as a platform separate from the Palace which they could use to successfully conduct their massive stabilisation initiative through provincial governors' offices.

82 In 2019, before my resignation, the Independent Directorate of Local Governance (IDLG) was responsible for 34 provincial governor offices, 34 provincial councils' offices (420 plus representatives), 387 district governor offices (364 official districts and the rest yet to receive parliament's approval), and more than 165 municipalities, not to mention 450,000+ formally registered villages in the country with IDLG approving the selection of village representatives.

83   Internal Independent Directorate of Local Governance document.
84   Bijlert, (2009).
85   Mashal, M. 2014. "The Men Who Run Afghanistan." *The Atlantic*. June 23, 2014.
86   Office of National Budget Annual 2010–11 Report. Afghanistan Ministry of Finance.
87   Author's Interview, December 4, 2010.
88   "Hamid Karzai Admits Office Gets 'Bags of Money' from Iran." *The Guardian*, 25 October 2020.
89   Rosenberg (2013).
90   Article 84 of the Constitution.
91   After much debate, on October 27, the cabinet passed the decree in which two Meshrano Jirga members were elected from each provincial council during their elections in early November 2005.
92   Karzai (1988).
93   See Ruttig (2011).
94   See Afghanistan Independent Human Rights Commission Reports.
95   Ibid.
96   Coghlan (2009).
97   See Beath, Christia and Enikolopov (2015).
98   Hewad (2011).
99   See Ruttig (2012).
100 Ibid.
101 Hewad and Ruttig (2013).
102 Ibid.
103 Kakar, J. H. 2013. "Hezb-i-Islami Hekmatyar Faaliyat haye Arghandiwal va Helal ra Shakhsi Khand." *Pajhwok News*, September 28, 2013.
104 Ghani (2009).
105 Sakhi (2014).
106 Author's conversation with several of these leaders reveals that some of them were waiting for Karzai's signal, which never arrived. This pushed them to join Abdullah Abdullah's campaign as his second vice president candidate.
107 According to Radio Azadi, at the side lines of the Shanghai Cooperation Organisation (SCO) summit in the Kyrghyz capital Bishkek on September 13, 2013, Karzai told Putin that one possible presidential candidate with them in the room, which many took as a signal for Karzai's support for Zalmai Rasoul. In a recent interview with *BBC Persian*, he revealed that he had voted for Ashraf Ghani. BBC Persian, "BBC Exclusive Interview with Hamid Karzai."
108 Hewad and Clark (2013).
109 "IEC Announces Preliminary Results of the 2014 Presidential Election Run-Off", press release, IEC, July 7, 2014. For a more detail insight leading up to the result announcement see Asia Briefing N°260, Afghanistan's Political Transition, October 16, 2016.
110 Rosenberg and Ahmad (2014).
111 Graham-Harrison, E. 2014. "Afghan Election Crisis: 'Stuffed Sheep' Recordings Suggest Large-Scale Fraud." *The Guardian*, June 22, 2014.
112 Ibid.
113 International Crisis Group report (2016).
114 Ahmad, A. 2014. "Afghan Candidate Stops Short of Forming Government." *New York Times*, July 8, 2014.
115 Aziz and Harooni (2014).
116 Gall and Rosenberg (2014).
117 Author's interview with people close to Abdullah, Karzai, and Ghani, Kabul, November 2014.

118 The first trip was on 12 July right after the mechanisms for the audit was proposed by IEC.
119 Norland (2014).
120 The U.S. Ambassador, James B. Cunningham and other American diplomats had met Ghani 39 times and Abdullah 42 times and Karzai 15 times to broker the deal. Ibid.
121 The Agreement was signed by Ashraf Ghani and Abdullah Abdullah and witnessed by UN Special Representative for the Secretary-General, Jan Kubis, and U.S. Ambassador James Cunningham. Those close to Karzai, as well as Karzai himself, privately accused the Americans of achieving their wish in creating a prime minister's position to weaken the power of the president. Karzai alleged that this was an American's plan in the making since the disputed 2009 presidential elections, hatched by Richard Holbrooke to ensure a weak presidency. Also, some of the former Jamiat leaders had advocated for the creation of a strong executive position since the 2003 Loya Jirga with the calculation that the position would most likely go to an ethnic Tajik from their group as the second dominant political force in the country. See "Balkh Governor Atta on Possible Karzai-Abdullah Power-Sharing Arrangements." U.S. Embassy Cable. 2009. October 16, 2009.
122 IEC Press Release, "IEC Announces Results of the 2014 Presidential Election Run-Off", IEC, September 21, 2014; Clark, K. 2014. "Elections 2014 (51): Finally, a Deal, but not yet Democracy." AAN, September 21, 2014.
123 U.S. Embassy "Agreement between the Two Campaign Teams Regarding the Structure of the National Unity Government." Kabul, July 12, 2014. The Agreement was signed by both leaders in front of the UN Secretary-General Jan Kubis and U.S. Ambassador James Cunningham. The Agreement was released by the U.S. Embassy on September 21, 2014.
124 Conversation with two diplomats in July 2016.
125 Mashal (2014).

6   The National Unity Government

Political order disruption and strains

Introduction

It was a blistering hot summer day in August 2017 as we started our lunch meeting on the fifth floor of the Independent Directorate of Local Governance (IDLG). The bursts of cool air from the air conditioner and the shade from the towering pine trees that encircled our office building were a welcome comfort. The three ministers, two deputies, and I were gathered to discuss the drafting process for the new municipality law. This was the president's latest policy reform fixation: reforming subnational administrations. In the two and half years of my assignment, I had witnessed up close how President Ghani's infatuation and passion frequently jumped from one reform agenda to another—often without seeing them through. His was a grand vision on paper but a jumble of unfinished business in reality or, as one Afghan colleague summed it up to me, using an Afghan proverb: "wetting a hundred heads but shaving one (*Sad sar ra tar kard, yak sar ra kal*)."

The technical discussion was short but productive, followed by lunch. The meal was sumptuous—a stark contrast to the less than 50 Afghani (just over 75%) daily food allowance in 2017 that government employees were allotted. Embedded in a strict culture of hospitality, an official's status and power were measured among his peers and subordinates by the quality of his food menu, among other things. Over lunch, at first with a bit of humour, one of the ministers complained about the worsening pain in his left arm and shoulder and talked about his recent visit to the doctor, who had prescribed anti-stress and anxiety medication. Sympathising with him, the other minister complained that he wasn't getting enough sleep because of the stresses of his job, brought on by the endless demands of the president and constant smear campaigns by his disruptive inner circle. By then, over two years into the presidency, many of his ministers and officials had accepted as normal President Ghani's behaviour of belittling and scorning them. A damning *Washington Post* profile characterised the president as an "autocratic micromanager" and a "remote academic with no feel for the common man," a perception reinforced by his opponents.[1]

Isolated within the palace walls, President Ghani prided himself on his long working hours—according to some 15–18 hours a day with a two-hour nap break

DOI: 10.4324/9781315161617-6

during the day—while disdaining his ministers for being incompetent, or not trying hard enough. Once he gave a presentation about local governance to 360-plus district governors who were in Kabul to attend the annual district governors' conference. At the end of his presentation, he proposed a series of governance-related questions and asked them to formally answer them in writing the next day. Two days later, on the final day of the conference, to everyone's surprise, he presented key trends, similarities, and differences by reading more than 4,500 pages—an unnecessary exercise that could have been left to subordinates at a time when the Kunduz Province was on the brink of collapse. This was just more evidence of what people perceived as his intellectual arrogance—not listening to or consulting with others—for which he had come under criticism, along with his elitist attitude towards everyday people. In a BBC interview, he once said: "I have no sympathy" for people fleeing the country after the 2014 crisis, when it seemed like Afghanistan would again spiral into civil war. They were guilty of "breaking the social contract,"[2] he claimed.

As the ministers' conversation continued, what struck me as illustrative of where Afghanistan was at that moment, which I also found deeply unsettling, was that its leaders had become consumed by how to gratify and entertain the president, one man among the many responsible for governing the country. Missing from these interminable internal dialogues was *the people* and how to serve them best. What was absent were fundamental questions of security and governance, the same issues that received so much lip service in their public rhetoric.

A few months later in May 2018, I found myself presenting the newly drafted subnational reform roadmap, titled Citizen-Centred Governance: A Roadmap for Subnational Reform, in a cabinet meeting. As I was walking towards the *Char Chinar* building where cabinet meetings were held, I ran into three young cabinet members. We briefly talked about a number of issues including the president's recent angry outburst. Looking at the cabinet agenda, one of them said: "Who should we pick on in today's meeting?"

At the time, I didn't pay much attention to the importance of this conversation. A few days later, at a dinner gathering, I listened to the same individuals boasting about the ingenious methods they employed to influence discussions during high profile meetings in an effort to elicit a negative reaction from the president against specific officials. It seemed that on this occasion, they succeeded in manipulating the president, from what they claimed, into disgracing the mayor of Kabul in front of his cabinet colleagues. When I probed, one of them explained how the president was easily triggered when references were made to specific topics and themes, in the case of the mayor by referring to the land and waste management failure. Apparently, once while flying over Kabul city, irritated with the mayor, the president had complained about the city's pollution and bad smell.

The incident, like the lunchtime conversation, was illuminating. Both demonstrated the degree to which governing within the highest echelon of power had become an exercise in manipulation and callous backstabbing, as key rules of the game for survival, and the degree to which Afghanistan's politicians were obsessed with securing their own positions.

This poisoned atmosphere reached new heights during the Ghani period. This chapter details the key events, power dynamics, tensions, and political network infightings during that time, from 2014 to the post-2019 presidential election's power-sharing agreement between Ghani and Abdullah Abdullah. It shows how the National Unity Government (NUG) was plagued by divisions, intimidation, and backstabbing which produced considerable dysfunction and political infighting. President Ghani's inconsistent reform agenda and ineffective management, particularly when it came to political networks and centres of power, undermined his grand vision to transform the Afghan state. His inability to trust others put him in a vulnerable position, especially when facing a shrinking power base from 2018 onwards. While the few who had the president's ear felt empowered to effortlessly manipulate him to their advantage—a small group of "yes-men" (and they were mostly men)—others' time and zeal were consumed by day-to-day crisis management, anxiety, and fear: fear of being humiliated in front of colleagues and subordinates for uttering the wrong idea or proposing a different recommendation to the one considered correct by the president.

From 2014 to the collapse of the Republic in August 2021, President Ghani called most of the shots and often dictated terms, often unsuccessfully. This chapter is therefore seen mainly through the lens of President Ghani's strategies, policies, and actions, applying four different prisms through which we may interpret them: First is Ghani-as-reformist, allied with young technocrats versus the old guards. In this guise, Ghani depicted himself as advancing along the same path as the reformist king, Amanullah Khan. He often made references to the "unfinished chapters" of Amanullah's reform agenda and his obligation to complete them.[3] Second, Ghani-as-visionary, who offered a vision for the future from Kabul to many officials and echelons of the state but failed to translate it into practice. As this chapter shows, he overpromised and underdelivered. Third, Ghani-as-nationalist, utilising populist rhetoric to appeal to urban, youth, and female constituencies in Afghanistan. This put him at odds with his fourth guise: Ghani-as-ethnocentric leader. As this chapter demonstrates, he was not shy of openly pursuing a policy of ethnic favouritism, favouring his ethnic Pashtun group in appointments and other privileges, and within them the Ghilzai tribal confederations. The latter was exacerbated by the structure of the NUG, which divided the government into two rigid political camps in which he saw himself as representing mainly the ethnic Pashtun constituency and the "patron" of ethnic Pashtun political networks while Abdullah represented mainly the ethnic Tajik, in particular the Panjshiris, and the interests of political networks north of Kabul.

This chapter proceeds as follows: Section 6.1 highlights political network restructuring as a result of the NUG power-sharing agreement as well as President Ghani's monopolisation of power around his Office (Section 6.2) and his attempt to sideline former jihadi networks in Kabul and the provinces (Section 6.3). This is followed by a section on the underlying sources of tensions within the NUG which exacerbated distrust and infighting. Section 6.5 examines the impact of ethnic polarisation and factionalism within political networks, and how this reverberated through the political order and affected the balance of power. Section 6.6 details the emergence of two important youth protest movements and President Ghani and his associates' attempts to crush them—a turning point after which protesters took shelter with traditional leaders. The subsequent two sections assess the NUG's relations with the legislature and opposition groups, including those within the administration. The final section highlights the post-2019 presidential election crisis, the impact of the agreed-upon power-sharing settlement on political network dynamics and infighting within them.

6.1 NUG power-sharing, ethnicity, and political network restructuring

The 2014 elections and the formation of the NUG—led by Ghani and Abdullah—facilitated a serious disruption in the power dynamics of political networks. The NUG agreement signed between the two camps was essentially intra-elite bargaining in a limited access order framework, whereby privileges were divided as incentives for political networks with access to state riches to avoid engaging in conflict with each other over spoils. The division of spoils was in full display in the appointment of cabinet members, governors, and other senior government officials behind the scenes immediately after the formation of the NUG. The cabinet became the source of intense competition between rival networks that had delivered votes and were now demanding state positions. The first 100 days of the NUG stalemate was a power struggle not just between the two camps centred around President Ghani and CEO Abdullah but also an internal power struggle *within* these camps over the distribution of state assets and privileges.

Under immense pressure, the new government finally settled on a list of 26 cabinet nominees (to be approved by Parliament) in November 2014, two months after the agreement of the NUG. Table 6.1 provides a list of 26 first-round cabinet nominees (including the ministries they were nominated to, the nominees' ethnic background, and their political patrons). Ashraf Ghani mostly nominated Ghilzai Pashtun elites, most with a civil society background and a Western education. Similarly (but not surprisingly), Abdullah Abdullah's own choice of nominees was biased towards Panjshiri and northern Kabul network members. Abdullah was under pressure from his camp—especially former Jamiatis, Mohaqqiq's Wahdat Mardom, and Arghandiwal's Hezb-i-Islami—to appoint their affiliates to cabinet posts. While he was successful in nominating the leader of Jamiat-i-Islami, Salahuddin Rabbani, to the post of Foreign Minister, Abdullah tried but failed to nominate two aides—both ethnic Tajiks from Panjshir province—for the post of Interior Minister. Ashraf Ghani was reported to have used his presidential veto to reject the candidates, arguing they lacked the necessary qualifications and expertise. The main grievance, however, was that the president did not want to appoint a Panjshiri as Minister of Interior, the one senior security position usually held by former Shura-i-Nezar commanders, with Abdullah's main choice being Atiq Baryalai. Abdullah had to settle with Nurul Haq Ulumi, a former communist, and one of the few ethnic Pashtun aides in his camp for the post.

Table 6.1 First round of cabinet nominees

Full name	Ministry	Ethnicity	Nominated by
Noor-ul-Haq Ulumi	Interior	Pashtun	Abdullah/former Communist Parchami/Abdullah
Sher M. Karimi	Defence	Pashtun	Ghani, former Communist Parchami
Salahuddin Rabbani	Foreign Affairs	Tajik	Abdulah/Jamiat leader
Eklil Hakimi	Finance	Pashtun	Ghani
Seyar Mahjoor	Justice	Pashtun	Abdullah
Mohd. Zalmai Yonusi	Education	Tajik	Abdullah—Atta M. Noor
Najiba Ayoubi	Women Affairs	Tajik	Ghani/Killid Group NGO
Firozuddin Firoz	Public Health	Tajik	Abdullah
M. Yaqub Haidari	Agriculture	Tajik	Abdullah—The Greater Council of North
M. Rahmanoghli	Economy	Uzbek	Abdullah
Ai Sultan Khairi	Information & Culture	Uzbek	Ghnai—Dostum
Faiz M. Osmani	Haj and Islamic Affairs	Turkmen	Ghani—Dostum
Nasir Durani	Rural Development	Pashtun	Abdullah—Mohammad Khan
Abbas Basir	Public Work	Hazara	Ghani—Karim Khalili
Faizullah Kargar	Counter-narcotics	Pashtun	Ghani
S.Hossain Alemi Balkhi	Refugees & Repatriation	Hazara	Abdullah—Mohaqqiq
Daod Shah Saba	Mines	Pashtun	Ghani
Qamaruddin Shinwari	Borders & Tribal Affairs	Pashtun	Ghani—Eastern Council of Tribes
Khatira Afghan	Higher Education	Pashtun	Ghani—Hekmat Karzai
A. Rahman Salahi	Energy & Water	Tajik	Abdullah—Herat/Jamiat
Barna Karimi	Communication	Hazara	Abdullah—Mohaqqiq
Sardar M. Rahimi	Industry & Commerce	Hazara	Abdullah—Mohaqqiq
Saadat M. Naderi	Labour, Social Affairs, Martyred, & Disabled	Hazara	Ghani—Sayed Mansoor Naderi family
Faizullah Zaki	Transport and Aviation	Uzbek	Ghani—Dostum
Shah Zaman Maiwandi	Rural Rehabilitation	Pashtun	Ghani—Noorzai
Rahmatullah Nabil	National Directorate of Security	Pashtun	Ghani—remained in his position (close Hamid Karzai)
Khalil Seddiq	Afghanistan Bank	Pashtun	Ghani

On 28 January 2015, the Lower House (*Wolesi Jirga*) approved only nine of the 27 cabinet nominees, including the head of Afghan Intelligence, Rahmatullah Nabil. In the final vote, the two ethnic Uzbek ministers and four ethnic Hazara ministers were all rejected, and the position of Ministry of Defence was left vacant. There were several reasons for the mass rejections. First, most MPs felt disappointed when NUG leaders failed to consult them on the list of nominees.[4] Second, Ghani put himself on a collision course with MPs when, during his 2014 inauguration speech, he directly criticised MPs for intervening in the key operations of the government, including "recommending employment, or [asking] to discharge or transfer staff within state institutions."[5] MPs were angry about the president's public criticism of them so early on in his administration, which was interpreted as signalling a serious change in the rules of the game. A February 2015 survey found that 59% and 70% of MPs were "dissatisfied" or "somewhat dissatisfied" with President Ghani and CEO Abdullah, respectively.[6] Third, and arguably, the most important reason for parliamentary discontent was the lack of bargains offered by most ministerial candidates. While some of the nominees dodged offering promises of jobs, projects, contracts, and positions to MPs, others, especially those with less funding and ministry projects, didn't spend money in return for votes—or their network patrons couldn't afford the huge sums of money required to purchase votes (see Chapter 8 for detailed operations of bargains in the House).

It took Ghani and Abdullah and their camps another four months to agree to the list of the remaining 16 cabinet nominees, on the eve of the Persian New Year, 21 March 2015. There was no deal agreed upon for the Ministry of Defence as the two leaders could not reach a compromise. It was believed that Abdullah was willing to make a compromise to let Ghani have his minister if he was willing to trade the Supreme Court *and* the Chief of Military Staff positions. Table 6.2 provides the list of the second round cabinet nominees.[7] The list reveals that Ghani was more accommodating and had softened his position towards Jamiat, Wahdat, Junbish, and Hezb-i-Islami patronage networks. A major feature of the NUG's five-year term would be that the government was run by acting ministers, who hardly saw themselves accountable to the legislature. Before the 2019 presidential elections, 15 ministers were acting, including the ministry of defence, interior, foreign, and finance.[8]

Overall, in the cabinet and other key positions, the balance of power tilted towards Western-educated and civil society networked elites most closely allied with Ghani during the elections—all ethnic Pashtuns and either technocrats or joining from the non-governmental organisations (NGO) sector. In the initial years, the traditional religious authorities and family-based networks led by Ishaq Gailani, Abdul Rasul Sayyaf, and Mojadaddi were sidelined. It was only after tensions between Abdullah and Ghani intensified in 2016 that the president made amends with them and his relations with Sayyaf improved. Ghani also appointed technocrats as governors in the major provinces of Herat, Kandahar, Kunar, Nangarhar, Kunduz, and others, positions usually offered to well-connected political network clients. As explained below, most of them failed to perform satisfactorily.[9]

The structure of NUG led to further ethnicisation of Afghan politics. Ghani's decision to appoint mainly fellow Pashtuns, and amongst them mainly Ghilzai

Table 6.2 Second round cabinet nominees

Full name	Ministry	Ethnicity	Nominated by
Abdul Raziq Wahidi	Telecommunication	Hazara	Abdullah—Mohaqqiq
Mahmood Baligh	Public Works	Hazara	Ghani, Danesh—Omran Group
Homayoon Rasa	Industry & Commerce	Hazara	Abdullah—Mohaqqiq
Abdul Bari Jahani	Culture & Information	Pashtun	Ghani
Asadullah Zamir	Agriculture & Livestock	Pashtun	Ghani—Ahmad Zia Masoud
M. Gulab Mangal	Borders & Tribal Affairs	Pashtun	Ghani
Abdul Sattar Murad	Economy	Tajik	Abdullah—Jamiat—The Greater Council of North
Mohamadullah Batash	Transportation and Aviation	Uzbek	Ghani—Dostum
Asadullah Hanif Balkhi	Education	Tajik	Abdullah—Governor Noor
Sa'adat Mansoor Naderi	Rural Rehabilitation	Hazara (Ismaili)	Ghani—Sayed Mansoor Naderi
Abdul Basir Anwar	Justice	Pashtun	Abdullah—Mohammad Khan
Salamat Azimi	Counter-narcotics	Uzbek	Ghani—Dostum
Farida Momand	Higher Education	Pashtun	Ghani—Hekmat Karzai
Nasrin Oriakhil	Labour, Social Affairs, Martyred, & Disabled	Pashtun	Ghani—The First Lady
Ali Ahmad Osmani	Energy & Water	Tajik	Abdullah—Herat
Dilbar Nazari	Women's Affairs	Uzbek	Abdullah—Governor Noor

Pashtuns, to positions of power and authority was perceived as ethnic bias. Almost all of the key positions around the president's office, including within his Administrative Office of the President, National Security Council (NSC), IDLG, and Chief of Staff, were ethnic Pashtuns.[10] Abdullah, on the other hand, appeared to favour fellow Tajiks over Pashtuns. Figure 6.1 charts the ethnic composition of staff in key administrative offices, including the Office of Administrative Affairs (OAA), the CEO's Office, Mohaqqiq's Office, and a list of presidential advisory posts at the end of 2015.[11] The clearest example of this ethnic fracturing is evident in the composition of the Administrative Office of the President (AOP). In the months after the 2014 elections, Ashraf Ghani appointed several of his network members to the AOP. A quick scan of its ethnic and ideological composition reveals a clear bias towards technocratic Ghilzai Pashtuns: 75% (or 21 appointees) versus 14% (or four appointees) ethnic Tajiks. To the presidential advisory posts, too, Ghani appointed mostly people of Pashtun origin: 69% (or 22 appointees) versus 19% (or six appointees) Tajik. Similarly, with Abdullah, cabinet nominations and appointees to the CEO's Office indicate a favouring of Tajik jihadis. However, at the CEO's Office,

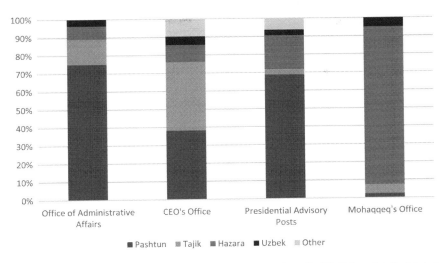

Figure 6.1 Ethnic composition of key administrative offices (in %) (More detailed data is included in the appendices (appendices 1, 2, and 3) to this study.)

Pashtun and Tajik appointees were equal in number at eight (or 38% each). And yet, Mohammad Mohaqqiq, too, appointed a majority of ethnic Hazara aides—87.5%, in fact—to his own office. This was the case across all sectors of the Afghan government. A study conducted by an Afghan newspaper in June 2016 found that 16 senior posts were filled by Pashtuns, 14 by Tajiks, two each by Uzbeks, Hazara and Turkman, and one Sayyed in 37 Afghan embassies (see Figure 6.2).[12]

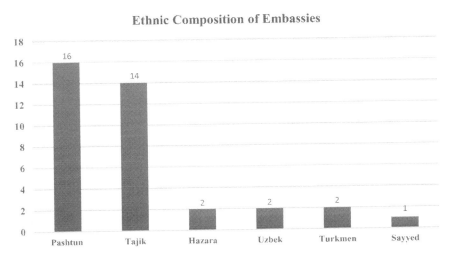

Figure 6.2 Ethnic composition of embassies in Afghanistan.

The ethnicisation of staff offices had three immediate effects. First, Ashraf Ghani set the tone by signalling—intentionally or not—to Abdullah and other network leaders that they were free to ethnicise staff appointments. Second, ethnic biases resulted in the reliance on a few key individuals, narrowing access to an already limited access order: Ghani, for example, was dependent on brokers such as Atmar, Rahimi, and Popal whose influence within the administration increased significantly. Third, among the initial restructuring that occurred during the NUG, the biggest winners were the Western-educated technocrats and the younger generation whom Ghani promoted to key positions in an attempt to sideline Jihadis and Karzai allies.

The incessant political and ethnic divisions and turmoil undermined the administration's ability to govern effectively and as discord and distrust increased, dysfunction became more pronounced. The NUG seemed unable to effectively respond to security, political, and economic crises. The fall of Kunduz (first in September 2015 and then in October 2016) to the Taliban; the near-collapse of Helmand in January 2016; and the fall of 72 police checkpoints in Uruzgan in less than two hours in September 2016 were a few examples of the breakdown in the Afghanistan National Security and Defense Forces (ANSDF) central command. The political situation adversely affected Afghan National Army (ANA) resource management, strategic planning for offensive operations at the zone level, and coordination across command structures. Based on my own working mandate with the security sector, by early 2018 the ANA leadership had been seriously politicised. President Ghani's drive to reform ANSDF leadership had led to a Pashtunisation of the Army and Police which alienated many of the non-Pashtun generals. In one decree, the president promoted 23 generals, among them 19 ethnic Pashtuns, two Tajiks, one Hazara, and one Uzbek, leading to a massive backlash within the Ministry of Defence (MoD) and considerable resentment amongst non-Pashtun officials, which subsequently and indirectly impacted soldier's morale and performance in the field.[13] From my observations attending the daily Ministry of Defence Joint Central Strategic Command, throughout 2018, the average estimate of the number of casualties (both martyred and wounded) recorded was between 120 and 150 soldiers per day (Figure 6.3).

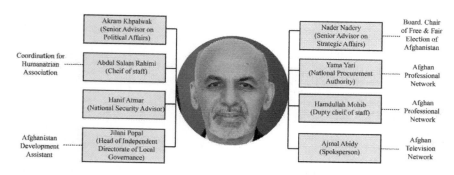

Figure 6.3 President Ghani's technocratic inner circle.

6.2 The underlying source of tension and discord

From the outset, tensions between the two camps (CEO Abdullah and President Ghani) strained. Both teams had a different interpretation of the Agreement. Abdullah considered the NUG a power-sharing compromise, whereas Ghani saw it as a coalition government.[14] Abdullah was under the impression that power would be shared equally between them, including a 50–50% share of government appointments; while Ghani and his advisors insisted that ultimate power, as defined in the constitution, resided in the presidency, including veto power over Abdullah's appointments.

By mid-2016, it became clear that the CEO position as pledged in the original agreement to formalise the position through a constitutional amendment Loya Jirga (Grand Assembly) in two years was unlikely to be legislated. Abdullah also showed little incentive to formalise his position either. First, the prerequisites for a constitutional *Loya Jirga*—that is, a legitimate parliament and district council representatives—were not in place. Second, both Abdullah and Ghani lacked the political capital to influence *Loya Jirga* results that would help set the political agenda. The risk was high and showed that the agenda could be derailed by spoilers like the former president and other disgruntled political network leaders such as Dostum, Mohaqqiq, Khalili, Arghandiwal, and others who wanted to see the NUG fail (discussed below).[15]

The key source of distrust and frustration was the political structure of the NUG. As a 50–50 power-sharing agreement, at least in the view of Abdullah, it produced two rigid camps, going against the logic of *networked governance* and institutional settings of deal-making and opportunism. The set-up made it difficult for the established bases of authority and networks of power to effectively manoeuvre and bargain, frustrating them further and exacerbating personal and institutional rifts between the aides of the two camps, each trying to undercut the other when it came to policy development and programme execution. In August 2015, President Ghani sacked four deputies of the Ministry of Labour and Social Affairs and Martyrs over allegations of widespread corruption. Abdullah Abdullah ordered the same individuals back to work arguing that the president had not consulted him on the sacking.[16] Such incidents became a frequent feature of the NUG; reforms at all levels of the government became highly politicised. The result was a fragmented government with two rigid camps with a daily rift between officials who were blocking each other's projects and initiatives.

Tensions between Ghani and Abdullah were further exacerbated in August 2016 when Abdullah declared Ghani "unfit for the presidency" in a press conference and accused him of not listening or including him in decision making.[17] What triggered the outburst was the appointment of Nader Nadery as the Head of Afghanistan Civil Service and Reform Commission without obtaining Abdullah's approval, replacing Ahmad Mujahed, an ally of Abdullah, a Jamiati and son-in-law of the late former president Rabbani. He was also annoyed that Ghani had been blocking his candidate, Fazal Ahmad Manawi, for the position of Attorney General.[18] A few months before the October 2016 international donors conference on Afghanistan in Brussels, a frustrated Ghani allegedly planned to abolish the CEO position by presidential decree, or at least the idea was being tested by the president's aides. But in the face of Western pressure, particularly from the U.S.A., the aides abandoned these efforts.[19]

6.3 Concentrating power in the palace

By early 2017, it was evident that Ghani was aggressively monopolising power and decision-making processes in the president's office. The Chief of Staff, Salam Rahimi, acted as gatekeeper, providing access to only his fellow network colleagues while bad-mouthing and undermining others. This created a complicated political atmosphere with concerns over who was in charge, considering that the president was often easily manipulated by his inner circle. Although difficult to verify, there were also many accounts of financial extortion from business leaders, companies, and officials. In one incident, according to two sources working on the Aria Residency Complex land acquisition and its phony contract with Kabul Municipality, a relative of one of the senior staff in the president's office allegedly used the government fact-finding report to extort money from the Complex's owners, Century Land Company, threatening to show the report to the president.[20] Accusation of extortion and corruption would become even worse after the 2019 presidential election when Fazl Ahmad Fazli would become the head of the Office of Administrative Affairs. Allegedly his networked clients in the Attorney General's Office and National Procurement Authority and other key positions would enable him to threaten rivals and extort resources as he wished.

After the election, the president's office, including the office of the Chief of Staff and Administrative Affairs Office of the President, was further expanded and given more functions, along with more staff. The President ruled that all policies had to be approved by the Administrative Affairs Office and the newly established High Councils, 11 in total, further concentrating power around the office of the president.[21] These Councils included Economic Development, Governance and Rule of Law, Justice and the Fight against Corruption, Human Resources, Water and Energy, and Urban Development, among others, and became the second most important bodies for decision making after the cabinet tasked with coordinating policy and monitoring development progress in key sectors. In early 2018, according to information provided to me, the President had over 150 advisors. Headed by the president's close aide, Hanif Atmar, the National Security Council (NSC), responsible for coordinating security policy, also expanded considerably, with two additional deputies and several new directorates. The new structure at the NSC mirrored the government, with key functions branching out to all sectors of the state. Many believed that Atmar was building his presidential election campaign within the NSC and, as we will see, contributed to his eventual fall (Figure 6.4).

The president also regularly restructured the administration to benefit his broader vision and goals in what his opponents claimed were power grabs under

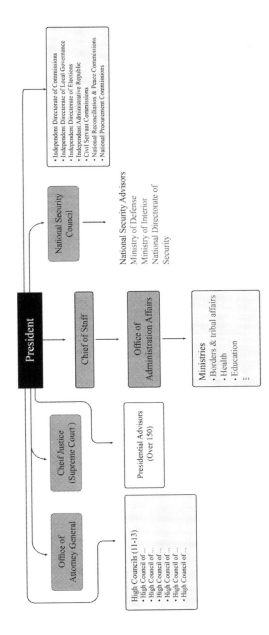

Figure 6.4 Structure of the centre of government.

the pretext of reform. The moves did indeed resemble attempts to concentrate power under the Presidency Office and his allies' ministries, often at the expense of the CEO's authority, by creating, merging, or dismantling government departments. In 2015, for instance, Ghani created a new office, the National Procurement Authority, centralising government procurement within his office. The argument was that corruption and mismanagement within ministry and provincial directorates' procurement systems had been a driving force for chronic sleaze.[22]

In other moves, the Afghanistan Investment Support Agency (AISA)—responsible for facilitating the registration, licensing, and promotion of all investments in Afghanistan—which had been headed by an Abdullah aide, was merged with the Ministry of Trade and Industries, controlled by the president's team.[23] Also, most Ministry of Economy functions went to the Finance Ministry headed by Ghani's close clienteles. In other examples, the Ministry of Transport, which was first divided into three different independent authorities (railways, aviation, and public transport), was amalgamated when Ghani's former Head of Procurement Authority was appointed minister in 2017. And in 2020, when Ghani came to power to serve his second term, one of his first decrees amalgamated three Ministry of Finance departments, including Customs and Revenues, within the Administrative Office of the President.

The increasing level of centralisation, along with the president's weakness as a manager and bad temper, proved to be a recipe for disaster. President Ghani's gross mismanagement of political networks shook the foundation of the networked state and the political order carefully established under Karzai. By relying on a small group of inner circle advisors, President Ghani reduced the prestige and authority of the cabinet and ministers. Some of these advisors, including Humayoun Qayoumi (Infrastructure and Development and later Finance Minister) and Ajmal Ahmadi (advisor on banking and economic development) acted as "super ministers," often bullying and bad-mouthing those they didn't like.[24] For instance, Qayoumi interviewed the nominee for the Ministry of Energy and Water and his approval was essential for the appointment. During his tenure as finance minister, he introduced three ministers to their offices, a tradition carried out usually by vice presidents, thus demonstrating his authority and power. This created considerable hostilities within the cabinet between those who were favoured and those who had little or no access to the president and his inner circle. The most recurrent criticism of Ghani was that the visionary technocrat lacked the political sense to navigate Afghanistan's complex political, ethnic, and tribal dynamics.[25]

6.4 Centre–periphery relations: disrupting the provincial order

President Ghani also tried to disrupt the established political order in the provinces. In the eastern region, where his ethnic Pashtun constituency stronghold was based, he came to rely on a group of technocratic governors and a few controversial tribal figures. In Nangarhar, he tried to sideline the Arsala family network, the Jamiat network led by Hazarat Ali, and other smaller provincial and district networks. Ghani's strategy was to promote the relatively weaker centre of power led by Fazal Hadi Muslimyar—later the Lower House Speaker and a close political and business associate of Abdul Rasul Sayyaf—and his Khugyani tribal elders against the Arsala family.[26]

Most of his young technocratic inner circle, including Hamdullah Moheb and Fazl Fazli, came from the Khugyani district. However, the Arsala family along with Hizb Islami and Jamiat continued to exert influence in Nangarhar and the eastern region. In 2016, as a demonstration of his military strength, he recruited Shinwari tribal elders to join an uprising to fight the estimated 900 Deash fighters in three districts of Kot, Achin, and Naziyan. And in the 2019 elections, in retaliation, the Arsala family led by Din Mohammad and Haji Zahir supported Abdullah. However, Haji Zahir maintained a strong coercive power in Nangarhar.[27]

In Khost, he initially relied on Humayoun Humayoun, an MP from the province, and in Paktika and Paktia on MP Mirza Khan Katawazi's family and tribe, both very controversial figures. The former was President Ghani's campaign manager in Khost during the 2014 elections but had a fall out with him in 2017 over Ghani's failure to offer him a major position. To reward Katawazi for his support in Paktika and Paktia, in June 2020 Ghani appointed Katawazi's younger brother as Head of the powerful IDLG office.

Ghani's link with Katawazi is fascinating. Katawazi was arrested, found guilty, and sentenced to five years in jail for fraudulently producing armoured vehicle registration plates.[28] According to his campaign manager, Katawazi registered US$500 million as his net assets at the Independent Election Commission (IEC). In March 2019, Ariana News showed documents that accused President Ghani of intervening in Katawazi's case and verbally ordering the Attorney General's Office (AGO) to set him free.[29] When the IEC asked the AGO for further evidence that Katawazi did indeed have a criminal record, in an official reply they confirmed that he did, but they had mistakenly forgotten to add his name to the list of people with a criminal background. In October 2018, the National Directorate of Security arrested Katawazi in the Hairatan port, in the Balkh Province, but he was set free on bail and allowed to run for parliament after President Ghani's direct intervention.

Many of these civilian appointments in the provinces by Ghani came with little consultation from key political networks and powerbrokers, disrupting established political orders. For example, Ghani's appointment of Mohammad Omar Safi, a Western-educated technocrat with little experience in government, as governor of the Kunduz Province in 2014 did not sit well with local government insiders and network leaders, predominantly Jamiat.[30] In Kunduz, primarily former Jamiat associates controlled key subnational positions including much of the *arbaki* militia and Afghan Local Police (ALP).[31] Kunduz's security architecture greatly influenced the reception Safi received when he took up office. Safi, a Pashtun, did not get along with the police chief, an ethnic Tajik, and a Jamiati associated with CEO Abdullah. Kunduz's well-documented factionalism led to infighting, with provincial security and administrative officials trying to undermine the new governor's authority. Unsurprisingly, the Taliban were able to exploit these disunities and overwhelm government forces to capture the city in September 2015 and again in 2017.

Other provinces did not fare better. In Herat, Ghani allied himself with the Head of the Provincial Council, Kamran Alizai, a controversial figure who had several criminal cases against him, accused of assassinating rivals and customs extortion. His case went twice to court in Kabul, but he was only mildly reprimanded with minor fines. Whether there was an intervention from the president, as his opponents suggested, or whether he paid substantial bribes, is difficult to verify. Over time, across most provinces, the dysfunction severely weakened the provincial administrations and eventually led to a loss of territory to the Taliban, which forced many pro-government militias to relocate to major urban centres or peri-urban districts. In the Parwan Province, he empowered the Greater Council of the North against the Panjshiris.[32]

Taken together, these suspect appointments and alliances along ethnic lines in multi-ethnic provinces such as Kunduz and Herat convinced Ghani's opponents that the president was using ethnocentric strategies against non-Pashtuns, and eventually boiled over into open conflict with northern strongmen Atta Governor Noor and Abdul Rashid Dostum.

6.4.1 Confronting the first vice president

Just a year after the NUG's inauguration, relations between President Ghani and his first vice president, Abdul Rashid Dostum, the leader of Junbish-i-Islami, became strained. Disgruntled with the president for not appointing his network clients and not including him in key decision-making processes, he left Kabul to settle in his hometown of Sheberghan. In the political and military manoeuvring that followed, Junbish-i-Islami organised several offensive operations in the northwest. In June 2016, his militias in Faryab allegedly conducted mass arrests of villagers, looting about 300 homes, killing suspected insurgents, and setting fire to houses and shops, most of them belonging to ethnic Pashtuns.[33] In October, Dostum's convoy was ambushed by the Taliban on its way to Faryab city in Ghormach district where he lost several of his men but was himself unharmed. He criticised the central government for failing to send reinforcements and air support. In another public interview, he accused the president of ethnic favouritism, saying, "if you speak Pashto, you are a good person. If from Logar [Ghani's birthplace] even better."[34] He fell short of directly blaming the President and instead claimed that he was captured by a small circle of self-interested individuals. The relationship further deteriorated when Dostum's Uzbek rival, the former governor Ahmad Ishchi, went on national television accusing the vice president and his bodyguards of illegally detaining and sexually assaulting him.[35] Junbish-i-Islami's office denied the accusations, saying they were designed to discredit him in the wake of the failed assassination attempt on him in Faryab.[36] Under international pressure, President Ghani asked the attorney general office to begin an investigation.[37] Eventually, under international pressure, and once again with the Turkish Embassy's mediation, Dostum was forced into exile in Turkey, leaving the future of Junbish-i-Islami in disarray.[38]

A year later, the arrest of a powerful Faryab province militia commander, a Junbish-i-Islami client, Nizamuddin Qaisari, along with his bodyguards by Afghan special forces angered Junbish supporters. It was not clear who made the decision to carry out the arrests.[39] A video circulated of Afghan special forces mistreating one of Qaisari's bodyguards, with reports emerging that Qaisari himself had been dangled from a helicopter by special forces. These reports fuelled outrage and led to protests in major northern cities.[40] Seizing the opportunity, the disgruntled Wahdat-i-Mardom, Junbish-i-Islami, and Jamiat-i-Islami networked, respectively, joined forces against Ghani, demanding Dostum's return to Afghanistan.[41] In July 2017, while Dostum was still in exile, the three strongmen network leaders formed a new opposition alliance called Etilaf-i-Nijat-e Afghanistan (Alliance for the Salvation of Afghanistan) at Dostum's house in Ankara in preparation for the next elections.[42]

Both Rabbani, the leader of Jamiat-i-Islami, and Abdullah Abdullah threw their support behind this plan. Massive demonstrations were organised by Junbish network supporters in major cities in the north in which supporters blocked the main highways. The blockade was so disruptive that, according to several accounts, the Americans had to pressure President Ghani to speed up negotiations with Dostum, fearing a prolonged crisis would seriously impede the NATO military supply chain.[43] On 22 July 2018, Dostum, after a year in exile, returned to Kabul as a hero amid cheerful greetings by his supporters, with a government delegation waiting for him at the airport.[44] In a fresh push to defy the president, Wahdat and Junbish threw their weight behind CEO Abdullah, representing a significant part of the old Jamiat network in the 2019 presidential elections.

By July 2021, Junbish and its leader were battered and exhausted fighting for its survival with his son surrounded in the Jawzjan Province and was only airlifted at the last minute. Junbish as one of the sturdiest political networks gradually lost the support of ethnic Uzbeks in the north as most of the militia vessel clients joined the Taliban over time and Junbish-i-Islami became a family-led enterprise. Losing the support of the people and lacking military and financial resources, Dostum, the leader of the once-powerful Junbish-i-Islami network, disgracefully fled to Uzbekistan in August 2021.

6.4.2 Challenging Jamiat network and Governor Noor in Balkh

In September 2016, tensions between Governor Noor—a key 2009 and 2014 Abdullah campaign financier, Jamiat's Chief Executive and Afghanistan's longest-serving provincial governor—and CEO Abdullah emerged over the latter's failure to push for full implementation of the NUG agreement, including formalising the position of prime minister. Governor Noor began cosying up to President Ghani and publicly criticising Abdullah.[45] He held a series of talks with Ghani's team to discuss joining the national government while retaining his influence and privileges in the Balkh Province. In October, Abdullah's former Jamiat allies at a dinner which included Governor Noor presented an ultimatum to Abdullah, asking him to stand up to the President or risk being "removed" or "abandoned."[46] Sustaining his pressure, in December 2016, Governor Noor insisted that the 2014 NUG agreement was signed between the President and Jamiat rather than with Abdullah specifically. This, he therefore claimed, justified his ongoing negotiations with Ghani, which were aimed at "breaking the current political impasse."[47] Abdullah's supporters accused Governor Noor of attempting to further his personal interests by making a deal with Ghani to "resolve his problems, which might relate to his bank accounts, or to [officially securing] his position [as governor of Balkh]."[48] Sensing an opportunity, and to exert maximum pressure on Governor Noor, Ghani's inner circle spread rumours in early 2017 that Governor Noor had to resign from his position as the Governor of Balkh or risk being removed and humiliated. During the ensuing stand-off, the president eventually appointed Eng. Daud as the new governor. After a month-long political impasse, an agreement was reached in which Governor Noor appointed his aide, Rahguzar as the new governor, Mirwais Balkhi as education minister, MP Farhad Azimi as ambassador to Kazakhstan, and Tahir Qaderi as deputy ambassador to New Delhi. Allegedly, part of the deal was also to appoint Governor Noor as the president's running-mate in 2019, an empty promise which did not materialise.

Governor Noor's deal with Ghani was seen as a betrayal, upsetting many of the hardcore former Jamiat leaders and followers. But it seemed the strongman was determined to throw himself into national-level politics. Initially, he spent money to unify the so-called "old Jamiat" around a weak and indebted Salahuddin Rabbani, the son of the assassinated leader. In his calculation, he needed Rabbani to rally former Jamiatis against Abdullah. He moved to Kabul to revive the party and organised regular meetings. He reached out to disgruntled non-Panjshiri networks, including the Greater Council of the North (Shora-i-Sarta Sari Shamali), Ismail Khan faction in Herat, Jan Ahmad and Mir Alam in Kunduz, Andarabi commanders and the Mohseni family in the Baghlan Province, and many others to unite everyone around the Jamiat party. But these efforts did not improve Governor Noor's political status against a strong Panjshiri network who cast a long shadow over national politics and the three provinces north of Kabul.

The crisis in the Jamiat network was at least in part a consequence of its own success over the previous decade. Even as they leveraged their network resources, and lined their pockets, the inability of former Shuray-i-Nizar Panjshiri commanders-turned-politicians to open up access to middle-ranking officials and commanders frustrated many like Governor Noor and Amrullah Saleh. The interests of all patronage networks within former Jamiat lay in avoiding the emergence of a strong leadership, a classic example of Fotini's argument that alliance formation is subject to the relative power balance between groups confronted by survival choices and fractionalisation. When confronted with the prospect of losing access to a safe resource, in this case the old Jamiat as a symbolic and historical platform for legitimation, the old leaders swallowed their pride and stuck with the old alliances, despite their diminishing appeal to the younger generation.

After his removal as governor, President Ghani's aides-de-camp effectively identified and eliminated most of Governor Noor's military and criminal network centres of power in Balkh and other provinces. Weakened and wounded, to survive and remain politically relevant, he backed President Ghani in the 2019 election. To add insult to injury, the former strongman of the north was reportedly cut off by Iran, too, though the veracity of the reports, some from officials at the National Security Council, is difficult to verify. But his drift towards Saudi Arabia and the UAE in 2018 suggest a break with Iran was in the making. By 2021, Governor Noor found himself desperately fighting for his survival in the face of a Taliban offensive. Lacking the resources to put up much of a fight, he shamefully fled to Uzbekistan in August 2021.

6.5   A lost opportunity: crushing revisionist youth protest movements

In 2016 and 2017, two important youth protest movements emerged, creating momentum for a new power dynamics away from the traditional leaders and their networked governance: the Enlightenment (Jobbesh-i-Roshanayi) and the Uprising for Change (Junbish-i-Rastakhiz-i-Taghir) movements.[49] As Bose, Bizhan, and Ibrahimi found in their studies, these movements were driven primarily by strong perceptions of injustice, exclusion from important policy-making and rapidly deteriorating economic and security conditions following the 2014 presidential elections and the drawdown of international troops.[50] Before they erupted, there were several attempts by young technocrats to set up youth-led organisations and networks but many were not sustained. In 2010, the Afghanistan 1400 and Afghanistan Analysis and Awareness (A3) youth networks emerged whose members included a combination of young public servants, former MPs, civil society representatives, and others. A3 functioned mostly as a *protection network*, primarily made up of young and ambitious government officials coming together to support and protect each other against bigger groupings within the state.[51] Green Trend was another youth movement formed by Amrullah Saleh in 2010 when he resigned as the National Directorate of Security (NDS) director. It made its first public appearance on 5 May 2011. Youth-led networks made little headway against the more entrenched political networks that have *safe positions* within the state.

6.5.1   The Enlightenment movement

On 16 May 2016, thousands of ethnic Hazaras protested on the streets of Kabul in one of the biggest demonstrations the city had seen, chanting "death to discrimination," demanding the 500 kV TUTAP electricity transmission line to be routed back through the Bamiyan Province, its original route before the government decided to reroute it through the Salang Pass north of Kabul.[52] The government argued that the shorter route would save money and time.[53] However, the People's High Council (Shuray-i-Aliy-i-Mardomi), the leadership body of the Enlightenment, argued this was yet another blatant example of bias against ethnic Hazaras who had benefitted little from post-2001 international state-building and development.[54] Many ordinary people directed their anger at President Ghani and saw the rerouting as a divisive indicator of his systematic discrimination against Hazara groups despite his rhetoric of national unity and balanced development.[55] The demonstration mirrored the success of the November 2015 demonstrations, known as the Tabassum demonstration, in which demonstrators succeeded in breaching the outer walls of the Palace.[56] To appease the Movement and calm the situation, the government issued a decree promising to postpone the project for six months, set up a commission (12 members, of which six would be ethnic Hazara) to review the entire plan, and build an alternative 220 kV power line to Bamiyan from the neighbouring Baghlan province.

On 23 July, with no changes in the government's decision, Enlightenment organised its second major protest, accusing the government of misleading them with the Review Commission, buying time while actively negotiating and bargaining with traditional political network leaders, including that of Wahdat-i-Islami of Karim Khalili and Wahdat-i-Mardom of Mohaqqiq, to weaken the movement. It seems that the fear many had of being susceptible to jihadi leaders and elites, who joined the movement so they could use it as a bargaining chip to advance their factional interests, came to pass.[57] By this time, most ethnic Hazara leaders, including Khalili, VP Danesh, and Mohaqqiq, had left the Movement, with many accusing them of selling themselves for financial gains. There were also major protests in other cities and more than 20 cities worldwide, including Washington, DC, and London.[58] In London, on May 12, protesters interrupted President Ghani's talk three times at the Royal United Services Institute (RUSI) in Whitehall, during his official attendance at the Anti-Corruption Summit, reflecting the deep sense of resentment and anger.[59] In Kabul, with no other route to reach the palace, the protesters set up tents in the historic Deh Mazang square. At noon, two explosions took place killing hundreds of innocent protesters, for which Islamic State of Iraq and Syria (ISIS) claimed responsibility.[60] The government indirectly blamed the organisers for going ahead with the planned demonstrations despite reports of a planned attack.

The twin explosions shook the movement to the core and had an irreversible impact on future civic movements and freedom of expression. As one civil society leader aptly put it: "They took the only power we had: our ability to mobilise the public and protest in major cities."[61] Enlightenment came under attack by powerful ethno-regional leaders who had made deals with the Palace and who saw the movement as a serious threat to their survival. Also, a lack of a clear strategy in its negotiations with the government and limiting itself to a single issue rather than broadening its appeal contributed to its gradual downfall. But arguably the most important reason for its collapse was internal distrust and jockeying over the leadership of the movement as well as mismanagement and embezzlement of funds raised through public donations. According to some estimates, the Hazara community in Australia fundraised over US$1.6 million for the victims of the attack on Enlightenment, showcasing the power of their mobilisation and unity.[62] There were a lot of accusations against Enlightenment leaders for abusing funds for personal use: purchasing armoured cars, and so on. By the end of the year, the movement was fractured by division, with some negotiating their way into the government and by 2018 there was nothing left but the name.

6.5.2 Uprising for Change movement

Uprising for Change materialised in response to the 31 May 2017 truck bombing close to the German Embassy, one of the deadliest attacks of its kind in Kabul.[63] Many Afghan government officials saw this attack as an attempt to overshadow and undermine the June 6 Kabul Peace meeting. Angered by the government's inability to ensure security, some civil society and urban youth representatives called for a rally on social media. On June 2, chanting "Khasta az marg ba soy-e arg" (Tired of deaths and forward to the Arg [the Presidential Palace]), hundreds of demonstrators marched towards the presidential Palace.[64] Close to the *Zanbaq* square in downtown Kabul, demonstrators were stopped by police and the president's Personal Protection Security (PPS), which used live ammunition, killing six protesters and wounding 30. Among those killed was the son of deputy speaker of the Upper House, M. Alam Ezedyar, a prominent Jamiat politician. The next day, protesters issued a statement, demanding the resignation of the president and the CEO, dismissal of security sector leaders, and the establishment of an interim government.[65] Over the next two weeks, protesters blocked the main roads leading to the palace, setting up at least seven tents at key junctions. The Uprising soon took an ethnic dimension with some Tajik leaders, such as Ahmad Zia Masoud and Latif Pedram, joining the protests, and issuing direct warnings to the government. In north Kabul, there were calls for arms and some armed youth from neighbouring provinces joined protesters in the capital. On June 13, the Panjshir Mujahedeen Council announced their support for the Uprising. Protests were organised in ethnic Tajik-majority provinces of Badakhshan and others, as well as some major Western cities, including London. Jamiat activists, who joined Uprising, brought their long-standing demand for full implementation of the National Unity Agreement and expressed other grievances.[66] The Uprising's resolution stated that "the great Tajik community is not represented in government leadership and decision-making," repudiating those who claimed to be representing them in the NUG as "demagogic and vote-selling people."[67]

Under pressure, the President tasked the Attorney General's Office to investigate the June 2 killings. On June 11, acting on AGO findings, Gul Nabi Ahmadzai, the Commander of Kabul Garrison, along with Kabul Police Chief, Hassan Shah Frogh, were suspended from their jobs. Nevertheless, inside the administration, many saw these rallies as motivated and coordinated by the president's opponents in an attempt to undermine the NUG as it faced a serious legitimacy deficit.[68] To turn the tide, the administration organised several gatherings in the palace, inviting a diverse group of people from Kabul city and its surrounding districts, in which the IDLG and Kabul municipality played a key role. In an offensive campaign, they argued that these demonstrations were harming public order and the economy because of the closure of roads and businesses. On June 19, security forces cleared out the final tent and Uprising gradually died out. One of the main reasons for its sudden collapse was the lack of organisational structure which prevented the movement from presenting a united front to deal with the government as well as the lack of charismatic leadership.[69]

Both these movements, Enlightenment and Uprising, emerged spontaneously and in response to specific government failures.[70] Whatever the reason and rationale for President Ghani's decision to confront them rather than listening and riding the tide of their reform demands, he put himself on a collision course with ethnic Hazara and Tajik groups, especially the youth constituency, for the next three years. Many youth leaders and pro-government officials would later stress that the president lost an opportunity to seize on these momentums by empowering these movements to help him sideline former jihadi rivals. Instead, the president and his aides sided with traditional leaders in crushing these movements. His actions were in contrast to his claim that he had been advocating for a "generational change" in Afghan politics and was implementing a strategy of appointing young people to key government positions. Besides, these confrontations exposed the depth of misinformation within the government with different network factions pushing their agenda on the president. More importantly, the ethnicisation of these movements and the inadequate and hurried response demonstrated the government's incompetence and malpractice. There was, however, little attempt and no sign by either movement—except initially some Enlightenment sympathy and attendance of its members in one or two gatherings of Uprising—to come together around their common agenda. They did little to bridge the ethnic fault lines in Afghan politics by working together and turning these movements into bigger political forces.

6.6 Ghani: opposition alliances and disorder

By 2017, all of the major political network leaders in the government, including CEO Abdullah and his deputy Mohaqqiq, the first vice president Dostum, Governor Noor, and the president's Special Representative on Reform and Good Governance, Ahmad Zia Masoud, were either dismissed or in opposition to the President. In April 2017, Ghani prematurely dismissed Ahmad Zia Masoud, the only senior ethnic Tajik and Jamiat leader on his team, further upsetting the ethnic balance in the composition of the government.[71] Addressing the 25th anniversary of Mujahedeen Day on April 18, Masoud called Ghani a "dictator" and a "control-oriented" individual. He continued to say that he regretted joining Ghani's campaign. "I apologise to all of you. I cut off all my relations with this government which is being led by four suspicious people."[72] However, this was not the first time Masoud had gone against his patron. He had made similar charges against Karzai before. By the end of 2018, most of Ghani's ethnic Pashtun allies and inner circle had left him, including Hanif Atmar, Jilani Popal, and Akram Khpelwak, seriously narrowing his political base.[73] All Ghani had left were a few young technocrats, including Fazl Fazli (chief advisor and after the 2019 election, Head of Administrative Affairs of the President), Hamdullah Moheb (NSC Advisor, replacing Atmar), Matin Bek (Head of IDLG), among others, an over-reliance on whom would almost cost him the election.

Ghani's relations with the Lower House, meanwhile, were strained throughout his presidency by his arrogance and inability to build a coalition of reform-minded MPs to back his agenda. In November 2016, in an unprecedented move, MPs tried to unseat 16 ministers for failing to spend 70% of their development budget.[74] Despite government's intervention to save some of the ministers, seven out of 16 were ejected, including the acting leader of Jamiat and Minister for Foreign Affairs, Salahuddin Rabbani, along with the Minister for Labour, Social Affairs and Martyrs & the Disabled, and Minister for Public Welfare.[75]

As the NUG fractured, several temporary alliances were formed centred around various powerbrokers who felt excluded from the decision making and resource-sharing processes. In one of the earlier attempts in August 2015, the former president, Sebqatullah Mojadaddi, and Karzai's former vice president, Karim Khalili, both of whom had supported Ghani during the elections, set up the High Council of Jihadi and National Parties (Shora-ye-Aali Ahzab Jihadi wa Mellie). In a more serious effort, in early 2016, a group of prominent former officials and leaders set up the Afghanistan Protection and Stability Council (APSC), led by Abdul Rasul Sayyaf as chairperson, Yunus Qanuni as deputy, and former Presidential aide Sadiq Modabber as head of the secretariat. Other prominent members included Ismail Khan and Omar Daudzai. However, the group disintegrated as 2019 elections neared. Daudzai joined Ghani's election campaign at the last minute, with many speculating foul-play and intimidation by Ghani's aides.[76] From 2018 onwards, Ghani made a pact with Sayyaf and through him recruited his network-client, Fazil Hadi Muslimyar, the Speaker of the Upper House. However, Ghani had to make huge concessions with perks like personal guards, monthly allowances. Sayyaf's client, Asadullah Khalid was awarded the Ministry of Defence in 2018. Also, both Sayyaf and Muslimyar's corrupt practices, including land grabs and extortion, were overlooked despite extensive and detailed reporting on them in Khost, Nangarhar, and Kabul provinces.

Another small group that emerged in 2016 was the New National Front of Afghanistan, formed on 14 January 2016, by Anwar ul-Haq Ahadi, a close supporter of Ghani's election campaign in 2014 who later had a falling out with the president. The New National Front highlighted the inadequacies of the NUG and actively demanded an early election, noting that the NUG was facing a "legitimacy crisis."[77] As always, none of these alliances translated into serious opposition to the NUG. As noted earlier, the Junbish-Wahdat-i-Mardom-Jamiat alliance (Etilaf-i-Nijat-e Afghanistan, Alliance for the Salvation of Afghanistan) was serendipitously formed in Ankara after the Qaisari incident and found a new life in light of the 2019 elections. It at least succeeded in putting forward a candidate in Atmar.[78] In a secret meeting in Dubai in early 2018 between Governor Noor and Atmar, a settlement was reached in which Governor Noor (Chief Executive Officer of Jamiat-i-Islami) would be the chief executive officer on Atmar's ticket and Mohammad Mohaqqiq (Wahdat-i-Mardom) and Abdul Rashid Dostum (Junbish-i-Islami) would act as his deputies.[79] The campaign ticket collapsed just a few weeks before the elections when the secret deal was disclosed after Governor Noor insisted on being in the campaign photos. Ethnic Pashtun allies of Atmar vehemently opposed the idea of having Governor Noor as the CEO. With both sides failing to compromise, Atmar's ticket collapsed.[80] In a last-minute alliance reshuffle, Wahdat-i-Mardom and Junbish-i-Islami networks joined Abdullah's team and Governor Noor joined Ghani's camp but did not openly campaign for him.

6.6.1 *Karzai and the NUG*

Former president Karzai was able to cast a long and destructive shadow over the NUG and the new post-2019 administration by spearheading one of the main opposition voices to the government. Karzai regularly met with disgruntled officials, generals, and tribal chiefs and allegedly encouraged his allies to exploit internal government divisions. For instance, before the second anniversary of the NUG, he publicly criticised its leadership on various issues ranging from foreign policy to governance, and privately advocated for organising a Loya Jirga to determine the future of the government. His aides publicly argued that the NUG faced a serious legitimacy crisis.[81] For instance, in a March 2015 interview with the *Guardian*, Karzai criticised President Ghani for his policy of reaching out to the Pakistani military for peace talks with the Taliban, saying, "We want a friendly relationship but not to be under Pakistan's thumb."[82] He also criticised the NUG for blaming him for everything. "[Ghani] is also a legacy of mine," he once quipped sarcastically. "Rather than going into the past, they should begin to deliver."[83] In one case, in early 2016, several former Karzai officials submitted a document to Obama administration officials arguing that the government is essentially "politically bankrupt," hence the title of the document, Chapter 11, referring to the American system of filing for bankruptcy.[84] At the time, both Omar Daudzai and Rahmatullah Nabil, former aides of President Karzai, were calling the government "illegitimate" in private meetings and lobbying to hold a *Loya Jirga* or organise an early election (see below).[85]

Ghani's aides alleged that Karzai had been actively working in the shadows to destabilise the government and exploit the ongoing crisis for a political comeback or line up one of his aides for the presidency.[86] They went as far as to suggest that the Enlightenment and Uprising movements were provoked by Karzai to further weaken the government.[87] Although such claims are difficult to substantiate, some of the Enlightenment Movement leaders had close links with Rahmatullah Nabil, the former Director of National Directorate of Security, and Karzai.

6.7 The 2019 presidential election: network dynamics and the political settlement

The building political dysfunction under the NUG culminated in the fiasco of the 2019 presidential election. The campaign season began inauspiciously on 28 July 2019, two months early, amid a cloud of political uncertainty because of the ongoing peace talks between the U.S.A. and the Taliban. Zalmay Khalilzad, the

U.S. special envoy, had earlier told Afghan stakeholders that elections should be suspended, given the need for the creation of an interim government following proposed intra-Afghan negotiations being discussed.[88]

As the election went ahead on September 28, Ashraf Ghani and Abdullah Abdullah once again stood against each other, accusing one another of fraud and political bullying. Low turnout and massive fraud put the legitimacy of the elections into question, as well as the future government. This time, former Governor Noor (CEO of Jamiat-i-Islami) shifted his support for Ghani after his fall out with Abdullah while Junbish-i-Islami and Wahdat-i-Islami (Karim Khalili) joined Abdullah's ticket following their strained relations with Ghani. Also, most members of the Greater Council of the North (Shuray-i-Ali Sartasar-i-Shamali) joined Ghani's camp after receiving huge concessions. To lure them, in 2017, President Ghani had offered two provincial governor positions (Farah and Parwan) and a ministerial position in the government. However, the biggest breakaway force from Abdullah was the Rawan-i-Sabz network led by Amrullah Saleh who joined Ghani's team, first as Minister of Interior in early 2019 and then as Ghani's first vice president.

After months of disputes over the counting of suspicious ballots, the IEC in a surprise move on 18 February 2020 announced Ghani as the winner with 50.6% of the vote (923,592 votes) and Abdullah at 39.52% (720,841 votes).[89] Both camps were locked in a dispute over the results. Abdullah declared the election invalid and threatened to announce a parallel government. On March 9, both leaders inaugurated their presidency in parallel, declaring themselves the elected president of the country. However, with the Americans attending Ghani's inauguration ceremony and not Abdullah's, the latter's support diminished, and he refrained from further escalatory steps.[90] Eventually, after six months of disagreements, under immense American pressure, Ghani was forced to enter a power-sharing arrangement again with his rival's camp.[91] President Ghani's thinly-attended May 2020 inauguration ceremony stood in stark contrast to Karzai's 2009 inauguration, attended by 14 foreign ministers, the President of Pakistan, and the vice president of Iran—a clear sign of the weakening position of the future administration. Once again, a last-minute power-sharing settlement had saved the country from the brink of collapse. The deal this time was mediated by Afghan leaders—the former president Karzai, Dawat-i-Islami leader Abdul Rasul Sayyaf, Wahdat-i-Islami leader Karim Khalili, and former Jamiat and former Shuray-i-Nizar commander Yunos Qanuni—under American pressure. The most significant difference was that the agreement did not include a CEO position for Abdullah. Instead, he became the Chairman of the High Council of National Reconciliation, essentially managing the Afghan peace process. Abdullah and his team would select half of the cabinet and as a measure of precaution, the president could not remove Abdullah's ministers.[92] Dostum would be promoted to the rank of Marshal. The selection of provincial governors would take place through a jointly agreed upon formula, which would become a major source of confusion and tension. The vagueness in the agreement's language led to Abdullah's outburst in July 2020, when Ghani appointed and reshuffled 12 governors, saying that he had not been consulted and became aware of it through media.[93]

It took over six months of political manoeuvring after President Ghani's swearing in and nearly four months after both leaders signed a power-sharing deal to agree on a cabinet list. Key positions of Ministry of Defence, interior and Head of National Directorate of Security would remain acting because both camps could not agree on the final choice of candidates. The elections brought Afghanistan to a new level of disunity. The unilateral American negotiations with the Taliban further exacerbated uncertainty. In early 2021, the power dynamics of political networks were spectacularly disrupted, as discussed in the concluding chapter, that each political network was making their own deal with the Taliban behind the scenes with no trust in each other. The atmosphere had become so uncertain that Afghanistan's powerbrokers went into survival mode, scrambling for ways to maintain their own relevance amidst a growing sense of impending doom.

Conclusion

The National Unity Government failed as a political structure to boost the legitimacy of, or confidence in, Afghanistan's institutions. It created two rigid political camps that went against the logic of the *networked state* that produced fluid power dynamics among competing political networks, allowing them to continuously negotiate bargains and deals. It fashioned absolute dysfunctionality and infighting which negatively impacted service delivery, economic growth, and the government's ability to combat an increasingly emboldened Taliban. The pace of appointments for key positions was exceptionally slow. It took seven months to get a full cabinet in place while in the first-year hundreds of important subnational positions were vacant. In the five years of the NUG, the key security ministries of Defence and Interior had each respectively gone through three to four ministers and acting ministers, which demonstrates the degree of political instability, at a time when the ANDSF was fighting a resurgence of Taliban and ISIS.

Continued strained relations between President Ghani and CEO Abdullah produced unceasing crises which at several points brought the state dangerously close to collapse. President Ghani's radical reform agenda, in the absence of a strong political base, put him on a collision course with a difficult and entrenched stack of powerbrokers. However, he did himself no favours; his arrogance, poor management, and inability to build a coalition of multi-ethnic, reform-minded networks, and leaders undermined his ability to deliver his agenda and translate his grand vision into reality, something that many of the younger liberal voices had hoped for. It was not necessarily his vision that was the problem but the way he attempted to achieve it. His reckless and impulsive decision making, without a well-thought-through strategy, meant that he made enemies on all sides who acted as spoilers to his programme. And as his legitimacy came seriously into question following the 2019 elections, rather than his technocratic and nationalist character, it was his ethnocentric nature that became more pronounced.

Arguably, his biggest failure was how he democratised the balance of power among key political networks and centres of power which Karzai had carefully managed. The visionary technocrat lacked the political sense to navigate Afghanistan's complex politics and network power dynamics. At one point, almost all of the key jihadi network leaders, except the second VP, were resentful and hostile to Ghani. As one senior foreign diplomat at the time described it: "If VP Danesh walks out too, the position of the president will be very precarious with a narrow political base around some young technocrats."[94] Consequently, as Ghani restructured the power balance at the state level, weakening and marginalising key former jihadi political networks, and perhaps most importantly, restricting their access to financial and political resources, his government became shrunken and shaken. As such, by 2021, the legitimacy of his administration and key political networks that could not deliver patronage was seriously questioned, exacerbating its underlying ethnic tensions.

In the aftermath of the Taliban takeover of Afghanistan, Ghani's legacy will likely take a severe beating. The fact that the president surreptitiously left the country at its time of greatest need was seen as an act of cowardice. Most Afghans did not accept the president's reasoning that he left to prevent a bloodbath in the capital. This lack of credibility, however, clouds some more nuanced realities. For instance, Ghani was determined to dismantle the networked politics that had dominated Afghanistan since the signing of the Bonn Agreement in 2001 and raise up Afghanistan's democratic institutions in its place.

The next three chapters delve more deeply into the question of why. They demonstrate how political networks' day-to-day institutional practices (or rules of the game) played out during moments of contestation and crisis. These case studies reflect different moments of competition, conflict and compromise, which provided platforms for horse-trading, coercion and intimidation, and politicisation of identities.

Chapter 7 shows how political networks competed and bargained to secure community votes. Chapter 8 explores the political economy of the *Wolesi Jirga*, one of the key democratic institutions of the state, by detailing how the 2010–2011 Special Court crisis unfolded and evolved. Chapter 9 exposes the day-to-day network practices of criminality, opportunism, and extortion by examining several key economic industries such as banking, the extractive industry, and logistics.

These cases highlight how liberal peace institutions became compromised by political networks. These network practices help uncover the complexity of governance and statehood in post-2001 state-building, shedding light on how competing political networks survived within the state and beyond.

Notes

1 Constable (2016).
2 Hakim, Y. 2016. "President Ghani Calls for Afghans to Remain in Country." *BBC*, March 31, 2016. Many on social media pointed out the fact that his children are living in the U.S.A. and his not returning to the country after completion of his education.
3 "Mr. Ashraf Ghani Speech on Darul Aman," 100 Anniversary of Independence Day speech. *Youtube*, August 23, 2019, https://www.youtube.com/watch?v=MQQE71IL5t4.
4 Sharan and Bose (2016).

5 See "President Ghani's Inauguration Speech," Administrative Office of the President, September 29, 2014.

6 Democracy International. 2016. *A Survey of the Afghan Parliament*, February 2016.

7 For a list of biographies of these ministers, visit Afghanistan Analysts Network Report. 2015. "Finally towards a Complete Afghan Cabinet? The Next 16 Minister Nominee and Their Bios (Amended)." March 24, 2015.

8 See Suroush, E. "Hukumat Sarparast ha: Kabine-I Hukumat dar 5 sal guzashta chera takmil nashod", *Etilaat Ruz*, 3 Sunbula 1398.

9 See for example, Matta (2015).

10 His Chief of Staff Salam Rahimi and his brother-in-law, Nader Nadery (senior advisor to the president on public and strategic affairs); Akram Ekhpelwak (chief advisor on political affairs), and National Security Council Advisor Hanif Atmar; Jilani Polal (Head of Independent Directorate of Local Governance), later Qayumi, Ahmadi, Fazl Fazli, and Hamdullah Moheb were all from the Pashtun community. Matin Bek who became the Head of IDLG was the only non-Pashtun in senior position within his circle—but he was appointed when Dostum was sidelined and many argued he was brought in to offset the Uzbek alienation.

11 Sharan and Bose (2016).

12 "Tarkibi Qawmi dar Nomayandagihaye Siyasi wa Qunsuli Afghanistan." *Etilaatroz*, June 28, 2016.

13 In November 2017, President Ghani issued a decree in which a seven-member board was announced—the President's Advisory Board on Senior Appointments in the Security Sector—composed of retired generals, which would be solely responsible for appointments of senior MoI, MoD, and NDS officials based on merit. This was described as a way of speeding up the process of appointments and decreasing tensions between the two leaders. The President's team, especially within the NSC, would exert significant influence over appointments in the security sector. Many complained that the screening lacked rigour and was often very politicised.

14 Bose and Ibrahimi (2014).

15 By early 2016, as tensions between Ghani and Abdullah intensified, Karzai was publicly demanding that a Loya Jirga be held to determine a future governing arrangement, which was unlikely to favour either the president or CEO.

16 "President Ghani Dismisses 4 Deputy Ministers at MoLSAMD." *ArianNews*, August 18, 2015.

17 "Afghan Chief Executive Abdullah Denounces President Ghani as Unfit for Office." *The New York Times*, August 11, 2016.

18 Bijlert (2016).

19 International Crisis Group (2017).

20 Author's conversation with two government officials working on the Aria Shahrak case, Kabul, September 2020. The author also saw a copy of the report, titled, "Barresi Motalebat Dawlat az Forush-e Apartman haye Shahrak Aria", dated February 20, 2016. It details how the Century Land Company signed a contract with Kabul Municipality on April 21, 2003 to turn 290 hectares of an informal settlement area into a residential complex. Among many issues, it found that the company was not formally registered with the ministry of industry and trade before winning the contract.

21 Author interview with two senior OAA staff, Kabul. August 22–23, 2015.

22 Farahi and Guggenheim (2020).

23 The Afghanistan Investment Support Agency (AISA) was responsible for facilitating registration, licensing, and promotion of investment.

24 Author's interview with a former minister, Kabul, July 2020.

25 Constable (2016).

26 The Mawlawi Khales family, a Khugyani which led the Jihadi Tanzim Hizb-Islami [Khales] in the 1980s had been therefore excluded from the post-2001 setup. Most of the Khugyani tribal elders joined the Taliban led by Anwar ul-Haq Mujahed, Mawlawi Khales's son.

27 This reportedly created tension between him and the NDS and Provincial Governor, Salim Khan Kundozi. His action eventually forced the National Directorate of Security to finance these uprising forces, which included 1,150 official roster (500 in Naziyan, 500 in Achin, and 150 in Kot, plus 200 Local Afghan Police in Kot alone). Internal Afghan government document. Author's access to daily Central Strategic Command material.

28 He was accused of falsifying the registration plates of 75 armoured cars. These are cars that are known as "zero key."

29 "Leaked Documents Show President Ghani 'Meddled' in Parliamentary Vote." March 24, 2019, https://ariananews.af/leaked-documents-show-president-ghani-meddled-in -parliamentary-vote/.

30 See for example, Matta (2015).

31 For a detailed analysis of Kunduz's fragmented security architecture see Goodhand and Hakimi, "Counterinsurgency, Local Militias, and Statebuilding in Afghanistan," 32–37.

32 The Council was composed of former commanders such as Amanullah Guzar, Haji Almas, Nasruddin Baryalai, commander Fazuludin Ayar, MP Iqbal Safi, MP Anwar Oryakhail, and MP Daud Kalakani, who broke away from Abdullah in an attempt to disrupt the dominance of the Panjshiris. The Council often failed to act as a united force given that they did not have a coordinated and long-term strategy. Their underlining motive was amassing financial assets and maintaining their status quo. People such as Amanullah Guzar, Haji Almas, Commander Jurat, and Governor Salangi played along all sides, without fully committing to anyone in order to maintain and protect their economic interests. Non-Panjshiri Jamiat leaders also tried to build an alliance with the Council to undermine the dominance of Panjshiris. In 2017, Governor Noor while in confrontation with Abdullah tried to unite the Council behind him. On 29 January 2017, Governor Noor attended a gathering of hundreds of elders in the Kharikhana district of Kabul city. The event was organised by commander Gul Haidar Khan, MP Haji Almas, commander Nasruddin Baryalai, commander Fazuludin Ayar, MP Iqbal Safi, MP Anwar Oryakhail, MP Daud Kalakani, and others who declared their support for Governor Noor in unifying the former jihadi Jamiatis.

33 See "Afghanistan, Forces Linked to Vice President Terrorise Villagers," Human Rights Watch, July 31, 2016.

34 "Abdul Rashid Dostum Remark," *Ariana News Channel*, October 26, 2016.

35 Mashal and Abed (2016).

36 See "Afghan Vice President Escapes Unhurt after Taliban Ambush Convoy," *Reuters*, October 17, 2016; "Taliban Ambush Vice President Gen. Dostum's Convoys in Faryab," *Khaama Press*, October 17, 2016.

37 "Proclamation December 17, 2016," attorney general's office, Kabul. A European Union Statement read: "The EU and its member states present in Kabul, Australia, Canada and Norway, call for a fair and transparent official investigation as regards reports of gross human rights violations and abuses against Mr. Ahmad Ishchi."

38 A month after Dostum's departure from the country, seeing an opportunity once they were out from under the shadow of their former leader, several dissidents and reform-ists within Junbish on 11 July 2017 launched a new political party, the New Movement of Afghanistan (Junbish-i-Nawin-e Afghanistan). The former governor of Jawzjan, M. Alem Sai, and the deputy to the old Junbish, emerged as the leading figures in the party along with the Aidin Group, a network of former Turkey-educated politicians, civil society leaders, and others. Known members were M. Alem Sai, Jamhir Anwari (ethnic

Turkmen and former minister of refugees, Hashim Ortaq (MP from Faryab), Nazari Turkmen (a former deputy speaker of the Lower House), Ezatullah Amed, Ahmad Ishchi, and Gul M. Pahlawan. In an interview for Kabul-based *Madaniyat* newspaper on 18 June 2017, he criticised the old party for being "monopolised by one family," adding that "no role is granted to people outside the family of General Abdul Rashid Dostum." Dostum aides described the new party as the "agents of the palace." For more details see AAN report, Ruttig, T. 2017. "Defying Dostum: A New Junbish and the Struggle for Leadership over Afghanistan's Uzbeks." *Afghanistan Analysts Network*, July 19, 2017.

39 The decision to arrest Qaisari was part of a broader government policy to push for the arrest of illegal armed militia groups and their commanders across the country. There were a lot of meetings at the NSC on this, where groups were identified, arrests prioritised, and strategies developed to take them down. The National Directorate of Security identified over 1,200 armed groups which varied in size from 10 fighters to 2,000. Later, the discussion moved to identifying a select group to send a clear message. The instruction from the President was clear that SSL leadership should identify commanders from diverse geographic and ethnic backgrounds to avoid being accused of targeting a specific community given the sensitivity of the political situation. However, some of the lists proposed, especially by one of the NSC deputy, an ethnic Tajik and a former Jamiat clientele, clearly went against one or two ethnic groups.

40 Mashal and Rahim (2018).

41 Author's interview with several officials, Kabul, July 2018.

42 Fitri, K. B., and N. Bashardost. 2017. "Three-Party Alliance in Turkey Draws Scorn at Home." *Pajhwok News*, July 1, https://www.pajhwok.com/en/2017/07/01/three-party -alliance-turkey-draws-scorn-home.

43 Conversation with two foreign diplomats and one Afghan official close to the Palace, Kabul, July 2018.

44 Norland, R. 2018. "Accused of Rape and Torture, Exiled Afghan Vice President Returns." *The New York Times*, July 22, 2018.

45 There were other rumours of Governor Noor's change of heart, including his fear of being removed from his long-held position as governor of Balkh where he had established and consolidated an expansive political and economic network. Another rumoured reason was that the Palace had threatened, or even attempted, to freeze Governor Noor's bank accounts and businesses in Dubai, Malaysia, and other places. It seems unlikely that the government had the legal expertise to do this, but it might have raised concerns about his accounts. All in all, the threats seemed to have worked in bringing Governor Noor closer to talks with the Palace. And if true, it inherently put him in a weak position in his negotiations with Ghani.

46 Interview with several frustrated Abdullah supporters, September 24–25, 2016, Kabul.

47 In an op-ed, Governor Noor wrote: "with the good intentions I have seen from the President, I feel that the only way to strengthen the government and improve legitimacy" is to "establish a common axis [*mehvar*] to end the current crisis." Noor, A. M. 2016. "Afghanistan's Situation Needs a Closer Political Grouping." *BBC Online*, December 18, 2016. The Jamiat under Rabbani leadership issued a statement on February 5, 2017, giving Governor Noor the green light to pursue its negotiations with Ghani.

48 "Fazel Sangcharaki's Interview," Freedom Radio, December 24, 2016. The latter goal, his formal appointment as governor in February, has been achieved. Crisis Group interview, Kabul, August 2016. A February 5 party statement, while emphasising the importance of implementing the NUG agreement, said the "Leadership Council of Jamiat recommends Ustad Atta Mohammad Governor Noor to continue to negotiate with the palace on behalf of the party and thus the council supports the negotiations."

49 For detailed account of the Enlightenment Movement see Hugueley, S. 2019. "Enlightenment Movement: Electricity and Citizenship in Afghanistan." *Radicle: Reed Anthropology Review*, Issue 4; and AAN reports 2 and 3.

50 See Bose, Bizhan and Ibrahimi (2019).

51 Protection networks are those that are small, often working within the government as technocrats, do not enjoy political support from ethno-regional patrons and are vulnerable to network bargain shocks and crises. They come together to share information, protect each other, and, if necessary, engage in disruptive politics to undermine their rivals to maintain their position. SAGE eventually became a protection network shifting away from being president Ghani's campaign machinery as rivalries increased among members.

52 Qazi, S. 2016. "Afghan Power Project Prompts Hazara Protest in Kabul." *Aljazeera*, May 17, 2016; Latifi, A. M. 2016. "An Ethnically Charged Dispute over Electricity Brings Protesters into Kabul's Streets." *Los Angeles Times*, May 16, 2016. TUTAP was an initiative funded by the Asian Development Bank to connect insular power grid inside the country as well as the neighbouring countries.

53 There was a lack of clarity surrounding how and why the decision was made to switch from Bamiyan to Salang. President Ghani's team insisted that the decision to change the route had been taken under the previous administration, which had some truth to it. In 2013, the Asian Development Bank's feasibility study of the Bamiyan pass, carried out by German consulting firm Fichner, recommended the Bamiyan route because "it would avoid the narrow space and difficulties along the Salang pass ... [the Salang pass] may have the advantage of slightly shorter time for construction and will have slightly less investment cost." The government's rationale, at least in rhetoric, was cost and time. There were also accusations that elements within the Brishna Company, the state-owned company, and the Ministry of Energy and Water had suggested to Fichner to recommend the Salang Pass option, persuaded the cabinet, and then fast-tracked the process to achieve their corrupt ends: to give the projects to partners outside government for implementation. On 3 May, the Minister of Water and Energy, Ali Ahmad Osmani, announced that the decision about the TUTAP route could not be changed because such a change would affect the plans for electricity supplies to 12 southern provinces. Mirwais Alemi, the Acting Director-General of Brishna warned that the project would be cancelled if it was delayed.

54 For years the people of Bamiyan were complaining that they were suffering from a "peace penalty", meaning the international community and Afghan government were neglecting peaceful provinces in favour of insecure areas. See Chapter 9 on the politics of aid.

55 Bjelica and Ruttig (2016).

56 See Qazi, S. 2015. "Afghans Protest 'Beheadings of Ethnic Hazara by ISIL'." *Aljazeera*, November 11, 2015.

57 Karimi, K. H., "Kucha Bazari ha: Az Chashma ba Charkhab."

58 "Skirmishes Over TUTAP: London-Based Afghans Launch Protest," *ToloNews*, May 13, 2016.

59 Sengupta, K. 2016. "Heckling of Afghan President at Anti-Corruption Summit Gives Glimpse of Country's Division." *Independent*, May 13, 2016.

60 "Kabul Explosion: IS 'Claims Attack on Hazara Protest," BBC. July 23, 2016.

61 Author's interview, Kabul, August 2016.

62 Author's conversation with several Enlightenment Movement representatives throughout 2016.

63 "Death Toll Rises after Kabul Bomb, Extensive Damage to Germany Embassy," *Deutsche Welle News*, May 31, 2017.

64 For a detailed account of events and dates see Afghanistan Analysts Network Team. 2017. "AAN Q&A: Tents and Bullets – The Crackdown on the Kabul Protests." June 23, 2017. Kabul: Afghanistan Analyst Network.

65 Ibid. There was another attack at the burial of the Ezedyar's son the next day which brought in more protesters. Abdullah Abdullah, who attended the funeral prayer barely escaped death.

66 Ibid.

67 Adili and Linke (2016).

68 Author's interview and observation in the government.

69 See Bose, Bizhan and Ibrahimi (2019).

70 Ibid.

71 Masoud had joined Ghani's ticket in the run-off election in 2014 and served as an important asset in balancing out ethnic dynamics. He was the only ethnic-Tajik and Jamiati and was promised that his position would function as a vice-presidency with special privileges and authorities. He was frustrated for not being consulted on key issues.

72 Ghubar, G. 2017. "Zia Masoud Apologises to Nation for Having Supported Ghani." *Tolonews*, April 28, 2017.

73 Sadly, history was repeating itself. Karmal's government in the 1980s also struggled with inclusive representation. It struggled to include more non-Parcham and non-communist officials and leaders in the government. The Soviets failed to convince Karmal to broaden his power base, enabling the Soviets to exit.

74 See International Crisis Group Report (2017).

75 Interviews with people close to Governor Noor revealed that he might have had a hand in the fall of Rabbani. The president's visit to Mazar following the inauguration of the Aqina railroad project in Faryab, during which he stayed at Governor Noor's house, was a significant step in the rapprochement between the two. After that visit, Governor Noor orchestrated Rabbani's impeachment by the Parliament as a way of showing he was "warming up" to Ghani. Author's interviews, October and November 2018.

76 Author's interview, Kabul, August 2019.

77 "Newly-Launched Party Calls for Fresh Presidential Polls," *Pajhwok News*, January 14, 2016.

78 Author's interview with several officials in Atmar campaign, Kabul, June 2020.

79 Author's conversation with one senior Mohaqqiq confidante, Kabul, June 2020.

80 Author's interview with several officials in Atmar campaign, Kabul, June 2020.

81 "Interview with Hamid Karzai," video, *The New York Times*, August 5, 2016; "Afghanistan is in Chaos. Is that What Hamid Karzai Wants?," ibid., August 5, 2016; "Hamid Karzai: Afghanistan in Danger of Sliding 'under thumb' of Pakistan'," *The Guardian*, March 9, 2015; "Hamid Karzai in his Retirement, Says of Afghanistan: 'We Should not Be Failing'," *Los Angeles Times*, December 27, 2016. Crisis Group interviews, National Security Council officials, Ghani's advisers and ministers, Kabul, August–November 2016.

82 "Hamid Karzai: Afghanistan in Danger of Sliding 'under thumb' of Pakistan," *The Guardian*, March 9, 2015.

83 "Hamid Karzai in His Retirement, Says of Afghanistan: 'We Should not Be Failing'," *Los Angeles Times*, December 27, 2016.

84 International Crisis Group Report (2017).

85 International Crisis Group Observation of Meetings & Interviews, Kabul, August–November 2016.

86 International Crisis Group interviews with National Security Council and Administrative Office of the President, 5–6 September 2016, Kabul; "Afghanistan is in Chaos. Is that What Hamid Karzai Wants," August 5, 2016.

87 Author's conversation with senior Ghani officials in the Palace and MoD.

88 Donati, Nelso, and Nissenbaum (2018). There was increasing pressure from the U.S. not to go ahead with elections, prioritising the peace process. Many, including president Ghani, argued that this went against the constitutional order and saving the repub-

lic for which Afghans and American had made huge human and financial sacrifices. The Americans deliberately created an ambiguous environment, giving mixed signals about the elections. The American stand contrasted with the positions some of its allies, including the EU, took, actively advocated for organising elections on time.

89 "Ghani Elected President of Afghanistan," *ToloNews*, February 18, 2020.
90 See Watkins (2020).
91 At least two provinces' provincial capitals in the north were occupied by Abdullah supporters. Frustrated by the political impasse, the U.S. State Department on March 2020 issued a statement announcing it would reduce its assistance by $1 billion in 2020 and threatened to reduce another $1 billion in 2021 if disputes were not resolved (https://www.state.gov/on-the-political-impasse-in-afghanistan/, retrieved on 9 September 2020).
92 For more analysis of the deal see Adili (2020).
93 "Sapidar Palace Surprised by New Governor Appointments," *Afghan Voice Agency*, July 8, 2020.
94 Author's conversation with a foreign Embassy diplomat, Kabul, October 2016.

7 Elections for sale

Manipulating identities and bargains

Introduction

"Where are you going!" shouted an irritated and gaudy voice. Startled, I hit my brakes and brought my barely moving car to a full stop, staring blankly into the angry face of a police officer. Not uttering another word, he turned his gaze towards another officer, a member of the national police judging by his uniform, who, just a few seconds earlier, had signalled I could pass. He spat a few angry words at him in Pashto. The officer shrugged it off, as if he didn't care, and walked away. It was 9 March 2020, the presidential inauguration day, when the two top rival candidates—incumbent president Ashraf Ghani and the former Chief Executive Officer (CEO) Abdullah Abdullah—were holding parallel swearing-in ceremonies amid disputed election results, one in the palace and the other in the CEO office, just a few hundred metres away. It was a tense day. I was on my way to visit a friend in Shahr-i-Naw, Kabul's lively downtown core. The roadblock leading to the city centre, where the palace was also located, was manned by four different security branches, a familiar arrangement on such days when the city was under threat. The officer who had shouted at me was from Public Protection Force based on his uniform. He was also an ethnic Pashtun. In the end, he ordered me to turn around and use an alternative route to get to the city centre.

The checkpoint was in Deh Mazang Square, where the Islamic State of Khorasan Province (ISKP) twin bombings targeting Enlightenment Movement demonstrators in 2016 had killed over 100 people.[1] As I turned around, I realised the Public Protection Force officer had let the two cars behind me go through but had stopped the third car. Knowing that any protest would not go anywhere, I parked my car on the other side of the road and continued to observe the situation for a few more minutes. As I watched, the national policeman, an ethnic Tajik who had originally permitted me to pass, waved, and gave me that knowing smile, the kind that says: "You are one of us."

The incident was telling and made me angry. The fact that Afghanistan's security forces suffered from a weak and precarious central command was relatively clear, but this incident reflected the broader spillover of political division and fragmentation. How could it be that one of the few institutions that Afghans across the political spectrum had hoped would escape ethnicisation was being

DOI: 10.4324/9781315161617-7

further polarised along ethnic lines? This would be one of the key contributing factors to the eventual tumbling of the Republic.

Afghanistan had had seven rounds of parliamentary, presidential, and provincial council elections since 2001.[2] Those elections were supposed to usher in an era of national unity. The U.S.A. and its allies had considered free and fair elections the principal indicator of their success in the country. At the Bonn Conference, holding presidential and parliamentary elections was one of the main four benchmarks of the Agreement, with the instructions that "free and fair elections are to be held no later than two years from the date of the convening of the Emergency Loya Jirga."[3] To achieve this, the international intervention had invested significant financial, technical, and political resources to prepare the ground for elections in Afghanistan. Still, all of Afghanistan's post-2001 elections had been marred by accusations of industrial-scale fraud, vote-rigging, and irregularities, which subsequently led to prolonged political crises.[4]

In the preceding chapters, I laid out the contours of how elections in the post-2001 networked state in Afghanistan had less to do with determining the will of the people and more with renegotiating resource allocation (political, social, and material) and renewing pact-making among powerbrokers. Presidential elections in particular serve as excellent *critical junctures* to better understand the process by which state and subnational political networks competed and contested under the veneer of ostensibly liberal-democratic elections.

This chapter begins with a high-altitude view of how the international community, and in particular the U.S.A., contributed to creating an environment in which elections were doomed to failure (Section 7.1). A series of elections which followed were premised on that basic principle: it wasn't the will of the people that mattered, but the best means of re-allocating resources such that some form of stability would be maintained. Section 7.2 provides an overview of the underlying sources from which election disputes arose and how political networks were able to trigger them for their benefits. Next, in Section 7.3, I explore alliance formation and propagation of patron–client bargains, rent-seeking, intimidation, and manipulation of Afghanistan's identity groups, those based on ethnicity, and reciprocity linking electoral actors, middlemen, and constituencies. Finally, in the conclusion, I offer a more substantive explanation for fraud and vote-rigging in the 2009 poll, which focuses on the nature of networked politics.

7.1 The U.S.A., the international community, and the veneer of democracy

The meddling of the U.S.A. and its international allies in Afghan elections was a perennial feature of the country's electoral cycle. The stakes were high, not only in Afghanistan but in many western nations too, where Afghanistan had become a signature foreign policy issue for any number of governments. In many cases, in Canada for instance, success or failure in Afghanistan could win or lose an election for the incumbent party. Thus, ensuring a stable political order and legitimate government in Kabul to help fight the Taliban insurgency and international terrorism ranked high on the political priorities of a wide swathe of western politicians, diplomats, and aid workers. The significant financial contributions by international donors also gave them huge influence over technical election processes, approaches, and the politics of the elections. More importantly, the perception of international backing, especially the U.S.A., for a candidate, even a small hint, was key in swaying political network alliance-building. Many political network leaders looked to the U.S.A. to signal which candidate is supported, with the expectation that the American-favoured candidate would eventually win.

In some elections, the Americans directly tried to influence the outcomes (2004 and 2009) while in others, when election outcomes were challenged, followed by a crisis, they directly intervened to settle disputes, always with an eye for their own interests. As discussed in Chapter 5, during the 2009 election, Richard Holbrooke, the U.S. administration's special representative for Afghanistan and Pakistan, openly interfered in the process to tilt it against Karzai. His strategy was to encourage several potentially strong ethnic Pashtun candidates to run as a way of splitting the Pashtun vote and forcing a run-off in which Karzai could be defeated.[5] Robert Gates, the defence secretary, described Holbrooke's attempt as a "clumsy and failed putsch," adding, "it was all ugly: our partner, the president of Afghanistan, was tainted, and our hands were dirty as well." The rift with Karzai continued to burden U.S.–Afghan relations until the end of the Karzai administration in 2014. The election was also overshadowed by a public rift between the U.S.A. and UN Secretary-General Ban Ki-Moon when the latter dismissed the United Nations Assistance Mission in Afghanistan (UNAMA) deputy, Ambassador Peter Galbraith, who was supported by the U.S. State Department and more specifically by Richard Holbrooke. Peter Galbraith had clashed with the head of UNAMA, Kai Eide, over Galbraith's forceful and public criticism of the Karzai team's fraud and manipulation.

In the 2014 election, the Americans were compelled to intervene in the election rift between the two main candidates, mediating a quick and highly fraught power-sharing settlement. The ad hoc, extra-constitutional arrangement produced the National Unity Government, without much unity to speak of, led by a president and a newly created CEO (supposedly the head of government). As Chapter 6 showed that the formula fuelled political network disunity and ethnic division, producing immense political chaos and instability within the state.

Finally, in 2019, the Americans were quick to cast a shadow over the freedom and fairness of the elections. Following the announcement of the election results, the then U.S. ambassador to Afghanistan, John R. Bass, reiterated his caution about the preliminary nature of the results, tweeting that "many steps remain before final election results are certified."[6] In another tweet, and a sign which many interpreted as the American view on the election, Ambassador Bass, commenting on the low turnout, stated,

> in our political culture, [such a victory with less than one million votes in a country of 30 million people] is not a commanding mandate. That is not a signal that a large majority of the people support whoever that person is.

Ambassador Bass called on the eventual winner to exhibit humility and govern inclusively.[7]

The American position was perplexing and vexing for Afghans. For [months] in the lead-up, the U.S.A. had undermined the vote while it curried favour with the Taliban in its bilateral negotiations. The negotiations themselves, excluding the Afghan government, sent the message that the elections would be meaningless once the Americans signed a deal with the Taliban. To then criticise the low turnout felt outrageously self-fulfilling. Moreover, the Americans' open rejection of the election's legitimacy had the devastating consequence of reinforcing the Taliban's assertion that the Ghani government, which ultimately claimed victory, was illegitimate, shaping their behaviour in the upcoming intra-Afghan talks.

The American demand to delay the election on behalf of their efforts to negotiate a way out of Afghanistan was also puzzling. Delaying the election would have amounted to violating Afghanistan's constitution, an awkward place for the U.S.A. to be considering the degree to which Americans consider their own constitution sacrosanct. To most Afghans, the demand was simply more evidence that the American priority was not elections but a political deal with the Taliban, even if that meant sacrificing democracy and the constitutional order. Many also believed that the American exit was tied to President Trump's own re-election campaign for an election he was desperate to win at all cost.

7.2 Underlying sources of election disputes

The 2004 presidential elections set the wrong tone for the next three elections, in terms of processes, management of electoral bodies, and the politics of elections. From early on, President Karzai saw election bodies as a toolkit for his election engineering, building a politically charged foundation for his advantage. The Joint Electoral Management Body (JEMB) Secretariat, set up in July 2003, responsible for managing the election, had 11 members (six Afghans and five internationals appointed by UNAMA).[8] Instead of ensuring impartiality and transparency, President Karzai appointed political allies to executive positions and as commissioners. Farook Wardak was appointed Director-General of the Secretariat. For the next two elections, Karzai would appoint loyal clients to the Independent Election Commission (IEC—the successor of JEMB)—politicising it and the Electoral Complaints Commission (ECC), as well as their Secretariats.[9] It became an established rule that whoever appointed the Head of Secretariat in the IEC would emerge as the winner given that the latter exercised vast supervision, oversight, and appointment powers within the IEC. Over the years, independent observation bodies, including the Free and Fair Election Forum of Afghanistan (FEFA), became politicised, further undermining the credibility of electoral bodies. FEFA was a 13-member Afghan NGO association that was set up in 2004 with considerable international training and financial assistance from the Washington-based National Democratic Institute (NDI).[10] In 2014, there were serious accusations that it had provided detailed technical assistance to Ghani's camp and its board members, which included people who later became Ghani's confidantes in his administration.[11]

Voter registration and over-registration became an endemic problem which Afghan leaders, especially incumbents, would use to justify wholesale fraud and vote-rigging. In the 2004 election, around 10.57 million voters received voter cards, excluding those in Iran and Pakistan, representing over 100% of what had been determined as the total estimated electorate.[12] It was evident that there was clear over-registration in some areas and under-registration in others, which would facilitate future ballot stuffing and fraud. There was significant over-registration in the southeast region (Paktia, Paktika, and Khost), at 133.6%, including 55% female registration, compared to 41.3% for the entire country and 29.9% in the south, a striking difference.[13] Six other predominantly Pashtun provinces (Laghman, Nangarhar, Kunar, Ghazni, Helmand, and Kandahar) were also reportedly over-registered, compared to only three predominantly non-Pashtun provinces—Balkh, Badghis, and Herat.[14] There were serious irregularities in the registration process, too, including multiple registration and registration of underage voters. This further politicised the voter registration processes which Karzai would later use to demand additional seats in the lower house and create new districts while upgrading others. The lack of a population census further enflamed election disputes.[15] The introduction of indelible ink in 2004 and biometric voter registration in 2018 and 2019 elections did not prevent multiple voting.

Elections were also exceptionally expensive in Afghanistan and became a major source of corruption, bargains, and rent-seeking—the only moment that bargains and rent-seeking flowed at all levels of Afghan polity and society. One senior international electoral staff member complained about the lack of funds for the 2004 elections, describing it as "running on fumes."[16] As Table 7.2 reveals, the combined cost for the 2004 elections, including preparations for first-time voter registration, civil engagement, and conducting the elections, totalled over $203 million, excluding the provision of security by Afghan and international military forces. The cost of the 2009 and 2010 presidential, provincial council, and parliamentary elections was around $500 million.[17] Although this was reduced substantially in 2019, it was still a high-priced operation for the country considering that the Afghan government allocated $90 million of the $149 million overall estimated cost.[18] Table 7.1 shows commitments made by donor countries and areas where money was spent and Table 7.2 illustrates the commitment made to the 2009 elections by donor countries with the U.S.A. shouldering most of the financial burden.

These factors contributed to wholesale election fraud, irregularities, and moments of rupture in post-2001 Afghanistan. In the 2004 election, the Impartial Panel of Election Experts reported more than 300 cases of abuse and intimidation out of a total number of 448 officially filed complaints. In the 2009 elections, the Independent Electoral Complaints Commission (IECC) disqualified 1.2 million ballots, of which 1 million belonged to the incumbent President Karzai and 200,000 to Abdullah Abdullah.[19] The absence of voter lists and databases

Table 7.1 The cost of elections in Afghanistan

Election type	Year	Cost
Presidential elections	2004	US$203 million
Parliamentary and provincial council	2005	US$173 million
Presidential elections and provincial council	2009	US$300 million (approx.)
Parliamentary elections	2010	US$200 million (approx.)
Presidential elections	2014	US$203 million
Parliamentary	2018	
Presidential elections	2019	US$149 million

These data were collected from Afghan Elections Project, Excel document titled "Funding status 5 Oct 04.xls," <https://www.elec%ons-afghanistan.org.af/>. United Nations Development Programme, 2004 Afghan Elections Project Budget, <https://www.elec%ons-afghanistan.org.af/>; 20 United Nations Development Programme, 2004 Afghan Elections Project Budget, <https://www.elec%ons-afghanistan.org.af/>. SIGAR notes that the combined funding budgeted for the 2004 and 2005 election was USD 416 million, presumably including all programs related to elections and funds made bilaterally and through UNDP (https://d2071andvip0wj.cloudfront.net/88-afghanistan-from-presidential-to-parliamentary-elections.pdf). See also the UN. 2019. "The Situation in Afghanistan and Its Implications for International Peace and Security, Report of the Secretary-General," 312, March 2019.

Table 7.2 United Nations and bilateral assistance for 2009 elections (US$ in millions)

UNDP Elect II project	
Voter registration	102.2
Election administration	229.0
Bilateral assistance	
United States	143.1
Canada	9.2
Denmark	1.7
Germany	0.4
The Netherlands	2.5
Switzerland	0.5
Total bilateral assistance	157.4
Total assistance	488.6

Note that donors like Japan, the United Kingdom, and EU made significant contribution in the UNDP pool.
Source: UNDP ELECT I and SIGAR.

was a serious shortcoming which led to over 20 million people receiving registration cards for the 2014 elections. Without such a roll, the exact numbers of ballots needed at polling sites could not be determined.[20] To address the issue of voter fraud, in 2018 all existing voter registrations were cancelled and voters were required to register with a new biometric system, which included both fingerprint and photo identification. Around 9.66 million people registered. The biometric system was a major headache and did not resolve the fraud. In the 2018

Table 7.3 Election turnout and fraudulent vote

Elections and year	Voter registration	Turnout	Fraudulent/ disputed vote
Presidential elections (2004)	9,716,413	8,129,940/ (83.66%)	104,404
Parliamentary and provincial council (2005)	12,500,000	5,882, 867 (valid votes)	—
Presidential elections and provincial council (2009)	12,430,644	5,918,741/ (47.61%)	1.2 million
Parliamentary elections (2010)	10,300,000	4,126,594/ (40.94%)	1.5 million
Presidential elections (2014)	20,845,988	7,018,049/ (33.67)	
Parliamentary (2018)	8,899,941	3,660,124	
Presidential elections (2019)	9,665,777	2,695,890	871,942

The data from 2004 to 2014 parliamentary elections are from The International Foundation for Electoral System (http://www.electionguide.org/countries/id/2/) and the 2018 and 2019 elections from the United Nations Election Support Project (UNESP) report; and NDI Afghanistan Election Data (https://afghanistanelectiondata.org/elections) (https://www.af.undp.org/content/afghanistan/en/home /projects/UNESP.html). The final turnout of the 2019 elections was announced as 1,823,948, which was disputed by Abdullah's team, which wanted at least 350,000 votes disqualified.
Source: IFES, UNESP report, Afghanistan Election Data.

parliamentary elections, the IEC received 18,577 complaints. In the 2019 elections, almost 1 million votes were disputed, of which the IEC disqualified around 872,000, this is in addition to an exceptionally low turnout, with the IEC putting the valid biometric turnout at below 1.7 million (18%) out of the 9.66 million voters[21] (Table 7.3).

In the 2019 presidential election, the IEC produced four sets of turnout data, attesting to the level of confusion and manipulation by staff.[22] According to one senior IEC official, at least 50% of the IEC voter registration database in 2019 could not be corroborated with voters' details (either missing or inaccurate details including misspelling of full names, father's name, and date and place of birth) and may have been fraudulent or invalid.[23] This was further exacerbated by widespread mishandling of the issuance of *tazkira* (ID cards). The Afghanistan Central Civil Registration Authority (ACCRA) issued up to 10 million new *tazkiras* before the 2019 elections. There were widespread reports of wholesale *tazkira* and voters' sticker (a unique identification bar code) purchases by local strongmen, candidates, and officials.[24] There were also thousands of fake *tazkiras* and voter stickers around, especially in major cities, that facilitated widespread fraud in the 2019 presidential elections. According to a Kabul IEC official, more than half of Kabul MPs in the 2018 parliamentary elections were involved in wholesale procurement of voter stickers and *tazkiras* from corrupt ACCRA and IEC officials which facilitated ballot stuffing.[25] According to a detailed analysis of voter registration by provinces, six provinces had less than 40% of eligible voters registered, while four provinces registered over 100% of their estimated eligible voters.[26]

Finally, one of the biggest shortcomings of elections in Afghanistan was the lack of strong dispute resolution mechanisms within the election framework, possibly deliberately overlooked by the Afghan government and its international backers. The government lacked an authoritative body that was impartial, credible, and resourced to resolve disputes and act with an exclusive appellate function.[27] Even after 2017, when the electoral law, after years of civil society lobbying, introduced a complaint mechanism, tasking the ECC to deal with complaints, the ECC's authority remained limited for the resolution of legal disputes, as evidenced by the 2019 and 2018 elections. Over the years, the ECC was sidelined by a more powerful and politicised IEC. As Afghanistan's disputed presidential elections showed, these disputes often went beyond formal legal complaints and appeal processes, which were often better addressed through regular consultation and mediation processes.

All these technical shortcomings contributed to setting a shaky foundation for democratisation in Afghanistan, leading to disputes, irregularities, and vote-rigging. Over the years, instead of correcting these flaws the Afghan government and international backers engaged in positive spin-doctoring, promoting the message that these elections were "good enough" considering the complex and challenging circumstances in which they were held. "Good enough" would become a measure of success for subsequent Afghan elections. And when disputes arose, the integrity of elections and democratisation would be surrendered to maintain political stability and order.

7.3   Alliance-building, opportunism, and bargains

Elections became key moments for rent-seeking, bargains, and opportunism impacted all levels of Afghan society from village to national politics. As the experience of the 2009 and 2019 presidential elections shows below, to win, candidates had to assemble the largest alliance of political networks and centres of power with whatever power resources they had available to them, in a series of power resource interdependencies. These required political and financial resources to mobilise constituencies and finance campaigns as well as utilising violent means and personal reputation to defend candidates when election outcomes were contested.

7.3.1   *State-level alliance-building and power resource interdependencies in the 2009 and 2019 elections*

In the 2009 election, Karzai and Abdullah emerged as the two main contenders. Karzai was successful in building the largest alliance. Pacts were negotiated that secured ethno-regional vote bank political networks: Wahdat-i-Mardom and Wahdat-i-Islami led by Mohammad Mohaqqiq and Karim Khalili, respectively, for the ethnic Hazara vote; Junbish network led by Abdul Rashid Dostum for the ethnic Uzbek vote; Ismail Khan's network in the western region for ethnic Tajik vote; the gang of seven powerbrokers in the south for the ethnic Pashtun vote (i.e., Sher Mohammad Akhundzada in Helmand, Jan Mohammad Khan in Uruzgan and his brother Ahmad Wali Karzai in Kandahar); the Arsala family network for the Nangarhar vote; and Hizb-i-Islami fractured group led by Abdul Hadi Arghandiwal and Afghan Millet network for some of the northern Pashtun votes.[28] In 2009, Karzai won most of the southern votes because of the power of his network, the gang of seven, including their coercive power to line up support from tribal elders and other influential provincial leaders, who in turn amassed votes from their communities.[29] The decision to allow Abdul Rashid Dostum to return from exile and then to enlist him in his camp showed Karzai's anxiety over enticing vote bank networks like him to join his side. The gang of seven in the south did not necessarily bring vote banks, but they had the power to use their influence and, if necessary, their intimidation and monopoly of the use of violence to coerce and pressure tribal elders and influential players to support Karzai. They and their associates had immense financial capital at their disposal to finance the entire campaign in the south as well as intimidate local businessmen to fund Karzai's campaign in the form of renting campaign offices, paying for TV advertisements, and sponsoring campaign rallies.

Family-based and religious-centred networks like Nazhat-i-Hambastagi led by Pir Gailani and Jabha-i-Nijat-Milli Afghanistan led by the former president Mojadaddi, Sayed Mansoor Naderi that led most of the Ismailis group, and Dawat-i-Islami led by Abdul Rasul Sayyaf were recruited for networking skills and religious legitimation. These networks were valued because of their close connection with the country's conservative circles and religious support networks, including in the justice sector amongst judges. From 2005, Sayyaf had spearheaded president Karzai's agenda in parliament as well as aiding the palace with its outreach efforts to Jihadi leaders and provincial commanders. Sayed Mansoor Naderi, who led the tight-knit family network of Naderis, had a solid vote of around 50,000 from his Ismaili Shia group and financially contributed to the campaign, paying for campaign gatherings and media outreach efforts. In a religiously conservative society like Afghanistan, no candidate wanted to be accused of lacking religious support or to have his religious credentials questioned. In the 2019 election, Ghani avoided a presidential TV debate on TOLO TV because of a last-minute tip in which it was rumoured that Hekmatyar, or the moderator, might ask the candidates religious questions.[30] As explained in Chapter 5, Karzai successfully enlisted Marshal Fahim (an ethnic Tajik), the most senior former Shuray-i-Nezar commander to run as his first vice-presidential running-mate, thereby splitting the so-called United Front alliance. Karzai and Fahim families would rally Afghan businessmen in Kabul Bank (see Chapter 9) and other key sectors to support his campaign. Karim Khalili (an ethnic Hazara and leader of Wahdat-i-Islami) remained with Karzai as his second vice-presidential running-mate again. As discussed in Chapter 5, Karzai strong-armed several prominent Pashtun candidates like Gul Agha Shirzai and Minister Anwarul Haq Ahadi, a son-in-law to Pir Gailani, not to run and thereby ensure the Pashtun vote would not be split.

Abdullah, on the other hand, struggled to recruit influential ethno-regional vote banks into his alliance. Governor Noor and Burhanuddin Rabbani, both Jamiat network affiliates, were the most high-profile potential recruits for the ethnic Tajik vote, but the latter did not publicly endorse him. Reportedly, Governor Noor financed most of Abdullah's campaign.[31] When relations between Abdullah and Governor Noor deteriorated in September 2016, Governor Noor privately complained about and regretted paying some of Abdullah's campaign finances. Abdullah's Pashtun, Hazara, and Uzbek supporters mainly consisted of relatively less influential political networks such as Haraka-i-Islami (led by Sayyed Hussein Anwari) and Hizb-i-Wahdat-i-Islami Millet (led by Qorban Ali Irfani) and others. Abdullah's running mates, Humayoun Wasefi (an ethnic royalist Pashtun) and Dr Ali Cheragh (an ethnic Hazara) as first and second deputies, respectively, were relatively unknown figures. The Pashtun network clientele that Abdullah managed to recruit were low-level officials including Farahi, Ulumi, and Gulobzoy, who during the campaign privately expressed their frustration for their lack of inclusion in campaign decision making.

Ten years later, in the 2019 elections, Ghani's disruption of the Karzai-era order had broadly and significantly restructured political networks and bargains. He had lost the support of the two leading ethno-regional vote bank political networks, Junbish and Wahdat-i-Mardom, as well as the Sayed Mansoor Naderi family network who initially joined Atmar's ticket and when his campaign collapsed to Abdullah Abdullah's. Other political networks including Gailani's family, Jamiat-i-Islami led by Salahuddin Rabbani, and Wahdat-i-Islami led by Karim Khalili sided with Abdullah Abdullah. The three main breakaways from Abdullah's campaign were Amrullah Saleh who joined Ghani's ticket as his first running-mate, Governor Noor who sided with Ghani but did not publicly campaign for him, and Arghandiwal, the Hizb-i-Islami splinter network leader. Sayyaf was stuck with Ghani because of several key positions it had secured including the Ministry of Interior, but also did not publicly campaign. Other ethnic Hazara network leaders like Mohammad Akbari, second vice president Sarwar Danesh, and Sadiq Modabber sided with Ghani in the hope they would be rewarded after the elections. In Kabul and its northern provinces, most of the Greater Council of the North network joined Ghani's team with huge concessions but failed to deliver the vote for Ghani. In the south, key figures that comprised Karzai's network in the south had been replaced following their deaths by Shah Wali Khan (representing the Karzai family and the Popalzai tribe) and Tadin Khan (the brother of notorious General Raziq from the Achikzai tribe which controlled most of the southern Kandahar). Shah Wali stayed impartial while Tadin Khan tacitly backed Ghani but did not openly campaign or use his power of intimidation to bring the tribes into line for him (Figure 7.1).

In these reciprocal power interdependency relations, network clients were not shy about making their deals public. For instance, in 2009, Mohammad Mohaqqiq, the leader of Wahdat-i-Mardom, publicly demanded at least four ministries for his group. Also, Mohaqqiq demanded an upgrade for the Jaghuri and Behsud districts into provinces. Abdul Rashid Dostum also demanded similar concessions. As an independent female MP from Kabul explained:

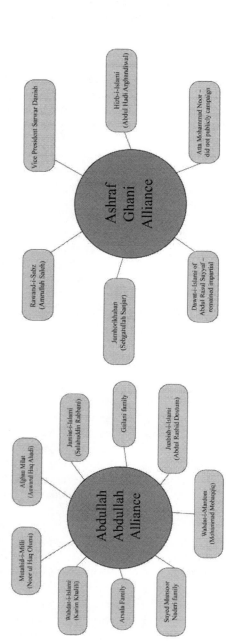

Figure 7.1 Political network alliances in the 2019 elections.

In the past these figures used to act like khans (chiefs), now they act as mediators between the candidate and the people. They and their *halaqat* [networks] are the key players within the system. They have money and resources including coercive power to win the vote. While the candidate pays the money to the main powerbrokers, they then distribute it down the chain to their cronies. They can also choose to appoint ministers like Mojadaddi. His son was appointed governor of Kabul city. The same goes for Junbish-i-Islami and Wahdat-i-Mardom who are demanding four and two ministries respectively.[32]

These patronage and bargaining practices were seen as mutually beneficial for the candidate and the network-clients. The ethno-regional patronage relations elicited by the election had extensive ramifications not just for the nature of governance in Afghanistan but the politico-administrative shape of the state itself. The decision to allow Dostum to return from exile in 2008 and 2018 just before the election and his ability to deliver votes, at least in certain provinces, was crucial for Karzai and Abdullah's vote. Client-networks led by leaders publicly campaigned for their patron-candidates. In their active campaigning, they manipulated the appropriate cultural symbols as well as articulated and advanced their ethno-regional groups' collective aspirations, as they defined them. Political leaders travelled widely across their regions to gather support in person. For instance, in 2009, in his first speech in his hometown of Jawzjan after returning from exile, Dostum declared:

If you like me or not, this is your personal choice. But when you come to Junbish, then support its decisions and its Muamela (political dealings). Let's stay united and do not let others exploit your sacrifices and your bloodshed. Let us stay with Hamid Karzai; and I, as your leader, ask you to come together and make sure that Hamid Karzai wins in the first round.[33]

Similarly, Mohaqqiq in the 2009 election told his supporters in Daikundi province:

If I knew among these 39 candidates a better one, I would have identified and told you to vote accordingly, my millet (nation). I have two demands from you, first your full participation in the election and second to vote for Karzai.[34]

Acting as a mediator or a campaign agent of the leading presidential candidates, political networks provided their staff and resources to help mobilise electorates. They used their own extended organisational patronage networks at the province, district, and village levels during the campaign. Campaigning usually involved assembling large gatherings, often with lunch and transport costs provided, private face-to-face meetings, organising rallies, distribution of campaign materials, gifts (e.g., headscarves for women or money for a local mosque) and passing around posters. In addition to their informal patronage networks, political networks were also able to utilise other forms of resources that they had at their disposals. In 2009, this included using TV and radio stations under their control to mobilise supporters and broadcast negative images of opposing contenders. Some of the most powerful networks had their own TV and radio stations, including Junbish-i-Islami, Wahdat-i-Islami, Wahdat-i-Mardom, Dawat-i-Islami to name a few. As Bashardost, the third-place presidential candidate in 2009, commented, "before they had a Kalashnikov, and now they have a TV [station]." In 2009, Abdullah could rely on Governor Noorin TV and Governor Noor TV channels, which were linked with Governor Noor. Newspapers like *Mandegar* and *Nokhost* also supported and advocated for Abdullah.

7.3.2 *Election entrepreneurs, bargains, and opportunism*

These bargains were not limited to state-level and ethno-regional-level political networks. There were so other actors, including district commanders, solidarity group (Qawm) elders, village chiefs and councils, and traders, overlapping, and often clients of political networks, who entered into bargains of one kind or another with subnational campaign managers and officials. As my ethnographic fieldwork during the 2009 election showed, local figures and representatives regularly approached different candidates, offering their support in exchange for jobs, development aid and even hard cash, partially side-lining the ethno-regional individual network ties. Martine van Bijlert, the Afghanistan Analysts Network analyst, made similar observations in her study of the election. "Communities, parties and solidarity groups go through several rounds of internal consultation and negotiation to make up their mind—in a process of communal decision making—about whom they will align themselves to," she noted. "Representatives are sent to sound out the various candidates in search of the best alliance or the best deal in exchange for the votes on offer."[35]

In these elections, local villagers, tribal representatives, and various professional associations from main cities, like shopkeepers' associations, carpet associations, writers and artists associations, and youth associations, would regularly visit each candidate, offering blocks of votes and in return asking for various demands like a new stadium, a social club, or other types of financial support. For instance, in one of the meetings, a female group claimed: "We represent Dasht-e-Barchi women. We have 300 voting cards ... we will continue [to work for] your campaign but we need your support [referring to financial support]."[36] Some candidates would commit to building a mosque or schools for communities. On another occasion, a group of boxers offered to provide security on Election Day if the candidate financially contributed to building their boxing club. Such offers were common. It is difficult to confirm whether such payments were actually made in the end but the fact that various groups would even consider seeking bargains openly indicates the degree to which such opportunistic practices were widespread.

These election entrepreneurs played a key role at all levels in Afghanistan's elections. The motivation to join the campaign offered by Karzai's deputy campaign manager in West Kabul in 2009 illustrates the extent to which bargaining and exchange down the line contributed to decision making:

My motivation to join was political networking as well as achieving a higher career position. I was recruited through Modabber's party [Karzai's former head of Office of Administrative Affairs and the leader of Ensejam-i-Millie] ... If I was not given the money, I would not have helped with Karzai's campaign.[37]

After the election, she complained bitterly that the client-network leader had not upheld his promise of either appointing her as the governor of the Ghor Province or giving her a senior position in the Afghan Embassy in Iran, which she was promised. Such promises were widespread, demonstrating the uncertainty and temporary nature of some of these promises. It shows how inconsistently these bargains resulted in payoffs but at the same time remained ubiquitous, perhaps because election entrepreneurship, like gambling, could result in windfalls for the lucky few. In some ways, campaigning resembled a cottage industry where individuals and groups could at least every few years count on the possibility of making some rent. Some, like a former Abdullah senior campaign official, described the system in trickle-down terms:

One hand operates over another [Dest balaye dest kar mekona—an Afghan proverb]. From the top to the bottom, there is an opportunity to make money. Most of these campaigners were there, not to make Abdullah win but to make money. It's like a business. Abdullah gets money from foreign countries, then he distributes it to his friends and cronies, and they distribute it to others. Even the poor benefit ... Everyday 1,000 people come here. I think they are all thieves and unemployed people who come from all provinces and they aim to get Abdullah's money. I do not think any of them do any campaigning once they get the money.[38]

Others, like this influential independent MP, described it as a financial and political marketplace:

For some, the election provided the best opportunity to make money. Some rented a small place or a political party used its office as a campaign-office claiming to have spent so much money. Their campaign was simple: gathering people at an especial venue, in some cases paying them to attend or offering them food. Some of my colleagues have received cars, money and gifts for their service.[39]

Still others, like Najiba Ayubi, the director of Killid Radio, a popular radio station in Afghanistan, viewed it more cynically as an avenue for swindlers to ply their trade:

Of course, there was some opportunist who wanted to make money out of these campaigns telling candidates that they have established a campaign headquarter in their districts or that they have distributed so and so many posters and leaflets, making fake invoices and receipts. Our reporters made several interesting observations. They were seeing the same person at one candidate campaign office one day and at another candidate's office the next day. These campaigns had a real business feeling to it.[40]

All of these descriptions, from my own observations, were true in different instances. In the 2009 elections, I observed representatives openly exchanging blocks of votes for up to $2,000. To complete such a transaction, local client-elites would be required to bring in a village's or a community's election cards. There were many cases of individuals from remote villages coming to Kabul headquarters providing dubious receipts and demanding reimbursement. One man showed a receipt saying, "I have been in Kabul for six days. I have established several campaigns in different districts of Herat province and I have spent $10,000." In some instances, provincial powerbrokers were also giving people money to attend rallies to show the patron a high level of support which would then help with their bargaining. In keeping with Bijlert's (2009: 14) findings, people were often invited to gatherings and conferences without knowing why they were there, simply to inflate the number of participants. As I observed, clients would often pay ordinary people up to 500 afghanis (a daily wage labourer at the time earned 300 afghanis) to attend gatherings to increase attendance and show sizeable support for the leader.

From a political–cultural perspective, candidates had to act more like a traditional Khan who had to provide hospitality and show generosity in distributing funds and resources. Projecting power and having support were seen as key to the candidates and their local backers' success. It was seen as generous and that your *distarkhan* (dinner table) was large enough to ensure that voters saw you as someone who could commit to his end of the bargain, even though this required spending a huge amount of money. Entertaining guests, providing meals, and hosting regular parties were key components of election campaigns, as Ayubi summarises:

> Wealth was not only important in terms of paying for campaign-related expenses, but also for giving the impression that a candidate is rich and influential and therefore more likely to be able to assist voters. People vote for people who have money because they will be useful and helpful and more influential.[41]

National NGOs and civil society also played a prominent role in election campaigns, especially in 2014 for Ghani. I identified four giants of service delivery NGOs who had established themselves as the gatekeeper to international money and funding, assisting Ghani's campaign.[42] Some allegedly made financial and technical contributions to Ghani's presidential bid. For instance, one NGO admitted to having taken on the responsibility for content production and producing campaign materials (e.g., newspapers, posters, leaflets, videos) and then helped distribute them across Afghanistan; another, which owned a media organisation and a series of non-profit radio networks, produced and broadcast election materials for the campaign. One election observation organisation that specialises in election monitoring and oversight was heavily involved in the Ghani campaign, providing election mapping, advice, and analysis free of charge. Most worked in the background; a few appeared on televised debates and chat shows to promote their candidate.[43] One NGO leader with extensive involvement in local governance reached out to key tribal leaders and village elders to recruit people to mobilise support through established campaign headquarters in provinces and districts. These NGO leaders were able to use their organisational and networking skills as well as their organisations' resources, including employees, for their candidate of choice. Consequently, many of these NGO leaders became part of Ghani's inner circle in his post-2014 administration.

7.3.3 Selling the state: state official clients and their power resources in the 2019 elections

The third venue where the presidential candidates contested for clients was the clients of political networks in the national and subnational administrations and bureaucracy. Prior to elections, the state was put on sale in exchange for election support—the most important currency available to an incumbent. This category of actors was not mutually exclusive of the informal networks discussed above but overlapped with them. In the 2019 elections, Ghani's campaign was centrally managed by some of his trusted advisors and cabinet colleagues who were de facto his campaign managers, including Fazl Fazly, Daud Governor Noorzai, Omar Daudzai, Matin Bek, and Hamdullah Moheb. Rivalry and tension between them over roles, functions, and funding distribution created immense confusion among provincial and district campaign managers.[44]

As argued in the previous chapter, in the post-2001 period both incumbents, both President Karzai and Ghani, were able to appoint many of their clients to key positions. Through the Independent Directorate of Local Governance (IDLG) and cabinet ministries, before the 2019 elections, Ghani and his campaign team in the government appointed over 240 district governors out of 364 formal ones, a significant number not to mention deputy governors and district and provincial police chiefs. For instance, to gain the support of people in Khost province, he appointed a deputy minister within his office and to satisfy the Greater Council of the North, he appointed their clients as governors of Parwan and Farah provinces as well as some of the district governors and police chiefs to expand their sphere of influence and their access to financial resources. The money gained by them could always find its way back to the campaign.

Such appointments became exceptionally frequent as the election date neared. Similarly, the second vice president appointed at least 15 advisors in his office to please different political groupings/communities within his ethnic group. The president's chosen first running-mate, Amrullah Saleh, reportedly tried to unseat a deputy minister at IDLG, and appointed one of his clients as deputy governor in the Bamiyan Province to secure the support of his fellow ethnic Tajik constituency. The IDLG became one of the main platforms for the president through which he would secure the loyalties of hundreds of elders and representatives from the provinces. Instructed by Matin Bek, the Director-General of IDLG and a close ally of President Ghani, IDLG organised official provincial governor, district governor, provincial council, and municipality conferences under the pretext of discussions on important local issues. However, informal gatherings and behind the scenes meetings were regularly held to reaffirm allegiances, and in some instances instruct allies about what measures. At the same time, the IDLG was also involved in securing the support of provincial council members while the State Ministry of Parliamentary Affairs, run by Farooq Wardak, worked to secure the support of MPs. The political groupings in parliament became an important support vote bank for the candidates.

During elections, provincial and district governors were instructed and pressured by Kabul to lobby for the incumbent in their meetings, showcasing the government's achievements.[45] In 2019, provincial governor clients organised several highly publicised shuras and events for their candidates with tribal elders, prominent politicians, civil society activist, and others under the pretence of consultation. These events were viewed by many as unofficial election campaign events and governors were not shy of openly advocating for a candidate. The local media branch of Radio and Television Afghanistan (RTA), the state-owned TV and radio station, was usually asked to cover these events. There were persistent indications during the campaigns that Afghan government resources were being improperly used for electioneering purposes. On 1 August 2019, the Electoral Complaints Commission (ECC) issued a written warning to both President Ghani and Chief Executive Abdullah for violating electoral campaign regulations, including using Afghan government facilities and financial resources for campaign purposes. In its warning, the ECC listed violations including the use of government vehicles and government equipment in campaign activities as well as the participation of high-ranking government officials at electoral gatherings.[46]

7.3.4 Election funding and reciprocity

A closer look at campaign finances is revealing. As in all democracies, election campaigns can become exceptionally expensive if a spending limit is not imposed in the law—not that this would have made much of a difference in Afghanistan. In the 2019 elections, an election manager in the Ghani camp described how finances worked to organise the final campaign event for Ghani:

> In our first meeting, the representative of these parties (local Ghani clients) told us that they can assemble up to 120,000 people in Ghazi stadium for the final campaign celebration. We realised this is not realistic both in terms of space and finances. We decided to invite 50,000. So, each party got between 2,000 and 5,000 invitation cards, and for each card we paid 500 Afghanis (around $8 at the time). On the event day, they couldn't gather 6,000 people but we had already paid them (a norm to pay in advance). It was embarrassing. We didn't know how to inform the president and at the last minute, we had to cancel the event.[47]

Moments like these were repeated hundreds of times across the country, with money paid for crowds of various sizes that only partially materialised. According to several conversations with Ghani campaign officials, President Ghani had over 70 large events in Kabul and the provinces. To pocket money from the corrupt practice of paying people to attend, each party involved exaggerated the size of the crowd they could mobilise. It was corruption on top of corruption. And the money available for the taking was substantial: the value of 50,000 invitations at 500 Afghanis each was just under $330,000.[48] At another event in Jalalabad, interviews revealed that Ghani's campaign distributed at least 120,000 invitation cards; less than one-third showed up.

A significant amount of money was pocketed by campaign staff at all levels: ethno-regional, community, and tribal leaders as well as many election entrepreneurs and election-brokers within the chain. For weeks after the election, Ghani's camp was reportedly consumed by blame-gaming and finger-pointing over election finances. Interviews and discussions revealed that in one vicious effort, several key campaign bosses had tried to blame one late-comer campaign manager for corruption and fraud. This led to an audit of this person's election finances, for which he could unofficially account for around 85% out of more than US$2.6 million.[49] The rest was probably pocketed in by that specific office campaign team. Ghani's campaign also supposedly spent around US$2.2 million on publications and advertisements including on Facebook and Twitter through one of his campaign offices which I toured which boasted its own "media room." That was just one office; there were many more. Both campaigns had hired hundreds of young people, often called "Facebook Chalawun [a negative description for those who run Facebook smear campaigns]," to run misinformation, fake news, and other disruptive practices against their opponents.[50] Many in Abdullah's campaign had complained about the lack of funds. As mentioned, Abdullah was not banking on elections happening in light of the U.S.–Taliban negotiations, so his campaign was ill-prepared. My best moderate estimate is that while Abdullah spent around US$2–5 million on his campaign, Ghani's expenditures were well above US$80 million.[51] However, estimates for Ghani's election expenditures varied between $50 million to over $150 million.

These soaring costs put pressure on candidates to find ways, including illegal means, to fund their campaigns. Election campaign funds in post-2001 Afghanistan came from several important sources and channels, almost all of them illegal. The first was national businessmen. For instance, interviews revealed that in the 2014 elections, the Alokozay Group of Companies and Azizi Bank had given over $30 million and $7 million, respectively, to Ghani's campaign. In June 2017, allegedly in return for the donations, the cabinet approved plans to allocate 143 acres of land to the Alokozay Group for a fraction of the estimated value of $350 million.[52]

Such election contributions are not in and of themselves against international norms or election laws in other democratic nations—though the amounts in play would violate funding limits in most. In most countries, it is illegal for a single company to contribute so much to an election campaign. In the U.S.A., one might be able to get around political donation limits by setting up SuperPacs. Indeed, Afghanistan does not stand alone in the world for scandals over election financing but the hidden motive and the nature of payments raise a lot of ethical questions. In another case, Mohammad Yousuf Ghazanfar, a successful businessman, endorsed Karzai in the 2009 presidential election and became his northern election campaign manager. According to a U.S. cable report dating 12 July 2009, Governor Noor confirmed that he had recently received two letters signed by Karzai asking the Balkh Customs Department to exempt Ghazanfar's company from paying duty on the import of the first 50,000 metric tonnes (MT) of fuel and then later, on another 30,000 MTs. Governor Noor said the letters were cleverly worded to make the exemptions seem legitimate. The exemptions totalled $12.8 million in customs revenues. Governor Noor suspected that some of that money would make its way back to Karzai himself in the form of campaign contributions from Ghazanfar. Similarly, in the 2019 elections, arguably one of the calculations for Ghazanfar as a choice for the third running-mate to President Ghani was his financial donation to the campaign. There were reports that money within the Ministry of Defence for several oil and gas contracts of Ghazanfar's which had been held up was finally released. This was convenient just before the campaigning began: many assumed the released money would go back into Ghani's campaign.[53]

If money corrupts elections, then Afghanistan's elections were a free for all of pocket-lining and patronage purchasing. The money, of course, had to come from somewhere, which will be discussed in more detail in Chapter 9, but for the purposes of winning elections, virtually every resource, from customs revenues to drug profits, was tapped. The incumbent, of course, always had the advantage as it was his networks which controlled most of those resources. Thus it was that an incumbent president never technically lost an election in Afghanistan.

7.3.5 Intimidation and coercion

The serious lack of impartiality and undue interference by local officials in the election process generated excessive intimidation against polling staff, candidate observers, tribal leaders, state officials, and others. In a complex web of relations and loyalties, police chiefs, provincial and district governors, and other state officials used their coercive resources to threaten and frighten rivals, limit their operations, and in some incidents, manufacture violence to ensure people could not access polling stations or that ballot boxes were destroyed on their way to the provincial capital.

During all elections, there were many reports of intimidation against election observers. In some areas, observers were denied access to polling centres, especially during the vote count. Others were coerced into signing paperwork saying they had not seen any irregularities. A reporter from Arman newspaper showed me video footage of intimidation by local district police in Wardak province in 2009 where ballot stuffing was widespread in favour of Karzai.[54] In 2014, there were reports that local powerbrokers had paid candidates' agents up to $2000 to secure their signatures approving the accuracy of the process and vote count despite massive ballot stuffing. In one incident, one senior campaign manager expressed his frustration that in Nangarhar his failure to buy the loyalty of a female observer in Abdullah's campaign was a blow to the campaign.[55] By 2019, it was evident that President Ghani's electoral camp was banking more on the strategy of buying votes for their success than actual campaigning.

These tactics were particularly effective for any candidate who had the widest alliance especially those political networks and powerbrokers with coercive and military resources. And the more clients in key security sector institutions such as district police chiefs, directors of the National Security Directorate, and local militiamen, the more the influence and bargaining power within the network and across election camps. With those resources at their disposal, they could systematically deploy intimidation against election staff and constituencies. Studies have highlighted how local election staff were often intimidated into cooperating with local officials in order to rig votes for their patrons.[56] The price of non-cooperation was often high, including detention and, in some cases, death, especially in rural areas where it was more difficult to remain anonymous and where district police chiefs, often linked to the local and central administration, tended to be the main channel of power and influence.

Local powerbrokers were valuable in other ways, too. For instance, in the 2019 elections, when biometric voter verification machines were brought in, local officials would manipulate machines and processes to stop people from voting, reporting a malfunction when it became evident that people's votes were swinging to their opponent's candidate. According to several sources, in one relatively safe district of Takhar, the polling stations were closed, and boxes transferred to the provincial capital at 11 am because it had become clear to which side the vote would swing—embarrassing a senior Ghani ally who couldn't secure votes in his home district. The incident was reported as a Taliban attack.

7.3.6 *Instrumentalising identity-based division and mobilising constituencies*

Candidate and political networks in their election campaigns further manipulated identity-based divisions to mobilise the vote. I have shown this elsewhere through the discourse analysis of election campaigns in the 2009 elections.[57] Candidates and their political network-clients in their rhetoric targeted issues that were important to particular ethno-regional groups. For instance, issues such as the problem of the Taliban threat and security provisions, the presence of foreign troops and the Durand line between Pakistan and Afghanistan were brought up for Pashtuns. To ethnic Hazaras, candidates addressed the Kuchi–Hazara land conflict, the construction of the Kabul–Bamiyan highway and the promise to make the two most populated Hazara districts of Jaghuri and Behsud into provinces. For Tajiks and Uzbeks, the issues of inclusion of jihadis in the government and social and political justice came to the fore.

Similarly, political networks also used these divisive tactics to provoke their constituencies to support their candidate. In the 2019 elections, Mohaqqiq often reminded ethnic Hazaras of the danger of voting for Ghani, portraying him as a Pashtun nationalist and a "disruptive force" who was on a collision course with other ethnic groups. Like Abdullah, his messages deployed ridicule as a tactic, in one speech representing Ghani as a pathological "liar" and adding that "as a liar, he has tied the hands of all other liars in history." This was an effective campaign strategy. For instance, Mohaqqiq reminded people that in 2014 Ghani had promised to create one million jobs in his first year in office but instead presided over a worsening of both security and the economy.[58] In 2019, leaders allied with Abdullah were also providing an ethnic subtext to their ordinary voters by portraying Ghani and his team as a disruptive force trying to destabilise the political order, especially in the northern regions.

Although such regional strategies are common in any large democracy, in Afghanistan they also had a clear ethnic basis and thus the potential for sparking conflict despite the rhetoric of "national unity." In these elections, the little policy that was discussed by candidates and political network-clients revolved around ethnically framed issues of political inclusion, social and political justice, and national unity. Substantive policy discussion was largely superfluous. For example, one of Abdullah's main policy proposals that at least addressed an overarching "national" issue was the transformation of the political system from presidential to parliamentary. However, in none of his speeches did he elaborate on the differences between the two or why the parliamentary system would be better for Afghanistan, (except to say that it would be better for the non-Pashtuns ethnic groups). Instead, he merely drew on the history of the demand among Jamiat leaders dating back to the Constitutional Loya Jirga in 2003.

President Ghani in addition to appealing to his ethnic Pashtun constituency tried to depict himself as a reformer and visionary leader with constant references to Afghanistan's history of reformist leaders, including individuals such as King Amanullah Khan. The 100th Independence Day celebrations, held at Darul Aman Palace, provided an excellent opportunity for Ghani to associate himself with the King Amanullah, continuing along the same path and "completing the unfinished chapter" of his reform vision. Others saw his administration's allocation of $4.5 million for events and celebrations throughout the year as an abuse of public funds in service to his election campaign.[59] His government instructed ministries to develop plans to celebrate Independence Day throughout the country. In another attempt to burnish his builder credentials, the president allocated funds to re-build most of the crumbling palaces in Kabul city and its surrounding districts, including Darul Aman Palace, as a way to demonstrate progress and development, in sharp contrast to the jihadis who he never failed to remind people had wrecked the city and the palace during the civil war. In retaliation, his opponents launched a massive social media campaign pointing out that Ghani's government had not rebuilt Mawlana Jalaluddin Rumi's birthplace or Ghazni city's iconic Ghaznavid monuments, which were in danger of collapse and represented an arguably more precious example of Afghanistan's rich history. Abdullah and his allies went even

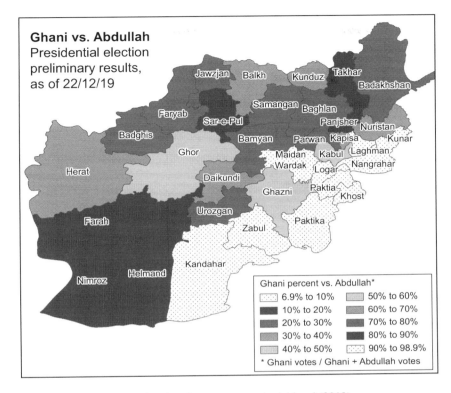

Figure 7.2 The ethno-regional voting map at provincial level (2019).

further, depicting the government's reconstruction efforts as reflective of one ethnic group's dominance over Afghanistan as they focused on the history of that
ethnic group rather than a genuine effort to protect the country's cultural diversity.

The 2019 (provincial level) election results (Figure 7.2) illustrate that the
results reflected the realities of ethnic division in Afghanistan. While Ghani
received most of his votes from the Pashtun south, Abdullah won most of his from
the northern, central, and western provinces where he was allied with prominent
ethnic Hazara, Uzbek, and Jamiat political networks.

Conclusion

Afghanistan's seven elections since 2001 represent different aspects of Afghan
political life in the post-2001 international intervention and state-building. It
demonstrates that elections ultimately served the interests of political networks
in further institutionalising network practices of power resource bargaining,
opportunism, backdoor deal-making, and identity politics, rather than achieving

the liberal peace goal of democratisation. During election campaigns, competing political networks manipulated identity divisions to mobilise their ethnic and tribal constituencies albeit unsuccessfully in the 2019 elections. The elections and their widespread fraud essentially undermined the integrity of democratic institutions and international liberal peace support, breeding doubt and scepticism among the Afghan people about the future of the country. In the eyes of many, Afghan elections were used to legitimise the dominance of political networks, and the political network settlement that ensued following each election helped produce the façade of political order within the state.

Elections in Afghanistan also illustrated that the state provided a framework for electioneering that ultimately ensured the incumbent, who controlled the majority of state resources, possessed an overwhelming advantage in terms of coercive and co-optive resources in the election campaign and in terms of corralling overall votes. The multi-dimensional account of the role of political networks and identity politics sheds new light on both the election and post-election bargaining. The patronage system practised during the election, when clients often tried to exaggerate the size of their vote banks, suggests a more nuanced explanation to the one often provided in the media that candidates and their networks were largely responsible for the gravity of fraud and vote-rigging committed. Having made unrealistic claims regarding the clusters of votes, candidates' clients were bound to manipulate the results to deliver on their promises. Bargains were made between candidate-patrons and client-networks at all levels, but they were often both immediately self-serving and subject to non-compliance. Indeed, impossible promises were made by both patrons and clients and election entrepreneurs. In these elections, candidates seemed to have offered to sell the state several times over with promises of posts, contracts, and aid which they were never able to deliver.

Elections in Afghanistan also exposed the double standard of the international interveners: on the one hand, they claimed to promote liberal values and agendas while at the same time employing illiberal means to achieve their ends. Illiberal practices that were overlooked by international counterparts, especially for achieving short-term political order and stability had serious implications for Afghanistan's nascent democracy, undermining the very objective of democratisation, institution-building, and a durable political order. When such practices were uncovered and debated, the attitude of international officials was shockingly unapologetic. As one former U.S. employee put it: "it's not like we can go without fuel for six weeks while we mount an investigation or try to replace our local procurer, right? Let the next U.S. staffer who shows up next year deal with it."[60]

In post-2019 Afghanistan, elections instead of a forum for airing grievances and offering solutions, they provided new conditions within which political network alliance-building and pact-making were re-negotiated and political settlements among elites were reached. From a networked governance perspective, challenging election outcomes was a convenient strategy for the losing alliance because, as discussed earlier, in a winner-take-all scenario they could force the winning side to negotiate a settlement, thereby ensuring their survival and relevance in the succeeding administration. In 2009, 2014, and 2019 elections,

Abdullah's team found it strategic to hedge their bets by challenging the outcomes of the elections far and wide. Interviews and conversations with several senior Abdullah officials suggested that the pressure to declare himself president in 2019 and hold his own inauguration came from its allied political networks in particular Junbish-i-Islami and Wahdat-i-Mardom.[61] Junbish's constituency power in the north and his network's disruptive power were evident.[62] And it was the leader of Wahdat-i-Mardom, Mohammad Mohaqqiq, reportedly frustrated by Abdullah's failure to protect his interests, who opened the door for a settlement with Ghani, classic evidence of *relative power balance* between groups confronted by survival choices both within and across alliances discussed in Chapter 2.[63] The Wahdat-i-Mardom preferred to defeat Ghani rather than risk being double-crossed at the hands of the stronger ally when cabinet and other key positions were bargained.

Notes

1 "Kabul Explosion: IS 'Claims Attack on Hazara Protest," *BBC*. July 23, 2016.
2 In 2005, the parliamentary and provincial council elections were held at the same time. In 2009 and 2014, presidential and provincial council elections were held at the same time. The scheduled 2015 parliamentary elections were organised in 2018 and there were no provincial council election after 2014.
3 The Bonn Agreement, Section I: 4.
4 Rosenberg and Ahmad (2014).
5 Gates (2014).
6 Bass, John. (@USAmbKabul), "2/3 It's Important for All #Afghans to Remember: These Results Are Preliminary. Many Steps Remain before Final Election Results Are Certified, to Ensure the Afghan People Have Confidence in the Results," December 22, 2019, https://twitter.com/USAmbKabul/status/1208664419657535493.
7 TOLOnews. 2020. "Outgoing US Ambassador John R. Bass Speaks of Afghan Peace, Elections, Corruption. [English]," January 1, 2020.
8 In the 2004 presidential election, UNDP was assigned with administering elections, including voter registration and strengthening the capacity of election organisations such as the Joint Electoral Management Body (JEMB) and the Interim Afghan Electoral Commission (IAEC). The UNDP/ELECT I (2005–2011), ELECT II (2012–2015), and UN Electoral Support Project (UNESP) (2016–2020) served as the mechanisms for international financial support for electoral processes. In 2005, at its peak, the JEMB Secretariat was staffed by 541 internationals and 179,384 nationals. UNDP/ELECT in June 2009 employed 44 international advisors assigned to IEC headquarters and 71 advisors at its regional and provincial offices. See SIGAR Report. 2009. "Strategy and Resources Needed to Sustain Afghan Electoral Capacity," September 2009.
9 The IEC, the ultimate authority on election, was formed with the Presidential decree (decree No. 23) without legislative approval.
10 Reportedly, FEFA received $350,000 for its monitoring activities for both presidential and parliamentary elections in 2009 and 2010. In the 2009 election, FEFA provided 2,300 observers in all 34 provinces.
11 Author's interview with several insider Ghani campaign officials, Kabul, March 2015.
12 The UN originally estimated there were 9.8 million eligible voters and later revised this to 10.5 million. See Reynolds and Wilder (2004).
13 UNAMA Electoral Component (UEC), "UEC Weekly Report: Week Ending August 26, 2004," in ICG Report, "Afghanistan: From Presidential to Parliamentary Elections," November 24, 2004.
14 Baldauf (2004).

15 The last (partial) census was conducted in 1979 and with only two-thirds of the population. In 2005, the population estimate varied widely from 22 million by the Central Statistics Office to 29 million by the CIA Factbook. Under the Bonn agreement, the UN was to carry out a census prior to any elections: "Request to the United Nations by the Participants at the UN Talks on Afghanistan … to conduct as soon as possible (i) a registration of voters in advance of the general elections that will be held upon the adoption of the new constitution by the constitutional Loya Jirga and (ii) a census of the population of Afghanistan, Bonn Agreement, op. cit., Annex III. At the same time, the electoral law directed the Central Statistics Office to "provide the latest official population figures or the estimated population of each province to the JEMB." The Central Statistics Office was in no way ready to conduct such a comprehensive census with limited technical and human capacity at the outset of the post-2001 period.
16 Background Briefing: Wolesi Jirga and Provincial Council Elections 2005, JEMBS.
17 Office of the Special Inspector General for Afghanistan Reconstruction (SIGAR) (2010: 1).
18 UN. 2019. "The Situation in Afghanistan and Its Implications for International Peace and Security, Report of the Secretary-General," 312, September 3, 2019, 2.
19 International Crisis Group Report. 2004. "Afghanistan: From Presidential to Parliamentary Elections," November 24, 2004.
20 Ibid; Reynolds Wilder (2004).
21 Adili, Bjelica and Ruttig (2019).
22 Ibid.
23 Author's private conversation with a senior IEC official, September 2019. This claim was further corroborated by a few other IEC Executive officials. Apparently in the 2019 elections, Abdullah Abdullah's name was not correctly entered into the database which, to the embarrassment of many, led to him being detained for a few minutes. He used to tell the story in amusement in many formal CEO meetings.
24 One IEC official noted that in Qarabagh district of Kabul, stickers were sold for 100–200 dollars and officials were paid to take *tazkira* machines to local districts for their constituency to get them IDs.
25 Author's interview, June 20, 2020, Kabul.
26 Worden (2018).
27 See Ahmadzai (2014).
28 Haji Din Mohammad was Karzai's national campaign manager while Haji Zahir became the Nangarhar Province campaign manager.
29 "Influential Pashtuns in Afghan Politics," US Embassy Cables, June 8, 2009.
30 Ghani unfortunately had suffered from many religious blunders in his five-year presidency. Once he made a mistake at a funeral prayer, and often recited religious verbs and sayings incorrectly.
31 According to the US embassy cables, Governor Noor told embassy representatives that he was financing most of Abdullah's campaign.
32 Author's Interview, Kabul, September 13, 2009.
33 Obtained from local media.
34 Obtained from local media.
35 Bijlert (2009: 13).
36 A group of 20 women at Abdullah's Shar-e-Naw campaign headquarter, August 15, 2009.
37 Author's Interview, Kabul, September 2, 2009.
38 Author's Interview, Kabul, September 4, 2009.
39 Author's Interview, Kabul, September 7, 2009.
40 Author's Interview, Kabul, September 14, 2009.
41 Ibid.
42 These NGOs were CHA (Salam Rahimi), ADA (Jilani Popal), DSHA (Zahir Shaheen), and others.

43 See Sharan and Bose (2016).
44 Eventually, it was agreed that Matin Bek through IDLG would work with provincial council members and Fazli to manage funding, Hamdullah Moheb the security institutions, Governor Noorzai the PR, and messaging.
45 "Provincial-Level Election Politiking," U.S. Embassy Cable, March 31, 2009.
46 UN. 2019. "The Situation in Afghanistan and Its Implications for International Peace and Security, Report of the Secretary-General," 306, September 3, 2019, 3.
47 Author's interview, Kabul, February 2020.
48 At 500 Afghanis per invitation, 50,000 invitations = 25,000,000 million Afghanis. The exchange rate at the time was 76 Afghanis on the dollar for a total of US$328,947.
49 Author's interview, Kabul, November 2019.
50 Author's interview with a senior Ghani campaign manager, Kabul, February 2020.
51 For instance, MP Ghoriani in Herat reportedly paid for most of Abdullah's campaign in Herat. He was on the list of governors. On June 12, parliament rejected the deal.
52 Salehi, Z. 2016. "Cabinet Approves Land Sale to Alokozay Group." *Pahjwok*, January 20, 2016. Wolesi Jirga speaker, Abdul Raouf Ibrahimi, assigned five commissions to investigate the sale of the land and said findings of the commissions showed the contract was signed between the government and the Alokozay Group in violation of the country's laws and national interests. *ToloNews*. 2017. "MPs Reject Govt Land Sale to Alokozay Company," June 12, 2017.
53 Interviews with several MoD officials revealed that the amount was over US$30 million.
54 Author's Interview, Kabul, September 7, 2009.
55 Conversation with a Ghani official who was involved as a senior campaign manager in 2014.
56 Bijlert (2009: 16–17).
57 See Sharan and Heathershaw (2011).
58 August 30, 2020, Kabul Loya Jirga tent, Farda Radio and TV, https://www.youtube.com/watch?v=NzeZZJUl6KY.
59 Almost two years before elections, decisions were made to set up a high committee (chaired by AOP, IDLG, and other ministries) to propose plans on key activities that should take place in cities and districts of the country. At IDLG, we collected hundreds of suggestions for activities from provincial governors' offices and instructions from AOP on what to do. These included academic seminars, flag waving ceremonies, collecting local heroic songs, and so many others. More than 20 ministries and directorates were involved in the organisation of the events.
60 Author's conversation with a former U.S. employee, February 1, 2021.
61 Author's interview with several officials in the Abdullah camp.
62 In 2018, in light of the Qaisari crisis, his supporters had blocked highways for weeks, seriously disrupting NATO's supply lines and the Afghan economy.
63 Author's interview with several Mohaqqiq confidantes.

8   Parliament as a grand marketplace

Alliance-building, auctions, and access

Introduction

In August 2018, I heard that Haji Ajmal and his father, Mir Rahman Rahmani, were running as candidates for the upcoming parliamentary elections for seats in Kabul and Parwan provinces, respectively. Haji Ajmal's father, Mir Rahman Rahmani, a jack-of-all-ideologies figure who started as a communist-era army official, turned jihadi commander during the civil war and finally transformed into a democratic parliamentarian and capitalist in the post-2001 era. The family had monopolised the energy sector by supplying petrol and gas to NATO forces in Afghanistan, and allegedly in the previous presidential elections has paid millions of dollars simultaneously to different campaigns to buy political protection and ensure his family's business survival.[1] By 2018, father and son had become so wealthy and powerful that they could add the ultimate layer of political protection: running for the Lower House themselves. Many would accuse both of essentially buying their seats, allegedly purchasing each vote for up to $50 (a daily-wage labourer in Kabul would earn less than $4 a day if one was lucky enough to find a job).

A few days earlier, a picture of Haji Ajmal along with General Miller, Commander of NATO's Resolute Support Mission and U.S. Forces-Afghanistan, and Ambassador John Bass, had been posted on the U.S. Embassy Facebook page praising the important role of Afghan youth in politics and business. Ajmal resourcefully spun the meeting in his social media posts to suggest the tacit support of the U.S. embassy for his candidacy. His post received harsh criticism from the Presidential Office, but it put the relatively unknown Ajmal on the national political map.

It wasn't the first time Ajmal had co-opted the Americans to serve his own ambitions. Indeed, from the very beginning of the American occupation of Afghanistan, he had carved out a place for himself with them. He was one of the first people recruited as an interpreter for the American military at Bagram airbase, when he was still a teenager. According to some accounts, he was hired by the Americans because of his father and uncle, both of whom had become *Jamiat-i-Islami* commanders responsible for the security of the airfield, reportedly to secure the loyalty of local commanders. Haji Ajmal was one of the many translators who acted as gatekeepers and middlemen to international military forces. Privately,

DOI: 10.4324/9781315161617-8

these interpreters would also run their own side businesses brokering deals, often with the knowledge of the Americans, in partnership with shady local logistics suppliers and businessmen. Translators mimicked strongmen, transforming themselves into businessmen, tapping into their inside access to people—foreign military or civilian—who could approve the distribution of obscene amounts of money without any oversight. Translators-cum-businessmen would become super-wealthy as the result of the American strategy of using their money as a "weapons system" that people would furnish them with a new label called the "9/11 millionaires."

In 2016, a contractor from the Naseri tribe described to me how he became one of the biggest trucking suppliers to NATO because of his partnership with one of the translators at the camp. He was charging $2000 for every truck, which cost him less than $500. Haji Ajmal, like many, would capitalise on his access to the camp and to NATO generals to become one of the early "9/11 millionaires" in post-2001 Afghanistan. The proximity of his village to the camp enabled his family to control access to the camp for Afghans. In the early days, they would allegedly charge daily-wage labourers a fee for permission to offer their services there. By 2014, Haji Ajmal (along with his family) would become one of the richest oligarchs in Afghanistan, on the back of international military intervention, monopolising the supply of fuel to NATO through many of his dubious and opaque companies.

I was amazed by the increasing number of Afghan businessmen like Haji Ajmal and his father running for the Lower House. It seems that people like Haji Ajmal, who himself was rather late into the political game, had realised that to maximise one's value in the networked state, and reap the benefits of foreign aid flows, one had to insert oneself into the theatre of democratic governance western donors wanted to see. The Lower House in post-2001 Afghanistan had become the major source of protection and security for political networks and their associates. The Afghan parliament then enabled political network leaders and their associates (e.g., businessmen, criminals, former officials) to expand their strategic socio-political positions and access to financial assets (legal and illegal) within the Afghan state and society. The parliament fell far short of Afghan and international donor expectations, the few were willing to shatter the warm illusion of democracy. As this chapter shows it emerged as the principal "political marketplace" and strategic "network-building arena" for political networks outside the state administration, linking state officials, local tribal and community elders, power brokers, licit and illicit commercial networks in Kabul, and the provinces into a complex web of power resource interdependencies, bargains, and loyalties.

This chapter is an attempt to capture additional vagaries of inter-network conflict, identity politics, and the opportunistic practices of patronage and rent-seeking to dominate the Afghan state by examining the power dynamics and daily operation of the Lower House. To do this, Section 8.2 offers an ethnographic study of the 2010–2011 Special Court (SC) crisis as a moment of rapture and how this then shaped power dynamics within the House.[2] The crisis was triggered when President Karzai established the SC with a presidential decree, and it proceeded to disqualify 62 sitting MPs (one-fourth of the Lower House) for fraud. This was seen by many as a direct and invasive attempt by Karzai and his clientele in the judiciary and the executive to subordinate the legislature. The SC crisis serves as a useful window into the broader political economy of the Lower House, governance, and statehood in post-2001 Afghanistan, including the impact of day-to-day network practices on political order and state stability. The first part of this chapter begins by detailing the political rationale behind the electoral law and how the system was put in place to serve the interests of political networks. It shows how subsequent parliamentary elections produced a parliament where a significant number of MPs won their seats through fraud and the illegal procurement of votes.

8.1 Assembling the house: composition, power dynamics, and strains

8.1.1 The single non-transferable vote: a political decision

The 2003 Constitutional Loya Jirga (grand council) agreed on a bicameral parliamentary system with two separate chambers: a 249-member elected Lower House (the House of the People, "Lower House") and an indirectly elected and appointed 102-member Upper House (the House of Elders, "Meshrano Jirga"). The 2004 drafters of the Constitution gave the Lower House fairly sufficient oversight and legislative powers to check the power of the executive branch.[3] However, the president remained the head of all three branches of the state, creating confusion and contention between the executive and legislature.

The new election system adopted for parliamentary and provincial council elections was the single non-transferable vote (SNTV), a decision that Karzai and his technocratic clients advocated, deceptively because of its simplicity for Afghans notwithstanding the technical difficulties associated with it.[4] But privately, their short-term calculation was that a more proportionate representation system might further empower and favour the already-established and organisationally strong jihadi political groupings that had the control of key subnational administrations and state positions.

As the experience of Afghanistan's three parliamentary elections proved, the SNTV was the worst possible choice for Afghanistan as it hindered the development of well-organised political parties that could whip organisational discipline within the House and appeal to a broad-based constituency. In Afghanistan, while the system easily accommodated and encouraged independent candidates, it led to internal political network fragmentation and discord when several candidates from the same network competed for the same vote—which could mean that they are potentially splitting their base and end up with neither getting a seat.

The problem became a lot more acute in Afghanistan given that there were no boundary demarcations for constituencies. It also further reinforced the politics of networking along with narrow identity-based interests and resource dependency-based alliance-building. Karzai's refusal to form a political party and his view that parliament should be subservient to the executive branch further undermined the house.

In subsequent elections, most candidates competed as independents despite a significant number being affiliated with former jihadi parties. In the 2005 elections, only 12% of candidates chose to give party affiliations despite direct political and financial support from their political networks.[5] However, this did not mean that political networks were not investing in their candidates. In the Herat Province in the 2005 election, it was reported that Ismail Khan backed a total of 11 male and four female candidates and according to one unconfirmed report provided $10,000 in financial support for the candidates' election.[6] Similarly in Nangarhar, the Arsala family backed five viable candidates and Hazrat Ali, the Jamiat associate, another five in provincial council elections. And because of the SNTV system, in which most votes were wasted, voters can only vote for one candidate and top voters win the seats regardless of what percentage of the vote they get. In Afghanistan, candidates were being elected with as little as 5% of the vote in their provinces. In the 2005 election, the leading candidate for the Kabul Province secured a mere 2% of the vote—11,158 out of 666,478 votes cast. And 26 of the elected Lower House legislators received less than 1% of the vote.[7]

In the absence of a national census, the Joint Electoral Management Board (JEMB), the body responsible for election monitoring and regulation, allocated provincial seats, calculated using the formula established in the 2005 Electoral Law. The estimates provided by the Central Statistics Office were highly political and misleading given that there had never been a census carried out in the country, setting the stage for pervasive political, ethnic, and tribal tensions in the years to come. For instance, Kabul and Herat received 33 and 17 seats, respectively, while smaller provinces like Nuristan, Nimruz, and the newly established Panjshir were guaranteed a minimum of two seats. This allocation remained the same despite considerable changes in the demographic composition of the country as the result of war and rapid urbanisation.

The approved Election Law and JEMB were powerless against powerful patronage, family-based, and strongmen networks who ensured their violent militia clients could stand in the 2005 parliamentary election. The Election Law explicitly stated that anyone associated with illegal armed groups or who had committed a crime was to be disqualified from running. However, the JEMB had no power to satisfactorily vet and thwart strongmen and violent militia commanders from running for seats. Nonetheless, most jihadi strongmen, including Abdul Rasul Sayyaf, Padsha Khan Zadran, and many others whose crimes were well documented by human rights groups were allowed to contest. A total of 5,800 candidates for both bodies (249 seats in the Lower House and just over 400 seats in the 34 provincial councils) were certified while only 45 candidates were refused because of connections with armed groups or for not giving up their government jobs.[8] The constitution also allocated at least 25% of the Lower House seats to women as part of the quota system, with a significant number of them being independent and not affiliated to key political networks.[9]

As a result of these factors, subsequent parliamentary elections during the Republic would be marred by mass vote-rigging and fraud. Election institutions would become politicised and at the service of the specific patron/alliance that had appointed them. Every election would result in major disputes and lead to month-long crises. For instance, the 2010 parliamentary election that we discuss in the second part of this chapter led to a year-long dispute while the 2018 parliamentary results were announced seven months after the election and President Ghani inaugurated parliament on 26 April in the absence of results from Kabul and Paktia.[10] Several electoral laws would be drafted and ratified with little attempt to resolve the underlying factors for disputes and election frauds.

8.1.2 The composition and structure of the Lower House over the years

Despite all of Karzai's efforts, the 18 September 2005 election produced a house captured by former jihadi *Tanzim* networks, including Afghanistan Nawin, Wahdat-i-Mardom, Junbish-i-Islami, Rabbani's Jamiat-i-Islami and Dawat-i-Islami, and other smaller ones (Table 8.1). According to an Afghanistan Research and Evaluation Unit (AREU) analysis of the composition of the House, approximately 133 of the 249 members fought in jihad and 113 were affiliated or belonged to former *Tanzim* groupings.[11] Of these, roughly 40 commanders were associated with armed groups, 24 members belonged to different criminal gangs, 17 were associated with drug trafficking, and 19 faced serious allegations of war crimes and human rights violations.[12] Another report found that in the second legislative elections in 2010, the number of MPs with a background in jihad had increased.[13] It seems that with further entrenchment in the system, these political networks had been able to utilise the strength of their organisational support and leverage identity politics to mobilise their constituencies.

Table 8.1 Political network composition in the Lower House

Political groupings	Leader	Estimated no of seats
Jamiat-i-Islami	B. Rabbani	25–30
Junbish-i-Islami	R. Dostum	23–25
Wahdat-i-Mardom	M. Mohaqqiq	20–25
Wahdat-i-Islami	K. Khalili	5–6
Afghanistan-i-Navin	Y. Qanuni	22–26
Dawat-i-Islami	R. Sayyaf	10–12
Muttad-i-Milli	N. Ulumi and other leftists	10–12
Afghan Millat	A. Ahadi	7–8
Mahaz	Gailani	6–7
Other Shia groups (Iqtedar-i-Millie, Harakat, Hizb wahdat)	M. Kazemi, M. Akbari, S. Jawed	5–6
Paywand-i-Millie	S. Masur Nadery	2

Source: mainly NDI, 2005 and AREU reports (National Democratic Institute Report (2005)).

Thus, instead of producing the hoped-for democratic plurality, Afghanistan's first parliamentary elections set the stage for conflict and contest between competing networks for the control of the state and constituencies. There was a small glimmer of hope that a more diverse political landscape would emerge overtime when, to everyone's surprise, 23 candidates with leftist or communist backgrounds, including 15 formerly affiliated with the People Democratic Party of Afghanistan (PDPA) such as Gen. Nur ul-Haq Ulumi and Gen. Sayed Mohammad Gulabzoy, were elected.[14] However, the intensity of divisions amongst leftists meant that they could not unite as a coalition and their power was further reduced in subsequent elections.

It seems that the majority of the MPs that did not associate themselves with the former jihadi networks—roughly 100—were either aligned with or subject to individual co-optation by Karzai's alliance before parliament passed a law enabling the establishment of political groupings.[15] This is roughly the same estimate that the AREU analysis of the composition of the House details, which divided MPs into three categories of pro-government (81 MPs), pro-opposition (84 MPs), and "non-alignment" or with no clear network affiliation (Isn't this a little bit at odds with the first sentence of this section? It doesn't seem like the Jihadis "captured" the House. It looks more like a pretty even split. Or am I missing something?) (84 MPs).[16] In terms of ethnic composition, Pashtuns comprised 43% (including ten seats allocated for Kuchis); Tajiks and Aimaqs 29%; Hazaras 16%; Uzbek and Turkmen 10%; and Baluch and Nurestanis 8 and 4%, respectively.[17] The Upper House had roughly the same ethnic distribution (35% Pashtun; 31% Tajik; 17% Hazara; 8% Uzbek and Turkmen; 3% Baluch, and 3% Nurestani).[18]

By the third parliamentary election in October 2018, the composition of the house was seriously restructured against key former jihadi political networks with a lot more MPs identifying themselves as independent. It saw a wave of young candidates register, with 60–65% of candidates under the age of 40. A majority were first-timers, a significant shift from the jihadi elders and commanders.[19] None of the major ethno-regional political network leaders including Sayyaf, Mohaqqiq, Qanuni, Dostum, and others ran for parliament. Instead, seeing that the political prestige of the House was diminishing, they put forward their children. A careful analysis of the composition of the new Lower House shows that most of these MPs were either young businessmen like Haji Ajmal who made their money through international contracting or were somehow affiliated with powerful financial networks. An analysis of the elected Kabul MPs and the Head of the 18 Parliamentary Commissions reveals the emergence of a new political class made up of those who no longer felt safe under the protection of traditional political network leaders for whom the House was an excellent protection platform. Interviews with several MPs suggested that this was partly because of the uncertainty generated following the U.S. military drawdown in 2014 as these elites strategised ways to shield their business assets and interests.

According to a study of the composition of the Lower House after the 2018 elections, of the 249 members, 22% (54) had a direct business background.[20] The same study categorised 37% (91 members) as having been MPs before but did not

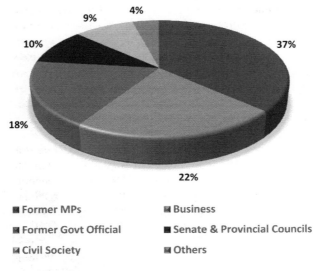

Figure 8.1 Composition of the House in 2018. Source: Khabarnama, 2020.

identify those who had business links. As the next chapter shows, more than 40 MPs were involved directly or indirectly in the mining industry, a clear indication that a significant number of MPs had side businesses or links with the business sector. One estimate suggested that 40% of Afghan parliamentarians had connections to the narcotics trade or other smuggling activities[21] (Figure 8.1).

8.1.3 The election of the leadership board of the Lower House: a contest

Political network fault lines became more pronounced during the election of the leadership of the House, a process which involved weeks of horse-trading and alliance-building by rival networks and alliances.[22] The political leadership of the Lower House was determined by MP votes and consisted of the Chair, elected for the entire term, two deputies, a secretary, and an assistant secretary, all elected for one year.

In 2004, Karzai struck a deal with former president Rabbani for his support in the 2004 presidential elections in exchange for the position of Chair of the Lower House after the 2005 parliamentary election. The deal fell apart when the former Shuray-i-Nezar commanders discovered the deal with Karzai. They subsequently staged an internal rebellion against Rabbani to force him to give up his hope of becoming House leader.[23] The different patronage and strongmen networks of former *Jamiat* then held its own internal vote in which Rabbani competed and was badly defeated by Qanuni—out of the more than 40 votes from the central committee, Rabbani reportedly got only two.[24]

Subsequently, Karzai's alternative choice for House Chair, Abdul Rasul Sayyaf, the leader of Dawat-i-Islami, went head-to-head with Yunos Qanuni. In a surprise move, Mohaqqiq, the leader of Wahdat-i-Mardom made a deal with the Palace to back Sayyaf with a promise of being voted in as the first deputy once Sayyaf was elected. He came under immense pressure from his own ethnic Hazara MPs and a wider network of clients for betraying his community, which had suffered immensely during the civil war of the 1990s at the hands of Sayyaf's militias.[25] Consequently, many of his Wahdat-i-Mardom network MPs sided with Qanuni. In the first round, out of the seven candidates, including three women (Sayyaf, Qanuni, Sayed Ishaq Gilani, Ulumi, Safia Siddiqi, Qadria Yazdan Parast, and Shukria Barekzai), no one secured a majority.[26] In the second round, only the top two candidates, Qanuni and Sayyaf, ran against each other. Qanuni was elected as Chair with 122 votes against Sayyaf's 117. With Sayyaf's defeat, the Mohaqqiq–Sayyaf deal was off and Mohaqqiq was defeated by Arif Governor Noorzai, an ethnic Pashtun from Kandahar and a President Karzai ally.[27] Fauzia Koofi, a female MP and an ethnic Tajik from Badakhshan, was elected the second deputy. Qanuni won with the backing of all Jamiat networks and ethnic Uzbek, Hazara, and Tajik political networks. In a conciliatory move, Qanuni and Ahmad Wali Masoud reportedly gave up their Afghanistan Nawin and Nohzat-i-Islami parties to re-join Jamiat-i-Islami under the leadership of Rabbani.[28]

Between the 2005 and 2010 parliamentary elections, Qanuni emerged as the main opposition leader to President Karzai. He proved effective and dynamic not only in galvanising support among MPs against the president on key issues but in blocking Karzai's policies inside and outside the house. His management was considered effective, including his skills as a "firefighter," dousing any crises that emerged, and his solid grip over legislative and oversight affairs and processes. He often sidelined Karzai appointees in the secretariat and worked hard to undermine Karzai clients and political agendas. For instance, in a display of power in September 2008, Qanuni garnered two-thirds majority support among MPs to override all of Karzai's vetoes, a significant defeat for the president.[29] His performance as an effective leader who could defy Karzai bolstered his position among the United Front (UF) coalition, who were looking for a candidate for the 2009 presidential election. However, the UF collapsed, as detailed in Chapter 5, and Qanuni threw in his lot with Abdullah Abdullah.

In the second parliament (2010–2018), Karzai became even weaker especially when he couldn't remove 62 sitting MPs—detailed in Section 8.2.

This meant that for Karzai to pass his legislation he and his team had to strike constant ad hoc bargains and build alliances. The contest was once again between Qanuni and Sayyaf, with almost the same alliance composition. Karzai utilised all the state resources and money to ensure Qanuni was not elected. After three rounds of voting, the process reached an impasse. An ad hoc commission from different political groupings was established to find an alternative solution. The commission's suggestion was to have a candidate from the ethnic Uzbek group who was not affiliated with both political alliances. The result was the election of Haji Abdul Rauf Ibrahimi, an MP from the northern province of Kunduz with close ties to both Hizb-i-Islami and Junbish, as the Chair of the House. However, Ibrahimi would prove to be a weak and indecisive leader, undermining the prestige and relevance of the House.

In the third legislature, the leadership board of the Lower House was essentially nothing but an "auction" with a three-way contest between Ghani's candidate, the so-called anti-Ghani alliance, and a network of interest-based businessmen. On 7 July 2019, after almost two months and four rounds of balloting, plagued by controversies and disputes, MPs elected Mir Rahman Rahmani, the father of Haji Ajmal detailed above, and an ethnic Tajik MP from Parwan, as the Chair.[30] Amir Khan Yar (an ethnic Pashtun MP from Nangarhar) was elected as the first deputy, Ahmadshah Ramazan (an ethnic Hazara MP from Balkh), as the second deputy, M. Karim Atal (an ethnic Pashtun from Helmand), as secretary, and Erfanullah Erfan (an ethnic Tajik MP from Kabul), as assistant secretary. All of them are wealthy businessmen controlling different sectors of the Afghan economy. There was a secret deal between Rahmani, Ahmadshah Ramazan, and Abbas Ibrahimzada for the second deputy position for Ramazan, an ethnic Hazara, in exchange for Hazara support for Rahmani. This election process was nothing short of an auction ("lelam"). The final price tag for the Chair seat reached somewhere between US$20 to 30 million, depending on who one spoke to[31] (Table 8.2).

The primary factor for the election of the Speaker was the measure of a candidate's wealth. It was in the fourth round, and after Rahmani and Wardak had financially outbid the opponents that they emerged as heavyweights with the ability to spend big. Interviews showed that the exchange varied from US$20,000 to 50,000 per vote, and in some cases armoured car. Rahmani outbid Wardak by a significant margin. During the election of the Board, the state Ministry of Interior internal report presented at the National Security Council, where I was present, estimated that over 2,000 armoured cars were distributed to MPs as gifts. Most of these were known as "zero key," meaning they were illegally imported without customs duties and lacked the necessary vehicle registration paperwork. The MPs had been pressuring security agencies to issue up to seven number plates (special number plates with the initial letters W and J—i.e., Lower House) for the MPs, a reflection of the number of armoured cars in distribution. But this caused a major security concern as it was argued that criminal networks could now easily hijack and traffic drugs in these high-profile vehicles.

All of the parliamentary commissions that were set up after the 2019 elections (except Naheed Farid who led the Women Affairs Commission) were presided over

Table 8.2 Four rounds of votes for Speaker of the House

Rounds	Competitors	Background
First	Mir Rahman Rahmani versus Kamal Naser Usuli	Both are rich businessmen. It was alleged that Usuli had the backing of the Palace while Jamiat (Abdullah) supported Rahmani
Second	Ahmad Jawid Jaihun versus Mir Afghan Safi	Both rich businessmen with Jaihun having business links to the first VP
Third	Khan Agha Rezayi versus Khan M. Wardak	Both rich businessmen with Rezayi a Panjshiri and security companies, Wardak owning the Khan Steel works
Fourth	Rahmani versus Wardak	Both exceptionally rich who had made it this far because of their ability to spend

by individuals with business links and deep financial pockets. Each Commission had between 10 and 25 members with MPs desperately competing to get into the most lucrative ones. These commissions were the best platforms through which MPs would extract rents from ministers and officials or intimidate them. This is shown in more detail in the below case study. The case study of the 2010 Special Court crisis offers an excellent window to observe the day-to-day functioning of the House.

8.2 The 2010–2011 election and the Special Court crisis

The root cause of the 2010–2011 Special Court crisis is the result of the 18 September 2010 parliamentary elections and the dispute that emanated from it. Fraud, vote-rigging, and insecurity further reduced Karzai allies' vote bank. The Independent Electoral Complaints Commission (IECC) received more than 3,000 complaints, with significantly higher levels of ballot stuffing, voter fraud, and intimidation in the Pashtun south.[32] The IECC ultimately disqualified 1.5 million ballots, an estimated quarter of the total votes, and disqualified 27 winning candidates due to electoral fraud, which Karzai took personally as an attack on his political base and clients.[33]

The results were a major setback for President Karzai and his allies. Some of Karzai's network nodes in the south, where Karzai's support was considered high, were either unable to win votes or local tribal jirgas had agreed on sending their own collective choices—an indication of tribal resistance to Karzai's gang of seven strongmen in the south. For instance, because of local tribal dynamics, Karzai's first cousin, Hishmat Karzai, didn't win a seat in Kandahar. In multi-ethnic provinces, insecurity and Taliban threats had forced the closure of polling stations in some provinces and in places where tribal competition could not be overcome, Karzai clients lost out. The worst was in Ghazni where lack of large tribal groupings (except the Andar tribe whose population and geography were facing serious threats by the Taliban) and entrenched rivalry among small tribes and mismanagement on the part of Karzai associates meant that not a single Pashtun candidate was elected.[34]

Immediately after the announcement of the election results, the Attorney General's Office (AGO) and Supreme Court (the heads of both organisations were members of Karzai's network) demanded a recount and accused the Independent Complaints Commissions of bias. Karzai had been using the Attorney General's Office as a whip to suppress and silence rivals. He also ordered the IECC to hold a new round of elections in the Ghazni Province to balance its ethnic composition.[35] In retaliation, the IECC certified the final election results on 1 December 2010, with United Nations Assistance Mission in Afghanistan (UNAMA) and other international donors promptly accepting them. Karzai's team accused the IECC head, Fazal Ahmad Manavi, an ethnic Tajik, and a former Jamiat member of manipulating the process against their camp—with some of them going as far as to say this was revenge for the 2009 presidential election disputes. The AGO issued an arrest warrant for three IECC staff, one of whom was a high-ranking official, accusing them of orchestrating mass fraud. With advice from the Supreme Court, Karzai issued a decree to set up a Special Court (SC) to re-investigate the

Table 8.3 The timeline of events

18 September 2010	Parliamentary Election was held
24 November 2010	Independent Election Commission (IEC) announced the results for 34 provinces except for Ghazni. 1.5 million votes were disqualified and 27 candidates were disqualified
24 November 2010	Attorney General's Office (AGO) and the Supreme Court demanded a recount and issued arrest warrants for three IEC staff
1 December 2010	In retaliation, IEC certified the final election results
21 December 2010	Karzai issued a decree forcing the creation of a Special Court
26 January 2011	Karzai agreed to inaugurate the Lower House if, in return, MPs allowed the SC to prosecute those who committed fraud
23 June 2011	SC issued its verdict disqualifying 62 sitting MPs
25 June 2011	MPs passed a vote of no confidence against the AGO and Supreme Court Judges
5 July 2011	MPs proposed to impeach the President
10 August 2011	Karzai backed down and issued a decree forcing the IEC to have the final say
21 August 2011	IEC announced the list of 9 MPs to be replaced
3 September 2011	The new 9 MPs were forcibly sworn in. The opposition called it a coup

IECC's list of disqualified candidates and other fraud cases. Eventually, on 26 January 2011, under intense pressure from international donors and disgruntled candidates (both those who won seats and those protesting), Karzai made a deal with the elected members to promptly inaugurate Parliament if in return the MPs agreed that the SC could pursue any criminal cases identified by the court.[36]

On 23 June 2011, the crisis resurfaced when the SC issued its verdict to disqualify 62 sitting MPs, one-quarter of the Lower House. Mohammed Mohaqqiq declared Karzai's attempt to implement the SC's verdict "an alarming danger" which went too far in "undermining all the Reshta [connections] built over the last ten years."[37] Two days later, in response, the Lower House passed a resolution denouncing the creation of the SC and declaring its decision illegal. This was followed by a vote of no confidence against the AGO and the Supreme Court judges. To coordinate efforts, an ad hoc Support for Rule of Law (SRL) coalition was established. At one point, MPs even discussed the possibility of impeaching the President. After two months of political manoeuvring, discussed below, and failing to generate enough support through deal-making and exchange, Karzai and his team backed down, issuing a decree giving the IECC the final authority to resolve the crisis. Ten days later, in a compromise, the IECC announced that only nine of the 62 MPs should be disqualified.[38] Clearly, a last-minute face-saving compromise was belted to avoid embarrassment for major political networks including president Karzai.

The next section seeks to identify some of the main client networks which both the Karzai and SRL networks relied on building an expansive alliance around the crisis (Table 8.3).

8.2.1 *Power dynamics of competing political networks*

8.2.1.1 *The Karzai alliance*

Having failed to secure substantial gains in the House, Karzai and his network allies were quick to activate their client networks and key nodes, including ministers, governors, and ethno-regional power brokers, to re-assemble an ad hoc alliance which would strengthen their positions vis-à-vis their strongmen opponents. Ethnographic fieldwork and interviews with dozens of key informants painted a fascinating picture of how Karzai's network operated around several influential state officials. These were Humayoun Azizi, the State Minister for Parliamentary Affairs; Hazrat Omar Zakhilwal, the Minister of Finance; Sadeq Modabber, the Head of the Office of Administrative Affairs; Ibrahim Spinzada, Deputy National Security Council (NSC); Rahmatullah Nabil, the then Director of National Directorate of Security; and Asadullah Khalid, the Minister for Border, Tribal, and Ethnic Affairs. By utilising state resources, including its coercive power and financial wealth, the Karzai network negotiated deals and exchanges to co-opt MPs. Although difficult to substantiate and confirm with absolute clarity, the rough picture that can be drawn suggests that during the crisis the State Minister for Parliamentary Affairs and Deputy Head of NSC functioned as "liaison officers" in pact-making. The finance minister sanctioned patronage payments to the Head of the Office of Administrative Affairs and Deputy of the National Security Council, Ibrahim Ispinzada, through code 91,[39] who distributed the bargained sum to the co-opted network leaders. The Attorney General's Office and Supreme Court judges acted as extensions of the executive for bringing people in line. MPs were open about how it all worked, summarised here by statements from MPs from Ghazni and Samangan:

> Intimidation was evident at all levels. If an MP was not ready to accept certain privileges, then he or she was threatened by the Special Court and the Attorney General's Office that they would be among the disqualified MPs. On the one hand, Karzai invites us to the Arg [palace] in an attempt to bribe us, and when we refuse, his ministers try to intimidate us.[40]

> The Ministry of Parliamentary Affairs has been lobbying hard in Parliament in favour of the executive branch. He acts as a facilitator while the Attorney General's Office plays the role of the prosecutor. Some of my colleagues who had relatives within the administration were warned if they did not support the Karzai team their family members would risk losing their positions.[41]

> The State Minister for Parliamentary Affairs has been facilitating privileges such as MP's bodyguards and houses. Some of these privileges have been allocated to them through the Ministry and the National Security Directorate for their guesthouse expenses, bodyguards, salaries and others. In provinces

like Kandahar and Helmand, Khalid has been making muamela [deals] with those that he can, whilst threatening others. I still receive calls from the Palace by Khurram [Karzai's Chief of Staff] threatening that they would do this and that to me and my family.[42]

These revelations highlight the level of intimidation used against some MPs. Several informants noted the key role played by the then Head of the National Directorate of Security, Rahmatullah Nabil, and the Minister for Border, Tribal, and Ethnic Affairs, Asadullah Khalid, in employing state coercive powers to threaten and intimidate opponents. It is widely reported in the Afghan media and confirmed by several senior members in the President's Office that some ethno-regional power brokers, including Abdul Rasul Sayyaf and Mohammad Mohaqqiq, had been regularly receiving extra security budgets, varying between 150 and 500 bodyguards per month, as well as other expensive gifts like armoured cars for their security.[43] As shown in Chapter 6, Asadullah Khalid, Jan Muhammad Khan and Ahmad Wali Karzai (assassinated in mid-2011) were instrumental in expanding and exerting Karzai's influence in the tribal south through intimidation and deal-making. Their control over key businesses, both licit and illicit, meant that they had the final decision as to who could gain access to state funds, services, and contracts. As one MP from Kandahar confided to me about the level of coercion his colleagues faced in Kandahar:

In all honesty, I am against the SC's decision. But if some of my friends don't support the government their commercial ertebatat [links] and ability to import goods from Pakistan would be significantly constrained. Ahmad Wali controls everything: the government, the customs, and security. If others do not support Karzai, they will risk losing their business.[44]

The Special Court crisis revealed that while the role of state-level networks and ethno-regional strongmen were important to connect patrons with MPs and other local actors, in a system where votes were anonymous and exchanges high, the temptation was great among MPs to attempt to make direct deals with patrons rather than go through their political networks. Karzai's main source of support was predominantly his ethnic Pashtun MPs. The Hizb-i-Islami under the leadership of Abdul Hadi Arghandival proved to be the most loyal and the largest bloc to support Karzai's decisions, with over 30 members as part of the Sabah parliamentary group (see below for more on these) in the Lower House.[45] Abdul Rasul Sayyaf's Dawat political network and his influence played a part. In post-2001, Sayyaf became Karzai's central power broker in the House. Twice he stood for the position of the Speaker of the House to represent the Karzai group; both times he fell short by only a few votes. In addition to these ethnic Pashtun powerbrokers, Karzai obtained the support of other ethno-regional power brokers in the parliament. For instance,

Sadiq Modabber (the Head of the Office of Administrative Affairs) sponsored a parliamentary group that backed the government amongst the ethnic Hazara MPs.

In the House, political network-patrons exercised some degree of control and hierarchy over their clients by establishing parliamentary groups (PGs). The provision for the formation of PGs was established in 2005, the first year of the Lower House, as a formal mechanism to encourage greater efficiency and organisation in plenary discussions in a highly fragmented and chaotic parliament. It was also aimed at assisting the establishment of interest groups and generating consensus around key issues and positions, transcending individual and ethnic interests and views.[46] De jure, a PG had to have at least 21 members and be inclusive of all ethnic, religious, and gender groups. The head of the PG had the advantage of attending the Lower House's executive meetings to decide parliamentary agendas. De facto, ethnographic fieldwork at some PG headquarters showed that the PGs were at best a form of patronage network centred around key political network leaders such as Abdul Rasul Sayyaf, Mohammad Mohaqqiq, Sadiq Modabber, Haji Zahir Qadir, Karim Khalili, and Abdul Hadi Arghandiwal. Also, some of them, like the Etemad (Trust) Group, were ethnically homogeneous in their composition, contravening the internal rules of the Lower House.[47] Each parliamentary group had at least one office/guesthouse close to the Lower House where they hosted visitors, financed by the patron. Various factors contributed to an MP's decision to join a PG: financial gains, political influence, ethnic and tribal affiliations, and legal and illegal business interests. As a female MP asserted:

> In the first month of the Lower House, Haji Zahir Qadir [the head of Peace Caravan PG and the leader of Support for Rule of Law coalition] approached me to join his group. He told me that he knew that I live in a rented house. He offered me $2000 per month if I joined his group.[48]

The financial dimension was one of the central contributing factors to the survival of a political group. Wafaey and Larson found that the main reason for the disintegration of Khat-i-Sewom (Third Line) and some other earlier, non-legacy/jihadi PGs was the absence of funds as well as internal rifts along identity-based lines.[49] For power brokers, the political and financial return was high (discussed in the next section), especially at moments of trading favours like electing a new Speaker or voting to approve a minister. Participatory observation and interviews with MPs revealed that during the crisis, the three main PGs—Sabah, Etemad, and Dawat—provided Karzai with the necessary client base. The patrons of these groups, Abdul Hadi Arghandiwal (later the Minister for Economy), Sadeq Modabber (the Head of the Office of Administrative Affairs), and Abdul Rasul Sayyaf (leader of Dawa-i-Islami), were key allies of Karzai in the post-2001 period (Table 8.4).

Table 8.4 List of parliamentary groups from 2010 to 2018

Groups name	Members	Chair	Deputy	Patron/affiliation
National League Group	11*	Ghulam Farooq Nazari	M. Farhad Sediqi	
Unification of Nation	15*	Saheb Khan	S. M. Akhond	
Peace Caravan	45	Haji Zahir Qadir	Nazifa Zaki	Haji Zahir Qadir/ Anti-Govt
Peace	20*	Obaidaullah Kalemzai	Rahima Jami	Pro-Govt
Rasalat (Pathway)	34	Abdul Baqi Malekzada	M. Sarwar Osmani	
Saba	28	Haji Almas Zahid	Sher Wali Wardak	Pro-Govt/Haji Almas
National Prosperity	18*	Safiullah Muslim	Nasir Ahmad Ghuriyan	
Enhancing Women Participation	22*	Fawzia Koofi	Wajhma Safi	Koofi/Jamiat
Voice of Justice	23	Shah Gul Rezayi	Chaman Gul Etemadi	
Free Afghanistan	29	Humayoun Humayoun	M. Reza Khoshak	
Independent	20*	L. Babakarkhail	A. Sabour Khedmat	

Source: The Official Website of WJ taken from AREU/(*registered but not officially formed).

8.2.1.2 The Support for Rule of Law (SRL) alliance

While the SRL opposition alliance in the House was purportedly formed to counter the Special Court decision to disqualify 62 MPs, its purpose was later revealed to be more complicated. Some MPs genuinely joined the coalition to check the ambitions of an intrusive president whom they saw as undermining the integrity of the House. Others, however, joined for self-preservation. The SC verdict found nearly 200 MPs had committed fraud to varying degrees during the election. The Attorney General and Supreme Court judges warned those MPs found guilty would face prosecution. The response was immediate and uncompromising: The parliamentary session on 25 June 2011 was dominated by tough statements from MPs, with references to "illegitimate government," "dictatorship," "mafia state," "corrupt government and its halaqat [circles]," "Jabbarkhan [cruelty]," and "Hakemiyat-e-Sultani [Sultanate-style governance]".[50] It was not clear how many MPs initially signed up for the SRL; the estimate varied from 140 to 180 out of 249. However, over time, as it became evident that no prosecution of MPs would follow, a significant number of MPs dropped out of the SRL while others were co-opted by the Karzai network through intimidation and the offer of rewards, as discussed above.

The most powerful central node in the SRL, around whom other dispersed anti-Karzai networks assembled, was Qadir's Peace Caravan, the largest opposition parliamentary group in the Lower House, with an estimated 40 MPs. As outlined in Chapter 4, the Arsala family had significant power in Nangarhar. With the new legislature and riding on the back of the SC crisis, Qadir established himself as a national figure in Kabul, beyond his family's base of power, in opposition to Karzai. During and after the crisis, the Karzai network made several attempts to discredit him and his family by accusing him of being involved in drug smuggling, kidnapping, and corruption—some of which were true. In January 2012, months after the crisis, he was elected the first deputy speaker of the Lower House, winning 140 votes, further consolidating his power in the House. In 2013, the Minister of Finance, a close ally of Karzai, accused Qadir of smuggling US$269 million worth of flour from Pakistan. In response, the next day Qadir declared to parliamentarians that he had more than US$350 million in his bank account, reminding the MPs how he had financially maintained them during the crisis.[51]

The SRL succeeded in building a powerful alliance against Karzai. It managed to draw support from some state-level and provincial political networks who were either disillusioned with Karzai's corrupt practices or felt betrayed by Karzai's false promises following the 2009 presidential elections. Amongst these was Abdullah Abdullah, Karzai's main contender in the 2009 presidential election. Following his defeat in the election, he was quick to capitalise on his 30% voting block by establishing the Coalition for Change and Hope. Several influential MPs, who were also members of Abdullah's Coalition, played a key role in the SRL coalition. Another important leader who supported the SRL, albeit privately, was Karzai's second vice president, Karim Khalili. Given Khalil's formal position in the executive, as well as his influence within the House as the patron of Saday-i-Adalat (Voice of Justice) parliamentary group, his support provided confidence to the opposition. Why Khalil supported the coalition was a purely number game: more people from his network were on the SC list of targeted MPs than any other individual network leader. He no doubt felt betrayed by Karzai.

The three main parliamentary groups at the disposal of the SRL—Peace Caravan (mostly ethnic Pashtuns), Saday-i-Adalat (predominately ethnic Hazaras), and the newly established Resalat (largely ethnic Tajiks), each with its own offices—were effective in mobilising MPs, arranging discussions and debate, and organising campaigns. The PGs functioned as a whip ensuring that MPs did stay committed to the cause.

The reasons for SRL's ability to defy Karzai's network were due to its rather inclusive internal organisational structure, which enabled better coordination efforts, and the leadership of its two speakers, Latif Pedram, a leftist ethnic Tajik MP from Badakhshan, and Asadullah Saadati, an ethnic Hazara and the MP from Daikundi. The SRL leadership council was a 17-member team. The two speakers proved skilful in establishing close relations with the main news outlets and TV channels in a successful public relations (PR) effort. In addition, most of the 18 parliamentary commissions within the Lower House, such as security affairs, women affairs, economic affairs, and others, were controlled by SRL-affiliated leaders, which gave them power over agenda setting and discussions within the House. The de jure roles of these commissions were to draft and review legislation and oversee the performance of relevant ministries. De facto, over years they became an important source of rent, deal-making, and sabotaging of rivals. At its height, the SRL became a real political threat to Karzai because of its control of parliamentary commissions. Latif Pedram, its speaker, described the SRL's strategy to me this way:

> The coalition presently controls 13 of the 18 select commissions in the Lower House and three Parliamentary Groups [PGs]. The Parliament Executive Team (PET), which is responsible for determining the agenda of parliamentary sessions, is comprised of both the head of Parliamentary Commission and PGs. We plan to create one or two more PGs to fully control the Lower House's agenda and its PET.[52]

The following section shows that what ensured the survival and longevity of SRL and Karzai's alliance in the House was rent and bargains more than anything else which became the key defining feature of the Afghan parliament—a grant marketplace for bargains and rent.

8.2.2 Rent-seeking, bargains, and opportunism

The SC crisis provided another excellent moment for rent-seeking, bargaining, and patronage practice that was propagated by Afghanistan's political economy of international intervention and state-building. Bargaining took place between multiple actors and layers of patronage, offering power brokers the bargains in exchange for their skills in buying loyalties and support with heavyweights and sometimes entire associates and group members. MPs were not shy of pointing out who had taken bribes or traded political favours privately and often accused each other of favouritism and connection with various actors. During the crisis, most bargains were made for financial gain, yet political privileges were also considered. Offers of government positions, state contracts, licenses, and gifts were widespread. Although it is difficult to estimate the amount of financial rewards offered to extend patronage, it was certainly extensive. As the following disclosures by two influential MPs show, the tactics used included both monetary rewards and personal safety in an insecure environment:

> The Jihadi leaders, ministers and governors would visit MPs' houses to make deals. These offers could include anything really from a simple bribe to covering the expenses of their guesthouses, to offering gifts like cars and installing family members in key positions. This is negotiated and agreed upon.[53]

Most of them [MPs] supported the government. The opposition is weak and powerless. When opposition members like myself are threatened what can we do? Mawlawi Tarakhel [MP] rigged 50,000 votes before the election for Karzai [referring to the 2004 presidential election] and he later confessed saying I did it because I got money and lands from the government and also because Karzai is the one who can provide me with security and safety. Another MP [who] supported Karzai, when asked why replied because he had been accused of killing 41 people so if he did not support him what guarantee was there that they would not kill him.[54]

Even international holidays and trips are decided based on which group you belong to. If you are not part of that group, you can never go. Karzai has 70-80 MPs on his side. They have their special meetings. The ministers sit with them often, bribing them by offering them trips abroad, gifts, and positions for their relatives.[55]

A political economy researcher documented similar layers of opportunism and bargaining among network-patrons and the network-client leaders. An informant reported to him that one powerbroker, usually considered of only moderate importance, "paid one car, or USD 10,000 for each vote he could convince MPs to give to [a certain more influential MP]; [this influential leader] then gave this amount back to him."[56] He also found that in some cases, power brokers invested their own money knowing that they could get a higher return later from their patron.

State officials were not the only ones involved in financial and political deal-making and corruption. During the SC crisis, following a rumour that the Azizi Bank had gone bankrupt, MPs scheduled an inquiry session to investigate the bank's financial position. Some MPs provided compelling evidence suggesting that the bank had been involved in illegal and corrupt business practices. As the day of the inquiry approached, tensions intensified. Amazingly, on the day itself, despite most MPs' earlier rhetoric of corruption and mismanagement, they voted overwhelmingly not to investigate the bank's financial dealings any further. Some MPs complained that others had taken bribes while some had been intimidated by political networks within the state that had close links with the bank. As one MP put it:

I fear for my life. Azizi Bank [i.e. people within the security apparatus with close links to the bank] has threatened me on many occasions. We have evidence that 450 million dollars were transferred to Dubai for purchasing property, and not a single penny has returned. The bank has also been involved in corruption in the oil business.[57]

A senior investigative officer at the High Office of Oversight and Anti-Corruption, confirmed these practices inside the Lower House:

Both Azizi Bank and Kabul Bank were heavily involved in bribing MPs in the parliament and in some cases making sure that nominated ministers are approved. We have evidence that Azizi Bank bribed MPs to make sure that certain appointed ministers get elected. As you can imagine, once these ministers are appointed, they have to get involved in corruption to pay back their debt. We know in one case, Kabul Bank spent nearly USD 200,000 to get its person elected.[58]

Most MPs interviewed pointed out that if the investigation had gone ahead, it would have exposed and implicated at least 100 MPs and a wide network of top officials. As Chapter 9 shows, in 2010, the investigation into the corruption of the largest bank in Afghanistan, Kabul Bank, revealed that it had become a virtual "Ponzi scheme" implicating over 103 MPs, governors, and ministers.

The reason for the intensification of MPs' deal-making lies in the political economy of the Lower House. MPs not only had to cover the cost of maintaining an office, staff, and other expenses, but they also had to fulfil several traditional political obligations for their constituencies, including providing a place for the constituents to stay while visiting Kabul, attending weddings, providing expensive gifts, offering food on feast days, and fulfilling religious obligations such as paying for a religious figure to recite the Quran.[59] The state also paid for two bodyguards and an assistant. It seemed that bargaining and exchange was a practical strategy that allowed MPs to survive and maintain their influence and social and political status. At the time, several MPs highlighted how some MPs had incurred debts to be elected. As one MP succinctly put it: "Some MPs have borrowed a lot of money to come to parliament, so they have to make deals to pay for their debt."[60] These bargaining and opportunistic practices were not considered corruption but more a survival strategy that had become the norm in an environment of uncertainty, elite distrust, and dysfunctional state institutions.

Also, from a cultural–political dimension, MPs were obligated to reciprocate because of the social obligation of family, kinship, tribe, qawm, and others. Constituents see their MPs first and foremost as part of the local patronage networks.[61] Before an election, often a discussion takes place among communities over who to send to parliament. Once in parliament, they are expected to help securing jobs and business contracts, lobbying for development projects, and providing political protection, among other services.[62] Such high expectations put MPs in a difficult situation. This is evident from one MP's reply when I asked for his reason for joining the Karzai network: "They are the dominant network. They are in power. If I do not establish a close relationship with them, how could I resolve my people's [constituents] problems when they come to Kabul?"[63] The ability of an MP to politically manoeuvre within complicated formal state institutions as well as informal local societal power structures and licit and illicit business networks was a determining factor in their survival success. To survive, they used different strategies with their local constituency. For instance, some MPs paid local elders some pocket money or got their sons jobs in the local administration. These local elders in return acted as their "goodwill ambassadors." Doing a favour for an influential community or tribal elder seemed an easier investment to maintain a good reputation than playing by democratic rules.

Interviews revealed that the expanding nature of these patronage practices stretched beyond Afghanistan's key players to include regional nations and the international community more broadly (see quote below). In 2010, the National Directorate of Security announced that over 120 MPs had links or received some kind of support from neighbouring Iran. A U.S. Embassy cable in 2009 highlighted the same concern, accusing the Iranians of routinely encouraging the parliament to support anti-U.S. policies and to put anti-American talking points on the agenda.[64] The same cable noted that Omar Daudzai, Karzai's Chief of Staff at the time, had asserted that, "in addition to financing Afghan religious leaders, Iran had provided salary support for some [Afghan government] deputy ministers and other officials, including 'one or two' even in the [presidential] palace."[65] Another cable in March 2009 noted how Iranians approached Mirwais Yasini, an MP from Nangarhar, to include a debate on the agenda on the status of coalition forces, which coincided with the visit of Iran's vice president to Kabul. Although Yasini claims to have declined, he faced the wrath of two pro-Iranian MPs who criticised him for betraying his country.[66]

Other countries also tried to influence MPs. The Indians designed and paid for the new parliament building, which was seen as a symbol of Indian–Afghan friendship. Prime Minister Modi attended the inauguration of the parliament in December 2015. At one point, the Chinese took as many as 100 MPs to China for exposure visits to enhance their influence, especially MPs from the northeast and southeast. The frequency of these trips became a major concern for the Afghan government. Western countries, meanwhile, provided financial and technical support to strengthen the capacity of the newly established parliament and parliamentarians.[67]

To conclude this section, the SC crisis highlighted several important characteristics of the nature of power dynamics of political networks and their day-to-day practices, and especially alliance-building. First, it suggested that alliance formations are fluid, unstable, and temporary. While a core set of political networks might be part of a broader alliance of common interests, they also compete with each other over influence, allegiances, state positions, and resources. The SC crisis laid bare how alliances were reshaped and restructured as events unfolded, the crises continued, local socio-political balances changed, and positions and resources shifted. In an environment of uncertainty and political network distrust in post-2001 Afghanistan, it seemed to be in the interests of political networks and their clientele to keep their motivations and intentions concealed and remain publicly ambiguous, especially in the Lower House. At the same time, as highlighted earlier, political networks utilised and manipulated the newly established and internationally sponsored formal state institutions, in this case the Lower House, to legitimise their network practices and strengthen their power within the state. Karzai and his allies in the government, having control over most of the state's resources, was able to rely on institutional organisations such as the Attorney General's Office (AGO) and the Supreme Court to defend and justify their decision in setting up the SC in the first place.

Conclusion

This chapter showed how the Afghan parliament came to serve the interests of political networks rather than the Afghan people and its diverse constituencies. It proved to be an excellent "networking arena" crossing old political boundaries where legal and illegal business and political lines merged, and business opportunities were cooked up and executed. The lack of political parties meant that horse-trading was a time-consuming and exhaustive process in which each MP had to be dealt with individually despite the introduction of parliamentary groups, which at times produced chaos and political instability. The parliament gave MPs the "power of access" to all levels and layers of government for personal profit. Bargains, rent-seeking, and intimidation became a key part of their practice of survival. The 2010–2011 Special Court crisis revealed that the House had become a grand marketplace for rent-seeking and bargains further reinforcing the consolidation of a networked state. The SC crisis also uncovered that Karzai's power was supreme if multiple and entrenched political networks allowed it to be. His ability to remove the 62 sitting MPs exposed the limits of his power. The anti-Karzai network groups sent a clear message that they were an essential part of the system for which Karzai must share the fruits of state resources and international patronage.

In practice, the Afghan parliament performed poorly in its constitutionally mandated powers and functions. An AREU 2019 report on the parliament found that in the three-legislature period of the Republic (2005–2021), the House had only drafted five laws on its own initiative.[68] Most of the bills were drafted by the executive branch and passed through decree with little oversight and deliberation from MPs. Parliament's oversight powers, specifically the right to exercise the no-confidence vote, in practice had been remarkably destabilising.[69] MPs were often accused of striking self-interested deals as a price for their affirmative votes on the budget. The only area where they performed relatively better was constituency services. However, some came under criticism for getting a cut for their service, came to be known by ordinary Afghans as "Commission Kari [Commission work]." Despite some gains in opening the civil space for MPs to resolve their differences through networking and discussions, albeit with occasional barbs and insults, the overall performance of the Afghan parliament remained shaky, and its reputation was shattered. One could argue that the legislature branch is as much responsible for the collapse of the Republic as other branches of the post-2001 state.

Despite these shortcomings, the Afghan parliament also opened the civil space for MPs to resolve their differences through networking and discussions, albeit with occasional barbs and insults. The next chapter examines the role of rent extraction and illegality in post-2001 Afghanistan by looking at three key economic sectors: banking, extractive industries, and customs.

Notes

1 "Afghan Translator Who Become a 9/11 Millionaire," *Juicy News*, March 25, 2015.
2 This chapter is based on four months of ethnographic fieldwork inside the Lower House from June to October 2011 as well as observations and interviews conducted in 2011 and some in early 2019.
3 For a detail description of Afghanistan's constitutional design, see Thier (2007); Kakar, Kraemer, and Raoofi (2017); Pasarlay and Mallyar (2019).
4 There are conflicting stories about who made the decision to accept SNTV. President Ghani at one point noted that this was Karzai's decision. But some put the blame on Ghani saying that from the several options on the table, Ghani reportedly questioned the ability of Afghans to comprehend a more complex system. The first proposed electoral law draft would have mandated a party list system. However, Karzai was against giving a greater role to political parties, despite international lobbying and advice.
5 According to an International Crisis Group (2005) report, the percentage was likely lower by election day since a list of those claiming such affiliation was then given to the parties for approval.
6 Leslie (2015).
7 Ibid.
8 See the EU Election Observation Mission final report, 12 November 2005: 22 more candidates were disqualified at a very late stage on the same grounds.
9 Specifically, 2,815 candidates, including 347 women, sought Lower House positions while 3,185 candidates, including 279 women, ran for provincial council positions.
10 "Kabul, Paktia MPs Sworn in Amid Problems in Parliament," *TOLOnews*, May 15, 2019.
11 Wilder (2005).
12 Ibid.
13 Hussaini and Faizi (2010).
14 Ibid, 6.
15 See National Democratic Institute Report. 2005. "The September 2005 Parliamentary and Provincial Council Elections in Afghanistan," 20,
16 Wilder (2005).
17 Ibid.
18 With the delay in district council elections, on 27 October 2005, the Cabinet passed a decree in which two members from the upper house were elected from each provincial council and on December 11, 2005, President Karzai announced his 34 appointees. For percentage of ethnic composition see NDI Report. 2005. "The September 2005 Parliamentary and Provincial Council Elections in Afghanistan," 20,
19 For a detailed account of the challenges in the 2018 parliamentary elections see Johnson and Ronald (2020); Johnson (2018); Hasrat-Nazimi, W. 2018. "Afghanistan Election: Can Young Candidates Turn Things Around?" *Deutsche Welle*, October 16, https://www.dw.com/en/afghanistan-election-can-young-candidates-turn-things-around/a-45905684.
20 Arefi, A., and F. Farhang. 2020. "Dawr-e-Hafdahom Majles-e-Nomayandagan: Entekhabat, Tarkib va Taghirat." *Khabarnama*, http://khabarnama.net/wp-content/uploads/2020/05/Afghanistan-Parliament-Research.pdf.
21 Schmeidl (2016).
22 The Chair administered the Lower House's sessions, set the agenda, supervised and monitored its budget, received reports from its commissions, and preserved its prestige (i.e., signed all contracts with legal entities). *Internal Rules of Procedure, Lower House*, art. 13 (2007), available at: thttp://wj.parliament.af/english.aspx (accessed 15 June 2018).
23 Author's interview with two Jamiat officials with knowledge of the event, Kabul, June 18, 2020.

24 Interviews with Jamiat leaders, June 2019. There was a lot of anger within Jamiat not only about the deal. Many felt that Rabbani's participation in the parliamentary election was below his prestige as a former president.
25 Author's interview and observations, August 2011. Many saw this as a betrayal as Sayyaf was responsible for starting the civil war against Wahdat in the 1990s and had committed atrocities against Hazara and Shia communities in West Kabul.
26 Qanuni received 108 votes, Sayyaf 88 and Gailani 16, Ulumi, 12, Barakzai 9, Yazdan Parast 6 and Seqqiqi 5. See Mujhda, A. W. et al. (2006).
27 Governor Noorzai is also related to Karzai's family. His sister was reportedly married to Karzai's younger brother.
28 "Afghan Parliament: Selection of Deputy Speaker," Wikileaks U.S. Diplomatic Cables, December 22, 2005.
29 US Cable. 2008. "Karzai's Ineffective Parliamentary Outreach," October 6, 2008.
30 For a detailed account of the four rounds and the controversies surrounding the election of the Chair see Adili, A. Y., and R. Sorush, "The Disputed Election of the Lower House's Speaker: A Story of a Balance of Power, Political Allegiance, and Money." Afghanistan Analyst Network, July 22, 2019.
31 Author's interview and private conversation with several parliamentarians, associates close to Rahmani, Wardak and Ramazan, Kabul, June 2019.
32 Bijlert, M. 2011. "Untangling Afghanistan's 2010 Vote: Analysing the Electoral Data." Afghanistan Analysts Network, *Briefing Paper* (3).
33 Ibid.
34 In 9 of the 19 districts in Ghazni, no votes were cast at all. See 2010 Election: Ghazni's Election Drama - It's the System (amended) (Afghanistan Analyst Network), http://aan-afghanistan.com/index.asp?id=1361.
35 Bijlert (2011).
36 Norland, R. 2011. "Karzai Agreed to Seat New Parliament." *The New York Times*, January 22, 2011, http://www.nytimes.com/2011/01/23/world/asia/23afghan.html?pagewanted=all.
37 Speech in the House, Observation on June 25, 2011.
38 Bijlert (2011).
39 This is one of the main discretionary budget codes which both presidents came to rely on to purchase loyalties. See Chapter 9 for more details.
40 Speech by a Ghazni province MP in the Lower House, Observation on August 24, 2011.
41 Speech by a Samangan province MP in the Lower House, Observation on August 24, 2011.
42 Author's Interview, Kabul, June 30, 2011.
43 Hakimi (2011).
44 Author's Interview, Kabul, July 24, 2011.
45 The 2010 Kabul Centre for Strategic Studies report identified the Hizb and its Sabah parliamentary groups as the most coordinated network in the House.
46 International Crisis Group (2006).
47 *Internal Rules of Procedure, Lower House,* art. 18 (2007), available, at: thttp://wj.parliament.af/english.aspx (accessed on 15 June 2018).
48 Interview 25, September 8, 2011.
49 Wafaey and Larson (2010: 9).
50 Author's observation in the Lower House on 25 June 2011.
51 Broadcast live on the National Radio Television of Afghanistan (https://youtube.com, http://www.youtube.com/watch?v=nst8M0Ftec4), 2013.
52 Author's Interview, Kabul, September 21, 2011.
53 Author's Interview, Kabul, June 24, 2011.
54 Author's Interview, Kabul, September 13, 2009.
55 Author's Interview, Kabul, September 12, 2009.

56 Coburn (2011).
57 Author's Interview, Kabul, July 16, 2011.
58 Author's Interview, Kabul, September 20, 2011.
59 As one MP put it, "There is this expectation from my constituency that now that I am in the parliament I must have made money and the least I can do for them is that when they come to Kabul, they stay at my guesthouse and I feed them. If I fail to provide, their perception of me changes as they think I have not been hospitable."
60 Interview 18, August 24, 2011.
61 See Coburn, N. 2011. "Political Economy in the Lower House: Sources of Finance and Their Impact on Representation in Afghanistan's Parliament." *Afghanistan Research Evaluation Unit*, May 2011.
62 Ibid.
63 Author's Interview, Kabul, August 29, 2011
64 U.S. Embassy Cables, February 3, 2010.
65 Ibid.
66 U.S. Embassy Cables, March, 2010.
67 USAID awarded the "Afghanistan Parliamentary Assistant Project" (APAP) to the State University of New York/Centre for International Development to design legislative programs and put in place processes and procedures for a representative and functioning parliamentary institution. A UNDP "Support for the Establishment of the Afghan Legislature" (SEAL) project offered assistance to develop both the technical and political skills of the members and the staff within the Parliament. These included basic office training, human rights, democracy, and budget oversight. There have been countless exposure visits offered by various countries to help parliamentarians learn and be influenced.
68 Pasarlay and Mallyar (2019). These laws were: the 2007 Law on National Reconciliation and General Amnesty, the 2014 Law on the Privileges and Immunities of the MPs, the 2016 Law on the Prevention of Harassment against Women and Children, the 2014 Law on Diplomatic and Consular Staff of Afghanistan and the 2017 Law on the Publication and Promulgation of Legislative Documents.
69 Ruttig (2016).

9 International money as a "weapons system," rent, and corruption

Introduction

Back in the summer of 2008 at Yamchi village in the Sar-i-Pul Province, while doing field research for Afghanistan Research and Evaluation Unit, I probed Baba Kohisaaf on the last thematic subject of my questionnaire: *International intervention and aid effectiveness*. I detailed Kohisaaf's hardships in the preface of this book. When I asked him about the impact of the international intervention and aid on his household, after a long pause he composed himself and sighed. "Two months ago, a German doctor came to the village clinic," he said finally. "Hearing about the doctor's presence, the Taliban came down from the mountains and killed him. A week later, the Germans distributed a sack of wheat and ten kilos of cooking oil per household in the village." He turned his gaze to the children playing by the mosque and continued: "I hope the Taliban kill another German, so we get another sack of wheat."

For years, Kohisaaf's statement haunted me. For Kohisaaf, killing had less to do with the taking of another human life, but maybe an act of striking back at the failure of the international community to live up to its promises. Still, the extreme cynicism with which he expressed this disappointment, and the "hidden transcript" behind it, puzzled me. As had been argued by others, it is in the embedded "cynical reasoning" and "hidden transcript" of these villagers that one may understand the irony of the post-2001 Western interventions.[1] This reflected a fundamental disconnect between the way the Western-led intervention and state-building project was being implemented and how its putative beneficiaries were experiencing it.

In post-2001 Afghanistan, the U.S.A. and its military allies employed a prosaic, quick-fix approach to nation-building, throwing money at things, and expecting instant results. Programmes such as the Provincial Reconstruction Team (PRT) became the extended arm of the U.S.A. and coalition partners' strategy to win "hearts and minds" in Afghan communities. As several studies have shown, this effort was counterproductive and failed to either increase support for coalition forces or improve the legitimacy of the Afghan state. For instance, whilst south and southeast Afghanistan, where most of the insurgency war was concentrated, received substantial aid, secured areas, including the Central Highlands, were

DOI: 10.4324/9781315161617-9

punished for the absence of violence. As one community elder in a remote district of the Bamiyan Province in early 2021 sarcastically put it; "We never realised when they [coalition forces] came and when they left."[2] The imbalance created more problems than any aid initiatives could solve. For many impoverished villagers at the receiving end of failed international strategies and initiatives, the war fashioned daily sufferings; for those ignored, its thinly stretched shadow reached them only intermittently in the form of the occasional subsistence assistance like cooking oil and wheat in Kohisaaf's village.

The problem was international money: it permeated all levels of society; it created a symbiotic relationship and entrenched an asymmetry of power dependency with a small group of elites who tacitly or inadvertently promoted the political and security interests of the U.S.A. and its allies rather than the broader interests of Afghanistan. The massive inflow of money post-2001 subsequently produced a new class of Afghan predatory entrepreneurs, local strongmen-turned-businessmen, contractors, bankers, and others who made their fortunes because of their association with, and hoarding of, international security and aid assistance. The international money and contracts fostered and facilitated an ecosystem in which corruption became the addictive drug sustaining a small group of elites and through them the entire Afghan Republic.

My own friends and colleagues were not immune to its allure. I recall one autumn night in 2018 when a former colleague dropped into my house for a visit. Later in the evening, as we sat down on the balcony to enjoy the breeze and watch the stars, my guest leaned forward and said: "You know, Doctor Jan, I have made so much money. I have flown first class. I have everything in my life that I could dream of." From the tone of his voice, I could discern that he was not telling me this out of pride but rather guilt. I had known him for more than ten years while he was working for a British-run organisation supporting civil societies in Afghanistan. In 2017, he had founded his own NGO. On another occasion he told me he had bought properties in the U.S.A. and in Turkey. As a former board member of the Afghanistan Civil Society Institute, I was not surprised by his revelation. I had heard many rumours and allegations about corrupt civil society leaders and fraudulent practices by some prominent NGOs which often acted as the gatekeepers to donors. My guest's story was merely one example of the constellation of problems dotting the country. The massive international flow of resources with little oversight blurred the line between civil society, the private sector, and the state. Opportunism and profiteering became the everyday rule of the game for survival.

In this chapter, I discuss how international money exacerbated opportunistic and corrupt practices in post-2001 Afghanistan and how this impacted statehood and the political order. The empirical cases show how illegality and corruption entangled actors, goods, and money in a complex labyrinth of profiteering and violence. Section 9.1 examines the massive flow of international money and its spell on the Afghan state. The following two sections (Sections 9.2 and 9.3) then demonstrate the interplay between key political and economic actors in the customs and banking sectors. Section 9.4 examines everyday illegality and criminality in the extractive industries—chromite extraction and timber exploitation in the Kunar Province and Lapis lazuli mines in Badakhshan. It highlights the emergence of a triangular relationship among state-level and local officials, insurgents, and traders whose access and control of resources funded both sides of the war. Section 9.5 examines the Taliban's financial sustainability and their success in winning the war. The final section discusses how attempts to battle corruption failed, overshadowed by a strategy focused on money as a "weapons system" and obsessions about short-term political stability/order for the principal purpose of counter-terrorism efforts at the expense of long-term democratic objectives and institution-building.

9.1 Weaponising international money and its spell on the Afghan state

From the outset, the U.S. political and military approach to the Afghan war and the ensuing façade of state-building was to employ its financial might as a "weapons system" to secure quick gains. The U.S. Army General in Afghanistan, David Petraeus, wrote in 2008 that the U.S.A. should consider *money* as a "weapons system," which it should use as "ammunition" in trying to win the insurgency war.[3] It empowered local strongmen, civil society activists, and others as allies for its "war on terror" objectives. International donors, particularly the U.S.A. and its military, but also NATO and other donor governments, became the biggest creditors of "rent" in the country.

International aid, both off-budget and on-budget, became the biggest source of funding for the Afghan government, creating massive interdependencies and rent. International spending shaped and reconfigured governance and statehood in post-2001 Afghanistan, exacerbating illegality, opportunistic behaviours, and corruption—as systematically reported over the years by the Special Inspector General for Afghanistan Reconstruction (SIGAR). An October 2020 SIGAR report estimated that over the previous 18 years, the United States had lost a staggering $19 billion in Afghanistan as a result of waste, fraud, and abuse.[4] The influx of sudden and enormous amounts of military and aid money from 2005 onwards with little due diligence, transparency, and accountability transformed political networks' underlying logic into a system driven by short-term and quick political access to the aid economy rather than the investment logic of a productive economy.[5]

The exact amounts provided by donors to support the Afghan Republic over the years remain unknown. According to one estimate, by 2013, at the peak of foreign intervention, military and non-military external assistance accounted for 95% of Afghanistan's GDP.[6] According to the latest 2019 World Bank report, aid and grants financed 75% of total expenditures despite the Afghan government's increasing revenue generation over the previous five years.[7] In 2019, government expenditure was around $11 billion, of which the government generated a mere $2.5 billion. One estimate put the cost of war for the U.S.A.—i.e., expenditures by both the U.S. military and Department of State—from 2001 to 2019 at around $978 billion.[8] The breakdown of the second quarter report of U.S. spending in 2019 shows that from $137 million, $86.38 million had gone

Table 9.1 U.S. government aid to Afghanistan/amount in billions

Funding sector	Amount
Security (including counter-narcotics)	86.38
Governance and development	35.85
Humanitarian aid	3.98
Civilian operations	11.64
Total	137.86

Source: SIGAR 2020 Second Quarter Report.

into the security sector and supporting the Afghanistan National Security and Defense Forces (ANSDF). The Afghan government allocated around 30% of its GDP to security, significantly higher than other low-income countries.[9] In terms of geographical disparity, the American military and United States Agency for International Development (USAID) poured millions of dollars of development aid into the south and southeast based on a misguided assumption that more aid would improve security.[10]

The irony is that a significant amount of the money deployed as the so-called "weapons system" was returned to the U.S.A. through contractors and their well-paid employees. According to the now-deceased Ambassador Richard Holbrooke, about 90% of U.S. aid "given" to Afghanistan came back to the U.S.A. in contractor fees.

The Afghan economy grew relative to the number of international forces on the ground. At the peak of international intervention when the U.S.A. had over 115,000 troops, the Afghan economy has a growth rate of 15% and with the 2014 drawdown it contracted significantly. The massive expenditures produced a thriving war economy industry which exacerbated corruption and private profiteering. As one commentator described it in 2010, "The virulent network of corruption … has grown with every bullet or meal consumed by soldiers and development workers brought in for the surge."[11] At the peak of the international military surge (2009–2012), NATO had over 800 small, medium, and large military bases scattered around the country serving 120,000 U.S. troops, excluding contractors.[12] The Bagram airbase just 40 km outside Kabul was one of the biggest camps and uniquely positioned as the epicentre of a whole host of shady and semi-shady business dealings. As the U.S. and NATO mission in Afghanistan deepened, the base became one of the biggest wartime assemblages of global military personnel, private companies, intelligence agencies, and other related organisations housing approximately 40,000 military personnel and civilian contractors at its peak in 2013.[13] Even after the drawdown in 2016, the U.S.A. had 9,800 uniformed personnel and more than 25,000 Pentagon contractors working for them—36% U.S. citizens, 41% Afghans, and the rest from other countries.[14]

Some expenditures, particularly logistics, were nakedly outrageous. According to a 2010 U.S. House of Representatives report, a single trucking company owner justified his charges by claiming that his income supported 20,000 people. At one point, U.S. military contracts were purchasing 6,000–8,000 truck shipments per month. Big military contracts, such as Host Nation Trucking (HNT), a massive initiative worth $2.16 billion to offload transportation logistics to local truck drivers and connect diverse groups of state and non-state actors and practices under one project turned out to be both a *remedy* (to the logistical quandary of moving around supplies for the NATO military mission and the Afghan military) and a *curse* in that it produced a system of perpetual violence at a sub-national level (discussed in detail below).

This massive flow of aid money, as well as the additional billions provided by NATO, created severe political and financial interdependencies which undermined the sovereignty of the Afghan state. This produced essentially a *rentier networked state*, in which political and economic networks fiercely competed against one another to capture and maintain "rent" as one of the key power resources needed for their survival, discussed in Chapter 2.[15] This was not new. As shown by Afghan historians, aid dependency and rent has been a key feature of statehood in Afghanistan. However, post-2001, the nature and scale changed dramatically.[16] As one analyst aptly put it in her article for an Afghan news outlet: international money became both "medicine and poison," essentially a paradox of dependencies, rent, and legitimacy deficit.[17]

International donors and their officials played a central role in fuelling corruption. Aid dependency meant that Afghanistan had to give up significant sovereignty to international donors in its domestic affairs, including policymaking—whether in terms of agriculture, local governance, counter-narcotics, or peace negotiations—budget allocation and even the appointment of senior government officials.[18] For instance, it became a norm that the Americans should have a say in the appointment of senior security sector officials. This was evident in early 2020 over the appointment of the Interior Minister when it was rumoured that the Americans were blocking certain nominees.[19] Aid dependency provided leverage to donor countries to use their funds as carrots against the Afghan state.[20] In a cruel twist, Afghan officials showed more accountability on some occasions to donors than to their own people while international donors and their officials, at least for the first decade of the intervention, were accountable to no one. Over the last decade or so of the intervention, American funding came under scrutiny by oversight agencies. For instance, the Special Inspector General for Afghanistan Reconstruction, set up in 2008 to provide independent and objective oversight of U.S. aid for reconstruction programmes to Congress, produced some damning investigative reports on their ineffectiveness over the years. It found massive waste, fraud, and abuse of funds, for instance in the multi-donor Afghanistan Reconstruction Trust Fund (ARTF), one of the largest sources of funding to Afghan government operations outside the security sector, established in 2002 and managed by the World Bank.[21] A 2018 SIGAR report highlighted the lack of transparency by the Bank, which it argued "puts billions of dollars at risk."[22] USAID officials had told SIGAR in September 2017 that the Bank could provide reasonable assurance that ARTF funding was reimbursing legitimate government expenditures[23] (Figure 9.1).

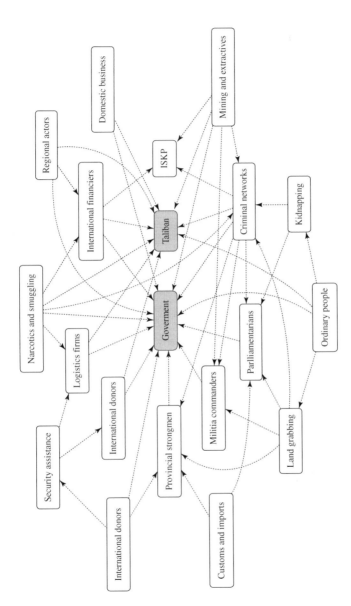

Figure 9.1 Visualisation of resource flows (Graeme (2020)).

Military contracting also indirectly benefitted the Taliban. NATO- and U.S.-contracted logistical and security companies, for instance, made regular protection payments to Taliban commanders and tribal elders to keep their operations safe.[24] For instance, a congressional report found that the Host Nation Trucking contract fuelled warlordism, extortion, and corruption, and was a significant source of funding for insurgents.[25] American officials estimated that around 10% of their logistics contracts went directly to insurgents.[26] A lawsuit by the families U.S. Gold Star servicemen serving in Afghanistan alleged that private security and logistical contractors were indirectly funnelling millions of dollars in payments to the enemy for protection that was then used by the group to attack American troops.[27] They alleged that "buying off the terrorists was the most efficient way to operate their businesses while managing their security risks—even though doing so jeopardized other American lives."[28] The *Host Nation Trucking* contract empowered hundreds of ethno-regional strongmen, militia leaders, insurgents, contractors, and private security companies. In some cases, the security companies' personnel were themselves involved in some of the attacks or were paying local militias for attacks to increase insurance costs and trucking fees. For instance, a government security report found that one of the local airlines was paying the Taliban to deliberately kidnap and harass passengers on their way to their provinces to create fear and thereby ensure their flights were at full capacity.[29]

International donor money sustained the Afghan state and most political and economic networks. The emerging *rentier networked state* therefore labelled a degree of political order, at least in Kabul while violence in provinces over access and control of key financial resources such as extractive industries continued. These financial flows and schemes discussed above were found in virtually every sector of Afghanistan's economic and security landscape. Two of the most lucrative were customs and banking. The next two sections show the overlap of economic and political networks post-2001 and how they worked in unison to syphon off billions, looking specifically at the Kabul Bank case as a Ponzi scheme.

9.2 Customs revenue and extortion

Customs revenues were one of the main sources of income for the central government and political networks and their associates in post-2001 Afghanistan. As shown in Chapter 3, post-2001 was almost immediately characterised by border customs, which generated the bulk of domestic revenues, being redirected to the coffers of regional strongmen networks. They imposed their own tariffs on goods, such as a 3% duty on all imported petrol and diesel.[30] Although the central government progressively imposed some degree of control over customs, regional and state-level networks continued to profit from access to customs revenues and extortion. An Afghan specialist on taxation estimated in 2010 that half of these revenues, both formal and informal, were still being collected by these networks.[31] Another UN study found that the largest bribe payments in Afghanistan went to

Table 9.2 Customs duties from imports (million Afghanis, BRT excluded)

Province	2014–2015	2015–2016	2016–2017
Herat	6,472	8,049	7,640
Nangarhar	5,398	5,967	5,747
Nimroz	3,753	4,753	5,233
Balkh	3,143	3,325	4,842
Farah	1,475	2,352	2,285
Faryab	1,395	647	338
Kandahar	1,007	1,726	2,004

customs officials.[32] Although the National Unity Government data for 1395–1397 showed a 9% increase in revenue compared to 2014 when Karzai was the president, the U.S. Institute of Peace report noted that the increase could be explained by inflation, exchange rate depreciation, and real growth of the economy.[33]

An investigation by Integrity Watch Afghanistan revealed that the National Unity Government (NUG) had done little to prevent leakages at customs,[34] despite giving the impression that it was going after those who pilfered its revenues. Moreover, what the data actually shows is that President Ghani's policy was selectively applied and was not an entirely neutral technocratic exercise to fight corruption as he purported.[35] As Table 9.2 suggests, customs revenues from Nangarhar and Faryab show almost no changes, whereas Balkh, Farah, and Kandahar increased by 50, 70, and 100%, respectively, by 2016–2017. As discussed in Chapter 7, customs revenues were closely associated and correlated with elections and election campaign funds, especially for incumbents (discussed below). In Balkh, Governor Noor, an ally of Abdullah, had publicly opposed Ghani and had threatened civil war. Influential figures in the Nangarhar Province who had backed Ghani in the 2014 elections went untouched and, similarly, in the Faryab Province Ghani's key election ally—the Junbish network—was rewarded for its support with declining enforcement of customs requirements.[36]

An investigative study of customs carried out by the Ministry of Finance in 2018 exposed the complex opportunistic web of relations and interests connecting MPs, provincial officials, the president's office, state-level network leaders and low-level customs and security officials, among many others.[37] The report found that most customs positions, from the director level to grade five, were bought off by MPs, provincial officials, and others for thousands of dollars. The case of the Farah Customs Office in 2018 and 2019 is telling. The Head of Customs' Office was an ethnic Baluch from the Rostaq district of Takhar in the North. His family was one of many settlers (known as *Naqelin*) in the 1940s who were forced to migrate from their homes in the south to the north. Reportedly, his appointment as the head of customs was facilitated through his political connection with the head of the Baghlan provincial council, who was a close ally of Abdullah Abdullah. To return the favour and show his loyalty to Abdullah, he reportedly made substantial financial contributions to Abdullah's presidential campaign in the Takhar Province in 2019. His personal wealth and connections to the upper echelons of power in Kabul, and his influence over the Independent Election Commission (IEC), had secured a seat for his sister in the Lower House, who was then able to secure additional political influence and protection for her brother.

The Ministry of Finance experienced one of the biggest shake-ups under the National Unity Government (2014–2019). Just 18 months before the elections, the Ministry of Finance had three deputy ministers of revenue and customs, three deputy ministers of administration; and three deputy finance ministers, the numbers that intimated the politicised and opportunistic nature of the appointments.[38] Many of President Ghani's opponents complained vehemently about the profiteering behind these appointments. In September 2020, an investigative report by a local newspaper found that 47 MPs had direct involvement in the appointments of half of customs department positions at the Ministry of Finance, getting their relatives and associates appointed or reshuffled to sit in key positions at the national, provincial, and municipality levels.[39] These appointments were made only after April 2020 when the new acting minister was appointed—a quick restructuring of positions in revenue-generating ministries and new opportunities for deal-making. The report argued that these appointments were made as part of a deal between the minister and MPs to secure a vote of confidence for him in the Lower House. Another opportunistic strategy was to facilitate and ease access to strategic customs for MPs' companies and those of their associates. It was widely known that customs, border police, transport, and other ministry officials kept fake records or declared bogus paperwork to pay less duty and other taxes. For instance, goods subject to heavy duties, such as construction and electronics goods, were often declared as toilet paper, the least taxed item. A study of illegal border crossings in Nimruz found that many fuel tankers had two "false tanks" with the equivalent of up to five metric tonnes (MT) of additional smuggled fuel (6,200 litres) smuggled across the border to Afghanistan.[40] A fuel tanker from neighbouring Iran crossing over at the Zaranj crossing officially weighed 33 MT (the equivalent of 28,520 litres). And Zaranj border crossing was relatively small compared to what was happening at other major customs crossings in the country.

The sheer scale of the money at play meant that customs revenues could be both a source of stability and violence in rural Afghanistan. My visit to Kandahar in August 2019 revealed that relations between Shah Wali Khan (President Karzai's brother) and Tadin Khan (Kandahar's Police Chief and brother of notorious Kandahar strongmen General Raziq) were strained, partly because of disputes over the Spin Boldak customs profit shares. Before Gen. Raziq's death in 2018, customs profits were distributed among them in an agreed-upon arrangement. In one of the efforts to go after former President Karzai's clients in Kandahar, in February 2016, the National Directorate of Security (NDS) arrested several Kandahari officials including the head of customs at the Spin Boldak border crossing on allegations of corruption. The detainees were released after an armed standoff with other elements of the security forces linked to Gen. Raziq.[41] The intelligence agency officers were able to obtain a video-recorded confession from the head of Customs, naming Gen. Raziq and other officials linked to the Karzai family as recipients of illegal profits.[42] This incident nearly sparked an all-out war within the provincial administration and was only resolved when a bargain was struck between President Ghani and Gen. Raziq about the latter's support for Ghani against the Karzai family network.

9.3 The Kabul Bank case: a Ponzi scheme

In early 2010, reports emerged that Kabul Bank had lost US$300 million due to mismanagement, cronyism, and dubious lending. Soon it appeared that the losses were the result of fraud, embezzlement, and mismanagement by the Bank's owners and could be as high as US$900 million, raising concerns that the bank could collapse and trigger a broad financial panic in Afghanistan.[43] The Bank was the prime channel for processing the $1.5 billion payrolls for the Afghan security forces and hundreds of thousands of government employees, leaving NATO and the Afghan government's efforts to fight the insurgency vulnerable. Like crucial institutions in many other countries, the bank was considered too big to fail.

Da Afghanistan Bank, Afghanistan's central bank, and American officials hired Kroll Advisory Solutions, a reputable international audit company, to conduct a forensic investigation. Its final report labelled the Kabul Bank a "well-concealed Ponzi scheme." As the report notes (Figure 9.2),

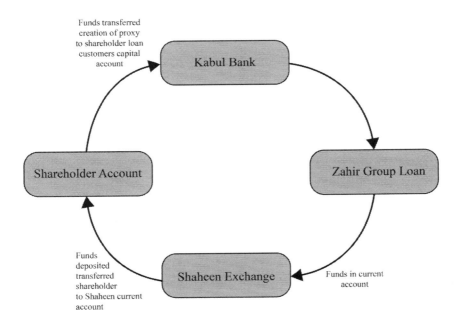

Figure 9.2 Movement of funds to shareholders.

Managers used the growth in depositors' funds to maintain the illusion of financial viability in the absence of any real-value creation and to mask the true purpose of the bank: to use depositors' funds to benefit the business ventures of a group of closely connected political and business leaders, without any apparent intention to repay the funds or provide the bank with returns on its investments.[44]

It became evident that the bank functioned as an extended arm of the state and its powerful network elites, including family members associated with the president, first vice president, and many others, offering them loans and personal grants. The money from the bank enabled political networks to purchase loyalty in parliament, to appoint associates as cabinet ministers, and to pay for election campaigns, among many other dubious schemes. The bank's corrupt practices and its web of connections involved ministers, senior government officials, MPs, Central Bank officials, and presidential candidates as well as many others (see Tables 9.3 and 9.4).[45] On the list of 200 people involved in receiving irregular loans from Kabul Bank were 103 former MPs who were receiving monthly paycheques from the bank,[46] bringing into question the entire bidding process for paying government staff salaries, which it had won.[47] Of the total estimated US$75 million dollars in bribes paid by the bank, a substantial portion had gone to MPs. My interview with several MPs and former bank officials revealed that most bribes were paid on behalf of the president's office, first vice president, and other powerful people in parliament to ensure nominated ministers received a vote of confidence.[48] The bank leadership saw its role in shaping the government as an investment, even allegedly paying off Abdullah Abdullah to withdraw from the run-off presidential vote in 2009, handing the presidency to Hamid Karzai.[49] The Bank's money was significant in getting Karzai elected in the 2009 elections, according to some former bank official's estimate well over 50 million, a significant amount of money for one of the poorest countries in the world.

The operation of the bank as a Ponzi scheme is revealing. Shareholders and many others linked with political elites had borrowed a substantial amount of

Table 9.3 Accounts due to the date of conservatorship from the main

Liable party	Principle of loans (US$)
Sherkhan Farnood	30,074,693
Khalilullah Firuzi	10,728,080
Abdul Fahim	2,309,539
Mahmood Karzai	5,773,988
Nesar Ahmad	1,328,006
Haji Taher (Amin jan)	4,607,344
Ghulam Farooq Naseeb	2,309,539
Hayatullah Nematullah (Kokcha)	1,154,910
Total	58,286,099

Source: Internal Kroll Memorandum and Supporting Documents.

Table 9.4 Kroll Report: final allocation of the loan book and status of recoveries

Type of borrower	Group name	Beneficiary	Total as of 31 August 2010 ($)
Senior officer	Zahir Ltd	Sherkhan Farnood	270,296,957.34
borrowings from	Feruzi: Various		94,344,199.40
Kabul Bank	assets		
Related party	Berham Behzad	Abdul Haseen Fahim	43,628,860,.65
borrowings	Limited		
fromKabul Bank	Concord Tobacco	Gulbahar Habibi	39,760,110.59
to individual	Mahmood Karzai	Mahmood Karzai	30,468,115.55
beneficiary of group	Nesar Ahmad	Sofi Nasar Ahmad	15,581,754.48
loan	Nesar Ahmad	M. Tahir Zahir	22,332,553.94
	Naseeb food	Ghulam Dawood	12,464,956.96
	industries	Naseeb	
	Dawi Group	Abdul Ghafar Dawi	39,035,794.57
	Najibullah payenda	Najibullah Payenda	1,771,472.58
	Hayutullah Kokcha	Hayutullah Kokcha	3,437,762.00
	KB advance salary	Shrukullah Shrukhan	2,026,304.43
Related party	Gas Group		121,232,314.41
borrowings from	Pamir Airways	Pamir Airways	88,291,139.69
Kabul Bank	Zakhira Ltd	Zakhira	22,859,150.90
to individual			21,459,199.43
beneficiary of group	Kabul Neft Ltd	Kabul Neft Co Limited	15,457,548.65
loan			
	Corporative	Corporative Hewadwal	
	Hewadwal		
	Gulbahar towers	Gulbahar towers	16,832,217.00
	Ariana Steel	Ariana Steel	1,529,059.00
Unrelated borrowers of	Normal customer	Various borrowers	74,074,028.16
Kabul Bank			
	Interest adjustment		(2,565,559.24)
			934,317,940.49

Source: Internal Kroll Memorandum and Supporting Documents.

money and then invested in other businesses, including Pamir Airways, Gas Group, Kabul Neft, Kabul Mine Companies, Gulbahar Towers, and others (see Tables 9.3 and 9.4). Following the money trail offers some fascinating insights. First, the loans concealed the true identity of the beneficiaries—accounts were opened in the names of proxies; loan applications, sanctioning, and monitoring records were fabricated; and the illusion of repayments of interest and principal was created by allocating funds from new advances using a variety of dodgy accounting techniques. Most of this money was then laundered outside the country, especially in Dubai, to purchase property, and from there to offshore accounts.[50] The borrowed funds were channelled through a second entity, Sherkhan Farnood General Trading—a company owned by the founder and Chairman of the Kabul Bank Board—the records of which were maintained at the Shaheen Exchange in Dubai and Zahir Group—again owned by Sherkhan Farnood. The Shaheen Exchange was used as an intermediary in the funding of share capital injections which enabled shareholders to conceal the true origin of funds.[51] The Kroll investigation found no written records/agreements between the bank and the borrower in the bank's loan books, but instead, found them in the Shaheen Exchange and Sherkhan Farnood General Trading loan books.

According to the Kroll investigation, at the point of conservatorship, $861 million of the loan book's content (over 92%) belonged to 19 individuals and their companies, and substantially for the benefit of 14 individuals who were not required to make any repayments (see Table 9.4). Table 9.3 shows the principal amount that seven of the main borrowers owed to the bank. The Kroll investigation puts the final amount at $86,843,81 with 12–17% interest. Sherkhan Farnood's breakdown of the loan was then given to 14 individuals, including Jamal Khalil (over $1.3 million), Dr. Jawed (over $1.16 million), and his wife Farida Farnood ($5.2 million). Shareholders had taken money out to invest in other businesses. In a separate loan, Farnood took out around $98 million to purchase and subsequently operationalise Pamir Airways in partnership with Qaseem Fahim, the first VP's brother, Mahmood Karzai, and others (see Table 9.4). His partner, Khalil Firuzi, the CEO, had borrowed over $94.3 million. The shareholders of Kabul Neft company—Farnood (30.5%), Qaseem Fahim (30.5%), Governor Noor (25%), and Kamal Nabizada (14%)—had taken out over $21.5 million. In Gas Group, which was owned by Farnood, Firuzi, Qaseem Fahim, and Mahmood Karzai, they had taken out close to $92 million. In Pamir Airways as shown in Table 9.5, seven shareholders had taken out over $88 million.

In 2012, the Afghan Supreme Court indicted 21 defendants in the Kabul Bank case with charges ranging from money laundering, public corruption, and fraud to negligence by regulators and bank officials.[52] In 2013, the Independent Joint Anti-Corruption and Evaluation Committee (MEC) report on Kabul Bank concluded that the indictment had excluded many key beneficiaries and participants in the

Table 9.5 Pamir airways beneficiaries

Ultimate Beneficiary	Stake (%)	Note
Sherkhan Farnood	34.77	Held through a stake in Kabul Holding Group
Mahmood Karzai	9.37	
Mohammed Tahir Zahir	7.12	
Ghulam Farooq Naseeb	3.19	
Hayatullah Kokcha	1.87	
Abdul Hussein Fahim	13.68	Held through Kabul holding Group and Zahir Walid Company
Zabiullah Shakhaini	30.00	Held directly

Source: Internal Kroll Memorandum.

scheme because of political interference from the top Afghan leadership.[53] Finally, in March 2003, the Special Tribunal for the Bank sentenced the former chairman, Sherkhan Farnood, and former CEO Khalilullah Feruzi to five years in prison and ordered them to return a combined $808 million.[54] In late 2014, President Ghani reopened the case and set up a new committee, called the Clearance Committee of Kabul Bank, to re-evaluate the Bank loans and charges. Very little of the money was recovered. Sherkhan Farnood, the Chairman of the Board, died in prison while his co-founder and CEO, Firuzi, was freed before the 2019 elections, with rumours that he had made a deal with the president through the first VP to buy his freedom and fund the election campaign.

9.3.1 A link with Afghanistan Investment Company

The Kabul Bank's list of debtors significantly overlaps with the Afghanistan Investment Company (AIC) set up in 2005. AIC was essentially a network of Afghan businessmen with close links to key political elites. In October 2005, 50 businessmen, both inside Afghanistan and from the diaspora, came together to form a consortium, the Afghanistan Investment Company, with the stated goal of attracting investments and investing in major infrastructure projects, including coal, fertiliser, construction, and energy in Afghanistan.[55] Reportedly, each member contributed half a million to buy shares in the company. It is quite likely that most of the funding came from Kabul Bank. At the time, the Executive board included Sherkhan Farnood as Chairman, Mahmood Karzai as Chief Executive Officer, and many others who were involved in the Kabul Bank scheme (see Table 9.6).

The Ghori cement plant linked to AIC is an interesting case, exposing how political and economic networks worked together to take over national industries but with no intention of investing in them. In 2005, AIC was in discussions with the Afghan government to invest up to US$250 million in the Greenfield cement plant in Pul-i-Khumri in the Baghlan province, known as the Ghori plant. AIC had registered a company called Afghanistan Cement Company. The Greenfield cement plant in Pul-i-Khumri never materialised because the Afghan government failed to provide a loan guarantee. It seems that the Exim Bank of China was willing to finance 85% of the project if the Afghanistan Cement Company could purchase Chinese equipment.[56] The company finally won the state-owned Ghori Cement factory contract in April 2007 which had two plants (Ghori 1 and Ghori II).[57] The project was then plagued by disputes over broken promises, unpaid levies, and contract violations. In early 2012, AIC claimed to have gone bankrupt and its promises to invest US$45 million in the project seemed to have been a ploy to win the bid.[58] The company did not build factory 3 as it had promised, after three years of winning the contract, clearly a breach of the agreement.[59] In 2011, Mahmud Karzai sold his shares to Azizi Hotek, the owner of Azizi Bank, to repay his loan to Kabul Bank.[60] In February 2017, the government abruptly cancelled the contract for the Ghori Cement factory. It argued that the company owed

Table 9.6 The Kabul Bank list of debtors[61]

Name	Position	Companies and affiliations
Sherkhan Farnood	Chairman	Chairman Kabul Bank
Mahmood Karzai	Chief Executive Officer	Head of Afghan American Chamber of Commerce and debtor to Kabul Bank; Karzai brother
Haseen Fahim	Vice-Chairman	brother of the powerful first Vice-President Fahim and half owner of Pamir Airways, Gas Group, and debtor to Kabul Bank
Abdul Ghafar Dawi	Chief Secretary	Chair of Dawi Groups and debtor of Kabul Bank
Habib Gulzar	Member	owner of the bottling facility licensed by Coca Cola Company and debtor to Kabul Bank
Rahim Safi	Member	Safi Industries and later Safi Airlines
Ehsan Bayat	Member	the Chairman of Afghan Wireless Communication Company, Ariana Television Network, Bayat Energy and others
Gulbahar Habibi	Member	Owner Gulbahar Tower and shopping mall and debtor to Kabul Bank
Mirwais Azizi	Member (jointed later after buying Mahmood Karzai shares)	Chairman of the Azizi Bank and the Azizi Hotak Group

millions of dollars in unpaid taxes and fees.[62] The new owner, Javid Jaihoon, the Chair of Afghanistan United Bank and reportedly a close business associate of the first VP, Amrullah Saleh, bought the shares of most of the initial investors when Kabul Bank went down.[63] He called the government's decision to cancel the project a "political decision," saying the company had paid all government fees and left cash in a bank that the government could take.[64] He went on to say that he had invested almost $60 million and brought it to near-full capacity. When Amrullah Saleh became the president Ghani's first VP, the case was suddenly resolved as they became part of the same election campaigns and a partner in the future government.

9.4 Contracting, collusion, and profiteering

The level of corruption and political network intervention in state contracting was also stunning. In 2015, President Ghani ordered the establishment of an ad hoc special oversight committee to investigate the Ministry of Defence (MoD) contracts, including one of the biggest fuel contracts awarded to two companies. The investigation looked at 12 contracts worth nearly $1 billion from fiscal years 2014 to 2016. The 24-page report, known as the *Farooqi Report*, was led by Hamidullah Farooqi, a former minister, with help from SIGAR and other U.S. officials.[65] It found serious collusion, price-fixing, and bribery amongst bidding companies, MoD senior officials, and staff of the Ministry of Finance Contracts Department, with intervention by some powerful political network leaders.

CCTV footage from a Dubai hotel revealed that, 10 days before the fuels contract deadline, six bidders met at a hotel hosted by Ghazanfar Gas Group to agree on a bidding strategy. The meeting was also attended by an MP from Balkh. They agreed to offer the MoD a high price and once any of them was awarded the contract, they would share the benefits. Only two companies were against the price fixing/collusion and left the meeting. Allegedly, Ghazanfar Gas Group and the MP offered one of the companies, the Afghan National Police, $6.5 million not to appear for the final contract bid, but it rejected the offer and filed a complaint to the relevant authorities. On the day of the bidding submission, the companies that had walked out of the internal deal could not make it to the MoD. Allegedly, one of the bidders was stopped by an intentional traffic accident and the other was stopped by Police District 10 personnel claiming they didn't have the proper license plate on their vehicle. Both incidents appear to have been part of a conspiracy to prevent them from bidding on the contracts. The bids were not only extremely high compared to the market price, but four bidders' prices were also virtually identical down to the fourth decimal, suggesting collusion. The investigation also found that two of the winning companies were not registered with the Ministry of Commerce at the time of bidding, but both the *Afghanistan Reconstruction and Development Services* (ARDS) offices and the MoD officials deciding on the contract ignored this report, indicating collusion with the contractors.

After more than a year of delays, the files of the companies, along with the MoD's procurement director, MoD assistant minister for technical and materials affairs, an MoD deputy minister, several officials at ARDS, and officials of the special procurements commission were submitted to the Anti-Corruption Justice Centre (ACJC) for investigation—a specialised court to combat serious corruption cases, under the direct supervision of the Attorney General. By September 2020, most of the people involved had been prosecuted except Ghazanfar, who became President Ghani's third deputy on his election ticket. According to a senior former official, the president needed Ghazanfar's financial contribution to his campaign, given that he had contributed substantially to previous elections—interestingly, to both winning tickets.

In another interesting case, in 2019 Da Afghanistan Brishana Sherkat (DABS), the main government-owned utility company, as part of a money-saving effort, connected 24 MoD and the Ministry of Interior (MoI) bases to the national electricity grid. Before this, millions of dollars were spent on diesel generators to power these bases. According to the DABS presentation to the cabinet, the government would save up to $180 million per year. It was agreed that the money-saving scheme is piloted at the Afghan air force base inside the Kabul airport. The pilot project failed after a few months of operations because it threatened to expose corruption; military officials and private companies (both national and international) collaborated to undermine it. The base's officials intentionally reported 17 power cuts in one month, arguing that the national grid was not reliable. DABS records showed only two power cuts during this time. They also harassed and threatened DABS personnel. The camp was using approximately 3 MW per hour, not the previously reported 20 MW per hour for which diesel was purchased. As a result, DABS officials were not allowed entry to the camp, and as of September 2020, MoI and MoD owed over 15.5 billion Afghanis to DABS which they refused to pay. The General-Director of DABS then came under heavy attack from MPs who had a connection to the fuel business, including the Speaker of the House and first VP. In August 2020, the DG of DABS was suddenly removed from his position.

9.5 The extractive industry: violence and disorder[66]

In 2010, American geologists estimated that Afghanistan had more than US$1 trillion in untapped mineral deposits, including iron, copper, cobalt, gold, and industrial metals like lithium (see Table 9.7).[67] The Afghan Ministry of Mines and Petroleum estimated this to be around US$3 trillion—a rather implausible figure.[68] However, between 2013 and 2015, Afghanistan's revenues from its mining sector averaged a trivial US$30 million annually, and there had been little improvement since.[69] A recent study by United States Institute of Peace (USIP) calculated that the government was losing US$50 million annually in revenues due to corruption and illegality in the sector.[70] A U.S. Department of Defence (DoD) analyst, Matthew DuPée, who has written widely on the politics of the extractive industry in Afghanistan warned that:

> Mining in a war zone such as Afghanistan cannot be of any use during periods of conflict—the lack of public and government control over the outcome,

Table 9.7 Projected and real net revenue contribution in US$, billion

Mineral/industry	Projected income USD
Copper (Aynak)	300–350
Iron (Hajigak)	400–600
Hydrocarbons (Amu Darya and Afghan-Tajik)	100
Gemstones	30–40
Construction materials	75
Coal	25
Total	930–1190

Table 9.8 Sample list of politically connected persons and their investments at the national level

Individual(s)	Association	Commodity	Nature of contract	Mine name
Governor Atta M. Noor	Partner as part of a consortium	Oil and gas exploration	Contract	Afghan Tajik
Zahir Qadir (Deputy Spokesperson of the Lower House)	Patron/illegal extraction	Talc powder	Illegal	Mines in Shirzad, Khogyani, & Goshta districts
Muslimyar (Head of Upper House)	Patron	Talc powder	Illegal	Shirzad
Feraidun Mommand (MP Nangarhar)	Illegal extraction/ monopoly	Jade, Serpentine, Nephrite		Goshta and Khas Kunar
MP Mirwais Yasini	Beneficial owner	Chromite	Legal/ illegal	Kunar and Kama
MP Zahid Almas	Hewad Brothers	Chromite	Contract	Kohi Safi
Zahir Saadat (MP Panjshir)	Illegal	Emerald	Illegal	Khenj
Mp Reza Khoshak	Family business	Coal	Contract	Garmake Gharbi (Herat)
Sayed Mansur Naderi	Contract	Gold	Contract	Dushi
Watan Group with CNPCI (Karzai family relative)	Amani Group	Oil and gas exploration	Contract	Sari pul
Ghazanfar Group	Ghazanfar Oil	Oil and gas	contract	Afghan Tajik
Bismillah Khan (Former Minister of Interior)	Patronage	Lapis	Illegal	Keran-Wa-Menjan (Badakhshan)

the adverse risk to investors, issues with infrastructure to include the lack of processing technologies and the impossibility of facilitating the movement of large amounts of products, all negate any positive political, economic outcomes that otherwise would be possible.[71]

Hopes that the Afghan extractive industry could generate billions of dollars for the country have faded. The sector, as the next three case studies below show, was thoroughly captured by local criminal networks and militia commanders affiliated with national and provincial political networks during the two decades of international intervention (see Table 9.8). The industry contributed to corruption, fuelling community grievances against the Afghan government and channelling support to the insurgency. Interviews with key officials suggest that over 40 members of parliament were involved in the mining industry, exposing the extent of the capture and the challenges any reform effort faced.[72] A report compiled by the Afghan mining ministry in 2012 showed over 1,400 sites where mines were illegally exploited.[73] This figure rose significantly in 2015 when representatives of the Afghanistan Natural Resources Oversight Network findings revealed that there were well over 2,000 illegal mining sites across the country—most of them small to medium size.[74] Most of the illegal operations were protected, if not directly owned, by powerful ethno-regional strongmen or national politicians, including members of parliament and provincial council members.

The following three case studies illustrate the perverse impact of the extractive industry, including violence and disorder, and the disruption of Afghanistan's tribal and community dynamics and relations. These cases reveal the significant level of violence the countryside experienced as the result of political network-clients competition and conflict over resources with serious repercussions on state stability. These cases, based on previous studies and augmented by additional interviews, highlight that violence was increasing in resource-rich districts, pushing locals into the arms of the Taliban.

9.5.1 Lapis lazuli extraction in Badakhshan

A detailed study by Global Witness in 2016 found that Haji Abdul Malek, a former Jamiat-i-Islami commander, had been in control of the Kuran wa Munjan lapis lazuli mine since the 1990s and had generated millions of dollars a year in profits.[75] Post-2001, Haji Malek used his hybrid position as a local district strongman as well as police chief, to wield significant power over the flow of resources within the district. His rival was Zalmay Mojadaddi, the Head of the 10th Directorate of the National Directorate of Security in Kabul under Karzai, responsible for all VIP protection, His brother, Asadullah, was the commander of the paramilitary Mining Protection Force for the mine.[76] Mojadaddi became an MP in 2005 and won a seat in the 2018 parliamentary elections. He was considered Karzai's "shadow viceroy" in Badakhshan, placing him in direct confrontation with former President Rabbani and other Jamiatis who supported Haji Malek.[77] Initially, however, it seems both of these local strongmen were getting along and enjoyed some sort of partnership, cooperating for their common interests. But from 2011 onwards, their relationship gradually soured as Mojadaddi strengthened his position in Kabul and subsequently his own home province of Badakhshan with support from Karzai. In an attempt to seize the mine and its revenues, Haji Ghulam Nassir—an ally of Mojaddadi—staged several violent skirmishes from March 2011 to May 2012, which provided the pretext to reassign Haji Malek as police chief to another district, Baharak.[78]

In February 2013, the central government awarded a 15-year mining contract for the Kuran wa Munjan mine to the Lajwardeen Mining Company, a generations-old, family-run import-export business, with the mine valued at US$125 million.[79] According to Global Witness findings, there was reportedly evidence of Mojadaddi's involvement in the contracting process. Yet, within 21 days of officially beginning its work, the company lost control of the mine to Haji Malek and his militiamen in January 2014, allegedly supported by Bismillah Mohammadi, the then MoD minister.[80] Over the years, Haji Malek had been making protection payments to various influential people, mainly Panjshiri leaders, to maintain his grip over the district and the mine. Haji Malek seized the mine under the pretext that the Taliban were threatening to take it over. Eight more clashes took place in 2014 between Haji Malek and commanders affiliated with Mojaddadi.[81]

Haji Malek's contention that the mines were under threat from the Taliban was based on some fact but likely a ploy. There is some evidence that a brief September 2013 seizure of the district capital where the mine is located by the Taliban was facilitated by Haji Malek. By November 2014, the Taliban had established a presence in strategic Yamgan district, exercising direct control over the northern edge of Kuran wa Munjan district, a few kilometres from the lapis mines. Haji Malek was also reportedly paying the Taliban protection money (almost half of all revenues) to safeguard his assets, giving the insurgent group the funds and space to thrive in what was once a peaceful province.[82]

In December 2015, the government decreed the termination of the Lajwardeen contract and offered reassurances to local commanders and influential players that they would not be removed. It also allowed "onetime" amnesty for lapis trucks to travel to Kabul and export their goods. The government accused the company of failing to implement the terms of the contract, failing to start extracting and having dubious links with Mojadaddi. The company, meanwhile, argued that they were caught in a broader rivalry that went beyond Badakhshan to include a network of competing players, from Badakhshan to Kabul politicians.[83] It accused the government of failing to hand over the mine and provide security. Ghani reopened the bidding process and proposed bringing the very same militia that ousted the legal contractor into the government framework. A New York Times article documents this episode and is scathing in its assessment. It reads that Ghani's actions set a dangerous precedent: "failing to protect a contractor from a seizure of assets and then legalizing the takeover."[84]

The lapis lazuli case shows how counterintuitive and complex extractive resources can be if local dynamics are not managed effectively. The state became dependent on a local strongman to guarantee security who made a tacit agreement with the Taliban for safe passage of goods. The squabbling over the mine meant that several districts surrounding it were destabilised, making space for the Taliban and putting communities in the unenviable position of having to choose between corrupt government officials and violent insurgents (Table 9.9).

Table 9.9 Lapis mine in Badakhshan

Lapis mining	
Export of lapis from Badakhshan, 2014	7,500 tons
Estimated value, 2014	$125 million
Export of lapis from Badakhshan, 2015	5,000 tons
Estimated value, 2015	$75 million
Armed groups mainly associated with Abdul Malek	
Revenue from lapis to armed groups associated with Abdul Malek, 2014	
Mine rent	$15.89 million
Security payments	$1.8 million
Road tolls	$290,000
Total revenue, 2014:	$17.98 million
Revenue from lapis to armed groups associated with Abdul Malek, 2015	$12 million
Armed groups mainly associated with Zulmai Mujadidi	
Revenues from lapis and tourmaline to armed groups mainly associated with Zulmai Mujadidi, 2014	
Baharak "contract"	$700,000
Road tolls	$700,000
Revenue from tourmaline mining under the PBIM contract (to Zekria Sawda)	$250,000
Total revenue, 2014:	$1.65 million
Mining income to these armed groups was not assessed for 2015 but was likely not significant	
The Taliban	
Revenues from lapis to the Taliban, 2014	
Direct payments from Abdul Malek	$750,000
Road tolls	$386,000
Total revenue, 2014:	$1.14 million
Revenues from lapis to the Taliban, 2015	$4 million
Revenues to the Taliban, 2016 (projected)	$6 million
Overall totals to armed groups	
Overall totals to armed groups, 2014 (not including $0.75 million transfer from Malek to Taliban)	$20 million
Overall totals to armed groups, 2015 (not including $4 million transfer from Malek to Taliban)	$12 million
Alleged transfers from one armed group to another are not included to avoid double-counting	
Afghan government	
Revenues lost from lapis by the Afghan government, 2014	$18.1 million
Potential revenues lost from lapis by the Afghan government, 2015	$10 million
Revenues lost from lapis by the Afghan government, since 2001	$100 million

Source: Global Witness.

9.5.2 Chromite extraction in Khas Kunar district

Historically, small-scale chromite extraction in the Kunar Province was undertaken by local communities that sold the multi-purpose mineral to local traders for export to Pakistan. The Khas Kunar mine was managed by five tribes (Mommand, Akhonzadas, Sahibzadagan, Saidan, and Miagan) who shared it through a self-regulating system of social ordering called *wand*.[85] Wand constitutes the administrative framework for political action, such as *shuras*.[86]

In 2010, as part of the U.S. military stabilisation initiative, the Defense Task Force for Business and Stability Operations (TFBSO) provided a chromite ore crusher used to process chromite to Governor Noor Mohammad and Farhad—the commander and deputy commander of the Afghan Local Police (ALP), respectively, in Khas Kunar.[87] The U.S. government, through TFBSO and USAID projects, had allocated close to US$500 million to support and prop up the extractive industries.[88] The TFBSO's stated mission was "economic stabilization to reduce violence, enhance stability and restore economic normalcy in areas where unrest and insurgency have created a synchronous downward spiral of economic hardship and violence."[89] However, as a 2016 SIGAR report found, these projects were a total failure. Broadly speaking, they did not have a unified strategy for the development of Afghanistan's extractive industry and did little to coordinate interagency activities. More specifically, they produced waste and mismanagement and empowered corrupt officials and violent forces.[90]

The project even helped commanders establish and register a company called Afghan Watandar. The rationale was to bring stability, peace, and self-reliance by turning pro-state armed groups into legitimate businessmen. As the Integrity Watch Afghanistan's (IWA) report finds, the Khas Kunar mine had a serious destabilising impact on the district.[91] It exacerbated conflict over the control of natural resources between the local tribal populations and the mining company owned by the ALP and, subsequently, the district spiralled into insecurity. As a result, the local population became more sympathetic to the Taliban in the area. Worse, the project disrupted the *wand* system, which had sustained socio-political order between the tribes as the inter-tribal conflict intensified—between the Mommand tribe who traditionally controlled a significant part of the mine and the ALP commander who was from the Akhondzada tribe. The ALP's control of the industry empowered other networks of illicit actors and helped establish new norms, business customs, and violent activities.[92]

9.5.3 Illegal timber exploitation

In 2010, the Natural Resources Counterinsurgency Cell (NRCC) valued Kunar province's timber at $828 million.[93] Historically, deforestation had been prevented by agreements between tribes and the central state, which allocated logging quotas. However, with the arrival of the Taliban and the Islamic State of Khorasan Province (ISKP) in the region, illegal timber cutting expanded

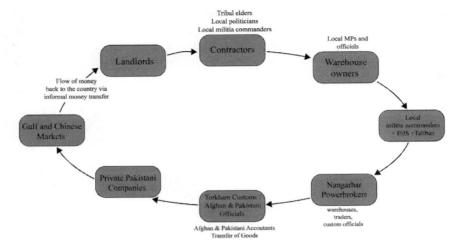

Figure 9.3 A mapping of the smuggling chain.

considerably, reaching scales that approached clearcutting. According to an internal Independent Directorate of Local Governance report, which I commissioned in late 2018, timber logging was carried out in at least 11 of the 15 districts of Kunar and illegally trafficked to neighbouring Pakistan, despite a government ban since 2006 (see Figure 9.3).[94]

In 2018, three MPs, one senator and six provincial council members were involved directly and indirectly in facilitating illegal trafficking or providing political protection to district officials and traders for illegal logging.[95] These *timber patrons* appointed their network-clients as district governors, police chiefs, and heads of provincial directorates to ensure their interests were protected. Some also had close links to powerful powerbrokers in the neighbouring Nangarhar province to secure additional protection.

The complexity of the timber exploitation network and processes in Kunar suggest the practice has been in place for many years and will likely outlive any specific government, merely changing power brokers as the power balances in Afghanistan shift. The Byzantine system begins with landowners (or in most cases tribal allotments) who are contracted with a trader for logging. Traders lend money to local labourers, often hired from nearby villages, who log and transfer timber on donkeys and horses from the mountain tops to privately owned warehouses. During the post-2001 period, these warehouses were either owned or protected by local MPs, provincial council members, and others. Since the fall of the Afghan government, it's unclear the role the Taliban now play in these networks. Before the Taliban takeover, however, armed groups, including the Taliban, as well as local militias (with links to local patrons) helped traders smuggle products on lorries to designated warehouses in Jalalabad city. Protection fees were paid. In some instances, people told Independent Directorate of Local Governance

(IDLG) that timber was transported in government ambulances and police and army pick-up trucks.[96] The role of accountants on both sides of the border was important in preparing all the necessary paperwork, including customs papers, receipts of payments, and others. Payments were often made in Pakistani cities such as Peshawar, including protection fees to the Taliban, ISIS, and even Afghan militia commanders, to specific accountants who then issued receipts which were shown as proof of payment.[97] Commissioners at the Torkham border crossing legalised the products by preparing and securing the trade permission certificate fee for formally registered timber, thus displaying the illegally logged timber as a legal good with Pakistani customs, including tariff fees.[98] Once the goods were in Pakistan, contractors sold the products to private companies at market price, who then traded them to Gulf countries and the Chinese. International payment transactions took place in the global market. Once goods were sold in the Pakistani market, contractors and traders then returned the payment to landlords and others within the network chain. Pakistani traders made the most financial gains from selling the goods on international markets.[99] In the entire process, the exchange currency for the market was the Pakistani rupee, even inside Afghanistan.

The timber industry shows the emergence of an entrenched relationship between government officials, insurgency groups, criminals, and traders which was transnational in nature. These cases also suggest that international state-building had a capricious effect on exacerbating violence and disorder in rural Afghanistan. In places like Khas Kunar and Kuran wa Munjan in Badakhshan, local communities welcomed and co-operated with insurgency groups who exploited the gap left by the disruption of the socio-political order.

9.6 Taliban insurgency, illegality, and revenues

The role of the Taliban in resource extraction, trafficking, and drug production is well documented.[100] The above cases and other studies suggest that the Taliban earned cash mainly by directly extracting resources, extorting money from mining companies and other sectors, charging security and transportation fees, and collecting *ushr*, a traditional tithe. American officials estimate that around 10% of their logistics contracts went directly to insurgents.[101] For instance, on 20 July 2020, the Taliban stopped "around 1000 oil tankers" in the Baghlan Province and drivers said they were charged 30,000 Afghanis (approximately US$390 based on 2 July 2020 exchange rate) for each vehicle before they were allowed to continue.[102] Zabihullah Mujahid, the former Taliban spokesman, did not deny this but said they had charged less and that they charged a "customs duty" in areas under their control in exchange for providing security.[103]

In this milieu, the Taliban were also directly and indirectly involved in mining. Rent from the illegal mining of lapis was split between local militias (supported by Afghan elites) and the Taliban. Similarly, Global Witness reported that the industry was fuelling the insurgency, threatening to turn the country's vast mineral wealth into a resource curse.[104] Their investigation in the Badakhshan Province revealed that in 2015 the Taliban taxed mining activities, including charging a transit fee to local powerbrokers and smugglers operating near the Tajikistan border. Global Witness estimated that between 2014 and 2015, illegal trade in lapis was worth about US$20 million, out of which armed groups made at least US$12 million, and the Taliban specifically around US$4 million. Global Witness further estimated that as of mid-2016, protection and taxation payments to the Taliban reportedly amounted to at least 50% of total revenues from the mines. Also, according to another study, the overall financial gain, directly and indirectly, from timber for the Taliban exceeded 20% of the total revenue.[105] Since the Taliban takeover of Afghanistan, and as of writing, it remained unclear how their revenues have been affected. In some ways, being an illegal armed group may have been more financially lucrative for the Taliban as it allowed the group to tap into illegal activities like timber and mineral smuggling. As the government in post-August 2021, they must now find ways to dismantle these networks and redirect revenues into state coffers.

The same is true for opium cultivation and the drug trade. As an insurgent group, drug trafficking was central to the Taliban's existence and their ability to fund their war.[106] The Helmand Province represents the world's largest centre of poppy cultivation in the world. The Taliban taxed opium production and were involved in smuggling both raw opium and processed heroin, as well as providing protection to traders. In Farah, they protected over 300 small-scale opium and heroin factories and smuggling across the border to Iran.[107] Afghan officials accused the Taliban of collecting about $400 million annually from narcotics. However, several leading experts, including David Mansfield, have cautioned against such numbers. Instead, his estimate is that armed actors on both sides of the conflict made opium profits of almost $40 million annually, with the Helmand Province generating half the revenue.[108]

The Taliban also operated an effective system of revenue collection, charging NGOs, local people, traders, and others *ushr*. In recent years, they were able to collect *ushr* at the outskirts of major cities like Ghazni and Kunduz. There were reports that in 2018 they would visit cities and districts regularly to collect their tax. A UN report found that in 2012, *ushr* was the main source of income for the Taliban in areas where farmers cultivated poppies.[109] In May 2016, when a drone strike killed the then Taliban leader, Akhtar Mansur, in Pakistan, feuds arose among the Taliban leadership over the $900 million that reportedly went missing from Mansur's bank accounts.[110] Although this is difficult to substantiate, figures even half that were an indication of their capacity to generate significant revenues to sustain their insurgency.

9.7 The façade of combating corruption

The Taliban's ability to generate such lucrative revenues was intimately connected to, indeed even sustained by, the inability of the Afghan state to tackle corruption. President Ghani described president Karzai's government as "a looting machine" questioning his resolve to combat graft and illegality.[111] However, throughout Ghani's own presidency, Afghanistan remained one of the most corrupt countries in the world, according to Transparency International, except for a brief period between 2015 and 2016.[112] In 2016, Integrity Watch Afghanistan's (IWA) National Corruption Survey found that an estimated $3 billion was paid in bribes in 2015, an almost 50% increase from 2014.[113] Such payments were paid to public servants (e.g., provincial officials, land registry officials, tax officials, customs officers, and others), judges and prosecutors, MPs and provincial council members, security officials, teachers, and even NGO staff to secure a job or a project.

International donors and the Afghan government's response to corruption was a façade as there was no serious political will to combat it. Instead, international donors and subsequent Afghan governments tacitly decided on employing quick technical fixes. After 2010, several anti-corruption institutions were set up on top of existing ones: the Independent Joint Anti-Corruption and Evaluation Committee (MEC) in 2010; the Corruption and Justice Centre (ACJC) in 2016; and the Ombudsperson's Office just before 2020 Geneva Conference. The latter never managed to establish a legal foundation or functional foothold before the government collapsed in 2021. In yet another initiative, President Ghani set up the National Procurement Authority (NPA) to centralise the procurement system within the President's Office of Administrative Affairs. In November 2016, the NPA claimed to have re-assessed around 2000 contracts, approving ones worth $3 billion while rejecting 90, "generating savings of $270 million." It claimed, "around 100 companies were also blacklisted."[114] However, complaints emerged about the centralisation of procurement, many accusing President Ghani and his closes aide of using the NPA as a "whip" to go after their opponents' companies and contracts.[115]

Legal institutions were equally complicit in facilitating corruption. In a damning report issued on 23 July 2020, Integrity Watch Afghanistan said that the ACJC had failed to handle major corruption cases in the country because of political interference and a lack of transparency in the selection of cases.[116] Similarly, the 2020 United Nations Assistance Mission in Afghanistan (UNAMA) anti-corruption report concluded that in 2019 the government's efforts to fight corruption had overall not been satisfactory.[117] The ACJC suffered from weak law enforcement support, as demonstrated in particular by a failure to fully execute all 255 arrest warrants pending for many years. Over 20% of the ACJC's trials were held in the absence of the accused. On 17 June 2020, the Pajhwok local news agency reported that the High Council of Rule of Law and Anti-Corruption had blocked MEC's publication of its report on the National Procurement Authority (NPA) because it exposed the rampant corruption in President Ghani's inner circle.[118] I interviewed several different company owners who, like my friend, alleged to have been approached by NPA staff before bidding processes, asking them for an 8–10% share of the total contract.[119] The UNAMA report essentially assessed that efforts to fight corruption under Ghani had backslid. The government response was that fighting corruption takes time, and that they were confronting strong and resilient networks.[120]

Despite the rhetoric, President Ghani evidently lacked the political will— and possibly the desire—as he surrounded himself with a small circle of corrupt officials who were constantly misinforming and manipulating him for their personal gains. As one MP bluntly put it:

> Look at the people the president has surrounded himself with. Farooq Wardak who made hundreds of millions out of schools and teachers' salaries; Amarkhel, whose audiotapes revealed how he facilitated wholesale fraud in the 2014 elections; Humayun Qayoumi who made millions before elections from Customs for Ghani; Eklil Hakimi who is known to have made money from phone credit cards; Fazl Fazli whom Amrullah Saleh [current First Vice-President] accused of interfering in the [2018 parliamentary] elections and moral corruption. Do you think with such people around him, he is serious about fighting corruption? Or maybe he needs such a network to do his dirty work?[121]

In the long list of priorities for international donors, the battle to curb corruption was most often sacrificed for the sake of counterinsurgency operations and political stability. As the SIGAR report found, the U.S. government was stuck in a dilemma between choosing to maintain a hard line against corruption or seeing its counterinsurgency efforts undermined as a consequence of cracking down on corrupt power structures. Instead of wrestling with these difficult issues, it turned its attention to other priorities.[122] As one political party leader commented,

> The international community has sacrificed justice for security and stability. They have sacrificed democracy and human rights for security. For them, it doesn't matter if Mullah Raketi [a Talib fundamentalist] comes to power or a corrupt official, as long as there is stability.[123]

Despite the lack of nuance, this statement captures how key figures within the Afghan state saw the international engagement in Afghanistan and worked towards manipulating it to their advantage.

From my experience working as a senior civil servant, donors' anti-corruption efforts, such as the 2014 U.S.–Afghan Compact (with five pillars, several benchmarks, and over 300 indicators), were nothing but mere lip service to technical issues that could be measured by benchmarks and indicators. The more fundamental structural issues were ignored, with western donors and officials slipping into the neo-colonial habit of exonerating their own shortcomings with a romanticised image of the indigenous, local, and irremediably predatory Afghan actor and a complacent population. It was a clever little rhetorical trick: deploying money as a "weapons system," which fostered corruption in the first place, and then employing slogans like "local ownership" and "participation" which put the blame for failure squarely on Afghans. For their domestic consumption, donors wilfully directed their attention to technical approaches, internal practices, and procedures to fight corruption. Sensing the lack of political will from the donors, Afghan politicians, including Karzai and Ghani, took few necessary steps—in some instances remaining complacent—in cases of Kabul Bank and others to recover stolen assets and prosecute their associates involved in embezzlement and fraud.

9.8 Resource flow: upward or downward?

The cases in this chapter and previous chapters have shown that state-level networks are often sustained by the upward flow of financial and political resources from provincial and district networks and officials. This runs counter to the argument put forward by neo-patrimonialists who consider such flows top-down. Kabul-based political leaders came under immense political and financial pressure from their local associates to survive and remain politically relevant so they could continue offering them political protection against competition in a complex marketplace. Sarah Chayes offers a compelling framework as to how this worked: local officials paid their bosses in provincial capitals, who then paid off someone else in Kabul to purchase or rent their position. A 2015 report on police chief appointments found that officials paid thousands of dollars to secure profitable appointments through intermediary powerbrokers and agents linked to network leaders in Kabul (see Table 9.10).[124] The more lucrative the position, the higher the price. During my work at the IDLG, there were several cases in which governors had procured their position within the system. One position in 2018 was allegedly sold to the highest bidder (over $250,000) amongst members of the Greater Council of the North following their collective deal with President Ghani—securing two governorship positions.[125] In another case, a cabinet position in early 2015 was sold to the highest bidder with the deal being made by an intermediary in Dubai. A businessman once explained to me how the system worked:

> I was partly involved in securing his position [district police chief] as I facilitated the down payment to the Kabul police chief. The district police chief collects daily fees from shops, businesses, street vendors, land agencies and people who are building skyscrapers [10 to 30 floors]. For instance, the fee for constructing each floor is $10,000 for which district municipality officials, land authority officials, police chiefs and others get paid. At the moment, in Shahr-i-Naw and other areas, you have to pay a protection fee to a particular criminal group linked to a member of the Kabul provincial council who rent out their armed men to the investor for the duration of construction. Now, these armed men have formed a connection with the police chief; if you don't pay them, you won't be allowed to construct your tower complex.[126]

Table 9.10 Price list of MoI appointments (advance one-off payments)

Position	Price US$
Provincial police chief	50,000–200,000
District police chief	20,000—50,000
Head of passport office (Kabul)	200,000
Head of department in MOI	100,000
Customs commander	100,000

Source: IWA: 2015.

The role of intermediary agents (*dalal* or *commissionkar*) like this businessman, who could sidestep bureaucratic difficulties and obstructionism (*Mushkel tarashi*), was visible and omnipresent across all levels of Afghan polity and society. The agents played a pivotal role in the chain of resource flows, facilitating bargains and purchases. A 2009 Integrity Watch Afghanistan report found that intermediary agents were charging around US$400 for vehicle registration and US$500 for company registration in 2009; between US$200 and $300 for a three-year passport that was legally priced at US$42 (2,100 afghanis); and between 8,000 Afghanis (US$160) and 20,000 Afghanis (US$400) for connecting to electricity lines in Kabul.[127] As Figure 9.4 shows, there was a potent circle of power and corruption in which political networks sustained themselves and maintained political order.[128] The primary objective of the political network in the circle of power resources was to improve its *purchasability* of state positions by spending money to gain access to another set of resources, even if this was achieved through various illegal means. In this vicious chain of dependencies, illegality and corruption seemed essential to the survival of political networks and consequently the Afghan state.

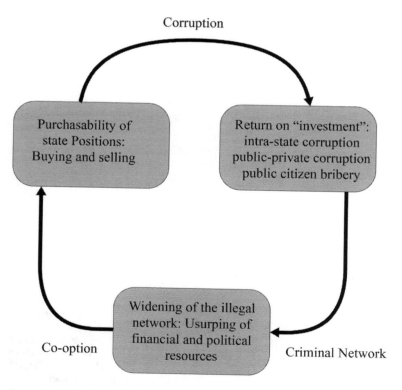

Figure 9.4 The circle of corruption and power.[129]

Conclusion

This chapter showed that international money used as a "weapons system" played an instrumental role in creating an environment of corruption and nefarious interdependencies in post-2001 Afghanistan. By partnering with malign political networks and strongmen, the international intervention exacerbated corruption in Afghanistan in its scale, scope, and depth, transforming Afghan polity and society.[130] In addition to all of the contributing factors, including decades of uncertainty, war, poverty, identity-based grievances, and weak rule of law, corruption in its magnitude and modern practices was deeply tied with international money and aid delivery as well as Afghanistan's clientelistic and customary patronage arrangements. International aid dependency meant that fighting corruption had to be sacrificed for the sake of political stability and state survival. As the case of Kabul Bank demonstrated, the bank and the people affiliated with it were too powerful for it to collapse and risk destabilising an already fragile state.

Illegality and corruption thus became essential to the survival of the state and to sustain political order. The extractive industry cases in this chapter illustrated that while existing political network practices may help explain political order at the macro-level, it is insufficient to explain why instability and violence raged in the countryside (micro-level). The timber exploitation and illegal mining cases showed how the state became thoroughly captured by economic and political networks that lubricated the gears of conflict, corruption, smuggling, money laundering, and international organised crime. In some places, this overlapped and intertwined with insurgency groups and their interests.

"Money as a weapons system" obscured responsibility and allowed everyone to get off the hook. President Ghani's government was too fragmented along ethnic and political lines and often used the fight against corruption as a tool to selectively go after its opponents. Ethnic network leaders were then successful in manipulating identity-based divisions and claimed to carry the banner of their ethnic and tribal interests. Karzai used to employ a politically meaningful, but somewhat vague term, *maslehat*, to justify his complacency with political networks.[131] His was the same argument employed by the international community: sacrifice long-term institutionalisation and democracy for short-term stability.

Notes

1 See Yurchak (1997); Scott (1985).
2 Author's interview, March 2021, Panjab district of Bamiyan province.
3 DOD, *Money as a Weapon System – Afghanistan (MAAWS-A): Afghanistan Reintegration Program (ARP)*, May 2011, 8–14.
4 This of course did not include the massive amounts of money going into the pockets of foreign contractors, consultants, and aid workers who were paid ludicrously more than their resumes and eventual job performances could justify. This kind of "legal" corruption has often been overlooked when calculating waste in Afghanistan.
5 Farahi and Guggenheim (2020).
6 Katzman (2013).

7 World Bank Report. 2019. "Afghanistan Public Expenditure Update." The World Bank Group, July 2019. In those countries' security spending stands at 3% of GDP. The same World Bank report noted that total budget expenditure on security was equal to around US$50 per capita compared to just US$21 per capita for infrastructure, US$17 per capital for education, and US$8 per capita for health.

8 Crawford (2019). "United States Budgetary Costs and Obligations of Post-9/11 Wars through FY2020: $6.4 Trillion." Costs of War Research Series, Brown University, November 13, 2019.

9 World Bank Report. 2019. "Afghanistan Public Expenditure Update." The World Bank Group, July 2019. In those countries' security spending stands at 3% of GDP.

10 See Fishstein and Wilder (2012).

11 Aikins, M. 2010. "Last Man in Kandahar." *The Walrus*, December 12, 2010.

12 Minnion, M. (2013).

13 Clark, E. 2015. "The 40,000 People on Bagram Air Base Haven't Actually Seen Afghanistan." *The Wired*, February 2015.

14 Peters, Schwartz, and Kapp (2017).

15 For a recent, excellent article on this see Kate Clark (2020).

16 See Saikal (2006); Shahrani (1990); and Rubin (2002).

17 Clark, K. 2020. "Both Medicine and Poison: The Paradox of Support to Afghanistan," *ToloNews*. June 21, 2020.

18 See Ghani, Lockhart and Carnahan (2005) and Ghani and Lockhart (2008).

19 Author's conversation with several ethnic Hazara leaders in June and July 2020.

20 The State department and the US Secretary of State were quick in 2019 to cut one-billion-dollar aid money to the Afghan government to exert pressure on Ghani administration just before the elections. This was discussed in chapter 6.

21 Up to December 2017, donors had paid over $10 billion to the Fund to provide direct assistance to the government.

22 SIGAR. 2018. "Afghanistan Reconstruction Trust Fund: The World Bank Needs to Improve How it Monitors Implementation, Shares Information, and Determines the Impact of Donor Contributions," April 2018.

23 Ibid.

24 Peters (2009).

25 See *Warlord, Inc.: Extortion and Corruption along the U.S. Supply Chain in Afghanistan* (2010), Report was prepared by the Majority staff of the Subcommittee on National Security and Foreign Affairs of the Committee on Oversight and Government Reform.

26 Roston, A. 2009. "How the U.S. Funds the Taliban." *Nation*, November 11, 2009.

27 Shortell, D. 2019. "Gold Star Family Lawsuit Alleges Contractors in Afghanistan Funneled Money to the Taliban." *CNN Politics*, December 28, 2019.

28 Ibid. The data for the lawsuit was based on confidential witnesses, as well as internal company documents, declassified intelligence, congressional testimony and reports, and press accounts.

29 Author's conversation with a senior security official.

30 Bizhan (2017:108-120).

31 Ibid.

32 Bisogno, E., et al. 2010. "Corruption in Afghanistan: Bribery as Reported by Victims," United Nations Office on Drugs and Crime.

33 See International Monetary Fund. 2020. "Sixth Review of Afghanistan's Extended Credit Facility." MoF, September 26, 2020; United States Institute of Peace. 2017. "Revenue Growth in Afghanistan Continues Strong but Future Uncertain." USIP, February 2017. In October 2014, when NUG took office, 1 US dollar was 57.57 Afghani. In December 2019, 1 US dollar is 78.30 Afghani. Also, in fiscal year 2018, according to SIGAR reports there was reports that AFN 4 billion (US$51 million) were transferred from the Central Bank to the Ministry of Finance as one-off revenues in an effort to show an increase in the revenues in an election year. See Special Inspector

General for Afghanistan Reconstruction, "SIGAR Quarterly Report, October 2018," SIGAR.

34 "People's Treasure: An Analysis of the Executive Budget Proposal of Afghanistan 2020," Integrity Watch Afghanistan, January 2020.
35 Smith (2020).
36 Ibid.
37 Internal Ministry of Finance document, 2018.
38 Byrd (2020).
39 Begzad, M. 2020. "Pshte Parde-e Tayinat dar Gomrokat: Nesfe Mamuran ba Zor 47 Nomayand-e Majles Tayeen Shodand." *Hashe Subh*, September 27, 2020.
40 Mansfield (2020).
41 Smith (2020).
42 Ibid.
43 Rubin, A., and J. Risen. 2011. "Losses at Afghan Bank Could Be $900 Million." *NYT*, January 30, 2011.
44 Internal Kroll Memorandum emailed to the Governor of Da Afghanistan Bank, subject title, Allocation of the Loan Book, June 4, 2012.
45 Zaheer, A., and A. Q. Siddiqui. 2011. "Kabul Bank's Corrupt Shareholders Named." *Pajhowk News*, April 27, 2011.
46 See Bijlert (2011).
47 Filkins, D. 2011. "The Afghan Bank Heist." *The New Yorker*, February 14, 2011.,
48 Author's interview, Kabul, August 2020.
49 Author's interview, Kabul, August 2020.
50 Internal Kroll Memorandum emailed to the Governor of Da Afghanistan Bank, subject title, Kabul Bank Loans for Shares and Capital Injections, June 4, 2012.
51 Ibid.
52 SIGAR. 2016. "Corruption in Conflict."
53 MEC, *Report of the Public Inquiry into the Kabul Bank Crisis*, 14–15.
54 "Kabul Bank Fraud: Sherkhan Farnood and Khalilullah Ferozi Jailed," *BBC News*, March 5, 2013.
55 "Afghanistan Investment Company Closing in on First Project," US Embassy Cable. 2006. February 26, 2006.
56 Ibid.
57 Under the contract, AIC agreed to invest an initial capital of US$45 million, both to rehabilitate the existing Factories 1 and 2 which had 330 and 1,000 tons of daily production capacity, respectively. Additionally, AIC's investment would mobilise more capital to build a new factory (3), with a 3,000-tons-per-day production capacity, by 2009. The company was also to pay US$1.04 per tons as royalty on the cement, fixed permanently. See Integrity Watch Afghanistan Report.
58 Tolo News. 2012. "Ghori Cement Plant Faces Bankruptcy," May 12, 2012, http://www .tolonews.com/en/business/6196-ghori-cement-plant-faces-bankruptcy (accessed December 24, 2013).
59 Integrity Watch Afghanistan. 2015. "The Plundering of Hope? Political Economy of Five Major Mines in Afghanistan," 2015.
60 Mahmud Karzai had secured a US$11 million loan for AIC through Azizi Bank. This close contact and support from Azizi Bank to the AIC was underpinned by a partnership between them in Onyx Construction, one of the biggest commercial and residential towers in Kabul.
61 Other Sources (Bayat Energy signed a contract with the Afghan government to build a gas-fired power plant in Jawzjan province to generate 200 MW of electricity. "Bayat Power Announces Three-Phase US$250M Investment Program to Accelerate Afghanistan's Gas-Fired Power Industry." *Prnewswire.com*, October 03, 2016. Habibi was arrested on 25 January 2012 accused of forging the signature of the first vice-president to construct the Gulbahar Centre Mall on government land and paying US$150,000

in bribes. He also reportedly owed US$27 million to Kabul Bank. "Owner of Gulbahar Tower Detained for Corruption Charges," Khama Press, January 25, 2012. Azizi was one of the main Afghan investors in the Dubai property market. "UAE's Azizi Records $350m Home Sales at Cityscape." *Arabian Business*, September 17, 2017).

62 MacKenzie, J., and H. Shalizi. 2017. "Major Afghan Cement Contract Cancelled in Investment Setbacks." *Reuters*, February 10, 2017.

63 According to his own estimate, his net worth was around $200 million. In addition to the Ghori Cement factory, he owned the United Afghanistan Bank, and a security company. "Football, Funfair and Fortunes: In Afghan Election, Money Talks," *Euronews*, December 9, 2019.

64 Ibid.

65 The author has seen a copy of this report and what follows is based on findings of the report.

66 The author would like to especially thank Mr. Javid Noorani for his detailed discussions on the sector and providing some of the empirical data included in this section, especially the mapping of networks and the mining sector.

67 United Press International (2012); Risen (2010).

68 Muhammadi, Z. 2010. "Afghanistan's Minerals Worth $3 Trillion." *Pajhwok Afghan News*, June 17, 2010; The Guardian. 2010. "Afghan Mineral Deposits Worth $3 tn Says Mining Official," June 18, 2010.

69 Najafizada E. 2015.The Taliban is Capturing Afghanistan's $1 Trillion in Mining Wealth." *Bloomberg*.

70 Noorani (2015).

71 Author interview with Matthew DuPée, email correspondence, January 24, 2017.

72 Author interview with Afghan mining expert, Kabul, June 2016. This figure is buttressed by a USIP report of 2015 (see Noorani 2015).

73 Cited in Noorani (2015: 9).

74 Tolo News. 2015. "Analysts: Over 2,000 Illegal Mining Sites in Afghanistan," June 24, 2015,

75 For details of this case study see Global Witness. 2016. "War in the Treasury of the People: Afghanistan, Lapis Lazuliand the battle of Mineral Wealth," June 2016.

76 Giustozzi and Orsini (2009).

77 Ibid.

78 There were several violent clashes against Haji Malek and the mine by a former jihadi commander named Haji Ghulam Nassir who reportedly had links to MP Mojaddadi which caused several police and civilian casualties.

79 The contract was dated 16 February 2013 http://mom.gov.af/Content/files/Limiston %20of%20badakh%20shan.pdf (in Dari – see Global Witness website for unofficial English translation).

80 Mashal, M. 2016. "Greed, Corruption and Danger: A Tarnished Afghan Gem Trade." *The New York Times*, June 5, 2016, https://www.nytimes.com/2016/06/06/world/asia /afghanistan-lajwardeen-mining-lapis-lazuli.html.

81 According to Global Watch report at least 24 people were killed and 24 injure in 2014 and 2015. Some of these attacks involved mortars, cannons, rocket-propelled grenades, and armoured venhicles.

82 Mashal (2016); O'Donnell, L. 2016. "Afghan Mineral Wealth Being Looted by Strongmen. Experts Say." *Associated Press*,

83 It seems that the company did not deny its association to Mujaddadi which created the tensions. While the company denied offering any shares to Mujaddadi, they acknowledged that they enlisted the support of powerful people like him; the reality of doing business in Afghanistan.

84 Ibid.

85 Integrity Watch Afghanistan (2013); *Wands* represent the division of geographical space between tribes and is determined on the basis of administrative sections—the *wand*—where each tribe and their jurisdiction of responsibility are known.

86 Krause (2013).
87 Zimmerman, Egel and .Blum (2016). http://www.rand.org/content/dam/rand/pubs/research_reports/RR1200/RR1243/RAND_RR1243.pdf.
88 TFBSO spent US$282 million on 11 projects while the USAID-run Mining Investment and Development for Afghan Sustainability (MIDAS) implemented three programmes that totalled US$206 million. TFBSO focused on five main areas of the mining sector: (1) mineral development, (2) hydrocarbon development, (3) enhancing access to energy resources, (4) village stability operations, and (5) capacity building at the Ministry of Mines and Petroleum (MoMP) and the Afghanistan Geological Survey (AGS). The aim of the USAID programme was to find potential investors who would work with Afghan businessmen, develop the actual infrastructure and geological research needed to exploit the mines, develop the capacity of the MoMP, manage tender processes, and otherwise secure extractive business deals. For more details see Special Inspector General for Afghanistan Reconstruction (SIGAR). 2015. "Afghanistan's Mineral, Oil and Gas Industries: Unless US Agencies Act Soon to Sustain Investments Made $488 Million in Funding is at Risk," SIGAR 15-55 Audit Report, April 2015, https://www.sigar.mil/pdf/audits/SIGAR-15-55-AR.pdf.
89 Ibid.
90 Special Inspector General for Afghanistan Reconstruction (SIGAR). 2016. "Corruption in Conflict: Lessons from the US Experience in Afghanistan," September 2016.
91 Integrity Watch Afghanistan (2013).
92 DuPée (2012).
93 Sexton, R. 2012. *Natural Resources and Conflict in Afghanistan*. Kabul: Afghanistan Watch. Kabul: July 2012.
94 "A Political Economy Study of Timber Logging in Kunar Province," *IDLG Report*, March 3, 2018.
95 Ibid.
96 Also see Bader, Hanna, Douglas, and Fox (2013).
97 Ibid. In 2010, people affiliated with Commander Malek Zarin were charging 3,500 Pakistani rupees for trafficking, whereas commander Jandad in South Kunar was charging 2,250 rupees.
98 In 2010, the trade permission certificate fee of formally registering timber as a legal good with Pakistani custom was 75,000 rupees for every 150 square metres. The commissioners were paying 50,000 for securing the trade permission certificate from the Pakistani customs.
99 In 2010, contractors were buying a good quality wood for 11,000 rupees for each square meter. This then sold for US$300 (25,000 rupees) in Dubai. See Trofimov, Y. 2010. "World News: Taliban Capitalize on Karzai's Logging Ban --- Move to Preserve Afghanistan's Forests Instead Turns Them Over to Militants." *Wall Street Journal*, April 10; and 2013.
100 See for instance, *Warlord, Inc.: Extortion and Corruption along the U.S. Supply Chain in Afghanistan* (2010), Report was prepared by the Majority staff of the Subcommittee on National Security and Foreign Affairs of the Committee on Oversight and Government Reform; Roston, A. 2009. "How the U.S. Funds the Taliban." *Nation*, November 11, 2009; Smith (2020); Peters (2009); Weigand (2017).
101 Roston, A. 2009. "How the U.S. Funds the Taliban." *Nation*, November 11, 2009.
102 ToloNews Tweet, July 20, 2020, https://twitter.com/TOLOnews/status/1285090890491494400.
103 Ibid.
104 Global Witness (2016).
105 Bader, H. R., C. Hanna, C. Douglas, and J. D. Fox (2013).
106 See Peters (2009); Mansfield (2018).
107 Internal IDLG report.
108 Mansfield (2019).

109 Wittig (2012). 'Letter Dated 4 September 2012 from the Chair of the Security Council
     Committee Pursuant to Resolution 1988 (2011) Addressed to the President of the
     Security Council," United Nations Security Council; also see Jackson, A. 2018. 'Life
     under the Taliban Shadow Government," Overseas Development Institute, https://
     www.odi.org/publications/11144-life-under-taliban-shadow-government.
110 Smith 2020.
111 CNN Amanpour. 2009. "Afghan Govt. A "Looting Machine"," November 20, 2009;
     retrieved July 29, 2020, https://www.youtube.com/watch?v=ppnY5jojtCQ.
112 https://www.transparency.org/en/cpi/2019/results/afg#details (accessed on 15 May
     2020); in 2019 Afghanistan dropped one spot to 173 out of 183.
113 "2016 National Corruption Survey," Integrity Watch Afghanistan, December 8, 2016;
     "Afghanistan in 2016: A Survey of the Afghan People," www.asiafoundation.org.
114 "Reforming the Procurement: The Journey So Far" (pdf presentation), prepared for
     the weekly Donor Stakeholder Meeting, Kabul, February 12, 2017.
115 The National Procurement Agency was subject to persistent accusations of corrup-
     tion. Many simply accused the president of using NPA as a way to punish those who
     opposed him while others levelled accusations of pressuring major companies who
     won contracts through the NPA to allocate a percentage of their earnings to the presi-
     dent's 2019 election campaign. A business friend explained on 21 July 2020 how NPA
     staff had approached him before the opening of bids, coming to his office, and asking
     him how much he was willing to pay to ensure he won the IT contract.
116 Rahimi, Z. 2020. "AGO, ACJC Failed to Pursue Major Corruption Cases: Watchdog",
     ToloNews, July 23, 2020. The ACJC is comprised of seven primary court and seven
     appellate court judges, 25 prosecutors and 12 Major Crimes Task Force investigators
     and administrative support staff.
117 United Nations Assistance Mission in Afghanistan. 2020. "Afghanistan's Fight
     against Corruption: Crucial for Peace and Prosperity," June 2020.
118 Sohaib, A. 2020. "MEC Report Being Blocked to Hide Graft in NPA." Pajhwok News
     Agency, June 17, 2020.
119 Author's interview, Kabul, May 2020.
120 International Crisis Group interviews, senior Palace officials, Kabul, November 2016.
121 Author's interview, March 2020, Kabul.
122 SIGAR. 2013. "Corruption in Conflict."
123 Interview 118, September 7, 2009.
124 See Ishaqzadeh and Giustozzi (2015).
125 Author's private conversation with officials close to the ethno-regional leader and to
     the minister, Kabul, August–September 2017.
126 Author's interview with a Kabul-based businessman, June 2020.
127 See Gardizi, M. 2007. "Afghans' Experiences of Corruption: A Study across Seven
     Provinces." Kabul: Integrity Watch Afghanistan.
128 Gardizi, Hussmann, and Torabi. (2010).
129 Source: Gardizi, Hussmann and Torabi, AREU Publication (This excellent point was
     made by Gardizi, Hussmann, and Torabi (2010). *Maslehat* means to "discuss" or
     "seek advice" and, in this context, to seek stability through inclusiveness and political
     compromise, even if this carries short-term costs).
130 SIGAR. 2016. "Corruption in Conflict: Lessons from the U.S. Experience in
     Afghanistan," September 2016. Also see Clark (2020).
131 This excellent point was made by Gardizi, Hussmann, and Torabi (2010). *Maslehat*
     means to "discuss" or "seek advice" and, in this context, to seek stability through
     inclusiveness and political compromise, even if this carries short-term costs.

10 The U.S.A. military exit and a spectacular collapse

Introduction

At the end of November 2021, just over three months after Afghanistan once again fell to the Taliban, I caught up with an Afghan friend in a café in Istanbul when we had a heated discussion about the reasons for the collapse of the Republic on August 15.

While a variety of factors contributed to the precipitous fall of Kabul, we kept coming back to the collective political and moral failure of the Afghan elites and the US–Taliban deal as the betrayal. Like thousands of Afghans in Turkey, we were now refugees residing in a country at best begrudgingly tolerant of our presence. As we discussed the collapse and the chaotic evacuations that followed, my friend recounted a story he had heard from the former Ambassador of Afghanistan to Qatar, Abdul Hakim Dalili.[1] A year before the collapse, apparently in preparation for an important meeting with the Taliban in Doha, the Ambassador had faced a dilemma: He had received frantic calls from every significant political leader inside the country demanding their own representative to be included in the room with Taliban. As an Abdul Rasul Sayyaf appointee, the Ambassador had first tried to accommodate his patron's instructions. Soon, however, more and contradictory instructions came from President Ghani's National Security Council Advisor, Hamdullah Mohib, as well as Hanif Atmar, the Foreign Secretary, Amrullah Saleh, the first Vice-President, Hamid Karzai, the former president, Abdullah Abdullah, the Head of the High Council for National Reconciliation, and so on. This horse-trading was happening despite the existence of a formal government negotiating team.

The explanation, my friend and I concluded, was that no one trusted a representative of a competing group to be alone in the room with the Taliban. The suspicion would continue to the very last days of the Republic, with competing political networks trying to strike private deals with the Taliban. Many international diplomats and analysts in Kabul and Doha saw these tensions as procedural and protocol arrangements. As this book illustrates, such infighting over presence and relevance were part of the political networks' daily strategy of survival within a *networked state*, and the political settlement with the Taliban was merely the latest political marketplace for survival. Ensuring a seat in a high-profile meeting would

DOI: 10.4324/9781315161617-10

serve several purposes with different audiences: to the Taliban, it would essentially showcase the networks' political relevance and influence over constituencies inside the country; to the Afghan public and more specifically to their ethnic and political base, inclusion in the process would illustrate the significance and weight of the leaders and their networks; meanwhile, all the Republic political leaders, particularly President Ghani, needed to also project the illusion of a singular and vertical state and a functioning Republic. The process became a performative act even though it had become clear to many by early 2021 that the Taliban were not serious about negotiations and were only buying time. As the U.S. military withdrawal approached, such enactments and performances became more absurd, further exacerbated by the hollowness of the state, as discussed below. Under immense pressure following President Biden's announcement in May to fully withdraw from the country on the 20th anniversary of the 9/11 attacks, whatever fragments of a government remained began to crumble. Political network clients, especially those at the subnational level, sensing the change in the political winds, began shifting their allegiances from their patrons and the Republic to the Taliban. Following the collapse, for months, the political conversation among Afghanistan was entirely dominated by accusations about different political leaders' and their representatives' secret dealings with different factions of the Taliban.

My friend and I talked about the political and military failures and more impor-tantly our collective moral failure as a nation. We reflected on the role of the post-2001 political and civil society elites, including ourselves, for not doing enough to save the Republic, for not adequately fighting against corruption, and for not more forcefully questioning the flawed US statebuilding agenda and the small Afghan elite circle that promoted and manipulated that agenda for their own survival. We agreed that the eroding legitimacy of political networks, the moral bankruptcy of political and civil society leaders, and subsequently the collapse of the Republic did not suddenly appear out of thin air; it was gradual and, most damningly, the warnings were plainly discernible. The continued corruption since 2001 that had been institutionalised under President Karzai had hollowed out state institutions; late and rushed attempts at reform by President Ghani were misguided at best and self-serving at worst leading to further fragmentation; and the American-led peace process delivered the final blow.

But the rot was already deeply rooted and perhaps already terminal well before President Donald Trump scratched his fibrillar signature onto the agreement. In May 2019, for instance, I found myself at the office of the Army Chief of Staff within the Ministry of Defence (MoD) to help coordinate the military campaign against the Taliban, who had entered Farah city in the southwest. The new MoD headquarters, a five-story building, was a confusing maze of corridors and offices. It had cost around $154.7 million to build and was marred by corruption and delay.[2] There were conflicting reports from Farah city that the provincial governor's building had already been captured by the Taliban and by 10 am fierce fighting was raging around the National Directorate of Security building. However, by 5 pm, the Taliban were pushed back to the outskirts of the city with the support of Afghan special forces and army units from the neighbouring Helmand province.

Late in the evening, an emergency National Security Council (NSC) video conference meeting was held to assess the situation and the damage done. During the briefing, the Farah army division commander blamed the failure on the shortage of 500 soldiers in his brigade size of 1,800 personnel. The Chief of Staff was quick to remind the commander that he had requested and received substantial supplies and equipment (clothes, ammunition, food, winter wood, fuel, etc.) for the full Tashkeel the previous month. An awkward silence followed, with every passing second exposing the naked truth of corruption. I anticipated the moment could come to something serious but the division commander was saved by an intervention of a general who re-directed the conversation to the role of Iranians in the attack on Farah province.

After the meeting, as we walked towards the outer gate of the Presidential Palace, I caught up with the Army Chief of Staff and politely asked him whether we should have investigated the issue. He simply walked off—not out of disrespect, I surmised, but out of awkwardness. Later I told the story to a trusted army colleague, at the time a two-star general, to seek his advice. His answer only compounded my concerns: "The reality is that Farah is not an exception," he told me. "The problem is everywhere and worse. Do you think if the Chief of Staff went after every provincial or corps commander who was corrupt and investigated each case you would have an army?" A year later, I found this army colleague at the international terminal of Kabul airport, lying down in a corner, too ill to sit down and in pain, without medical attention; not even a special treatment or a special pass at the VIP section of the airport—the price a three-star general pays for serving his country with dedication and honesty. He was severely wounded at the battle in the north commanding the Afghan special forces, and he was on his way to Turkey for treatment.

I knew about ghost soldiers but had not realised the magnitude of the problem. In 2020, in its assessment of four southern provinces, SIGAR had found that 50–70% of personnel at police stations were ghost officers.[3] It was clear that security institutions, like the rest of the Afghan state, had become largely hollow. Corruption in key sectors of the country had become the biggest existential threat to Afghanistan and its survival, far more than the threat of the Taliban. As Gen. John Allen warned in his testimony before the U.S. Senate in 2014, seven years before the Republic's collapse, "For too long, we focused our attention solely on the Taliban... They are an annoyance compared to the scope and the magnitude of corruption with which you must contend."[4] Everyone ignored the warning, including the Americans. In May and June 2021, a few months before the collapse, I was contracted to do a political economy mapping of the Ministry of Interior by the German aid agency, GIZ. What I found was shocking: central command within the ministry and police forces had collapsed as early as July, largely because of a last-minute shake-up of over 60 leadership positions in Kabul alone by President Ghani and his National Security Advisor, Hamdullah Mohib. Some inferred from these last-minute leadership changes in the heat of a losing battle with the Taliban that President Ghani and his inner circle were in some way preparing to hand over the ministry to the Taliban in a last-ditch bargaining effort to save their skin.

This is not to suggest that the collapse of the Republic was, as some American apologists have argued, inevitable due to the failure of leadership on part of Afghans. Indeed, what I will show in this concluding chapter are some of the key contributing factors that led to the collapse and how they were a function of the fragility of Afghanistan's endogenous political networks, which were themselves the product of failed American policy. Drawing on this book's central arguments, I demonstrate that the collapse was not months but years in the making. It was the culmination of many gradual failures rooted in the last two decades of flawed U.S.A misguided counter-insurgency efforts masked as statebuilding: America's reliance on corrupt strongmen and their militia networks, President Karzai's unwillingness to prioritise institution building preferring to govern through patronage, and the political economy of a *networked state* illustrated by active and short-sighted profiteering of the Afghan elite from the international intervention, institutionalizing corruption and impunity, eroding public legitimacy and support.

The U.S.A. withdrawal deal was essentially an announcement of the end of the partnership between the U.S.A. in its counter-terrorism effort with the small pack of Afghan leaders and political networks. Since the survival of these networks had become so solely dependent on external factors i.e. the U.S.A.'s military engagement and significant U.S. military expenditure and contracting, the withdrawal essentially pulled the rug from under the Afghan Republic. Subsequently, this set in motion the breakdown of the existing fragile order and set the conditions for the swift collapse of the Afghan Republic.

In the second part of this chapter, I explore some of the implications that stem from the theoretical and empirical claims of the book relevant to future studies of international state-building, political networks, and institutional studies. I briefly situate the key findings of this book within broader theoretical contexts and investigate the application of the political network approach beyond Afghanistan, with an eye to avoiding sweeping assertions but instead pointing out where additional research is required.

10.1   International military intervention and state-building in post-2001 Afghanistan: a self-defeating effort

On 15 August 2021, the Afghan government and large parts of the state, including its army and police, came tumbling down like a house of cards. The Afghan Republic collapsed after President Ghani's disgraceful exodus from the capital, despite a last-minute deal engineered to save Kabul and the state.[5] Most analysts were privately giving the Republic between six months to two years of survival. In April 2021, the U.S. intelligence agencies' annual review warned President Biden that if U.S. troops left Afghanistan before a power-sharing deal was agreed upon, the country could fall to the Taliban within that timeframe.[6] The Chairman of the Joint Chiefs, Mark Milley, in a May press conference, warned that "it's not a foregone conclusion, in my professional military estimate, that the Taliban automatically win and Kabul falls, or any of those kinds of dire predictions."[7]

Those assessments proved spectacularly wrong and the precipitous collapse of the Afghan Republic has now become the subject of belligerent debate in Washington, Brussels, London, and other capitals, as well as among Afghans. Most policymakers in Western countries have placed the collapse squarely at the feet of the Afghan state, in particular its corrupt elites and the failure of the Afghan National Défense and Security Forces to put up a fight. These explanations, mostly politically motivated, acquit the U.S.A. and its flawed military and political strategies, including the damaging 2020 U.S.–Taliban deal.

10.1.1 Hubris and flawed strategies

Throughout its two decades of military intervention, the U.S.A. had no well-thought-out *strategy* and its *objectives* continually shifted to suit different administrations' framing of the Afghan war, driven by the electoral cycles in Washington, DC, rather than the realities on the ground. Objectives were always framed by U.S. interests in its War on Terror campaigns and constantly evolving, shifting from state-building to stabilisation, to killing the al Qaida leadership to counterinsurgency and regional stability in which the priority was to have some "good Afghan guys" as counterterrorism partners, rather than building lasting state institutions. Throughout the last two decades of U.S. military intervention, the overall Afghanistan policy was dictated by two overarching *foci*: troop numbers and arbitrary military withdrawal dates regardless of conditions on the ground, which fashioned inconsistent and short-term goals. As Whitlock demonstrates in his book, *The Afghanistan Papers: A Secret History of War*, the war in Afghanistan from the very beginning was marred by a lack of clarity of objectives, deception, ignorance, and hubris. As the war dragged on, American political leaders "avoided accountability and dodged reprisals that could have changed the outcome or shortened the conflict. Instead, they chose to bury their mistakes and let the war drift."[8] Administration after administration failed to recognise missteps and adapt, and each leadership continued with the same old tools and means.

Development programmes and state-building were also framed by the overarching objective of U.S. interests in the War on Terror, not the interest of Afghanistan. As discussed below, aid and state-building enriched a small group of Afghan elites while leaving many Afghans behind, like Kohisaaf in Yamchi village (discussed in the Preface), wondering what the true purpose of the foreign intervention was. In another change of objectives, in early 2018, the Trump administration decided to exit Afghanistan by striking a deal with the Taliban in a nakedly political effort to generate a policy win before the 2020 U.S. presidential elections. And in April 2021, the newly elected Biden administration justified its decision to fully withdraw from Afghanistan based on the questionable logic that the nation's original goal of killing Osama bin Laden had been achieved a decade ago in Pakistan and that al Qaida had lost its capabilities in Afghanistan.[9] He went on to say that the U.S. objective was never nation-building, suggesting this was mission creep. Yet, from the start by militarily removing the Taliban and trying to achieve its "War on Terror" objectives, the U.S.A. committed to rebuilding the Afghan state and sustaining it including its bloated army and police through its strategy of money as "weapons system."

Inconsistent objectives and shifting signposts meant that the U.S.A. and its allies were never able to focus on addressing the root causes of the Afghan conflict, including Taliban sanctuaries in Pakistan, widespread corruption within the Afghan state exacerbated by massive but often poorly directed aid flows, and weak rule of law. For instance, from 2004 onwards, despite overwhelming evidence about the role of the Pakistani Inter-Services Intelligence (ISI) in supporting and funding the Taliban, including providing sanctuaries, Washington never sufficiently pressured the Pakistani government, and even worse, played along in keeping all of this from the American public, as shown in the 2020 Washington papers. Washington also continued to partner with corrupt Afghan officials to secure short-term military gains whilst undermining rule of law, justice, and formal institutions. As part of their approach to using their money as a "weapon system," the Americans preferred to partner with opportunistic political networks that could use international money including contracts to sustain themselves, play along with the unspoken but quickly established rules of the game, and create some illusion of stability and order.

Many Western accounts of the war make the point that U.S. policy on Afghanistan was incoherent or never settled, but as this book has partly shown, for Afghans, there was a remarkable consistency in how different U.S. administrations pursued their policies, the tools they turned to, and the methods they applied. If the war's strategy or its aims were never consistent, the way it was implemented and its impact on the lives of Afghans certainly were as the stories in this book show.

Most Afghans resented and were angered at the U.S. reliance on warlords and corrupt political leaders in their chief pursuit: counterterrorism. The brutality of the war and atrocities committed by local commanders across the country further undermined the legitimacy of the historically powerful political networks. The Afghans saw the state as an extension of the U.S. in its counterterrorism and "war on terror" effort above all with little accountability to them. Certainly, the political model adopted at the Bonn Conference and the 2002 Loya Jirga by the U.S.A and Afghan elites including President Karzai disfranchised ordinary Afghans of voice and representation. This led to a hollowed-out state that responded to the needs and objectives of the U.S.A. more than the Afghan people.

As the war dragged on and the Taliban extended control over larger parts of the countryside, rumours and conspiracy theories about the real intention and purpose of the U.S. military and political intervention circulated among Afghans. Ordinary Afghans could not comprehend that a ragtag insurgent group could keep the world's most powerful armies at bay. Statements such as "if they [Americans] wish, they could defeat the Taliban—but they have other intentions" were common in public squares as well as government offices. The official narrative proposed by the U.S.A. and the Afghan government also stopped making sense in the minds of many American soldiers and their Afghan counterparts fighting the Taliban. For many, the Taliban itself had become an illusion, veiled in a fog of ideology, criminality, and insurgency. In the autumn of 2016 in Jalalabad city in eastern Afghanistan, for instance, while I was interviewing local officials for a report for the International Crisis Group, a local official branded local Taliban fighters as *destmal* ['handkerchief'], explaining:

> The Taliban are partly a guise, readily available for anyone who wants to wash their dirty hands of their *jorm* ['illegal practices']. Criminals on both sides [the Taliban and the Afghan Republic] use the Taliban brand to carry out their illegal practices.

In his district, a powerful former Mujahedeen family and their loyal subnational administrative officials, drug traffickers, smugglers, and criminals were regularly instigating conflict in the name of the Taliban, and sometimes in coordination with local Taliban commanders, to profit from insecurity. And yet despite knowledge of the family's illegality as shown in this book, the U.S. military and Afghan intelligence agency continued to fund them and hire their tribal militias at astronomical rates to fight against the Islamic State of Khorasan Province (ISKP) and the Taliban.

10.1.2 *Money as a "Weapon System" and its drawdown*

The overall U.S. political and military approach to the Afghan war was even more problematic when its financial might was used as a "weapon system" to "get things done," driven by the desire to secure quick gains. The magic wand of international money, including aid, cast a mesmerising spell over the Afghan state and its officials, corrupting the very fabric of Afghan society and polity.

As shown in this book, international money helped consolidate political networks and centres of power through the distribution of contracts and access to funds. In the immediate post-2001 Afghanistan, donor strategies protected, financed, and entrenched key regional strongmen who helped the U.S.A. in its War on Terror efforts. These regional strongmen and militia vassal networks in turn provided the façade of political stability at the provincial levels. A U.S. House of Representatives report questioned the strategy of relying on regional strongmen as it undermined building formal state institutions and democratisation.[10] Empowering corrupt leaders and officials meant a shrinking space for reform-minded liberal and civil society voices who tried to carve a political space for a more open-access society.

The money as a "weapon system" approach fostered and facilitated an ecosystem in which corruption became the addictive drug sustaining the Afghan state. As one development expert described it in 2020:

> With access to virtually unlimited funds, Afghanistan became a proving ground where everybody agreed on the goal, but nobody agreed on the means. The country was a riot of half-designed, never-finished projects, competing

programs, and everybody's favourite great new idea to test. Nearly two decades later and with tens of billions of dollars having been spent, the government calculates the poverty rate to be 55 per cent. The unemployment rate is
24 per cent.[11]

The long-lasting impact of international money and contracting was the creation of a complex chain of interdependencies between a small group of Afghan
elites, like Haji Ajmal and my former colleague at the Independent Directorate
of Local Governance (detailed in the previous chapter) in Kabul, the provinces
and their international allies—an addiction that remained difficult to eradicate.
This small class was also effective in exploiting and manipulating the system to
their personal, political, and economic advantages and inadvertently promoted
the political and security interests of the U.S.A. and its allies rather than those of
Afghanistan. In this expansive chain of interdependencies, most senior government officials remained highly dependent on the Afghan state and its *destarkhan*
("tablecloth") for survival in terms of security and livelihood in the form of
armoured cars, rent, bodyguards, and perks. With this money as a "weapon system," international donors held the Afghan state, NGOs, and political and military leaders hostage; the Afghan state subsequently held its rank and file hostage;
and the chain extended down through the system, including local communities,
as shown in Chapter 7. My former boss at the Independent Directorate of Local
Governance (IDLG) had over 100 security personnel for his security and three
to four armoured cars—mostly to showcase his political muscle rather than to
ensure his safety. Despite the private criticism of international aid and Afghan
government leaders, officials like my boss who was a significant beneficiary of
the administration's largess could never publicly condemn the administration. As
one Afghan expert wistfully summed it:

> we failed because of our financial and political dependence on the Afghan
> state and international donors and their projects; if an MP complained in par-
> liament about a minister or a donor, he/she was showered with contracts and
> projects [to shut them up].

This was a moral collapse on the part of Afghan elites, whether they were in the
Karzai or Ghani administration's inner circle, or working as a public servant, civil
society, or the security sector.

As such, international military intervention and the state-building that followed
became self-defeating in its effort to build effective Afghan state institutions
and democratisation.[12] As the empirical chapters in this book underscored, the
U.S.A. and its allies sacrificed institutionalisation and democratisation, the fight
against corruption and justice for political stability and maintaining order, by
empowering and enriching patronage, strongmen, and family-based networks.
The story of the Rahmani family recounted in the previous chapter was a prime
example: as the U.S.A. in the Bagram airbase depended on Baba Jan for the
security of the base, his nephew and brother became the dominant suppliers of

oil and gas to the base. They became the most powerful people in the district and the province. The money that the commander and brother made subsequently went into the pockets of the Taliban as payment for safe passage, which in turn made the NATO military further dependent on the family for logistics. The profit made by the two brothers far outweighed any capacity-building or rule of law assistance received by the district and provincial administration. Such contracting practices may not have amounted to corruption in a strictly legal sense, but it set the rule that power and profit are derived more from operational and financial links to the U.S. military and aid money than formal economic activities.

While privately key donors criticised the consolidation of the *networked state* and its corrupt practices, publicly they had little option but to rationalise the outcome through the circulation of liberal peace discourses, legitimising the Afghan state and international state-building to maintain and justify their military engagement. The reply of a senior NATO coalition official when asked about Gul Agha Shirzai's illegal practices provides evidence of this: "We know he is corrupt. But we have to ask ourselves: Has he crossed a sufficient number of red lines that we've got to deal with it? So far, he doesn't appear to have."[13] This also reveals the double standards of Western intervention, which on the one hand claimed to be promoting liberal values and agendas and at the same time employing illiberal means to achieve their ends. Such rationales also questioned the intention and legitimacy of the war in the eyes of the Afghan people, and subsequently widened the gap between the government it was sponsoring and the general population, especially in rural Afghanistan.

These factors more broadly played an overarching role in the failure of the U.S. mission in Afghanistan and the eventual collapse of the Afghan Republic. The U.S.A. was never the committed partner it claimed to be; its objectives and strategies constantly shifted, sending confusing messages to the Afghan political class and the general population. The Afghan state and its officials, including those outside the state (e.g., civil society organisations, media, and communities), remained utterly dependent on foreign funding for their survival. Like all addicts, when in late 2020 it became apparent that the state, the Afghan army and police, and the economy was on a path towards eventual collapse and the supply of funding would be dramatically reduced, if not cut off altogether, panic set in with Afghan elites. The 2020 U.S.–Taliban deal became the watershed moment when the networked state began to eat itself.

In other words, it was international aid and military expenditures, comprising money as a "weapon system" and representing important sources of patronage for political networks that was more important for deterring political disorder and instability in the last two decades than having U.S. troops stationed in the country as a means of deterring a Taliban takeover. Evidently, the 20 years of international military interventions were built to fail like an empire of mud that when the military, political, and financial support was pulled off, it disintegrated rapidly, which exposes the nature of the intervention and its supposedly state-building efforts.

10.2 The U.S.–Taliban deal: demoralising ANDSF and undermining the already strained informal order

After 18 months of intense negotiations, led by Zalmay Khalilzad, the U.S. peace negotiator, the United States, and the Taliban reached an agreement on 29 February 2020. The U.S.A. offered an extraordinary concession: full withdrawal by May 2021, surrendering almost all its military, diplomatic, and financial leverage without any serious assurances or concessions. It also forced the Afghan government to make similar concessions, despite not only being excluded from the negotiations but also suffering the ignominy of not even signing the deal.[14] The deal was essentially a "hasty exit," which set the terms of full American troop withdrawal from Afghanistan by May 2021.[15] In exchange, the Taliban committed to not harbouring or supporting international terrorist groups in Afghanistan. However, it quickly became apparent that with the U.S.A. giving up its leverage so quickly and easily, the Taliban had little incentive to seriously negotiate with its Afghan counterparts before the U.S. exit.

The most serious impact of the U.S.–Taliban deal was that it tipped the balance of power in favour of the Taliban, undermining the overarching policy of maintaining a "hurting stalemate" between the Taliban and the Republic—a status actively favoured and lobbied for by policymakers in some embassies and international agencies. Ideally, a "mutually hurting stalemate" arises when actors in conflict feel they cannot achieve victory, that the deadlock is mutually painful, and the pain can rise sharply if nothing is done about it.[16] The argument goes that this can eventually force both sides to cease fighting and engage meaningfully in peace settlement negotiations. With international leverage (diplomatic, financial, and military) shrinking and a military exit timeline in place, it became evident that the Taliban's thinking had passed the hurting stalemate phase and that they were using delaying tactics in the intra-Afghan negotiations to wait out the American withdrawal while pushing for military advancement, if not a full takeover. By early 2021, the Taliban was in a triumphalist mood, boasting that they had defeated the U.S.A. and NATO and forced the world's premier superpower into signing an agreement with them. Thus, they began posturing as the "government-in-waiting," showing little incentive to negotiate a deal with their Afghan counterparts.

The deal and the planned withdrawal also demoralised political and security officials and hampered their ability to deter Taliban attacks. President Biden's 14 April 2021 announcement that all U.S. military forces would depart Afghanistan by the 20th anniversary of the September 11 attacks, regardless of the conditions on the ground, further emboldened the Taliban and incentivised them to increase their attacks in pursuit of a battlefield victory. Morale was further demolished as the Afghan government became incapable of supplying key military bases and checkpoints in peri-urban districts surrounding major cities—chiefly because of Afghan leadership incompetence and poor planning as well as the withdrawal of U.S.-funded logistics and maintenance contractors. In May, it was widely reported that the Afghan government was transferring cash to base commanders to purchase ammunition and weapons from the black market.

More importantly, the 2020 U.S.–Taliban deal further strained the already elusive informal order amongst political networks and the centres of power, supercharging their survivalist instincts. The Karzai era held fragile informal order, and the established rules of the games were already strained because of President Ghani's policies, which were explained in detail in Chapter 6. While Karzai tried to govern through entrenched political networks, treating them as intrinsically linked to stability and state survival, including their role as formidable spoilers, President Ghani instead did everything to humiliate and marginalise them. Disgruntled and sensing imminent downfall, especially with the drying out of international money, political network leaders began hedging their bets by reaching out to their military and social power bases while engaging with regional patron-states for future support and protection.

However, this was already too late to generate enough support among local constituencies, especially as their financial resources contracted. In addition, political networks, especially jihadi networks-turned-patronage networks, had already lost considerable political legitimacy and support over the years as they limited access to family members and a handful of loyal clients, shifting away from being broad-based political networks with access relatively open across various communities and groupings. As shown in Chapter 7, this was particularly the case after the 2018 and 2019 parliamentary and presidential elections and the ensuing power-sharing agreements. Prominent jihadi political networks within the old Wahdat, Jamiat, and Junbish had become increasingly family-based in structure and access. This was the *tragedy of political networks* in post-2001 Afghanistan, aggravated by the international money as "weapon system": political network leaders had lost their reputation and trust in the eyes of the people. In other words, as this book has shown political networks lost two of the four key power resources to survive: (1) social capital and maintaining durable ties to local communities for mobilisation, and (2) coercive military capacity—important in times of conflict and major crisis. The other two power resources are: maintain and consolidate political power within the state, and accumulate financial gains to buy loyalties. Political networks in the words of Azoy, after 2019, lost two important qualities of social capital: *haisiyat* (character) and *itibar* (credit).[17] Limiting access to extended family members and a few individuals and overplayed horse-trading within the political marketplace over the years had a major reputational cost which jeopardised their survival. They quickly lost the support of tribes and ethnic groups. In the absence of both qualities, political networks were politically bankrupt and incapable of galvanising support to defy Taliban advances. The public saw them as the political networks and President Ghani with little legitimacy worth risking their lives for.

In more "fragmented" political landscapes like Kunduz, Takhar, and Kandahar provinces, where there was no clear-cut political network that could guarantee a degree of political cohesion, subnational clients, tribal elders, and militia commanders began shifting their allegiance in favour of the Taliban. They concluded that the Taliban were likely to come out on top. This was not new. In multi-ethnic and tribally diverse provinces like Kunduz and Kandahar, with a higher degree of permeability between the government and the Taliban, militia commanders had always found space to switch sides. What we witnessed in the last days of the Republic was what Maley has described as a "cascading effect" which ultimately led to Afghanistan's rapid collapse.[18] By July 2021, over a quarter of all districts have fallen to the Taliban in less than one and half months. A month later, the Afghan Republic collapsed.[19]

10.3 A gamble or horrid intention? The ethnicisation of the security sector and collapse of central command—the case of the Ministry of Interior

Frequent changes in the security leadership in 2020 and 2021 and last-minute restructuring of security ministries weakened the effectiveness of the ANDSF as well as seriously disrupted the command-and-control structure to defend major cities.

My political economy mapping of Ministry of Interior in May–July 2021, commissioned by an EU-funded project, revealed the precariousness of the situation. In the months leading to the collapse, President Ghani, and his National Security Advisor (NSA), Hamdullah Mohib, pushed ahead with appointments of loyal clients within the security sector that favoured their ethnic Pashtuns, mostly from Ghani's ethnic Ghilzais. In May 2021, they pressed on with one of the most visible wholescale reshufflings and restructuring of the MoI, which further polarised the Afghan security forces along ethnic lines and demoralised the forces. Ghani forced Interior Minister Andarabi to resign and appointed Hayatullah Hayat in his place, an ethnic Pashtun with no experience in policing, only to be replaced in June 2021 with Abdul Sattar Mirzakwal. Hayat's appointment was politically motivated to help reshape the patronage networks inside the MoI in favour of President Ghani and his narrow inner circle, including Mohib. During his short tenure (just over two months), over 30 out of around 60 key Director-General (DG) and director-level positions within the ministry in Kabul were replaced, and subsequently, some of the departments saw significant changes in the composition, especially in Audit, the Major Crime Task Force, and Criminal Investigation Department. All of the new appointments were allies of Mohib.[20] To some, President Ghani's Pashtunisation of the MoI was seen to be driven by his calculation that the ministry could be used as a "bargaining chip" in future power-sharing settings—and most likely to be handed over to the Taliban. Later, many non-Pashtun political and security officials would accuse him of preparing the ground for an ethnic Pashtun Taliban handover, especially to his fellow Ghilzai Haqqani network. As this book has shown, the instrumentalising ethnic and tribal division was used as an effective tool to galvanise constituency support. If truly intended for the purpose of galvanising Pashtun support or preparing the ground for the Taliban takeover to save their skin, it seems this attempt backfired spectacularly for Ghani and his inner circle.

A year before the collapse, in one of the widest restructurings of MoI at the subnational level, Mohib and the first vice president had pressed for the appointment of 230 district police chiefs (out of 364 total), replacing them with the army and intelligence commanders and officials. They claimed that the goal was to disrupt corrupt criminal networks within the MoI. Many questioned the timing and the stated intentions, seeing it as an attempt by the NSC and first VP's office to consolidate their authority and power before one last effort to negotiate with the Taliban. This proved to be an ill-considered policy with serious implications for the further militarisation of the police force, seriously undermining the ability of police to counter the Taliban offensive. While it might have removed a few corrupt and incompetent police chiefs, it not only contributed to the breakdown of central command, but also detached the police from the communities they were serving in an already divided and fragile country along ethnic and tribal lines (most of the former police chiefs enjoyed close relationships with communities stretching as far back as the days of Jihad; most of them were also network clients of key political networks). The newly appointed police chiefs received little local support and by July 2021, most fallen districts were ones led by these former army commanders.

Taken together, these elements of *networked state* logic provide a more nuanced understanding of the collapse of the Republic than what has been proposed by U.S. policymakers. The apercu from Ernest Hemingway's 1926 novel *The Sun Also Rises* best sums this up: When asked, "How did you go bankrupt?" the reply was: "Two ways. Gradually, then suddenly." President Karzai and Ghani administrations, and the political networks that governed post-2001 Afghanistan, became gradually bankrupt as they lost credibility in the eyes of the public, and when international money dried up with the U.S. exit, the collapse came abruptly and swiftly.

10.4 The networked state and statehood: a summary

The empirical chapters in this book showed that post-2001 Afghan state institutions, rebuilt and re-assembled with international support, were thoroughly captured by endogenous power networks. They came to exist in the shadows of and in subordination to political networks and their associates. As Chapters 3 and 4 demonstrated, once the empowered political networks held different parts of the Afghan state as *safe positions*, they began circumscribing access and privileges, as well as resources—political, social, financial (domestic and international, licit, and illicit), and military—for their members and the communities they claimed to represent. The state and political networks became essentially indistinguishable from one another; the empowered networks masqueraded as the state. This is not to say that state institutions and community structures were irrelevant, but they were made less meaningful as the result of competition for power, conflict, and compromise between rival political networks, their day-to-day practices, and the rules of the game in which they operated. The post-2001 state was thus constituted as a state by its accumulation of informal exchange and international financial and discursive support, as shown in Chapters 6, 7, and 8. In this way, political networks formed an internationally supported government which operated as a state in a system of patronage, rent, and illegality. The Afghan state provided a framework for inter-network competition, compromise, and accommodation made manifest in identity-based divisions, patron–client relations, coercion, and the expropriation of public resources for personal gain. Indeed, the state itself exacerbated this problem as it provided the primary incentive structure for inter-network competition. The subsequent instrumentalisation of identity-based divisions became sources of power for political networks, and a mask to conceal their illegality and corrupt practices on a day-to-day basis.

I have demonstrated that these networks mutually reinforced several important *network practices* (or rules of the game) such as patron–client relationships, rent-seeking, and instrumentalisation of identities, which became essential to political network survival. Thus, the nature of international state-building in contemporary Afghanistan contained multiple layers of contradiction—often deliberate—and conflicting national and international objectives, "progressing" to build a schismatic state rooted in political networks while fostering profiteering and opportunism for those in possession of it. Despite continued violence and disruption in the countryside, including an active insurgency from 2004 onwards, informal order emerged, or at least the façade of it, increasingly in major urban centres. However, with the re-emergence of the Taliban and their domination of the countryside from 2014 and loss of territory to them, most pro-government clients, including militia commanders, relocated to provincial capitals or peri-urban districts. The shrinking geographical space and access to resources as the result of President Ghani's policies after 2014 to some degree destabilised President Karzai era established rules of the games and recognised power dynamics, and as a result, further reduced historically powerful jihadi political networks into family-based networks desperate to survive under difficult circumstances.

Chapter 3 revealed that the consolidation of a *networked state* was historically and sociologically grounded in Afghanistan's modern state formation and therefore not a new feature of Afghan politics and statehood. The state and political networks (be they tribal, clan-based, family-based, or modern organisational structures) have been mutually constitutive throughout Afghanistan's modern state formation. The founder of the Durrani Kingdom established the foundation of a *networked state* that his successors built upon and further expanded. The post-2001 state-building efforts were not divorced from this earlier tradition of statehood and the state was transformed around key political networks and centres of power that came to compose the state regime. As before, the state functioned like a *distarkhan* (tablecloth): large, expansive, and the most inclusive of major political networks and centres of power. While President Karzai kept access open to most actors, including his political rivals, by performing like a *Khan*, his successor president Ghani reduced access to a handful of elites and groups, alienating others and contributing to the collapse of the Republic in August 2021.

Post-2001 Afghanistan, as constructed at the Bonn Conference by the international community, primarily the U.S.A., was unique, however, in that it emerged as a politically consensual framework in the form of a *networked state* where the needs and interests of political networks were accommodated but not the needs of the public. The *networked state* intertwined political networks and their clientele at all levels in a complex interdependency of resources where financial, political, social, and coercive powers were distributed across the state in a Byzantine system of bargains—both top-down and bottom-up. While the alliance-patron depended on the support of network leaders, these leaders relied on the backing of their local and regional clientele to mobilise support and exercise a degree of control over the collection and allocation of resources. This relationship was reciprocal and mutual. The resource bargaining between the alliance-patron and political network leaders ensured the distribution of power and wealth resources among the network clients at the local and regional levels. Provincial and district authorities depended on the support of their network leader for protection and often channelled resources upwards to their patrons to protect and maintain their position and privilege. They often shaped, nudged, persuaded, and in some cases dictated policies and strategies to their patrons. The outcome was unruly but nonetheless provided a framework for resource flows that constituted the post-2001 state and helped maintain its informal order and survival. It also helped limit violence, at least at the national level within a tacitly agreed upon institutional setting, while a degree of violence over control of local administrations and resources continued in the countryside. This produced a mixed picture in which political stability at the macro-level (national) was ensured while a *managed* level of political instability and violence at the micro-level (provincial and district) was encouraged, benefitting all parties, including the Taliban. Violence and competition over key strategic state resources in the periphery were managed to ensure it did not translate into all-out conflict and war between groups within mutually understood and well-functioning rules of the game. Thus, political networks were successful in projecting the façade of political order, at least at the national level.

At the subnational level, political networks, especially strongmen networks and their militias, made themselves indispensable to post-2001 Afghan politics and the international community because of their control over resource flows and readily available access to violence, including clients in the Afghanistan National Defence and Security Forces. The environment that facilitated their activities, however, was the product of international military strategy, which adopted "money as a weapon system," thereby sustaining the addictions of the Afghan state, political networks, and their elites. Money was the drug that kept Afghanistan's networks performing the democratic dance for the international community, even as democratic institutions were transformed into mere props.

10.5 Informal order and state survival: its relevance and applicability

The goal of this book was to show how the nuts and bolts of a *limited-access order* and its emerging state work on a day-to-day basis and thus contribute to a broader understanding of political order and state transformation. The empirical chapters showed that for a political network to survive, it must perform at least two of the following functions:

- Co-opt or eliminate rivals to consolidate power
- Accumulate wealth for rent distribution
- Maintain strong ties with local communities to strengthen a constituency power base
- Amass the capacity and resources to coerce and intimidate.

In Afghanistan, these functions were achieved through network practices of patron–client relations, rent-seeking, manipulation of identity-based divisions, and intimidation and violence. The empirical evidence suggests that the ability of political networks to achieve these functions varied. Although Karzai and his network enjoyed an expansive patronage system and accumulated significant wealth and power, he lacked a strong link with any ethnic constituency—except maybe his Popalzai tribe in the south through his brother. Thus, during the presidential elections of 2009 and 2014, he had to purchase constituency support and votes by relying on vote bank political networks such as Junbish-i-Islami and Wahdat-i-Mardom led by Abdul Rashid Dostum and Mohammad Mohaqqiq. As shown in Chapter 8, the failure of Karzai and his networked associates in 2010 to unseat the 62 sitting MPs despite being the top player in the system demonstrated his dependency on ethno-regional, patronage, and family-based networks. Political network leaders were able to deliver a strong message to Karzai and his team that their power rests largely on their support, despite enjoying international legitimacy as the head of state and as a patron with control over the distribution of state funds (Figure 10.1).

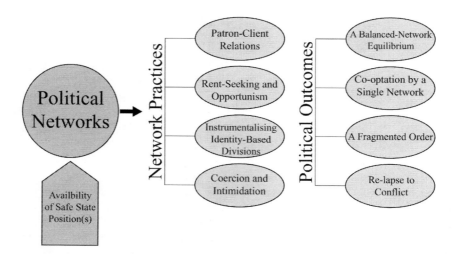

Figure 10.1 Informal order and political outcomes.

The experience of Afghanistan reveals that in terms of political order and state survival in conflict and post-conflict settings—particularly relevant once the international military withdraws from the host country—we are likely to see four different potential outcomes: (1) a balanced network equilibrium; (2) co-optation by the dominant network (the emergence of a regime); (3) a fragmented authority; and (4) relapse into an anarchic civil war.

As the experience of post-2001 Afghanistan, including its modern history of state formation, demonstrates, the ideal outcome that would benefit all political networks is collaboration and the creation of a *balanced network equilibrium*, where each political network respects the other's spheres of influence and relies on other's power resources for survival. This is aligned with Douglas North's framing of limited-access order where elites establish a coalition through which they limit access to privileges of the empowered political networks, thereby creating incentives for cooperation rather than trying to outmanoeuvre each other. The logic is simple: violence reduces political rents, especially international aid. This also fits with the logic of game theory: cooperation will produce outcomes that are more favourable to parties involved than when parties compete.[21] Collaboration is perceived as the management of differences between competing networks or a continuous "negotiating process" between them over key policies, objectives, and strategies within the state.[22] Agranoff and McGuire suggest that network collaboration raises the potential for more rational decision-making.[23] Operating within a *networked state* in which a balanced network equilibrium was the dominant outcome from 2001 to 2014, political networks demonstrated a degree of discretion and flexibility over key decision-making processes and goals, maintaining the established balance with the understanding that not doing so was likely to harm their interests.

During his two terms in office, President Karzai was successful in maintaining a relatively balanced equilibrium among competing political networks and centres of power both in terms of sharing power and dispensing international funds. He saw himself primarily as the patron-in-charge, a traditional Khan, whose principal responsibility was ensuring the functioning of the rules of the game to guarantee political stability. And it seems that most of the major political groups accepted the established status quo, showing no serious intention to destroy the established order. While every single presidential election post-2001 was challenged, there was never a serious fear that political alliances would go so far as to destabilise the system. In the established power equilibrium, political networks became more entrenched and respectful of each other's spheres of influence and their power resource interdependencies. Indeed, the fact that Afghanistan's only two presidents post-2001—Hamed Karzai, who was imposed by the Americans at the Bonn conference, and Ashraf Ghani, who emerged because of Karzai's support—faced no serious political contenders outside the jihadi networks is telling of the rigidity and exclusivity of the established system.

When collaboration fails, the next best outcome in a conflict-driven or post-conflict state-building where there is an asymmetry of power resources is the establishment of a *hegemonic regime-state network*, often in the form of a hegemonic authoritarian regime. As has been noted by Abdulkader Sinno, co-optation is a strategy employed by a more powerful party to offer positive sanctions to key members of other threatening networks in return for accepting the norms of interaction desired by the dominant party.[24] The empirical chapters in this book uncover the astonishing amount of bargaining to purchase loyalties within an environment of multiple alternative networks. However, as Piattoni reminds us, the best resource buyer in a patron–client network is usually a political actor with access to government resources, most often the incumbent authority.[25] Once the power of one individual network exceeds the power of all political networks combined, the emergence of a regime becomes imminent. In post-2001 Afghanistan, President Karzai and his associates, in government twice, (2002 to early 2005 and then from 2009 to 2010) tried unsuccessfully to consolidate their grip over the Afghan state and possibly to move towards establishing a single-networked regime-state at the expense of others through a combination of repression and co-optation strategies. However, both times they had to back down, faced with powerful ethno-regional strongmen networks who controlled vast political, military, financial, and social resources and under international pressure. As Chapter 8 detailed, Karzai was quick to appease ethno-regional networks and their clients in the Lower House following his failed attempt to unseat 62 sitting MPs in 2010.

The experience of Afghanistan showed that international intervention and state-building fashions a *networked state* which is fragmented and dispersed. The immediate post-2001 intervention in Afghanistan resembled a *fragmented order* in which regional strongmen networks exerted their independence, barely acknowledging Kabul's authority. International intervention produced fragmentation in which the Afghan state was divided into several competing authorities with their own administrations, army, police, and fiscal policies—the third political outcome in conflict and post-conflict settings. In Afghanistan, this did produce a degree of political order, but violence was significantly high with competing strongmen and their militias over control of territory and resources in the provinces. The power dynamics under President Ghani and National Unity Government from 2014 onward was another form of a moderately fragmented order in which the state was divided into two rigid political camps, which undermined the logic of a networked state with little room for compromise.

The final and worst political outcome is the *relapse into an anarchic civil war*. This happens when political network distrust reaches a level that leaves no room for collaboration, when there is no dominant network that could co-opt opponents and when the international military exits without establishing some kind of external deterrent against total collapse. This was the case in post-1992 Afghanistan following the collapse of the Soviet-backed regime. In the post-August 2021 Taliban takeover, we have not yet seen inter-network conflict in the absence of a serious threat against the Taliban; however, if the economic situation worsens and the dominant groups within the Taliban in Kabul try to centralise power in the next few months, we are likely to see fraction and internal conflict within the Taliban-networked groupings.

These political outcomes arguably could be applied to other conflict-driven and post-conflict countries that have either experienced international intervention and state-building or externally mediated power-sharing agreements. Post-conflict states like post-1991 Cambodia, post-2003 Iraq, post-1999 Tajikistan, and Post-2000 Kosovo are excellent cases where competing political groups have managed to constitute a complex peace, which has gradually become more authoritarian and controlled by a single dominant network. In Iraq, it was president Nouri al-Maliki (2006–2014) who tried to build an extensive political network with the help of Iran-backed Shia militias, moving towards dictatorship, until he fell out of favour.[26] In Tajikistan, Emomali Rahman and his vassals have emerged as the hegemonic force from 2005.[27] In Cambodia, Hun Sen's ruling coalition, beginning in 1979, established dominance over rival networks within the Cambodian People's Party, and after the 2015 death of Chea Sim, the head of a rival faction paved the way to the transition to hegemonic authoritarianism in 2018.[28] Both of these political outcomes tend to produce political stability and subsequently state survival, even though in most cases this is achieved with a significant degree of violence.

The collapse of the Soviet Union in Tajikistan in 1991–1993 produced a fragmented order and a brief but bloody civil war. Post-Gaddafi Libya emerged as a fragmented order with several competing strongmen controlling different parts of the country with the backing of external players, both regional and international. Post-1992 Afghanistan and current Somalia are also examples of such situations, the eventual outcome of which is state collapse and conflict.

10.6 Theoretical considerations for understanding state and international state-building

One must of course always be wary of drawing broad generalisations from a single case study. This book has attempted to show how specific features of the Afghan state and society interacted with an internationally managed state-building project to produce a fragmented political order premised on the logic of networked governance. The contours of the Afghan state are specific to Afghanistan. It is, however, worth exploring the broader theoretical contributions of this study to how we understand the state, state formation, and international state-building.

The first and foremost assumption that must be interrogated is that international state-building in fragile and post-conflict contexts like Afghanistan produces a *unitary* state, or more specifically a politically and vertically organised and all-encompassing entity. What was fashioned in Afghanistan was a *networked state* that was fragmented and diverse in nature, where power was assembled and flowed through endogenous political networks in power resource interdependencies. Formal state institutions and structures were constituted by informal political networks and functioned under their shadow. Thus, as argued in the introduction of this book, employing a political network approach to the study of state and international state-building helps us shift our conceptual focus from the institutional and structural effect to the informal *networked character* of the state and international state-building. Furthermore, seeing the state as *multiple* and *networked* helps us to go beyond the empirical categorisation of the state as either "weak," "strong," "fragmented," or "failed." In Afghanistan, the state has been characterised variably as "weak central power but strong local powers" or "strong at the centre but weak at the local."[29] These categorisations are misleading. As the example of the post-2001 Afghan state shows, post-conflict states are both weak and unstable according to the empirical definitions of statehood—exercising weak autonomy and authority and exhibiting feeble capacities to provide basic services to citizens—and relatively strong and stable in their effects on everyday life. This is not a paradoxical situation if we use a network lens to understand statehood and international state-building. As Reeves has noted about the Central Asian Fergana valley, "these paradoxes and puzzles [of state weakness] arise from an initial assumption that the state 'ought', in both normative and descriptive senses, to be singular rather than multiple entities."[30] And similarly as Agnew asserted, once the concept of the state is freed from the "territorial trap," we can see that international intervention generates a complex networked state rather than the ideal of a vertically organised and territorially encompassing sovereign entity.[31]

Second, the Afghanistan case suggests that we need to shift our focus from the behavioural aspect of state-building to the daily *performance* of the actors that constitute the state. Afghanistan's political networks came to masquerade as the state, producing the impression of an organisation that is singular and vertical. Political networks within the state were effective in portraying themselves as the state through symbolic and material images manifested through the organisation of social and political spaces, which bestowed upon them the necessary domestic and international legitimacy. It also enabled them to naturalise their authority and represent themselves as superior to the formal institutions and structures of the state. However, as the day-to-day functioning of the post-2001 state demonstrated, the state does not stand apart from or in opposition to society; rather it is intertwined and embedded in it. This is in line with recent anthropological studies of the state in Central Asia that question the nature of spatiality and argue that we investigate the "everyday" performance of actors to understand statehood and governance.[32] And as shown in the empirical chapters, political order and state survival are best understood in the everyday *practices* and *performances* of political networks and their power dynamics within the state and society.

Third, we ought to pay more attention to the *co-constitutive* and *networked mode of governance* of international state-building. As marginally shown here, international state-building creates interdependencies with a small group of local networked elites in reassembling and transforming the state. International military engagement, aid, and development projects connect a diverse group of actors in a global assemblage of existence which bind together drug traffickers, private security firms, international contractors, military commanders, customs officials, criminals, and even insurgents in a complex system of interdependencies and flows of resources. Although this book touched on these features, a more systematic account of the co-constitutive power dynamics of international-local relations is yet to be produced with a particular focus on the *network character* of state-building.

10.7 The end of an era: uncertainty and instability

An era ended on 15 August 2021 with President Ghani's sudden departure from Afghanistan. The Commander-in-Chief fled the country during its hour of need, ceding power to the Taliban[33] and leaving behind most of his cabinet and close allies, including Sarwar Danesh, the second vice president, Matin Bek, his Chief of Staff, Salam Rahimi, his confidante, former Chief of Staff, Hanif Atmar, his Foreign Minister, and Ajmal Ahmadi, the Central Bank Chief. On the heels of Ghani's departure, a delegation of high-profile politicians, including Ahmad Zia Masoud, the former first vice president, Rahman Rahmani, the Head of Lower House, Mohammad Mohaqqiq, and Yunos Qanooni left on a chartered flight for Islamabad, just before the airport was overrun by desperate Afghans. Ajmal Ahmadi's tweets summed up the mood: "disorienting and difficult to comprehend … it did not have to end this way. I am disgusted by the lack of any planning by Afghan leadership. I cannot forgive him [Ghani] for creating that without a transition plan."[34] In the last NSC Council meeting a day before the fall, it became evident that most of Kabul's police chiefs had abandoned their posts, leaving the city almost unguarded. It's difficult to know what was going through Ghani's head in that meeting but one can imagine a degree of paranoia setting in: after years of being fed false information, the realisation must have dawned on the president that his power, which he thought was unassailable, was crumbling around him. His ministers, who had up until then been deferential, were now openly criticising him for his failures. A week after his escape, his team issued a letter briefly explaining and justifying his last-minute, humiliating departure. The feeble face-saving attempt failed. The world was shocked by Ghani's lack of empathy for his fellow citizens as the chaotic scenes at the Kabul airport unfolded. As one commentator put it: "[He] remembered to mention his valuable sandals, pyjamas, laptop, notebooks, and books, but forgot to say even a word about the tragic fate of his compatriots."

But to lay the entirety of blame at the feet of Ashraf Ghani would be vastly understating the breath-taking extent of culpability. As this book has demonstrated, the collapse of the post-2001 Afghan state was made all the more likely the moment U.S. negotiators muscled through a governing system in Afghanistan at the 2001 Bonn Conference which served their interests, not the interests of the Afghan people. That original sin precipitated much of what followed and led ultimately to another moment of state collapse in Afghanistan's long history of vicious cycles of collapse.

The present moment, however, should not be seen as a mere repeat of history. The Taliban now face the challenges of governing a country and society that has changed significantly since they were last in power in the 1990s. The newly installed regime in Kabul has remained authoritarian and extremist, suppressing basic human rights, particularly for women and girls and religious minorities. The caretaker government, announced in September, was all male, almost entirely Pashtun (32 out of 34 ministers), and all clerical, a major setback to those hoping for a more inclusive government reflecting Afghanistan's complex social and geographical realities. The primary goal of the new caretaker government composition was clearly designed to ensure internal cohesion rather than international legitimacy.[35] However, if one applies the logic of the *networked state*, the Taliban government is unlikely to last long, especially if the structure of the state remains centralised in Kabul, further marginalising diverse ethnic groups and tribal and community structures from key decision-making processes and political representations. We are likely to see a fragmentation of order and possibly a civil war, the worst of the outcomes outlined above. The Taliban lack a conceptualisation of the state in terms of its functions and what it is supposed to do, in part because of its own lack of competencies and in part because of the failure of the Bonn agreement to codify a cohesive system of governance.

In the absence of a modern governing framework, civic and political rights have been significantly shrunk, especially for women. Vulnerable groups like ethnic Hazaras, who have long been persecuted, have faced forced displacement in several provinces, systematic discrimination, and mass killings since the Taliban takeover. The Taliban have struggled to provide basic services to the Afghan people. The country is facing its worst "humanitarian catastrophe" in its history, with the Taliban focusing on further restricting women from public spaces rather than addressing humanitarian and economic challenges.

After two decades of international engagement and development, Afghanistan remains one of the poorest, most violent, and most corrupt countries in the world. Even before the Taliban takeover, the poverty rate stood at 47.5% and the country faced a humanitarian catastrophe.[36] In August 2021, the World Food Program calculated that 14 million Afghans were on the brink of starvation.[37] United Nations Secretary-General, Antonio Guterres, reiterated on August 30 his "grave concern at the deepening humanitarian and economic crisis" in Afghanistan, warning that food stocks could run out by the end of the month.[38] And in September 2021, the United Nations Development Programme (UNDP) warned that 97% of Afghans could plunge into poverty by mid-2022.[39]

At the international and regional levels, the U.S.'s humiliating defeat in Afghanistan sent a strong signal to other jihadi groups across the world and international terrorists that the world's superpower could be defeated if they remain patient and true to the cause. Afghanistan is likely to emerge once again as a "regional security complex" in which its neighbours, in particular Pakistan, Iran, India, Russia, and Central Asian Republics, start supporting their clients against others. Thus, the ripple effects of the failure to create a stable Afghanistan will continue to be felt globally for the foreseeable future.

Notes

1 In the chaotic evacuation following the collapse of Kabul city, the Americans had flown out over 115,000—one-third being families and relatives of the notorious Khost Protection Force (KPF) who were called in at the last minute to safeguard the outer perimeter of the Kabul airport. The KPF was a clandestine Afghan force operating as part of the covert operations of the Central Intelligence Agency (CIA), involved in grave abuses and extrajudicial killings of innocent people. The Human Rights Watch

2019 did a damning report on their operations in 2019, titled, "They have shot many like this."

2 According to SIGAR, the original estimated price was $48.7 million, and it was to be completed in 18 months. The eventual cost was $154.7 million, or more than three times the original estimated cost and it took five years to complete. See SIGAR February 2016 report titled "Afghan Ministry of Defense Headquarters: $154.7 Million Building Appears Well Built but Has Several Construction Issues that Should Be Assessed," SIGAR 16-16 Inspection Report, February 2016.

3 "Quarterly Report to the United States Congress," SIGAR Quarterly Report, July 30, 2020, 4.

4 John Allen, testimony before the U.S. Senate Foreign Relations Subcommittee on Near Eastern and South and Central Asian Affairs, hearing on "A Transformation: Afghanistan Beyond 2014," April 30, 2014, 28.

5 Several accounts so far have detailed a last-minute deal between the Taliban in Doha and Ghani's administration in which both sides would declare a two-week ceasefire in exchange for Ghani's resignation. Some of the former government officials have pointed to Ghani and his NSC's treachery, corruption, and delusions resulting in the sabotaging of last-minute talks with the Taliban. They have noted that as a radical Ghilzai Pashtun, Ghani couldn't bear the thought of handing over power to Kandahari Durranis or the thought of giving the transition of power to Abdullah Abdullah and former president Karzai, his rivals. Some of Ghani's supporters, on the other hand, note that Ghani was strategic in his decision to hand over Kabul to the Haqqani network to carve division within them for future use. Only history will tell us the reason for his escape and the content of the last-minute deals. What is evident is that historically, no military force in Afghanistan has ever committed to negotiating over a prize so valuable as the control of Kabul city, and therefore one must not overplay this. Certainly, Zalmay Khalilzad was quick to sell this as a last attempt to save the Afghan Republic and to get himself off the hook. See for instance, Kabul's collapse followed a string of intel failures, defence officials say, https://www.politico.com/news/2021/08/16/kabul-afghanistan-collapse -intel-failures-505101.

6 "Annual Threat Assessment of the US Intelligence Community," Office of the Directorate of National Intelligence, April 9, 2021.

7 Losey (2021).

8 Berger (2021).

9 Ryan and DeYoung (2021).

10 See *Warlord, Inc.: Extortion and Corruption along the U.S. Supply Chain in Afghanistan* (2010), Report was prepared by the Majority staff of the Subcommittee on National Security and Foreign Affairs of the Committee on Oversight and Government Reform.

11 Farahi and Guggenheim (2020).

12 See Aikins (2010).

13 Hodge (2012).

14 The Afghan government was pressured to release over 5,000 Taliban prisoners – ten days after the signing of the deal. The prisoner exchange created an immediate dispute. The Taliban insisted on getting 5,000 of their colleagues released, and 5,000 whom they alone would choose. The Afghan government, not a signatory to the document, argued that the agreement said "up to 5,000," a ceiling, and that it was up to the Afghan government who to let go. After months of disputes and under immense pressure from the Americans, the Kabul government released over 5,000 prisoners amongst them some notorious drug traffickers that the Americans had captured including the drug kingpin, Governor Noorzai, and a number of terrorists that were involved in the killing of French and Australian citizens. See Sediqi (2020).

15 See Miller (2021); Duffy (2021); Haqqani (2019); Maley (2021).

16 For the literature on "hurting stalemate" see Zartman (1989 and 2009); Lilja (2011); and Pruitt (2007).
17 Azoy (1982).
18 For details see Maley (2021).
19 See Clark and Ali (2021).
20 This draws on a private study commissioned by GiZ in May–July 2021 and written by the author.
21 See Axelrod (2006).
22 See Williams (2002: 115) and Bardach (1998: 232).
23 Agranoff and McGuire (2007: 157).
24 Sinno (2008: 55)
25 Piattoni (2001).
26 See Dodge (2012).
27 Heathershaw (2011)
28 Cock (2010); Loughlin (2021); Norén-Nilsson (2016).
29 See Saikal (2006); Weiner and Banuazizi (1994).
30 See Reeves (2007: 11).
31 On territorial trap see Agnew (1994).
32 See Reeve (2007); Collins (2002); Schatz (2004).
33 The last picture of President Ghani taken in Afghanistan before his escape is revealing. He was sitting in his residence's garden, known as Palace One, reading a book—maybe the last remedy to calm his nerves. Three helicopters were waiting nearby in the Palace compound, ready to fly him, his wife, NSA Moheb, and AOP chief Fazl Fazli out. This was while the defence minister was told the president would be visiting the ministry.
34 Ajmal Ahmady tweet.
35 Bijlert (2021).
36 The World Bank. 2021. "Afghanistan Development Updates April 2021: Setting Course to Recovery," April 2021. *UN News*, September 1, 2021.
37 Duncan and Clark (2021).
38 "UN Chief Warns of 'Humanitarian Catastrophe' in Afghanistan." *Aljazeera*, August 31, 2021.
39 UNDP. 2021. "97 Percent of Afghans Could Plunge into Poverty by Mid-2022." UNDP, September 9, 2021.

Bibliography

Adamec, L. W. 2005. *Historical Dictionary of Afghan Wars, Revolutions, and Insurgencies*, 2nd edition. Lanham: Rowman & Littlefielld.

Adili, A. 2020. *End of the Post-Election Impasse? Ghani and Abdullah's New Power-Sharing Formula*. Kabul: Afghanistan Analyst Network. May 20, 2020.

Adili, A. 2020. *Afghanistan's 2019 Elections: (29): A Statistical Overview of the Preliminary Results*. Kabul: Afghanistan Analyst Network. February 8, 2020.

Adili, A., J. Bjelica, and T. Ruttig. 2019. *Afghanistan's 2019 Election (20): Even Lower Turnout Figures*. Kabul: Afghanistan Analyst Network. October 22, 2019.

Adili, A., and L. Linke. 2016. *The Politics of Opposition: A Challenge to the National Unity Government?* Kabul: Afghanistan Analyst Network. October 27, 2016.

Afghanistan: Forces Links to Vice President Terrorize Villagers. 2016. New York: Human Rights Watch. July 31, 2016.

Ahmad, A. 2014. "Afghan Candidate Stops Short of Forming Government." *New York Times*, July 8, 2014.

Ahmadzai, A. 2014. *Impartiality Critical to Ensuring Afghanistan's Election Credibility*. Kabul: The Asia Foundation. April 2014.

Ahram, A. I., and C. King. 2012. "The Warlord as Arbitrageur." *Theory and Society* 41: 169–86.

Agnew, J. 1994. "The Territorial Trap: The Geographical Assumptions of International Relations Theory." *Review of International Political Economy* 1 (1): 53–80.

Agranoff, R., and M. McGuire. 1997. "Multi-Network Management: Collaboration and the Hollow State in Local Economic Policy." Unpublished manuscript, School of Public & Environmental Affairs. Bloomington, IN: Indiana University.

Agranoff, R., and M. McGuire. 2003. *Collaborative Public Management: New Strategies for Local Governments*. Washington, DC: Georgetown University Press.

Agranoff, R., and M. McGuire. 2007. *Managing within Networks: Adding Values to Public Organizations*. Washington, DC: Georgetown University Press.

Aikins, M. 2010. "Last Man in Kandahar." *The Walrus*, December 12, 2010.

Alger, C. F. 2005. "Expanding Involvement of NGOs in Emerging Global Governance." In *Subcontracting Peace: The Challenge of NGO Peacebuilding*, edited by O. P. Richmond, and H. F. Carey. Aldershot: Ashgate Publishing, 3–18.

Allina-Pisano, J. 2009. "How to Tell an Axe Murderer: An Essay on Ethnography, Truth and Lies." In *Political Ethnography: What Immersion Contributes to the Study of Power*, edited by E. Schatz. Chicago, IL: University of Chicago Press, 53–73.

Alter, C., and H. Hage. 1993. *Organizations Working Together*. Newbury Park, California: SAGE.

Anderson, M. B. 1990. *Do No Harm: How Aid Can Support Peace-or War*. London: Lynne Rienner.

Anderson, J. L. 2005. "The Man in the Palace." *The New Yorker*, May 30, 2005.

Anderson, S. A. 2010. "The Enforcement Approach to Coercion." *Journal of Ethics & Social Philosophy* 5 (1):1–31.

Ardant, D. P. 2013. *Battle Studies: Ancient and Modern Battle*. Lavergne, TN: Forgotten Books.

Arnold, A. 1985. *Afghanistan: The Soviet Invasion in Perspective*. Stanford, California: Hoover Institution Press.

Arnold, A. 1994. "The Ephemeral Elites." In *The Politics of Social Transformation in Afghanistan, Iran and Pakistan*, edited by M. Weiner, and A. Banuazizi. New York: Syracuse University Press, 35–71.

Astill, J. 2004. "Civil War Fear as Afghan City Falls to Warlord." *The Guardian*, April 9, 2004.

Autesserre, S. 2010. *The Trouble with the Congo: Local Violence and the Failure of International Peacebuilding*. Cambridge: Cambridge University Press.

Axelrod, R. 2006. *The Evolution of Cooperation: Revised Edition*. London: Basic Books.

Aziz, M., and M. Harooni. 2014. "U.S. Warns Afghans not to Form Parallel Government." *Reuters*, July 8, 2014.

Azoy, G. W. 1982. *Buzkashi: Game and Power in Afghanistan*. Philadelphia, PA: University of Pennsylvania Press.

Baldauf, S. 2004. "Afghans Vote, Ready or Not." *Christian Science Monitor*, October 8, 2004.

Bacon, E. E. 1958. *Obok: A Study of Social Structure in Euroasia*. New York: Wenner-Gren Foundation for Anthropological Research.

Bader, H. R., C. Hanna, C. Douglas, and J. D. Fox. 2013. "Illegal Timber Exploitation and Counterinsurgency Operations in Kunar Province of Afghanistan: A Case Study Describing the Nexus among Insurgents, Criminal Cartels, and Communities within the Forest Sector." *Journal of Sustainable Forestry* 32 (4): 329–53.

Baiza, Y. 2013. *Education in Afghanistan: Development, Influences and Legacies since 1901*. London: Routledge.

Banks, M. 1987. "Four Conception of Peace." In *Conflict Management and Problem Solving: Interpersonal to International Applications*, edited by J. D. Sandole, and I. Sandole-Staroste. London: F. Pinter, 259–274.

Barabasi, A.-L. 2003. *Linked: How Everything is Connected to Everything Else and What it Means*. New York: Plume.

Barber, B. 1983. *The Logic and Limit of Trust*. New Brunswick: Rutgers University Press.

Bardach, E. 1998. *Getting Agencies to Work Together*. Washington, DC: Brooking Institute Press.

Barfield, T. 1990. "Tribe and State Relations: The Inner Asian Perspective." In *Tribes and State Formation in the Middle East*, edited by P. Khoury, and J. Kostiner. Berkeley, CA: University of California Press, 153–82.

Barfield, T. 2012. *Afghanistan: A Cultural and Political History*. Princeton, NJ: Princeton University Press.

Barkey, K., and S. Parikh. 1991. "Comparative Respective on the State." *Annual Review of Sociology* 17: 523–49.

Barnes, J. A. 1972. "Social Networks." *Addison-Wesley Module in Anthropology* 26: 1–29.

Barnes, C. 2005. "Weaving the Web: Civil Society Roles in Working with Conflict and Building Peace." In *People Building Peace 2, Successful Stories of Civil Society*, edited by P. van Tongeren M. Brenk, M. Hellema, and J. Verhoeven, 7–24. London: Lynne Rienner.

Barnett, M., and C.Zurcher. 2009. "'The Peacebuilder's Contract: How External Statebuilding Reinforces Weak Statehood'." In *The Dilemmas of Statebuilding: Confronting the Contradictions of Postwar Peace Operations*, edited by Roland Paris and Timothy D. Sisk, 37–66. London: Routledge, 23–52.

Barth, F. 1969. "Pathan Identity and Its Maintenance." In *Ethnic Groups and Boundaries: The Social Organization of Cultural Difference*, edited by F. Barth. Boston, MA: Little, Brown & Co, 9-38.

"The Inauguration of the Anti-Corruption Justice Center in Afghanistan". 2016. BBC June 30, 2016.

BBC Exclusive Interview with Hamid Karzai (translation). 2016. BBC Persian. January, 2016.

Beath, A., F. Christia, and R. Enikolopov. 2015. "The National Solidarity Program: Assessing the Effects of Community-Driven Development in Afghanistan." *Policy Research Working Paper* No. 7415. Washington, DC: World Bank.

Beaumont, P. 2002. "US Pulls Out Karzai's Military Bodyguards." *The Guardian*, November 24, 2002.

Begzad, M. 2020. "Poshte Parde-e Tayinat dar Gomrokat: Nesfe Mamuran ba Zor 47 Nomayand-e Majles Tayeen Shodand." *Hashte Subh*, September 27, 2020.

Beissinger, M. 2002. *Nationalist Mobilization and the Collapse of the Soviet State*. Cambridge: Cambridge University Press.

Bellamy, A. J., and P. D. Williams. 2011. *International Peacekeeping*. Cambridge: Polity.

Belloni, R. 2001. "Civil Society and Peacebuilding in Bosnia-Herzegovina." *Journal of Peace Research* 38 (3): 163–80.

Berdal, M. 2009. *Building Peace After War*. London: International Institute for Strategic Studies.

Berger, J. 2021. "The Afghanistan Papers Review: Superb Expose of a War Built on Lies." *The Guardian*, September 5, 2021.

Bethany, M. 2015. "The Failed Pilot Test: Kunduz' Local Governance Crisis." June 5, 2015.Kabul: Afghanistan Analysts Network.

Beugelsdijk, S., and S. Smulders. 2003. "'Bridging and Bonding Social Capital: Which Type is Good for Economic Growth?'." In *The Cultural Diversity of European Unity*, edited by W. Arts, J. Hagenaars, and L. Halman, Leiden: Brill, 275–310.

Bevir, M., and R. A. W. Rhodes. 2004. *Interpreting British Governance*. London: Routledge.

Bezhan, F. 2013. "The Emergence of Political Parties and Political Dynamics in Afghanistan 1964–73." *Iranian Studies* 46 (6): 921–41.

Bhatia, M. 2007. *Afghanistan, Armed Groups, Disarmament and Security in a Post-War Society*. London: Routledge.

Bhatia, M., and M. Sedra. 2008. *Afghanistan, Arms and Conflict*. London: Routledge.

Bijlert, M. 2009a. *How to Win an Afghan Election: Perceptions and Practices*. Afghanistan Analyst Network.

Bijlert, M. 2009b. *The Cabinet List*. Kabul: Afghanistan Analyst Network. December 24, 2009.

Bijlert, M. 2011a. *A New Result for the Parliamentary Election?* Kabul: Afghanistan Analyst Network.

Bijlert, M. 2011b. *Untangling Afghanistan's 2010 Vote: Analysing the Electoral Data*. Kabul: Afghanistan Analyst Network.

Bijlert, M. V. 2011c. *The Kabul Bank Investigations: Central Bank Gives Names and Figures*. Kabul: Afghanistan Analyst Network.

Bijlert, M. 2011a. "Untangling Afghanistan's 2010 Vote: Analysing the Electoral Data." *Briefing Paper* (3). Kabul: Afghanistan Analyst Network.

Bijlert, M. 2011b. *A New Result for the Parliamentary Election?* Kabul: Afghanistan Analyst Network. August 21, 2011.

Bilert, M. 2014. *Elections 2014: Final Results' Timeline Trumps Transparency.* Kabul: Afghanistan Analyst Network.

Bijlert, M. 2016. *Afghanistan's National Unity Government Rift (2): The Problems That Will Not Go Away.* Kabul: Afghanistan Nanalyst Network. September 6, 2016.

Bijlert, M. 2021. *The Focus of the Taleban's New Government: Internal Cohesion, External Dominance.* Kabul: Afghanistan Analyst Network. September 12, 2021.

Billiet, J., and B. Cambre. 1999. "'Social Capital, Active Membership in Voluntary Associations and Some Aspects of Political Participation'." In *Social Capital and European Democracy,* edited by J. Van Deth, M. Maraffi, K. Newton, and P. Whiteley. London: Routledge, 240–62.

Bizhan, N. 2017. *Aid Paradoxes in Afghanistan.* London: Routledge.

Bjelica, J., and T. Ruttig. 2016. *Power to the People (3): Perspectives from Bamiyan.* Kabul: Afghanistan Analysts Network. June 5, 2016.

Bliesemann de Guevara, B. 2008. "The State in Times of Statebuilding." *Civil Wars* 10 (4): 350–70.

Bliesmann de Guevara, B. 2012. *Statebuilding and State Formation: A New Framework of Analysis.* London: Routledge.

Bogason, P., and T. A. J. Tooner. 1998. "Comparing Networks." *Public Administration* 76 (2): 205–407.

Boone, J. 2009. "Afghan Election Chaos as Abdullah Pulls Out of Run-Off." *The Guardian,* November 1, 2009.

Bose, S., N. Bizhan, and N. Ibrahimi. 2019. *Youth Protest Movements in Afghanistan: Seeking Voice and Agency.* Washington D.C.: United States Institute of Peace.

Bourdieu, P. 1991. *Language and Symbolic Power.* Cambridge: Polity.

Bourdieu, P., and J. C. Passeron. 1977. *Reproduction in Education, Society and Culture.* London: Sage.

Boutros-Ghali, B. 1992. *An Agenda for Peace: Preventing Diplomacy, Peacemaking and Peacekeeping.* New York: United Nations.

Boutros-Ghali, B. 1993. *Report on the Work of the Organisation from the Forty-Seventh to the Forty-Eight Session of the General Assembly.* New York: United Nations.

Boutros-Ghali, B. 1995. *Supplement to an Agenda for Peace.* New York: United Nations.

Bradsher, H. S. 1999. *Afghan Communism and Soviet Intervention.* Karachi: Oxford University Press.

Brahimi, L. 2007. "State Building in Crisis and Post-Conflict Countries." In *7th Global Forum on Reinventing Government,* Building Trust in Government, June 26–29.

Brubaker, R. 2006. *Ethnicity Without Groups.* Cambridge, MA: Harvard University Press.

Brubaker, R., and F. Cooper. 2000. "Beyond 'Identity'." *Theory and Society* 29 (1): 1–47.

Brulliard, K. 2009. "In Nod to the U.S., Karzai to Keep Current Ministers in Top Cabinet Jobs." *Washington Post,* December 19, 2009.

Burt, R. S. 1980. "Models of Network Structure." *Annual Review of Sociology* 6: 79–141.

Burt, R. S. 1992. *Structural Holes: The Social Structure of Competition.* Cambridge: Cambridge University Press.

Burt, R. S. 2005. *Brokerage & Closure: An Introduction to Social Capital.* Oxford: Oxford University Press.

Burton, M., and J. Higley. 1987. Elite Settlements. *American Sociological Review* 52 (3): 295–307.

Burton, M., and J. Higley. 1989. The Elite Variable in Democratic Transitions and Breakdowns. *American Sociological Review* 54 (1): 17–32.

Buzan, B., and O. Weaver. 1990. *The European Security Order Recast: Scenarios for the Post-Cold War Era*. London: Pinter.

Buzan, B., and O. Weaver. 2003. *Regions and Powers: The Structure of International Security*. Cambridge: Cambridge University Press.

Byman, D. L. 2002. *Keeping the Peace: Lasting Solutions to Ethnic Conflict*. Baltimore, MD: John Hopkins University Press.

Byrd, W. 2020. *Dismembering Afghanistan's Ministry of Finance*. Washington, DC: United States Institute of Peace. March 31, 2021.

Campbell, S., D. Chandler, and M. Sabaratnam. 2011. "Introduction: The Politics of Liberal Peace." In *A Liberal Peace: The Problems and Practices of Peacebuilding*, edited by S. Campbell, D. Chandler, and M. Sabaratnam. London: Zed Books, 1–9.

Caplan, R. 2005. *International Governance of War-Torn Territories*. Oxford: Oxford University Press.

Caroe, O. 2000. *The Pathans: 500 B.C.-A.D. 1957, (reprint of 1958 edition)*. London: Kegan Paul International.

Gossman, P. 2005. *Casting Shadows: War Crimes and Crimes against Humanity: 1978–2001*. The 2005 Afghanistan Justice Project Report.

Chandler, D. 2006. *Empire in Denial: The Politics of Statebuilding*. London: Pluto Press.

Chandler, D. 2010. *International Statebuilding: The Rise of Post-Liberal Governance*. Oxon: Routledge.

Chandler, D. 2011. "The Uncritical Critique of 'Liberal Peace." In *A Liberal Peace: The Problems and Practices of Peacebuilding*, edited by S. Campbell, D. Chandler, and M. Sabaratnam. London: Zed Books, 174–190.

Chatterjee, P. 2009. "Afghanistan: Paying Off Warlords, Anatomy of an Afghan Culture of Corruption." *TomDispatch*, November 17, 2009.

Chayes, S. 2006. *The Punishment of Virtue: Inside Afghanistan after the Taliban*. New York: Penguin Publishing.

Chayes, S. 2015. *Thieves of State: Why Corruption Threatens Global Security*. New York: W.W. Norton.

Cheng, C., and D. Zaum. 2011. *Corruption and Post-Conflict Peacebuilding: Selling the Peace? Case Series on Peacekeeping*. Abingdon: Routledge.

Chesterman, S. 2002. "East Timor in Transition: Self-Determination, State-Building and the United Nations." *International Peacekeeping* 9 (1): 45–76.

Chesterman, S. 2004. *We, the People: the United Nations, Transitional Administration and Statebuilding*. Oxford: Oxford University Press.

Chopra, J. 2000. "The UN's Kingdom of East Timor." *Development and Change* 33 (5): 979–1000.

Christia, F. 2012. *Alliance Formation in Civil Wars*. Cambridge: Cambridge University Press.

Clark, K. 2013. *A Yes, a Maybe and the Threat of Migration: The BSA Loyi Jirga's Last Day*. Kabul: Afghanistan Analyst Network. November 24, 2013.

Clark, K. 2020. *The Cost of Support to Afghnaistan: New Special Report Considers the Causes of Inequality, Poverty and a Failing Democracy*. Kabul: Afghanistan Analysts Network. May 29, 2020.

Clark, K., and O. Ali. 2021. *A Quarter of Afghanistan's Districts Fall to the Taliban amid Call for a 'Second Resistance'*. Kabul: Afghanistan Analysts Network.

Coburn, N. 2010. *Connecting with Kabul: The Importance of the Wolesi Jirga Election and Local Political Networks in Afghanistan*. Kabul: Afghanistan Research and Evaluation Unit.

Coburn, N. 2011a. *Political Economy in the Wolesi Jirga: Sources of Finance and Their Impact on Representation in Afghanistan's Parliament*. Kabul: Afghanistan Research and Evaluation Unit.

Coburn, N. 2011b. *Bazaar Politics: Power & Pottery in an Afghan Market Town*. Stanford, CA: Stanford University Press.

Coburn, N. 2016. *Losing Afghanistan: An Obituary for the Intervention*. Stanford, CA: Stanford University Press.

Cock, R. A. 2010. External Actors and the Relative Autonomy of the Ruling Elite in Post-UNTAC Cambodia. *Journal of Southeast Asian Studies* 41: 241–65.

Coghlan, T. 2009. "The Taliban in Helmand: An Oral History." In *Decoding the New Taliban: Insights from the Afghan Field*, edited by A. Giustozzi. London: Hurst, 118–31.

Coleman, J. S. 1990. *Foundations of Social Theory*. Cambridge, MA and London: Harvard University Press.

Coll, S. 2004. *Ghost Wars*. New York: Penguin Press.

Collins, K. 2002. "Clans, Pacts and Policies in Central Asia." *Journal of Democracy* 13 (3): 137–152.

Constable, P. 2016. "Afghanistan has Many Problems: Its President Maybe One of Them." *Washington Post*, September 2, 2016.

Cooley, A., and J. Sharman. 2015. "Blurring the Line between Licit and Illicit: Transnational Corruption Networks in Central Asia and Beyond." *Central Asia Survey* 34 (1): 11–28.

Cordesman, A. 2010. *How America Corrupted Afghanistan: Time to Look in the Mirror*. Washington, DC: Centre for Strategic & International Studies, 11–28.

Cordovez, D. and Harrison, S. 1995. *Out of Afghanistan: The Inside Story of the Soviet Withdrawal*. Oxford: Oxford University Press.

Cousens, E. M., and C. Kumar. 2001. *Peacebuilding as Politics: Cultivating Peace in Fragile Societies*. Boulder: Lynne Rienner Publishers.

Cramer, C., and J. Goodhand. 2002. "Try Again, Fail Again, Fail Better? War, the State, and the 'Post-Conflict' Challenge in Afghanistan." *Development and Change* 33 (5): 885–909.

Crocker, C. 2003. "Engaging Failed States." *Foreign Affairs* 82 (5): 32–44.

Croker, C., O. Hampson, and P. Aall. 1996. *Managing Global Chaos: Sources of and Responses to International Conflict*. Washington, DC: United States Institute of Peace Press.

Curtin, P. D. 1984. *Cross-Cultural Trade in World History*. Cambridge: Cambridge University Press.

Darlymple, W. 2013. *The Return of a King: The Battle for Afghanistan*. London: Bloomsbury Publishing.

Davis, A. 1998. "How the Taliban became a Military Force." In *Fundamentalism Reborn?*, edited by W. Maley. London: Hurst Publications, 43–71.

De Waal, A. 2009. "Mission without End? Peacekeeping in the African Political Marketplace." *International Affairs* 85 (1): 99–113.

DeMars, E. W. 2005. *NGOs and Transnational Networks: Wild Cards in World Politics*. London: Pluto Press.

Diehl, P. F. 1994. *International Peacekeeping*. Baltimore, MD: Johns Hopkins University Stationary Office.

Dobbins, J. 2008. *After the Taliban: Nation-Building in Afghanistan*. Sterling, VA: Potomac Books.

Dodge, T. 2017. *Iraq: From War to a New Authoritarianism (The Adelphi Series)*. London: Routledge.

Dodd, M., and J. Kelly. 2009. "ADF Plays Down Warlord's Role on Crucial Supply Chain." *The Australian*, April 28, 2009.

Dolatabadi, B. A. 2001. *Shenasname Afghanistan*. Mashad: Erfan Publishing.

Donati, J., C. Nelso, and D. Nissenbaum. 2018. "U.S. Considers Asking Afghanistan to Suspend Presidential Election." *The Wall Street Journal*, November 13, 2018.

Dorronsoro, G. 1995. "Afghanistan's Civil War." *Current History*. 94 (588): 36–49

Dorronsoro, G. 2012. "The Transformation of the Afghanistan-Pakistan Border." In *Under the Drones: Modern Lives in the Afghanistan-Pakistan Borderlands*, edited by S. Bashir, and R. D. Crews. Cambridge, MA: Harvard University Press, 30–44.

Dorronsoro, G. 2012. *Waiting for the Taliban in Afghanistan*. South Asia: The Carnegie Papers.

Doyle, M. 1983. "Kant, Liberal Legacies, and Foreign Affairs - Part 1." *Philosophy and Public Affairs* 12 (3), 205–35.

Doyle, M. W., and N. Sambianis. 2000. "International Peacebuilding: A Theoretical and Quantitative Analysis." *American Political Science Review* 94 (4): 779–801.

Doyle, M. W., and N. Sambianis. 2006. *Making War and Building Peace: United Nations Peace Operations*. Princeton, NJ: Princeton University Press.

Duffield, M. 1997. "NGO Relief in War Zones: Towards an Analysis of the New Aid Paradigm." *Third World Quarterly* 8 (3): 527–542.

Duffield, M. 1999. *Global Governance and the New War: The Merging of Development and Security*. London: Zed.

Duffield, M. 2007. *Development, Security, and Unending War*. Cambridge: Polity.

Duncan, H., and K. Clark. 2021. *Afghanistan's Looming Economic Catastrophe: What Next for the Taliban and the Donors?* Kabul: Afghanistan Analyst Network, September 6, 2021.

DuPée, M. 2012. "Afghanistan's Conflict Minerals: The Crime-State-Insurgent Nexus" *Combating Terrorism Center (CTC) Sentinel*. February 16.

Dupree, L. 1969. "Afghanistan and the Unpaved Road to Democracy." *Royal Central Asian Journal* 56 (3), 272–290.

Dupree, L. 1973. *Afghanistan*. Oxford: Oxford University Press.

Dupree, L. 1979. *Red Flag over Hindu Kush, Part 1: Leftist Movement of Afghanistan*. American Universities Field Staff Reports Asia No. 44. American Universities.

Dupree, N. 1989. "Seclusion or Service: Will Women have a role in the Future of Afghanistan." *The Afghanistan Forum*. Occasional Paper 29. New York.

Du Picq, A. 2013. *Battle Studies: Ancient and Modern Battle*. Lavergne, TN: Forgotten Books.

Durch, W. J. 1994. "Introduction." In *The Evolution of International Peacekeeping*, edited by W. J. Durch. Basingstoke: Macmillan, 1–15.

Edwards, D. 2002. *Before the Taliban: Genealogies of the Afghan Jihad*. Berkeley, CA: University of California Press.

Edwards, L. M. 2011. *The Afghan Solution: The Inside Story of Abdul Haq, the CIA and How Western Hubris Lost Afghanistan*. London: Bacteria Press.

Eide, K. 2012. *Power Struggle over Afghanistan: An Inside Look at What Went Wrong and What We Can Do to Repair the Damage*. New York: Skyhorse.

Eide, K. 2014. *Afghanistan and the US: Between Partnership and Occupation*. Oslo: Peace Research Institute Oslo (PIRO).

Eilstrup-Sangiovanni, M. 2009. "Varieties of Cooperation: Government Networks in International Security." In *Network Politics: Agency, Power and Governance*, edited by M. Kahler. New York: Cornell University Press, 43–63.

Eilstrup-Sangiovanni, M. 2017. "Global Governance Networks." In *Oxford Handbook of Political Networks, Global Governance Networks*, edited by Victor, J.N., Montgomery, A.H., and Lubell, M. Oxford: Oxford University Press, 689–714.

Elphinstone, M. 1972. *An Account of the Kingdom of Caboul* (first edition 1815). Karachi: Oxford University Press.

Emadi, H. 1991. "A Historical Perspective on the Durand Line and the Future of Afghanistan-Pakistan Relations." *World Review* 30 (3): 5–12.

Emadi, H. 2010. *Dynamics of Political Development in Afghanistan: The British, Russian and American Invasions*. New York: Palgrave MacMillan.

Emirbayer, M., and J. Goodwin. 1994. ""Network Analysis, Culture, and the Problem of Agency." *American Journal of Sociology* 99: 1411–54.

Erlanger, S. 2001. "A Nations Challenged: Negotiations; Talks in Bonn End with Deal on Leadership for Afghans." *New York Time*, 5 December 2001.

Evans, M., and Davies, J. 1999. "Understanding Policy Transfer: A Multi-Level, Multi-Disciplinary Perspective." *Public Administration* 77 (2):361–85.

Evans, P., D. Rueschemeyer, and T. Skocpol. 1985. *Bringing the State Back in*. Cambridge: Cambridge University Press.

Faccio, M. 2006. "Politically Connected Firms." *American Economic Review* 96 (1): 369–86.

Fange, A. 2002. *The Emergency Loya Jirga: Hopes and Dissapointments*. Kabul: Afghanistan Analyst Network.

Farahi, G. 2001. *De Demokrasi aw Jamhuryat pa Kalono ke 1963–1978*. Peshawar, 161.

Farahi, K., and S. Guggenheim. 2020. *Pathways for Post-Peace Development in Afghanistan*. Washington, DC: United States Institute of Peace, Special Report No. 487, November 2020.

Fearon, J. F., and D. Laitin. 2004. "Neotrusteeship and the Problem of Weak States." *International Security* 28 (4): 5–43.

Featherstone, A. B. 2000. "Peacekeeping, Conflict Resolution and Peacebuilding: A Reconsideration of Theoretical Framework." *International Peacekeeping* 17 (20): 190–217.

Field, G., and J. Higley. 1973. *Elites and Non-Elites: The Possibilities and Their Side Effects*. Boston, MA: Routledge & Kegan Paul.

Fields, M., and R. Ahmed. 2011. "A Review of the 2001 Bonn Conference and Application to the Road Ahead in Afghanistan." *The Institute for National Strategic Studies*, National Defense University, May 2011.

Filkins, D. 2010. "With US Aid, Warlord Builds Afghan Empire." *The New York Times*, June 5, 2010.

Finsveen, E., and W. van Oorschot. 2008. "Access to Resources in Networks: A Theoretical and Empirical Critique of Networks as a Proxy for Social Capital." *Acta Sociologica* 51 (4): 293–307.

Fishstein, P., and A. Wilder. 2012. *Winning Hearts and Minds? Examining the Relationship between Aid and Security in Afghanistan*. Boston: Feinstein International Centre: Tufts University.

Fisman, R. 2001. "Estimating the Value of Political Connections." *The American Economic Review* 9 (14): 1095–102.

Forsberg, C. 2010. *Politics and Power in Kandahar*. Washington DC: Institute for the Study of War.

Fortna, V. P. 2003. "Inside and Out: Peacekeeping and the Duration of Peace after Civil and Interstate Wars." *International Studies Review* 5 (4): 97–114.

Foschini, F. 2011. "The Enteqal Seven (4): Herat, the Seeds of Fear." June 2. https://www.afghanistan-analysts.org/the-enteqal-seven-4-herat-the-seeds-of-fear/.

Foschini, F. 2011b. *How Outside Interference Politicised the Achin Land Conflict*. Kabul: Afghanistan Analyst Network.

Foschini, F. 2012. *Land Grabs in Afghanistan (1): Nangarhar, the Disputed Orangeland*. Kabul: Afghanistan Analyst Network.

Foschini, F. 2013. *Back to Stopgap Appointments? The Story behind the Replacement of Herat's Governor*. Kabul: Afghanistan Analyst Network.

Foschini, F., and O. Ali. 2013. *A New Round of Anti-Shirzai Protest in Nangarhar*. Kabul: Afghanistan Analyst Network. April 25, 2013.

Fukuyama, F. 2004. *State-Building Governance and World Order in the 21st Century*. New York: Cornell University Press.

Gall, C. 2006. "Nation Faltering, Afghans' Leader Draws Criticism." *The New York Times*.

Gall, C., and M. Rosenberg. 2014. "Anxious Moments for an Afghanistan on the Brink." *The New York Times*, July 14, 2014.

Gallaghy, T., R. Kassimir, and R. Latham. 2001. *Intervention & Transnational in Africa: Global-Local Networks of Power*. Cambridge: Cambridge University Press.

Gardizi, M. 2007. *Afghans' Experiences of Corruption: A Study across Seven Provinces*. Kabul: Integrity Watch Afghanistan.

Gardizi, M., K. Hussmann, and Y. Torabi. 2010. *Corrupting the State or State-Crafted Corruption? Exploring the Nexus between Corruption and Subnational Governance*. Kabul: Afghanistan Research and Evaluation Unit.

Gate, R. 2014. *Duty: Memoirs of a Secretary at War*. New York: Alfred A. Knopf.

Ghafour, H. 2003. "Anarchy, Ambition Collide in Kabul." *The Globe and Mail*, August 12, 2003.

Ghani, A. 2009. "Kick Out Karzai: We Deserve a Second Chance." *London Times*, August 20, 2009.

Ghani, A., and C. Lockhart. 2008. *Fixing Failed States: A Framework for Rebuilding a Fractured World*. Oxford: Oxford University Press.

Ghani, A., C. Lockhart, and M. Carnahan. 2005. *Closing the Sovereignty Gap: An Approach to Statebuilding*. Working Paper 253, London: Overseas Development Institute.

Ghubar, M. G. M. 1981. *Afghanistan Dar Masire Tarikh* (first edition 1968). Qum: Payam-I-Muhajir.

Giustozzi, A. 2000. *War, Politics and Society in Afghanistan*. London: Hurst & Company.

Giustozzi, A. 2004. *Good State vs. Bad Warlords? A critique of State-Building Strategies in Afghanistan*. London: Crisis States Research Centre.

Giustozzi, A. 2005. *The Ethnicisation of an Afghan Faction: Junbish-I-Milli From its Origins to the Presidential Election*. London: Crisis States Research Centre.

Giustozzi, A. 2007. "War and Peace Economies of Afghanistan's Strongmen." *International Peacekeeping* 14 (1): 75–89.

Giustozzi, A. 2008. "Bureaucratic Façade and Political Realities of Disarmament and Demobilisation in Afghanistan." *Conflict, Security and Development* 8 (2): 169–192.

Giustozzi, A. 2009. *Empires of Mud: Wars and Warlords in Afghanistan*. New York: Oxford University Press.

Giustozzi, A. 2011. "Armed Politics in Afghanistan." In *The Peace In Between: Post-War Violence and Peacebuilding*, edited by M. Berdal, and A. Suhrke. London: Routledge, 153–172.

Giustozzi, A., and Governor NoorUllah. 2007. "The Inverted Cycle: Kabul and the Strongmen's Competition for Control over Kandahar, 2001–2006." *Central Asian Survey* 26 (2): 167–184.

Giustozzi, A., and D. Orsini. 2009. "Centre-Periphery Relations in Afghanistan: Badakhshan between Patrimonialism and Institution-Building." *Central Asian Survey* 28 (1): 1–16.

Glatzer, B. 1983. "Pashtun Nomads and the State." In *The Conflict of Tribe and State in Iran and Afghanistan*, edited by R. Tapper. London: St. Martin's Press, 212–232.

Glatzer, B. 1998. "Afghanistan: Ethnic and Tribal Disintegration." In *Fundamentalism Reborn*, edited by W. Maley. London: Hurst & Co., 167–181.

Global Policy Forum. 2002. *Procedures for Afghanistan's Emergency Loya Jirga*. April. Accessed March 28, 2020.

Global Witness. 2016. "War in the Treasury of the People: Afghanistan, Lapis Lazuli and the Battle for Mineral Wealth." London: Global Witness Report.

Gompelman, G. 2001. *Winning Hearts and Minds? Examining the Relationship between Aid and Security in Afghanistan's Faryab Province*. Boston, MA: Feinstein International Centre. January 2001.

Gopal, A. 2014. *No Good Men among the Living: America, the Taliban and the War through Afghan Eyes*. New York: Metropolitan Books.

Goodhand, J. 2002. "Aiding Violence or Building Peace? The Role of International Aid in Afghanistan." *Third World Quarterly* 23 (5): 837–859.

Goodhand, J. 2004. "From War Economy to Peace Economy? Reconstruction and State Building in Afghanistan." *Journal of International Affairs* 58 (1): 155–174.

Goodhand, J. 2005. "Frontiers & Wars: The Opium Economy in Afghanistan." *Journal of Agrarian Change* 2: 191–216.

Goodhand, J and M. Sedra. 2010. "Who Owns the Peace? Aid, Reconstruction, and Peacebuilding in Afghanistan." *Disaster* 34 (1): 78–102.

Goodhand, J. 2011. "Corrupting or Consolidating the Peace? The Drug Economy and Post-Conflict Peacebuilding in Afghanistan." In *Corruption and Post-Conflict Peacebuilding: Selling the Peace?*, edited by D. Zaum, and C. Cheng. London: Routledge, 146–163..

Goodhand, J., and A. Hakimi. 2014. "Counterinsurgency, Local Militias, and Statebuilding in Afghanistan." Washington DC: United States Institute of Peace, Peaceworks Report No. 90.

Goodson, L. 2003. "Afghanistan's Long Road to Reconstruction." *Journal of Democracy* 14 (1). 89–102.

Goodson, L. 2005. "'Building Democracy After Conflict: Bullets, Ballots, and Poppies in Afghanistan." *Journal of Democracy* 16 (1): 24–38.

Graham-Harrison, E. 2014. "Afghan Election Crisis: Stuffed Sheep." *The Guardian*. June 22.

Granovetter, M. 1974. "The Strength of Weak Ties." *American Journal of Sociology* 78 (6): 1360–1380.

Granovetter, M. 1985. "Economic Action and Social Structure: The Problem of Embeddedness." *American Journal of Sociolog* 91 (3): 481–510.

Gregorian, V. 1969. *The Emergence of Modern Afghanistan*. Stanford, CA: Stanford University Press.

Grewal, D. S. 2009. *Network Power: The Social Dynamics of Globalization*. London: Yale University Press.

Gulette, D. 2007. "'Theories on Central Asian Factionalism: the Debate in Political Science and its Wider Implications." *Central Asian Survey* 26 (3): 373–387.

Hakimi, A. 2011. *The Parliament Must Work to Institutionalise Democracy.* Kabul: Bamdad News Agency.

Hakimi, A. 2012. *The Changing Nature of Power and Sovereignty in Afghanistan.* Policy Research Project, CIDOB.

Hakim, Y. 2016. "President Ghani Calls for Afghans to Remain in Country." *BBC,* March 31, 2016.

Hameiri, S. 2007. "Failed States or a Failed Paradigm? State Capacity and the Limits of Institutionalism." *Journal of International Relations and Development* 10 (2): 122–149.

Hameiri, S. 2012. "Mitigating the Risk to Primitive Accumulation: State-Building and the Logging Boom in Solomon Islands." *Journal of Contemporary Asia* 42 (3): 405–426.

Hammersley, M., and P. Atkinson. 1983. *Ethnography: Principles in Practice.* London: Tavistock Publications.

Hampson, F. O. 1996. *Nurturing Peace: Why Peace Settlements Succeed or Fail.* Washington, DC: US Institute of Peace.

Hanifi, J. M. 2004. "Editing the Past: Colonial Production of Hegemony Through the "Loya Jerga" in Afghanistan." *Iranian Studies* 37 (2): 295–322.

Hanifi, J. M. 2011. "Review Essay: Vending Distorted Afghanistan Through Patriotic 'anthropology'." *Critique of Anthropology* 31 (3): 161–184.

Hanifi, S. M. 2011. *Connecting Histories in Afghanistan: Market Relations and State Formation on a Colonial Frontier.* Stanford, CA: Stanford University Press.

Hanson, J. K., and R. Sigman. 2011. *Measuring State Capacity: Assessing and Testing the Options.* Annual Meeting of the American Political Science Association.

Hardin, R. 1995. *One for All: The Logic of Group Conflict.* Princeton, NJ: Princeton University Press.

Heathershaw, J. 2008. "Unpacking the Liberal Peace: The Merging of Peacebuilding Discourses." *Millennium - Journal of International Studies* 36 (3): 597–621.

Heathershaw, J. 2009. *Post-Conflict Tajikistan: The Politics of Peacebuilding and the Emergence of Legitimate Order.* London: Routledge.

Heathershaw, J., and D. Lambach. 2008. "Introduction: Post-Conflict Spaces and Approaches to Statebuilding." *Journal of Intervention and Statebuilding* 2 (3): 269–289.

Heinz, J. P., E. O. Laumann, R. H. Salisbury, and R. L. Nelson. 1990. "Inner Circles or Hollow Cores? Elite Networks in National Policy Systems." *The Journal of Politics* 52 (2): 356–390.

Held, D. 1998. "Democracy and Globalization." In *Re-Imagining Political Community,* edited by D. Archibugi, and D. Held. Stanford, CA: Stanford University Press:3–15.

Helman, G. B., and S. R. Ratner. 1992. "Saving Failed States." *Foreign Policy* 3-20.

Helmke, G., and S. Levitsky. 2004. "Informal Institutions and Comparative Politics: A Research Agenda." *Perspectives on Politics* 2 (4): 725–740.

Hersh, S. 2004. "The Other War." *The New Yorker,* April 12, 2004.

Herring, E., and G. Rangwala. 2006. *Iraq in Fragments: The Occupation and its Legacy.* London: Hurst.

Hewad, G. 2013. *Elections or National Consensus: Which One Wins?* Kabul: Afghanistan Network Analysts.

Hewad, G. 2011. *The New National Front: A Dark Horse Returns—With Three Riders.* Kabul: Afghanistan Analyst Network. December 1, 2011.

Hewad, G., and T. Ruttig. 2013. *Narrower than Expected: Political Opposition Presents "Electoral Union of Afghanistan".* Kabul: Afghanistan Analyst Network. August 29, 2013.

Hewad, G., and K. Clark. 2013. *Dancing to Power: Getting an Afghan Presidential Ticket Together*. Kabul: Afghanistan Analysts Network. September 30, 2013.

Hobbes, T. 2017. *Leviathan*. London: Pengium Classics

Hodge, N. 2012. "US finds Graft by Favored Afghan Leader." *Wall Street Journal*.

Hodgeson, G. 2004. *The Evolution of Institutional Economics: Agency, Structure and Darwinism in American Institutionalism*. London: Routledge.

Hopkins, B. D. 2008. *The Making of Modern Afghanistan*. London: Palgrave Macmillan.

Human Rights Watch. 1991. "Afghanistan: The Forgotten War: Human Rights Abuses and Violations of the Laws of War Since the Soviet Withdrawal." *A Human Rights Report*. February 1, 1991. New York: Human Rights Watch, 125–130.

Human Rights Watch 1991. *Human Rights Abuses and Violations of the Laws of War since the Soviet Withdrawal*. New York: Human Rights Watch.

Human Rights Watch. 1998. "The Massacre in Mazar-i Sharif." November 1998. New York: Human Rights Watch.

Human Rights Watch. 2001. *Everybody Lives in Fear: Patterns of Impunity*. New York: Human Rights Watch.

Human Rights Watch. 2001. "Massacres of Hazaras in Afghanistan." *Human Rights Watch*. New York: Human Rights Watch.

Human Rights Watch. 2003. *Killing You is a Very Easy Thing for Us*. New York: Human Rights Watch.

Human Rights Watch. 2019. *They Have Shot Many Like This': Abusive Night Raids by CIA-Backed Afghan Strike Forces*. New York: Human Rights Watch.

Huntington, S. 1984. "Will More Countries Become Democratic?" *Political Science Quarterly* 99 (2): 193–218.

Hussaini, A., and N. Faizi. 2010. *The Composition of the New Parliament*. Kabul: Kabul Centre for Strategic Studies.

Huxham, C., and S. Vangen. 2005. *Managing to Collaborate*. London: Routledge.

Ibrahimi, N. 2017. *The Hazaras and the Afghan State: Rebellion, Exclusion and the Struggle for Recognition*. London: Hurst.

ICISS. 2001. *The Responsibility to Protect*. Ottawa, ON: International Development Research Centre.

Ignatieff, M. 2002. "Nation-Building Lite". *The New York Times Magazine*, July 28, 2002.

Ishaqzadeh, M., and A. Giustozzi. 2015. *Senior Appointment and Corruption within the Afghan MoI: Practices and Perceptions*. Kabul: Integrity Watch Afghanistan.

Independent Election Commission. 2011. "The 2010 Parliamentary Election Result."

International Crisis Group. 2002. *The Loya Jirga: One Small Step Forward*. Brussels/Kabul: Asia Briefing 17.

International Crisis Group. 2003. "Afghanistan: The Constitutional Loya Jirga." *Asia Briefings* No: 29. Kabul/Brussels: 12 December 2003.

International Crisis Group. 2003. "Afghanistan's Flawed Constitutional Process." *Asia Briefings* No: 56. Kabul/Brussels: 12 June 2003.

International Crisis Group. 2006. *Afghanistan's New Legislature: Making Democracy Work*. Kabul: ICG. Asia Report 116.

International Crisis Group. 2005a. *Political Parties in Afghanistan*. Kabul: ICG. Asia Briefing 39.

International Crisis Group. 2005b. *Afghanistan Elections: Endgame or New Beginning*. Kabul: Asia Report 101. July 21, 2005.

International Crisis Group. 2012. *Afghanistan: The Long, Hard Road to the 2014 Transition*. Kabul: ICG. Asia Report 236.

International Crisis Group. 2015. *The Future of the Afghan Local Police*. Kabul: ICG. Report. 268.

International Crisis Group. 2016. *Afghanistan's Political Transition*. Kabul: ICG. Asia Briefing 260.

International Crisis Group. 2017. *Afghanistan: The Future of the National Unity Government*. Kabul: Report No. 285. April 10.

Isaacs-Martin, W. 2013. "Chromite Extraction in Kunar: Factor of Instability." Kabul: Integrity Watch Afghanistan.

Jabri, V. 2010. "War, Government, Politics: A Critical Response to the Hegemony of the Liberal Peace." In *Palgrave Advances in Peacebuilding: Critical Developments and Approaches*, edited by O. Richmond. London: Palgrave Macmillan, 41–57.

Jackson, A. 2014. "Politics and Governance in Afghanistan: The Case of Nangarhar." Working Paper 16, Kabul: Afghanistan Research and Evaluation Unit.

Jackson, M. 2008. *Social and Economic Networks*. Princeton, NJ: Princeton University Press.

Jackson, R. H. 1990. *Quasi-States: Sovereignty, International Relations and the Third World*. Cambridge: Cambridge University Press.

Jackson, R. H., and C. G. Rosberg. 1982. "Why Africa's Weak States Persist: The Empirical and Juridical in Statehood." *World Politics* 35 (1): 1–24.

Jacoby, T. 2007. *Understanding Conflict and Violence*. London: Routledge.

Jacobson, G. 2010. "A Tale of Two Wars: Public Opinion on the U.S. Military Interventions in Afghanistan and Iraq." *Presidential Studies Quarterly* 40 (4): 585–610.

Jalali, A. 2003. "Afghanistan in 2002: The Struggle to Win the Peace." *Asian Survey* 43 (1): 174–185.

Jarstad, A. K., and T. Sisk. 2008. *From War to Democracy: Dilemmas of Peacebuilding*. Cambridge: Cambridge University Press.

Jawad, K. 2011. "Is the 'Bulldozer' Running Out of Fuel?" *Afghanistan Today*.

Jeong, H. W. 2005. *Peacebuilding in Post-conflict Societies: Strategy and Process*. Boulder, CO: Lynne Rienner Publishers.

Jessop, B. 2000. *The Strategic Relational theory of the State*. Seoul: Han-ul Publishing.

Johnson, C., and J. Leslie. 2004. *Afghanistan: the Mirage of Peace*. London: Zed Books.

Johnson, T. H. 2006. "The Prospect for Post-Conflict Afghanistan: A Call of the Sirens to the Country's Troubled Past." *Strategic Insights* 5 (2).

Johnson, T. H. 2017. "The Illusion of Afghanistan's Electoral Representative Democracy: The Case of Afghan Presidential and National legislative Elections." *Small Wars & Insurgencies* 29 (1): 1–37.

Johnson, T. H. 2018. "The Myth of Afghan Electoral Democracy: the Irrigularities of the 2014 Presidential Election." *Small Wars & Insurgencies* 29 (5): 1006–39.

Johnson, T. J., and B. Ronald. 2020. "An Examination of Afghanistan's 2018 Lower House Elections: Chaos, Confusion and Fraud." *Journal of Asian Security and International Affairs* 7 (1): 57–100.

Johnson, T., and C. Dandeker. 1990. "Patronage: Relation and System." In *Patronage in Ancient Society*, edited by A. Wallace-Hadrill. London: Routledge, 219–238.

Kaarianinen, J., and H. Lehtonen. 2006. "The Variety of Social Capital in Welfare State Regimes: A Comparative Study of 21 Countries." *European Societies* 8: 77–57.

Kahler, M. 2009. *Network Politics: Agency, Power, and Governance*. Ithaca, NY: Cornell University Press.

Kakar, H. 1997. *Afghanistan, the Society Invasion and the Afghan Response*. Berkeley, CA: University of California Press.

Kakar, H. 2006. *A Political and Diplomatic History of Afghanistan*. Leiden: Brill.

Kakar, K., T. Kraemer, and H. Raoofi. 2017. *Evolution of the Executive Branch in Afghanistan: A Look Back and Recommendations on the Way Forward*. Kabul: Afghanistan Research and Evaluation Unit.

Kaldor, M. 1999. *New and Old Wars: Organised Violence in Global Era*. Cambridge: Polity Press.

Kalyvas, S. 2001. "'New' and 'Old' Civil Wars: A Valid Distinction?" *World Politics* 54: 99–118.

Kaneko, I., and K. Imai. 1987. "A Network View of the Firm." 1st Hitotsubashi Stanford Conference: Tokyo, Japan.

Kapferer, B. 1972. *Strategy and Transactions in an African Factory*. Manchester: Manchester University Press.

Kaplan, R. 1994. "The Coming Anarchy: How Scarcity, Crime, Overpopulation and Disease are Threatening the Social Fabric of Our Planet." *Atlantic Monthly* 44–74.

Karzai, H. 1988. "Attitude of the Leadership of Afghan Tribes towards the Regime from 1953–1978." *Central Asian Survey* 7 (2): 33–9.

Katzman, K. 2013. *Afghanistan: Politics, Elections, and Government Performance*. Congressional Research Service Report RS21922, Washington DC: Congressional Research Service Report.

Katzman, K. 2013. *Afghanistan: Post-Taliban Governance, Security, and US Policy*. Washington, DC: U.S. Congressional Service Report.

Kaufmann, C. 2000. "Possible and Impossible Solutions to Ethnic Civil War" *International Security*. 20(4): 136–175.

Kaufmann, D., K. Aart, and P. Zoido-Lobaton. 1999. *Governance Matters*. The World Bank Policy Research Working Paper 2196, Washington, DC: The World Bank Policy.

Kazemi, S. R. 2014. *Money, Jobs and Mutton Soup: Pre-Election Discourses in a Herat Township*. Kabul: Afghanistan Analysts Network. February 3. https://www.afghanistan -analysts.org/money-jobs-and   -mutton-soup-pre-election-discourses-in-a-herat-to wnship/.

Khagram, S. 2006. "Possible Future Architectures of Global Governance: A Transnational Perspective/Prospective." *Global Governance* 12 (1): 97–117.

Khalilzad, Z. 2016. *The Envoy: From Kabul to the White House, My Journey Through a Turbulent World*. New York: St. Martin's Press.

Khalilzad, Z. 2010. "Lessons from Afghanistan and Iraq." *Journal of Democracy* 21 (3): 41–9.

Khan, M. H. 2000. 'Rent-Seeking as Process." In *Rents, Rent-Seeking and Economic Development: Theory and Evidence in Asia*, edited by M. H. Khan, and K. S. Jomo, 70–144. Cambridge: Cambridge University Press.

Kelly, J. 2009. "Long Road to Tarin Kowt." *The Australian*, April 28, 2009.

Kickert, W. J. M., E-H. Klijn, and J. Koppenjan. 1997. *Managing Complex Networks: Strategies for the Public Sector*. London: Sage.

Kilduff, M., and W. Tsai. 2003. *Social Networks and Organizations*. London: Sage Press.

Kitchelt, H., and S. I Wilkinson. 2007. "Citizen-Politician Linkages: An Introduction." In *Patrons, Clients, and Policies: Patterns of Democratic Accountability and Political Competition*, edited by Kitchelt, H. and S.I. Wilkinson. Cambridge: Cambridge University Press, 1–49.

Klijn, E.-H., and J. F. M. Koppenjan. 2000. "Public Management and Policy Network: Foundations of a Network Approach to Governance." *Public Management* 2 (2): 135–158.

Klijn, E.-H., and J. F. M. Koppenjan. 2004. *Managing Uncertainties in Networks*. London: Routledge.

Klijn, E.-H., and C. Skecher. 2007. "Democracy and Governance Networks: Compatible or Not?" *Public Administration* 8 (3): 587–608.

Knack, S., and P. Keefer. 1997. "Does Social Capital Have an Economic Pay-Off? A Cross-Country Investigation." *Quarterly Journal of Economics* 112 (4): 1251–1288.

Knoke, D. 1990. *Political Networks: The Structural Perspective*. Cambridge: Cambridge University Press.

Kooiman, J. 1993. *Modern Governance: New Government-Society Interactions*. London: Sage.

Krasner, S. 2004. "Sharing Sovereignty: New Institutions for Collapsed and Failing States." *International Security* 29 (2): 85–120.

Krause, K. 2013. *Armed Groups and Contemporary Conflicts: Challenging the Weberian State*. London: Routledge.

Krueger, A. O. 1974. "The Political Economy of the Rent-Seeking Society." *American Economic Review* 64 (3): 291–303.

Kwon, H. 2010. *The Other Cold War*. New York: Columbia University Press.

Ladwig III, W. C. 2017. *The Forgotten Front: Patron-Client Relationships in Counterinsurgency*. Cambridge: Cambridge University Press.

Lake, D., and W. Wong. 2009. "The Politics of Networks, Interests, Power and HR Norms." In *Network Politics: Agency, Power and Governance*, edited by M. Kahler. Ithaca, NY: Cornell University Press, 127-150.

Lakhani, S. 2013. *Extractive Industries and Peacebuilding in Afghanistan: The Role of Social Accountability*. Special Report 339, Washington DC: United States Institute of Peace.

Lamond, G. 1996. "Coercion, Threats, and the Puzzle of Blackmail." In *Harm and Culpability*, edited by A. P. Simester, and A. T. H. Smith, 215–38. Oxford: Clarendon Press.

Laumann, E. O., P. Marsden, and J. Galaskiewicz. 1977. "Community-Elite Influence Structures: Extension of a Network Approach." *American Journal of Sociology* 83 (3): 594–631.

Laumann, E. O., and F. U. Pappi. 1976. *Networks of Collective Action: A Perspective on Community Influence System*. New York: Academic Press.

Le Billon, P. 2008. "Corrupting Peace? Peacebuilding and Post-Conflict Corruption." *International Peacekeeping* 15 (3): 344–361.

Lederach, J. P. 1997. *Building Peace: Sustainable Reconciliation in Divided Societies*. Washington, DC: United States Institute of Peace Press.

Lee, J. L. 2018. *Afghanistan: A History from 2060 to the Present*. London: Reaktion Books.

Leslie, J. 2015. *Political and Economic Dynamics of Herat*. Peaceworks No. 107, Washington, DC: United States Institute of Peace.

Lezhnev, S. 2005. *Crafting Peace; Strategies to Deal with Warlords in Collapsing State*. Lanham, MD: Lexington Books.

The Liason Office. 2004. *Justice and Security: Practices, Perceptions, and Problems in Kabul*. Kabul: The Liason Office.

Lin, N. 2000. "Inequality in Social Capital." *Contemporary Sociology* 29: 785–795.

Loughlin, N. 2021. "Beyond Personalism." *Contemporary Southeast Asia* 43 (2): 241–64.

MacGinty, R. M. 2010. "Hybrid Peace: The Interaction between Top-Down and Bottom-Up Peace." *Security Dialogue* 41 (4): 391–412.

MacGinty, R. M. 2011a. *International Peacebuilding and Local Resistance: Rethinking Peace and Conflict*. Basingstoke: Palgrave.

MacGinty, R. M. 2011b. "Hybrid Peace: How Does Hybrid Peace Come About." In *A Liberal Peace: The Problems and Practices of Peacebuilding*, edited by S. Campbell, D. Chandler, and M. Sabaratnam. London: Zed, 121–38.

MacGinty, R. M., and O. Richmond. 2009. *The Liberal Peace and Post-War Reconstruction: Myth or Reality?* London: Routledge.

Malejacq, R. 2020. *Warlord Survival: The Delusion of State Building in Afghanistan*. Ithaca, NY: Cornell University Press.

Maley, W. 1997. "The Dynamics of Regime Transition in Afghanistan." *The Central Asian Survey* 16 (2): 167–84.

Maley, W. 1998. "Introduction: Interpreting the Taliban." In *Fundamentalism Reborn? Afghanistan and the Taliban*, edited by M. Maley. London: Hurst & Company.

Maley, W. 2002. The Afghanistan Wars. New York: Palgrave MacMillan, 1–28.

Maley, W. 2003. "Institutional Design and the Rebuilding of Trust." In *From Civil Strife to Civil Society: Civil and Military Responsibilities in Disrupted States*, edited by W. Maley, C. Sampford, and R. Thakur, 163–79. Tokyo: United Nations University Press.

Maley, W. 2006. Rescuing Afghanistan. London: Hurst & Company.

Maley, W. 2018. "Institutional Design, Neopatrimonialism, and the Politics of Aid in Afghanistan." Asian Survey 58 (6): 995–1015.

Maley, W. 2021a. *Transition in Afghanistan: Hope, Despair and the Limits of Statebuilding*. Oxon: Routledge.

Maley, W. 2021b. *The Afghanistan Wars*, 3rd edition. London: Macmillan/Red Globe Press.

Maley, W. 2021c. *Afghanistan on the Brink of an Abyss*. Occasional Paper 181. Sydney: The Centre for Independent Studies. July 2021.

Malikyar, H., and B. Rubin. 2002. *Centre-Periphery Relations in the Afghan State: Current Practices, Future Prospects. Centre on International Cooperation*. New York: New York University.

Mandell, M. P. 2002. Getting Results Through Collaboration: Networks and Network Structures for Public Policy and Management. London: Quorum Books.

Mann, M. 1986. The Sources of Social Power Volume 1. Cambridge: Cambridge University Press.

Mansfield, D. 2014. A State Built on Sand: How Opium is Undermining Afghanistan. London: Hurst & Co.

Mansfield, D. 2019. *The Sun Cannot be Hidden by Two fingers: Illicit Drugs and the Discussions on a Political Settlement in Afghanistan*. Kabul: Afghanistan Research and Evaluation Unit.

Mansfield, D. 2020. *Catapults, Pickups and Tankers: Cross-Border Production and Trade and How it Shapes the Political Economy of the Borderland of Nimroz*. Kabul: Afghanistan Research and Evaluation Unit.

Maoz, Z. 2010. *Networks of Nations: The Evolution, Structure, and Impact of International Networks*. Cambridge: Cambridge University Press.

Marks, Z. 2013. *The Internal Dynamics of Rebel Groups: Politics of Material Viability and Organizational Capacity –RUF*. Unpublished PhD Dissertation, Sierra Leone: University of Oxford.

Marsden, M. 2015. "From Kabul to Kiev: Afghan Trading Networks in the Former Soviet Union." *Modern Asian Studies* 49 (4): 1010–48.

Marsden, M., and P. Anderson. 2020. "Introduction to the Special Issue: After Trust." *Global Networks* 20 (1): 697–707.

Marten, K. 2012. *Warlords: Strong-Arm Brokers in Weak States*. Ithaca, NY: Cornell University Press.

Martinez-Diaz, L., and N. Woods. 2009. *Networks of Influence? Developing Countries in a Networked Global Order*. Oxford: OUP.

Marx, M. 1998. *Making Race and Nation: A Comparison of South Africa, the United States and Brazil*. Cambridge: Cambridge University Press.

Mashal, M. 2016. *Greed, Corruption and Danger: A Tarnished Afghan Gem Trade*. The *New York Times*. June 5.

Mashal, M. 2014a. "Hamid Karzai: 'I Didn't See a War in Afghanistan – I Saw a Conspiracy', An Exit Interview with the Afghan President." *The Atlantic*, June 23, 2014.

Mashal, M. 2014b. "The Men Who Run Afghanistan." *The Atlantic*, June 23, 2014.

Mashal, M., and F. Abed. 2016. "Afghanistan Vice President Accused of Torturing Political Rival." *New York Times*, December 13, 2016.

Mashal, M., and N. Rahim. 2018. "Video of Afghan Forces Abusing Detainees Emerges as Protests Simmer." *NYT*, July 13, 2018.

Matta. 2015. *The Failed Pilot Test*. Kabul: Afghanistan Analyst Network. June 5, 2015.

McChesney, R. D. 1991. *Waqf in Central Asia*. Princeton, NJ: Princeton University Press.

McChrystal, S. 2011. "It Takes a Network: The New Front line of Modern Warfare." *Foreign Policy Magazine*, February 21.

McGuire, M. 2002. "Collaborative Public Management: Assessing What We Know and How We Know It." *Public Administration Review* 66 (1): 33–34.

Medard, J. F. 1982. "The Underdeveloped State in Tropical Africa: Political Clientelism or Neopatrimonialism?" In *Private Patronage and Public Power: Political Clientelism in the Modern State*, edited by C. Clapham. London: Frances Pinter, 162–92.

Mendel, J. 2010. "Afghanistan, Networks and Connectivity." *Geopolitics* 15 (4): 726–751.

Middlebrook, P., and M. Sedra. 2005. *Revisioning the International Compact for Afghanistan*. Washington, DC: Foreign Policy in Focus.

Mielke, K., C. Schetter, and A. Wilde. 2011. *Dimensions of Social Order. Empirical Fact, Analytical Framework and Boundary Concept*. Working Paper Series of the Centre for Development Research, No. 78. Centre for Development Research.

Migdal, J. 1988. *Strong Societies and Weak States: State-Society Relations and State Capabilities in the Third World*. Princeton, NJ: Princeton University Press.

Migdal, J. 2001. *State in Society: Studying How States and Societies Transform and Constitute One Another*. Cambridge: Cambridge University Press

Miller, P. D. 2020. "Ending the "Endless War"." *Atlantic Council*, March 26, 2020.

Milward, H. B., and K. G. Provan. 2000. "Governing the Hollow State." *Journal of Public Administration Research and Theory* 10 (2): 359–380.

Milward, H. B., and K. G. Provan 2003. "Managing the Hollow State: Collaboration and Contracting." *Public Management Review* 5 (1): 1–18.

Ministry of Finance. 2011. "Office of National Budget Report." http://mof.gov.af/en#.

Minnion, M. 2013. "Economy Built around ISAF and Impact of Withdrawal," unpublished report for United Nations Development Programme.

Mitchell, J. C. 1969. *Social Networks in Urban Situations: Analyses of Personal Relationships in Central African Towns*. Manchester: Manchester University Press.

Mitchell, T. 1991. "The Limits of the State: Beyond Statist Approaches and Their Critics." *The American Political Science Review* 85 (1): 77–96.

Mitchell, T. 1999. "Society, Economy, and the State Effect." In *State/Culture: State-Formation after the Cultural Turn*, edited by G. Steinmetz. Ithaca, NY: Cornell University Press, 76–97.

Monge, P. R., and N. S. Contractor. 2003. *The Theories of Communication Network.* Oxford: Oxford University Press.

Monsutti, A. 2004. "Cooperation, Remittances, and Kinship among the Hazaras." *Iranian Studies* 37 (2): 219–40.

Monsutti, A. 2014. "Trust, Friendship and Transversal Ties of Cooperation among Afghans." In *Local Politics in Afghanistan: A Century of Intervention in the Social Order*, edited by C. Schetter, 147–62. London: Hurst Publishers.

Morgan, G. 1986. *Images of Organisations.* London: Sage.

Morgan, L. H., and C. Levi-Strauss. 1969. *The Elementary Structures of Kinship.* Boston, MA: Beacon Press.

Mosca, G. 1939. *The Ruling Class.* New York: McGraw-Hill.

Motlagh, J. 2010. "Kandahar Air Base: Part Afghanistan, Part Jersey Shore." *Time*, July 5, 2010.

Mousavi, S. A. 1997. *The Hazaras of Afghanistan: An Historical, Cultural, Economic and Political Study.* New York: St Martin's Press.

Mueller, J. 2004. *The Remnants of War.* Ithaca, NY: Cornel University Press.

Muhammadi, Z. 2010. "Afghanistan's Minerals Worth $3 Trillion." *Pajhwok Afghan News.*

Mujhda, A. W., N. A. Nawidy, S. Khan, A. W. Mujhda, N. A. Naweedi, and S. Khan. 2006. "Afghan Parliament: Expectations, Challenges and Opportunities." *Policy Perspectives* 3 (2): 61–81.

Mukhopadhyay, D. 2009. *Warlords as Bureaucrats: The Afghan Experience.* Washington DC: Carnegie Endowment for International Peace.

Mukhopadhyay, D. 2014. *Warlords, Strongman Governors, and the State in Afghanistan.* Cambridge: Cambridge University Press.

Murtazashvili, J. 2015. "Gaming the State: Consequences of Contracting out Statebuilding in Afghanistan." *Central Asia Survey* 34 (1): 78–92.

Murtazashvili, J. B. 2016. *Informal Order and the State in Afghanistan.* New York: Cambridge University Press.

Murtazashvili, J. B., and I. Murtazashvili. 2021. *Land, the State, and War: Property Institutions and Political Order in Afghanistan.* New York: Cambridge University Press.

Naadim, B. A. 2016. *Spin Boldak Customs Manager among Several Detained.* February 23.

Najafizada, E. 2015. "The Taliban is Capturing Afghanistan's $1 Trillion in Mining Wealth." *Bloomberg.*

National Democratic Institute Report. 2005. *The September 2005 Parliamentary and Provincial Council Elections in Afghanistan.* Kabul: National Democratic Institute.

Narten, J. 2009. "Dilemmas of Promoting 'Local Ownership': The Case of Postwar Kosovo." In *The Dilemmas of Statebuilding: Confronting the Contradictions of Post-War Peace Operations*, edited by R. Paris, and T. D. Sisk. London: Routledge, 252–284.

Natsios, A. S. 1995. "NGOs and the UN System in Complex Humanitarian Emergencies: Conflict or Cooperation?" Third World Quarterly. 16:405-419.

Neumann, R. 2015. *Failed Relations between Hamid Karzai and the United States.* Special Report 373, May 2015. Washington, DC: United States Institute of Peace.

Noelle, C. 2016. *State and Tribe in Nineteenth-Century Afghanistan: The Reign of Amir Dost Muhammad Khan.* London: Routledge.

Noorani, J. 2015. Afghanistan's Emerging Mining Oligarchy. Special Report No. 358, Washington, DC: United States Institute of Peace.

Norén-Nilsson, A. 2016. *Cambodia's Second Kingdom: Nation, Imagination, and Democracy.* Ithaca, NY: Cornell University Press.

Nordland, R., and J. Sukhanyar. 2017. "Afghanistan Police Surround Vice President's House." *New York Times*. February 21.

Nordstrom, C. 2001. "Out of the Shadow." In *Intervention and Transnationalism in Africa: Global-Local Networks of Power*, edited by T. Gallaghy, R. Kassimir, and R. Latham. Cambridge: Cambridge University Press, 216–239.

Nordstrom, C., and A. C. G. M. Robben. 1996. *Fieldwork Under Fire: Contemporary Studies of Violence and Culture*. Berkeley, CA: University of California Press.

North, D. 1990. *Institutions, Institutional Change and Economic Performance*. Cambridge: Cambridge University Press.

North, D. 2009. *Violence and Social Orders: A Conceptual Framework for Interpreting Recorded Human History*. Cambridge: Cambridge University Press.

North, D. C., J. J. Wallis, and B. R. Weingast. 2009. *Violence and Social orders: A Conceptual Framework for Interpreting Recorded Human History*. Cambridge: Cambridge University Press.

Nozick, R. 1969. "Coercion." In *Philosophy, Science, and Method: Essays in Honor of Ernest Nagel*, edited by S. Morgenbesser, P. Suppes, and M. White, 440–72. New York: St. Martin's Press.

Nunan, T. 2016. "The Anti-Colonial Origins of Humanitarian Intervention: NGOs, Human Rights." *Jadaliyya*. September 15, 2016.

O'Donnell, L. 2016. *Afghan Mineral Wealth Being Looted by Strongmen, Experts Say*. April 14. http://bigstory.ap.org/article/0427c669a4824bb9bbe5ab2a0f4341d2/afghan -mineral-wealth-being-looted-strongmen-experts-say.

Ober, J. 2011. *Karzai's Court*. Foreign Policy, The AF-Pak Channel.

Ohanyan, A. 2008. *NGOs, IGO, and the Network Mechanisms of Post-Conflict Global Governance in Microfinance*. Basingstoke: Palgrave Macmillan.

O'Mahony, A., M. Priebe, B. Frederick, J. Kavanagh, M. Lane, T. Johnston, T. S. Szayna, J. P. Hlavka, S. Watts, and M. Povlock. 2018. *US Presence and the Incidence of Conflict*. Santa Monica, CA: RAND Corporation.

Oneal, J. R., and B. Russett. 1999. "The Kantian Peace: The Pacific Benefits of Democracy, Interdependence, and International Organisations." *World Politics* 52 (1): 1–37.

Ostrom, E. 1990. *Governing the Commons: The Evolution of Institutions for Collective Action*. Cambridge: Cambridge University Press.

O'Toole, L. J. 1997. "Treating Networks Seriously: Practical and Research-Based Agendas in Public Administration." *Public Administration Review* 57 (1): 45–52.

Ottoway, M., and A. Lieven. 2002. *Rebuilding Afghanistan: Fantasy versus Reality*. Policy Brief 12, Washington, DC: Carnegie Endowment for International Peace.

Owen-Smith, J., and W. W. Powell. 2007. *Networks and Institutions, The Sage Handbook of Organizational Institutionalism*. New York: Sage.

Paffenholz, T. 2010. *Civil Society and Peacebuilding. A Critical Assessment*. London and Boulder, CO: Lynne Rienner.

Pareto, V. 1935. *The Mind and Society: A Treatise on General Sociology*. New York: Dover.

Paris, R. 1997. "Peacebuilding and the Limits of Liberal Internationalism." *International Security* 22 (2): 54–89.

Paris, R. 2000. "Broadening the Study of Peace Operations." *International Studies Review* 2 (3): 27–44.

Paris, R. 2004. *At War's End: Building Peace After Conflict*. Cambridge: Cambridge University Press.

Paris, R. 2009. "Understanding the 'Coordination Problem' in Postwar Statebuilding." In *The Dilemmas of Statebuilding: Confronting the Contradictions of Postwar Peace Operations*, edited by R. Paris, and D. Sisk. London: Taylor & Francis, 53–78.

Paris, R. 2011. "Critiques of Liberal Peace." In *A Liberal Peace: The Problems and Practices of Peacebuilding*, edited by S. Campbell, D. Chandler, and M. Sabaratnam. London: Zed, 31–54.

Partlow, J., and C. Whitlock. 2011. "Karzai Demands NATO Stop Bombing Homes." *Washington Post*, May 31, 2011.

Pasarlay, S., and Z. Mallyar. 2019. *The Afghan Parliament: Constitutional Mandate versus the Practice in the Post 2001 Context*. Kabul: Afghanistan Reserach and Evaluation Unit.

Peters, G. 2009. How Opium Profits the Taliban. Washington: United States Institute of Peace.

Peters, G. 2009. *Seeds of Terror: How Heroin is Bankrolling the Taliban and al Qaeda*. New York: Thomas Dunne Books.

Peters, H., M. Schwartz, and L. Kapp. 2017. "Department of Defense Contractor and Troop Levels in Iraq and Afghanistan: 2007–2017." *Current Politics and Economics of the Middle East* 8 (4): 449–63.

Piattoni, S. 2001. "Clientelism in Historical and Comparative Perspective." In *Clientelism, Interests, and Democratic Representation: The European Experience in Historical and Comparative Perspective*, edited by S. Piattoni. Cambridge: Cambridge University Press, 1–30.

Pieterse, J. 1997. "Sociology of Humanitarian Intervention: Bosnia, Rwanda and Somalia Compared." *International Political Science Review* 18 (1): 71–93.

Podolny, J. M., and K. Page. 1998. "Network Forms of Organization." *Annual Review of Sociology* 24: 57–76.

Poullada, L. 1973. *Reform and Rebellion in Afghanistan: Kinf Amanullah's Failure to Modernise a Tribal Society*. Ithaca, NY: Cornell University Press.

Powell, W. 1990. "Neither Market nor Hierarchy: Networks Forms of Organizations." *Research in Organizational Behaviour* 12: 295–336.

Powell, W., and L. Smith-Doerr. 1994. "Networks and Economic Life." In *The Handbook of Economic Sociology*, edited by N. J. Smelser, and R. Swedberg. Princeton, NJ: Princeton University Press and Russell Sage Foundation, 368–402.

"Presidential and Provincial Councils Elections: Afghanistan. 2009. Elections—Final Certified presidential Results by Vote Order." *Independent Election Commission*.

"Presidential and Provincial Councils Elections: Afghanistan. 2014. Elections—2014 Elections Results." *Independent Election Commission*.

Provan, K. G., G. Keith, and P. Kenis. 2008. "Modes of Network Governance: Structure, Management, and Effectiveness." *Journal of Public Administration Research and Theory* 18 (2):229–252.

Provan, K. G., M. A. Veazie, L. K. Staten, and N. I. Teufel-Shone. 2005. "Utilization of Network Analysis for Strengthening Community Partnerships in Health and Human Services." *Public Administration Review* 65: 603–613.

Pugh, M. 2004. "Peace-Building and Critical Theory." In *Peace Operations and Global Order*, edited by A. Bellamy, and P. Williams. London: Routledge, 39–58.

Pugh, M. 2006. "Crime and Capitalism in Kosovo's Transformation." In *Kosovo between War and Peace*, edited by T. B. Knudsen, and C. B. Laustsen. London: Routledge, 116-134.

Pugh, M., N. Cooper, and J. Goodhand. 2004. *War Economies in a Regional Context: Challenges of Transformation*. London: Lynne Rienner.

Putnam, R. 1976. *The Comparative Study of Political Elites.* Englewood Cliffs, NJ: Prentice-Hall.

Putnam, R. 1993. *Making Democracy Work: Civic Traditions in Modern Italy.* Princeton, NJ: Princeton University Press.

Radio Free Europe/Radio Liberty. 2002. "Afghanistan: Karzai to Announce Decision on Paktia after Pakistan Trip". February 8, 2002.

Rasanayagam, J. 2011. *Islam in Post-Soviet Uzbekistan: The Morality of Experience.* Cambridge: Cambridge University Press.

Rashid, A. 2000. *Taliban.* London: Pan Books.

Raverty, H. G. 1888. *Notes on Afghanistan and Part of Baluchistan.* London: Eyre & Spottiswoode.

Reeves, M. 2007. *Border Work: An Ethnography of the State at its Limits in the Fergana.* PhD Thesis: University of Cambridge.

Reeves, M., J. Rasanayagam, and J. Beyer. 2014. *Ethnographies of the State in Central Asia: Performing Politics.* Bloomington, IN: Indiana University Press.

Reforming Public Institutions and Strengthening Governance: A World Bank Strategy. 2000. Washington, DC: The World Bank.

Reidy, D. A., and W. J. Riker. 2008. *Coercion and the State.* Amsterdam: Springer.

Reilly, B. 2001. *Democracy in Divided Societies: Electoral Engineering for Conflict Management.* Cambridge: Cambridge University Press.

Reilly, B. 2002. "Democratic Validation." In *Contemporary Peace Making: Conflict, Violence and Peace Processes,* edited by J. Ginty, and M. R. Darby. Basingstoke: Palgrave., 245–255.

Reno, W. 2001. "How Sovereignty Matters: International Markets and the Political Economy of Local Politics in Weak States." In *Intervention & Transnational in Africa: Global-Local Networks of Power,* edited by T. Gallaghy, R. Kassimir, and R. Latham. Cambridge: Cambridge University Press, 197–215.

Reno, W. 1998. *Warlord Politics and African States.* Boulder, CO: Lynne Reinner.

Reynolds, A., and A. Wilder. September 2004. *Free, Fair and Flawed: Challenges for Legitimate Elections in Afghanistan.* Kabul: Afghanistan Research and Evaluation Unit Briefing Paper.

Rhodes, R. A. W. 1981. *Control and Power in Central-Local Government Relations.* Farnborough, Hants: Gower.

Rhodes, R. A. W. 1997. *Understanding Governance: Policy Networks, Governance, Reflexivity and Accountability.* Buckingham: Open University Press.

Rhodes, R. A. W. 2006. "Policy Network Analysis." In *The Oxford Handbook of Public Policy,* edited by M. Moran, M. Rein, and R. E. Goodin. Oxford: Oxford University Press, 425–447.

Rhodes, R. A. W. 2007. "The New Governance: Governing without Government." In *Public Governance, Theories of Governance,* Vol. 1, edited by M. Bevir. London: Sage, 423–45.

Rhodes, R. A. W., and D. Marsh. 1992. *Policy Networks in British Government.* Oxford: Oxford University Press.

Ribot, J., and N. L. Peluso. 2003. "A Theory of Access." *Rural Sociology* 68 (2): 153–81.

Richmond, O. 2004. *The Transformation of Peace.* Basingstoke: Palgrave Macmillan.

Richmond, O. 2005. "The Dilemmas of Subcontracting the Liberal Peace." In *Subcontracting Peace: The Challenges of the NGO Peacebuilding,* edited by O. Richmond, and H. Carey. London: Ashgate, 19-35.

Richmond, O. 2007. "Critical Research Agendas for Peace: The Missing Link in the Study of International Relations." *Alternatives* 32 (2): 247–274.

Richmond, O. P. 2008. "Reclaiming Peace in International Relations." *Millennium: Journal of International Studies* 36 (3): 439–470.

Richmond, O. P. 2011a. *A Post-Liberal Peace*. London: Routledge.

Richmond, O. P. 2011b. "Resistance and the Post-Liberal Peace." In *A Liberal Peace: The Problems and Practices of Peacebuilding*, edited by S. Campbell, D. Chandler, and M. Sabaratnam. London: Zed, 138–155.

Rigby, A. 2001. "Humanitarian Assistance and Conflict Management: The View from the Non-government Sector." *International Affairs* 77 (4):957–966.

Risen, J. 2010. *U.S. Identifies Vast Mineral Riches in Afghanistan*. New York Times. June 13.

Robinson, S. 2002. "Karzai's Kabul: Fit for a King?" *The Times*, April 18, 2002.

Roitman, J. 2001. "New Sovereign? Regulatory Authority in the Chad Basin." In *Intervention and Transnationalism in Africa: Global-Local Networks of Power*, edited by T. Gallaghy, R. Kassimir, and R. Latham. Cambridge: Cambridge University Press, 240–263.

Roitman, J. 2003. "Unsanctioned Wealth: Or, the Productivity of Debt in Northern Cameroon." *Public Culture* 15 (2): 211–237.

Rosenberg, M., and Ahmad, A. 2014. Afghan Candidate Alleges Voting Fraud By Karzai and Aides. New York Times. June 17.

Rosenberg, M. 2013. "Afghan Leader Confirms Cash Deliveries by CIA." *New York Times*, April 28, 2013.

Rotberg, R. 2002. "Failed States, Collapsed States, Weak States: Causes and Indicators." In *State Failure and State Weakness in a Time of Terror*, edited by R. Rotberg. Washington, DC: Brookings Institute.

Rothchild, D. 1970. "Ethnicity and Conflict Resolution." *World Politics* 21 (4): 597–616.

Roy, O. 1984. "The Origins of the Islamist Movement in Afghanistan." *Central Asian Survey* 3(2): 117–127.

Roy, O. 1989. "Afghanistan: Back to Tribalism or on to Lebanon." *Third World Quarterly* 11 (4): 70–82.

Roy, O. 1988. "The Origins of the Afghan Communist Party." *Central Asian Survey* 7 (2): 45–74.

Roy, O. 1990. *Islam and Resistance in Afghanistan, Second Edition*. Cambridge: Cambridge University Press.

Roy, O. 1995. *Afghanistan from Holy War to Civil War*. Princeton, NJ: The Darwin Press.

Rubin, A., and R. Nordland. 2011. *"KabulBank is Portrayed as a Private A.T.M for Afghanistan's Elite." The New York Times*.

Rubin, B. 1992. "Political Elites in Afghanistan: Rentier State Building, Rentier State Wrecking." *International Journal of Middle East Studies* 24 (1): 77–99.

Rubin, B. 1994. "Afghanistan in 1993: Abandoned but Surviving." *Asian Survey* 34 (2): 185–190.

Rubin, B. R. 2002a. *The Fragmentation of Afghanistan: State Formation and Collapse in the International System*. New Haven, CT: Yale University Press.

Rubin, B. R. 2002b. "A Blueprint for Afghanistan." *Current History* 101:153–157.

Rubin, B., and H. Malikyar. 2002. *The Politics of Center-Periphery Relations in Afghanistan*. New York: Center on International Cooperation, New York University.

Rumsfeld, D. 2011. *Known and Unknown: A Memoir*. New York: Penguin Group.

Ruttig, T. 2009. "Loyi Paktia's Insurgency: The Haqqani Network as an Autonomous entity." In *Decoding the New Taliban: Insights from the Afghan Field*, edited by A. Giustozzi. London: Hurst 57–88.

Ruttig, T. 2011. *Who was Jan Mohammad Khan*. Kabul: Afghanistan Analysts Network. July 18, 2011.

Ruttig, T. 2012. *Ambiguity Reiterated: The 20 Parties 'Democracy Charter'*. Kabul: Afghanistan Analyst Network. September 26, 2012.

Rutting, T. 2016. *Parliament Kicks Out Ministers Again: A Multi-Dimensional Power Struggle*. Kabul: Afghanistan Analyst Network.

Ruttig, T. 2020. *Flash from the Past: The 1950 Kabul Students Union and its Impact on the Post-WWII Opposition Movement*. Kabul: Afghanistan Analyst Network.

Ryan, M., and K. DeYoung. 2021. "Biden Will Withdraw All U.S. Force from Afghanistan by September 11, 2021." *The Washington Post*, April 13, 2021.

Sabaratnam, M. 2011. "The Liberal Peace? An Intellectual History of International Conflict Management, 1990–2010." In *A Liberal Peace: The Problems and Practices of Peacebuilding*, edited by S. Campbell, D. Chandler, and M. Sabaratnam. London: Zed, 245–264.

Sahlins, M. 2013. *What Kinship Is – And Is Not*. Chicago, IL and London: The University of Chicago Press.

Saikal, A. 2002. "Afghanistan After the Loya Jirga." *Survival* 44 (3):47–56.

Saikal, A. 2005. "Afghanistan's Weak State and Strong Society." In *Making States Work: State Failure and the Crisis of Governance*, edited by I. Chesterman, and R. C. Thakur. Washington, DC: United Nations University Press.

Saikal, A. 2006. *Modern Afghanistan: A History of Struggle and Survival*. London: I. B. Tauris & Co. Ltd.

Sakhi, G. 2014. "The Elections and Political Realignments in Afghanistan." Kabul: Danish Institute of International Studies. May 2014.

Santiso, C. 2001. "Good Governance and Aid Effectiveness: The World Bank and Conditionality." *The Georgetown Public Policy Review* 7 (1): 1–22.

Schatz, E. 2004. *Modern Clan Politics: The Power of "Blood" in Kazakhstan and Beyond*. Seattle, WA: University of Washington Press.

Scheepers, P., M. Te Grotenhuis, and J. Gelissen. 2002. "Welfare States and Dimensions of Social Capital: Cross-National Comparisons of Social Contacts in European Countries." *European Societies* 4: 185–207.

Schetter, C., R. Glassner, and M. Karokhel. 2007. "Beyond Warlordism: The Security Architecture in Afghanistan." *Internationale Politik und Gesellschaft (International Politics and Society)* 2: 136–53.

Schmitt, E., and C. Gall. 2004. "Karzai is Sworn in, Citing a 'New Chapter' for Afghanistan." *New York Times*, December 2004.

Schmeidl, S. 2016. "The Contradictions of Democracy in Afghanistan: Elites, Elections and 'People's Rule' Post-2001." *Conflict, Security & Development*, 16: 575–94.

Schneider, V., and D. Hyner. 2006. "Security in Cyberspace: Governance by Transnational Policy Networks." In *New Modes of Governance the Global System: Exploring Publicness, Delegation and Inclusiveness*, edited by M. Koening-Archibugi, and M. Zurn. New York: Palgrave Macmillan, 154–176.

Schneider, D. M. 1984. *A Critique of the Study of Kinship*. Ann Arbor, MI: The University of Michigan Press.

Schramm, C. 2010. *Afghanistan's Most Important Natural Resource*. Wall Street Journal.

Schweizer, T., and D. R. White, eds. 1997. *Kinship, Networks, and Exchange*. Cambridge: Cambridge University Press.

Schuman, M. 1995. "Managing Legitimacy: Strategic and Institutional Approaches." *Academy of Management Review* 20 (3): 571–610.

Scott, J. 1969. "Corruption, Machine Politics, and Political Change." *The American Political Science Review* 63 (4): 1142–58.

Scott, J. C. 1972. "Patron-Client Politics and Political Change in Southeast Asia." *The American Political Science Review* 66 (1): 91–113.

Scott, J. C. 1976. *The Moral Economy of Peasant: Rebellion and Subsistence in Southeast Asia*. New Haven, CT: Yale University Press.

Scott, J. C. 1985. *Weapons of the Weak: Everyday Forms of Peasant Resistance*. New Haven, CT: Yale University Press.

Scott, J. C. 1990. *Domination and the Art of Resistance: Hidden Transcripts*. New Haven, CT: Yale University Press.

Scott, J. C. 1998. *Seeing Like a State: How Certain Schemes to Improve the Human Condition Have Failed*. New Haven, CT: Yale University Press.

Scott, J. D. 2000. *Social Network Analysis: A Handbook, Second Edition*. Newbury Park, CA: Sage Press.

Sediqi, A. Q. 2020. "Australia, France Object to Release of Final Taliban Prisoners." *Reuters*, August 17, 2020.

Sending, O. J. 2011a. "The Effects of Peacebuilding: Sovereignty, Patronage and Power." In *A Liberal Peace: The Problems and Practices of Peacebuilding*, edited by S. Campbell, D. Chandler, and M. Sabaratnam. London: Zed, 55–68.

Shahrani, M. N., and R. Canfield. 1984. *Revolutions and Rebellions in Afghanistan*. Berkeley, CA: Institute of International Studies.

Shahrani, N. 1990. "Afghanistan: State and Society in Retrospect." In *The Cultural Basis of Afghan Nationalism*, edited by E. W. Anderson, and N. H. Dupree. London: Piner Publisher, 41–49.

Shahrani, N. 1998. "The Future of the State and the Structure of Community Governance in Afghanistan." In *Fundamentalism Reborn?: Afghanistan and the Taliban*, edited by W. Maley. London and New York: Hurst & Co. and New York University Press, 212–242.

Shahrani, N. 2002. "War, Factionalism, and the State in Afghanistan." *American Anthropologist* 104 (3): 715–722.

Sharan, T. 2011. "The Dynamics of Elite Networks and Patron-Client Relations in Post-Bonn Afghanistan." *Europe-Asia Studies* 63 (6): 1109–1127.

Sharan, T. 2013. "The Dynamics of Informal Networks and Statehood in Post-2001 Afghanistan: A Case Study of the 2010–2011 Special Election Court Crisis." *Central Asian Survey* 32 (3): 336–352.

Sharan, T. 2014. *Solution to Afghan Election Crisis Lies in Elite Power-Sharing*. July 10. https://theconversation.com/solution-to-afghan-election-crisis-lies-in-elite-power-broking-28986.

Sharan, T., and J. Heathershaw. 2011. "Identity Politics and Statebuilding in Post-Bonn Afghanistan: The 2009 Presidential Election." *Ethnopolitics* 10 (3–4): 297–319.

Sharan, T., and S. Bose. 2016. "Political Networks and the 2014 Afghan Presidential Election: Power Restructuring, Ethnicity and State Stability." *Conflict, Security and Development* 16 (6): 613–633.

SIGAR. 2010. *Lessons Learned in Preparing and Conducting Elections in Afghanistan*. Washington DC: Office of the Special Inspector General for Afghanistan Reconstruction.

Special Inspector General for Afghanistan Reconstruction (SIGAR). 2015. "Afghanistan's Mineral, Oil, and Gas Industries: Unless US Agencies Act Soon to Sustain Investments Made $488 million in Funding is at Risk." SIGAR 15–55 Audit Report. April.

Special Inspector General for Afghanistan Reconstruction (SIGAR). 2016. "Corruption in Conflict: Lessons from the US Experience in Afghanistan."

Special Inspector General for Afghanistan Reconstruction (SIGAR). 2017. "Quarterly Report to the United States Congress." January 30.

Simonsen, S. 2004. "Ethnicising Afghanistan? Inclusion and Exclusion in Post-Bonn Institution Building." *Third World Quarterly* 25 (4): 707–739.

Sinno, A. 2008. *Organizations at War in Afghanistan and Beyond.* Ithaca, NY: Cornell University Press.

Sisk, T. 1996. *Power Sharing and International Mediation in Ethnic Conflicts.* New York: Carnegie Corporation of New York.

Sisk, T. 2001. "Violence: Intrastate Conflict." In *Managing Global Issues: Lessons Learned,* edited by P. J. Simmons, and J. O. Chantal. Washington, DC: Carnegie Endowment for International Peace, 534–563.

Sisk, T. 2009. "Pathways of the Political: Electoral Processes after Civil War." In *The Dilemmas of Statebuilding: Confronting the Contradictions of Postwar Peace Operations,* edited by R. Paris, and T. Sisk. London: Routledge, 196–224.

Slaughter, A. M. 1997. "The Real New World Order: The State Strikes Back." *Foreign Affairs* 76 (5): 183–198.

Slaughter, A-M. A. 2009. *New World Order.* Princeton, NJ: Princeton University Press.

Smith, G. 2013. *The Dogs are Eating Them Now.* Toronto: Knopf Canada.

Smith, G. 2020. *Resource Flows and Political Power in Afghanistan.* London: Overseas Development Institute.

Sriram, C. L. 2009. "Transitional Justice and the Liberal Peace." In *New Perspectives on Liberal Peacebuilding,* edited by E. Newman. Tokyo: United Nations University Press, 112–130.

Stedman, S. J. 1997. "Spoiler Problems in Peace Processes." *International Security* 22 (2):5–53.

Steuter, E., and D. Wills. 2011. "Making the Muslim Enemy: The Social Construction of the Enemy in the War on Terror." In *The Routledge Handbook of War and Society,* edited by S. Carlton-Ford, and M. G. Ender, 250–70. London: Routledge.

Stewart, S. 2012. *Democracy Promotion and the 'Colour Revolution'.* New York: Routledge.

Stockman, F. 2009. "Karzai's pardons nullify drug court gains." *Boston Globe.*

Stone, D. 2000. "Non-Government Policy Transfer: The Strategies of Independent Policy Institute." *Governance: An International Journal of Policy and Administration* 13 (1). 45–62.

Stone, D. 2001. *Learning Lessons, Policy Transfer and the International Diffusion of Policy Ideas.* Warwick: Centre for the Study of Globalisation and Regionalisation.

Suchman, M. C. 1995. "Managing Legitimacy and Institutional Approaches." *The Academy of Management Review* 20 (3): 571–610.

Suhrke, A. 2009. "The Danger of a Tight Embrace: Externally Assisted Statebuilding in Afghanistan." In *The Dilemmas of Statebuilding: Confronting the Contradictions of Postwar Peace Operations,* edited by R. Paris, and D. Sisk. London: Taylor & Francis, 227–251.

Suhrke, A. 2012. *When More is Less: The International Project in Afghanistan.* London: Hurst.

Suhrke, A. 2013. "Statebuilding in Afghanistan: A Contradictory Engagement." *Central Asian Survey* 32 (3): 271–286.

Suhrke, A., K. B. Harpviken, and A. Strand. 2004. *Conflictual Peacebuilding: Afghanistan Two Years After Bonn*. CMI. Oslo: International Peace Research Institute.

Sukhanyar, J., and R. Norland. 2014. "In Prison Release, Signs of Karzai's Rift with U.S." *New York Times*. February 13, 2014.

Suroush, E. 2017. "Shikayat Farmande Peshin Police Kabul ba Wazir Dakhela: Yak Nomayande Majles ke Ghazeb Zamin ast, Tahdidam Mekonad." *Etilaat Roz*, 9 Aqrab, 1397.

Suroush, E. 2018. "Hukumat Sarparast ha: Kabine-I Hukumat dar 5 sal guzashta chera takmil nashod." *Etilaat Roz*, 3 Sunbula 1398.

Swedberg, R. 1994. *The Handbook of Economic Sociology*. Princeton, NJ: Princeton University.

Synovitz, R. 2002. "Afghanistan: Rift in Government Surfaces over Killing of Minister." *Radio Free Europe*, February 21.

Tadjbakhsh, S. 1993. "The Tajik Spring of 1992." *Central Asia Monitor* 2 (2): 21–29.

Tajdbakhsh, S. 2011. *Rethinking the Liberal Peace: External Models and Local Alternatives*. London: Routledge.

Tapper, R. 1983. *The Conflict of Tribe and State in Iran and Afghanistan*. New York: St. Martin's Press.

Tarzi, A. 2003. "A Victory for Karzai or a Masked Plea for Help?" *Radio Freedom*, May 23, 2003.

Tawana, S. M. 1989. "Glimpses into the Historical Background of the Islamic Movement in Afghanistan, Part (4)." Peshawar: *AFGHANews* (15 May 1989).

Tchalakov, M. 2013. *The Northern Alliance Prepares for Afghan Election in 2014*. Report No. 10, Institute for the Study of War.

Thier, A. 2007. "The Making of a Constitution in Afghanistan." *New York Law School Law Review* 51: 557–79.

Tomsen, P. 2011. *The Wars of Afghanistan: Messianic Terrorism, Tribal Conflicts, and the Failures of Great Powers*. New York: PublicAffairs, 641–42.

"Afghan Mineral Deposits Worth $3 tn Says Mining Official." 2010. *The Guardian*.

Tierney, J. F. 2010. *Warlord, Inc.: Extortion and Corruption along the U.S. Supply Chain in Afghanistan*. Collingdale: DIANE Publishing Company.

TOLO News. 2015. *Analysts: Over 2,000 Illegal Mining Sites in Afghanistan*. June 24.

TOLO News. 2017. *Ghani Fired Top Aide for Reforms and Good Governance*. April 17.

Tsai, W. 2001. "Knowledge Transfer in Intra-Organizational Networks: Effects of Network Position and Absorptive Capacity on Business Unit Innovation and Performance." *Academy of Management Journal* 44: 996–1004.

Tsai, W., and M. Kilduff. 2003. *Social Networks and Organizations*. London: Sage.

Tullock, G. 1967. "Welfare Costs of Tariffs, Monopolies and Theft." *Western Economic Journal* 5: 224–32.

UNDP. 2009a. "Elections and Conflict Prevention: A Programming Guide." United Nations Development Programme. Bureau for Development Policy. Oslo: Oslo Governance Centre.

UNDP. 2009b. "Assessment of Development Results: Evaluation of UNDP Contribution to the Islamic Republic of Afghanistan." United Nations Development Program Evaluation Office.

United Nations. 2000 *Report of the Panel on United Nations Peace Operations*. Brahimi Report, New York: United Nations General Assembly.

United Nations. 2002 *Report of the Special Committee on Peacekeeping Operations: Comprehensive Review of the Whole Question of Peacekeeping Operations in All Their Aspects.* UN Doc. A/56/863. 11 March, New York: United Nations.

United Nations Office on Drugs and Crime (UNODC). 2004. *Afghanistan Opium Survey 2004*, November 2004.

UN Security Council Report. 2002. *The Situation in Afghanistan and its Implications for International Peace and Security.* (A/56/1000 S/2002/737). New York: UN Security Council Report.

UN Security Council. 2002. *Loyi Jirga a Truly Representative Sample of Afghan Society.* (SC/7429), New York: UN Security Council Report.

UN Security Council. 2012. *From Arbaki to Local Police: Today's Challenges and Tomorrow's Concerns.* Kabul: Afghanistan Independent Human Rights Commission.

UN Security Council. 2014. *Fourth Report of the Analytical Support and Sanctions Monitoring Team Submitted Pursuant to Resolution 2082.* New York: United Nations Security Council.

United Nations Economic and Social Council. 1999. *Report on the Situation of Human Rights in Afghanistan.* (E/CN.4/1999/40), Geneva: United Nations Economic and Social Council (Commission on Human Rights).

United Press International. 2012. USGS Surveys Afghan Natural Resources". United States Geological Survey. International. July 18, 2012.

U.S. Diplomatic Cables. 2006. "Karzai: A Lame Duck President." *Wikileaks*, July 17, 2006.

Uzzi, B. 1997. "Social Structure and Competition in Interfirm Networks: The Paradox of Embeddedness." *Administrative Science Quarterly* 42: 35–67.

Van Oorschot, W., and W. Arts. 2005. "The Social Capital of European Welfare: The Crowding Out revisited." *Journal of European Social Policy* 15: 5–26.

Volgelsang, W. 2008. *The Afghans.* London: Wiley-Blackwell.

Wafa, A. W. 2008. "Former Warlord in Standoff with Police at Kabul Home." *New York Times*, February 4, 2008.

Wafaey, H., and A. Larson. 2010. *The Wolesi Jirga in 2010: Pre-Election Politics and the Appearance of Opposition.* Kabul: Afghanistan Research and Evaluation Unit.

Wakil, A. 1396. *Az Padshahi Motlaqa Ela Suqute Jamhuri Demokratik Afghanistan*, 2nd Edition. Kabul: First Volume.

Waldman, A. 2004. "Officials Killed as Strife Grows in Afghanistan." *The New York Times*, March 22, 2004.

Wasserman, S., and K. Faust. 1994. *Social Network Analysis: Methods and Applications.* New York: Cambridge University Press.

Watkins, A. 2020. *Afghan Leaders End Political Impasse.* Brussels/Kabul: International Crisis Group, May 20, 2020.

Watson, P. 2004. "U.S. Hand Seen in Afghan Election." *Los Angeles Times*, September 23, 2004.

Watts, D. J. 2004. *Six Degrees: The Science of a Connected Age.* London: WW Norton & Company.

Wedeman, B., and J. Bittermann. 2001. "Afghan Leaders Look Beyond Taliban." *CNN*, November 28, 2001.

Weinbaum, M. G. 1977. "The Legislator as Intermediary: Integration of the Center and Periphery in Afghanistan." In *Legislatures in Plural Societies: The Search for Cohesion in National Development*, edited by A. F. Eldridge, 95–121. Durham, NC: Duke University Press.

Weinbaum, M. G. 1972. "Afghanistan: Nonparty Parliamentary Democracy." *Journal of Developing Areas* 7 (1): 57–74.

Weigand, F. 2017. "Afghanistan's Taliban – Legitimate Jihadists or Coercive Extremists?" *Journal of Intervention and Statebuilding* 11 (3): 359–81.

Weiner, M., and A. Banuazizi. 1994. *The Politics of Social and Transformation in Afghanistan, Iran and Pakistan*. New York: Syracuse University Press.

Weingrod, A. 1968. "Patrons, Patronage, and Political Parties." *Comparative Studies in Society and History* 7 (3): 377–400.

Weiss, T. G., D. P. Forsythe, and R. A. Coate. 1994. *The United Nations and Changing World Politics*. Boulder, CO: Westview Press.

Wilder, A. 2005. *A House Divided: Analysing the 2005 Afghan Election*. Kabul: Afghanistan Research Evaluation Unit.

Williams, P. 2002. "The Competent Boundary Spanner." *Public Administration* 80 (1): 103–124.

Williams, B. G. 2010. "Abdul Rashid Dostum and the Mazar i Sharif Campaign: New Light on the Role of Northern Alliance Warlords in Operation Enduring Freedom." *Small Wars & Insurgencies* 21 (4): 610–632.

Williams, B. G. 2013. *The Last Warlord: The Life and Legend of Dostum, the Afghan Warrior Who Led US Special Forces to Topple the Taliban Regime*. Chicago, IL: Chicago Review Press.

Wimmer, A., and C. Schetter. 2003. "Putting State-Formation First: Some Recommendations for Reconstruction and Peace-Making in Afghanistan." *Journal for International Development* 15 (5): 726–741.

Woods, N., and Martinez-Diaz, L. 2009. *Networks of Influence? Developing Countries in a Networked Global Order*. Oxford: Oxford University Press.

Worden, S. 2018. *Afghan Election Conundrum (13): New Voter Registry too Good to Be True*. Kabul: Afghanistan Analysts Network.

The World Bank. 1992. *Governance and Development*. Washington, DC: World Bank.

Yunas, F. 1997. *Afghanistan: Political Parties, Groups, Movements and Mujahideen Alliances and Governments 1879–1997*, Vol. 2, Peshawar: Indus Publications, 566–576.

Yunas, F. 2002. *Afghanistan: A Political History - Vol 5*. Peshawar: Indus Publications.

Yurchak, A. 1997. "The Cynical Reason of Late Socialism: Power, Pretense, and the Anekdot." *Public Culture* 9 (2): 161–188.

Zartman, I. 1995. *Collapse States: The Disintegration and Restoration of Legitimate Authority*. Boulder, CO: Lynne Rienner.

Zartman, W. 1989. *Ripe for Resolution: Conflict and Intervention in Africa*. Oxford and New York: University Press.

Zartman, W. 2009. "'Conflict Resolution and Negotiation'." In *The SAGE Handbook of Conflict Resolution*, edited by J. Bercovitch, V. Kremenyuk, and W. Zartman, New Delhi: SAGE, 322–38.

Zaum, D. 2007. *The Sovereignty Paradox: The Norms and Politics of International Statebuilding*. Oxford: Oxford University Press.

Zimmerman, D. 1981. "Coercive Wage Offers." *Philosophy & Public Affairs*: 10 (2): 121–45.

Zimmerman, S. R., D. Egel, and I. Blum. 2016. "Task Force for Business and Stability Operations: Lessons from Afghanistan." Santa Monica: RAND Corporation.

Zurcher, C. 2011. "The Liberal Peace: A Tough Sell?" In *A Liberal Peace: The Problems and Practices of Peacebuilding*, edited by S. Campbell, D. Chandler, and M. Sabaratnam. London: Zed, 69–88.

Index

Abdullah, Abdullah 80–81, 84, 131, **149**, 188, 229
Administrative Office of the President (AOP) 162
Afghan elites 48, 261, 273, 277–78, 280–81
Afghan Millat 121, 123–24, 128, 218
Afghan National Army (ANA), 164
Afghan Special Forces 84, 171, 274–75
Afghan Transitional Administration 107
Afghanistan Analysis and Awareness (A3) youth networks 173
Afghanistan Central of Civil Registration Authority (ACCRA), 194
Afghanistan Civil Service and Reform Commission 165
Afghanistan Civil Society Institute 239
Afghanistan Investment Company (AIC) 251
Afghanistan Investment Support Agency (AISA) 168
Afghanistan National Defense and Security Forces (ANDSF) 34, 164, 241
Afghanistan Protection and Stability Council (APSC) 177
Afghanistan Reconstruction and Development Services (ARDS) 253
Afghanistan Reconstruction Trust Fund (ARTF) 242
Ahmadi, Ajmal 168, 293
aid: agencies 15; delivery regime 62; dependency 242
Ajmal, Haji 214–15, 219, 222, 280
Allen, John 275
alliance formation 28, 38–39, 64–65, 122, 172, 189
al-Qaida 77, 95, 100, 277
Amarkhel, Ziaulhaq 147
American exceptionalism 136
American military intervention 52, 55, 102

American policy interests 75
Amin, Hafizaullah 55–56
Andewali 13, 16, 44
Anglo-Afghan war, 21
Anti-Corruption Justice Centre (ACJC) 253
Armitage, Richard 75
Arsala family 64, **80**, 93–94, 127, 168, 169, 196, 229
Attorney General's Office (AGO) 169, 223, 233
Australian 48, 99
Azizi Bank 205 231–32, 251–52

Bagram airbase 42, 76, 83, 214, 241, 280
Bagram prison 136
Bahir, Ghairat 145
balanced network equilibrium 289
Barekzai tribe 80, 108, 141, 221
Bass, John R. 190–191
Bek, Matin 177, 203–04, 293
Biden, Joe 6, 274, 282
Bilateral Security Agreement 141
Bonn Agreement 1–2, 17, 53, 66, 95
Bourdieu, Pierre 12, 45
Brahimi, Lakhdar 74–75
Britain 15
budget code 92, 142
Bush administration 1, 118
Buzkashi 17

Canada 15, 189, 193
Central Intelligence Agency (CIA) 1, 135
Central Statistics Office 123, 217
Chairman of the High Council of National Reconciliation 179
chapan 77
Chayes, Sarah 10, 265
Cheney, Dick 118

China 233, 251
chromite extraction 240, 259
civil society networks 31
Civil Society Organizations (CSOs) 31
co-constitutive 12, 16, 292
coercion 28, 30, 35, 44–45, 94, 101, 206, 226, 286
coercive military capacity 283
Coercive provincial 90
coercive resources 34, 93, 137, 206
Cold War ideologies 52
collaboration 4, 289–90
collaborative governance 15
Commanders' Council (Shura Sar ta Sari) 63
communist party 7, 29, 53, 56
communist regime 7–8, 23, 52, 61, 63
Community Development Councils (CDCs), 142
conflict: management 2–3; internecine 64; intrastate 48
conscription 21
conservative clerics 21
constitutional decade 52–53, 60
Constitutional Loyi Jirga 13, 62, 102, 104, 165, 208, 216
constitutional monarchy 53
Constraints, formal 40
contested field 17, 37, 48
Cooperation Council of Political Parties and Coalitions of Afghanistan 143–44
Corruption and Justice Centre (ACJC) 263
corruption, fight against 166, 280
Council of Supreme Popular Settlement 67
counterinsurgency 1, 259, 264, 277
counter-terrorism mission 101, 108
counterterrorism 15, 79, 277–78
coups 22–23, 52, 55
cousin rivalry (Tarburwali) 20
criminal networks 43, 87–88, 91, 222, 243, 255, 285
customs revenues 64, 96, 98, 100–101, 127, 206, 244–46
Cyprus groups 2

Da Afghanistan Bank 247
Da Afghanistan Brishana Sherkat (DABS) 253
Dalili, Abdul H. 273
Darul Aman Palace 208
Daudzai, Omar 86, 134, 136, 177–78, 203, 233
Dawat-i-Islami network 96

deal-making 41, 119, 165, 209, 224, 226, 230, 232, 246
Defense Task Force for Business and Stability Operations (TFBSO) 259
Democracy Charter 143
Democratisation 7, 109, 195, 210; process 17
destarkhan (tablecloth) 106, 280, 286
destmal ('handkerchief') 279
Disarmament Demobilisation, and Reintegration (DDR) programme 83
discrimination, systematic 174, 294
dispute resolution mechanisms 195
Dobbins, James 74
donor aid money 14
Donor Coordination Assistance 62
Dostum, Abdul Rashid, 34–35, 57
drug trade 17, 37, 99, 118, 262
Dubai 177, 231, 249–50, 252–53, 265
Durand Line Agreement 21
Durrani Kingdom 19–20, 286
Durrani, Ahmad S. 19–20

economic resources 29, 34
Eide, Kai 136, 190
Eikenberry, Karl 136
election: finances 205; law 120, 143, 217
Electoral Complaints Commission (ECC) 191
electoral system, proportionate 143
Electoral Union of Afghanistan 144–45
electoral: crisis 146; patronage 41; system 143, 194
elites, predatory 17
emergency Loyi Jirga 62, 102, 189
enactment, 40
Enlightenment Movement (Jobbesh-i-Roshanayi) 173
Ensejam-i-Millie network (National Harmonisation) 101
entrenched economy 42
entrenched leadership 19
ethical discourses 15
ethnic constituency mobilisation 35
ethnic divisions 9, 164
ethnic favouritism 158, 170
ethnic polarisation, impact of 158
ethnic solidarity, 4, 58–59, 92
ethnic violence 33
ethnicisation: of Afghan politics 161; of staff offices 164
ethno-regional: political networks 101; solidarity 2; strongmen 133, 226, 244, 256, 290

Etilaf-i-Nijat-e Afghanistan (Alliance for the Salvation of Afghanistan) 171
European Union 131

Facebook Chalawun 205
factional infighting 23, 56
factionalism 7, 52–56, 67, 125, 158, 169; impact of 53; networked 23; political 68
factionalism, elite 7
Fahim, Qasim, M. 76, 81, 108
Farnood, Sherkhan 248–51
Farough, Haji 127
Fazly, Fazl 203
financial patronage 57
First Anglo-Afghan war (*1839–1842*) 19
fractionalisation 38–39, 65, 122, 172
fragmented order 78–80, 89, 102, 290–91
fragmented state 102
France 22
Free and Fair Election Forum of Afghanistan (FEFA) 191

Gailani, Pir 122, 126, 144, 149, 196
Galbraith, Peter 136, 190
Gates, Robert 136, 190
Geneva Accords 56, 66
Geneva Conference 263
Georgia 31
Germany 14–15, 62, 74–75, 193
Ghani, Ashraf 58, 104, 119, 139, **149**, 158, 170, **209**
Ghazanfar Group 135, 255
Ghazanfar, Banou 135
Ghazanfar, Mohammad Y. 206
Ghilzai confederation 20
Ghilzai Pashtuns 54, 162
Ghori cement plant 251
Ghulam Muhammad Niazi 60
Gilani, Sayed A. 2
global assemblage 14
complex global assemblage, 14
Global Witness 256–58, 261–62
Gorbachev, Mikhail 56
government-in-exile 53
Granovetter, Mark 5
Greater Council of the North 172
Green Trend 173
guilt society 13

haisiyat (character) *see* social capital
Harakat-i-Shamal (the Movement of the North) 58
Harmony Group 126

Hazara 9, 173, 207, 294
hegemonic regime-state network 289
Helmand province 99, 142, 164, 262, 274
Herat province 64, 95–96, 107, 128, 217
Hezb-i-Wahdat-Islami (the Islamic Unity Party) 66
Hezb-i-Watan 57
Hizb-i-Islami 60–61, 221
Holbrooke, Richard 135–36, 190, 241
Host Nation Trucking (HNT) 242, 244
Hughes, Karen 118
humanitarian catastrophe 294
Humayoun, Humayoun 169
hurting stalemate 282
hybrid authority 6, 8, 101
hybrid forms of peace 16

identities, politicisation of 9, 11
identity division 23
identity-based conflict 14
identity-based divisions 29, 38, 46, 207, 286, 288
Ideological forces 21
illegible budget 140
illiberal practices 210
Independent Administrative Reform and Civil Service Commission of Afghanistan (IARCSC) 139
Independent Directorate of Local Governance (IDLG) 46, 129, 156, 203, 280
Independent Election Commission (IEC) 131, 146, 169, 101, 246
Independent Joint Anti- Corruption and Evaluation Committee (MEC) 250, 263
Informal access 12–14
informal economy 43
informal institutions 11, 40, 44, 67
informal order 16, 99, 282–83, 286–87
informal rules 40
insecurity 88, 223, 259, 279
institutional design 14
institutional theory 2–3
institutionalisation 14, 280; of identity-based, 29, 286
insurgency group 1
Integrity Watch Afghanistan (IWA) 245, 259, 263, 266
interim government 66–67, 75, 100, 102, 175, 179
intermediary agents (dalal or commissionkar) 266
international aid 31, 41, 48, 62, 240, 280–81, 289; money 14, 42

International Crisis Group 235–36, 279
International military forces 42, 101,
    192, 214
International Monetary Fund (IMF) 4
international patronage 29, 31, 55, 58,
    98, 234
International Security Assistance Force
    (ISAF) 1, 79
international-local power 16
inter-network competition 286
inter-network fighting 56
Inter-Service Intelligence (ISI) 60
Intimidation 44
Islam 21, 60, 64, 95–96, 101, 130
Islamabad Accord 67
Islamic Republic 103
Islamic State of Iraq and Syria (ISIS) 174
Islamic State of Khorasan Province (ISKP)
    188, 259, 279
Islamism 21, 60
Islamist groups 53
Islamist tanzims 33, 60
itibar (credit) 34, 283

Jabbar, Abdul 130
Jabha-i-Nijat-Milli Afghanistan
    (Afghanistan National Liberation
    Front) 122
Jabha-i-Tafahom-e-Melli-i-Afghanistan
    (the National Understanding Front of
    Afghanistan) 122
Jamiat-i-Islami (the Islamic Society) 60
Jamiati-Islami tanzim 96
Jareer, Humayoun 2
jihadi tanzim networks 124, 218
Joint Election Monitoring Body
    (JEMB) 123
Joint Electoral Management Body (JEMB)
    120, 191
Junbish militiamen 91
Junbish network 39, 82, 92, 120, 171,
    195, 245
Junbish-i-Islami 67, 143, 145, 171, 178

Kabul Bank 196, 231–32, 244, 247–52, 264
Kabul civil war 67
Kabul Military Academy 55
Kabul University 53, 55, 60
Kalakani, Habibullah 21–22
Kandahar provinces 15, 283
Karmal, Babrak 23, 54, 56
Karzai, Hamid 35, 76, 118
Katawazi, Mirza K. 169

Kemalist-style modernisation 21
Kerry, John 147
KGB 56
Khalili, Karim 75, 100–101, 174, 197, 229
Khalilzad, Zalmay 74, 103, 106, 118,
    178, 282
Khalq 23, 53–56, 61
Khan, Abdul R. 21
Khan, Amanullah 21, 58, 96, 107, 141,
    158, 208
Khan, Daud, 22–23, 52, 55, 60
Khan, Dost M. 19
Khan, Habibullah 21
Khan, Ismail 95, 107
Khan, Nadir 22
Khan, Sher Ali 19
Khas Kunar mine 259
Khat-i-Sewom 227
Khost Protection Force (KPF) 95
King, Charles 8
kinship-based networks 29, 31, 101
Kroll investigation 250
Kunduz province 157, 164, 169, 221

Lajwardeen Mining Company 257
lapis lazuli 240, 256–57
Lapis lazuli mines 240
Latif Pedram 149, 175, 229–30
leadership, effective 32–33
leftist political 53
leftist revolution 55
Legal institutions 263
legitimacy, representational 46
Legitimacy: external 36, 45; domestic 56;
    political 9, 35, 46, 283; problems of
    139: representational 46
liberal peace 14–15, 17–18, 210, 281
limited-access order 18, 65, 287, 289
limited-access state 18
local government 141–42, 169
Loose-knit networks 5
Lower House (Wolesi Jirga) 84, 123, 161
Loyi Jirga (Grand Assembly) 2, 165

malek (village elder) 139
Malek, Haji A. 256
maleks (village elders) 36
Mansfield, David 262
Mansur, Abdul H. 104
Mansur, Akhtar 262
Marxist-Leninists 61
Masoud, Ahmad S. 58, 60, 63, 67, 79,
    102, 143

Masoud, Ahmad W. 118, 126, 133, 221
Masoud, Ahmad Z., 122, 130–31, 145,
 175–76, 293
mass violence 23, 55, 64
Mazar-i-Sharif 9, 58, 89–92, 107
Mehdi, Mohiuddin 104
military contracting 244
Military Council 59, 63, 67
military wing of Jamiat (the Shuray-i-
 Nezar) 76
militia groups, 29, 46, 92
Millet network 137, 146, 196
Milley, Mark 276
9/11 millionaires 215
mining sector 58, 143
Ministry of Border and Tribal Affairs
 (MoBTA) 141
Ministry of Defence (MoD) 85, 92, 129,
 164, 253, 274
Ministry of Hajj and Religious
 Affairs 142
Ministry of Interior (MoI) 59, 142–43,
 197, 222, 253, 275, 284
Ministry of Mines 143, 254
Ministry of Parliamentary Affairs 126,
 140, 204, 225
Ministry of Rehabilitation and Rural
 Development (MRRD) 142
mistrust 32, 106, 122
moderates 21
modernisation 21–23
modernist-nationalists 21
Mohaqqiq, Mohammad 35, 125, 129, 163,
 197, 208, 220, 226
Mohib, Hamdullah 169, 176, 203, 273,
 275, 284
Mojadeddi, Sebghatullah 59, 129–31, 177
monopolisation 81, 96, 158
Mujahedeen Day 102, 176
Mujahid, Zabihullah 261
Musahibans 22
Muslim Youth Organization (Sazman-i-
 Jawanan-i-Musulman) 60
Muslim 5, 21, 60, 228
mutually hurting stalemate 282

Nadery, Nader 165
Najibullah regime 23, 59, 64
Najibullah, Mohammad 56, 58, 67
Nangarhar province 93, 124, 127, 245
Naqibullah, Mullah 97–99, 108
narcotics trade 93, 220
National Democratic Front 122

National Democratic Institute (NDI)
 123–25, 191, 218, 235
National Directorate of Security (NDS) 85,
 140, 173, 246
national elites 7
national level 12, 38, 140, 242, 255, 287
national NGOs 202
national patrimony 16
National Procurement Authority (NPA) 86,
 88, 166, 168, 263
national reconciliation policy 57
National Security Council (NSC) 85, 140,
 162, 166, 225, 275
National Solidarity Programme 142
National Understanding Front 122–23, 125
National Unity Government (NUG) 58,
 120, 148, 190, 245–46, 290
National Unity Government
 Agreement 148
nation-building experiment 139
Natural Resources Counterinsurgency Cell
 (NRCC) 259
Nazhat-i-Hambastagi (the National
 Solidarity Movement) 122
neo-patrimonial political system 10
nepotism 13, 81, 89
network collaboration 289
network effectiveness, 12, 35–36
network structures 4
network, timber exploitation 260
network-as-governance 3–4
network-as-relations approach 3
networked governance 2–3, 28, 40, 64–65,
 67, 165, 173, 210, 291
networked insurgency 61
networked kingdom 19–20
networked politics 2–3, 7, 9–14, 54, 56,
 67, 189
networked regime 55
networks, technocratic 28, 30–31, 45, 54, 62
Neumann, Ronald 136
Newsweek 92
Niazi, Muhammad 60
Nongovernmental organisations (NGOs)
 15, 30–31, 62, 202, 239, 262, 280
Noor, Atta M. 35, 38, 89, 149, 259
North Atlantic Treaty Organisation
 (NATO) 1, 135
Northern Alliance (NA) 1–2, 17, 75,
 104, 106

Obama administration 135–36, 178
Obama, Barrack 133, 135–36, 147, 178

obstructionism (Mushkel tarashi) 266
open-access network 96
open-access order 18
open-access state 18
opium cultivation 118, 142, 262
opportunism 195, 200, 209, 230–31, 239, 286
organisational studies 2–3
Organisations at war 4
Osama bin Laden 277

Pakistani Inter-Service Intelligence (ISI) 60
Pamir Airways 249–50, 252
Parcham (banner) 23, 53–56, 86
Paris, Ronald 14
Parliament Executive Team (PET) 230
parliamentary groups (PGs) 126, 227
parliamentary system 104, 143, 208, 216
Pashto 22, 170, 188
Pashtu Tulane 22
Pashtun nationalism 22
Pashtun Tarburwali 32
patronage networks 29
patron-client relations 9
patu 76
Payman-i-Kabul (Kabul Accord) 123
Peace Caravan 227–29
People's Democratic Party of Afghanistan (PDPA) 23, 29, 53, 125, 129
People's High Council (Shuray-i-Aliy-i-Mardomi) 173
performance 12, 292
Personal Protection Security (PPS) 175
Peshawar Accord 67
Peshawar groups 66–67
Petraeus, David, 240
police force, militarisation of 285
policy, elite bargain 7
policymaking 173, 242
Politburo 54–56
political access 13, 240
political capital 34, 59, 165
political economy 41, 216, 230–32, 237, 275–76, 284
political instability 18–21, 180, 234, 287
political liberalisation 53
political marketplace 86, 215, 273, 283
political network approach 11–12, 276, 291
political network-patrons 227
political order, façade of 18, 37–38, 48, 89, 210, 287
political parties 13–14, 54

political resources 31, 34–35, 100, 189, 265
political stability 22, 119, 195, 240, 264, 279–80, 287, 289, 291
political *tanzims* 33, 64
politics of difference 10
Popal, Ghulam J. 137
Popalzai tribe 76, 98–99, 142
positional goods 14, 76
power resource 11, 36; diversity of 33
Power, Monopolisation of 96, 158
power-sharing agreement 5, 55, 158, 165
presidential system 104, 106
profiteering 239, 241, 246, 252, 276, 286
protection: fees 34, 84, 87, 95, 260–261; network 173; payments 244, 257
protectionist policy 102
provincial council (PC) 120, 123, 126, 138–139, 143, 217
provincial leadership council 89
Provincial Reconstruction Teams (PRTs) 37, 238
provincial-level network elites 94
Public Protection Force 188
public resources, expropriation of 286
purchasability 266

Qadir, Haji A. 64, 75, 93, 102
Qadir, Jamal, 127
Qanuni, Yunus, 75, 81, 86, 105, 177
qawm 12, 200, 232
Qayoumi, Humayoun 168
Hilal, Qutbuddin 145

Rabbani, Burhanuddi 60, 63, 77, 84, 129, 143, 196
Rabbani, Salahuddin 149, 159–60, 172, 177, 197
Radio and Television Afghanistan (RTA) 204
Rahmani, Mir R. 214
Rasoul, Zalmai 146
Rawalpindi Accord 63
reciprocity 10, 12, 41, 189, 204
Reconstruction Trust Fund 140, 242
regional conflict complex 52
regional stability 277
regional strategies 208
regional strongmen networks 37–38, 126, 129, 137, 244, 290
relative power balance 39, 65, 172
religious support networks 196
rent creation 18

rentier networked state 242, 244
rentier state 14, 16
repression strategy 106
reputational cost 6, 283
resource interdependency 11, 32–33, 36, 39
resource: extraction 48, 101, 139, 261; illegal 43, 85, 129 Taliban in 261
Revolutionary Organisation of the Toilers of Afghanistan 123
rival political networks 17, 79, 85, 285
Rome group 2, 17, 75, 94, 102
Rumsfeld, Donald 77, 118

Sabit, Abdul J. 130
Saday-i-Adalat 229
Sadiq, Mirwais 107
safe positions 48, 79, 89, 101, 173, 285
Saleh, Amrullah 81, 130, 147, 197, 203, 252
Sarabi, Habiba 101
sardars 20–21, 23
Saudi Arabia 66, 173
Sayyaf, Rasu A. 35, 60, 122, 177, 196
SAZA 123
Scott, James 41
Second Anglo-Afghan war (1878–1880) 19
Second President *see* Khalilzad, Zalmay
sectarianism 21
self-organised kleptocracy 119
self-perpetuating system 89
Senior Afghan Government Employee (SAGE) network 32
Shah, Zahir 2, 22, 52, 141
Shamali plains 79
Sharik-o-Dawla 20
Shia groups 66, 124, 218
Shirzai, Agha. G. 64, 80, 94, 97, 99, 108, 127, 196, 281
Shura-i-Qiyadi (Leadership Council) 67
Shuray-i-Bozorg-i-Shamali (Ground Council of the North) 81
Shuray-i-Democracy (Council of Democracy) 123
Shuray-i-Nezar commanders 75, 77–78, 81, 83, 220
single non-transferable vote (SNTV) 216–217
Single-authority structure 6
Sinno, Abdulkader 4, 290
social capital 3, 12–13, 18, 85, 283
social resources 34, 93, 290
sovereignty gap 16
Soviet intervention 23, 56

Soviet Union 22, 29, 34, 52, 55–56, 66, 93, 291
Spanta, Rangin D. 122–23, 128, 133–34
Special Court (SC) 215, 223; crisis 216, 229–231, 233–234
Special Inspector General for Afghanistan Reconstruction (SIGAR) 14, 240
spoilers 7–8, 15, 32, 165, 180, 283
state bureaucracy 48, 55, 81
statebuilders 29
statebuilding: process 15, 36; fragmented 15, 48; networked character 3, 12, 16, 291
state-level powerbrokers 133
state-society relations 21, 52, 55–56
strongmen-based networks 8, 29, 33
Strongmen-based political networks 31
Student Union 53, 60
subnational administrations 122, 137, 139, 148, 156, 203, 216
subnational level 29, 36–37, 44, 48, 88, 140, 274, 284, 287
Subnational strongmen 129
Support for Rule of Law (SRL) coalition 224, 229; opposition alliance 228
Supreme Court 161, 223–25, 234, 250

Tabassum demonstration 174
Tajik 21, 59, 104, 145, 162, 175, 195, 205
Taliban insurgency 9, 46, 53, 190, 261
Taliban sanctuaries 278
tanzims 63, 79, 101
Taraki Nur M., 23, 54–55
taxation 21, 244, 262
tazkiras 194
Thieves of the State, 10
Tilly, Charles 4
timber 240, 259–262; patrons 260
traditional hierarchical structures 4
traditional political organisations 5
tragedy of political networks 283
transgovernmental networks 4
Transition Council (Shura-i-Intiqali) 67
translators 214–215
Translators-cum-businessmen 215
Transparency International 263
tribal chiefs 19–23, 61, 139, 178
tribal dynamics 20, 97, 141, 168
tribal khan (chief) 119
tribal society 34
Turkey 130, 170, 239, 273, 275
Turkmen 92, 125, 219
Turko-Mongol empires 19
Turko-Mongol governance system 20

U.S. embassy 90, 214
U.S. Institute of Peace 245
U.S. Provincial Reconstruction Team 98
U.S. Special Forces 1, 91, 95
U.S.-Afghan Compact 264
U.S.-Afghanistan Bilateral Security
    Agreement 136
U.S.-Taliban deal, 17–18, 277, 281–83
UAE 173, 252
ulama 67, 128
ulema (religious leaders) 103
United Front (Jebha-i-Millie) coalition 129
United Front (UF) 130, 221; coalition
    126, 129
United Nations Assistance Mission in
    Afghanistan (UNAMA) 131, 190,
    223, 263
United Nations 4, 62, 74, 98, 118, 131,
    190, 193–94, 223, 263
United States Agency for International
    Development (USAID) 62, 241
Upper House (the House of Elders,
    Meshrano Jirga) 216
Uprising for Change (Junbish-i-Rastakhiz-
    i-Taghir) 173
Uprising for Change 173, 175
ushr 261–262

USSR 4
Uzbek 82, 92, 125, 133, 146, 209, 221
Uzbeki 106
Uzbekistan 90, 171, 173

violent criminal enterprises 84
vote-rigging 189

Wahdat network 100–101
Wahdat-i-Mardom 35, 143
wand system 259
War on Terror 1, 48, 77, 240, 278;
    objectives 48
Wardak, Farook 126, 191
Waseta 12–13, 16, 44, 119
Washington DC, 174, 277
Waste 157, 240, 242, 259
weapons system 14, 215, 240
Western-style democracy 2
Wolesi Jirga 91, 93, 123, 128, 161
World Bank 4, 15, 140, 142, 240, 242
World Food Program 294

Zadran, Padsha K. 80, 94, 108, 124, 217
Zahir, Haji 93–94, 108, 124, 127–28, 169,
    227–28
Zanbaq square 175